India Studies in Business and Economics

The Indian economy is considered to be one of the fastest growing economies of the world with India amongst the most important G-20 economies. Ever since the Indian economy made its presence felt on the global platform, the research community is now even more interested in studying and analyzing what India has to offer. This series aims to bring forth the latest studies and research about India from the areas of economics, business, and management science. The titles featured in this series will present rigorous empirical research, often accompanied by policy recommendations, evoke and evaluate various aspects of the economy and the business and management landscape in India, with a special focus on India's relationship with the world in terms of business and trade.

More information about this series at http://www.springer.com/series/11234

Purnamita Dasgupta · Anindita Roy Saha ·
Robin Singhal
Editors

Sustainable Development Insights from India

Selected Essays in Honour of Ramprasad Sengupta

Springer

Editors
Purnamita Dasgupta
Institute of Economic Growth
University of Delhi Enclave
Delhi, India

International Centre for Integrated
Mountain Development (ICIMOD)
Kathmandu, Nepal

Anindita Roy Saha
Department of Economics
Indraprastha College for Women,
University of Delhi
Delhi, India

Robin Singhal
School of Liberal Studies
Dr. B. R. Ambedkar University Delhi
Delhi, India

ISSN 2198-0012 ISSN 2198-0020 (electronic)
India Studies in Business and Economics
ISBN 978-981-33-4829-5 ISBN 978-981-33-4830-1 (eBook)
https://doi.org/10.1007/978-981-33-4830-1

This Springer imprint is published by the registered company Springer Nature Singapore Pte Ltd.
The registered company address is: 152 Beach Road, #21-01/04 Gateway East, Singapore 189721, Singapore

Foreword

I have known Ramprasadda ever since I can remember. He was, I think, the only Ph.D. student my father ever had, a fact made more remarkable by the fact that my father, Dipak Banerjee, halted his education after his B.Sc. I suspect that in today's more regulated environment this could not happen, but it seemed to have worked wonderfully. My father, an economic theorist, and Ramprasadda, who combined an interest in mathematical economics with an interest in how real industries work, would talk for hours, or at least that is how I remember it, going between abstract models, the many nuances of the steel industry and the general state of Bengal, which I gathered was not too good. Ramprasadda's Ph.D. research was on the steel industry, and as in everything else, his command over details of the industry was amazing, a fact that I know from my father's reaction after he left, which was part proud and part a bit stunned by the barrage of information he had just been exposed to. Interestingly, I think this exposure got my father much more interested in the economics of actual industries and he eventually did some work with the Bureau of Industrial Costs and Prices about the coal industry, if my memory serves me right.

Many years later, when I was deciding between JNU and Delhi School for my Master's, I remember talking to Ramprasadda. He did not pretend to be objective—he was a professor at JNU—but his response was typically gentle and thoughtful. I went to JNU.

At JNU he taught planning, which, if truth be told, was not my favourite subject. It had the disadvantage of living inside a reality that seemed very different from ours, where the government is able to dictate what happens in every corner of the economy. But he also taught a set of special lectures on nonlinear programming which stuck with me. We also met often in the house of Gauri and Tapas Majumdar, a JNU institution, where many of us would congregate several evenings a week, shamelessly inviting ourselves to Gaurimashi's wonderful food, Tapasmesho's wide-ranging and witty conversation, and the warmth and kindness that both of them radiated.

Then, alas, I left for the USA and we stopped meeting. Interestingly, it is significantly after this, at an age when many scholars slow down a bit, that Ramprasadda's research seems to have gone to an entirely different level. Reinventing himself as an economist of natural resources and the environment, he has become one of the country's most prominent and prolific scholars on the subject. These days, I run into him occasionally, at the India International Center, always with Sheiladi, his wonderful wife (who also managed to finish a Ph.D. at an age when most people retire), and as always, he is full of energy and excitement about the work he is doing. A festschrift for a scholar like him is just a way station, a stepping stone on the way to do even better things. Congratulations Ramprasadda!

Abhijit V. Banerjee
Department of Economics
Massachusetts Institute of Technology
Cambridge, USA

Abhijit V. Banerjee Co-recipient of The Sveriges Riksbank Prize in Economic Sciences in Memory of Alfred Nobel 2019; Ford Foundation International Professor of Economics, MIT.

Preface

This book is a festschrift in honour of Prof. Ramprasad Sengupta, Emeritus Professor, at the Centre for Economic Studies and Planning (CESP), School of Social Sciences (SSS), Jawaharlal Nehru University, New Delhi. Prof. Ramprasad Sengupta was an outstanding teacher at CESP for more than three decades and a pioneer in research in the economics of energy, environment and sustainable development in India. Environmental and resource economics in India has made a short but distinguished journey pioneered by the first movers among whom Prof. Ramprasad Sengupta holds a distinguished position. He inspired his fellow travellers among Indian economists and helped in nurturing generations of students and researchers. He embellished this endeavour with innovative research and set an example in collaborating on issues of sustainability both within and outside the government. This volume brings together a wide repertoire of authors and their writings on niche areas related to development, energy, environmental, ecological and resource economics. As editors of this book, we are extremely happy to present this collection of essays, in a humble effort to honour him as our teacher and mentor.

The career of Prof. Ramprasad Sengupta shines with academic brilliance and professional accomplishment of the highest order. As a student at the prestigious Presidency College and Calcutta University, he has been a winner of the University medals for academic excellence. Before joining CESP, JNU, he served at the Centre for Economic Studies, Presidency College, Kolkata. He had a distinguished tenure at CESP during 1976–2012 with occasional stints elsewhere. He held the position of Sukhamoy Chakravarty Chair Professor of Planning and Development at CESP during 2010–2012. He has also served as the Dean, School of Social Sciences, at JNU during 2004–2005. In his illustrious career, he has held several faculty positions within and outside India. This includes the position of Professor of Economics at the Indian Institute of Management Calcutta, the Centre for Development and Environment Policy, and visiting faculty at the National Institute of Public Finance and Policy and Ambedkar University, Delhi. He has held prestigious international assignments as a visiting honorary professor, researcher and scholar at the University of British Columbia, Vancouver; University of Calgary, Alberta; University of

Hamburg; University of Kobe; University of Pennsylvania, Philadelphia; University of Applied Sciences, Osnabrück; University of Birmingham; Erasmus University, Rotterdam; Boston University and University of Twente. He has been a Senior Fulbright Scholar and Fellow of the Shastri Indo-Canadian Institute. He has been the Mahatma Gandhi National Fellow of the Indian Council of Social Science Research with affiliation at the Centre for Studies in Social Sciences, Kolkata.

Beyond teaching and university positions, Prof. Ramprasad Sengupta has made significant contributions through his professional associations with the government and public sector. He has been Advisor (Modelling) at the Planning Commission during 1986–1989 for the development of energy policy model for the Indian economy. He has been Member of the Working Groups for the Ninth, Tenth and Eleventh Five-Year Plans for the steel sector and the Twelfth Plan for education. He has been on the expert committees of the University Grants Commission several times. He has been Director (independent) at the Steel Authority of India Limited and Consultant cum Advisor to the Bureau of Indian Costs and Prices. He has been an honorary advisor in the ministries of steel and power for many years.

Prof. Sengupta has served on governing bodies, research and academic committees of many universities and institutes, such as Indian Statistical Institute, Delhi; Indian Institute of Sciences, Bengaluru; Delhi School of Economics; Institute of Economic Growth, Delhi; Indira Gandhi Institute of Development Research, Mumbai; Visva Bharati, Santiniketan; Centre for Development Studies, Thiruvananthapuram; Madras School of Economics, Chennai; University of Calcutta and Jadavpur University, Kolkata. He has been a founding member of the Indian Society for Ecological Economics and is a member of several professional bodies in economics and econometrics at the national and state levels.

Besides publishing extensively in journals of repute, he has authored three books which may be considered fundamental in understanding the nuances of environmental and ecological economics. He has directed a large number of studies and projects at central as well as state levels in the steel, power and transport sectors. Rooted deeply in the fundamental principles of economics, these studies have led to findings and insights relevant for pursuing new areas of enquiry in the tradition of economic research in India.

A large number of students have had the good fortune to have received his mentorship and guidance as a research supervisor in the Ph.D. and M.Phil. programmes at JNU. He has also examined dissertations and theses at premier institutions of the country, especially in the domains of sustainable development, energy and environmental economics.

Prof. Ramprasad Sengupta belongs to that genre of intellectuals who can traverse from economics to literature and from mathematics to religion with equal ease and expertise. That the foundation of economics is laid fundamentally in the principles of philosophy, laws of physics and lessons from history, was at the core of his interdisciplinary understanding of the subject. Starting a journey from conventional topics in development economics and economic planning, he expanded the research horizon to include areas such as steel and energy that were lesser known at the time, without losing sight of the core disciplinary strengths. Subsequently, his work in the areas of environment, ecology and sustainability came to be respected and well accepted among the new directions of economic research in the country. His profound knowledge of several disciplines led him in his own research, as well as in mentoring his students to pursue a holistic understanding of the subject.

A description of his achievements would be incomplete without an acknowledgement of his and Sheiladi's open house policy towards his students, whether on festive occasions for feasting and the famous Bengali "adda", or in liberal invitations to sample the finest music, literature and poetry from renowned artists and writers who would visit their home in the JNU campus. We do hope that the collection of essays in this volume, which is built on the generous contributions from leading scholars in their respective fields, will prove useful in furthering Prof. Sengupta's passion for excellence in pursuit of academics.

Delhi, India

Purnamita Dasgupta
Anindita Roy Saha
Robin Singhal

Acknowledgements

Our sincerest gratitude goes to all the authors who have come forward to join us in preparing a tribute to Prof. Ramprasad Sengupta. The esteemed contributors of this book have been either his students or his associates in various academic capacities. Their scholarship, expertise and long experience in the chosen fields have enriched this volume. We are grateful to all of them for taking time out of their busy schedule, especially while managing disruptions on the personal and professional front owing to the COVID-19 pandemic to make this book a reality.

Prof. Sengupta had wide-ranging academic interests, and there would always be the potential for scholars to contribute on different aspects. As editors, we honed in on the theme of sustainability and development as an appropriate focus area for this book. We would like to record our appreciation of all those who have encouraged us in this endeavour, based on their past and present associations with Prof. Sengupta. We are extremely grateful to Prof. Abhijit Vinayak Banerjee for taking the time to write a foreword for the book.

Our heartfelt thanks go to the Publishing Editor, Nupoor Singh, and the production team of Daniel Joseph Glarance, Jayanthi Narayanaswamy and their team members at Springer Nature for taking care of every detail to give the final shape to this book. Without their constant support and guidance at every stage, this book would not have been possible.

Finally, we thank all our well-wishers, at home and at work, who have stood by us through this journey.

Contents

Editors and Contributors

About the Editors

Dr. Purnamita Dasgupta Chair Professor in Environmental and Resource Economics at the Institute of Economic Growth, Delhi, is currently on leave as Theme Leader, Ecosystem Services, ICIMOD. She has been visiting professor at University of Cambridge, UK and Johns Hopkins University, USA. Her teaching and research focus on the relationship between environment and economic development. Her research assignments include CLA of the IPCC and IPSP, author HIMAP, Advisor IPCC's Scientific Steering Group on Economics, Costing and Ethics; CARIAA and the Association of Commonwealth Universities, UK. She has contributed to modelling for India's NDCs and NATCOM processes, drafting regulation on e-waste, natural resource accounting for the CAG, Supreme Court committee on NPV for Forests, committee to evolve environmental standards, among others. She has published in journals such as *Climatic Change, PLOS One, Environment and Development Economics, Environmental Development, Environmental Health Perspectives.*

Dr. Anindita Roy Saha is Associate Professor at the Department of Economics, Head of the Department of Environmental Studies and Coordinator of the Centre for Earth Studies at Indraprastha College for Women, University of Delhi. She is a visiting faculty at the Department of Environmental Studies, Faculty of Science, University of Delhi. She has been associated with Jawaharlal Nehru University, Ambedkar University Delhi, Nalanda University, Indira Gandhi National Open University and Amity University in various capacities. She completed her Master's and Ph.D. degrees from CESP, JNU. Her area of specialization is environmental and resource economics that has evolved from energy economics during her doctoral research. She has been engaged in research guidance and published several articles in reputed national and international journals. Beyond academics, she is engaged in popularizing environmental education and community sensitization.

Dr. Robin Singhal is Assistant Professor of Economics at the School of Liberal Studies, Dr. B. R. Ambedkar University Delhi. He works in the area of energy economics, environmental and resource economics and issues relating to Economics of Infrastructure. He has been a visiting faculty for Master's Programmes in Environmental Studies and Resource Management, and Climate Science and Policy at the TERI School of Advanced Studies, New Delhi and the Executive Energy Management Programme at the Management Development Institute, Gurgaon. He has also been associated in various academic and professional capacities with the Department of Environmental Studies, University of Delhi; School of Inter-Disciplinary and Trans-Disciplinary Studies at Indira Gandhi National Open University, New Delhi; Punjab School of Economics at Guru Nanak Dev University, Amritsar and DAV University, Jalandhar. He has published in reputed journals and presented his research at several conferences.

Contributors

Sk. Md. Azharuddin is a Ph.D. candidate at the Centre for International Trade and Development (CITD), School of International Studies, Jawaharlal Nehru University. He was awarded an M.Phil. degree from the same centre. He also holds an MA in Economics from the School of Economics, University of Hyderabad, Hyderabad, and a B.Sc. (Hons) in Economics from the University of Calcutta, Ramakrishna Mission Residential College, Narendrapur, Kolkata. His research areas include macroeconomics, growth theory, new Keynesian economics, energy and environment and international trade.

Dr. Kaushik Ranjan Bandyopadhyay is Associate Professor at IIM Lucknow (IIML). Currently, he is Chairperson of the PGPSM programme and heads the Centre for Business Sustainability at IIML. He is Member of the Board of Directors of Enterprise Incubation Centre (EIC) at IIM Lucknow. Prior to his current role, he has been Principal Policy Advisor with International Institute of Sustainable Development (IISD), Expert with International Centre for Trade and Sustainable Development (ICTSD) Geneva, Senior Consultant with Tata Trusts and Associate Professor at The Energy and Resources Institute (TERI) School of Advanced Studies. He has also taught at United Nations University (UNU-IIST), Faculty of Management Studies (FMS), Delhi University and been Japanese Society of Promotion of Science (JSPS) Visiting Scholar at Asian Growth Institute (AGI), Japan.

Dr. Sangeeta Bansal is Professor at the Centre for International Trade and Development, Jawaharlal Nehru University. Her main research interests are in environmental economics, nutrition and game theory. She is Co-editor of the journal *Resource and Energy Economics*, Editorial Board Member of *International Review of Environmental and Resource Economics* and has served on the editorial board of *Environmental and Development Economics*. She is a recipient of the Fulbright Research

Fellowship in 2013–2014 to visit University of California, Berkeley, USA. She has provided consultancy to various national and international organizations. She holds a Ph.D. in Economics from Indian Statistical Institute.

Dr. Manoj Bhatt is Faculty at Department of Economics, University of Jammu. He has more than nineteen years of teaching and research experience in different universities which include Department of Business Economics, University of Delhi (South Campus), and Department of Economics at Doon University, Dehradun. He also worked briefly at National Institute of Public Finance and Policy, New Delhi. He has done MA, M.Phil. and Ph.D. from Jawaharlal Nehru University (JNU), New Delhi. He specializes in energy economics and has written various articles in the area. Recently, he has also completed a study granted by Reserve Bank of India (RBI), Mumbai.

Gaurav Bhattacharya is a Ph.D. candidate at the Centre for International Trade and Development (CITD), School of International Studies, Jawaharlal Nehru University. After completing his MA in Economics from CITD, he was awarded an M.Phil. degree from the same centre. Previously, he received a B.Sc. (Hons) in Economics from the University of Calcutta, Scottish Church College, Kolkata. His research interests include microeconomics, energy and environment, international trade and political economics.

Dr. Surya Bhushan currently teaches Economics at the Development Management Institute (DMI), Patna, India. Previously, he worked with Accenture, a global management consultancy company, for almost a decade. He obtained an MA, M.Phil. and Ph.D. in Economics from the Centre for Economic Studies and Planning (CESP), Jawaharlal Nehru University (JNU), New Delhi, India. His widely cited publications include works on agricultural productivity; the impact of technological change on growth and poverty; environmental issues in agriculture; livelihoods and rural non-farm economy and the role of agriculture in economic development.

Dr. Chetana Chaudhuri is currently associated with Public Health Foundation of India, Gurugram, India. Her areas of interest are energy and environment, health and development economics. She has published research papers in books and reputed journals. She has done Ph.D. in Economics under the supervision of Prof. Ramprasad Sengupta and Prof. Krishnendu Ghosh Dastidar, Centre for Economic Studies and Planning (CESP), JNU, New Delhi. She has more than 9 years of experience in academic research. Previously, she was associated with Institute of Economic Growth (IEG), National Institute of Public Finance and Policy (NIPFP), Asian Institute of Transport Development (AITD), and SYLFF, Jadavpur University.

Dr. Indrani Roy Chowdhury is currently Associate Professor (Economics) at the Centre for the Study of Regional Development (CSRD), School of Social Science, Jawaharlal Nehru University. Her areas of specializations are health economics and environmental economics, and she has earned her publications in many peer-reviewed journals. She did her Ph.D. in Environmental Economics from the Centre for International Trade and Development, School of International Studies, Jawaharlal Nehru University, and M.Phil. in Economics from Jadavpur University. She has more than 18 years of teaching and research experience, and prior to her position in JNU, she had served in the Department of Economics, Jamia Millia Islamia, National Institute of Public Finance and Policy, Council for Social Development.

Dr. Nandini Das is currently Postdoctoral Project Research Personnel at the Global Change Programme of Jadavpur University, Kolkata, India. Her research interest is in the field of climate change mitigation and environmental sustainability with a special focus on transition of the electricity sector. She takes interest in energy security, energy efficiency, SDGs and multi-level climate governance and air pollution. She is currently Chapter Scientist with IPCC WGIII 6th Assessment Report, focusing on demand-side mitigation measures. She completed her Ph.D. in 2019 from the Department of Economics, Jadavpur University. Her doctoral research deals with alternative pathways for low-carbon growth and its financing mechanisms in Indian context. She has seven peer-reviewed publications including articles and chapters. She is also working on scenario building exercise for IDEEA model.

Dr. Somit Dasgupta is former Member (Economic and Commercial) of the Central Electricity Authority and originally belonged to the Indian Economic Service (1984 batch). He has served in various government departments since his first posting in 1986 but for most of his career, and he has served in power-related departments/discharged responsibilities related to power. He has served for more than 25 years in the power sector having done stints in the Ministry of Power, Niti Aayog, the Delhi Electricity Regulatory Commission and the Central Electricity Authority. He holds a Ph.D. from JNU, and the subject of his dissertation was "Power Sector Reforms in India". After superannuating from the government, he is currently associated with the Indian Council for Research on International Economic Relations (ICRIER) as Senior Visiting Fellow and also works as a newspaper columnist, writing on power sector-related issues.

Dr. Ananya Ghosh Dastidar is Associate Professor at the Department of Finance and Business Economics, University of Delhi, and has a doctorate in Economics from CESP, JNU. She started her teaching career at the Department of Economics, Delhi School of Economics. Her research interests are in the areas of international economics and development economics. She has published widely on macroeconomic issues in development, income distribution, structural transformation and international trade. Her recent publication includes the edited volume (co-editors, Rajeev Malhotra and Vivek Suneja) “Economic Theory and Policy amidst Global Discontent”, a festschrift volume in honour of Professor Deepak Nayyar.

Dr. Vikram Dayal is Professor at the Institute of Economic Growth, Delhi. He is author of “Quantitative Economics with R: A Data Science Approach”, published by Springer. He has published research on a range of environmental and developmental issues, from outdoor and indoor air pollution in Goa, India, to tigers and Prosopis juliflora in Ranthambore National Park. He received his doctoral degree from the Delhi School of Economics, University of Delhi.

Dr. Nilanjan Ghosh is Director, Observer Research Foundation, Kolkata. His previous positions include Senior Fellow at ORF Kolkata, Senior Vice President and Chief Economist at MCX (I) Limited (Mumbai) and Professor of Econometrics at the TERI School of Advanced Studies (New Delhi). He holds a Ph.D. degree from IIM Calcutta and has held visiting faculty positions at various universities across the globe, e.g. Linnaeus University (Sweden), Uppsala University (Sweden), Massachusetts Institute of Technology (USA) and Stanford University (USA), at various points in time. He advised WWF India to set up their ecological economics practice and also served as Vice President of the Indian Society for Ecological Economics.

Dr. Kajleen Kaur is Assistant Professor at Sri Guru Gobind College of Commerce, University of Delhi. She has an experience of 20 years in teaching, and her areas of interest include macroeconomics, microeconomics and money and financial systems. She has presented research papers at various national and international conferences including IIM Calcutta, IIFT, TERI University besides others and has been thrice awarded with the Best Paper award. Her research papers have been published in reputed journals. Recently, she mentored a students' team from her college for RBI Policy Challenge: 2020 which won Best Paper in the region and stood second in the North Zone.

Dr. K. S. Kavi Kumar is currently Professor at Madras School of Economics, Chennai. He has about 24 years of experience in research, teaching and industries. After receiving bachelor's and master's degrees in Engineering, he completed his Ph.D. in Development Economics in 1998 from Indira Gandhi Institute of Development Research, Mumbai. He has been associated with various international and national institutions including the World Bank, International Institute for Applied Systems Analysis, Potsdam Institute for Climate Impact Research, GIZ, British High Commission, Tata Energy Research Institute and Institute of Economic Growth for various research assignments. During 2008–2015, he had coordinated the activities of the Centre of Excellence in Environmental Economics supported by the Ministry of Environment, Forest and Climate Change, Government of India.

Dr. Surender Kumar is Professor at the Department of Economics, Delhi School of Economics, University of Delhi. He had been Visiting Fellow at the University of Illinois at Urbana-Champaign (USA) and Senior JSPS Fellow at the Yokohama National University, Yokohama (Japan). He has been working with a concentrated focus on environmental and resource economics and climate change and energy economics. He also extends his ambit of research to productivity and efficiency measurement and applied econometrics. He has authored five books and extensively published in reputed journals. He teaches courses on applied environmental policy and applied production analysis.

Dr. Amitabh Kundu currently has advisory positions at Research and Information System for Developing Countries, World Resources Institute and Oxfam India. He was Professor and Dean of the School of Social Sciences at Jawaharlal Nehru University, Member of National Statistical Commission and chaired the Post Sachar Evaluation Committee and the one for estimating Urban Housing Shortage. He was Regional Advisor on Poverty at UNESCWA, Beirut, and Consultant to Sri Lankan Government on Population Census. He chairs the committee overviewing survey for Swatch Bharat Mission (Rural). He has been Visiting Professor at the University of Amsterdam, Sciences Po, Maison des Sciences de L'homme Paris, University of Kaiserslautern and University of Wuerzburg, Germany, and Director at various institutes in India. With about 35 books and 300 research articles to his credit, he also serves on the editorial boards of *Manpower Journal*, *Urban India* and *Indian Journal of Labour Economics*, among others.

Hasan Mahmud is Bangabandhu Chair Researcher at the Asian Institute of Technology (AIT), Thailand, and Doctoral Student with the Sustainable Energy Transition Program, AIT, since 2018. Bangabandhu Chair was established in AIT by the Government of Bangladesh to conduct research on sustainable energy solutions for Bangladesh. He is on deputation from Sylhet Gas Fields Limited (a national company for natural gas exploration and production), Bangladesh. He has worked in national gas producing company for nine years. He graduated with B.Sc. engineering degree in Chemical Engineering from Shah Jalal University of Science and Technology, Sylhet, Bangladesh, in 2007 and obtained M.Sc. engineering degree in Petroleum Engineering from Bangladesh University of Engineering and Technology, Dhaka, Bangladesh, in 2009.

Dr. Sugata Marjit is First Distinguished Professor of the Indian Institute of Foreign Trade. Formerly, Vice Chancellor at Calcutta University and RBI Professor and Director at CSSS Calcutta, he has also held positions as Sukhamay Chakravarty Professor at CESP, JNU, New Delhi, and visiting professorial positions at well-known universities in Europe, USA and Australia. He has published widely in reputed journals including *American Economic Review*, *Journal of Economic Theory*, *Journal of International Economics*, *European Economic Review*, *Journal of Economic Behavior and Organization*, *Economic Theory*, *Oxford Economic Papers*, *NATURE Climate Change*, *PLOS One* and *Indian Journal of Physics*, to mention a few. His books and edited volumes have been published by OUP, CUP and Springer Nature. Recipient of the Mahalanobis Gold Medal and the VKRV National Prize, he was a university-wide Distinguished Visiting Fellow of Queen Mary, University of London. He edits the *South Asian Journal of Macroeconomics and Public Finance.*

Dr. Meeta Keswani Mehra is Professor of Economics at the Centre for International Trade and Development (CITD), School of International Studies, Jawaharlal

Nehru University (JNU). She has been Chairperson of the Centre in December 2013–2015 and January 2018–2020. A Ph.D. from the Indian Statistical Institute, Delhi, she teaches macroeconomics, open-economy macroeconomics, environmental economics and regulatory economics at JNU since 2004. Her research lies in the interface of growth theory, international trade, energy economics, environment and climate economics, politics of regulation and political business cycles. She has published widely in reputed journals including *Environmental and Resource Economics*, *Research in Economics*, *International Economic Journal* and *Current Opinion in Environmental Sustainability*, among others.

Dr. Suryaprakash Mishra works with the National Law University, Delhi (NLUD). He teaches Economics/Law and Economics. He has earned his Ph.D. (Economics) from the Centre for Studies in Social Sciences, Calcutta (CSSSC), and an M.S. (Applied Economics and Statistics) from Clemson University, USA. For over a decade, he has been with the leading and prominent national law universities in India, such as NALSAR, Hyderabad, and NLU, Delhi. He has academic publications in internationally leading publications outlets on various sub-disciplines of economics such as microeconomic theory, industrial organization, development economics, international trade, poverty and inequality and public finance/economics.

Sayanangshu Modak is Junior Fellow at Observer Research Foundation, Kolkata. His research involves themes like transboundary water governance, hydro-diplomacy and flood risk management and explores the interface of science and policy for the effective governance of river basins. He has previously worked as Project Manager in Foundation for Ecological Security where he researched on water commons in the semi-arid landscape. He also tracks issues related to natural resource management and environmental sustainability. He has a B.Sc. (Hons.) in Geography from Presidency University, Kolkata, and an M.Sc. in Water Policy and Governance from the Tata Institute of Social Sciences, Mumbai.

Dr. Saptarshi Mukherjee is Associate Professor of Microeconomic Theory at IIT Delhi. He graduated from the Indian Statistical Institute (Delhi). He works on mechanism design, social choice, game theory and bounded rationality and teaches microeconomics, game theory and mathematical economics. He has published in journals such as *Journal of Economic Theory*, *Games and Economic Behavior*, *Energy Policy*, *Economics Letters*, *Social Choice and Welfare* and *Theory and Decision*.

Dr. Tapaswini Nayak currently teaches in the Department of Economics at P. N. Autonomous College (Utkal University), Odisha. Prior to this, she was a Ph.D. research scholar in Jamia Millia Islamia (Central University), New Delhi, and is a recipient of doctoral fellowship award from Indian Council of Social Science Research, New Delhi. Her research interests include environmental economics, health economics and development economics. She has published her research work in peer-reviewed international and national journals such as *Ecology, Economy and Society—The INSEE Journal*; *Environment, Development and Sustainability Journal* and *International Journal of Big Data Mining for Global Warming*. She has also presented many research papers in international and national conferences.

Dr. Anusree Paul is Associate Professor in Economics at BML Munjal University in School of Commerce and Economics. She has more than eleven years of teaching and research experience in the field of international trade and health economics. She has worked on various projects funded by the British High Commission, UGC, ICSSR, Oxfam International, etc. Her research areas are applied econometrics, international economics and health economics. She has published papers in various peer-reviewed journals. She is proficient in statistical analysis and software like Stata, EViews, Gretl and MATLAB.

Dr. M. Rahul is Indian Economic Service Officer and currently Deputy Director in the Ministry of Finance, Government of India. Previously, he has also worked in the Reserve Bank of India. He received his doctorate in Economics from Jawaharlal Nehru University, New Delhi. He was a recipient of Ford Foundation Scholarship while pursuing his Master's from the same university. He also received the ecbi-Oxford Fellowship to attend Oxford Seminar and Fellows Colloquium on climate change negotiations in 2018. His research areas cover a wide range of economic issues covering climate change, environmental economics, economics of open-source software and other policy issues.

Dr. Moushakhi Ray is associated with teaching in an undergraduate degree college for the past nine years. She is presently Assistant Professor in the Department of Economics at Siliguri College (government sponsored), Darjeeling, India. She obtained her Ph.D. in 2018 on "Technology, Competition and Finance-Implications for Trade in Imperfect Markets". Her research interests are in the areas of theoretical and empirical studies in international trade, credit market along with issues of sustainable development. Her major publications include "Credit constraints, fragmentation and inter-firm transactions" in *Asia-Pacific Journal of Accounting and Economics* (2014), "Export profitability, competition and technology" in *International Review of Economics and Finance* (2017).

Dr. Joyashree Roy currently inaugural Bangabandhu Chair Professor at AIT, Thailand, has been with the Economics Department at Jadavpur University. Awarded National Fellow of the ICSSR, she was Ford Foundation Postdoctoral Fellow at LBNL, Berkeley, USA, and Founding Advisor of the Global Change Programme and Ryoichi Sasakawa Young Leaders Fellowship Fund (SYLFF) Project, Jadavpur University. She has been the author in IPCC's Nobel Peace Prize Panel and Global Energy Assessment and Member of the winning team of Prince Sultan Bin Aziz award for water. Currently a CLA of the IPCC's 6th assessment cycle, she has to her credit over 120 peer-reviewed journal articles, authored and edited books. Her research interests include economics of pollution and climate change, modelling energy demand, economy-wide models and water quality demand, pricing, sustainable development, natural resource accounting, valuing environmental services including coastal ecosystems, informal sector concerns, Bangladesh economy and energy policy.

Dr. Shalini Saksena Associate Professor in the Department of Economics, DCAC, University of Delhi, graduated from the Delhi School of Economics and completed her Ph.D. from CESP, Jawaharlal Nehru University. Her main areas of specialization and interest include environmental and social sustainability and inclusive growth and development. She has had the opportunity to work on a couple of consultancy assignments with the World Bank and the Asian Development Bank and as Project Investigator of projects backed under Delhi University's Innovation Project Scheme (2013–2015 and 2015–2016). She has published her research work in national and international journals.

Dr. Md. Zakaria Siddiqui works at Gulati Institute of Finance and Taxation, Kerala. His research focuses on Indian public policy debates such as modern energy services, nutrition transition, calorie norm for poverty, women in labour market, scientific diaspora and development and democracy and minorities. He has published in academic journals such as *World Development*, *The Journal of Development Studies*, *Health Policy and Planning*, *Public Health and Nutrition* and *Energy Policy*. He was trained at Centre for Development Studies (CDS), Thiruvananthapuram, Centre for Economic Studies and Planning (CESP), Jawaharlal Nehru University (JNU), and Center for Operations Research and Econometrics (CORE), Belgium.

Dr. Anup Sinha is currently Chairman, Bandhan Bank Limited, and Chief Mentor of Heritage Business School. Prior to this, he was Professor of Economics at IIM Calcutta for over 25 years. Educated at Presidency College, Kolkata, University of Rochester, New York, and University of Southern California, Los Angeles, his academic interests and publications are in the areas of macroeconomic policy, development strategies, sustainable development and ethics. He has taught at Presidency College, University of Calcutta, Indian Statistical Institute and held visiting appointments at University of Southern California, Washington University, in St. Louis, Curtin University of Technology at Perth and Kyoto University. He has served three terms on the Board of Governors of IIM Calcutta. A recipient of the Best Faculty Award from the alumni of IIM Calcutta during 2004 and 2005, in 2012, 2014 and 2015, he was chosen as the Most Popular Teacher by outgoing MBA students.

Shreya Some is currently working as Scientist in IPCC-WG-III Technical Support Unit. Her research interests include emission trend analysis, sustainability and co-benefits of adaptation and mitigation options. She has worked as Contributing Author in Chap. 5 of the IPCC Special Report 1.5 and WRI ocean report—The Ocean as a Solution to Climate Change: Five Opportunities for Action. She is an exchange scholar at the Technical University, Freiberg, Germany, funded by the UGC-DAAD-PPP 2019–2021. For a short while, she has worked as Business Analyst with Wipro Technologies (India) and was Summer Intern at Reserve Bank of India (Kolkata). Her Ph.D. thesis is on "Economics of Greenhouse Gas Emission Mitigation: A Study of the Indian Agricultural Sector" which is due for submission at the Department of Economics, Jadavpur University, India. In 2015, she completed master's degree in Economics from Jadavpur University.

Kavitha Srikanth is Research Analyst and works in the Environmental and Resource Economics Unit at the Institute of Economic Growth, New Delhi. At the institute, she has experience working on projects relating to environmental finance mechanisms and environmental valuation, which were conducted for various organisations such as the 15th Finance Commission, The Nature Conservancy and the Foundation for Ecological Security. She is a graduate in accounting and finance and a postgraduate in economics with specialization in environmental and resource economics. Her research interests involve exploring issues relating to financing for the environment.

Dr. Nawin Kumar Tiwary is Assistant Professor in the Department of Environmental Studies at Indraprastha College for Women, University of Delhi. He completed his master's degree in Environmental Studies and Ph.D. in Ecology and Conservation from the Department of Environmental Studies, Faculty of Science, University of Delhi. He has been actively involved in ecological and biodiversity research with a special interest in the evolutionary and behavioural ecology of birds, urban ecology, wetland studies and habitat modelling. He has published several high impact research articles in journals of international repute. As an avid birdwatcher, he is also involved in popularizing field ornithology and has made several presentations and talks on related topics.

Introducing Contemporary Development and Sustainability Concerns for India

Purnamita Dasgupta, Anindita Roy Saha, and Robin Singhal

1 The Why Question

1.1 Rationale for the Book

The journey towards achieving an economy where societal well-being is unequivocally centre staged requires thinking about the path that will be charted till the year 2030 and well beyond it. This is the year for which countries have adopted targets related to the Sustainable Development Goals (SDGs) and is also the year of focus for the much discussed Nationally Determined Contributions (NDCs) in the Paris Agreement. The severe shock posed by COVID-19 has for some constituencies rung the alarm bells for focussing on sustainability as a core principle for development—economic, social and environmental—in the near term and the long term. For many though, it has resurrected single-minded pursuit of economic growth as the need of the hour.

While much has been achieved with economic growth, as Stiglitz (2019) reminds us, *there is ample room to change the quality of growth, to reduce its environmental impact significantly* (Stiglitz, 2019). This presents an opportune moment in time to

P. Dasgupta (✉)
Institute of Economic Growth, University of Delhi Enclave, Delhi, India
e-mail: purnamita.dasgupta@gmail.com

International Centre for Integrated Mountain Development (ICIMOD), Kathmandu, Nepal

A. R. Saha
Department of Economics, Indraprastha College for Women, University of Delhi, Delhi, India
e-mail: aroysaha@hotmail.com

R. Singhal
School of Liberal Studies, Dr. B.R. Ambedkar University Delhi, Lothian Road, Kashmere Gate, Delhi, India
e-mail: rbnsinghal@gmail.com

P. Dasgupta et al. (eds.), *Sustainable Development Insights from India*,
India Studies in Business and Economics,
https://doi.org/10.1007/978-981-33-4830-1_1

revisit the debates, and for researchers as writers, to don the responsibility of *dredging up to the light our dark and dangerous dreams for the purpose of improvement* (Steinbeck, 1962).

This book is an attempt to further the discussion on the continued coexistence of synergies and incompatibilities, between sustainability and conventional economic development, in a world that considers itself to be plunged into a crisis as never before.

1.2 The Enduring Relevance of Sustainable Development

Principles of equity and fairness in distribution of resources, maintaining planetary health, the call for climate justice and economic growth that respects the planetary boundaries have found increasing acceptance over the last few decades. The global sustainable development goals were a major effort to recognise that developmental goals need to be in sync with each other, and to centre stage the relevance of people and planetary well-being. This book probes some contemporary issues that will help in understanding the sustainability narrative in India. The topics explored include the complex challenges at the interface of development and environment, and the conservation of natural resources in the face of conventional developmental approaches. The discourse further extends to the role of economic modelling, governance and institutions, in the theory and practice of sustainability across different sectors and decision-making agents in the economy. It aims to examine, analyse and interpret the topical issues that not only persist in demanding resolution as outstanding concerns for policymakers but emerge as new challenges such as those posed by climate change in building a resilient society. It thus collates past learnings with new understanding, combining views about the big picture with specialised core analytical contributions.

2 The How Question

The abundance of perspectives and multitude of dimensions that scholars have associated with the term sustainable development is unrivalled by any other terminology linking environment and development. It is no easy task to knit together nor to pick and choose some topics as having greater salience over others. However, the editors' task in putting together this book was made easy by contributions from leading scholars. Our contributors were forthcoming in offering their scholarship, and the chapters reflect the foremost challenges and opportunities as "natural fits" for an edited volume on sustainable development. The chapters have been organised into four themes, namely:

- The Big Picture: Evolving Perspectives
- The Energy Scenario: Dilemmas and Opportunities

- Sustainability Cross-Cuts: Developmental Aspects
- Externality Empirics: Knowledge and Practice.

2.1 *The Big Picture: Evolving Perspectives*

The rationale for initiating a discussion on sustainable development with the big picture is self-explanatory in today's context. The Brundtland Commission, in its pursuit of a global agenda for change, had early on identified that the concern was for three interlocking crises that the globe faced: an environmental crisis, a developmental crisis and an energy crisis (WCED, 1987). The three key advisory panels set up on energy, industry and food security to support the commission's work had strong participation from India. That integration is the key to advancing well-being is also well recognised in the framing of the Sustainable Development Goals (SDGs); that action in one area will affect outcomes in others, and that creativity, knowhow, technology and financial resources from all of society are necessary to achieve the ambitious SDG targets (Goals et al., 2020). The system view is as critical as the specifics of associations and causes that lead to resilient sectoral solutions and sustainability in society. The grounded realities of the science–policy interface are equally critical to achieving success in pursuing the goal of sustainable development.

2.2 *The Energy Scenario: Dilemmas and Opportunities*

The energy sector has been a key player in discussions of sustainability, especially for India where significant technological advances in conventional forms of energy supply coexist with fairly low levels of per capita energy consumption. Energy policy grapples with formidable challenges in balancing efficiency, equity and sustainability issues in striving to achieve energy security. The dominant share of fossil fuels in the primary energy mix on the one hand and increasing import dependence for meeting the primary energy needs for a growing economy on the other manifests in a gradual pacing of the much-needed transformation and adaptation of India's energy system. The range of topics in the energy sector on which scholarship has emerged is vast. There can be no two opinions that the attainment of sustainability in the Indian context will depend on the concerted efforts in the energy sector to deal with several of its dilemmas and exploit the potential opportunities.

2.3 *Sustainability Cross-Cuts: Developmental Aspects*

The mainstreaming of sustainability aspects into topics conventionally perceived to fall in the preeminent domain of development is inevitable for the transition to a sustainable economy. One such dimension involves resorting to a framework of the circular economy, compared to a linear one, that gives due considerations to the feedback impacts on the natural environment emanating from the process of economic growth and development. This, in turn, implies that the strategies in pursuit of economic growth and development in emerging economies such as India should lay adequate emphasis in terms of its quality through protecting the interests of the vulnerable sections of the population, promoting resilience of production systems, the evolution of the institutional and governance structures and envisioning the economy-wide impacts of the transitioning phase. Such considerations, however, if ignored can create much disquietude for well-being, not only in the long term but also undermine the peace and tranquillity in the immediate and near term, a necessary prerequisite for economic progress and prosperity.

2.4 Externality Empirics: Knowledge and Practice

Externalities are core to the discussions of sustainability in economics. The unaccounted environmental effects of production and consumption are often ignored in the science and practice of conventional economics. Bad outputs and negative externalities are integral to the economic systems which in turn pose threats to life on the planet. Production spillovers such as environmental degradation, resource depletion, ecological imbalance and so on are serious concerns in the face of the current climate crises and sustainability threats of the economic system. Different types of environmental hazards emanating from different economic activities need policy attention and institutional intervention of varying degrees in designing the appropriate mitigation strategies. The trends in behaviour, knowledge and practice provide inputs to address the issues related to environmental externalities in the larger backdrop of sustainable production, consumption and overall development.

3 The What Question

This section presents a brief description of the contents of each chapter, highlighting the main points and arguments made by the respective chapter authors.

3.1 The Big Picture: Evolving Perspectives

The dilemma faced by developing countries in fast-tracking economic well-being, which undeniably can deliver substantially on several other fronts of social progress, is how to address the trade-offs in prioritising immediate needs over longer-term sustainability considerations. Economic growth has no doubt helped to address several concerns such as poverty, but as the size of the cake has grown, increasingly the distribution of the cake has raised troubling questions for social well-being, including environmental impacts. Climate change has since emerged as a major challenge that threatens to sharpen existing inequities while creating new ones, adding layers of complexity to conventional focus on economic growth and its fallouts. If climate action is often considered to be something that may be postponed for the present, the COVID-19 pandemic was a rude awakening, interpretable as an environmental shock. While its implications for economic and social well-being are here to stay for a while, it prompts thinking on whether the shock could lead to the much desired, across the board big nudge for a sustainable future.

In the specific context of India, the immediate concerns can appear overwhelming, many of them interconnected. A key within country concern for development and well-being is urbanisation—it has become a talking point for researchers for its own merits as well as because of its linkages with other socio-economic concerns. Getting the basics right in how we measure and relate to it is important. An equally important concern is how market structures help or hinder the cause of economic progress which again links with several aspects of both international and domestic agencies through trade, competitiveness, access to finance and technology. Understanding the role of policy in supporting synergistic interconnections for sustainable development is most crucial in ensuring that a multitude of goals can be met in the pursuit of sustainability. In the broader framework, monetary policy along with other policy forms has its role to play, more so when the focus is on economic recovery with a human face.

In the forward-looking paper titled "Fast-Growing Developing Countries: Dilemma and Way Forward in a Carbon-Constrained World", Joyashree Roy, a well-known expert on climate change issues, collaborates with co-authors Nandini Das, Shreya Some and Hasan Mahmud to reflect on the dilemmas and the way forward for the countries moving on a fast growth path in the current world facing severe environmental challenges. The calculation and comparison of national progress are still dominated by the conventional metric, namely the gross domestic product (GDP). While some countries recorded more than seven per cent annual GDP growth rate in this century, many others experienced the same in the last century. Roughly thirty percent of human settlements in the countries traditionally classified as developing have already followed the path of economic progress shown by the highly industrialised countries of today. Their journey in the post-World War II period has proved successful in improving individual quality of life. They are on the way to adopting more solutions for improving social as well as environmental quality. So, the real question is about the remaining seventy per cent who as a country group are the true representatives of the global south. The question of broader equity and justice demands that there can be no denial of progress for this part of the world, given that no difference exists in human aspiration levels in any part of the globe. The faster is the movement towards bridging the gap, the faster will be the attainment of peace and harmony in a society that can wisely deliver the global common good. There is a growing realisation that these debates are emerging mostly due to the changing climate and carbon constraints in this part of the world. This in turn may delay the basic development process further and bring in greater inequity while experts search for better alternative development strategies. So, the fast-developing countries will need to maintain high economic growth rates merely for providing universal access to a decent life. The authors have presented two short case studies of India and Bangladesh. Poised for fast growth, Bangladesh is setting some new examples of social transformation unlike many predecessors during the last century. The narrative of Indian progress so far has been along the incremental path of growing energy efficiency and inducting renewable energy within the chosen option to show how it can transform ambition into reality.

In his paper titled "Looking Beyond the COVID-19 Pandemic: What Does Our Future Hold?", Anup Sinha presents a topical discussion on an inclusive and sustainable future, weaving a narrative with masterly subtlety, clarity and objectivity in the post-pandemic world. While elaborating on the various impacts of and responses to the COVID pandemic, the author focusses on the idea of the pandemic as a complex environmental shock. The pre-pandemic, global economic slowdown in 2019 where carbon emissions did not fall in spite of a situation of slackening demand coalesces with many other issues such as increasing authoritarianism, inequality and weakening of environmental laws, to set the stage. The chapter discusses wide-ranging economic, political, social and environmental impacts attributable to the pandemic, subsequent control measures and the policies introduced by different countries, leading to a discussion on possible futures. The economic impacts in relation to output, jobs, investment and stock markets, social implications of the pandemic and social distancing measures, impacts on human behaviour and mental health, and various monetary and fiscal policy actions undertaken by different countries, especially the policy responses in China, USA and India are presented in some detail. In particular, the positive and negative impacts on the environment are elaborated upon. The lessons for society as we live through the pandemic are mapped, and the possible alternative futures that can emerge are discussed. The lessons include reducing the ecological footprint and consumerism, improving policy responses, global sharing of innovations, technological developments, access to affordable education and health care, and the need for transcending entrenched identities. In terms of the future, three options are presented: business-as-usual as though the pandemic had not occurred; a taking over by authoritarian regimes; and the evolution of a more sustainable system. What will the future be? In the wise words of the author: "It is for us as citizens to decide how much we assert our agency, communicate with one another, and restart the world".

Amitabh Kundu's paper on "Identification of Urban Centres for Conducting Population Census; Need for Combining GIS with Socio-economic Data" is a combination of rigorous empirical analysis and an adept review of the conceptual issues involved in identification of urban centres and determining their boundaries. A renowned expert on urbanisation, the author brings his experience to bear in taking a critical look at the prevailing procedures of distinguishing urban centres from rural areas (and related terms), proposes new approach for a real classification and details out an interesting operational methodology to address the current deficiencies in the system, followed in South Asian countries in conducting their population census. The chapter provides insights into the current international practices with respect to the definition of urban areas and criteria used for areal classification globally, with focus on South Asian countries (Sri Lanka, Pakistan, Bangladesh and India). An examination of the methodologies used by global institutions for delimiting urban centres' boundaries and estimating urban population—OECD methods, the framework used in World Development Report and the e-Geopolis project—reveals the importance of combining the GIS data with socio-economic statistics obtained through census, survey or administrative records for capturing the dynamics of recent developments. It demonstrates the relevance of the GIS data, illustrating how existing census procedures fail in including settlements having high current population density and expanding built-up areas within the urban frame. The fourfold criteria proposed for areal classification are based on a selection of a few from a range of demographic and socio-economic indicators and combining these with information built through satellite imagery. The method proposed is illustrated with a case study of Sri Lanka, comparing results with their official estimates. The chapter makes a valuable contribution by integrating the GIS technology with socio-economic data and highlights how existing estimates of urban population would change as a result of the new approach, as practised in a few countries.

"Competition, Technology, Innovation and Exports: Contemporary Theoretical Insights" by Sugata Marjit, Suryaprakash Mishra and Moushakhi Ray is an important contribution to this book as it brings to the fore key enduring and emerging issues of relevance for economic development in India. This scholarly contribution bears the imprint of Marjit's exceptional achievements in the field and provides an invaluable, updated review of theoretical frameworks and critical understanding on the role of competition in innovation and export decisions, along with technology and financial factors. Topics covered include firms' choice of collusion or competition and the role played by technology in this choice, innovation incentives and decisions by firms, the role of competition and technology on the export profitability of the firms, credit market and firm behaviour. Important insights are gained. Replacing constant marginal costs with increasing marginal costs in models for behaviour of firms has important implications for market structure and welfare outcomes and on firms' innovation and export decisions. The inclusion of financial factors in an explicit manner when looking at export decisions of firms facing credit constraints is another key consideration. Expansion of smaller firms is hampered by finance cost constraints, while these very constraints support domination by the larger firms. In conclusion, the authors state that "the assumption of credit market perfection and linear costs both have deterred a healthy growth of the literature in trade and industrial organization".

The pursuit of economic growth is considered critical for eradicating poverty and undertaking redistributive measures for addressing inequality concerns (SDGs 1 and 10). Managing inflation, especially food inflation, lies at the core of strategies designed to end hunger and achieve food and nutrition security (SDG 2). Ananya G. Dastidar and Kajleen Kaur make a meaningful contribution as they seek to evaluate the performance of monetary policy in terms of its effectiveness in influencing the rate of economic growth and controlling inflation for India in their essay titled

"An Evaluation of Monetary Policy in India: A Sustainable Development Perspective". The authors take up an interesting issue that has a wide-ranging appeal in the current context. The ongoing COVID-19 pandemic poses unprecedented challenges in achieving the SDGs, especially in mitigating poverty, inequality and ensuring food and nutrition security. The massive socio-economic disruptions caused by the pandemic across the world have adversely affected the functioning of the economic systems, increased volatility in financial systems owing to greater risks and uncertainties, and impacted the access to essential goods and services. They review the various transmission channels for the monetary policy in terms of their effectiveness for the Indian economy. On the basis of an extensive literature review, they conclude that there has been relative importance of the interest rate and credit channels, while asset price and exchange rate channels seem to appear relatively ineffective in affecting aggregate output in the post-liberalisation period. The chapter underscores the relevance of supporting institutions and of business and consumer confidence in influencing the level of consumption, private investments and job creation through monetary policy. In the advent of the global financial crisis, it is observed that the advanced economies seem to be using the policy rate to stabilise the output gap, whereas, in the emerging economies, it is the stabilisation of headline inflation, especially food inflation that seems to be a central concern. The chapter explores the prospects of monetary policy during the ongoing pandemic in stabilising the Indian growth momentum and combatting the severity of a potential recession and overcoming the adverse impact on well-being. The authors also emphasise the need for further research to inform the policy debate in this regard.

3.2 *The Energy Scenario: Dilemmas and Opportunities*

It is crucial to develop an understanding of the reform process that has been underway for this vital sector of the economy since the 1990s and to explore its key achievements such as the reforms in the power sector and gains from energy efficiency. The electrification of households and meeting their cooking energy needs through clean fuels is a pressing need. In the context of increasing mechanisation and intensity of resource use, sustainability of the agricultural sector is inextricably linked to the fostering of green growth. Further, the unprecedented crises that have unfolded in the wake of the COVID-19 pandemic have far-reaching implications for the business environment as well as the smooth functioning of the energy sector owing to the globally integrated energy markets. It is crucial that the vulnerability of the institutions such as energy markets should be assessed for making them resilient.

In an enquiry into the journey of the power sector reforms, Somit Dasgupta presents an insightful discussion on its evolution over time and the architecture behind this process in the chapter titled "The Genesis of Electricity Reforms in India and the UK, Its Repercussions and the Way Forward". The Indian power sector came down to almost a dead end in the 1980s with huge losses incurred by the state electricity boards. This justified the initiation of the reform process in the 1990s. It involved several amendments to the electricity laws, tweaking the role of the Central Electricity Authority and a Common Minimum National Action Plan for Power in the first phase of reforms. Subsequently, the second phase witnessed a couple of acts such as the Electricity Regulatory Commissions Act, 1998, and the Electricity Act, 2003. The author has made a comparison between India and the UK in the power sector restructuring programme with specific reference to competition. The major features of the latter include the unbundling of the utilities, separation of distribution and retail, the introduction of retail competition, creation of a power pool, initiation of contract for differences and the introduction of the New Electricity Trading Arrangement. The author brings his considerable experience and knowledge of the sector to opine that the Indian restructuring programme has been one of mere unbundling into separate entities which failed to make any material difference in terms of efficiency and growth. The chapter contains a description of how the power sector performed in India after restructuring was done and the contribution of the regulatory bodies in this process. The regulatory bodies have not been adequately proactive as in the case of the UK and have degenerated into passive organisations doing the government's bidding. The author suggests a way forward to improve the functioning of the distribution sector, and the recommendation is one of privatisation of the distribution companies. It is strongly felt that the public-owned discoms can never deliver efficiently due to the lack of accountability which gets further complicated on account of government interference. Therefore, competition and privatisation of distribution are keys to success, along with the simultaneous creation of markets for both generation and retail, along with the strengthening of our regulatory institutions.

Different states responded to the national policy reform agenda differently and evolved policies to suit their local economic and sociopolitical conditions. The political climate and institutional structures prevailing in the states play a crucial role in the effectiveness and success of the implementation of national policies. Md. Zakaria Siddiqui skilfully weaves varying institutional dimensions in presenting the case of the electricity sector reforms in the Indian state of Bihar in his essay titled "Embeddedness of Economic Reforms in Regional Political Climate: A Case of Delayed Reforms in Bihar's Electricity Sector". The story of Bihar's power sector performance can be characterised by two significant factors, namely change in the government and bifurcation of the state. The previous political regime is known to have practised a well-articulated strategy of "state incapacity by design". It is interesting to note that this state-motivated destruction of public sector is deeply rooted in caste politics, a dominant social institution in Bihar. Since the public sector bureaucracy was dominated by the so-called upper caste officials, a political party that represents the marginalised poor found it suitable to paralyse the bastion of the privileged, the economic cost of which became very high. Uninterrupted power supply became a luxury commodity for the people in the wake of systemic failure of the power sector. The scenario changed with a change in the political climate when the incumbent head of the state took up the electricity sector reforms with high priority. Several measures have been taken so far in the spirit of good regulatory governance. The electricity sector of Bihar ventured into the expansion of network and consumers, designated critical role of the holding companies after unbundling, introduced a pool of distribution franchisees, outsourced the process of revenue collection and so on. On the one hand, subsidies have been provided to retain the domestic consumers, and financial resources have been made available at opportune time on the other. Several organisational changes and coordination between political and executive leadership have led to a remarkably better performance of the sector. Use of renewable resources has been given a boost as part of a larger national and global agenda. The recent records of the power sector are a welcome change, though delayed, in the history of the state.

Energy-efficient behaviour is a vital strategy in a carbon-constrained world for decoupling the process of economic growth from energy use and achieving sustainable energy use. In the context of developing economies, there arises a need for suitable policy interventions for promoting such behaviour and thereby ensuring concerted efforts towards bridging the energy efficiency gap. Efficient energy consumption behaviour across economic sectors would be instrumental in reducing the energy intensity of the gross domestic product and can also contribute to climate goals. Sangeeta Bansal and M. Rahul present a focussed and well-balanced discussion on the various policy measures that have been adopted by the government of India to promote energy efficiency across energy-consuming sectors in their chapter "Towards an Energy-Efficient Economy: Policy Measures by Government of India". They attempt an interesting expert assessment of the energy efficiency programmes and policies and the choice of economic instruments resorted to in bridging the energy efficiency gap for the Indian economy. The institutional framework for energy efficiency in India is based on the Energy Conservation Act, 2001, subsequently amended in the year 2010, which led to the creation of the Bureau of Energy Efficiency (BEE). Several programmes have been initiated by the BEE covering a wide range of sectors (namely households, buildings, electrical appliances, demand-side management in agriculture and municipalities, as well as micro, small and medium enterprises and large industries), and set of economic instruments adopted includes subsidies, standards and labelling, cap and trade scheme as well as information dissemination programmes. They report that as per the official estimates, the total cost savings and CO_2 emission reduction achieved in India through the implementation of energy efficiency schemes stood at Rs.53,000 crores and 108.28 million tonnes (MT) in 2017–18 and that increased to a level of Rs.89122 crores and 151.74 MT, respectively, for 2018–19. Further, based on an extensive literature review of studies assessing the efficacy of India's energy efficiency schemes, the authors make interesting policy suggestions in this regard for the times ahead.

Access to affordable clean energy is one of the announced goals of sustainable development (SDG 7). Lack of adequate, affordable and clean energy services often lead the households to vicious cycles of deprivation, lower-income and unhealthy living conditions. The use of the modern forms of energy is essential to eradicate poverty, improve the economic condition, generate employment opportunities and promote sustainable human development. Although there has been a significant increase in the use of clean fuels for cooking in recent years, a large part of rural India is continuing with the use of unclean fuels like biomass (fuelwood, dung cake, etc.) and kerosene in their households. Chetana Chaudhuri uses statistical inference techniques to investigate whether the households are actually climbing the energy ladder by switching fuels or are they stacking multiple fuels despite an access to clean energy "Climbing Energy Ladder or Fuel Stacking in Indian Households: A Multinomial Logit Approach". The study finds that rural households often stack multiple fuels and do not switch completely to cleaner fuels. Such choices are based on a multitude of considerations, such as affordability, accessibility, monthly per capita expenditure and ownership of cultivable land on the one hand and several socio-economic conditions on the other. Some interesting insights are presented. Family size, occupational category, social groups such as caste and religion, age, gender and educational level of the heads of the households are some of the determining social factors in the rural sector. On the other hand, rich households in urban areas tend to use cleaner fuels such as LPG and kerosene, while poor households rely mostly on the traditional forms of energy. The energy ladder is more observable in the urban areas where the household shifts from unclean fuels to clean fuels with increases in income and standard of living. Biomass is considered to be a polluting fuel because of the associated risk of indoor pollution. Chaudhuri recommends greater use of biomass in the long run in view of its renewable and biodegradable nature. The use of biomass can be promoted through use in pollution-less devices and technologies, such as biomass briquettes, biogas and improved chullahs. Necessary infrastructure, proper maintenance and lowered capital cost of installation can make this fuel option commercially viable and economically attractive, over and above being an environmentally sustainable option.

Manoj Bhatt and Surya Bhushan have examined an extremely relevant concern, namely the intensity of energy usage in the agricultural sector in various states of India in the post-WTO period. The picture sketched in the investigation titled "Understanding Energy Use in Indian Agricultural Production System in Post-WTO Period" demonstrates that spatial and temporal distributions of agricultural productivity vary markedly across the Indian states. The post-reform and post-WTO decade of the 2000s have been unprecedented for Indian agriculture. On the one hand, the sector recorded 3.8% annual growth in value-added since 2004–05 which is the highest since 1950–51. On the other hand, the absolute number of cultivators and agricultural labourers started to fall for the first time in the history of Indian agriculture. The challenges of sustaining food security and promoting growth seem more difficult now than in the past. Sustainable production in agriculture is facing challenges with a decline in the quality of land and water. Moreover, Indian agriculture has undergone some structural shifts in terms of the composition of the input–output mix, such as energy, labour and so on. Human labour, animal labour and electricity are important inputs to agricultural production. Recently, there have been significant changes in farm power availability. There has been a rise in the use of electricity and fossil energy accompanied by a decline in that of agricultural workers and draught animals. Differences in agriculture and infrastructure are the largest sources of inequality among the various regions of India. Further, the results indicate that the highly productive states have seen a negative response of animal labour and chemical fertiliser use in food grain production. Despite some significant changes in the overall structure and intensity of energy consumption in Indian agriculture in the last ten years, the regional disparity persists across the Indian states. The authors' intensive analytical discourse concludes that there is a greater need for introducing technological change involving energy-efficient farm machinery, electricity and human labour. Additionally, initiatives must be taken for promoting alternative renewable sources of energy involving technologies, institutions and policy measures.

Kaushik Ranjan Bandyopadhyay analyses with qualitative acumen the impact of the novel coronavirus disease on the global oil market in the chapter titled "COVID-19 and the Big Oil Price Crash: Exploring the Anatomy". COVID-19 has affected the world in several ways ranging from ecology and environment to multiple sectors of the economy. The oil market is one such area that witnessed a big price crash during the periods of worldwide lockdown. Crude oil prices have fallen drastically since the beginning of 2020 driven by the lethal economic contraction caused by the pandemic. The suspension of an OPEC-NOPEC (OPEC+) deal due to the defection of the Russians and the eventual price war waged by Saudi Arabia led to a protracted disequilibrium and volatility in the world oil market. Several energy companies turned bankrupt, and the so-called American energy dominance got battered. This resulted in huge job losses and weakening of the financial institutions that have been backing these industries. The coupling of unprecedented demand and supply shocks tested the oil market and its storage capacity to the limits. The current chapter offers scrutiny of such issues and imbalances that have been building in the system dynamics of oil markets. There was a serious crisis of physical storage capacity to park the excess global oil supply, leading to upward pressure on land storage costs worldwide and raising the rate of crude oil maritime shipping. The escalating glut of oil made global storage capacity (onshore plus offshore) gradually reach its limits and created more volatility in the market. Bandyopadhyay, in his discourse on this topical issue, is apprehensive about the possibility of a return to "normal" for the energy sector that has been bruised by the historically steepest slide in crude prices. With the emerging trends of "work from home" under the "new normal", the oil demand from the transport sector and energy demand from the offices for cooling and heating purposes may remain low. As a result, the volatility of the oil sector may continue for a long time.

3.3 Sustainability Cross-Cuts: Developmental Aspects

One of the central themes in the pursuit of sustainable development is to ensure the co-evolution of the human systems and the natural systems over time and space while promoting resilience, stability and diversity. In the context of economic systems, this implies fulfilling development objectives while maintaining social cohesion. On the environmental front, it involves putting in place an efficient governance system facilitating the sustenance of the productive capacity of the economy (inclusive of its natural capital base) while addressing the conflicts between the ecological and economic sectors.

Ecological limits threatening human existence and economic prosperity are the reality of the twenty-first century. With the growing realisation of the possible limits to growth, Sustainable Development Goal 12 spells out a target of ensuring sustainable consumption and production patterns, thereby laying down the path towards a sustainable economy. Globally, the concept of circular economy (CE) is being propounded as an effective means of ensuring sustainable consumption, production and waste management patterns for the future. This can potentially foster the preservation of the natural resource base by ensuring optimum resource utilisation, waste management and minimisation of the negative environmental externalities caused by anthropogenic action. In this context, Robin Singhal presents an in-depth review of the conceptual foundations of the CE as a "Recourse to the Circular Economy: The Path Ahead". This is based on the idea that the economy is a closed and circular system, subject to natural boundaries and circular interlinkages. It becomes a sustainable system, wherein wastes generated get recycled, just as in the case of the natural systems. He further analyses the scope and methodological framework of CE in terms of its interlinkages with other fields such as industrial ecology and ecological economics. However, Singhal feels that the critical third dimension of sustainable development, namely social sustainability, remains lacking in these integrations while economic and environmental dimensions are resorted to in terms of linkages. Finally, the author has critically evaluated the recent initiatives taken by the Government of India towards the adoption of resource efficiency and circular economy. Putting forth an economic perspective towards CE, he has highlighted some thought-provoking potential hindrances in its mainstreaming from the point of view of the economic methodology followed in the neoclassical tradition of environmental and resource economics. The author concludes that there is an urgent need to move beyond the techno-centric and business-oriented understanding of CE to a framework that attempts to integrate the socio-economic realities and development priorities of the developing nations. The governments will have to carefully handle the trade-offs involved in public policy interventions, business environment and social acceptance during the intervening transition phase.

While coal has great economic significance, it has major environmental externalities and adverse health impacts. Ambient air pollution originating in the coal mining areas impacts the environment and economy severely in the form of health externalities. Longer exposure to air pollution leads to high morbidity, increased respiratory illness, asthma, high blood pressure, reduced lung functions, heart diseases and many more. The global economic cost of air pollution has been estimated to be approximately 3.3% of the world's GDP and the estimated costs of ambient air pollution alone accounted for 5.4% of India's GDP in 2018. In the chapter titled "Ambient Air Pollution and Respiratory Illness: A Study in Opencast Coal Mining Region of Odisha", Indrani Roy Chowdhury, along with her co-authors, Anushree Paul and Tapaswini Nayak argue convincingly that the economic cost is underestimated, as pollution hazards in many mining infested remote corners of India are left unaccounted in the estimation. The mining regions of India, mostly located in the vast tracts of remote forests inhabited by the marginalised tribal people, face the greatest environmental externalities and adverse health impacts. The authors have studied the pattern of concentration of ambient air pollution in the open cast coal mining region of Mahanadi Coal Fields (MCL), Angul-Talcher in Odisha and the associated vulnerability of the people living in the proximity of the mining region towards respiratory illness (RI). It has been observed that the probability of self-reported RI episodes is negatively affected by the distance to mine, and is positively affected by seasonality, socio-economic parameters, health indicators and demographic determinants. The study further examines the determinants of the mitigating expenditure on RI undertaken by the people in the vicinity of the mining region. Health expenditure incurred on RI was found to be determined by the incidence and/or severity of RI, proximity to healthcare facilities and the overall health status. These findings provide some policy relevant insights into the adverse health externalities of open cast mining that are often ignored behind the obvious positive economic impacts of mining in developing countries characterised by laxer environmental regulations, weak institutions and disorganised civil societies.

K. S. Kavi Kumar in the chapter "Rice Production Systems and Drought Resilience in India" investigates the resilience of the rice production system in India with respect to the derived stressors of climate change such as drought. Using a district-level data set covering more than 300 districts spread across 20 Indian states over five decades, the study empirically investigates the extent of the impact of different drought conditions on rice yield and assesses the role of irrigation facilities in reducing such vulnerabilities. One of the deleterious effects of climate change is expected to unfold in the case of the agricultural sector having far-reaching implications for the human economy. Despite a declining trend in the contribution of the agriculture sector to the nation's gross domestic product, the vulnerabilities of food systems in the context of developing economies such as India are bound to have adverse socio-economic implications. A large percentage of the total workforce still depends upon this sector for their livelihood, and the resilience of this sector in the wake of climate change holds critical importance for several of the public programmes aimed at the attainment of the Sustainable Development Goals such as eradicating poverty (SDG 1), ensuring food security (SDG 2) and reducing inequalities (SDG 10). With his substantial expertise and experience in climate change-related policy issues in agriculture, Kavi Kumar finds that the rice yield has shown resilience to drought conditions across India but observes significant regional disparities. Also, the role of irrigation in ameliorating the adverse effects remains limited to the low and moderate drought conditions compared to severe droughts. It further underscores the need for augmenting farm management strategies as an effective means for dealing with severe droughts and emphasises the promotion of technology adoption through concerted efforts in the times ahead.

In the chapter titled "Water Disputes in the Cauvery and the Teesta Basins: Conflictual Federalism, Food Security, and Reductionist Hydrology", Nilanjan Ghosh and Sayanangshu Modak postulate that the water conflicts in India are essentially the results of three major policy-driven factors. These include the federal structure of the nation where water has been made part of the state list, the wrong delineation of the food security policy with food security being viewed through the lens of production and procurement of high water-consuming crops like rice and wheat, and finally the lack of an integrated ecosystem approach to understand the land–water–food nexus in the water policy of the nation. Management of natural resources is a major exercise in governance and that of the "fugitive" resource water is particularly complex because of its transboundary nature. The recent definition of transboundary waters incorporates waters crossing boundaries of any form, ranging from the international level to the most micro-level of the society including the sectoral boundaries. In fact, the most recent form of transboundary water conflicts occurs between the economic sector and the ecosystem sector, as human interventions over flow regimes for meeting short-term economic needs result in substantial losses for downstream ecosystems. Despite the imminent rationale and the traditional understanding that river basins are the ideal natural units for planning and management of surface water resources, there has been an equally dominant idea and evidence of fragmenting the basins for governance based on jurisdictions that were human-centric and solely focussed on the reductionist view of water as a stock of resource. The arguments have been elaborated in this paper with expositions from two transboundary water conflicts, namely the interstate water conflicts over River Cauvery involving Tamil Nadu, Karnataka, Kerala and Puducherry and the conflicts over River Teesta at various levels, such as Bangladesh–India, centre–state and economy-ecosystem. Nilanjan Ghosh partners with his co-author, to bring to bear his substantial experience with water governance and policy in arguing for a paradigm change from the reductionist approach to a holistic approach towards water governance, embedded in the emerging thinking of Integrated Water Resource Governance at a basin scale.

Meeta Keswani Mehra, Saptarshi Mukherjee, Gaurav Bhattacharya and Sk. Md. Azharuddin in their chapter "Renewable Energy in India: What It Means for the Economy and Jobs" conduct a very relevant and contextual empirical investigation of the linkages between important macroeconomic and demographic variables with renewable energy deployment in India covering the period from 1990 to 2016. The transformation and adaptation of energy system is one of the essential prerequisites in realising sustainable development goals. It is believed that the mainstreaming of renewable energy sources and technologies would not only yield environmental benefits but also their increased deployment would have stronger backward and forward linkages comparable to fossil energy for an economy. The purpose of the study is to explore both the long-run association between renewable energy deployment and major macroeconomic variables and developing an understanding of the potential short- to medium-term economic implications of the ongoing COVID-19 pandemic, along with capturing the overall energy transitions in India. The future projections of renewable energy generation and associated capacity and job creation are made for the period up to 2042 under three different scenarios, namely business-as-usual (i.e. continuation of the past trends and policies with no significant structural breaks), pessimistic scenario (a situation wherein all the key driving macroeconomic variables move in a manner in future years such that they adversely affect renewable energy diffusion) and an optimistic scenario (wherein the movement of the driving variables is such that these encourage a higher growth of renewable energy than the business-as-usual scenario). The analytical framing leads them to some interesting and policy relevant findings. The authors suggest that on the one hand factors such as a higher economic growth rate, a higher return on investment and a more remunerative tariff structure for renewable energy would expedite the deployment of renewable energy, while on the other hand, factors such as a higher fiscal deficit, higher subsidies to fossil energy and energy imports will retard the pace of its diffusion in the country. Given that a higher population level or higher energy access could imply greater reliance on fossil energy vis-à-vis renewable energy, there arises a need for a greater policy push for switching to renewable energy.

3.4 Externality Empirics: Knowledge and Practice

One way of considering economic growth and its resultant ecological threats is to adjust the estimates of the standard economic indicators for the impact on the natural environment given its role as a source and a sink. The true macroeconomic scenario can be understood only with adequate knowledge about the country's resource base and the condition of the associated ecosystem services. There is also a definite need for pro-environmental behaviour at the community level with regard to their decisions on production and consumption. Individual behaviour and community action must be based on the requisite knowledge about the concerned environmental issues, often supported by beliefs, instincts and sensitivity. In a world ridden with the uncertainty of outcomes, particularly in cases of environmental shocks and health issues, people rely on causal inferences for taking decisions about their actions. Everyday environmental problems, such as pollution, need to be analysed in a larger framework where socio-economic parameters indicate the true nature of people's short-term concerns and long-lasting impacts on health and overall existence on the planet. Appropriate policies for enhancing people's awareness, changing lifestyles and encouraging collective action can help combat environmental challenges and show the pathway towards a sustainable world. Science, state and society need to play a coordinated role in this regard.

In the chapter titled "Embracing Natural Resource Accounting in India: Some Reflections", Shalini Saksena discusses the limited scope and coverage of national accounts based on SNA and the conceptual framework and scope of the System of Integrated Environmental and Economic Accounting (SEEA). With the rising levels of production and consumption, recent economic growth is pushing the ecosystems towards their critical limits set by the availability of natural resources and environmental services. There is a growing realisation in the global community about the need to undertake prompt and effective measures to offset resource depletion and environmental degradation in order to sustain long-term growth. This has led to the search for appropriate indicators and accounting measures beyond the conventional macroeconomic indicators of economic growth such as GDP or GDP per capita. The conventional approach to the preparation of national accounts in most countries is primarily based on the System of National Accounts (SNA). Over the years, the accounting framework and methodology of SNA have been comprehensively updated in view of the evolving environment–economy interactions and occurrence of new phenomena in the world. However, SNA is conceptually based on the neoclassical market theory and it focusses on the key indicators that are based mostly on short-run Keynesian macro-models and not on any long-run growth theory and/or models. The SNA seems to be inadequate for obtaining information on the various determinants of growth and for measuring a country's sustainable development appropriately. Sustainability analyses require mainstreaming of a system of natural resource accounting that integrates information on the environment–economy interactions. The SEEA, adopted by the UNSD in 2012, provides the conceptual framework for understanding such interactions. This first international statistical standard for environmental–economic accounting framework along with its standardised methodology serves as a ready reckoner for countries trying to mainstream natural resource accounting. In this comprehensive and well-researched chapter, Saksena argues that widespread adoption of SEEA has the potential to support critical global initiatives such as the monitoring of SDG indicators, the post-2020 biodiversity agenda and the international climate policy. The Indian narrative on the initiatives by the government towards mainstreaming of natural resource accounting has also been critically evaluated by the author which she feels has been sporadic, albeit noteworthy and encouraging.

Anindita Roy Saha and Nawin Kumar Tiwary in their chapter "Environment and People: Reflections on Perception, Education and Behaviour" bring in fresh thinking on emphasising the need for incorporating social norms, competitions, group dynamics and other key insights from behavioural economics within the framework of environmental policy for raising people's environmental consciousness. In general, the pursuit of the goals of sustainable development calls for fundamental changes in the lifestyles and adopting pro-environmental behaviour in economic decision-making for affecting the much imperative transformation in the consumption patterns and production systems. Despite wide-ranging differences in the socio-economic indicators of well-being across countries and stark disparities in the standard of living within nations, the progress in traversing a path to sustainability as an international development agenda requires a reorientation of the people's value system to live in harmony with nature and curb their tendencies for wealth accumulation and consumerism at the expense of the natural environment. This necessitates concerted efforts towards raising environmental consciousness in general and imparting environmental education in particular. The authors argue that environmental consciousness is an outcome of specific psychological parameters or constructs related to an individual's inclination to participate in pro-environmental behaviour. An individual's pro-environmental behaviour can be strengthened in turn by general beliefs, certain attitudinal instincts and sensitivity that may be enriched by information, knowledge and training. In this regard, they convincingly highlight the role and importance of environmental education in ensuring both the enhancement of the discipline-specific environmental knowledge of students and facilitating the development of environmental thinking for realising sustainable development. Further, they carefully underscore the critical role played by major institutions such as educational institutions, family and public forums (such as media, non-governmental agencies and civil society organisations) in building a sustainable and resilient community through the promotion of environmentally responsible behaviour on the one hand and enhancing the awareness and preparedness for disasters on the other. Against this backdrop, they also discuss interesting findings in the Indian context from a set of three studies carried out in the National Capital Territory (NCT) of Delhi to provide relevant insights into the perception, education and connectedness of the members of the civil society through curriculum, training and information.

In a captivating discussion on "Uncertainty and Causality in Public Policy: The Cases of Heart Disease and Climate Change", Vikram Dayal uses the analytical framework of uncertainty and causality to examine cases of health issues, such as heart disease and climate change. Uncertainty is a key feature of the current world, and probability is the natural language of uncertainty. While considering the courses of action, uncertainty is faced along with some issues of causality. Causal inferences can provide the necessary information required for undertaking action. While causality is a law-like necessity, probability connotes exceptionality, doubt and lack of regularity. Expected utility in human action depends on both utility and probability, although the latter may be hard to assess. An economic framework that considers well-being over time points to the importance of an assessment of the physical impacts and the importance of the uncertainty of such impacts. Decisions about treatment for disease and combating climate change involve a deep structural uncertainty about what may go wrong and what potential damages are possible for the patient and the planet, respectively. Causal inference may inform us about both and thus help in making calculations that precede our actions. The author skilfully weaves into the narrative that while causality has a key role to play, there may be other factors, such as beliefs, communications and literacy that are crucial behind personal assessment and action. People may have good intuitive knowledge, beliefs and opinions instead of clear evidence and information. All these may be instrumental in creating a knowledge base, necessary for policy design, people's action and collective response to the uncertain events. Conditional probability, availability of knowledge, effective communication and people's perception can help take action in cases such as heart disease as well as climate change. Decisions to change lifestyle, prevent damage, reduce risk and delay action depend on the understanding of the complex issues pertaining to health threats and environmental challenges.

The study titled "Unbundling Air Pollution Concerns: A Closer Look at Socio-economic Factors" by Purnamita Dasgupta and Kavitha Srikanth examines the importance of considering socio-economic characteristics in managing air pollution. Air pollution has several adverse impacts on human health, labour productivity and agricultural yield and reduces profits to employers and businesses. It is a matter of great concern in India as it has increased in severity and spread over the last couple of decades, with several cities experiencing poor air quality for several months in the year. Particulate matter concentrations frequently exceed the National Ambient Air Quality Standards. Pollutant concentrations vary substantially in terms of the type of pollutant, geographical topography, meteorological conditions, natural capital endowments, transboundary conditions, demographic features and socio-economic characteristics. Consequently, states and cities in India are not similarly positioned to handle mitigation of air pollution. The authors examine the empirical relationship between air pollution and variables such as income, urbanisation, industrialisation, energy consumption, social development and green cover. Tackling pollution effectively depends on a host of interdependent factors, and engaging with both the supply and demand sides is critical. The drivers of change could be technological, social or economic in nature. The findings suggest that socio-economic determinants need to be explicitly accounted for and demand-side measures derived thereby tailored to deal with specific underlying economic causes at the state (or city) level, where decisions on economic activities and public sector resource allocations are taken. The authors also indicate that there is huge potential to tap into the synergies between air pollution reduction and climate mitigation, which holds across the spectrum of states covered in the analysis. The insights drawn from the paper make an important contribution to widen the analytical framework of the climate change discourse as well as in putting forth a more nuanced understanding to the current measures being considered to tackle pollution such as the National Clean Air Programme.

Given the laws of thermodynamics, it is argued that the negative externalities are not an exception rather in fact an inherent and general part of the production and consumption process. Consequently, the internalisation of such external costs remains fundamental to the realisation of sustainable production. The conventional production modelling approach, however, assumes free disposability of bad outputs similar to the free disposability of desired outputs and inputs. This assumption is untenable in the scenario where the scale and nature of anthropogenic activities across the world are being held accountable for the climate disturbances and threatening ecological order. Surender Kumar in the chapter "Modelling Production of Bad Outputs: Theory and Empirics" focusses on the issue of modelling bad or unintended outputs from the production process within the domain of applied production analysis and questions the conventional modelling approach given their assumption of free disposability of bad outputs and consequently the treatment of bad outputs as conventional inputs in the production modelling. He presents a salient discussion around the notion of weak disposability and costly disposability that has served as the basis of different production modelling approaches to account for bad outputs—joint production approach and by-production approach, respectively. Besides providing a comprehensive review of empirical techniques for the estimation of technology functions, this chapter further presents an insightful discussion on the estimation of shadow prices of bad outputs (such as carbon emissions) along with the productivity and efficiency estimates for the Indian thermal power sector. Such empirical applications of the modelling of bad output framework in turn reflect that it not only provides reliable estimates of the production processes but can also provides useful information on various public policy parameters for designing incentive-compatible environmental policy.

4 Concluding Remarks

The present collection of essays brings together central themes and key issues in the sustainable development discourse, of special significance in the developing country context. While no single book on the topic of sustainability can hope to be exhaustive in its coverage, the chapters in this collection present a fair mix of diversity and inclusivity of subjects. Sustainability will perhaps remain one of the largest challenges for humankind, and many attempts to push the boundaries of knowledge will continue. Scholarly contributions, practitioners' experiences and behavioural change from stakeholders will chart the path towards our common sustainable future. In this context, the discussions put forth are a combination of certain theoretical aspects and empirical findings on sustainable development for the Indian economy. This volume is a contribution to the ongoing and enduring journey of academic debate in sustainability and economic development with an understanding that the twenty-first century dawned on India with the highest growth rate being experienced since independence. However, there is an urgent need for her to adhere to the goals of attaining economic efficiency and equity while subscribing to the notions of sustainability. At the times, when the world is coming to terms with the increasing episodes of feedback impacts from the natural environment on the human systems, it becomes necessary to traverse a path of economic progress and prosperity in a sustainable manner. The contributions in this volume, thus, are a humble attempt to put forth thoughtful considerations deeply rooted in the socio-economic complexities and understanding embedded in the institutional environment of the world's largest democracy that conditions her pursuit of the sustainable development agenda.

References

Stiglitz, J. (2019, December 9). *The guardian. Fighting the climate crisis need not mean halting economic growth.* https://www.theguardian.com/business/2019/dec/09/climate-crisis-economic-growth-green-economy.

Steinbeck, Nobel Banquet speech. (1962). Retrieved October 2, 2020, from, https://www.nobelprize.org/prizes/literature/1962/steinbeck/25229-john-steinbeck-banquet-speech-1962/.

Sustainable Development Goals, UNDP. Retrieved October 2, 2020, from, https://www.undp.org/content/undp/en/home/sustainable-development-goals.html.

WCED, World Commission on Environment and Development. (1987). *Our common future*. Oxford: Oxford University Press.

The Big Picture: Evolving Perspectives

Fast-Growing Developing Countries: Dilemma and Way Forward in a Carbon-Constrained World

Joyashree Roy, Nandini Das, Shreya Some, and Hasan Mahmud

1 Introduction

The reporting and comparing national progress are still dominated by single metric of gross domestic product (GDP). In pre-COVID-19 period, countries like Bangladesh were experiencing ~ >7% annual GDP growth rate in this century, while many others experienced that in the past century (Mahmud & Roy, 2020). While China experienced high GDP growth of 8.26% annual average between 2009 and 2017, Costa Rica 3.47% annual average between 2009 and 2019, Finland 0.11% annual between 2009 and 2019 and some faced even negative growth rate (Greece—2. 81% annual average between 2009 and 2017), India's average annual GDP growth rate was ~7% during 1995–2007. IPCC report clearly shows that income growth per capita is contributing more compared to population growth to decadal emissions growth (Fig. 1) (IPCC, 2014). Question is do people want more products? Or do people want a healthy,

J. Roy (✉)
Asian Institute of Technology, Khlong Nueng, Thailand
e-mail: joyashreeju@gmail.com

J. Roy · N. Das
Global Change Programme, Jadavpur University, Kolkata, India
e-mail: nandiinii.das@gmail.com

S. Some
Global Centre for Environment and Energy, Ahmedabad University, Ahmedabad, India

Department of Economics, Jadavpur University, Kolkata, India
e-mail: ayerhs7891@gmail.com

H. Mahmud
Sustainable Energy Transition, EECC/SERD, Asian Institute of Technology, Khlong Nueng, Thailand
e-mail: hmplus02@gmail.com

P. Dasgupta et al. (eds.), *Sustainable Development Insights from India*,
India Studies in Business and Economics,
https://doi.org/10.1007/978-981-33-4830-1_2

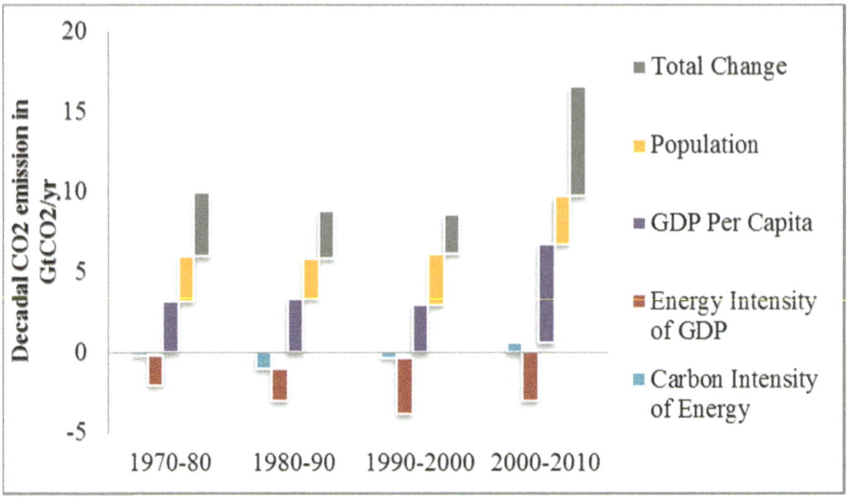

Fig. 1 Decomposition of the change in total emissions from fossil fuel combustion. *Source* (IPCC, 2014) (adapted)

cohesive, equitable, peaceful life? Global debates about how Global South (a highly contested concept) (Hayward & Roy, 2019) might rise over the course of the next one, two and three decades and Global North manage their irresponsible consumption (Schor, 2005) by the time the global population growth will be peaking, need more deeper analysis and reflection. In reality, there is vast literature (Golley & Meng, 2012; Chancel & Piketty, 2015; Jorgenson et al., 2019) which is trying to see this debate in terms of reducing inequity in consumption and access to good life (Hayward & Roy, 2019). Roughly, 30% of human settlements in traditionally classified developing countries have already followed the path of economic progress of the now highly industrialized countries in the Post-World War II period and have proved successful in improving individual quality of life and are on the way to adopting solutions for improving social and environmental quality (Singer, 2018). If we talk of broader equity and justice, there can be no denial of progress for the remaining 70% who in fact as a group are true representation of the Global South following various definitions provided in the literature (Hayward & Roy, 2019; Rao et al., 2019; Rao & Pachauri, 2017).

Many believe that if these debates are emerging mostly due to changing climate and carbon-constrained world, they are going to delay the basic development process for the less developed world further and lead to more inequity while experts search for alternative development pathways. It is also well understood that fast-developing countries will need to maintain this initial phase of high economic growth rates merely for providing universal access to a decent living. This is seen by many as a threat to increasing impact on climate change. However, recent research shows otherwise. Decent living standards for everyone in developing countries can be met with just 10% of the total energy consumption by the USA in 2020 (Rao et al., 2019; Millward-Hopkins et al., 2020).

Can fast-developing countries of this decade avoid what was known as the most efficient examples of land-use patterns in human settlement design, in which a strip of road provides space for multiple basic service delivery compatible infrastructure, including water supply pipelines, transport and mobility, telecommunications, drainage and sewerage, a grid-based electric supply, transmission and distribution network, street lighting and avenue plantation? What can be the options for human settlement design and living patterns for the half of the world? Today, when frustration is leading to social conflicts over lack of access to basic facilities, the first political step becomes adoption of the establishment of grid power connectivity, provision of public transport system and comfortable homes with basic service access. It is easy to see that lack of adequate infrastructure kills aspiration. Potatoes, tomatoes, garlic, onions, and other vegetables and fruits are left to rot in many villages in India and Bangladesh and in many less developed countries because of lack of on the farm cold storage facilities. Food processing industries are not able to move to the point of produce because of lack of reliable, adequate, productive power connections. Life therefore remains stuck at subsistence level, and the day ends with sunset. This has nothing to do with aspiration levels but with basic needs for a dignified living. Hot summer days of 40 °C and 98% humidity take a toll on life and labor productivity (NATCOM, 2018). It is not that hot tropical countries in South and South-East Asia do not want air-conditioned spaces. Nor can any ethical consideration be put forward to say that they should not aspire to have space cooling as they become affluent enough to afford it, on the grounds that it will mean increased global warming. These are the minimum aspirations for well-living and for productive thinking. What needs to be answered is how to provide these services with new innovative service delivery mechanisms. Today, thanks to improved irrigation facilities and advanced agricultural equipment, India produces no fewer than a dozen top-quality varieties of rice, cereals, mangoes and so on. If strategically managed, these resources would be able not only to feed India's own population but also to feed large parts of the rest of the world. The much-bruited adverse impact on soil quality and water table levels are misrepresentations of the environmental concerns: they result from a lack of investment in natural capital, i.e. the environmental resources management. Experiences in the field give grounds for hope; when orchards are seen replacing paddy cultivation in some of the degraded lands of Punjab in India, drip irrigation is replacing flooded irrigation, and vegetables and horticulture are bringing in more cash and adding diversity to dietary habits. However, these changes are propagating but not at an exponential rate which deserve attention.

We present in the sections below how the two neighbouring developing countries are navigating on their own despite the climate change and GDP growth in early development phase dilemma and are raising ambitions in tandem: *a way forward for development in a carbon constrained world*. Indian progress so far has been on incremental path of energy efficiency with cumulative positive impact through relative decoupling renewable energy growth to show how it can in reality enhance ambition

(Das & Roy, 2020). Indian agriculture also plays its role here. Adopting new activities that reduce non-energy-related emissions without reducing yield provides various other sustainable development-related co-benefits (Some, 2020) as well. These aid in achieving GDP growth in a sustainable way, as Indian agriculture contributes ~ 17% to India's GDP. Bangladesh poised for fast economic growth to catch up with developed country status (Mahmud & Roy, 2020) is setting some new examples of social transformation unlike many past century predecessors and holds a promise for leapfrog in sustainable energy transitions.

2 India's Achievements and Scope for Enhancing Contribution

2.1 In Energy Matters

Low-carbon strategies gained importance in Indian policy documents as well as a part of both environmental and developmental concerns. India is home to one-sixth of world's population but accounts for only 6.8% of global energy use and consumes only 5.25% of electricity produced globally (Enerdata, 2018). Economic development without proportional expansion of carbon emissions has become one of the major challenges in today's development strategy in India. Study shows that for both primary and secondary energy-related emissions, rising economic activity and fossil fuel intensity of these activities are the two dominant factors for increase in emission from various economic sectors in India (Dasgupta & Roy, 2002; Dasgupta & Roy, 2017). During the period 1990–91 to 2014–2015, the overall energy intensity in India declined from 0.007 Mtoe per billion INR of GDP to 0.004 Mtoe per billion INR of GDP with annual average decline of 2% (GoI, 2016). Industrial sector is found to be the highest contributing sector in CO_2 mitigation by reducing its energy intensity (Dasgupta & Roy, 2017). Apart from industrial sector, service sector has also contributed positively in reducing CO_2 emission by reducing energy intensity. This change is also boosted by the structural shift in the economic sectors. India is moving away from energy-intensive industries to relatively non-energy intensive industries (Das, 2019). Share of agriculture in GDP has gone down during 1990 and 2015, thereby reducing energy intensity by 5% (RBI, 2017). Share of service sector has also increased from 51 to 67% during study period (RBI, 2017). Service sector is less energy intensive with average energy intensity of 0.002 Mtoe/Rs billion of output compared to industry with average economy-wide energy intensity of 0.016 Mtoe/Rs billion. However, fuel mix with increasing share of non-fossil sources which has proved to be important mitigating factors for many countries is showing limited impact in Indian context across all the sectors. Primary reason is high domestic reserve of coal and socio-technical regime that influences the decisions towards maintaining the high share of coal in total energy use which is around 80%.

Power generation is still the most strategic sector in India from the perspective of economic and social development as well as from GHGs emissions (Das & Roy, 2020). When landscape-level pressures through global discourse are building stronger towards ending the use of coal in energy supply sector by 2050, it is becoming increasingly important for India to transform its energy supply sector towards a low-carbon one. Hence, the opportunity for low-carbon future of power sector in India lies in reducing energy intensity with introduction of more energy-efficient technology combined with low/no-carbon fuel mix at an exponential rate. Indian power sector is diversified in terms of different primary energy sources used in generation. Still dominant source is fossil fuels, mainly coal. Installed capacity categorized as thermal power, consists of coal, oil and natural gas accounts for nearly 67% of total installed capacity in India as on March, 2017 (CEA, 2017a).

Increase in share of variable renewables like solar and wind along with hydro and nuclear-based power generation is a very important part of Indian energy policy. Capacity of renewable electricity generation in India has annually grown by 38%, and its generation has shown even a higher annual growth rate of 45% during 1990–2015 which is highest among all the other sources (CEA, 2017a). India is running one of the largest committed renewable capacity expansion programmes in the world. India aims to achieve 175 GW of renewable energy capacities by 2022 (INDC, 2015) from 42.85 GW as on March 2016 (CEA, 2017b). At present, cumulative capacity of renewable energy sources contributes to almost 17.5% which is 57.25 GW of total installed capacity 326.83 GW in India (Fig. 2) (CEA, 2017a). The share of renewable grid capacity has increased over 13% between 2002 and 2015, and the installed capacity of grid-connected renewable energy has touched 38.1 GW in December 2015 with an increase of 18% from last year. Installed capacity of off-grid captive power from renewable sources has crossed 1.23GW (INDC, 2015). Though wind continues to dominate grid-connected power in India, solar power has shown the highest expansion of more than 100% increase. Untapped potential for overall non-fossil energy in India is more than 1000 GW which shows huge growth potential for renewable energy in India, and Government of India has set a target of more than 200 GW capacity by the year 2022 from all the non-fossil sources. Renewable sources contribute to almost 17.5% of total installed capacity in India (CEA, 2017a). The installed capacity of grid-connected renewable energy has touched 38.1 GW in December 2015 with an increase of 18% from the previous year. Installed capacity of off-grid captive power has crossed 1.2 GW. According to Indian Renewable Energy Status Report, 2014, total renewable energy potential from various sources in India is almost 250 GW. The untapped market potential for overall renewable energy in India is more than 200 GW that shows huge growth potential for renewable energy in India (NREL, 2014). This growth rate is particularly significant for solar energy.

Among other non-fossil sources, large hydropower is an important source of power generation in India. In 2015, hydropower share in total installed capacity was 17% (46.1 GW); out of that small hydro consists of 9% (4.1 GW) and large hydro is 91% (41.99 GW).

(INDC, 2015). At the end of March 2017, installed capacity from hydro was 44.5 GW which comes second after thermal power, accounting for 14% of the

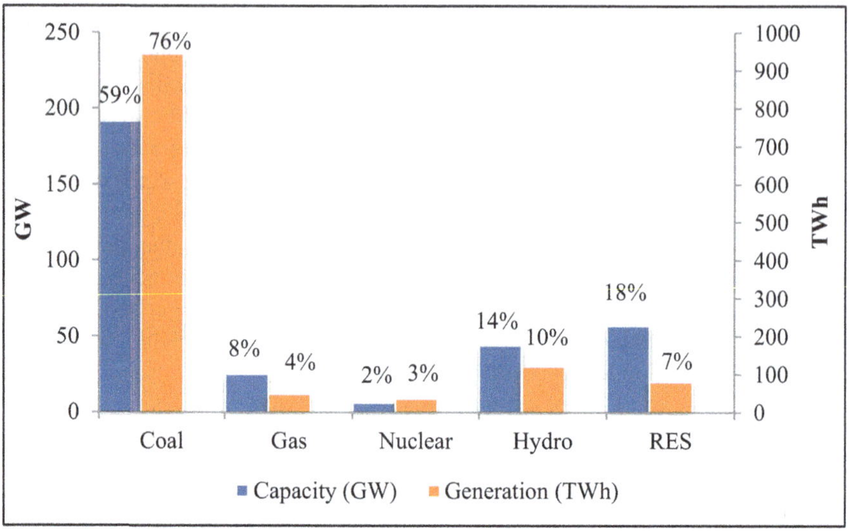

Fig. 2 Share of installed capacity and generation of different fuels (March 2016). *Source* (CEA, 2017a)

total installed power. Share of hydro in total capacity and also in generation started to decline since 1984–85 (CEA, 2017b). This falling capacity of hydro is mainly replaced by wind and solar. Nuclear-based capacity is given the foremost priority in India due to advantage of indigenous technology. The highest rate of annual growth from 2013–14 to 2014–15 in installed capacity was for nuclear power (20.92%) (GoI, 2016). With a 2% share in current installed capacity, total installed capacity of nuclear power in operation is 5.78 GW. In 2017–18, another 1.5 GW of capacity addition is expected to be happening. Additionally, six reactors with an installed capacity of 4.3 GW are at different stages of construction. It is expected to achieve 63 GW installed capacity by the year 2032. But this is highly dependent on the supply of the fuel (INDC, 2015) (Fig. 2).

Falling electricity intensity of the Indian economy at the end user point is one of the important contributors in the fall of CO_2 emission from power generation. It is estimated that during the study period (1990–191 to 2014–15), electricity-GDP elasticity in India is 0.85, and overall energy-GDP elasticity is 0.72 (CEA, 2017a; RBI, 2017). This implies that change in GDP is faster compared to change in energy and electricity. Cumulative effect of declining electricity intensity of the economy resulted in a decrease of 91.90 million tonne of CO_2 (Das, Low Carbon Growth: Alternative Pathways for India, 2019). During 1998–2015, falling electricity intensity acted as an inhibiting factor in CO_2 emission reduction by 35 and 76 million tonne, respectively (Das, Low Carbon Growth: Alternative Pathways for India, 2019). During this period, the ratio of change in electricity generation to change in GDP was below unity for a considerable period of time (Fig. 3). This implies that one unit of GDP can be increased by using less than one unit of expansion of electricity generation. This has

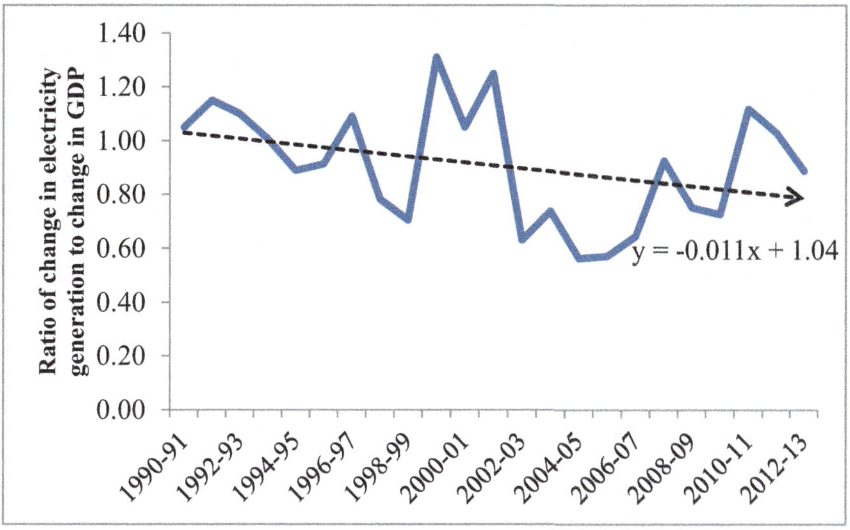

Fig. 3 Change in electricity intensity of GDP in India during 1990–2013. *Data Source* (CEA, 2017b; RBI, 2017)

resulted from enhanced efficiency of electrical appliances and resulting reduction in consumption of electricity. Government of India has introduced several policies to promote efficient use of energy under the Energy Conservation Act 2001 (EC Act). Bureau of Energy Efficiency (BEE) was set up as the statutory body to facilitate the implementation of the EC Act and promote energy efficiency in all sectors of the economy (Das & Roy, 2020). Ministry of Power through BEE has initiated a number of measures for standards and labelling of equipment and appliances, energy conservation building codes for commercial buildings and energy consumption norms for energy-intensive industries (Ministry of Power, GoI, 2018). These initiatives have contributed in falling electricity intensity per unit of GDP in India (Roy et al., 2018).

Emission coefficient, a measure of energy efficiency in fossil-based power generation (Shrestha et al., 2009), is another important factor which acts as an inhibiting factor on CO_2 emission reduction. Since 1991, decline in emission coefficient led to a fall in emission of CO_2 by 11 million tonne. Plant load factor (PLF), which is the ratio of actual output to optimum output of thermal power plants, is another important parameter of operational efficiency of thermal power plant. In Indian thermal power plants, PLF is declining over time. A study of Central Electricity Authority has shown that the reason behind this falling PLF of thermal power plant is due to increasing capacity of renewables and hydro and any increase in renewable electricity generation is mostly replacing the thermal generation (CEA, 2017b).

Following the discussion, it is evident that targeted policy in combination with technology choice can change the level of emissions from the power generation sector. Such actions and policies in energy sector can help in managing emissions in desired direction along with economic growth. In the past decade, India has seen how positive policy environment can foster effective change in case of use of LPG expansion. To improve the availability and access of clean cooking fuel, the Government of India adopted a policy package for the expansion of LPG connection comprising many complementary schemes which resulted in a shift from traditional biomass to the adoption of modern cooking fuel for 80 million households in rural India (Dabadge et al., 2018). According to a study of NITI Aayog of India, the demand of electricity in building and transport sector is going increase at a rate of 5.4–6.4% under different economic growths (NITI Aayog, 2016). The transition of cooking fuel from biomass to LPG has a scope for scale up and a significant potential for the transition towards an emission-free cooking with use of electricity as cooking fuel.

2.2 *In Non-Energy Matters: Indian Agriculture*

Indian agricultural sector has potential for adoption of new activities which not only increase yield but also help in mitigating GHG emissions. Indian agriculture offers the highest global mitigation potential from paddy cultivation (USEPA, 2019; Beach et al., 2015). India has adopted the National Mission for Sustainable Agriculture (NMSA) in 2010 which aims to reduce agricultural GHG emission. Other aims include improving food security, protecting natural resources like land, water, biodiversity and genetics and making agriculture climate resilient. All these objectives are related to Sustainable Development Goals (SDGs). There are several agricultural practices or mitigation options already in practice, but in smaller scale that can reduce non-energy-related GHG emission and provide SDG benefits. Here, we provide three such examples: changing paddy water management practices and planting practices; efficient use of nitrogenous fertilizer and climate-smart agriculture (CSA).

Adopting paddy cultivation practices like alternate wetting and drying (AWD), direct seeded rice (DSR) and system of rice intensification (SRI) can increase productivity by 35–40% (Deelstra et al., 2018; Kakumanu et al., 2018) depending on location. SRI provided a world record rice yield of 21.16 tons/ha (Kassam & Brammer, 2013) in Bihar. These practices help in reducing GHG, especially methane emission. Imbalanced used of nitrogenous fertilizer (urea) has increased nitrous oxide emission (Some et al., 2019). Studies (Basak, 2016; Datta et al., 2017) suggest that applying neem oil-coated urea reduces GHG emissions by 13% as compared to urea alone. Furthermore, efficient use of nitrogen fertilizer is possible by using smart technologies (e.g. optical sensors), as well as by changing the method of application (e.g. deep placement). Use of optical sensors in northern states of India has reported increasing wheat productivity by 0.20–0.53 t/ha, and nitrification inhibitors have increased maize production by 0.150–0.520 t (Basak, 2016). Climate-smart agriculture practices such as rice-shrimp cultivation, agroforestry and use of water management technologies ensure better livelihood security by increasing productivity, farm income and boosting employment opportunities (Sikka et al., 2018). A study based on Punjab reveals that CSA reduces GHG emission intensity by 34% (Groot et al., 2019).

Some (2020) has explicitly shown from extensive literature review that adoption of these new activities (mitigation actions) provide various SDGs-related co-benefits. For example, adoption of SRI requires less fertilizer (Kassam & Brammer, 2016), so it reduces water pollution through leakage of agro-chemicals (catering to SDG 6 and 14) (Rockström et al., 2017). Efficient use of nitrogenous fertilizers saves energy (SDG 7) due to reduction in application of fossil fuel-dependent synthetic fertilizer (Kritee et al., 2015) and also reduces leaching, thereby reducing water pollution (SDG 6 and 14), and hence aids in sustainable production (SDG 12). CSA practices sustain soil health (SDG 2 and 12) (Parihar et al., 2018), save water and increase water productivity (SDG 6) and improve energy use efficiency and energy productivity compared to traditional practices (SDG 7) (Groot et al., 2019). Therefore, to pave the path towards sustainable development of Indian agriculture, scaling up these new activities is a must.

There are few barriers (Table 1) that can impede this scaling up in India because of the economic background and landholding of Indian farmers. But the literature suggests that these barriers can be solved through expert consultation and multi-stakeholder partnerships. For instance, recently, farmers are opting out of the SRI practice mainly due to high initial cost and physical difficulties in using tiny seedlings along with the risk of seedling loss due to pest attack (Berkhout et al., 2015). But government initiatives like Joint Action Initiative on SRI (JaiSRI) in Telengana provide subsidies as guarantee against the risk of implementing these new SRI practices which incentivizes farmers to adopt SRI and also provide trainings to farmers.

Some et al. (2019) has shown link between fertilizer policy intervention and nitrous oxide emissions. Therefore, policy has a major role to play. Government of India (GoI) has mandated the production (both indigenously produced and imported) and use of neem-coated urea (as it reduced nitrous oxide emission) since 2016 but might need bigger push to ensure effective implementation. Besides policy, scaling up of new activities like efficient use of nitrogen fertilizer needs government intervention through a combination of appropriate financial incentives and awareness mechanisms. Community-based extension services and demonstration projects are also helpful to promote necessary knowledge required in adopting these new activities. Krishi Vikas Kendras (KVKs), the agricultural extension centres in India associated with the Indian Council of Agricultural Research (ICAR), are organizing short training programmes on balanced use of fertilizers for farmers and suppliers in various parts of India. The main impediment in upscaling CSA practices is high transaction cost (Westermann et al., 2015), high upfront costs of machinery, lack of site-specific scale-appropriate machinery in some locations, the traditional mindset on crop establishment and farm management of the farmers (Groot et al., 2019; Kakraliya et al., 2018; Sapkota et al., 2015). Government has started providing field-specific data to the farmers through mobiles or smart phones for better decision making related to amount of input use. But wide-scale scaling up of CSA in India needs data-driven technology generation process in Indian NARS (National Agricultural Research System) (Rao, 2018) so as to facilitate assimilation of field-specific

Table 1 Productivity increase, emission mitigation and barriers to adoption of new activities in Indian agriculture

New activities (mitigation options)	Productivity increase in India (per ha or %)	GHG emission mitigation (in % compared to conventional practices)	Barriers to widespread scaling up
Changing paddy water management practices and planting practices	35–40%[a]	~ 30%[b]	– Lack of proper financial and market-driven incentive for adoption and scaling up of this practice – Lack of capacity building of farmer
Efficient use of nitrogenous fertilizer	Wheat: 0.20–0.53 t/ha [c]	10–15%[b*]	– High cost for small landholders. High upfront cost – Access to information regarding such technologies
Climate-smart agricultural practices	Maize: 60–70%[d]	34%[e]	– Expensive for small landholders and small holdings do not generate adequate income to apply such technologies – Farmers may find it unattractive because they may have lower yield in the first year of adoption due to in-expertise in handling new technologies – Government extension agents have limited knowledge about the tools and techniques available for using CSA technologies in small land holding

Note Compiled by authors using the following sources: [a](Kakumanu et al., 2018; Deelstra et al., 2018), [b](Pathak et al., 2014), [c](Basak, 2016)-reported for optical sensors, *Site-specific N-use; [d](Chan et al., 2017); [e](Groot et al., 2019)-reported emission intensity data, conveying data-driven agronomic knowledge to farmers and government extension agents for proper decision making. For this to be effective, joint participation of Government and private sectors plays pivotal role. Therefore, scaling up of these agricultural activities will help in achieving sustainability in agriculture and pave the path towards sustainable development.

3 Bangladesh

Bangladesh with ~160 million people has attained lower middle-income country status in 2015 with ~6.5% yearly GDP growth rate over the last decade and attained over 8% growth in the 2019 (WB, 2019). This remarkable progress is driven by export, remittance, private consumption and investment, agricultural development (Asian Development Bank, 2018; LR Global Research, 2017; Rahman, 2016). The country represents a unique success story of the development from 1990 to 2016 with significant progress in the social development indicators. Poverty (headcount ratio at $1.90 a day) reduced from 44.7 to 14.5% (Fig. 4a), fertility rate came down from 4.3 to 2.1 birth per woman (Fig. 4b), infant mortality rates declined from 95.9 to 28.3 per 1000 live births (Fig. 4c), maternal mortality ratio declined from 569 to

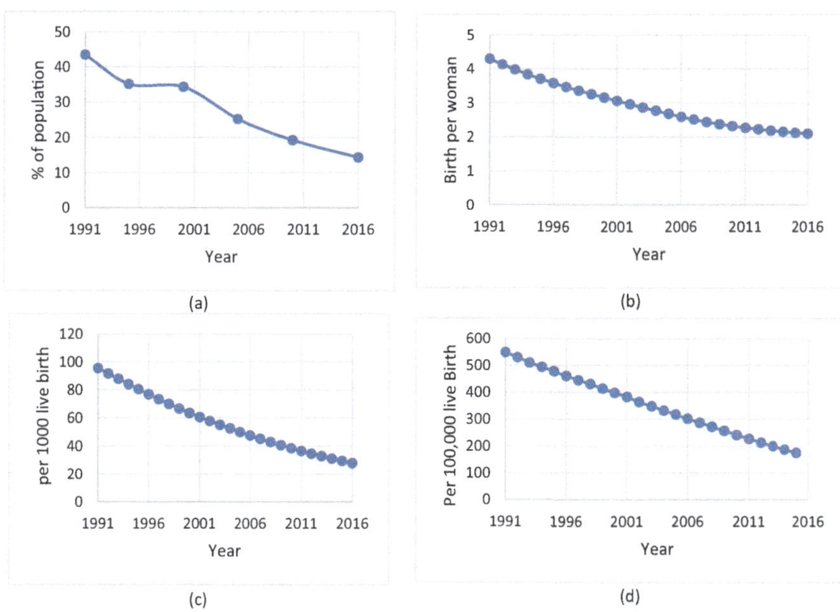

Fig. 4 Trend in **a** poverty, **b** fertility, **c** infant mortality and **d** maternal mortality rate of Bangladesh 1990–2016. *Source* (WB, 2019)

176 per 100,000 live births (Fig. 4d), achieved gender parity in school enrolment. (WB, 2019).

Analysis shows that the achievement of the export-oriented labor-based garments industry and the flow of remittance from labor migration are the drivers of social development in Bangladesh and ultimately raised the earnings and human capital at the grass-root level within the nation. The women-targeted microfinance programmes and the NGO-led social mobilization intensified this success (Al-Muti, 2014). Vision of digital Bangladesh by 2021 emerged in 2008 to enable Information and Communication Technology (ICT) penetration in all sectors of economic activity to act as powerful technology led disruption to advance the socioeconomic development. (Access to Information Program, 2009; Palak, 2015). For managing this disruptive economic transformation, multi-directional change has been planned, and policy push is supporting the growth of the power sector, social changes, especially women empowerment, girls education, children's health improvements (life expectancy is now 72 years), population growth reduction, NGO participation in development sector and microcredit programme stimulating social interactions and involvement of rural women in economic activity (Basu, 2018; Mahmud et al., 2013).

Evidence clearly shows the rise of Asian economic power centres in the past century like Singapore, South Korea, Malaysia, China which fueled their growth by heavy dependence on fossil fuel. Bangladesh is although not a major exception but one advantage which the country enjoys over India and China is due to the domestic natural endowment of natural gas as opposed to coal which has so far been fueling the economic growth. Figure 5 shows the comparative analysis of energy and GDP growth rates of these countries in their fast economic growth phase (mentioned in

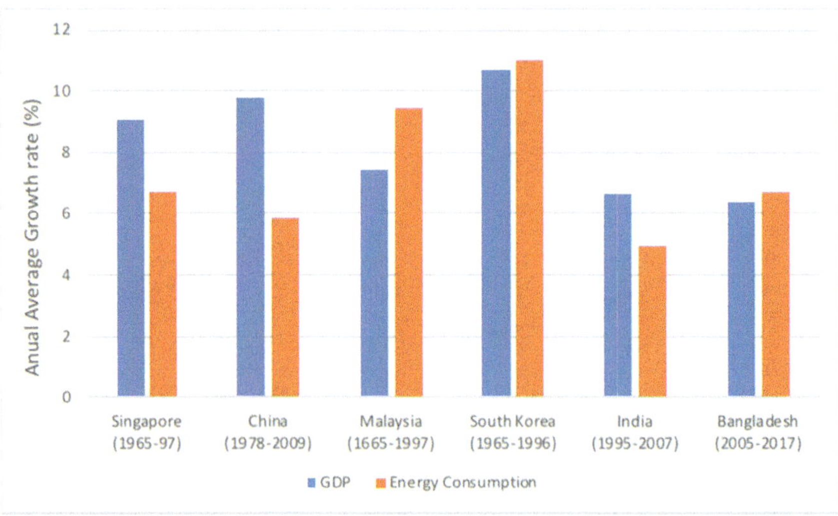

Fig. 5 Energy and GDP growth rates in fast-growing phase of selected Asian countries. *Source* Adapted from Mahmud and Roy (2020)

the bracket the country name). Historically, Singapore full filled its primary energy demand from imported oil and China from both imported and locally produced coal, gas and oil. Again, Malaysian energy support comes from locally produced oil although with time it balances the consumption of oil, gas and coal. South Korea's initial industrialization was supported by imported coal, and with time, energy mix has been diversified to oil, coal, gas and nuclear energy. Bangladesh as a late comer in the development process is supporting the fast growth phase with locally drilled natural gas and with some imported refined oil. Extraction, transportation infrastructure, manpower development and institutions, regulatory mechanisms and price subsidy were centred around increasing penetration of gas in total energy mix. With declining local gas reserve over time, the country started to import natural gas from 2018 to meet its growing demand. Coal share is increasing since 2005. The energy mix was changed from 71% gas, 25% oil, 3% coal and 1% hydro in 2005 to 69.3% gas, 22.69% oil, 7.09% coal, 0.71% hydro and 0.3% renewables in 2017 (BP 2018). Development context today in the world has moved to the goal of sustainable development, especially after adopting the agenda titled "Transforming our world: the 2030 Agenda for Sustainable Development" in 2015 UN general assembly. Around the same time, Paris agreement has been signed by the countries including Bangladesh. In the energy supply sector, Bangladesh is uniquely positioned in the region which can with global cooperation within Paris and Agreement and as an actively participating country in 2015 globally accepted common future defined by the Sustainable Development Goals (SDGs) framework. Through technology partnership, it can move away from natural gas at the end of its life to make a technically feasible transition to geothermal and hydrogen fuel economy and by strategically using the comparative advantage of the existing drilling and gas distribution network (Roy et al., 2020).

While Bangladesh adds new capacities in power sector and other energy service demands over next two decades, it can align to satisfy multiple goals under three broad categories: social, economic and environmental. In sustainable energy sector development, high target of energy supply growth is seen at the same level with high energy efficiency growth and energy security (UN, 2007, 2020; Vera & Langlois, 2007). Unless enhanced supply is simultaneously synergistic with social goals of equity in access, affordability and environmental goals of clean air, water, etc., twenty-first-century energy sector development will not be consistent with sustainability goal. These are also linked to high decent job creation goal. Bangladesh economy now is trying to catch up with the similar pattern and rate of economic growth as other fast-growing economic countries in the region during their rapid growth era of the past century. Therefore, significant growth in energy sector is inevitable and needs to be assured.

As the country's domestic resource endowment of natural gas is depleting due to historical dependence and limited reserve, the country is currently struggling with the persistent problem of the gas-based energy system and how to make transition more sustainable in future (Broerse & Grin, 2017). The major transition in energy sector to gas-based energy sector happened in 1975 in Bangladesh with nationalization of the gas fields (Petrobangla, 2016). From multilevel perspective landscape level changes through adoption of global collective actions towards sustainability where Bangladesh is also a party (MOEF, 2015), the pressure is building up for

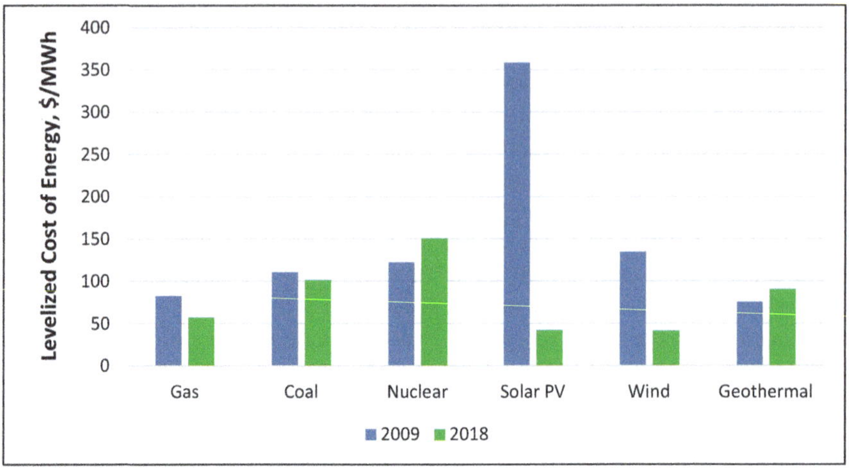

Fig. 6 Levelized cost of energy. *Source* Data used from (Lazard, 2020)

change. However, this is also coinciding with national level need for diversification of almost monolithic natural gas-dominated sector. So, the past cheap fossil fuel-driven regime of Asian fast-developing countries of past century is an old narrative which is changing very fast and needs to be articulated to the decision maker and political level so as to break away from persistence of the problem from fossil fuel dependence. Wind and solar technologies are also becoming competitive now in global market place in terms of levelized cost of energy (Fig. 6).

In Bangladesh, besides supply-side transition, there is huge scope of transition in demand-side sectors for Bangladesh which can provide faster economic growth, job creation and emission reduction, and energy conservation is through enhancement of energy efficiency. While many countries could combine higher economic activity growth rate with relatively lower energy sector growth rate due to conscious choice of relative decoupling strategy mostly through energy efficiency programmes (Das & Roy, 2020), Bangladesh has not mainstreamed energy efficiency yet within sectoral policies, technologies and human capacity building. Bangladesh is in a much advantageous position than other fast-growing countries from the past century as only 15% of the future energy sector is currently locked-in on fossil fuel path (Roy et al., 2020). Increase in energy efficiency in end use sector and a variety of clean/renewable energy penetration for achieving SDG 7 target by 2030 provides enormous scope for Bangladesh. Bangladesh while taking off in next couple of decades can take advantage of multidimensional global developments in the energy sector.

4 Concluding Remarks

Fast economic growth in the next two decades and need for energy to fuel the growth are essential for providing basic decent living standards to people of Bangladesh and India. The current dominant fossil fuel path dependency is only for 25–30% of the economy. Major growth in energy sector will happen now through the next two decades. Both the countries are already breaking away from the past development precedents of Asian developed countries and embarking on sustainable development pathway, but exponential scaling up of efforts is needed both in supply and demand sectors. These potentials for energy sector growth provide unique opportunity for economic growth and employment generations. There is need for international cooperation in technology and investment in innovation and institution building for managing this sustainable transition in energy sector with global common goal. These growth rates are required for providing universal access to a decent living for all. India already enjoys low per capita emission due to dietary habits based on locally grown agricultural produce and low per capita meat consumption approximately 5 kg per capita a year, compared to 120 kg in the USA and 80 kg in Germany (Roy & Pal, 2009). India's ~10% of urban households own a car; car sharing is a lifestyle in India, 42% still use a bicycle, and motorized two-wheelers are used by 35% of urban households, per capita CO_2 emissions are less than 2 metric tons (MT) (Roy et al., 2018). For Bangladesh, per capita emission is less than 1.3 MT, compared to 17 MT in the United States, 7 MT in the EU and 6.7 MT in China. India for very long time could manage to keep per capita emission at very low level due to its developmental choices. Industries have begun to adopt cleaner production to maintain global competitiveness in India (Roy, Dasgupta & Chakraborty, 2017; Roy, 2007). A five-fold increase in energy growth can now produce 20-fold activity growth thanks to energy-saving technology. Policies related to agriculture have started focusing on GHG emissions from agricultural practices and implement strategies like neem-coated urea, adopting climate-smart technologies that can help in reducing it. These examples can help in the global search for alternative sustainable development narratives for many fast-developing countries and developed countries who are locked in high emission trajectory from the past century.

Acknowledgements Joyashree Roy and Hasan Mahmud acknowledge the support of Bangabandhu chair endowment of the Ministry of Foreign Affairs, of the Government of Bangladesh (#MoU AIT-GoB) at the Asian Institute of Technology, Thailand. The endowment is provided to conduct research primarily on Energy Sector of Bangladesh.

Nandini Das duly acknowledges Global Change Programme, Jadavpur University, for the financial and infrustructural support to carry out her research work. Shreya Some acknowledges the financial assistance received under Senior Research Fellowship from University Grants Commission (UGC) of India.

References

Access to Information Program. (2009). Digital Bangladesh Concept Note. Dhaka: Access to Information Program, Prime Minister Office. Retrieved March 30, 2019, from https://a2i.gov.bd/wp-content/uploads/2017/11/3-Concept_Digital_Bangladesh_2009.pdf.

Al-Muti, S. (2014). Asis foundation. Retrieved from asis foundation: https://asiafoundation.org/2014/06/25/bangladeshs-development-surprise-a-model-for-developing-countries/.

Asian Development Bank. (2018). *Asian Development Outlook 2018*. Metro Manila, Philippines: Asian Development Bank.

Basak, R. (2016). Benefits and costs of nitrogen fertilizer management for climate change mitigation Focus on India and Mexico (Issue 161). www.ccafs.cgiar.org.

Basu, K. (2018, April 25). Why is Bangladesh's economy booming? Retrieved from Livemint: https://www.livemint.com/Opinion/6avW0qZka0ZT1cVaT0UEPK/Why-is-Bangladeshs-economy-booming.html.

Beach, R. H., Creason, J., Ohrel, S. B., Ragnauth, S., Ogle, S., Li, C., et al. (2015). Global mitigation potential and costs of reducing agricultural non-CO_2 greenhouse gas emissions through 2030. *Journal of Integrative Environmental Sciences, 12,* 87–105. https://doi.org/10.1080/1943815X.2015.1110183.

Berkhout, E., Glover, D., & Kuyvenhoven, A. (2015). On-farm impact of the system of rice intensification (SRI): Evidence and knowledge gaps. *Agricultural Systems, 132,* 157–166. https://doi.org/10.1016/j.agsy.2014.10.001.

Broerse, J. E. W., & Grin, J. (2017). *"Introduction," in toward sustainable transitions in healthcare systems*, 1st ed., J. E. W. Broerse & J. Grin (Eds) (pp. 11–11). New York: Taylor and Francis.

BP. (2018). Statistical review of world energy-all data, 1965–2019. Retrieved from: https://www.bp.com/en/global/corporate/energyeconomics/statistical-review-of-world-energy.html.

CEA. (2017). *Growth of electricity sector in India from 1947–2017*. New Delhi: Ministry of Power, GoI.

CEA. (2017). *19th electric power survey report*. New Delhi: Ministry of Power, GoI.

Chan, C., Sipes, B., Id, A. A., Zhang, X., Laporte, P., Fernandes, F., Pradhan, A., Chan-dentoni, J., & Roul, P. (2017). Efficiency of conservation agriculture production systems for smallholders in rain-fed uplands of India : A transformative approach to food security. *Land, 6*(58). https://doi.org/10.3390/land6030058.

Chancel, L., & Piketty, T. (2015). Carbon and inequality: From Kyoto to Paris: Trends in the global inequality of carbon emissions (1998–2013) & prospects for an equitable adaptation fund.

Das, N. (2019). *Low Carbon Growth: Alternative Pathways for India*. Ph.D. Thesis, Jadavpur University.

Dasgupta, M., & Roy, J. (2002). Energy Consumption in India: An indicator analysis. *Development Alternatives, 12*(10), 12–14.

Dasgupta, S., & Roy, J. (2017). Analysing energy intensity trends and decoupling of growth from energy use in Indian manufacturing industries during 1973–1974 to 2011–2012. *Energy Efficiency, 10*(4), 925–943.

Dabadge, A., Sreenivas, A., & Josey, A. (2018). What has the Pradhan Mantri Ujjwala Yojana achieved so far? *Economic & Political Weekly, LII, 1*(20), 69–75.

Das, N., & Roy, J. (2020). India can increase its mitigation ambition: An analysis based on historical evidence of decoupling between emission and economic growth. *Energy for Sustainable Development, 57*(2020), 189–199. https://doi.org/10.1016/j.esd.2020.06.003.

Datta, A., Santra, S. C., & Adhya, T. K. (2017). Environmental and economic opportunities of applications of different types and application methods of chemical fertilizer in rice paddy. *Nutrient Cycling in Agroecosystems*. https://doi.org/10.1007/s10705-017-9841-2.

Deelstra, J., Nagothu, U. S., Kakumanu, K. R., Kaluvai, Y. R., & Kallam, S. R. (2018). Enhancing water productivity using alternative rice growing practices: A case study from Southern India. *Journal of Agricultural Science, 156*(5), 673–679. https://doi.org/10.1017/S0021859618000655, https://doi.org/10.1007/s10640-008-9223-y.

Enerdata. (2018). *Global energy statistics yearbook*. Retrieved September 06, 2018, from https://yearbook.enerdata.net/total-energy/world-consumption-statistics.html.

GoI. (2016). *Energy statistics*. Ministry of Statistics and Programme Implementation.

Golley, J., & Meng, X. (2012). Income inequality and carbon dioxide emissions: The case of Chinese urban households. *Energy Economics, 34*(6), 1864–1872.

Groot, A. E., Bolt, J. S., Jat, H. S., Jat, M. L., Kumar, M., Agarwal, T., & Blok, V. (2019). Business models of SMEs as a mechanism for scaling climate smart technologies : The case of Punjab, India. *Journal of Cleaner Production, 210,* 1109–1119. https://doi.org/10.1016/j.jclepro.2018.11.054.

Hayward, B., & Roy, J. (2019). Sustainable living: bridging the north-south divide in lifestyles and consumption debates. *The Annual Review of Environment and Resource, 44*(6), 1–9.

INDC. (2015). Intended Nationally Determined Contribution. GOI.

IPCC. (2014). *Climate change 2014 synthesis report summary for policymakers*. Chembridge & NY: Chembridge University Press.

Jorgenson, A. K., Fiske, S., Hubacek, K., Li, J., Mcgovern, T., Rick, T., … Zycherman, A. (2019). Social science perspectives on drivers of and responses to global climate change. *WIREs Climate Change*, https://doi.org/10.1002/wcc.554.

Kakraliya, S. K., Jat, H. S., Singh, I., Sapkota, T. B., Singh, L. K., Sutaliya, J … Jat, M. L. (2018). Performance of portfolios of climate smart agriculture practices in a rice-wheat system of western Indo-Gangetic plains. *Agricultural Water Management, 202*(July 2017), 122–133. https://doi.org/10.1016/j.agwat.2018.02.020.

Kakumanu, K. R., Kaluvai, Y. R., Balasubramanian, M., Nagothu, U. S., Kotapati, G. R., & Karanam, S. (2018). *Adaptation to climate change: Impact of capacity building*. India: Irrigation and Drainage. https://doi.org/10.1002/ird.2275.

Kassam, A., & Brammer, H. (2013). *Commentary Reply to Sumberg, 179*(2), 186–187. https://doi.org/10.1111/geoj.12010.

Kassam, A., & Brammer, H. (2016). Environmental implications of three modern agricultural practices: Conservation agriculture, the system of rice intensification and precision agriculture. *International Journal of Environmental Studies, 73*(5), 702–718. https://doi.org/10.1080/00207233.2016.1185329.

Kritee, K., Nair, D., Tiwari, R., Rudek, J., Ahuja, R., Adhya, T., et al. (2015). Groundnut cultivation in semi-arid peninsular India for yield scaled nitrous oxide emission reduction. *Nutrient Cycling in Agroecosystems, 103*(1), 115–129. https://doi.org/10.1007/s10705-015-9725-2.

Lazard. (2020). "Lazard's levelized cost of energy analysis-Version 12.0," 2018. Retrieved on 10, 2020, from https://www.lazard.com/media/450784/lazards-levelized-cost-of-energy-version-120-vfinal.pdf.

LR Global Research. (2017). *Bangladesh economy 2017*. Retrieved from lrglobalbd.com: https://www.lrglobalbd.com/wp-content/uploads/2017/07/LR_GLOBAL_INSIGHTS_BANGLADESH_ECONOMY-2017-1.pdf

Mahmud, M., Asadullah, M. N., & Savoia, A. (2013). Bangladesh's achievements in social development indicators explaining the puzzle. *Economic & Political Weekly, 44,* 26–28.

Mahmud, H., & Roy, J. (2020). Sustainable energy sector for fast growing economy like Bangladesh: How relevant are the past Asian precedents? *International Energy Journal, 20*(Special Issue 3A), 381–394.

Millward-Hopkins, J., Steinberger, J. K., Rao, N. D., & Oswald, Y. (2020). Providing decent living with minimum energy: A global scenario. *Global Environmental Change, 65,* 102168.

Ministry of Power, GoI. (2018). Energy efficiency. Retrieved November 11, 2018, from https://powermin.nic.in/en/content/energy-efficiency.

MOEF. (2015). Intended Nationally Determined Contributions (INDC). Retrieved on June 14, 2020, from https://www4.unfccc.int/sites/ndcstaging/PublishedDocuments/BangladeshFirst/INDC_2015_of_Bangladesh.pdf.

NATCOM. (2018). A case-study based assessment of economic cost of impact of heat stress on labour productivity and adaptation in selected building and transport sector. Global Change Programme-Jadavpur University.

NITI Aayog. (2016). India Energy Security Scenario 2047. *Niti Aayog*, GoI.

NREL. (2014). *Indian renewable energy status report.*

Palak, Z. A. (2015, March 10). Towards Digital Bangladesh: 24th Anniversary of The Daily Star (Part-1): supplements: Home: *The Daily Star*. Retrieved March 30, 2019, from The Daily Star Web site: https://www.thedailystar.net/supplements/24th-anniversary-the-daily-star-part-1/towards-digital-bangladesh-72925.

Parihar, C. M., Parihar, M. D., Sapkota, T. B., Nanwal, R. K., Singh, A. K., Jat, S. L., et al. (2018). Long-term impact of conservation agriculture and diversified maize rotations on carbon pools and stocks, mineral nitrogen fractions and nitrous oxide fluxes in inceptisol of India. *Science of the Total Environment, 640–641,* 1382–1392. https://doi.org/10.1016/j.scitotenv.2018.05.405.

Pathak, H., Bhatia, A., & Jain, N. (2014). *Greenhouse gas emission from Indian agriculture: Trends, mitigation and policy needs.* New Delhi: Indian Agricultural Research Institute. https://krishi.icar.gov.in/jspui/bitstream/123456789/32431/1/GreenhouseGasEmissionfromIndianAgricultureHPathaketal%20%281%29.pdf.

Petrobangla. (2016). Anual Report 2016, Dhake, 2016. Retrieved on August 10, 2020. https://petrobangla.portal.gov.bd/sites/default/files/files/petrobangla.portal.gov.bd/annual_reports/f63a2fc1_5c56_4a07_9c0c_03827a254846/2020-01-15-19-14-d636a153a8062a0e4dccf99c941cf9c8.pdf.

Rao, N. D., & Pachauri, S. (2017). Energy access and living standards: some observations on recent trends. *Environmental Research Letters, 12*(2). https://doi.org/10.1088/1748-9326/aa5b0d.

Rao, N. D., Min, J., & Mastrucci, A. (2019). Energy requirements for decent living in India. *Brazil and South Africa. Nature Energy, 4*(2019), 1025–1032.

Rao, N. H. (2018). Big data and climate smart agriculture—status and implications for agricultural research and innovation in India. *Proceedings of Indian National and Scientific Academy, 84*(3), 625–640. https://doi.org/10.16943/ptinsa/2018/49342.

RBI. (2017). *Handbook of statistics on Indian economy.* Reserve Bank of India.

Rockström, J., Williams, J., Daily, G., Noble, A., Matthews, N., Gordon, L., et al. (2017). Sustainable intensification of agriculture for human prosperity and global sustainability. *Ambio, 46*(1), 4–17. https://doi.org/10.1007/s13280-016-0793-6.

Rahman, M. (2016). *Bangladesh sconomy in 2021—Prospects and challenges in a globalized world economy.* Tohoku: International Graduate School of Accounting Policy (IGSAP) Research Forum, Tohoku University.

Roy, J. (2007). De-Linking Economic Growth from GHG Emissions through Energy Efficiency Route: How Far Are We in India? *Bulletin on Energy Efficiency, 7,* 52–7.

Roy, J., Dasgupta, S., & Chakraborty, D. (2017). Realizing long–term transitions towards low carbon societies. In: Lechtenbohmer S & Knopp K (Eds), *Deep Decarbonistion in Industries: What does it mean for India?*, Wuppertal Spezial, Wuppertal Institute, *53,* 88–91.

Roy, J., & Pal, S. (2009). Lifestyles and climate change: link awaiting activation. *Current Opinion on Environmental Sustainability, 1,* 192–200. https://doi.org/10.1016/j.cosust.2009.10.009.

Roy, J., Chakravarty, D., Dasgupta, S., Chakraborty, D., Pal, S., & Ghosh, D. (2018). Where is the hope? Blending modern urban lifestyle with cultural practices in India. *Current Opinion on Environmental Sustainability, 31,* 96–103. https://doi.org/10.1016/j.cosust.2018.01.010.

Roy, J., Mahmud, H., Assadi, M., Iman, N., & Nikpey, H. (2020). Moving beyond gas: Can Bangladesh leapfrog and make the energy transition just by exploring the role of geothermal energy and gas infrastructure? *International Energy Journal, 20*(Special Issue 3A), 395–410.

Sapkota, T. B., Jat, M. L., Aryal, J. P., Jat, R. K., & Khatri-Chhetri, A. (2015). Climate change adaptation, greenhouse gas mitigation and economic profitability of conservation agriculture: Some examples from cereal systems of Indo-Gangetic Plains. *Journal of Integrative Agriculture.* https://doi.org/10.1016/S2095-3119(15)61093-0.

Schor, J. B. (2005). Sustainable consumption and worktime reduction. *Journal of Industrial Ecology, 9*(1–2), 37–50.

Shrestha, R. M., Anandarajah, G., & Liyanage, M. H. (2009). Factors affecting CO_2 emission from the power sector of selected countries in Asia and the Pacific. *Energy Policy, 37*(6), 2375–2384.

Sikka, A. K., Islam, A., & Rao, K. V. (2018). Climate-smart land and water management for sustainable agriculture. *Irrigation and Drainage, 67*(1), 72–81. https://doi.org/10.1002/ird.2162.

Singer, M. (2018). Climate change and social inequality: The health and social costs of global warming. Earthscan.

Some, S. (2020). Exploring mitigation interventions and SDGs links : Evidences from Indian agriculture. https://www.researchgate.net/publication/340777417_Exploring_Mitigation_Interventions_and_SGDs_links_Evidences_from_Indian_agriculture#fullTextFileContent.

Some, S., Roy, J., & Ghose, A. (2019). Non-CO_2 emission from cropland based agricultural activities in India: A decomposition analysis and policy link. *Journal of Cleaner Production, 225,* 637–646. https://doi.org/10.1016/j.jclepro.2019.04.017.

UN. (2007). United Nations forum on energy efficiency and energy security for sustainable development: Taking collaborative action on mitigating climate change. Retrieved on August 10, 2020, from https://sustainabledevelopment.un.org/content/documents/1474aide_memoire.pdf.

UN. (2020). Transforming our world: The 2030 agenda for sustainable development, A/RES/70/1, 2015. Retrieved on August 10, 2020, from https://www.unfpa.org/sites/default/files/resource-pdf/Resolution_A_RES_70_1_EN.pdf.

USEPA. (2019). *Greenhouse gas emissions projections greenhouse gas emission projections.* https://www.epa.ie/pubs/reports/air/airemissions/ghgprojections2017-2035/2018_Seminar_GHG_Projections_to_2035.pdf.

Vera, I., & Langlois, L. (2007, June). Energy indicators for sustainable development. *Energy, 32*(6), 875–882. https://doi.org/10.1016/j.energy.2006.08.006.

Westermann, O., Thornton, P., Förch, W., Aggarwal, P. K., Araba, D., Barón, D. M., … Zougmoré, R. (2015). Reaching more farmers innovative approaches to scaling up climate-smart agriculture CGIAR Research Program on Climate Change, Agriculture and Food Security (CCAFS) (No. 135; Issue 135). www.ccafs.cgiar.org.

World Bank. (2019). Data bank. World development indicator. Retrieved from The World Bank web site: https://databank.worldbank.org/data/reports.aspx?source=2&series=EG.USE.PCAP.KG.OE&country=#.

Looking Beyond the COVID-19 Pandemic: What Does Our Future Hold?

Anup Sinha

1 Introduction

This paper is about COVID-19 and its effects on the world economy and society. The pandemic is a classic example of a complex environmental shock. It is likely to take a heavy toll in terms of human lives, health and well-being, as well as livelihoods and incomes. The pandemic, as I write this, is already into the eighth month, and there is no clear evidence when this will taper off so that one can talk about a post-COVID-19 world. There is a possibility of a vaccine but it is not known when it will be available on a mass scale and how effective it might be. Treatment is still arbitrary and uncertain with doctors trying out different combinations of drugs. There are parallel narratives about the medical evidence and its interpretation. The scientific community, the policy-makers and big business are revealing their vested interests much to the confusion and anxiety of the ordinary citizen. There are conspiracy theories too about how the virus spread and who were responsible for it. Different heads of state have responded differently to these doubts and ambiguities. Stories emerging out of nations are different too. This impact on health is something that human society has not seen in a century since the influenza epidemic of 1918. In terms of the impact on the economy, the data are gradually becoming as alarming as it was during the Great Depression of the 1930s. The two combined is a unique and unprecedented phenomenon.

In this paper, I have treated the pandemic essentially as an environmental problem that could be likened to (or even related to, as we may find out someday) climate change and the associated increase in pathogens. Section 2 discusses the economic and environmental trends in the world just before the onset of the COVID-19

The author is indebted to Runa Sarkar for valuable comments on an earlier draft.

A. Sinha (✉)
Heritage Business School, Kolkata, India
e-mail: anup.aks@gmail.com

P. Dasgupta et al. (eds.), *Sustainable Development Insights from India*,
India Studies in Business and Economics,
https://doi.org/10.1007/978-981-33-4830-1_3

pandemic. Section 3 discusses the impact of COVID-19 on economy, environment and society, on human life and health along with the different policy responses adopted by nations. In Sect. 4, I discuss the lessons that are being learnt while living through the pandemic. These lessons might change over time, and it is not clear how they will be absorbed and appreciated by diverse segments of society. However, they are valuable. This is followed by Sect. 5 where I discuss alternative futures that are possibly emerging from the lessons learnt during the pandemic. However, the pandemic could also turn the future world more dystopian—politically, environmentally and economically. It is for us as citizens to decide how much we assert our agency, communicate with one another and restart the world. Section 6 concludes the essay.

2 The World Economy and Environment Before COVID-19

The year 2019 was a year when the global economy began to show distinct signs of economic slowdown. This was the result of a combination of factors. Investment optimism had declined, leading to a fall in economic growth and incomes leading to a further decline in demand. World trade had been affected adversely from the trade war declared by the USA on China and some other economies, causing large-scale disruptions in the international flow of goods and services. This also contributed to a lack of optimism about future growth and potential for new investments. Economic inequality had risen to levels unprecedented in modern times. Labour as a class was much less organized, and many rights and privileges had been eroded by the growth of casual and contract work in the gig economy. Central banks tried to push recovery by cutting interest rates but were not successful as the "animal spirits" of investors refused to respond positively. In a result to stimulate growth, many governments tried to dilute the implementation of environmental laws and regulations. Governments were less concerned about climate change and biodiversity loss. The trends observed in new technologies were more about labour-saving strategies through the use of data analytics, machine learning and artificial intelligence. New technologies with energy saving and carbon reducing features were relatively scarce. Finally, there was a phenomenon observed in many big and powerful economies of the world, where democratically elected leaders were found wanting in protecting democracy and civil rights. Authoritarianism was on the rise with strong leaders showing little respect for dissent and contrarian views.

According to the United Nations World Economic Situation and Prospects Report, dated 19 January 2020, global economic growth in 2019 was 2.3%, the lowest for the decade. The global rate of growth was 3.2% in 2017 and 3.0% in 2018. Trade disputes had increased tariffs, which reduced international trade and investments leading to a slowdown. Aggregate demand contraction softened oil prices and commodity prices, especially those of industrial use metals. China and India, the two fastest growing large economies, were experiencing slowdowns too. China's growth had declined from 6.6% in 2018 to 6.1% in 2019. In India, GDP growth was 5.7% in 2019. The

GDP growth rate had been slowing down for ten successive quarters by the end of the calendar year 2019. Before the start of the pandemic, most projections of the global growth rate of income and trade for 2020 were lower than actual growth achieved in 2019.

An updated version of the UN World Economic Situation and Prospects Report (dated May 13, 2020) projected that with the onset of COVID-19, the revised estimates for world economic growth were a negative 3.2%, with the developed market economies shrinking by 5% and developing market economies by 0.7%. The International Monetary Fund (IMF), in its World Economic Outlook of January 2020, found that in 2019 all major economies had slowed down. This included the USA, China, India, the European Union, Brazil, Russia and Mexico, along with countries of the Gulf Cooperation Council. The IMF also found that some other nations such as Argentina, Venezuela, Iran, Libya, Turkey and Sudan not only slowed down, but were severely stressed. It was the same almost everywhere: investments fell, growth slowed down as firms became cautious about new spending on machinery and equipment, and consumers were wary about spending on durables. The consumer non-durables sector, and to some extent, the services sector kept a low growth rate going.

The World Economic Outlook Update (IMF July 2020) showed revisions made in projected growth rates after the advent of COVID-19. World economic growth was projected to shrink to 4.9%, with the developed market economies shrinking by as much as 8% and the emerging market economies experiencing a negative growth rate of 3%. China was the only major country expected to have a positive rate of growth of 1%, and India was expected to shrink by 4.5%. World trade was expected to decline by 0.9%.

As far as the natural environment was concerned, 2019 saw, despite the Paris Accord and a slowdown in global demand, no decline in carbon emissions in the world. The total global carbon emissions of 33.3 Gigatonnes of carbon dioxide were the same for 2018 and 2019. This was after two years of increase during 2016 and 2017 from 32.1 Gigatonnes to 32.7 Gigatonnes, respectively. Climate change from the emissions, made in the past as well as emissions made currently, has contributed to a rise in average global temperatures by over 1 °C. Large and growing economies like China and India have committed themselves to keeping global warming to within 2 °C. Hence, a 2° increase is almost given with the best of mitigation strategies like afforestation, switch to wind and solar power from coal to natural gas, increases in safe nuclear power and new technologies to reduce dependence on fossil fuels. The threat of climate change is real and persistent, and perhaps one little piece of hopeful news was that carbon emissions had at last begun to flatten out for the first time in the last thirty years.

To sum up, 2019 was a year where the global economy was showing distinct signs of trouble, and the trends in natural environmental damage were far from being free from posing a serious danger to human health and well-being. Economic slowdown, astonishing inequalities, rising authoritarianism, climate change and biodiversity loss presented an ideal ambience for the perfect storm called COVID-19.

3 The Pandemic and Its Effects

3.1 The Medical Evidence and Surprises

At some point of time in December 2019, doctors in Wuhan, China, began to report an unknown type of influenza or pneumonia which many people were having, and that standard treatments were not working. In few days, it was detected as a new strain of the coronavirus, a type of severe acute respiratory syndrome (SARS) virus labelled SARS-CoV-2. It was also referred to as the novel coronavirus and the disease was named COVID-19. The genetic sequence was mapped by early January 2020. The disease began to spread rapidly from China to a large number of countries, especially to Europe and USA. There was a New Year celebration in Wuhan where many people, some non-resident Chinese included, congregated. Most of these people contracted the disease. While many recovered fast with only mild influenza-like symptoms, some exhibited severe respiratory distress and a few succumbed to the disease. The Director General of the World Health Organization visited China to look into the spread of COVID-19 but did not make any statement regarding the possible dangers from the spread of this infectious disease.

It was much later, on 11 March 2020, that the World Health Organization declared a pandemic caused by COVID-19. The disease is believed to have zoonotic origins and has close genetic similarity to bat coronaviruses, suggesting it emerged from the virus-carrying bats. There is no evidence yet to link an intermediate animal reservoir, such as a pangolin, to its introduction to humans. The virus shows little genetic diversity, indicating that the spillover event introducing SARS-CoV-2 to humans is likely to have occurred in late 2019. The WHO advised all people to avoid crowded places, wear masks and practice social distancing by maintaining at least one metre's distance between two people.

A number of unusual things about the disease began to be observed by then. Epidemiological studies estimated that each infection resulted in 1.4–3.9 new ones when no members of the community were immune and no preventive measures were taken. This rate of contagion was considered unusually high, much higher than the earlier SARS. Secondly, there were a lot of people who were infected but showed symptoms after a long lag of four or even seven days. These asymptomatic carriers were even more dangerous because they would not be consciously avoided. The third fact emerging was that people over 60 years of age and having co-morbidities such as type-2 diabetes, hypertension, kidney ailments and chronic obstructive pulmonary disorders (COPD) were likely to show severe symptoms and high fatality rates. Finally, it was obvious that a vaccine would take a long time, and in the interim there was no treatment using existing drugs that worked in curing the ailment. In short, the evidence and the data were too little and too confusing. Within the community of medical practitioners and researchers, there were parallel and often conflicting hypotheses asserted about the disease, its degree of danger and the warranted line of treatment.

Table 1 Comparison of cases and deaths

Country	Cases	Deaths
USA	5,997,163	183,069
Brazil	3,862,331	120,828
India	3,621,245	64,469
World	25,225,985	846,405

Source The Johns Hopkins University Coronavirus Tracker coronavirus.jhu.edu/map.html accessed on August 31 12.30 p.m

The spread of the disease was so swift and widespread that doctors and policy-makers had no time to reflect or strategize as to what would be the best responses. Most governments announced "lockdown" or closures of all non-essential activities like shops and markets, gyms and theatres, schools and colleges and all offices barring essential services. In some nations, like in India, there was a strict and complete lock-down that closed all economic activities, and there was a curfew declared restricting citizens from going out of their homes. In other nations like the USA, the restrictions were not effectively announced or followed. Some states were strict while others had virtually no restrictions at all. In Europe, many countries followed the strict lock-down model, while in many other nations it was largely left to the wisdom of citizens to behave in a responsible manner. All nations began to report the incidence of the disease. The world had not experienced such a severe pandemic since the influenza epidemic of 1918–20. By the end of August 2020, the global data of COVID-19 infections along with the three worst affected countries in terms of total caseloads were as given in Table 1.

3.2 Economic Impact

The pandemic came as a severe shock to markets and economic production. International travel and tourism came to a sudden halt. Hotels and bars and restaurants were shut. Shops and malls were closed as were factories. At the retail level of trade, only food items and medicines were allowed. Offices, schools and colleges were closed as people stayed home to avoid infections. Theatres showing films or playhouses for drama were closed. Suddenly, the global economy came to a grinding halt. Health-care workers on the other hand were stretched to their limits as the number of patients increased and health infrastructure in most countries came under severe strain. There was a shortage of gloves and protective wear and intensive care equipment like ventilators.

First, economic production slowed down to an alarming level. Firms shut down or went out of business altogether as the disease continued to spread and lockdowns began to be extended. This led to large-scale lay-offs and loss of jobs. Those who were lucky to retain their jobs had to take substantial pay cuts or remained edgy as to when their turn for retrenchment would come. Unemployment figures skyrocketed in most countries to levels not witnessed since the Great Depression of the 1930s. In the USA, for instance, unemployment climbed by 14 million, which was more than the additional unemployment experienced in the country during the Great Recession of 2007–08 (Kochhar 2020). In India, unemployment climbed by 20 million during the period April to June 2020 (Ghosh et al. 2020).

While unemployment increased in all countries, there were differences in the impact depending upon the extent and efficacy of social safety nets. In Europe, the impact was less than in the USA. In the latter country, many of the social security benefits had been reduced over the years as government support was thought to be too expensive and only induced laziness in recipients of state aid. In countries like India where there is massive inequality accompanied by widespread poverty and deprivation, there is hardly any built-in fiscal measures that can count as social insurance barring the public food distribution system and the work guarantee scheme under the (Mahatma Gandhi National Rural Employment Guarantee Act) MGNREGA. This ensures a minimum of 100 days of work at a preannounced minimum wage. The bulk of India's workers (estimated to be about 85%) are in the informal sector with no rights and benefits. Many of them are temporary migrant workers who move from villages to far-off urban centres to work as daily wage earners on oral contracts. They do not have job security of any sort and often stay in temporary shanties or urban ghettos. They are not covered by the public distribution system, and many do not even have proper identity cards as citizens.

When the lockdown was announced in India by the prime minister, a notice of only four hours was given. Suddenly millions of migrant workers not only were left without a job, but were stranded without food. Hence, a large part of these many millions started to go back to their own villages which in many cases were hundreds of kilometres away. Since no public transports like trains and buses were allowed to ply, they began to walk. One of the most striking images of poverty and hunger was that of millions of Indians walking on highways and roads to reach home. Some had to go a hundred kilometres while some others travelled anywhere up to seven hundred kilometres. Some died on the way, some collapsed, and few of the migrant workers gave birth on the way, while others lost their newborns. These hitherto invisible Indians were perhaps unknown to, or ignored by, the ruling elites.

There was a lot of talk in the media about the necessity of this lockdown that the medical practitioners were insisting on, to contain the disease and related deaths. Some economists claimed that the shutdown could claim equal or perhaps even more deaths from hunger and other diseases brought about by unemployment. In the advanced economies of the world, the debate was between loss of lives and the loss of livelihoods. In India, it was between the "visible" loss of lives from the virus and the "invisible" loss of lives from hunger.

The nature of the shock to the global economy was complex. The first effect was that of a sudden disruption of supply and supply chains across the economies of the world. This came at a time, as I had mentioned earlier, when the global economy was weak and sluggish. The disruption in supplies led to closures and the release of a large number of workers. This obviously had a severe adverse effect on demand. With stagnating and falling consumer demand and the general outlook for the immediate future looking gloomy, nobody was willing to invest, which aggravated the crisis. In India, the financial system was already suffering from large amounts of uncovered bad debts. In such a situation, banks, for instance, fearing opportunistic behaviour from potentially bad borrowers were unwilling to lend, and the demand for credit was also low. The shock led to a vicious cycle of low supply, low demand and low growth, low off-take of credit coupled with massive unemployment and unprecedented closure of small and medium enterprises. The pandemic and its economic effects had other consequences too. It affected social values and beliefs, political positions and individual well-being even without being infected.

Surprisingly, stock markets were not crashing anywhere. In the USA, it was distinctly doing very well, while in most other countries there was increased volatility but there was no downward trend visible. Nobody knows how long the disruption will continue, yet there are people who seem to be confident of a quick and decisive recovery from the recession in terms of what is called a V-shaped recovery, once the pandemic dies down. Obviously, policy responses emerged to counter the economic shock. They were qualitatively as well as quantitatively different in different countries.

3.3 Social and Political Impact

The social impact of the pandemic was initially marked, the world over, by a callousness and overconfidence that the whole thing was being hyped up by the medical community. Some saw even a conspiracy to sell a vaccine; some thought it was deliberately let loose by the Chinese from Wuhan to dominate the world. These kinds of attitudes and narratives soon got replaced by a sense of panic and fear realizing that the disease was really infectious, and some people were actually dying from it. Gradually the wearing of masks caught on, as did the washing of hands more frequently and the use of hand sanitizers. Social distancing, as recommended by doctors and governments, were a bit more difficult for a couple of reasons. The first was the inherent tendency of human beings to be together and socialize. Hence, sea beaches, parks, markets, places of worship, restaurants and social functions like marriages, drew people close together in large numbers. The second was the lack of space in densely populated urban areas and in crowded cities of the developing world. People living in crowded tenements and narrow lanes had no way of keeping a metre's distance between two individuals.

Next, there was widespread anger and suspicion about people who were infected and people who were likely to be asymptomatic carriers. These people, including healthcare workers like doctors and nurses, were hounded from their homes. They were considered too risky to have as next-door neighbours. They were treated as untouchables. These effects varied from nation to nation, and even within a country there were variations of these reactions in different parts. In some countries, there were still many people who thought it was all hype. National leaders like Bolsonaro in Brazil and Trump in the USA actually defied medical advice by either not wearing masks, or not practising social distancing. Their supporters kept behaving as if there was no pandemic at all (Galea and Alcalde 2020).

Political responses were varied (Nath 2020). Most nations cracked down when the disease began to spread with strict "lockdown" in almost all economic and social activities. The degree of strictness varied though, as did the duration of the closures. There were debates within the medical community, especially among epidemiologists, regarding the efficacy of strict lockdowns. Governments were obviously confused. In India, a strict lockdown was followed. Even as I write this essay, international and domestic travel and tourism are still down to a tiny fraction of the pre COVID-19 levels. Governments found this to be a good opportunity to trace the activities of citizens so as to keep track of potential infections spreading. However, it was also helpful in increasing the surveillance over citizens and keeping a tab over other kinds of activities, especially political, being carried out. In all countries of the world, the pandemic caused heavy disruption in economic activity (Miller 2020). The poor were hit the hardest both from the pandemic as well as from loss of incomes and jobs. In some countries, the ethnic minorities suffered more in terms of infections and deaths. The medical calamity got inextricably tied up with politics. The economic loss and the huge strain on public health systems forced the political establishment to react. It would be disastrous not to do so. Designing and funding a recovery package would mean finding appropriate means to alleviate immediate suffering and also open opportunities to quickly rebuilding the economy with new livelihood and employment opportunities. It would mean a great strain on fiscal resources in rich countries and poor.

3.4 The Environmental Impact

COVID-19 and the associated lockdowns in economic and social activities had positive as well as negative effects on the natural environment. The full extent of these effects is yet to be measured, and some of the consequences are told in terms of anecdotal evidence and what was perceptible to the naked eye. The effects were globally observed in varying degrees since 213 nations have been affected by the virus (Schuijers 2020). A major beneficial effect observed was the reduction in air pollution since many manufacturing units were closed, road and air travel were drastically cut, a large number of oil refineries were shut, and coal consumption had fallen. Some preliminary estimates suggest that in the European Union, particulate matter (PM 2.5) and nitrogen oxides (NOx) emissions fell by 20–30% in the first month of the pandemic-induced closures. In China during February 2020, carbon dioxide emissions fell by 200 million metric tons compared to the emissions in February 2019.

Another benefit from the stay at home restrictions imposed by governments helped clean water bodies like the canals of Venice or the sea beaches of France and Spain. It is expected that fish stock growth will be higher since the quality of water would be better in rivers as well as coastlines. Environmental noise measured in decibels fell significantly with lower traffic movements. Road accidents declined too as highways and roads were nearly empty. Ecological footprints fell since international mobility of goods and people were suddenly reduced. This, in turn, enabled local producers of food and other essentials to enjoy improved sales. A number of wild animals and birds were spotted in deserted urban areas seemingly comfortable with no signs of humans or vehicles to frighten them. Pakistan took this opportunity of healing the environment by putting unemployed people to work in planting 10 billion trees as part of a social and environmental campaign (Zambrano-Monserrate, Alejandra Ruano, & Sanchez-Alcalde, 2020).

However, there were negative effects too. The most serious of these has been the huge increase in waste, as recycling was virtually stopped from the fear of infections spreading from reused materials. Of the increased waste, a large part is considered biohazardous. Also waste management has been disrupted in many places as it was not sure whether there was contaminated refuse in garbage piles. Indeed, in some countries of Europe households were prohibited from sorting their own garbage in the fear that some people could end up spreading the virus in the process. Many companies have repealed their own bans on disposable bags by going back to single use packaging. With reduced movement of people, environmental policing has slackened. This has led to a spurt in crime such as poaching of rare wildlife or the felling of trees. It is claimed that deforestation has increased sharply in Brazil. It might be noted though that this might have happened even without the pandemic since the president of Brazil officially endorsed clearing up the rainforests. In many other countries like India, governments have diluted the environmental clearances required for large projects where environmental damage was more likely to occur. It reflects an effort to please big business and facilitate the ease of doing business by small and medium enterprises. This will, governments believe, help a quick recovery from the economic effects of the pandemic.

3.5 The Human Costs of the Pandemic

The prolonged lockdown and the uncertainty about what the future holds have affected all individuals, in varying degrees, in terms of their lifestyles and their behaviour patterns. The first, and most obvious impact, is the rise in stress and anxiety about health and incomes. The lockdown turned out to be a virtual home imprisonment where even visits by friends, relatives and neighbours were a source of unease and fear about infections. Many families had to cope with children at home, partners having lost their job or source of income and a sharply increased work stress for those who had to go out like health care workers. Two kinds of emotions have become dominant in the pandemic: anger and a low-grade depression. Those who fell ill and were lucky to have recovered are likely to feel helpless in not being able to comprehend why they fell ill. Those who had to be quarantined developed a sense of isolation and loneliness (Dubey et al., 2020). Those who did not survive the illness left a deep scar of sorrow and despair in the minds of their close relatives and friends.

Domestic violence is reported to have increased across the world as have incidences of suicides.

A number of people have tried to exploit the vulnerability of other people and passed around fake news, false narratives about how the disease came about and how it spreads and peddling treatments that were to say the least, therapeutic misadventures. In India, various Godmen claimed cure from the disease through ingestion of cow's urine, or some herb that carried the saliva of the quack. Some of them could not prevent having the disease themselves, and in the process of their blind superstitious beliefs put a number of people into danger of contracting the disease. Many alternative medicines have been suggested through the Internet along with innumerable preventive, immunity-boosting diets. Social media and the Internet have become, according to the Director of WHO, a "coronavirus infodemic".

Some parts of society have been hit by overwork and strain like frontline healthcare personnel such as doctors, nurses, paramedics, policemen, bankers and delivery people. The psychological effects on these people, who are much more vulnerable to infections, are twofold. One is that they often face social rejection as untouchables and are often asked to leave their residences and go somewhere else. The other constant fear they live with is the higher chance of their being asymptomatic carriers of the virus and infecting their loved ones at home including partners, children and old parents.

Children stuck at home, without games even on television, and without being able to go to school or play in the neighbourhood park, have faced problems. Anger and tantrums have increased, and many sensitive children might be left with indelible scars from the pandemic. A simple example will suffice to show how the world of adults can create lasting behavioural impressions on children. The pandemic has introduced extensive use of the thermal gun to record the body temperature of people trying to enter office buildings or public spaces. The hand-held device is held by one adult and pointed like a gun at the middle of the forehead of the person whose temperature is being checked. Other adults do not show any apprehension nor do they try to stop the person from pointing the gun-like device. The child can easily process this image as shooting a gun at another person's forehead is acceptable social behaviour.

The other sections of society badly hit are the marginalized communities of migrants, homeless, slum dwellers and prison inmates. Their abilities to practise social distancing or adopt basic hygienic rules are extremely limited. The poor and deprived are always the worst hit in times of disasters. In such situations, rational behaviour is often replaced by herd behaviour where everyone feels comfortable in being led and identifying with a common enemy. Hence, the pandemic has seen significant increase in xenophobia, communalism and racism. One important upshot of the social impact of the pandemic is that old patterns of accepted behaviour have been disrupted. New practices are being tried out. This implies that the barriers around stereotypical behaviour have broken down. These often take extremely long to change. Disasters and upheavals break them down decisively. It is a moment of social inflection. New patterns emerge. Whether the new patterns are forward-looking and harmonious, or they are myopic and dissonant is anybody's guess at the moment.

3.6 The Economic Policy Responses

With the economies of most nations coming to a grinding halt, for the first time since the Great Depression, both advanced economies and developing economies are in recession. Governments and central banks have responded to the pandemic and the economic crisis using both fiscal and monetary tools on a scale that the world has not witnessed before. A recent paper (Benmelech & Tzur Ilan, 2020) estimated the determinants of fiscal and monetary policies during the COVID-19 crisis. It was found that high-income countries announced larger fiscal interventions than lower-income countries. It was also found that a country's credit rating is the most important determinant of its fiscal spending during the pandemic. High-income countries entered the crisis with historically low interest rates and as a result were forced to use non-conventional monetary policy tools. These findings raised the concern that countries with poor credit histories and those with lower credit ratings, in particular, lower-income countries have not been able to deploy fiscal policy tools effectively during the pandemic. As a result, they have been pushed into using interest rate policies and other monetary policy tools such as loan moratoriums or guaranteed credit and soft loans without collaterals as instruments to kick start the economy.

The differences in policy emphasis can affect the speed of recovery. The reason is quite straight forward. I have already argued that the shock to supply quickly spilled over into a severe demand contraction. Hence, the policy to trigger recovery would have to focus on demand stimulation that would restore the confidence of producers and investors. If, on the contrary, the supply side is focussed on by polices where cheap money and easy credit are made available, the producers would not increase capacity utilization and capital expenditures since they were not sure of future demand. The additional liquidity in the economy would fuel inflation and speculative activities in financial markets. If fiscal policy has been used more effectively by rich economies to directly stimulate demand, then their recoveries would be likely to be faster than that of poor countries that relied more on private debt in the fear of their sovereign ratings being downgraded.

A quick look at the strategies used by USA, China and India will suffice in this context. The USA declared a large fiscal stimulus of $2.3 trillion which was 11% of its GDP. Coronavirus Aid Relief and Economic Security (CARES) Act provided enhanced unemployment benefits, widened the food safety net and prevented corporate bankruptcy and mechanisms for writing off or deferring small business debts. About $483 billion of the fiscal package went directly for the protection of wages and salaries, and healthcare support was enhanced. As far as monetary policy was concerned, the Federal Reserve Bank dropped policy rates by 150 basis points in March 2020 and reduced the cost of funds at the discount window. It also declared that it would make open market purchases of government securities as and when necessary. The Federal Reserve has been buying corporate papers directly and indirectly through financial agencies. Clearly, the basis of the stimulus for recovery was focussed more on direct demand creation rather than on supply side easing of liquidity constraints. Yet it was ready to use monetary policy when the additional demand for credit started to be discernable following growth in aggregate demand.

China's fiscal policy stimulus was 4.5% of GDP which was to the tune of RMB 4.6 trillion. This package of incentives for demand contained larger doses of public investment, significant tax waivers and accelerated disbursements of government dues to citizens and corporates. China also used its monetary policy tools to support easy credit, with large doses of liquidity injection through open market operations and reverse repos. The policy rate was reduced by 50 basis points. Around RMB 1.8 trillion was targeted directly to support the credit needs of manufacturing units producing necessities like food and medical supplies. Unsecured loans were allowed under certain conditions, and banks were allowed a higher tolerance for non-performing assets. China used a judicious mix of fiscal and monetary tools in ensuring that production and employment were minimally affected, especially in sectors like food and medical supplies. In these sectors, demand was not a problem but supply constraints were. Hence, in these sectors monetary policy had a specific role to play. In other cases, the demand stimulus was the main trigger. It may be noted that China was defending itself from a drastic fall in its reputation as a responsible economy after the perception mounted that it had in some way contributed to the global spread of the virus. China was trying to ensure that there was no serious flight of direct foreign investment as a fallout of the trade war with USA.

In India, though the government claimed that its (rather late) stimulus package was worth around 10% of GDP, the direct fiscal demand generating component was only 1.9%. The unspoken fear was that the fiscal deficit would spin out of control leading to a downgraded sovereign rating. Direct support was given to the poorest of the poor in terms of free public distribution of cereals and other food, cooking gas and direct cash transfers. The government also helped the middle class and the well to do through the deferment of tax collections. This has been considered to be too little too late. However, the government expressed a view that cash transfers and tax cuts are not spent, but rather saved for future use. On the monetary policy front, the promise of loans and guarantees on loans was very large, much larger than the fiscal policy package. This was to the tune of 4.9% of GDP in the form of shored up credit lines for the micro, small and medium enterprises (MSMEs). The Reserve Bank of India has, since March 2020, reduced its repo and reverse repo rate by 115 and 155 basis points. It also reduced the cash reserve ratio for banks, along with the liquidity coverage ratio and increased the marginal standing facility.

A moratorium on loan repayment was announced for a total of six months from 1 March 2020 to 31 August 2020. Once the moratorium is lifted, borrowers would have to pay their dues with interest, as well as interest accrued on the late payment. This particular clause has been frowned upon by courts in India. During April 2020, the RBI, along with additional monetary easing, announced a TLTRO-2.0 (funds to be invested in investment grade bonds, commercial paper and non-convertible debentures of NBFCs); special refinance facilities for rural banks, housing finance companies and small and medium-sized enterprises; a temporary reduction of the liquidity coverage ratio (LCR) and restriction on banks from making dividend payments; and a standstill on asset classifications during the loan moratorium period with 10%

provisioning requirement and an extension of the time period for resolution timeline of large accounts under default by 90 days. Clearly, the Indian policy-makers have depended heavily on the supply side through credit flows to stimulate growth and economic activity. The direct demand stimulation has been significantly lower in India as compared to the USA and China. This is well brought out by the latest data on GDP for different countries for the April–June quarter of 2020. While China grew by a paltry 3.2%, India's performance was the worst among the G-20 nations with a contraction of 23.9%. USA was somewhere in between with a contraction of 9.5%.

4 The Unfolding Lessons from the Pandemic

The pandemic has forced lifestyle changes on all people. There has been talk of a new normal in the sense that these restrictions such as work from home will remain even after the pandemic is over. The longer the restrictions last and the more prolonged the fear of contracting the disease becomes, human beings will begin to realize important life lessons taught by COVID-19. For instance, the disease caused by the virus found in nature affects all. However, trends show that people with lower incomes and deprived minorities get affected more and are more likely to die from the disease. This means that while all are equal in nature, social hierarchies and inequalities tend to create an unjust distribution of the costs. The pandemic has made people learn to live with much less material goods than what they were used to before the pandemic hit. Of course, the rich would feel the pinch more than the poor in deprivations like not being able to take an international vacation, or go to luxurious restaurants for dinner. The core of this lesson is that consumerism as promoted by the free market economy is largely irrelevant in terms of basic requirements for living. The human ecological footprint has been forced to be reduced with lower movements in international goods and services during the lockdown periods. People also realized that basic needs can be met through local resources to a very large extent: food, shelter and clothing and other necessities of life. There is also a realization that with the lockdown of most economic activities, nature looked rested and rejuvenated. It was clear that human interventions in nature do cause terrible degradations (Dasgupta, 2020). It is also clear that nature can be cleaned up but ethically it cannot be done so with higher unemployment and closures of factories and plants.

There are a number of lessons emerging from governments' reactions in terms of policies and packages to ameliorate the suffering caused by the pandemic. One thing was clear from the responses of all nations is the fact that when pushed to an emergency, the state can dole out cash transfers to poor and adversely affected people without necessarily having a fiscal crisis. Indeed, the actions taken during the pandemic may turn out to be a nascent embryonic pilot project for the introduction of universal basic income in the future.

Two other significant lessons revolve around the importance of healthcare facilities that all citizens can access at reasonable costs, and the ability to have uninterrupted, universally accessible education services. Countries from USA to India have all experienced a shortage of healthcare infrastructure in terms of equipment, beds, hospitals, paramedical staff, nurses, medicines or doctors. A well-planned healthcare plan at affordable costs is of paramount importance for any caring society. Education is also equally important. In India, for instance, it is well known that access is not universal, and where access can be made, the quality is far below par. During the pandemic, there had to be a quick shift to digital platforms for uninterrupted classes. However, it was found that a significant proportion of children and young students did not have access to the Internet or to smart devices like a cell phone or laptop. A plan for universal education with flexible technologies is needed across the world. The digital platforms provide new challenges to pedagogies and teaching tools. This is true for rich and poor nations alike. The lacunae in health care and education have been very acute and costly.

In the times of what some refer to as de-globalization and a return to trade protection, there is a lesson that even though humans can reduce their ecological footprints quite significantly without many tears, in the realm of ideas and knowledge the global arena is still the most desirable. For instance, medical research on drugs, the search for a vaccine and the analysis of the pandemic data are best shared around the world. Technologies, new ideas and innovations are still inherently goods with global positive externalities. Hence, international cooperation in these fields is vital for benefits to be shared equitably around the world. Also, certain problems like controlling the pandemic, mitigating climate change or increasing the chances of nuclear disarmament can only be carried out through international dialogues and mutual understanding.

Finally, the pandemic is leaving human beings with one important philosophical lesson. The disease affects all of us independent of race, religion or nationality. Identities are irrelevant as far as nature is concerned. In the age of rising authoritarianism and xenophobia, this is important. Religious beliefs have also been hit to the extent that one's belief in God or superhuman powers could not save even priests getting the infection. In fact, governments had to prevent by edict congregation of worshippers in temples, mosques, synagogues and churches.

People have multiple identities, and these are subject to change with changes in the preferences of an individual. One can change one's religion and one's nationality. One can change less important identities too like being someone's partner, or supporting a particular football team or political party. Indeed, in today's world of science, one can change one's gender too. However, one identity is immutable as along as one is alive is that of being a human being. This is very evident when one looks at the world of medical science. There is no separate diagnosis or treatment for a Dalit and a Brahmin, or black or white individual. This lesson, if learnt well, can ease a lot of tension around the world.

Can these lessons teach us ways of making the post-COVID-19 world a better place or are these lessons mainly transitory, and once the pandemic dies down, will people rapidly return to business as usual of the pre-pandemic days? It is obviously difficult to predict, and the world can turn out be better in some respects and worse in others. Some social and economic trends may continue while others may get reversed. However, one thing has undoubtedly happened. The barrier to changing human behavioural patterns has been broken decisively with the advent of the pandemic. It is a hard barrier to crack through policies alone. It is the fear of death and disease that forced the issue. Hence, resetting the world economy and society may not be an impossible task after all.

5 Imagining Alternative Futures

The COVID-19 has suddenly exposed the fragility and structural weaknesses of the existing economic system built upon free markets and liberal politics of parliamentary democracy. Some sore spots were already visible before the pandemic as I discussed earlier in the paper. Liberalism was becoming a dirty word in the authoritarian right-wing political lexicon. Free markets and globalization were up for challenge from an inward looking, xenophobic populism that was spreading across the world. The weaknesses exposed were long known in the textbooks of economic development but hardly observed in public policy and the ruling political ideologies of ultra-nationalism and the fear of the immigrant. The stunning inequalities in income and wealth that kept rising beyond imagination, the lack of assured basic health care for most, the poor access and quality of education for the poor and the deprived, the fragility of jobs and incomes, the systematic degradation of the natural environment and the restricted domain of civil rights and liberties all were ignored by policy-makers as an inevitable outcome of market efficiency or at best, a temporary adjustment problem which would disappear if left to itself as the economy continued to grow in terms of GDP.

I have discussed the lessons learnt from COVID-19 and the possibilities. However, it is not clear to what extent societies would be courageous enough to reset the world. Much would depend on the longevity of the virus and the size of the toll it finally takes. On this there could be different combinations of responses by civil society and the state that would determine the broad categories of outcomes. If business and markets are weak and so is the state in terms of governance and regulations, the transition to the post-COVID world would be a chaotic one. If the state is weak but businesses are strong and influential, the outcome will be business as usual. These two outcomes are likely to be costly and the world would become a worse place in terms of the festering fragilities. One the other hand, a strong state with a weak civil society would mean low rates of growth and economic recovery but potentially leaving the system with a better distribution of goods and services so that the poor are better off. I am using the word potential to flag the fact that a strong state post-COVID could be an authoritarian one and whether that government decides to bring reforms for redistribution or uses force to supress any civil disturbances is unknown and not easy to predict. Finally, a strong civil society with a strong state could potentially work out a better long-term strategy of inclusive development on the assumption that civil society displays strategic foresight about a more stable world. Once again, under this scenario, it is difficult to predict how things would shape up. The world could be a more difficult place to live in, somewhat of a combination of Huxley's Brave New

World and Orwell's 1984. It could also be a new economy where the prime objective would be to protect human beings and the planet they inhabit with adequate resources and rights for all. This description does not rule out basic changes. One possibility is that a post-COVID chaotic transition actually throws up new rules and norms, and institutions are tweaked to benefit all. It would mean that power structures change with new social classes getting more influence in policy-making and legislation.

Fundamentally, three exhaustive alternatives might emerge from the four combinations I described. First would be a situation where people act as if the pandemic had never happened. The second alternative is the consolidation and comeback of strong authoritarian states whose policies would be hard to predict. The third possibility remains the emergence a newly evolved system where people and the planet could be looked after in a sustainable fashion.

There is a strong possibility of a change in the global food supply chains. The international food market is controlled by a few giant corporations from fields to supermarket shelves. They sell organic and healthy foods at high prices to the rich and sell hamburgers and pizzas and other junk foods at very low prices for the vast majority of poor and even middle-class people. The mantra is that the world needs to produce more for feeding a growing population of 9–10 billion people this century, hence grow more for less value. This has never benefited poor farmers across the world. Now people are much more concerned and aware of healthy food and realized the importance of wellness and immunity. This might help consumers focus more on what they eat and where the food comes from. There is no aggregate shortage of food. The current food availability is said to be enough to feed 12–14 billion people instead of only the 7.5 billion inhabiting the planet today.

One trend will continue from the pre-COVID times, whatever kind of post-COVID world emerges. That trend is the rapid development of biotechnology and nanotechnology. The advent of machine learning and artificial intelligence will be used to do three distinct things. The first will be to restrict wastage and use of energy to ensure that the artifices of the new technology will be environment friendly and energy efficient. The second test of a new technology would be how it can displace human labour, especially repetitive tasks that can be done by robots without failure, at reduced costs and with no errors. The third test would be if the new technology can keep learning and adapting in dynamically changing work environments. These changes are likely to affect the energy sector too. Rapid evolution of battery technologies will allow the transport sector's emissions to be reduced, resulting in a significant improvement of the quality of air one breathes.

The existing trend of these changes can only be accelerated after COVID-19 dies down. New jobs requiring new skills will be required but many older traditional jobs will be lost. These jobs will not be limited to low skilled jobs, but also include high skilled jobs like that of doctors, engineers, project managers, professors and accountants to name only a few. This new world of technology will create new jobs which require accomplished skills in data analysis and keeping data secure, creative content making for new industries like virtual reality and virtual tourism and entertainment. Technological developments described above would also create a very large unemployable class of useless people. How society treats and looks after this class would determine the quality of life. There would be a strong need to provide some assured basic income to this class.

6 Conclusion

This paper discussed the pandemic as a complex environmental shock and the systemic disruptions caused by it. These disruptions are likely to take a heavy toll on economies and societies. The world after COVID would be a different one from the world before COVID. There are possibilities of change for a better, more humane world emerging from the wisdom gathered out of experience (OECD, 2020). The changes could also be for the worse. Some things are almost certain to happen: there will be labour displacing technological changes and the emergence of mass unemployment. Governments are likely to become more authoritarian. The outcomes can be of various kinds; some much better than the others. Much depends on what societies choose. This statement is itself somewhat vacuous at the end of a rather long essay about COVID. However, it must be noted that the sheer possibility of having alternatives and to move for the betterment of the world by leaving old baggage behind is not something that happens often in history. Change is usually incremental and gradual. Periods of rapid disruptions are rare and revolutionary. The COVID moment is one such exceptional instance in human history. Liberalism is on its way out since it is no longer able to solve the world's problems. There is no alternative at the moment. The struggle to find an alternative to it will continue. It is likely to result in a conflict between the agency of human beings seeking to build their own lives and the powers seeking a return to a promised but non-existent golden past, by consolidating tyrannical forces of control and suppression. It will not be a classical class conflict under capitalism. Nonetheless, it would be a widespread and complex social upheaval.[1]

References

Benmelech, E., & Tzur-Ilan, N. (2020, July). *The Determinants of Fiscal and Monetary Policies during the COVID-19 Crisis.* NBER Working Paper Series WP 27461. Retrieved on August 31, 2020, from https://www.nber.org/papers/.

Dasgupta, P. (2020, June 5). *Coronavirus shows we must change our economy to recognize that human wealth depends on nature's health.* Retrieved on August 31, 2020, from independent.co.uk/news.

Dubey, S. et al. (2020). *Psychosocial Impact of COVID-19.* Retrieved on August 31, 2020, from nebi.nlm.nih.gov/pmc/articles PMC 7255207.

[1] I have extensively used news reports from a variety of publications, the internet, especially the You-tube, and television. The sources are too numerous to record exhaustively. These sources have informed me about news and facts and debates in the course of the pandemic.

Galea, S., & Abdalla, S. (2020, June 12). *COVID-19 pandemic, unemployment and civil unrest*, JAMA (pp. 227–228).

Ghosh, A., et al. (2020). How India is dealing with COVID-19 pandemic. *Science Direct Sensors International, 1*, 1–8.

IMF. (2020a). *World Economic Outlook April 2020*. Washington D.C., USA.

IMF. (2020b). *World economic Outlook Update*. Washington D.C., USA.

Kochhar, R. (2020). *Unemployment rose higher in three months of COVID-19 than it did in two years of the Grate Recession*. Retrieved on August 31, 2020, from pewresearch.org/fact-tank/2020/6/11/.

Miller, C. (2020, March 5). *COVID-19 Crisis: Political and Economic Aftershocks* Foreign Policy Research Institute. Retrieved on August 31, 2020, from frpi.org/2020/03/COVID-19.

Nath, A. (2020). *The Impact of COVID-19 on Global Politics: It is all in the response*. Retrieved on August 31, 2020, from https://trendsresearch.org/insight/.

OECD. (2020, June 10). *Political responses to COVID-19: Strategic foresight for the covid-19 crisis and beyond: Using futures thinking to design better public policies*. Retrieved on August 31, 2020, from oecd.org/coronavirus/policy responses/.

Schuijers, L. (2020, April 18). *COVID-19 is an opportunity to reset our environmental future Design*. Retrieved on August 31, 2020, from pursuit.unimelb.edu.au/design.

UN. (2020). *World economic situation and prospects report*, New York.

Zambrano-Monserrate, M., et al. (2020). *Indirect Effects of COVID-19 on the Environment* (pp. 1–4). Science Direct Science of the Total Environment, Elsevier.

Identification of Urban Centres for Conducting Population Census; Need for Combining GIS with Socio-economic Data

Amitabh Kundu

1 Preamble

In my general conversation with Professor Ramprasad Sengupta, I have often noted that he prefers using robust dataset, up-to-date information and statistical rigour, than the grandeur of modelling. Besides using well-verified datasets, he would go for the latest information and accept a delayed paper submission if that helped in updating the data. Once, he expressed surprise and strong displeasure at Indian Population Census using decade old data in identifying the urban centres for an upcoming Census operation. As the Census towns for 2011 must be identified well before canvassing the Census schedule, there was no way that the current data on population, size, density and non-primary workforce of the year 2011 can be used for notifying the towns. However, the fact that the information of 2001 Census is used to identify the new Census towns of 2011, with marginal discretion left to Directorate of Census Operations, made him uncomfortable with the methodology.

Ramprasad is a great supporter of technology for improving quality of information. I believe the work I did to improve the information base for identification of urban centres and generate an alternate estimate of urban population for Sri Lankan government, using GIS technology, would reduce his discomfort—at least to a small extent.

A. Kundu (✉)
World Resources Institute and Research and Information System for Developing Countries, New Delhi, India
e-mail: akundu.jnu@gmail.com

P. Dasgupta et al. (eds.), *Sustainable Development Insights from India*,
India Studies in Business and Economics,
https://doi.org/10.1007/978-981-33-4830-1_4

2 Introduction

The magnitude of any measurable attribute of a unit becomes meaningful only when that is placed in relation to the value of other units or those of the same unit at different points of time. It would be considered high or low, good or bad, etc. only through comparisons. In a large country, cross-sectional or temporal comparison of attributes of its constituent areal units, therefore, is possible only when there is a system to build statistics, articulating the attributes in a standardised manner. Hence, having a system of data collection to capture the relevant attributes meaningfully across the micro units and over time would be important, despite wide diversity or disparity that may exist within the country. Furthermore, for temporal comparisons, it would be important to ensure that the essence of the attribute does not undergo significant change, as a result of social and economic dynamism. However, when the attribute has undergone changes over time, one would have to alter the indicator and the method of collecting the information so that the essence is appropriately captured in the base and terminal year.

The concepts on which information are collected at national, regional and sub-regional levels in a country has to meet another requirement, besides ensuring temporal and cross-sectional comparability. The information set generally constitutes the basis for designing policies and programmes. Since the objectives of policy intervention are to alter specific attributes in all or certain targeted regions, monitoring of progress becomes mandatory. That can be done only when temporally and cross-sectionally comparable statistics are available. The areal classification system used in building the database in a country must, therefore, match the concepts and categories constituting the basis of policy intervention.

Understandably, there will be additional issues of comparability across the countries. The World Development Report (WDR, World Bank 2009), despite having to deal with the problems of making data on urbanisation comparable across countries, states categorically that "each country can have its own definition of urban centre for designing and monitoring its urban related programmes". The task of areal classification and identification of urban centres along with delimitation of their boundaries in any country becomes challenging since it involves ensuring comparability within and across the countries and also to meet the requirements of policy at regional and national level. International comparability is desirable but unfortunately most countries have not been able to achieve that in any satisfactory manner.

3 Objectives of the Study

The key objective of the paper is to critically analyse the present system of areal classification system into urban, rural (and in some cases semi-urban, estate sector or rurban) in countries in South Asia and propose a new operational methodology that addresses the current deficiencies. The proposed criteria meet the needs of policy making without sacrificing temporal and cross-sectional comparability of the data. The new criterion is based on a review of the international practices and examination of the best practices. The proposed definition and the system of classification could constitute the basis for the future Population Censuses in developing countries. In addition, this could be applied in the national level surveys, undertaken at regular intervals. Furthermore, the new data gathering and compilation system would make it possible to construct at least a select set of key indicators, with some amount of disaggregation and reaggregation of information, for the years in the recent past, so as maintain continuity with the past dataset.

The key objectives of the present study are (a) review current and best international practices with respect to the definition of urban and rural areas, (b) analyse the data from previous Population Censuses and other relevant sources to propose new definitions for areal classification, (c) analyse the ground level situation with the new definitions and show how existing Census procedures fail in including settlements having high current population density and built-up area, (d) analysis of how estimates of urban population, provided by the previous surveys and Censuses would change as a result of the new definition.

4 Review of International Practices with Respect to the Definition of Urban and Rural Areas

The Population Division of the United Nations (UNPD) brings out compendiums on urban population at regular intervals, giving data since 1950 and projections up to 2050. It obtains the basic information from different countries that are collected as per the definitions adopted by their national statistical system, often designed to meet the requirements of their own policies and programmes. Population Censuses are the most commonly used sources of data for UNPD, although estimates obtained from Population Registers or administrative statistics are also incorporated for a few countries.

It is important to note that the urban definitions employed for Census or other major surveys vary widely across countries and in many cases among different agencies within a country. Furthermore, the definitions change over time due to changed socio-economic context or a shift in policy perspective. There have been a few efforts by UN agencies to produce globally comparable estimates of urban population with uniform criteria to define urban areas through commissioned studies and by globally networked projects, using satellite imagery of land cover, night-time lights, etc., and combining these with socio-economic data, at spatially disaggregated level. These, however, have not been able to generate time series data for different countries on a comparable basis. In fact, UNPD has not pursued the goal of evolving a common global definition of an urban settlement since it believes that "national statistical offices are in the best position to establish the most appropriate criteria to characterise urban areas in their respective countries". The exceptions are when countries lack in

Table 1 Percentage of Urban Population in Sri Lanka for different years obtained from WUP 2011 Revision

	1980	1985	1990	1995	2000	2005	2010	2015	2020
Per cent urban	18.8	18.0	17.2	16.4	15.7	15.1	15.0	15.5	16.4

"clear definitions or historical changes prevent to reconstruct consistent time series". Adjustments in the figures, provided by the national level agencies, are made mostly for the purpose of ensuring consistency of the estimates across time within a country and not for inter-country comparisons.

Sri Lankan case may be referred here for illustrative purposes. The World Urbanisation Prospects (WUP) (2011 Revision) reports the percentage of urban population to be 17.2, 15.5 and 16.4 for the years 1990, 2015 and 2020, respectively, for the country. Understandably, these interpolated and extrapolated figures are based on the information provided by the Department of Census and Statistics (DCS), Sri Lanka, for the years 1981 and 2001. It is important to note here that Population Census could not be conducted in 1991 and the figures from 2012 Census were not available to the UN at that time. Building on the premise of a sharp decline in the figures from 21.2 to 13.1% during 1981–01, as reported by the Census, the time series data were constructed and smoothened by UNPD, determining the figures as given in Table 1.

It may be observed that the UNPD stipulated a uniform decline by 0.8 percentage point for each of the three quinquennial periods after 1980. For the subsequent two periods viz. 1995–2000 and 2000–2005, the decline was taken as 0.7 and 0.6, respectively. The World Bank Report entitled Leveraging Urbanisation in South Asia, too, suggests that the share of urban population fell in Sri Lanka between 2000 and 2010, based on this limited data.

These figures, however, stand revised in WUP 2014 Revision, as the new data became available from the Census of 2012, at the time of its preparation. The figures for 1990 and 2014 have been placed at 18 and 19% by this latest WUP, to bring these in line with the urban percentage figure of 18.2%, as determined by the national Census of 2012. Furthermore, the optimism reflected in projecting the urbanisation level to double during 2015–30 in WUP 2014 can be explained primarily by the urban growth reported by the Census during 2001–12. It is, thus, evident that the WUP makes adjustments in the estimates of certain countries, based on the data made available by their national level agencies. These, however, have been only to ensure temporal consistency for the countries and not for comparability across countries, where there appears to be a serious problem, as noted above.

An important limitation of the urban data has been underlined by UNPD itself. It argues that an increase in the number of urban centres and extension of their areas are common phenomena always taking place in the process of the country's economic development. Understandably, keeping urban and rural units fixed or their boundaries unaltered for a long span, pending administrative decisions at a high level, are likely to underestimate the urban population, at any given time. It has long been recognised that, given the variety of situations in the countries of the world, it is not possible or

Table 2 Criteria applied singly or in conjunction with other criteria for identification of urban areas in different countries

	Singly	Along with Adm./demo criteria	Along with Adm./demo, eco and urban criteria	Along with other criteria	Total
Demographic	48	24	49	59	196
Administrative	64	24	30	54	172

desirable to adopt uniform criteria to distinguish urban areas from rural areas (see United Nations, 1967 and 1969) or to delimit the boundaries of the agglomerations in a mechanical fashion. Owing to these two factors, urban data, as reported by UNPD, based on the information obtained from national level agencies, underestimate the urban population for a number of developing countries.

An overview of the definitions of urban centres has been attempted here based on the compilation of information in WUP 2011 as also details available in the relevant websites in different countries. It is noted that four criteria have been used globally in area classification. These are: (a) administrative (decision by concerned ministry or department based on civic status, revenue, need to bring a settlement under a programme etc. or as per certain statute), (b) population threshold (c) economic (proportion of workers employed in non-agricultural sectors, tax collected outside agriculture etc.) and (d) urban services (infrastructure such as paved roads, electricity, piped water or sewers; presence of education or health services). Each of these has been used independently as well as in conjunction with the other criteria. Furthermore, these criteria have also been used along with some other criteria, reflecting functional characteristics, as may be seen in Table 2.

It may be noted that out of the 231 countries for which urban data are available from World Urbanisation Prospects (WUP) 2011 and the current websites of the governments, in case of 26, the definitional issues cannot be analysed since these (a) either have the entire population of the country declared as urban or (b) have no definition for urban centres or (c) employ definitions without any clarity. Among the remaining 205 countries that use unambiguous criteria, 196 (96%) use demographic while 172 (84%) use administrative criterion, singly or in conjunction of other criteria. However, only 64 (31%) among all countries depend totally on administrative criteria for defining the urban centres and Pakistan and Sri Lanka are among them. Similarly, 23% of the countries totally depend on demographic criteria, mostly gathered through Population Census. A global review of the definitions, thus, suggests that administrative and demographic criteria are the ones that are in common use.

One would infer from this overview that the countries that use only the administrative criterion and do not take into consideration urban processes taking place due to economic and infrastructural development, changes in workforce structure and functional characteristics of the settlements, etc., would fail to identify emerging urban centres and, thereby, tend to underestimate the level of urbanisation. The other factor, responsible for urban undercount, is keeping the official boundaries of cities and towns fixed or expanding these only with considerable time lag which tantamount to ignoring demographic growth outside the official urban limits (UNESCAP, 2013). These are the factors responsible for the Census figures failing to assess the settlement level dynamics and underestimate urban growth with respect to both territory and population in South Asia (UN, 2014). The countries that, besides the statutory towns that are identified as per administrative orders, employ criteria relating to population, density, economic functions, availability of certain infrastructure and amenities for identifying other urban centres would broaden the canvass and can report urbanisation levels closer to ground reality. It is important to note that the Censuses in India and Bangladesh attempt to capture the dynamics of development, reflected in changes in socio-economic characteristics in an institutionalised manner by combining the two criteria to identify urban centres.[1]

It would be useful to have a closer look at the definitions in the South Asian countries as many among these, besides sharing a common geography, also have a common colonial history that impacted on the administrative and legal systems, even after their Independence. In the context of urban data for Pakistan, which, as per the World Bank Report, is experiencing serious problems due to messy urbanisation, a common concern shared by researchers, administrators and planners, both at national and city levels, has been that the actual "city populations were higher than what official data reports".[2] They have made a strong case for probing into the issue of definition, specially the changes introduced in the 1981 Census, leading to abandonment of demographic and economic criteria in favour of using only administrative judgement.[3] Leading Pakistani demographers and social scientists had commented and raised questions on the apparently low urban population reported in the 1998 Census, considering it inconsistent with economic trends and evidence-based research. These concerns are similar to those expressed with regard to urban data in Sri Lanka, as discussed below. Currently, Pakistan is considering ways by which urban population can be correctly determined, without which it has been difficult to design and implement a balanced strategy of urbnisation and address the problem of spatial disparity in provisioning of basic amenities. As per the World Bank Report, Pakistan is urbanising faster than the whole of South Asia, their growth rates in urban population being 3.1% and 2.7%, respectively. Agglomeration index computed in the World Development Report (WDR 2009) suggests that urban figures for all South Asian

[1]Buettner (2014) notes that out of these 231 countries, 121 have adopted a single criterion while 84 have used a combination of two or more criteria. Among the single criterion users, 64 countries have adopted purely administrative criteria, 48 have adopted population size/density related criteria while in nine countries, the classification is based on solely urban functional characteristics. Among the combinations, most common is that of administrative and population size/density, followed by population size/density and economic criteria and population and functional characteristics.

[2]Reza Ali, Haque, Husain and Arif, 2013. "Estimating Urbanisation", The Urban Gazette, December, 2013.

[3]"An estimate of 361 places with a population of 5,000 or more that were considered rural in the 1998 Census actually had urban characteristics better than many places considered urban in the Census; if their population is considered urban, this would add another 6.5% to the 1998 urban population of Pakistan" (Arif, 2003).

countries are much higher than those officially reported, that constitute the data base for UNPD. The maximum difference is seen in case of Sri Lanka.

In Bangladesh, urban areas are centres having over 5000 people, "with such amenities as metalled roads, improved communication, electricity, gas, water supply, sewerage, sanitation and also having comparatively higher density of population with majority population in non-agriculture occupations". These include city corporations, (administered by the Local Government Division under City Corporation Act, 2009), cities having population 1,00,000–49,99,999, towns having population less than 1,00,000 and *paurashavas* (administered by local government under Paurashava Act, 2009). In addition, all *upazila* headquarters which are not *paurashavas* and the 17 unions located within Dhaka Metropolitan Area are treated as urban on the basis of their functional characteristics. It is, thus, evident that both administrative and socio-economic criteria are used in Bangladesh in areal classification.

India, after Independence inherited the Census traditions from British period like Pakistan and Bangladesh. After Independence, however, it has gone towards strengthening the system of data linked identification of urban centres rather than state or provincial governments declaring these under their statutes in an ad-hoc manner. The statutory towns are those that are declared to be so by the provincial governments. The criteria they adopt are not very transparent and vary across provinces. Their decisions are often based on level of infrastructure, revenue earning capabilities etc., besides the usual demographic and workforce linked criteria. A large part of the responsibility of identifying urban centres (45% of them being Census towns), however, falls on the Census organisation, using the following criteria.

(a) Population size of 5000 and above
(b) Population density of 400 per km^2
(c) 75% of the male workforce being outside agriculture.

Understandably, several among the statutory towns do not meet the three demographic thresholds, proposed above. Importantly, many of the Census towns, too, do not satisfy these criteria. The Directorates of Census Operations have been given the right and responsibility to exercise discretionary judgement for identifying settlements as towns, based on their pronounced urban characteristics. The Census organisations have been assigned this responsibility for addressing the problems arising out of non-application of uniform criteria by the provincial governments to identify the statutory towns and bringing in certain amount of standardisation.

Countries in South Asia and across the globe are realising the usefulness of using demographic and functional criteria along with administrative judgement in identifying urban centres. The governments in these countries, nonetheless, would like to retain the powers of identifying urban centres in the context of meeting the needs of their regional development strategy as and when required and not to abdicate the total responsibility to Census organisations.

5 Exploring Methodologies for Delimiting Boundaries of Urban Centres and Estimating Urban Population

A methodology for identifying urban centres and delimiting their boundaries depends on the theory of development—an understanding and explanation of the dynamism of the development process and its manifestations in space. Urbanisation, in the context of economic development in a globally linked market, has been conceptualised in terms of the areas and population "that can both benefit from and contribute to agglomeration economies".[4] It has often been taken to imply the coverage of areas of high "economic density", defined in terms of output per square kilometre. Unfortunately, information on economic density or gross product at a disaggregated spatial scale—such as a district or a settlement—is not available in most developing countries. Data from different parts of the globe, however, suggest that economic mass or output density is strongly correlated with population density, lending support to the proposition that the concentration of population in urban areas lead to conglomerations of economic actors. The gradient of population density with distance from the city centre would then approximate corresponding gradient of economic density. Uneven distribution of population reflects "bumpiness" of economic geography which is inevitable in countries adopting market linked development. The neoclassical theory stipulates that development is always accompanied by rising density in select locations making the surface of economic development uneven. Furthermore, distance intermediated by technology determines the travel time which can be used in drawing the boundaries of outreach of the development dynamics in a region. The percentage of people commuting for economic reasons to the nearest settlement of high economic density and thereby accessing to economic opportunities can then be used as the criterion for delineating the limits of a city region.

The methodologies for areal classification within this theoretical framework would involve identification of urban core, based on settlement of "sizeable population" and then determination of the periphery of the agglomeration based on population density, continuity of the built-up area and functional measures such as travel time for commutation or the share of population commuting to the city core on a regular basis (Chomitz et al., 2005, Uchida and Nelson, 2008). Total urban population can then be worked out by aggregating the population of the core and periphery. Such standardisation of the definition of urban areas helps in inter-country comparison of the economic, social and environmental performances of metropolitan cities and making a comparative assessment of the process of urbanisation.

Several attempts have been made by global institutions to assess the trends and pattern of urbanisation within this methodological perspective. These stipulate metropolitan areas as polarised network systems determined through population size, density and intensity of interactions among constituent "local units". The methods adopted by the institutions vary significantly in terms of their choice of indicators, threshold values for each of these and use of the administrative boundaries. The

[4]This provides the rationale for using the criteria of population density and accessibility to a sizable market for building up an agglomeration index. See World Bank (2009).

common point in these methods is that they use information pertaining to commutation or interaction to capture the degree of relationships among densely inhabited core and their neighbouring areas—that are physically separated, but economically integrated—to define the metropolitan regions.

One innovative approach within this theoretical perspective is that of Organisation for Economic Cooperation and Development (OECD) which has evolved a "harmonised definition" for "functional economic units" that are comparable across countries. The methodology has been approved by the OECD Working Party on Territorial Indicators in 2011. It takes the building blocks, the smallest administrative units for which national commuting data are available (OECD, 2013), as the primary areal units. It uses population density to identify "urban cores" or "high-density clusters", while the hinterland is delimited based on the information on the share of population, commuting to the core on a regular basis.

High-density clusters of contiguous grid cells (1 kmX1Km), with a density of at least 1500 inhabitants per square kilometre, constitute the core. In case of low density countries like Canada and United States, the threshold is brought down to 1000 people per square km. Furthermore, while the OECD methodology uses municipal bodies as the constituent units of high-density cluster, in the case of USA, these are the counties.

Importantly, urban high-density clusters extend much beyond the administrative borders of the cities. A municipality would be a part of an urban core if at least 50% of its population lives within the urban cluster. All the cities in the OECD are not characterised by contiguity in built-up development. An important innovation of this methodology is that it can delineate urban areas with a polycentric structure. The final step of the methodology consists in delineating the hinterland of the metro areas defined as the "worker catchment area" for the labour market, outside the densely inhabited core. Urban hinterlands are defined comprising all municipalities with at least 15% of their employed residents working in the urban core. Understandably, non-contiguous municipalities are not included in the hinterland.

A similar framework has been applied in the WDR 2009 in proposing a measure of agglomeration—agglomeration index—based on a uniform definition of "urban centre", following a variant of the Chomitz et al. (2005) and Uchida et al. methodology. It locates "sizable settlements" as the urban centres for "agglomerated areas" based on population density criterion while their boundaries are determined based on a cap on the time taken for the residents to travel to the centre. For being identified as an urban centre, a settlement must have certain minimum population size and minimum density. The settlement for which the travel time to the sizable settlement is less than a specified limit would constitute the hinterland of the settlement. Hinterland is delineated by considering grid cells with an area of 1 square kilometre as the basic units. These would be considered as urban, agglomerated, or dense if they satisfy the criteria of (a) population density exceeding 150 persons per square kilometre, (b) having access to a sizable settlement with population above 50,000 inhabitants, identified as urban centre, and (c) time threshold of 60 min to reach the sizable settlement by road. The density and travel time thresholds are those employed in Chomitz et al. (2005). The procedure for computing the population residing in the agglomerations

Table 3 Percentage of urban population based on the compilation of UNPD and agglomeration index of the world bank in South Asian countries

Country	Country specific definition UNPD (WUP 2011)	Uniform definition agglomeration index (WDR 2009)
Bangladesh	23.2	48.0
India	28.7	52.4
Pakistan	33.2	53.6
Sri Lanka	15.7	38.2

in a region or country, thus, involves five steps: (a) identification of sizable settlements, (b) creation of population density grids, (c) identification of grid cells that satisfy the above three criteria, (d) aggregation of grid cell populations, and finally, (e) determination of the boundaries of the agglomeration. This mapping is done using data from the Global Rural–Urban Mapping Project (GRUMP). Understandably, an agglomeration, comprising the core and the hinterland as per this methodology, may not coincide with any administrative unit in a country. The proportion of the population in the agglomerations to that country's total population is the agglomeration index, a summary measure of the proportion of the population living in areas of high density.

This method helps in building a measure of settlement concentration, facilitating cross-country comparison, which can be used as a proxy for the level of urbanisation. It is quite revealing that the urbanisation level inferred from the agglomeration index for all South Asian countries are much higher than reported by the World Urbanisation Prospects. The former are higher than the latter by 20 percentage points but the figure is more than double in case of Sri Lanka (Table 3 and Graph 1).

It is important to note that the estimated value of the "agglomeration index" is sensitive to the choice of the population threshold, noted above. When the threshold is taken as 50,000, the value of the agglomeration index works out as 52%. However, when 100,000 is taken as the minimal settlement size, the figure is 44% only. The other underlying assumption in the methodology is that a settlement must be within one hour of travel distance from the core or the sizable settlement in order to be included in the agglomeration. This implicitly assumes that the success of urbanisation strategy in a region depends on accessibility of its settlements to metrocities or other agglomerations. The validity of this assumption needs to be examined in the context of less developed countries before adopting the methodology for identification of urban centres. Building metropolis centred transport and institutional system, as attempted in some of the Latin American and East Asian countries for the success of capitalism, can, however, turn out to be not only expensive but counterproductive in South Asia.

The e-Geopolis project is yet another significant initiative designed with the objective of building up comparable urban data for all countries of the world over the last two centuries, using a uniform definition. Three different sources of information are used in building the database: (a) Population Censuses from over 200 countries/territories covering about two centuries, (b) information on 2 million geo-referenced "local units" (places, villages, cities, towns, places, etc.) and (c) high definition satellite images delineating built-up areas. Now, an "agglomeration" is defined as a morphological body of continuous built-up areas with gaps not exceeding 200 m between buildings/blocks (excepting parking areas, roads, graveyards, mines, rivers, etc.) and a population threshold of 10,000 inhabitants. Total urban population in a country is determined by aggregating the population of all the agglomerations.

Information on agglomeration is already being collected in about 50 countries as a part of their national statistical system. In case of others, it is estimated by the e-Geopolis team. A "local unit" is defined as the country's smallest administrative division for which official statistics are available along with its geographical coordinates. A built-up area of an agglomeration can extend over several local units. A local unit is included in the agglomeration if 50% of its built-up areas are part of the main built-up area. The first version of e-Geopolis database was brought in public domain as early as in 1990s. Its objective is to update information of all agglomerations using the information from satellite images on a regular basis.

It is important to note that all the methods discussed above use the conventional Census along with the GIS data to determine the agglomerations, thereby capturing population in the peripheries of the central city or town, although the population threshold for determining the urban core vary significantly. A settlement as per the methodology can be considered urban only if it has continuity of built-up areas with the core settlement. It is, however, observed that many of the developing economies are experiencing significant in-situ urbanisation through transformation of rural to urban units. Many of them are located in distant areas, have little access to infrastructural facilities of any agglomeration and owe their growth to their own dynamics rather than support of the global or the national market.

Emergence and growth of small and medium towns, interacting with the people in their immediate hinterland for collection of primary products and delivery of basic services, through an alternative and often more time intensive modes of transportation and absorbing the dispossessed rural migrants searching for livelihood, in several Asian countries, thus, reflects developments outside mainstream urbanisation. Labour supply driven sectoral diversification is the key factor behind the growth of many of these towns, as noted above. Location of large industrial units, universities, hospitals, residential complexes, etc. in public or private sector, is the other important factor. A few of these settlements are able to take advantage of the demand support from the adjacent industrial or commercial units and exogenous investment. Much of their growth, however, is attributed to the struggle of the local population to find livelihood for themselves, reflecting endogenous growth potential.

Given this definite evidence of in situ urbanisation, it would be important that a "theory of development and system of measuring urbanisation" is built from below by exploring the internal dynamics of the settlements and local level institutions, instead of defining urbanisation solely in terms of linkages with global and national market. This puts a question mark on the advocacy of a uniform system of identifying urban areas based on density and access to national/global market through agglomerated development. It would be important to build up a database for the settlements with obvious development potentials, based on their current level of sectoral diversification and the degree of interaction with neighbouring rural areas for promoting sustainable development.

6 Proposing a System for Areal Classification: Criteria for Identifying Urban Centres

A number of global institutions, including development cum banking institutions have argued that the percentage of urban population in many of the countries in South Asia are outliers when analysed in relation to their per capita income, percentage of non-agricultural workers, infrastructure, energy consumption, etc. These stands away from the regression line determined empirically, using information from all countries. It was noted above that urbanisation levels, as suggested by the agglomeration index constructed by WDR 2009 are much higher and the official figures grossly underreport the phenomenon.

Unhappiness with the urban data is reflected in numerous policy statements made in government documents, research papers and media reporting in these countries. It is generally argued that not recognising the urban territories officially is coming in the country's way of achieving its full growth potential. Furthermore, not having the urban status is impacting adversely on the realisation of political rights, participation in economic activities and building of right based relationship between the citizen and the state. It also affects composition of revenue base and access to federal government resources resulting in serious disparities in the level of basic amenities between the core and periphery of the cities. Also, it is argued that bestowing urban status on a settlement could result in higher efficiency in governance and greater capacity to acquire land and other resources for development projects. Given this perspective, the policy thrust of the government on urban development is understandable. However, for the success of various missions and programmes related with urban development, appropriate classification of rural and urban areas would be extremely important.

The dissatisfaction with the stringent system of identifying urban centres and the low percentage of urban population thus determined in South Asia have led researchers and institutions propose definitions based on a number of socio-economic indicators. The global overview of the definitions suggests that population size, reflecting the magnitude of agglomeration economies, is a key indicator in defining an urban centre. Provisioning of basic services like a common market, school, bank, etc. requires certain scale of operation for economic viability. In view of this, many countries have specified 2000 or 5000 as the minimum threshold population per square kilometre as a critical criterion reflecting urbanity. However, in South Asian context with massive physiographic diversity, smaller settlements may exist. In fact, such settlements have emerged around large cities or in hilly areas. Considering all this, it would be important to have low population threshold like 500 as the first criterion for a locality or village for inclusion into urban frame.

A reasonable sized market requires certain mass of people and density that can be taken as a proxy for "market thickness". High density also provides an opportunity for creation of pool of skills needed for diversifying production base. Density of 400 persons per square kilometre can, therefore, be proposed as the minimum population density necessary for an urban centre in Asia. It is indeed true that countries in continents of America, Australia and Europe have lower density thresholds as their overall population densities are low. However, countries with higher densities like Bangladesh, India also accept the threshold as 400 per square kilometre. For countries like Sri Lanka, proposals are made to lower the density requirements one notices that a large part of the population here is concentrated in a few districts where urban density below 400 per square kilometre would be undesirable.

An indicator of employment diversity, reflecting non-agricultural alignment of the local economy, has been adopted as a mandatory criterion in a large number of countries. There is, indeed, a strong case for inclusion of an indicator pertaining to diversification of economic activities, reflecting a shift away from agriculture to industry and services. In the absence of information on total non-agricultural employment, the number of workers in government, semi-government and private establishments to the total employees above 15 years of age can be considered appropriate in defining urban centres in certain countries. It would, however, be desirable to have the percentage of total non-agricultural employment, including those in informal sector, as a criterion for identifying the urban centres in Asian countries, that have a high incidence of informal employment. In India, the threshold is kept at a high level of 75%, simply because it is applied to the male workforce. If the criterion is applied to the total workforce, the figure would be close to 55%, since the participation of women outside agricultures in India is very low. Similar is the case of Sri Lanka. A village having more 55 or 60% of workforce outside agriculture can then be considered as the third criterion for defining an urban centre.

Keeping the data constraints in view, scholars have suggested incorporation of access to certain basic amenities pertaining to improved drinking water and energy, etc. as a criterion for defining urban centres. Importantly, it is not the level or quality of services that should distinguish an urban from a rural habitat as service quality in many towns in Asian countries are worse than in rural areas. What should distinguish them is the source of energy and water or the technology for their provisioning since that have implications for the requirement of open space within a habitation. The argument is that if the households, for example, depend on ponds rivers, well, etc. for drinking water or has traditional source of energy, it would involve a large area per person, signifying rural living conditions.

There are, however, arguments against considering source of energy and water as critical indicators of urbanity since this depends on physiographic conditions that vary significantly across and within countries. Also, there are town planning norms stipulating mandatory open spaces within the cities although these have not been implemented uniformly across provinces and cities. More importantly, if the idea is to identify urban areas as those that have less area per person, this must be done by taking indicators such as density, built-up areas or the households living in flats or multi-storied apartments. Also, the definition linking rural areas with traditional sources of energy or water would not be in line with the policies and programmes to provision these services through modern technology and using non-traditional sources, irrespective of their rural or urban status. Finally, this would mean making a significant departure from the criteria being adopted by different countries and global institutions, as discussed above. In view of all these, it would be worthwhile not to include any criterion pertaining to level of basic amenities or the source of energy or technology for providing these, for identifying urban centres.

A settlement meeting the above mentioned three criteria but performing no nodal function through interaction with neighbouring settlements and having no critical social and economic infrastructure may not be included in the urban frame. One must, however, include an indicator, reflecting interactions of a settlement with its neighbouring areas, that reflect its centrality or nodality of a village. Alternately, one may propose that the latter must have at least one facility reflecting spatial interaction. Importantly, nodality and interaction of settlements has been considered important but only with the neighbouring large cities to draw urban boundaries or in working out the agglomeration index. WDR considered travel time of one hour from the urban core as the threshold limit for drawing agglomeration boundaries. However, for transitional economies in South Asia, with a dominant primary sector, proximity and interaction would have to be considered also in terms of providing facilities for trade and other services or access to bank and high or middle level educational institution.

In the context of Sri Lanka and Bangladesh, one may propose that a settlement must have at least 15 trading and service establishments per thousand population or have any one of the facilities such as a common market, bank, high school, etc. for being considered as an urban centre. It may, however, be argued that a settlement having connectivity with its neighbouring settlements or providing nodal services may not be relevant in the context of those in the hinterland of large cities or in the development corridor connecting two cities. These settlements, characterised by high density and large percentage of built-up areas, need not perform such nodal functions for their neighbouring areas since the settlements in the hinterland may avail these facilities at the central city.

Given this perspective, it is proposed that the settlements with 500 or more persons but not meeting the non-agricultural employment and interaction criterion should be considered as urban if they have very high population density and corresponding built-up area. The threshold for high population density can be taken as 1000 per square kilometre. The peripheral areas in American and European cities work out to be one-tenth of that in the core.[5] The core in the large cities in Sri Lanka (also India) has population density of around 10,000 which provides a rationale for taking the cut-off point of 1000 for declaring a locality as a part of urban agglomeration. Furthermore, the average built-up area in Asian cities is taken to be between 30 and 40%. If the data are generated through high resolution imagery, 30% of built-up area can be considered to be adequate for being counted as a part of an agglomeration. The methodology and the computational details for identifying urban centres and

---

[5] World Bank (2015)

the estimates of urban population are presented in the following section, taking Sri Lanka as a case study. Information on built-up area is obtained from the Facebook, as processed at the Centre for Earth Sciences Network, Earth Institute, Columbia University.

7 Determining the Level of Urbanisation in Sri Lanka in 2012 Employing the Proposed Definition: An Illustrative Case

An attempt is made in this section to compute the percentage of urban population for the year 2012 based on the available data, using the methodology of areal classification, proposed above and compare it with the official estimate. The objective is to make a case for the adoption of this methodology for the upcoming Census of 2021 in Sri Lanka as also in other Asian countries.

A two-stage approach has been followed taking *Grama Niladhari Divisions* (GNDs), the smallest areal units for which official statistics are available in Sri Lanka, to build the database. In the first stage, the units satisfying all the four criteria discussed above have been identified and their population is worked out. In the second stage, additional urban centres have been identified based on the same population threshold of 500 but an enhanced density criterion of 1000 per square kilometre and a built-up area criterion of 30%. Neither the workforce threshold nor the interaction criterion has been applied at the second stage.

The Directorate of Census and Statistics (DCS) in Sri Lanka has compiled spatially disaggregated database for a large number of variables from pre-listing operations, regular Census and economic Census for 14,022 GNDs, pertaining to the year 2012. The four criteria, as discussed in the preceding section, have been applied sequentially, the roadmap for which is elaborated below in Table 4. It was observed that in case of a large number of GNDs, no information was given with regard to population and a number of other variables. Excluding these generally uninhabited settlements as also those having population less than 500, a set of 12,881 GNDs have been selected to begin an iterative exercise. Only 56.11% of the units satisfy the criterion of population density of 400 per square kilometre as 5653 GNDs got disqualified by the density criterion. Of the remaining 7228 GNDs, 51.90% are noted as having the threshold level workers of 55% in government/semi-government and private establishments and thereby qualify by the third criteria.

Among the 3751 GNDs having the required threshold population, density and non-agricultural employment, as high as 86.6% qualify by the interaction criterion at the fourth level of screening. One can, thus, see that 23.16% of the GNDs possess all the stipulated urban characteristics. The share of these GND units in the total population of the country, however, is even higher, since their population size is larger than the average. These GNDs have above six million inhabitants in total

Table 4 Iterative process of screening the GNDs through application of fourfold criteria articulating urban features stage I

No of GNDs	Stage 1 (S1) population criterion >=500	Per cent to total in S1	Stage 2 (S2) density criterion >=400	Per cent to Total in S2	Stage 3 (S3) non-ag. employee >=55% criterion	Per cent to total in S3	Stage 4 (S4) interaction criteria any one (a) 15 or more trading est. per 1000 persons, (b) common market, (c) bank, (d) school		Per cent to total in S4	Per cent meeting and not meeting all criteria to total GNDs
Satisfy	12,881	91.86	7228	56.11	3751	51.90	(a) 20 or more trading, etc. or (b)common market and bank, or (c) school	3248	86.59	23.16
Do not satisfy	1141	8.14	5653	43.89	3477	48.10		503	13.41	76.84
Total	14,022	100.00	12,881	100	7228	100.00	Total	3751	100.00	100.00

Note At level 1, GNDs having population below 500 are excluded. Level 2 filters out those reporting population density less than 400 per square kilometre. The percentage of employees in government, semi-government and private establishments above 55% is the selection criterion at level 3. At level 4, the GNDs that meet the first three criteria are screened to find whether these had either (a) more than 15 trading and service establishments per thousand population, or (b) common market or (c) bank or (c) school against the national figure of 20 million. The level of urbanisation in Sri Lanka in 2012 at the first stage, thus, works out as 29.72%.

Policy makers, administrators and researchers working on Sri Lanka have often noted that many of the large cities have expanded beyond their municipal limits that have not been bought within the urban frame, as discussed above. These areas are characterised by high population density, high percentage of built-up areas. Many among these, nonetheless, do not satisfy the interaction or interlinkage criteria. It has been argued above that the system of areal classification must bring these units within the urban fold. An attempt is made in the second stage to identify such GNDs and consider bestowing "urban" status on them through, once again, a similar iterative process, as discussed below.

At the first iteration in stage 2, 12,881 GNDs having population above 500 have been identified, as was done in stage 1. The units have been tested against the second criterion of density of 1000 per square kilometre. As many as 4536 GNDs in the country satisfy the population density criterion but a few among these have population size below 500. The units with qualifying level of values in both have been placed against the third criterion, the percentages of built-up areas of over 30%. The number of GNDs satisfying all the three criteria works out to be 2064 only (Table 5). As per the stipulations discussed above, the DCS could consider all these units as urban. It must, however, be pointed out that many among these have already qualified as urban by the fourfold criteria in stage 1, as discussed above. Cross classification of the GNDs identified by the two approaches reveals that of these 2064 GNDs, 1001 units are already in the urban list, prepared in stage 1. Consequently, only 1063 units need to be added to the list. As many as 4311 or 30.74% of the GNDs in Sri Lanka can, thus, be declared as urban.

It is important to note that the additional units that qualify as urban by the sheer strength of population size, enhanced density and built-up area constitute only 7.58% of the total units. The population in these settlements, however, is as large as 2.8 million, comprising 13.81% of the total population. Adding this number with the figure computed earlier, based on the fourfold criteria, the total urban population in the country would be over 8 million which is 43.54% of the total population.

Table 6 presents summary statistics of this exercise giving the number and population of the GNDs identified as urban in stage I applying the fourfold criteria and the additional units and their population identified in state II, by applying the threefold criteria.

The distributions of the 3248 urban GNDs identified in stage I and 1063 additional GNDs identified in stage II across the provinces are presented in Table 7. Clearly there is concentration of "urban" GNDs in western, central and southern provinces, accounting for over 75% of "urban" units in Sri Lanka. The western province alone has over 58% of its GNDs as urban while the percentage figures are 30, 25 and 23 in case of southern, central and north western provinces. Sabaragamuwa on the other hand records a modest share of 16% only.

Table 5 Iterative process of screening the GNDs meeting population, high density and built-up area criteria: stage II

No. of GNDs	Iteration 1 (It.1) population criterion >=500	Per cent to total in (It.1)	Iteration 1 (It.2) density criterion >=400	Per cent to total in (It. 2)	Iteration 3 (It.3) built-up area (30%)	Per cent to total in (It. 3)	Iteration 4 (It.1) any of the four interact criterion	Per cent to total in (It. 4)	Per cent meeting and not meeting all criteria to total GNDs
Satisfy	12,881	91.86	7228	56.11	2064	28.56	1001	48.50	7.14
Do not satisfy	1141	8.14	5653	43.89	5164	71.44	1063	51.50	92.86
Total	14,022	100.00	12,881	100	7228	100.00	2064	100	100.00

Table 6 GNDs identified as urban through state I and stage II and their population shares for the year 2012, based on population and economic Census data in Sri Lanka

	Urban GNDs and additional GNDs	Percentage to the total GNDs	Urban population in GNDs	Percentage to total population
Stage I	3248	23.16	6,051,641	29.72
Stage II	1063	7.58	2,812,470	13.81
Total	4311	30.74	8,864,111	43.53

8 Key Issues in Areal Classification and Recommendations

It is generally accepted that urban populations in countries of South Asia, as officially reported, do not reflect the ground reality. There is a long standing demand for proper area classification in the government circles, among industrialists and businessmen and within civil society, which would (a) bring urban data of the country in line with global data and (b) provide right spatial frame and rural urban classification for launching a strategy for rapid and balanced development in the country. The views are shared by a large number of administrators and researchers.

One important issue in operationalising a scheme of areal classification is to determine the level of disaggregation at which identification of urban areas would be made. Census block or a hamlet may be too small a unit. A *Pradeshiya Sabha* (PS), *Tehshil* or even a village would in many cases be too large a unit since it has significant variations within it. In view of all this, it is proposed, for example in Sri Lanka, to consider GNDs as the basic units of analysis. This would enable retaining much of the information on spatial variation.

In cases of expansion of cities into its surrounding areas, impacting on the nature of activities, spatial interdependencies etc., it would be desirable that the Census organisation declares the identified areas, thus identified, as urban. This implies that the urban agglomerations, covering the central city and surrounding areas, coming under administrative bodies like PS, *tehshil*, district or state bodies would function without disrupting the existing governance system. Under specific programmes of the central and provincial governments, the central city can be asked to take up responsibilities for the expanded territory for which additional funds can be allocated. In special cases, a separate agency such as Metropolitan Development Authority can be created with limited functions and responsibilities vis-à-vis the agglomeration.

The application of this schema to Sri Lankan data for the year 2012 has been presented as a case study. Needless to mention that one or more of the indicators and their proposed threshold levels can be changed in different countries, based on an informed discussion with policy makers, administrators and researchers, as also availability of data. For example, the economic indicator for identification of urban centres should ideally be the percentage of workers outside agriculture. Unfortunately, the data at that level of disaggregation have not been compiled with adequate robustness in certain countries. It is recommended that the information on the number

Table 7 Percentage distribution of the GNDs and their population, identified as urban in stage I and stage II across provinces

	Total GNDs	Stage I GNDs identified as urban as per fourfold criteria	Per cent to total urban GNDs in Iteration I	Population in the identified GNDs	Per cent to total urban pop	Stage II additional urban GNDs identified by threefold criteria	Per cent to total additional urban GNDs	Population in the additional GNDs	Per cent to total additional urban pop
Western	2496	848	26.1	2,442,124	40.4	598	56.3	2,009,110	71.4
Central	2223	420	12.9	683,988	11.3	90	8.5	172,652	6.1
Southern	2121	531	16.3	693,484	11.5	102	9.6	138,908	4.9
Northern	893	198	6.1	282,175	4.7	48	4.5	84,931	3.0
Eastern	1076	283	8.7	435,125	7.2	163	15.3	273,630	9.7
North Western	2158	490	15.1	606,661	10.0	45	4.2	92,047	3.3
North Central	988	190	5.8	319,793	5.3	3	0.3	4961	0.2
Uva	886	108	3.3	221,923	3.7	6	0.6	14,507	0.5
Sabaragamuwa	1148	180	5.5	366,338	6.1	8	0.8	21,724	0.8
Total	14,022	3248	100	6,051,611	100	1063	100	2,812,470	100.0

of workers engaged in non-agricultural activities must be computed from the pre-listing schedule of the Census. Alternately, the labour force survey should be designed in a manner so that this information at settlement level is estimated with statistically acceptable level of standard error. When this percentage of non-agricultural workers to the total adult workforce is determined in a robust manner, it should replace the percentage of government, semi-government and establishment workers, employed in the illustrative case of Sri Lanka, for defining the urban centres. Similarly, the data on built-up areas can be updated when more recent data become available from the latest satellite imagery.

It is indeed not mandatory for the government to depend on the Census organisation to identify new urban centres or suggest expansion of the boundaries of the existing corporations or municipalities. All the governments in South Asian countries, under their urban development-related legislations, can easily declare any number of urban and municipal councils, so that urbanisation level is set optimally to meet the policy requirements or becomes compatible with the global scenario. It would, nonetheless, be desirable that their Census organisations are assigned this responsibility since they have the technical capacity to organise the necessary data and exercise the appropriate judgement regarding the weightages to be assigned to the selected indicators and specify their cut-off points to define "urbanity". Or else, the decisions are likely to be perceived as ad-hoc and based on political considerations. There are policies, programmes and allocations in the system, linked to the rural urban classification. Proper identification of the areal status would immediately entitle the settlements to their administrative and legal powers and help access the allocated funds.

After the Census organisation in a country identifies the new towns and determines the boundaries of the existing urban centres, it would be for the government to recognise the proposed schema, give statutory recognition to the newly identified Census towns and accept agglomerations as planning/developmental units. That would automatically entitle the new urban areas to all the administrative and financial provisions, existing in the country, and facilitate the government's task of designing and implementing a development strategy for urban agglomerations.

9 Recommendations

1. The Census and Statistics Organisation (CSO) in most countries are professional bodies with technical competence. It must be assigned the responsibility of proposing simple transparent and standardised criteria for areal classification, rather than relegating to a government department or ministerial discretion. The former should take the responsibility of exercising appropriate judgement with regard to the choice of indicators and determining the threshold levels to define "urbanity".
2. A fourfold criteria for identification of urban centres is suggested for consideration of CSOs, to be applied at village level, as presented below:

   (a) The minimum population size of 500 or more
   (b) Density of 400 persons per square kilometre
   (c) Percentage of workers outside agriculture to the total workers aged 15 years to be at least 50%
   (d) Trading and service establishments to be at least15 per 1000 population or existence of at least one facility like a common market, bank or a high/middle school

3. The urban villages, contiguous to the existing urban centres, should be declared as parts of urban agglomeration. This implies that the agglomerations would comprise the central city and several urban villages. It would not be mandatory to bring the village under the central municipality or corporation for all administrative purposes. Indeed, they retain their rural body, if their merging with the urban body is administratively difficult. However, under specific programmes of the central and provincial government, the central city or a metropolitan authority can be asked to take up the responsibilities for the expanded territory for which additional funds can be allocated.
4. After the CSO identifies the Census towns and determines the urban agglomerations, it would be for the government to slowly provide statutory recognition to the newly identified towns and the expanded boundaries.
5. The government, as per the requirements of its development strategy, can declare new urban centres from time to time that may or may not meet the criteria, proposed by the CSO. These settlements should immediately be accepted as statutory urban units by the CSO.
6. Countries may retain threefold areal classification—urban, rural and estate in Sri Lanka or Urban, semi-urban and rural as proposed in Pakistan—as these are required for designing or implementing a specific programme of the governments. However, for other policy contexts and global comparisons, it should be possible to merge estate and semi-urban unit data with those of rural or urban settlements, based on their characteristics.

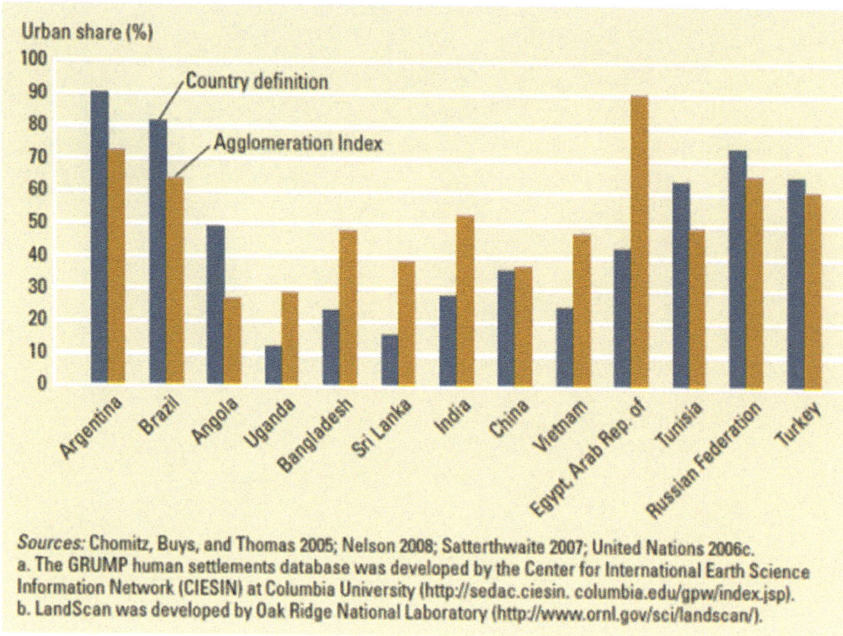

Graph 1 Agglomeration index computed by world bank for developing countries for the World Development Report 2009

References

Arif, G. M. (2003). Urbanisation in Pakistan: Trends growth and evaluation of the 1998 census. In I. Kemal & Mahmud (Eds.), *Population in Pakistan: An analysis of the 1998 population and housing census*. Islamabad, PIDE.

Ali, R., Haque, N., Husain, I., Arif, G. M. (2013, December). Estimating urbanisation. *The Urban Gazette*.

Chomitz, K. M., Buys, P., & Thomas, T. S. (2005). *Quantifying the rural-urban gradient in Latin America and the Caribbean*. World Bank Policy Research Working Paper 3634. Washington D.C: World Bank. https://documents.worldbank.org/en/publication/documents-reports/documentdetail/417881468226751166/quantifying-the-rural-urban-gradient-in-latin-america-and-the-caribbean.

Uchida, H., & Nelson, A. (2008). *Agglomeration Index: Towards a new measure of urban concentration*. Background paper for World Development Report 2009. Washington D.C: World Bank. https://openknowledge.worldbank.org/bitstream/handle/10986/9039/WDR2009_0008.pdf?sequence=1.

World Bank. (2015): Demographia World Urban Areas (12th ed., 2016).

Competition, Technology, Innovation and Exports: Contemporary Theoretical Insights

Sugata Marjit, Suryaprakash Mishra, and Moushakhi Ray

1 Introduction

In this essay, we discuss new theoretical insights in understanding certain enduring and emerging issues in the context of industrial organization and trade and more specifically on the role of competition in determining innovations and exports. Technology and finance are also critical in this context and hence are also included. Two major contributions are incorporating increasing marginal costs rather than working with constant marginal costs, as has been the universal norm with the models of industrial organization and explicitly including financial factors in decisions to export

*This paper is written in honour of Prof. Ramprasad Sengupta, an excellent economist, a reputed and caring teacher to many and a very close personal friend, more like an elder brother to me since my days at JNU. Depth of his knowledge, commitment and sincerity as an academic scholar and above all humility as a human being make him a very special person in our profession. This paper has benefitted from discussions with Dyuti Banerjee, Hamid Beladi, Reza Oladi, Arijit Mukherjee and Lei Yang and presentations of related papers at IIM Ahmedabad, CSSSC, IGIDR, Universities of Monash, Nottingham, Queensland, Washington, St. Louis, Dresden, City University of Hong Kong, WEA meeting in Singapore, etc. The usual disclaimer applies.

S. Marjit (✉)
Indian Institute of Foreign Trade, Kolkata, India
e-mail: sugata@iift.edu

CTRPFP (CSSSC), Kolkata, India

CES-Ifo, Munich, Germany

S. Mishra
National Law University, Delhi, India
e-mail: misra.suryaprakash@gmail.com

M. Ray
Department of Economics, Siliguri College, Siliguri, India
e-mail: rmoushakhi@gmail.com

P. Dasgupta et al. (eds.), *Sustainable Development Insights from India*,
India Studies in Business and Economics,
https://doi.org/10.1007/978-981-33-4830-1_5

when firms face credit constraints. We discuss variety of results and provide intuitive outline of the theoretical models which have been referred. Several interesting infrequently answered queries are addressed.

Competition, technology and innovation are highly complex phenomena, and so is their interaction. In an oligopolistic set-up, generally the firms are faced with two choices, namely to form a collusion among themselves or to compete with each other. The literature has umpteen number of contributions where the said choices of the firms are analysed using game-theoretic models. Linear demand constant marginal cost framework has been extensively used. However, this framework shows that technology has no role to play as far as above-stated choices of the firms are concerned. Celebrated textbooks of Tirole (1988), Gibbons (1992), Shy (1996), Martin (2001), etc., show that the collusive is only driven by the discount factor.

However, altering the above framework by replacing the constant marginal cost assumption by increasing marginal cost offers very novel insights not only with regard to the final outcome of collusion or competition and welfare (Marjit et al., 2017) but also has implications for innovation (Misra, 2019) and export decision of the firms (Marjit & Ray, 2017). While Marjit and Ray (2017) analyse the export profitability of firms for a given level of technology and credit constraints, Misra (2019) addresses the issue of innovation incentives for firms with respect to the evolutionary dynamics of technology and competition.

The paper proceeds as follows. Section 2 reviews the literature pertaining to firms' choice of collusion or competition and then highlights the role played by technology in the said choice, while 2.1 reviews the literature pertaining to the innovation decision by the firms. Section 3 surveys the literature on the role of competition and technology on the export profitability of the firms and then also highlights the literature focusing on credit market and firm behaviour. Section 4 concludes.

2 Technology and Market Structures

In the context to the firms' decision to collude, until the very recent past in the literature, the critical discount factor determining the collusive or competitive outcome(s) was equal to a constant, $\frac{9}{17}$ (Gibbons, 1992). Studies addressing the firms' choice to collude or compete were using the linear demand constant cost framework, and the above stated result had been the generally accepted conclusion. We change the basic framework in the analysis of the firms' choice to collude or compete and derive significantly different results. We maintain the same linear demand but consider quadratic costs instead of the constant costs and conclude that technology improvement has the potential to alter market structures. These alterations in market structures have welfare and policy implications. We show that not only our results are very different from the ones in the literature but also our generalization of the analysis from the two-firm Cournot duopoly to the n-firms Cournot oligopoly gives a new set of results with regard to both the impact of technology on collusion and thus on market structures and also the act of innovation by the firms.

Firms take strategic decisions regarding collusion. Various considerations that the firms may have regarding their decision to collude could be but not limited to homogeneity/heterogeneity of the product, symmetries/asymmetries in costs, etc. The issue of collusion has been addressed from various perspectives like product differentiation (Deneckere, 1983; Wernerfelt, 1989; Chang, 1991; Ross, 1992; Symeonidis, 2002; Collie, 2006; Weibull 2006), asymmetric firms (Harrington, 1989) and cheap talks (Campbell, 1998; Miralles, 2010).

Deneckere (1983) analysed duopoly supergames with heterogeneity in goods. Working with a multi-product demand function in a repeated game set-up, he derived trigger strategy equilibrium in both Bertrand set-up (i.e. price setting supergames) as well as in Cournot set-up (i.e. quantity setting supergames). The degree of product differentiation is measured by an exogenously given parameter embedded in the demand functions. The least or the minimum discount factor supporting the maximum joint profit as a subgame perfect Nash equilibrium is a measure of the ease of collusion. This minimum discount factor is shown to be non-monotonically related to the substitutability between the goods. He found that when goods are very close substitutes or complements, trigger strategies of firms are more conducive to tacit collusion between the firms in supergames in Bertrand set-up (i.e. price setting supergames) as against in Cournot set-up (i.e. quantity setting supergames). However, the exact opposite happens, i.e. the situation is reversed, in case of moderate or poor substitutability between the goods. The welfare implications of his results are in contrast to those of the static situation where higher welfare always comes about by the Bertrand set-up (i.e. the price setting strategies) as against the Cournot set-up (i.e. the quantity setting game). It is suggested that the exact opposite welfare implications may come about for very close substitutes or complements.

In a simple supergame, Wernerfelt (1989) analysed tacit collusion in Cournot set-up with differentiated goods. In the context of optimal punishments, he analysed the effect of product differentiation on the maximum degree of tacit collusion, where the focus is on the analysis of conditions under which tacit collusion is easily brought about by production differentiation. He found that the net effects, which depend upon the temptation to cheat and the penalty effects, depending upon which dominates, could go either way.

Basing his paper on Hotelling's (1929) spatial competition framework, Chang (1991) analysed the relationship between the degree of product differentiation and the firms' ability to collude in price setting games, i.e. the Bertrand set-up. It is shown that the least or the minimum discount factor that is required to support the joint profits of the firms as a subgame perfect Nash equilibrium is a monotonically increasing function of the substitutability between the products; i.e. it monotonically increases as the products become better and better substitutes. This result is in contrast to the findings of Deneckere (1983) that the minimum discount factor is non-monotonically related to the substitutability between the goods. The optimal collusive price in Chang (1991) is shown to decline (and thus the joint profits cannot be supported) when the substitutability between the product increases. The paper's ultimate finding is that as the substitutability between the goods increases it is tougher for the firms to collude in price setting games.

Engaging with product differentiation and the stability of the cartel, Ross (1992) presented two models in which differentiated goods are being supplied by the cartels. Using a supergame-theoretic model of collusion, he analysed the effects on the stability of cartels that are brought about by the differing levels of product differentiation. The paper focused on how the increased product homogeneity has a positive impact on both, the benefits due to defection from a collusive agreement as well as the quantum of punishments following such defections. Results due to his supergame-theoretic analysis revealed that when finding an agreement is unproblematic, product differentiation may not hamper the stability of the cartel. The overall effect on the stability of the cartels, however, is not unambiguous. Finally, by making use of product differentiation model, contrary to the view from the literature, he shows that the stability of the cartels may be inversely related to product homogeneity; i.e. product homogeneity can diminish cartel stability.

Symeonidis (2002) also worked on cartel stability, but with multi-product firms. For a market which is horizontally differentiated, he examined the implications of the presence of multi-product firms on the stability of collusion. He found that in Cournot set-up (i.e. quantity setting supergames), for any arbitrarily given number of firms, the critical discount factor, above which collusion is rendered sustainable by means of trigger strategies by the firms, is an increasing function of the variety of goods produced by the firms. Thus, for a given number of firms, the critical discount factor increases as the number of varieties of goods produced by the firms increases. As a result, the likelihood of collusion diminishes. Generally, similar results come about in case of Bertrand set-up (i.e. price setting supergames) as well. However, these results may not hold in cases when the number of firms is small and the products are close substitutes.

Collie (2006) and Weibull (2006) worked with convex cost in their analysis of collusion by firms. Collie (2002) engaged with collusion in differentiated duopolies with quadratic costs (linear marginal cost) and compared the sustainability of collusion under Cournot and Bertrand duopoly with differentiated goods. He showed that if the marginal cost is sufficiently increasing, then for any degree of product substitutability, collusion is more easily sustainable in a Cournot set-up than in a Bertrand set-up. Weibull (2006) generalized the Bertrand model from linear cost to convex cost functions. He analyses price competition in both the static (one shot game) set-up, where the firms interact just once, and the dynamic (repeated game) set-up, where the firms interact repeatedly over and over again over uncertain future. He showed that there exists an interval of prices in equilibrium in both the static and the dynamic set-ups. He hinted that firms may earn huge profits and that their profits may be increasing in their production costs.

Considering the discount factors of the firms, with regard to collusion, Harrington (1989) analysed collusive behaviour of firms. Specifically, he investigated the collusive behaviour of the firms which are asymmetric in their discount factors. He developed a selection criterion which not only generates a unique collusive outcome but also respects the incentive compatibility constraints. This criterion leads to a unique collusive outcome in terms of output and prices. It is not important for the firms to have high discount factors for self-enforcing collusion; rather, what is important is that the firms have long-run view. Optimal collusive outcome is characterized by a unique relationship between output quotas and the discount factors of the firms. At the equilibrium, there are strictly ordered output quotas and the firms with relatively low discount factor get a disproportionately high share of the market demand. Also, in the event of collusion, the firm's discount factor inversely impacts its output quota and its profits.

Campbell (1998) and Miralles (2010) analysed the issue of collusion through cheap talk. Campbell (1998) studied coordination and the self-enforcing collusion in simultaneous second-price auctions characterized by entry costs and focused on the ranking mechanism. Initially, the bidders indulge in pre-play communication whereby they publicly signal their rankings of the objects to be auctioned. Thereafter, each bidder decides as to in which auction she/he would participate. Finally, the bidder pays the entry cost and participates in the auction. Campbell (1998) worked with two-bidder case and showed that there always exists a full comparative cheap talk (a truthful ranking revelation) equilibrium. As the number of objects to be auctioned gets large, the above mechanism leads to asymptotically fully efficient collusion.

Miralles (2010) based his study on Campbell (1998). He extended and analysed the above-said mechanism with more than two bidders. He has two prominent results: namely, (1) an enhancement in the number of objects (to be auctioned) leads to a full comparative cheap talk equilibrium yielding asymptotically fully efficient collusion and (2) partial comparative cheap talk equilibrium always exists. Through numerical examples he also suggests that even in event of fewer objects to be auctioned, full comparative cheap talk equilibria are pretty common.

In analysis of collusion with the context of homogeneous goods with constant marginal cost, the main contributions are from Gibbons (1992), Martin (2001), Shy (1996) and Tirole (1988). They show that the existence of collusion or Cournot competition as the subgame perfect equilibrium (SPE) in an infinitely repeated game is independent of the level of technological advancement. Collusion is shown to depend only upon the magnitude of the discount factor(s) of the concerned firms.

Marjit et al. (2017) show that changing the assumption of constant marginal cost to increasing marginal cost drastically alters the result and has other interesting implications for cost reducing technological improvement. Specifically, they show that in an infinitely repeated game framework, technological improvement increases the critical discount factor, above which collusion is the SPE. Hence, as technology improves and reaches a certain level, the SPE market structure switches from collusion to Cournot competition generating additional welfare gains. So, the infeasibility of an alteration of market structure that is present under constant marginal cost set-up is removed by the increasing marginal cost assumption. Thus, they show as to how market structures can evolve with technological changes. As technology improves, it gets difficult to maintain collusion and hence innovation leads to competition. But potential does exist to explore opposite results when innovation leads to market concentration. This may happen when one party wins the R and D race, but, ex ante if the outcome is symmetric, i.e. all firms can win the race, with constant MC nothing really changes in terms of incentives to collude, but with increasing MC the result is different.

Lahiri and Ono (2004) focused on trade and industrial policy under international oligopoly. They deeply analysed the industrial and trade policies in a framework where many countries are involved with each other for the purposes of trade. Under the imperfect competition conditions, they analysed various trade policies, industrial policies and R&D subsidies in a market characterized by Cournot oligopolistic interdependence among the agents, in production. Their first chapter is closely related to our work. In this chapter, they analyse an oligopolistic industry having finite number of firms with asymmetric costs rendered by asymmetric technology levels. They categorized the firms as major (efficient) or minor (less efficient) firms. They showed that, at an average, the elimination of minor firms raises the efficiency of the firms, in terms of production, in the industry. It also increases the degree of oligopolistic market structure (the competition economics literature sees this as hampering of competition) leading to reduction in the aggregate output and increase in the price and thus, as a result, a reduction in the consumers' surplus. The authors showed that such an improvement in the efficiency in production over all enhances aggregate welfare and addresses the problem of misallocation of production by diverting/shifting production from the minor (less efficient) to major (efficient) firms. They suggest that a tax-cum-subsidy policy that favours major (efficient) firms and adversely affects the minor (less efficient) firms is better than a tax-cum-subsidy policy that favours the minor (less efficient) firms and adversely affects the major (efficient) firms as the former enhances aggregate welfare by correcting the problem of misallocation of production while the latter hampers aggregate welfare by distorting production by misallocating it.

Outsourcing at international level has grown significantly over the recent years. The literature has focused mainly on explaining the make or buy decision of the firms. However, not much has been said about the said (make and buy) decisions of the firms. Analysing cooperation among the final goods producers in the product market, Beladi and Mukherjee (2012) offered a new logic for bi-sourcing. By bi-sourcing, they refer to a situation when the producer of a final good engages in both buying the inputs from a seller from the input market and producing the input himself. They observed that the market structure with regard to inputs is the primary determinant of bi-sourcing. If the input market is perfectly competitive or if there are symmetric input suppliers engaged in Bertrand competition without capacity constraint, the price of input obtainable from the outside sellers would be low and equal to the marginal cost of production and thus there would not be any incentive for bi-sourcing and the firm would buy its input from outside. But, if the input market is imperfectly competitive then the market power of the outside input supplying firms enables them to charge a price higher than the marginal cost of production and thus the final good producing firm would produce some amount of input in-house along with buying from outside, i.e. bi-sourcing would emerge. They also showed that bi-sourcing (certain amount of in-house input production), even when the marginal cost of the in-house production of input is more than that of the outside input supplier, enhances consumers' welfare as against complete outsourcing the inputs to a firm with lower marginal cost of production.

Crucial insights with regard to the outcomes of international negotiations on enforcement of patents in the southern countries are provided by Mukherjee and Sinha (2013). They worked with a North–South trade model and analysed the impacts of the southern patent protection on the innovation, profits and welfare of the southern countries. They, in the presence of southern innovation, challenged the justification of the blanket approach for patent protection in the developing countries. Considering international negotiations for efficient global patent regime, they showed that patent harmonization is neither necessary nor sufficient. Their result that the stronger southern patent protection may not benefit the north contrasts that of Grossman and Lai (2004). There would always be cooperation between the firms as it would increase their profits through creation of monopoly and elimination of imitation in the industry through scrapping off the incentive of the firms to compete with each other. However, the overall impact on the aggregate welfare is not unambiguous and immediate due to the induced trade-off between the incentive for innovation and the higher market concentration. The cost of southern innovation and the degree of substitutability between the products are the main factors which drive the impact of the southern patent protection on both a country's and the world's welfare.

Motivated by empirical findings regarding joint venture breakdown, Marjit and Raychaudhuri (2004) worked with asymmetric capacity costs and joint venture buyouts. They developed a simple model, basing it on the asymmetric access to capital, synergy and the size of the market. Level of demand or the market size plays a significant role in their analysis. A low level of demand or a smaller market size leads to the formation of joint ventures, while a sufficient enhancement in the level of demand or the market size always breaks down the joint venture and leads to a buyout. Their model also predicts the likely effects of tariff polices. For instance, if a reduction in the tariff levels in an industry by the government results in a reduction in the demand levels or the market size faced by the existing firms. And thus, as a result in turn, their theory predicts that the stability of joint ventures should be enhanced.

The long-run implications of international outsourcing and R&D for the consumers are analysed by Marjit and Mukherjee (2008). They developed a simple Cournot oligopoly model with an innovator who is also the potential outsourcing firm and showed the effect of outsourcing on the investment on R&D. They showed that international outsourcing and the investment on R&D may be either substitutes of each other or complementary to each other. They showed that outsourcing increases the investment on R&D in both small and highly competitive product markets while it decreases the investment on R&D in large markets. However, if under exporting, the outsourced firm is very efficient technologically, then outsourcing would hamper consumer surplus through reduced investment on R&D. They suggest that in the event of skill differential among the workers, the outsourcing that reduces the investment in R&D will take place in the relatively low-skilled industry. Outsourcing would further depress the investment in R&D if the outsourcing of the unskilled jobs decreases the effective costs of the skilled workers through enhancing their efficiency as against the situation that outsourcing does not affect the effective costs of the skilled workers.

Analysing the impact of outsourcing of production on the magnitude and composition of the investment in R&D of the home country, Beladi and Mukherjee (2013) had set up a model in which a multinational firm and a local firm compete in the developing country while producing heterogeneous or differentiated goods. They assumed that the cost of R&D does vary with outsourcing. They showed that outsourcing reduces the process R&D of the multinational firm in the large markets when the firm only conducts the process R&D. This happens due to the substitution effect between outsourcing and the process R&D. However, outsourcing emerges as a complement to product development when the multinational firm conducts both product and the process R&D, under certain conditions. However, this happens due to the complementary effect between outsourcing and product R&D. Thus, outsourcing emerges as a substitute to process R&D while a complementary factor to the product R&D. Their analysis hints that international outsourcing has disparate effects on process innovation and product innovation.

Continuing contributions to the long trending voluminous literature on technology transfer and patents in the developing world, two recent papers deal with restrictive policy and endogenous R and D and on patent rights, innovation and outsourcing in a vertical chain. Hong et al. (2016) extending Kabiraj and Marjit (2003) show that restrictive policy may facilitate technology transfer, but can hurt the country in the longer run by affecting innovations of the foreign firms. Beladi et al. (2016) argue for strong IPRs for increasing the incentive of the imitator to do *R* and *D* in the intermediate stage, leading to the more efficient outcome.

Bandyopadhyay et al. (2014) worked with international oligopoly, barriers to outsourcing and domestic employment. They, in an international oligopolistic set-up, where two developed nations produce a homogeneous good and compete with each other to sell the good in a third country, analysed as to how domestic employment is affected by the barriers to outsourcing. They showed that an outsourcing tax unambiguously makes the domestic labour cheaper, but the effect of the outsourcing tax on employment is not unambiguous. This happens due to strategic considerations. Considering international policy interdependence, they showed that a unilateral tax (subsidy) raises the domestic employment of the country; however, in Nash policy equilibrium, this may be counterproductive. They finally showed that both an increased product differentiation and a credit crisis worsen the employment effects of an outsourcing tax. Their results are robust in both, the Cournot and the Bertrand set-ups.

2.1 Innovation Incentives

Incentives to innovate have been analysed from various angles such as product differentiation, horizontal—Bester and Petrakis (1993) and vertical—Bonanno and Haworth (1998), profit incentives—(Yi, 1999; Delbono & Denicolò, 1990). This literature suggests that different measures of competition affect the firms' incentives to innovate in different ways.

Market structures and innovation have occupied the centre stage in the innovation literature since 1943 (Schumpeter's Capitalism, Socialism, and Democracy). The

'Schumpeterian trade-off'—perfectly competitive firms perform well in the sense of efficient allocation of resources (in the static sense) but poorly in terms of innovation, and have been dominant in many contributions (Sylos-Labini 1969; Scherer 1980; von Weizsacker 1980, Nelson & Winter, 1982; Kamien & Schwartz, 1982). Thus, the optimal market form seems to be the one having elements of monopoly.

However, later it was shown that perfect competition was more conducive to innovation than monopoly as there are more incentives for perfectly competitive firms to innovate as against a monopolist (Arrow, 1962). This is so because the monopolist already makes profits before innovation while the perfectly competitive firm just recovers its costs. Belleflamme and Vergari (2011) present a unified framework, whereby various sources of competition interact and shape the firm's incentives to innovate. They study the intensity of competition on innovation incentives and argue, in consonance of the existing literature (both, theoretical (Scherer (1967b), Barzel (1968), and Kamien and Schwartz (1972, 1976) and empirical (Mansfield, 1963; Williamson, 1965; Scherer, 1967a) that in contrast to the diametrically opposite and extreme cases of perfect competition and monopoly, the intermediate market forms may offer higher innovation incentives. However, they (Belleflamme & Vergari, 2011) qualify their findings by stating that different market forms create different incentives for innovation in different industries.

Tandon (1984) extends the Dasgupta and Stiglitz (1980) approach for analysis of the trade-off between static and dynamic efficiency. Optimal market structure or optimal degree of concentration is the main focus in answering the questions, '*are barriers to entry in addition to those created by R&D desirable?*' He finds the answer to be in the affirmative.

Traditional view suggests that entry of a firm in a market decreases the profit of the incumbent firms. However, introduction of R&D activities may lead to conclusions in contrast to the traditional view. Ishida et al. (2011) show that entry of a firm with a less efficient technology enhances both the R&D investment and the profit of the incumbent firms (which have a more efficient production technology). Entry in the presence of marginal cost differences decreases welfare in Cournot oligopoly set-up if the constant marginal cost of the entrant is sufficiently higher than those of the incumbents (Klemperer, 1988; Lahiri & Ono, 1988). Thus, this literature again is in contrast to the conventional view that entry enhances welfare, and may not hold in Cournot oligopoly set-up. There is also a part of the literature focusing on asymmetry due to differences in firm-level R&D capabilities. Interested readers may see Gallini (1992), Bester and Petrakis (1993), Mukherjee (2002), Mattoo et al. (2004) and Mukherjee and Pennings (2004, 2011).

Some studies have also shown that entry of firms may enhance the incumbent firms' profits. Working with a sequential move model in an asymmetric (marginal cost) Stackelberg set-up, Mukherjee and Zhao (2009) show that an inefficient follower (entrant) increases the profits of the incumbent firms (two) which, though, are heterogeneous in their efficiencies, but are relatively more efficient compared to the follower (entrant). However, similar results are also obtained by Coughlan and Soberman (2005), Chen and Riordan (2007), and Ishibashi and Matsushima (2009), but the difference is that they use simultaneous moved models.

Misra (2019) considers generalization of the increasing marginal cost linear demand model and shows that the profit of a colluding firm is always an increasing function of technological improvement; i.e. a cost reducing technological improvement always enhances an individual firm's profit under collusion. However, the same may not hold under Cournot competition; as in this situation, innovation may not be rewarding. The results indicate that cost reducing technological improvement: (i). unambiguously increases a firm's profit under collusion and (ii). increases a firm's profit under Cournot oligopoly iff there are at the most three firms in the market. Only if there are three or lesser firms, a cost-cutting technological improvement increases an individual firm's profit with certainty, else not. Thus, there would be conditional innovation by the firms, i.e. innovation contingent upon the number of firms in the market and the level of technology. Specifically, if the technology is already advanced and competition intensifies then firms would not innovate. This is very different from a Cournot model with constant marginal cost where cost-cutting innovation is always profitable. The author captures a dynamic interaction of technology with the possibility of innovation via the intensity of competition. It is shown that the intensity of competition and welfare may not have the usual (direct) relationship and 'monitored competition', wherein initially (at initial stages of innovation) competition is encouraged and then (at later stages of innovation) curtailed, to encourage innovation and thus welfare, as a suitable policy measure.

3 Exportability, Credit Market and Innovation

So far, the analysis is confined to the firms' behaviour in a domestic market leaving the possibility of export out of the purview. This section reviews the literature that concentrates on the export market along with domestic outlets. More specifically, the thrust is on two issues in the field, namely (a) the effect of competition and technology on export profitability of firms and (b) the role of credit market in the study of firm behaviour when export possibilities are allowed.

The central point of debate in the context of the role of 'competition' is whether the introduction of competitive forces in an otherwise restrictive economy would usher in economic development. The question is examined in the micro-context by way of evaluating the relationship between export profitability and competition. In this field, Clougherty and Zhang (2009) study the relationship between domestic rivalry and export performance on the basis of the world airline industry. Their paper develops a theoretical model with two markets—one domestic and the other international—dealing in a single industry. It highlights that the domestic rivalry enables domestic firms to improve and innovate the production process. As a result, they get a large share in the export market. In their paper, some measure of export performance (e.g. world market share, net exports, export revenue) is regressed on some measure of domestic rivalry (e.g. four-firm concentration ratio, Herfindahl–Hirschman index, instability in market shares) at the industry-wide level of analysis. Data from the world airline industry is used to test the impact of domestic rivalry on export performance. A fixed panel-and-period effect regression model is used here,

$$
\begin{aligned}
&\text{International} - \text{Market} - \text{Share}_{it} = b_0 \\
&\quad + b_{1*}(\text{International} - \text{Market} - \text{Share})_{it-1} \\
&\quad + b_{2*}(\text{International} - \text{Market} - \text{Share})_{it-2} \\
&\quad + b_{3*}(\text{Domestic} - \text{Competitors})_{jt} \\
&\quad + b_{4*}(\text{Domestic} - \text{Market} - \text{Share})_{kt} \\
&\quad + b_{5*}(\text{Domestic} - \text{Network})_{kt} + b_{6*}(\text{Merger})_{kt} \\
&\quad + b_{7*}(\text{Foreign} - \text{Rivalry})_{kt} \\
&\quad + b_{8*}(\text{Domestic} - \text{Competitor} - \text{Network})_{kt} \\
&\quad + b_{9*}(\text{Home} - \text{Competitors})_{it} \\
&\quad + b_{10*}(\text{International} - \text{Competitors})_{it} + \varepsilon_{it} + \alpha_i + \gamma_t
\end{aligned}
$$

where i indexes an airline's international country-pair market (433 of them), j indexes the nineteen countries, k indexes the thirty-seven airlines, t indexes time, αi represents the fixed panel-specific effect and γt captures the fixed period-specific effect.

Some studies in the literature focus extensively on the relationship of competitiveness and exports. In one of such studies by Barua, Chakraborty and Hariprasad (2010), an attempt is made to examine the interrelationships between entry and competitiveness in a consistent oligopolistic market framework. The basic theoretical model underlying the current empirical exercise is based on the segmented market hypothesis as put forward in a series of papers by Agarwal and Barua (1993, 1994, 2004). The main arguments of these papers are that entry liberalization would result in (a) increase in aggregate exports, (b) reduction in industrial concentration, (c) decrease in price-cost margin and (d) increase in social welfare. It is an empirical analysis on the basis of firm-level data for 14 sectors in India over 1990–2008. The model assumes that the firm behaves like a discriminating oligopolist between domestic and foreign markets. It is also assumed that the firms belonging to an industry produce a homogeneous product and all of them play the Cournot competition. From the first-order maximization condition of profit maximization subject to demand function, the price-cost margin is calculated. One of the central observations in the study is that the price-cost margin rises over the years 1990–1995 with the decline in concentration ratios. The paper concludes that India's liberalization results in lowering the concentration ratio and escalating the price-cost margin. This in turn signifies a better performance of export-oriented firms.

Das and Pant (2006) use a leadership model to underscore that the new industrial policy in India is not able to foster competition by facilitating the expansion of small firms. This is indicated by the calculation of markups. The model shows that the markups of small firms are higher than those of larger firms. The relevance of 'competition' evolves in various literatures including the paper of Das and Pant (2006). The issues of competitiveness, export intensity and productivity are empirically analysed through the estimation of markups in Barua, Chakraborty and Hariprasad (2010) and Das and Pant (2006). Again, the paper by Clougherty and Zhang (2009) uses the concept of market shares to denote domestic rivalry. In their paper, the effect of domestic rivalry is studied using the Herfindahl index. The Herfindahl index as a measure of concentration is also adopted in Calkins (1983). On the other hand, the price-cost margin is used as a proxy for the degree of competition in Aghion et al. (2008), Martins et al. (1996) and Borg (2009). However, these indices of measuring the degree of competitiveness fail to account for the reallocation of market shares in the economy.

In the milieu of 'technology', a rich literature has been developed on the relationship between trade and technology, and the majority of them on the causation from former to latter. The argument is that by importing products and services that embody new technology, the host country is able to introduce foreign technology in home production. A number of studies identify these so-called R&D spillovers as one of the major benefits of trade. For example, Eaton and Kortum (1996) and Bernstein and Mohnen (1998) estimate R&D spillovers from the USA to Japan juxtapose to that from Japan to the USA and suggest the former's predominance. Coe and Helpman (1995) show that for 1971–90, R&D expenditures that G7 undertook yielded 30% gain in total factor productivity in smaller industrial countries. This study has, however, been modified/extended in many respects. Thus, a specification error in one of their regressions is identified, and also the measure of R&D spillovers is modified, by Lichtenberg and van Pottelsberghe de la Potterie (1996, 1998).

Perla et al. (2015) develop a model trade-induced technology diffusion in line with Perla and Tonetti (2014). Considering the prevalence of both backward and advanced technologies in the domestic economy, they show how under the scope of better export opportunities and the pressure of foreign competition, the domestic firms adopt better technology and thus speed up technology diffusion. Trade-induced technology upgradation is also discussed in Pavcnik (2002) and Holmes and Schmitz (2010).

Keller (2000) presents a model highlighting the pattern of a country's imports in intermediary goods as an important explanation of its growth of productivity. The underlying logic is that more a country imports from technological leaders, better would be the scope of technology diffusion. This theoretical position is found valid in an empirical test on eight OECD countries over the period 1970–1991. The paper also discusses the implication of its findings for developing countries.

There are a number of studies on the effects of trade on technology in the context of economic reforms in developing countries. Thus, for example, Muendler (2004) investigates Brazil's trade liberalization for 1990–93 and underscores that foreign competition enhanced the firm-level productivity significantly. The elimination of inefficient firms under competitive pressures also increased the industry's aggregate productivity. A related field of study is the assessment of the impacts of regional free trade agreement on the diffusion of technology. In this field, the study of Bustos (2011) seeks to find out the effect of MERCOSUR, a regional free trade agreement, on the advancement of technology by Argentinean firms during 1992–96. Treating technology and exporting choice, the study suggests that revenue addition by trade integration induces exporters to adopt better technology. In particular, its empirical test shows faster technological upgradation for the industries that enjoyed higher tariff reductions in Brazil.

A number of studies are undertaken to relate the nature of trade and technological change to shed light on the emergence of wage gap in the industrialized nations (for the wage gap, see Reenen, 2011). Ekholm and Ulltveit-Moe (2001) develop in this field a model of imperfect competition with heterogeneous firms using modern and traditional technologies. High fixed costs are involved in the former with low variable costs. Remaining in the domain of intra-industry trade theory, the article shows that market integration expands the extent of market for individual firms and hence higher profitability for modern firms, relative to that for traditional firms. The consequent shift in technology dampens the wage rate for unskilled labour working in traditional sector. The question of trade-induced wage gap in the industrialized countries is also theoretically investigated in detail by Krugman (1985).

While the above literature assesses the impact of trade on technological development, some recent works discuss the impacts of technological development on trade. In this field, Marjit and Ray (2017) analyse the effects of competition and nature of technology on export profitability of firms in two different circumstances of 'price discrimination' and 'absence of price discrimination'. They use an oligopoly framework to closely determine the export incentive of firms in the midst of increasing competition and improving technology. They use firm-level data on India to support their theoretical underpinning. A fixed effect panel regression is used to empirically suggest the significant impact of technology (measured by the expense involved in capital–labour ratio) and competitiveness (measured by Herfindahl index and price-cost margin) on export profitability (measured by export earnings-to-sales ratio of firms) of firms. Results indicate that an increase in competition increases the export profitability of firms, when the nature of technology is 'good', in both the presence and absence of price discrimination. However, if technology is 'bad' it might or might not increase the export profitability. In the latter case, the paper highlights that in the presence of price discrimination there is a critical level of technology ($\tilde{s}$) such that $s < (n - 5)/2$. That is, below the threshold level exports appear to be profitable whereas it is not the case beyond the threshold level. The theoretical finding suggests that in the absence of price discrimination, at a given value of competitiveness, exports appear to be profitable for firms only if $s < (n - 3)$. This condition for export profitability in the absence of discrimination implies that the market structure should consist of at least four firms.

In recent years, the issue of 'credit market' is discussed in the context of competition and trade. The focus of attention in many such studies is certainly imperfect competition—a field that is bolstered by the works on monopolistic competition by Krugman (1979, 1980) and Lancaster (1979, Lancaster 1980a, 1980b), and on oligopoly by Brander and Spencer (1981). These studies have initiated an immense volume of theoretical literature. There is a rich body of literature on the effects of credit constraints in the decision-making process of a firm. In an environment of credit constraints, Stiglitz and Weiss (1981) discuss about credit rationing as a screening device in the process of giving loan to the industries. However, the rejected borrowers may apply for loans at a higher interest rate. The paper identifies the case where the interest rates equate the demand for loanable funds to the supply of funds. They demonstrate that the capital market may also be characterized by credit constraints because of the adverse selection problem. Their observation is that such constraints may take the form of limiting the number of loans that a bank provides, because imperfect information in the capital market leads to the failure of such financial instruments as increasing the interest rate, or else, scaling up the collateral requirements.

Kerr and Ramana (2009) argue that the credit constraint issue is all the more acute for new firms. The financial crisis of 2007–08 has exacerbated the problem of credit constraints, as it has further reduced the access to credit for many firms. In this context, Bandyopadhyay et al. (2014) develop a methodology for analysing the problem of credit constraints and employment in an oligopoly model. The central issue is, indeed, how credit-constrained firms can resolve the problems of insufficient credit.

Manova et al. (2011) highlight empirically that credit constraints restrict the international trade and affect the pattern of multinational activity. Their paper analyses the impact of credit constraints on firms' export decision and the pattern of FDI. Under these considerations, firm export is regressed on the interaction of proprietorship status of firms and the financial liability of sectors. The fixed effect regression is used in this context. Their paper includes two control variables, viz. the interaction of firms' size with the sectors' financial vulnerability and the interactions of firms' ownership status with the sectors' research and development, contract, physical capital and human capital intensity. Their paper is built on the assumption that, compared to manufacturers producing for the domestic market, exporting firms depend more on the external source of fund. This trend is explained by three factors. First, an entry into the global market necessitates extra expenses since the fixed trading costs are involved in studying the profitability of potential markets, market-specific investments, etc. Second, the cross-border shipping delivery requires longer time, which, in turn, heightens the working capital requirement for exporters. Third, the risks underlying transnational manoeuvres involve trade insurance for the exporters.

We should also refer here to Antras and Caballero (2009) which develops a general equilibrium model in a Ricardian continuum framework with heterogeneity of asset ownership. The paper clarifies the link between credit market imperfection and credit rationing, emphasizing that imperfections in the credit market can be characterized by credit rationing, though all of the borrowers with varying amount of assets may not face a binding credit limit.

Deardorff (2000) discusses the role of trade liberalization in service industries in stimulating trade in both services and goods. The paper identifies the role of trade in service in a model of international industrial fragmentation. In the presence of regulations and restrictions, the service costs of international fragmentation should be high. Trade liberalization in this field can, therefore, stimulate the fragmentation of production in both goods and services, thereby increasing the volume of international trade, as also the gains from trade. Deardorff (2000) argues that fragmentation allows countries to specialize in specific areas of production processes where they have comparative advantages. Coordinating such comparative advantages internationally, the world economy can gain in terms of productive efficiency.

In the context of fragmentation, Matsuyama (2005) analyses the effects of credit constraints on the pattern of international trade in the North–South framework. He finds that the North, which enjoys a better credit market, specializes and exports in sectors that severely suffer from agency problems, whereas, in the presence of credit market imperfections, the South specializes and exports in those areas where such problems are less felt.

The issue of fragmentation is also discussed in Nocke and Thanassoulis (2014), Meisenzahl (2011) and Jones and Marjit (2001). Jones and Marjit (2001) confirm that the older generation would fail to survive without local protection due to inefficient technology. The older generation, therefore, resists the exposure to foreign culture and international fragmentation in production. They argue that an alliance of the members of the younger generation with the foreigners would promote local production in those fragments. The paper by Marjit et al. (2014) discusses the issue of fragmentation in output in the process of alleviating the problems of credit constraints. They consider two theoretical frameworks, viz. 'with production fragmentation' and 'without production fragmentation'. Their study uses the following incentive constraints for buyers and sellers, respectively, in the case of 'with fragmentation', respectively.

$$\frac{1}{2}P - \frac{1}{2}P^{\sim} + \frac{1}{2}P + \left(k - \frac{1}{2}\alpha\right)(1+r) > P - \alpha(1+r) + k(1+r)$$

$$\frac{1}{2}P^{\sim} + \left(k - \frac{1}{2}\alpha\right)(1+r) > P - \alpha(1+r) + k(1+r)$$

which indicate that it is profitable for a firm to produce in fragments in imperfect credit market.

Cetorelli and Peretto (2000) develop a dynamic general equilibrium model of capital accumulation where credit is intermediated by banks operating in a Cournot oligopoly. Credit market is split into two segments—one in which loans are screened and only high-quality entrepreneurs have access to credit and the other in which banks extend credit indiscriminately to all entrepreneurs. The paper establishes that, under certain plausible conditions, the market structure of the banking industry that maximizes the steady-state income per capita is neither competitive nor monopoly—it is an intermediate oligopoly.

The impacts of financial underdevelopment and credit constraints on export decision of firms are studied in Meisenzahl (2011), Matsuyama (2008) and Manova (2008). Meisenzahl (2011) uses a comprehensive data set on business credit decisions and contracts to examine the importance of financial constraints in the evolution of firm-size distribution. The paper adopts three measures of firm size to examine firms' decision on applying for credit, (i) number of employees, (ii) volume of sales and (iii) net worth. His empirical investigations establish that financial constraints can account for the evolution of firm-size distribution. In particular, firms without access to credit are small and, hence, those firms exhibit a lower rate of growth in employment, although they are highly labour-intensive. Older firms, on the other hand, enjoy relatively greater access to credit. But they present low values for average leverage as well as for the net worth multiplier. In this regard, a model of financial constraints that Meisenzahl (2011) develops is capable of providing the explanation of these empirical findings. The policy implication of the study is this: small firms are subject to financial constraint though they enjoy higher productivity, and create more jobs; hence, by providing additional external finance, the productivity advantage of such firms can be harnessed, and also the generation of employment is maximized. Hence, the sanction of additional external finance to those firms is desirable from the welfare point of view.

Matsuyama (2008) investigates the macro-dynamics of credit market imperfection. His paper uses agents' utility function, the borrowers' objective function, profitability constraint and borrowing constraint to interpret the credit worthiness of borrowers. Matsuyama (2008) uses partial equilibrium model with homogenous agents to determine the aggregate capital stock available at the initial period. It is often argued that general equilibrium analysis of credit market imperfections fundamentally requires heterogeneous agents. But practically, credit market transactions can take place among homogeneous agents if there are some indivisibility constraints.

Manova (2008), however, examines the impact of liberalization in the equity market on the export behaviour of firms using panel data. His paper suggests that liberalization increases exports disproportionately more in those financially vulnerable sectors where more external funds are used, or fewer collaterizable assets are employed.

The nature of financial system in a country determines the export share of industries. The effect of financial development on export share has been studied in several papers. Beck (2003) argues both theoretically and empirically in a H-O framework that financially developed countries enjoy comparative advantages in those industries where the external source of finance is more predominant. Such countries have, therefore, higher export shares in those industries.

In Minetti and Zhu (2011), the impact of credit rationing on firms' export is evaluated. After controlling for productivity and other relevant attributes of firms, and also accounting for the endogeneity of credit rationing, the study estimates that the probability of opting for exports is lower by 39% for credit-rationed firms. The firm-level empirical analysis in this paper is closely related to Manova (2013) and Chaney (2016). While Manova and Chaney share the same view about the extensive margin of export, they hold divergent views about the effect of credit constraints on the intensive margin. However, Minetti and Zhu (2011) use a binary variable (C) that equals 1 if the firm faces credit rationing and 0 otherwise. They examine the effect of credit rationing on the probability of exporting using the following expression.

$$\pi_i^* = \alpha_1 + \beta_1 C_i + Z_i \gamma_1 + \varepsilon_i;$$

π_i^* represents the difference between firm i's operating profits when exporting and its operating profits when not exporting. This difference is determined by firm characteristics (e.g. productivity) and by credit constraints. C_i is a binary variable that equals 1 if firm i faces credit rationing, 0 otherwise; Z_i is a vector of controls for firm characteristics that may affect firm i's operating profits; ε_i captures the unobserved firm attributes and any other unknown factor that may also affect π_i^*. Their study suggests that credit rationing depresses domestic sales, and that firms with a high liquidity ratio are more likely to export. That is, the probability of opting for exports is higher for firms with a higher leverage ratio and lower cash flow. Credit rationing is found to have a statistically significant, negative effect on exporting.

Kapoor et al. (2012) also study the impact of credit constraint on exporting firms. Drawing reference from Melitz (2003), this paper argues that if causality runs from credit constraints to exports, financial sector reforms in emerging economies that improve the accessibility to credit for exporting firms can play a very significant role in promoting export-oriented growth in the economy. The paper exploits two exogenous policy changes in India that affected the availability of subsidized direct credit to small-scale firms. Using firm-level data from 1990 to 2006, it studies the behaviour of exporting firms on the basis of some key variables like total sales, total export earnings, total bank borrowing, etc. Difference-in-difference estimation strategy is used to estimate the causal impact of credit constraints on exporting firms.

In this context, we should refer to Banerjee and Duflo (2008) who focus on firms that are exporters in the manufacturing sector. In spirit with Banerjee and Duflo (2008), the study of Kapoor et al. (2012) suggests that when new firms are classified as belonging to the priority sector, both credit-constrained and credit-unconstrained firms would be willing to absorb more credit if it is cheaper than other sources of credit. A constrained firm would use this credit primarily to expand output/sales whereas an unconstrained firm would use this credit to substitute for other expensive sources of credit.

As an extension to these studies, Beladi et al. (2017) discuss the role of credit market imperfection in determining the export behaviour of an economy. Their paper highlights that credit rationing in the presence of asset inequality affects the level of production and the pattern of trade. Using a Ricardian general equilibrium framework, they prove that more equal asset distribution may reduce the output of the credit-intensive sector as redistribution to the bottom of the ladder fails to promote entrepreneurs. That is, in contrast to a conventional H–O–S model, their paper posits the possibility that an economy with relatively equal distribution of asset ownership might import capital or credit-intensive good and also export capital. The issue of export incentives is also investigated.

Marjit and Ray (2020) study export incentives of credit-constrained firms in the presence of credit rationing. They carve a relationship between the nature of technology, the degree of competition and the export incentive of a firm in an imperfect credit market. The theoretical and empirical findings suggest that the increase in the degree of competition increases the export profitability of firms, when only present period is concerned. But an increase in competition might not escalate the export profitability of firms, when both past and present time periods are considered in the life cycle of a firm. The study shows that the role of competition is impacted by the intensity of capital accumulation and the initial level of wealth. Greater local competition before the entry of firms in the export market hurts export incentive by limiting cash flows and asset build-up. Thus, low domestic profit due to competition allows firms to look for export opportunities but lower cash flows hurt such incentives.

4 Concluding Remarks

A number of studies have discussed the issues of competition, technology and innovation in the context of firm behaviour. In an oligopolistic set-up, firms can either collude among themselves or else compete with each other. These choices of firms have been studied using the game-theoretic approach. However, technology occupies a crucial place in studying such behaviour of firms. Technological improvement alters market structure and provides export incentives to firms. The innovations should thereby have welfare implications where policy-makers are interested. Technological improvement that accompanies with a higher degree of credit market competition increases the export profitability of firms. But such an innovation improves firms' profitability in the domestic market only when 'monitored competition' prevails. However, introduction of credit market in such scenarios makes the subject more realistic. Indeed, the nature of credit market that firms are subject to determines the behaviour of firms in the global market. Thus, the issue of credit market imperfections (or credit rationing) that finds relevance in some recent papers can further be extended to other forms of market organizations.

Two major sets of results that have come out in recent times point towards the role of increasing costs in collusion and innovation of firms in oligopoly and credit market imperfection as an impediment towards exports. Finance and cost constraints both deter expansion of smaller firms and encourage domination of big players. The assumption of credit market perfection and linear costs both have deterred a healthy growth of the literature in trade and industrial organization.

References

Agarwal, M., & Barua, A. (1993). Trade policy and welfare in segmented markets. *Keio Economic Studies, 30*(2), 95–108.

Agarwal, M., & Barua, A. (1994). Effects of entry in a model of oligopoly with international trade. *Journal of International Trade and Economic Development, 3*(1), 1–13.

Agarwal, M., & Barua, A. (2004). Entry liberalization and export performance: A theoretical analysis in a multi-market oligopoly model. *Journal of International Trade and Economic Development, 13*(3), 287–303.

Aghion, P., Braun, M., & Fedderke, J. (2008). Competition and productivity growth in South Africa. *Economics of Transition, 16*(4), 741–768.

Antras, P., & Caballero, R. J. (2009). Trade and capital flows: A financial frictions perspective. *Journal of Political Economy, 117*(4), 701–744.

Arrow, K. J. (1962). *Economic welfare and the allocation of resources for invention, in national bureau of economic research, the rate and direction of inventive activity* (p. 1962). Princeton: Princeton University Press.

Bandyopadhyay, S., Marjit, S., & Yang, L. (2014). International oligopoly, barriers to outsourcing and domestic employment. *Canadian Journal of Economics/Revue CanadienneD'économique, 47*(4), 1372–1386.

Banerjee, A. V., & Duflo, E. (2008). What is middle class about the middle classes around the world? *Journal of Economic Perspectives, American Economic Association, 22*(2), 3–28.

Barua, A., Chakraborty, D., & Hariprasad, C. G. (2010). *Entry, competitiveness and exports: Evidence from firm level data of Indian manufacturing*. MPRA Paper 22738, University Library of Munich, Munich.

Barzel, Y. (1968). Optimal timing of innovations. *Review of Economic Studies, 1*(3), 348–355.

Beck, T. (2003). Financial dependence and international trade. *Review of International Economics, 11*(2), 296–316.

Beladi, H., & Mukherjee, A. (2012). Market structure and strategic bi-sourcing. *Journal of Economic Behavior & Organization, 82*(1), 210–219.

Beladi, H., Marjit, S. & Misra, S. (2017). *Inequality, Structure of Production and International Trade–The Role of Credit Market Imperfection*. CESIFO Working Paper No. 6307, CESifo.

Beladi, H., Marjit, S., Xu, X., & Yang, L. (2016). Strategic enforcement, intellectual property rights and contractual R&D. *Economic Inquiry, 54*(4), 1904–1917.

Belleflamme, P., & Vergari, C. (2011). Incentives to innovate in oligopolies. *The Manchester School, 79*(1), 6–28.

Bernstein, J. I. & Mohnen, P. (1998). International R&D spillovers between U.S. and Japanese R&D intensive sectors. *Journal of International Economics, 44*(2), 315–338.

Bester, H., & Petrakis, E. (1993). The incentives for cost reduction in a differentiated industry. *International Journal of Industrial Organization, 11*, 519–534.

Bonanno, G., & Haworth, B. (1998). Intensity of competition and the choice between product and process innovation. *International Journal of Industrial Organization, 16*, 495–510.

Borg, M. (2009). Measuring market competition in the EU: The markup approach. *Bank of Valletta Review, 39*, 20–31.

Brander, J. A., & Spencer, B. J. (1981). Tariffs and the extraction of foreign monopoly rents under potential entry. *Canadian Journal of Economics, 14*(3), 371–389.

Bustos, P. (2011). Trade liberalization, exports, and technology upgrading: Evidence on the impact of MERCOSUR on argentinian firms. *American Economic Review, 101*(1), 304–340.

Calkins, S. (1983). The new merger guidelines and the Herfindahl-Hirschman index. *California Law Review, 71*(2), 402–429.

Campbell, C.M. (1998). Coordination in auctions with entry. *Journal of Economic Theory, 82*(2), 425–450.

Cetorelli, N., & Peretto, P. (2000). *Oligopoly banking and capital accumulation*. Working Paper Series WP-00-12, Federal Reserve Bank of Chicago.

Chaney, T. (2016). Liquidity constrained exporters. *Journal of Economic Dynamics and Control, 72*(C), 141–154.

Chen, Y. & Riordan, M.H. (2007). Price and Variety in the Spokes Model, *Economic Journal 117*, 897–921.

Chang, Myong-Hun. (1991). The effects of product differentiation on collusive pricing. *International Journal of Industrial Organization, 9*(3), 453–469.

Clougherty, J. A., & Zhang, A. (2009). Domestic rivalry and export performance: Theory and evidence from international airline market. *Canadian Journal of Economics, 42*(2), 440–468.

Coe, D. T., & Helpman, E. (1995). International R&D spillovers. *European Economic Review, 39*(5), 859–887.

Collie, D. R. (2002). Prohibiting state aid in an integrated market: Cournot and Bertrand oligopolies with differentiated products. *Journal of Industry, Competition and Trade, 2*, 215–231. https://doi.org/10.1023/A:1021532508081.

Collie, D. R. (2006). Collusion in differentiated duopolies with quadratic costs. *Bulletin of Economic Research, 58*(2), 151–159.

Coughlan, A. T. & Soberman, D.A. (2005). Strategic segmentation using outlet malls. *International Journal of Research in Marketing, 22*, 61–86.

Das, S., & Pant, M. (2006). Measuring market imperfection in manufacturing sector: Theory and evidence from India. *Journal of International Trade and Economic Development, 15*(1), 63–79.

Dasgupta, P. S., & Stiglitz, J. E. (1980). Industrial structure and the nature of innovative activity. *Economic Journal, 90*, 266–293.

Deardorff, A. V. (2000). *International provision of trade services, trade, and fragmentation.* Discussion Paper No. 463, School of Public Policy, The University of Michigan, Ann Arbor.

Delbono, F., & Denicolò, V. (1990). R&D investment in a symmetric and homogeneous oligopoly. *International Journal of Industrial Organization, 8*, 297–313.

Deneckere, R. (1983). Duopoly supergames with product differentiation. *Economics Letters, 11*(1–2), 37–42.

Eaton, J., & Kortum, S. (1996). Trade in ideas: Patenting and productivity in the OECD. *Journal of International Economics, 40*(3–4), 251–278.

Ekholm, K., & Ulltveit-Moe, K. (2001). *Relative wages and trade-induced changes in technology.* CEPR Discussion Paper No. 2677.

Gallini, N. T. (1992). Patent policy and costly imitation. *RAND Journal of Economics, 23*, 52–63.

Gibbons, R. (1992). *Game theory for applied economists.* Princeton University Press.

Harrington, J. E., Jr. (1989). Collusion among asymmetric firms: The case of different discount factors. *International Journal of Industrial Organization, 7*(2), 289–307.

Holmes, T., & Schmitz, J. (2010). Competition and productivity: A review of evidence. *Annual Reviews of Economics, 2*(1), 619–642.

Hong, H., Marjit, S., & Peng, C. H. (2016). *Oxford Economic Papers, 68*(4), 1107–1119.

Hotelling, H. (1929). Stability in competition. *The Economic Journal, 39*(153), 41–57.

Ishibashi, I. & Matsushima, N. (2009). The Existence of Low–end Firms may Help High–end Firms, *Marketing Science, 28*, 136–147.

Ishida, J., Matsumura, T., & Matsushima, N. (2011). Market competition, R&D and firm profits in asymmetric oligopoly. *Journal of Industrial Economics, 59*, 484–505.

Jones, R. W., & Marjit, S. (2001). The role of international fragmentation in the development process. *American Economic Review, 91*(2), 363–366.

Kabiraj, T., & Marjit, S. (2003). Protecting consumers through protection- the role of tariff induced technology transfer. *European Economic Review, 47*(1), 113–124.

Kamien, M. I., & Schwartz, N. L. (1972). Timing of innovations under rivalry. *Econometrica, 40*, 43–60.

Kamien, M. I., & Schwartz, N. L. (1976). On the degree of rivalry for maximum innovative activity. *Quarterly Journal of Economics, 90*, 245–260.

Kamien, M. I., & Schwartz, N. L. (1982). *Market structure and innovation* (p. 1982). Cambridge: Cambridge University Press.

Kapoor, M., Ranjan, P., & Raychaudhuri, J. (2012). *The impact of credit constraints on exporting firms: Empirical evidence from India.* Available at SSRN: https://ssrn.com/abstract=2023068.

Keller, W. (2000). Do Trade Patterns and Technology Flows Affect Productivity Growth? *World Bank Economic Review, 14*(1), 17–47.

Kerr, W. R. & Ramana, N. (2009). *Financing constraints and entrepreneurship.* NBER Working Paper No. 15489.

Klemperer, P. (1988). Welfare effects of entry into markets with switching costs. *Journal of Industrial Economics, 37*(2), 159–165.

Krugman, P. (1979). Increasing returns, monopolistic competition, and international trade. *Journal of International Economics, 9*(4), 469–479.

Krugman, P. (1980). Scale economies, product differentiation, and the pattern of trade. *The American Economic Review, 70*(5), 950–959.

Krugman, P. (1985). A 'technology gap' model of international trade. In K. Jungenfelt & D. Hague (Eds.), *Structural adjustment in developed open economies. International economic association series* (pp. 35–61). London: Palgrave Macmillan.
Lahiri, S., & Ono, Y. (2004). *Trade and industrial policy under international oligopoly*. Cambridge University Press.
Lahiri, S., & Ono, Y. (1988). Helping minor firms reduce welfare. *Economic Journal, 98*, 1199–1202.
Lancaster, K. (1979). *Variety, equity, and efficiency: Product variety in an industrial society*. New York: Columbia University Press.
Lancaster, K. (1980a). Intra-industry trade under perfect monopolistic competition. *Journal of International Economics, 10*(2), 151–175.
Lancaster, K. (1980b). Competition and product variety. *Journal of Business, 53*(3), 79–103.
Lichtenberg, F., & Pottelsberghe de la Potterie B. (1996). *International R&D spillovers: A re-examination*. NBER Working Paper No. 5668, Cambridge.
Lichtenberg, F., & Pottelsberghe de la Potterie, B. (1998). International R&D spillovers: A comment. *European Economic Review, 42*(8), 1483–1491.
Manova, K., Wei, S., & Zhang, Z. (2011). *Firm exports and multinational activity under credit constraint*. NBER Working Paper No. 16905.
Manova, K. (2008). Credit constraints, equity market liberalization and international trade. *Journal of International Economics, 76*(1), 33–47.
Manova, K. (2013). Credit constraints, heterogeneous firms and international trade. *Review of Economic Studies, 80*(2), 711–744.
Mansfield, E. (1963). *Size of firm, market structure, and innovation* (pp. 556–576). LXXI: Economy.
Muendler, M. A. (2004). *Trade, technology, and productivity: A study of Brazilian manufacturers 1986–1998*. CESIFO Working Paper No. 1148, CESifo.
Martins, J. O., Scarpetta, S., & Pilat, D. (1996). Mark up pricing, market structure and the business cycle. *OECD Economic Studies, 27*, 71–105.
Marjit, S., Misra, S., & Banerjee, S. (2017). Technology improvement and market structure alteration. *Economics Bulletin, 37*(2), 1106–1112.
Marjit, S., & Mukherjee, A. (2008). International outsourcing and R&D: Long-run implications for consumers. *Review of International Economics, 16*(5), 1010–1022.
Marjit, S., Yang, L., & Ray, M. (2014). Credit constraints, fragmentation and inter- firm transactions. *Asia-Pacific Journal of Accounting and Economics, 22*(1), 94–103.
Marjit, S., & Ray, M. (2017). Export profitability, competition and technology. *International Review of Economics and Finance, 47*(C), 35–45.
Marjit, S., & Ray, M. (2020). *Asset level heterogeneity, competition and export incentives: The role of credit rationing*. CESifo Working Paper No. 8208, CESifo.
Marjit, S., & Raychaudhuri, P. (2004). Asymmetric capacity costs and joint venture buy-outs. *Journal of Economic Behaviour and Organization, 54*(3), 425–438.
Martin, S. (2001). *Industrial organization: A European perspective*. Oxford University Press.
Matsuyama, K. (2005). Credit market imperfections and patterns of international trade and capital flows. *Journal of the European Economic Association, 3*(2–3), 714–723.
Matsuyama, K. (2008). Aggregate implications of credit market imperfections. *NBER Macroeconomics Annual, 22*, 1–60.
Mattoo, A., Olarreaga, M., & Saggi, K. (2004). Mode of foreign entry, technology transfer, and FDI policy. *Journal of Development Economics, 75*, 95–111.
Meisenzahl, R. (2011). *Can financing constraints explain the evolution of firm size distribution?—New evidence from US small business*. Washington DC: Federal Reserve Board.
Melitz, M. J. (2003). The impact of trade on intra-industry reallocations and aggregate industry productivity. *Econometrica, 71*(6), 1695–1725.
Minetti, R., & Zhu, S. C. (2011). Credit constraints and firm export: Microeconomic evidence from Italy. *Journal of International Economics, 83*(2), 109–125.
Miralles, A. (2010). Self-enforced collusion through comparative cheap talk in simultaneous auctions with entry. *Economic Theory, 42*, 523–538.

Misra, S. (2019). *Three essays on credit markets and industrial organization* (A doctoral dissertation submitted to the Faculty of Arts), Jadavpur University, Kolkata.
Mukherjee, A. (2002). Subsidy and entry: The role of licensing. *Oxford Economic Papers, 54,* 160–171.
Mukherjee, A. & Pennings, E. (2004). Imitation, patent protection, and welfare. *Oxford Economic Papers, 56*(4), 715–733.
Mukherjee, A., & Pennings, E. (2011). Unionization structure, licensing and innovation. *International Journal of Industrial Organization, 29,* 232–241.
Mukherjee, A., & Sinha, U. (2013). Patent protection, southern innovation and welfare in a North-South trade model. *Economica, 80*(138), 248–273.
Mukherjee, A. & Zhao, L. (2009). Profit Raising Entry. *Journal of Industrial Economics, 57*(4), 870.
Mukherjee, A. & Zhao, L. (2017). Profit Raising Entry. *Journal of Industrial Economics, 65*(1), 214–219.
Nocke, V., & Thanassoulis, J. (2014). Vertical relations under credit constraints. *Journal of the European Economic Association, 12*(2), 337–367.
Nelson, R. R., & Winter, S. G. (1977). Dynamic competition and technical progress. In Bela A. Balassa & Richard R. Nelson (Eds.), *Economic progress, private values and public policy: Essays in Honor of William Fellner* (p. 1977). Amsterdam: North- Holland.
Pavcnik, N. (2002). Trade liberalization, exit, and productivity improvements: Evidence from Chilean plants. *The Review of Economic Studies, 69*(1), 245–276.
Perla, J., & Tonetti, C. (2014). Equilibrium imitation and growth. *Journal of Political Economy, 122*(1), 52–76.
Perla, J., Tonetti, C., & Waugh, M. (2015). *Equilibrium technology diffusion, trade and growth,* NBER Working Paper No. 20881, Cambridge.
Reenen, J. V. (2011). *Wage inequality, technology and trade: 21st century evidence.* CEP Occasional Paper 28, Centre for Economic Performance, LSE.
Ross, T. W. (1992). Cartel stability and product differentiation. *International Journal of Industrial Organization, 10*(1), 1–13.
Scherer, F. M. (1967a). *Market structure and the employment of scientists and engineers* (pp. 524–531). 57: American Economic Review.
Scherer. F. M. (1967b). Research and development resource allocation under rivalry. *Quarterly Journal of Economics, 89,* 359–94.
Scherer, F. M. (1980). Industrial market structure and economic performance, 2nd edition. *Chicago: Rand and McNally.*
Schumpeter, J. (1943). *Capitalism, socialism, and democracy.* London: UnwinUniversity Books.
Shy, O. (1996). *The industrial organization.* The MIT Press.
Stiglitz, J. E., & Weiss, A. (1981). Credit rationing in markets with imperfect information. *American Economic Review, 71*(3), 393–410.
Sylos-Labini, P. (1969). *Oligopoly and technical progress.* Cambridge: Harvard University Press.
Symeonidis, G. (2002). Cartel stability with multi-product firms. *International Journal of Industrial Organization, 20*(3), 339–352.
Tandon, P. (1984). Innovation, market structure, and welfare. *The American Economic Review, 74*(3), 394–403.
Tirole, J. (1988). *The theory of industrial organization.* The MIT Press.
Von Weizsacker, C. C. (1980). *Barriers to entry.* Berlin: Springer-Verlag.
Weibull, J. W. (2006). *Price competition and convex costs* (No. 622). SSE/EFI Working Paper Series in Economics and Finance.
Wernerfelt, B. (1989). Tacit collusion in differentiated Cournot games. *Economic Letters, 29*(4), 303–306.
Williamson, O. E. (1965). Innovation and market structure. *Journal of Political Economy, 73,* 67–73.
Yi, S.-S. (1999). Market structure and the incentives to innovate: The case of cournot oligopoly. *Economics Letters, 65,* 379–388.

An Evaluation of Monetary Policy in India: A Sustainable Development Perspective

Ananya Ghosh Dastidar and Kajleen Kaur

1 Introduction

This chapter attempts to evaluate the performance of monetary policy in terms of its effectiveness in influencing the rate of economic growth and controlling inflation. The importance of these two policy objectives comes to the fore, especially when viewed through the lens of the Sustainable Development Goals (SDGs) of the United Nations. Growth is critical for combating poverty and undertaking redistributive measures to mitigate inequality within nations (SDGs 1 and 10), whereas managing inflation, especially food inflation, lies at the core of strategies designed to end hunger and achieve food and nutrition security (SDG 2). The performance evaluation undertaken in the paper is based on a review of relevant literature in the Indian context, focusing especially on the post-liberalization period.

Assessing monetary policy through the lens of sustainable development may be uncommon, but its relevance can hardly be questioned. Given the centrality of monetary policy measures in the Indian government's response to the economic pandemic wrought by COVID-19, perhaps such appraisal is needed now, more than ever before.

The authors would like to thank the editors for this opportunity to contribute to this volume in honour of Prof. Ramprasad Sengupta, one of the finest economists in our country. In particular, the first author, who has been a student of Professor Sengupta at JNU, is extremely grateful to him for the many lessons he imparted in class and through his exemplary sincerity as a teacher and practitioner of the discipline. The authors would especially like to thank Soumyen Sikdar for extremely helpful comments and suggestions on an earlier draft. Lastly, the usual disclaimer applies.

A. G. Dastidar (✉)
Department of Finance and Business Economics, University of Delhi, University of Delhi South Campus, New Delhi, India
e-mail: agdastidar@gmail.com

K. Kaur
Sri Guru Gobind Singh College of Commerce, University of Delhi, New Delhi, India
e-mail: kajleen@rediffmail.com

P. Dasgupta et al. (eds.), *Sustainable Development Insights from India*,
India Studies in Business and Economics,
https://doi.org/10.1007/978-981-33-4830-1_6

The discussion is structured as follows. To begin with, a brief overview of the conduct of monetary policy in India provides the necessary background for the remaining analysis (Sect. 1). The effectiveness of monetary transmission in affecting aggregate demand and output in the Indian context, especially in recent times, is examined thereafter (Sect. 2). The phenomenon of inflation, especially food price inflation and the efficacy of monetary measures in controlling it, is discussed next (Sect. 3). Findings from the literature are then used to assess recent liquidity measures of the Indian government for economic revival in pandemic times (Sect. 4). This is followed by concluding remarks.

2 Monetary Policy in India: An Overview

Monetary policy in India has seen it all! It has made a transition from a past marked by financial repression and fiscal dominance to the present where, in keeping with standard international practice, flexible inflation targeting was formally adopted since 2016 (Ray, 2013; Das, 2020; Dua, 2020).

The 1970s and 1980s were marked by fiscal dominance, wherein monetary policy almost entirely played a supporting role in financing fiscal needs. Reforms, introduced in the late 1980s decade, marked a break from the past and ushered in the era of *monetary targeting* which lasted for a decade, from 1988 to 1998. Under this regime, the central bank strived to maintain a target with respect to the quantum of money in the economy, an effort largely undermined by the issue of ad hoc treasury bills mainly under fiscal pressures. The need for reining in the fiscal deficit was increasingly felt ever since the country introduced sweeping economic reforms since 1991 and opted for a market-oriented, globalized pathway to growth. Monetary reforms kept pace,[1] by freeing the central bank from fiscal dominance[2] and crafting a transition to enhanced reliance on market-oriented, price-based, indirect instruments, from the direct measures used earlier on. These changes marked the Reserve Bank of India's (RBI) formal adoption of a *multiple indicator approach*, which lasted from

[1]Recommendations of landmark committees such as the Chakravarty Committee in 1985, Narasimham Committees (I and II) in 1991 and 1998, the Tarapore Committee in 2006, the Raghuram Rajan Committee in 2008 and the more recent Urjit Patel Committee in 2014 (which led to setting up of Monetary Policy Committee in 2016) have profoundly influenced the path of monetary reforms in India. These have also been shaped by detailed recommendations made by various Working Groups constituted by the RBI from time to time (e.g. Working Group on Sterilization in 2003, Working Group on Operating Procedure of Monetary Policy in 2011, etc.).

[2]Prohibition on the issue of fixed interest, ad hoc treasury bills since 1997–98, steady reduction in the statutory liquidity ratio or SLR (from 38.5 in 1990 to its statutory minimum of 25% by 1997) and enactment of the FRBM Act in 2003 (which put a stop to direct government borrowing from RBI 2006–07 onwards) were three important milestones that served to limit automatic fiscal accommodation by monetary policy. The first contributed to emergence of a market for government securities and transition to market-based interest rates (even as it raised cost of borrowing for the government). The third enhanced 'space' for using monetary policy by reducing the scope for monetization and imposing strict constraints on size of the fiscal deficit (Ray, 2013).

1998 till its official transition to inflation targeting in 2016 (see Dua, 2020). Monetary policy has since, strived to maintain a reasonable output gap (actual minus potential output) along with price and exchange rate stability, no mean challenge, in the face of volatile capital flows in a fast globalizing economy.

The most important development between 1998 and 2016 has been the emergence of interest rates as the chief tool of monetary intervention, a noticeable shift from the prior reliance on bank rate and cash reserve ratio (CRR) by the RBI. Liquidity adjustment facility (LAF), a cornerstone of monetary policy over this period, was used extensively to make temporary and swift adjustments in liquidity within the banking system mainly using the repo and reverse repo rates.[3] This process culminated in the evolution of the repo rate as the benchmark policy rate, determining the baseline cost of borrowing in the economy today.

The theoretical underpinning of the recent policy stance of the RBI can be traced back to the influential Taylor rule, which captures the way forward-looking central banks frame interest rate policies, by taking into account inflationary expectations (based on the Phillips Curve) and the impact of real interest rates on output (based on dynamic IS curve) (Carlin & Soskice, 2015). According to the simple, closed economy Taylor rule, central banks set nominal interest rates to achieve a real interest rate target, as output (especially investments) responds to the real rate, typically with a lag. Therefore, central banks choose nominal policy rates optimally by minimizing the deviation of actual inflation from target, subject to a reasonable output gap. Based on this underlying concept and historical data pertaining to policy rates set by the US Federal Reserve, John Taylor (1993) proposed a rule for setting nominal interest rates. The simplest version of the Taylor rule is captured by the following equation:

$$i = \pi + r * + \beta_1(\pi - \pi *) + \beta_2(y - y*)$$

where i is the nominal interest set by the central bank, r^* is the equilibrium real interest rate, π and π^* are the actual and target rates of inflation, respectively, and y and y^* are logarithms of actual and potential output levels (representing percentage change), respectively. According to the original rule, the coefficients β_1 and β_2 are positive and as a rule of thumb, equal in magnitude (i.e. $\beta_1 = \beta_2 = 0.5$). The rule thus proposes setting a higher interest rate, whenever inflation is above its target (i.e. a positive inflation gap ($\pi - \pi^*$)), and/or output is above its potential or full employment level (i.e. a positive output gap ($y - y^*$)). In other words, it calls for tight money policy when inflation or output gap is positive and monetary easing when the gaps are negative. When the economy experiences ‘conflicting’ goals such as stagflation (i.e. low growth and high inflation), the relative weights vary. The magnitude of the weights assigned to the inflation gap and output gap essentially

[3]The repo (short for repurchase) and reverse repo rates are used by the RBI, under the LAF to temporarily inject and withdraw liquidity, respectively, into and from the commercial banking system. The collateralized transactions involve lending to and borrowing from the commercial banks against government securities. These stand reversed within a very short time span as they simply involve digital entries, with no change in title of the holder of the securities used for the transactions.

indicate central banks' tolerance for deviations of output vis-à-vis inflation from respective targets.[4]

Inflation targeting (IT) has been widely criticized, yet it has been widely adopted by central banks around the world! The theoretical premises of the DSGE (dynamic stochastic general equilibrium) models based on forward-looking agents with rational expectations have borne the brunt of the criticism (see e.g. Blanchard & Gali, 2005). Indeed, 'real targeting' of employment growth or real GDP or investment growth has been suggested as alternatives to this approach (Epstein, 2003). By and large, in the developed world, inflation targeting seems to have worked though, especially by keeping fiscal dominance (and political interference) at bay, except for a brief period after the 2008 global financial crisis, when central banks across Europe and the USA opted for unconventional monetary measures (Ray, 2013).

The smooth functioning of IT, it has been repeatedly pointed out, calls for fiscal discipline, central bank autonomy, highly developed financial markets and supporting infrastructure (Hu, 2006; Mishra and Mishra, 2009; Sengupta, 2014). Therefore, IT may be somewhat unsuitable in the context of emerging nations like India (Jha, 2008; Kanan, 1999; Kumail et al., 2012).[5] After the implementation of wide-ranging financial reforms, however, there was greater consensus regarding its applicability in the Indian context (Sengupta, 2014; Singh, 2006), despite significant non-monetary influence on the inflation rate (Katkhate, 2006).

While India formally adopted an inflation target of 4% (within a 2% point range of 2–6%) in 2016, in practice, monetary policy seems to have broadly followed the Taylor rule right through the 2000s decade. However, evidence suggests that policy rates in India remained well below levels compatible with the Taylor rule (RBI, 2013), in line with global trends (Hofmann and Bogdanova, 2012), reflecting concerns regarding macroeconomic stability. Large interest differentials with the rest of the world could have triggered volatile capital (especially portfolio) inflows and jeopardized exchange rate and overall financial stability. Indeed, the responsiveness of policy rates to exchange rate fluctuations, rather than to inflation or output gap, has been noted across a wide spectrum of emerging economies (Mohanty and Klau, 2004).

Apart from the exchange rate and financial stability, interest rate setting by the RBI has mainly been shaped by concerns about growth and inflation. Evidence is mixed regarding the relative importance of these two objectives. The literature is replete with studies that have found interest rate movements responding relatively more to the output gap (Banerjee & Bhattacharya, 2008; Chand & Singh, 2006; Inoue & Hamori, 2009; Jha, 2008; Kaur, 2016; Ranjan et al., 2007; RBI, 2002) and even nominal income (Virmani, 2004), in the Indian context. Overall, the change in monetary policy stance with respect to inflation targeting is confirmed. For instance,

---

[4]E.g. higher magnitude of the weight for inflation gap indicates that the central bank cares more about inflation than unemployment. So it is more likely to raise interest rates to curb inflation when it exceeds target, even if that comes at the cost of lowering output and raising unemployment (Carlin & Soskice, 2015).

[5]It has also been suggested though that Taylor rule is appropriate for emerging economies only after suitable modifications (Taylor, 2000).

an influential study by Mohanty and Klau (2004) finds monetary policy responded more to the inflation gap between 1988 and 89 and 2008–09, compared to the period 1950–51 to 1987–88, when it was more responsive to the output gap. The study also finds asymmetry in policy response, which showed greater sensitivity to positive (i.e. actual inflation higher than target) than negative deviations of inflation from target. There is, however, substantial variation regarding the length of lags in the response of output and inflation to change in policy rates and exchange rates.[6] Findings in the literature are influenced by choice of the dataset, precise time period and overall empirical strategies adopted in the paper (more on this in the following section), with some studies recording policy effectiveness (e.g. OstaEraghi, 2015) and others ineffectiveness (e.g. Singh & Kalirajan, 2006), in controlling inflation and the output gap.

There have also been concerns regarding the possible persistence of fiscal pressure on the conduct of monetary policy, despite financial reforms. For instance, RBI (2013) and Raj et al. (2011) both find evidence of a rise in interest rates associated with increases in fiscal deficits. This underscores the need to analyse monetary policy in an expanded Taylor framework that includes both fiscal and exchange rate variables in the Indian context. Kaur (2016) is a recent attempt in this direction.

Challenges facing monetary policy in open economies, with flexible exchange rates and near-perfect capital mobility (especially highly volatile, short-term, portfolio flows), are well understood in theory and clearly articulated in the standard Mundell–Fleming model (see Sikdar, 2013 for a lucid exposition). Time and again, the RBI has risen to the occasion to handle crises, as demonstrated by its response to the 2008 financial crisis and taper tantrum that followed. However, as the following discussion shows, misgivings persist regarding its ability to rein in inflation and influence crucial real sector variables such as private business investments.

3 Monetary Policy: Impact on Aggregate Demand and Output

Discussions on the link between monetary and real variables have a long history. The classical quantity theory of money forged a direct link between money supply and inflation. In the purely classical world, the role of money was 'neutral' and output was determined by the forces of demand and supply, under the assumptions of flexible wages and prices. It was the Keynesian analysis that brought to the fore the role of interest rates in linking the monetary and real sectors of the economy.

[6]E.g. Lags in the effect of interest rate changes on the output gap range from two to three quarters (Mohanty, 2012; Patra & Kapur, 2010) and on inflation, from three quarters (Mohanty, 2012) to as much as two years (Chand and Singh, 2006). Real appreciation of the rupee has also been found to lower output with a lag of two quarters (Patra and Kapur, 2010).

3.1 Monetary Transmission: Basic Issues and Concepts

Monetary transmission refers to the manifold ways in which monetary variables affect real outcomes (Mishkin, 1995). Traditionally, monetary policy transmission is seen to occur via the *interest rate channel.* That is, monetary policy expansion lowers the real interest rate, which in turn reduces the cost of borrowing, triggering expansion in interest-sensitive components of aggregate demand, especially business investments and household spending on consumer durables and housing.

Empirical evidence indicates that change in interest rates can also affect the supply side through a change in borrowing costs, leading to the *cost channel* of monetary transmission, (Barth and Ramey, 2001; Chowdhury et al., 2006; Gaotti and Secchi, 2006; Henzel et al., 2009). A rise in real interest rates can lead to inflation by raising the cost of borrowing, making working capital relatively costly and leading to a rise in goods prices—this is known as the *price puzzle.* This may also lead to a cutback in output, adding to the contractionary effect from the demand side. However, it may increase the labour intensity of production via substitution effects and contribute to a rise in demand for labour and wages. In turn, this may result in second-round increases in the price of labour-intensive goods, like food. Through this channel, monetary policy may affect output, employment as well as inflation.

The *credit channel*, which emphasizes the supply of and demand for credit and asymmetric information in financial markets, works through changes in *bank credit* and via *balance sheet* effects. Expansionary monetary policy leads to higher deposit creation, enhancing banks' lending capacity, leading to higher credit disbursal and increases in investment and aggregate output, under the *bank credit channel.* The *balance sheet channel* works through the effect of monetary expansion on the borrowers' balance sheets, i.e. firms' balance sheets. Typically, firms with low net worth find it difficult to borrow from banks, especially in the presence of information asymmetries that enhance risks due to adverse selection and moral hazard. Monetary expansion lowers interest rates, raises equity prices and hence net worth of firms, making them more credit-worthy. It thereby enhances the flow of credit to firms, raising business investments, output and employment. Monetary easing also improves firms' cash flows, an important source of financing, leading to higher corporate investments. Internal finance is absolutely critical for investments, especially in the presence of credit constraints.

The *asset price channel* pertains to the impact of monetary policy on prices of real and financial assets. Expansionary monetary policy (i.e. fall in interest rates) lowers returns on bonds and raises equity prices and price of real assets (e.g. land, housing, etc.). The rise in asset values creates positive wealth effects, raising spending by firms and households, especially on durables and real estate (since borrowing costs are lower). Further, an increase in equity prices raises the market value of firms, leading to a rise in business investments, as explained by Tobin's q theory, where 'q' is the ratio of firms' market value to the replacement cost of capital. A rise in market value, relative to the cost of capital, induces capital formation (Sikdar, 2006).

The *exchange rate channel* of monetary transmission has assumed importance with the growing internationalization of economies. In open economies, monetary expansion reduces interest rates on domestic bonds, making foreign bonds relatively more attractive and leading to capital outflows. The resulting depreciation of domestic currency (with flexible exchange rates) raises net exports and output, by giving a competitive edge to domestic goods.

Different channels may assume importance in an economy, depending on the institutional context and extent of financial development. The importance of the Keynesian interest rate channel has been emphasized, especially in the context of developed economies. There is evidence of strong interest rate transmission to aggregate demand in well-functioning, developed financial markets (Bernanke, & Blinder, 1992; Christiano, & Eichenbaum, 1992; Dale, & Haldane 1995; Gerlash & Smets, 1995; Ramaswami & Slok, 1998; Fiore 1998; Favero et al. 1999; Mojon & Peersman, 2001; Smets & Wouters, 2002; Taylor, 1995; Norris & Floerkemeir, 2006). However, the presence of policy shocks and financial frictions can render the interest rate channel ineffective (Bean et al., 2002). Time can also be a factor as Berananke and Gertler (1995) show that the interest rate while effective in the short run may not be so over the long run.

The credit channel has also been found to be very effective (Bernanke & Blinder, 1988). However, with financial deepening and innovations, there is a decline in the importance of banks and the bank lending channel in the process (Romer & Romer, 1990; Edwards & Mishkin, 1995). Empirical evidence supports the greater effectiveness of the interest channel over the credit channel (Ramey, 1993). The importance of the exchange rate channel has also been stressed, especially in studies pertaining to euro areas (Obstfeld & Rogoff, 1995; Adolfson, 2001; Smets & Wouters, 2002; Gali & Monacelli 2005; Jardak & Wrobel, 2009).

For emerging economies, the evidence is mixed regarding the importance of the interest rate and credit channels, where studies contend, the absence of well-organized financial markets tends to weaken the interest rate channel (Bhattacharya et al., 2019). With banks still being chief sources of credit, the bank lending channel is often quite important in these economies. However, certain structural characteristics, especially the existence of informal markets, place limits on the relevance of formal channels of monetary transmission in such economies.

3.2 The Indian Experience

Monetary policymaking in India has made a gradual, fundamental transition from the pre-1990s regime of administered interest rates to a market-based system today where the repo rate has emerged as the primary tool of monetary intervention. Empirical evidence on the effectiveness of the interest rate channel, however, is mixed, partly due to the sensitivity of results to the choice of the study period and empirical techniques.

The Interest Rate Channel The importance of the interest rate channel of transmission is well established in the literature on India, especially for the post-LAF period (Anand et al., 2010; Aleem, 2010; Khundrakpam & Jain, 2012; Mohanty, 2012; Patra & Kapur, 2010; Sengupta, 2014; Singh & Kalirajan, 2006), with some estimates attributing to it as much as half the effect of monetary policy on GDP (Khundrakpam & Jain, 2012). However, serious issues have been raised with respect to pass-through of policy rates to lending and deposit rates of commercial banks in India. While few studies do find evidence of significant pass-through of policy rates (Singh, 2011), most others find it very slow, incomplete and asymmetric. In India, commercial banks' lending rates tend to respond more to policy rate hikes rather than to cuts, and the opposite holds true with deposit rates that respond more to cuts than to hikes in the benchmark policy rate (Das, 2015; Mishra et al., 2016; RBI, 2014).

An interest rate puzzle has also been observed in the case of India (Kaur & Dastidar, 2019). Such a puzzle exists when output is unresponsive to the interest rate, or when higher interest rates and higher growth rates go together, or when a fall in interest rate fails to revive economic growth (Nelson, 2000, 2002; Reinhart & Sbrancia, 2011). This may be observed when aggregate demand is driven by factors other than the cost of borrowing, such as consumer confidence, positive changes in the investment climate, electoral cycles, fiscal expansion in response to global shocks (such as the financial crisis) and so on. However, it may also follow due to misspecification of the IS curve in empirical studies (Furher & Moore, 1995; Nelson, 2002).[7]

Empirical evidence on the responsiveness of households' spending decisions to changes in the interest rates is limited in the Indian context. While private savings behaviour has been explored (e.g. Agrawal et al., 2010; Athukorala & Sen, 2004; Loayza & Shankar, 2000), there is a dearth of studies that specifically estimate the interest elasticity of household consumption in India. There is some evidence to indicate that consumption may be substantially affected by the change in deposit rates. A series of policy changes between 2001 and 2004 allowed banks to offer higher interest rates on time deposits held by senior citizens. Analysis of consumption behaviour of households before and after this change found the rise in deposit rate caused a significant dip in the consumption of affected households, in the short run (Kapoor & Ravi, 2009).[8] The magnitude of inter-temporal elasticity of substitution

[7]For instance, results depend on whether a forward-looking or backward-looking specification is used for the IS curve in empirical models. Moreover, use of restricted forms of the IS equation that ignore relevant factors such as real exchange rates and asset prices which also affect aggregate demand (especially private investments) may also lead to misspecification.

[8]Kapoor and Ravi (2009 and 2010) exploit the natural experiment presented by this policy change and analyse two rounds of NSSO data, classifying households on the basis of age (e.g. households in which the head is a senior citizen and those where the head is below 60 years of age). Using a regression discontinuity approach, Kapoor and Ravi (2009) estimate substantial short-run impact of the hike in deposit rates on consumption expenditure on non-food, non-essential items (including durables, education, clothing, travel, medicine, etc.). However, consumption resumes its average value in the longer run, which they surmise this could be due to income effects (i.e. higher interest income leading to higher consumption in the long run). Using a difference-in-difference estimator, Kapoor and Ravi (2010) compare consumption of two groups of households (those where head is

(which measures the impact of expected real interest rate on current consumption) was estimated to be greater than 1 (Kapoor & Ravi, 2010). This indicates substantial interest sensitivity of consumption, with a reduction in current consumption likely if interest rates on savings and fixed deposits are raised. Does this mean that a cut in deposit rates will necessarily lead to a rise in consumption? This is not at all clear.

In India, a steady fall in deposit rates in recent years has gone hand in hand with a change in financial asset holdings by households (RBI, 2020). There is a rise in the share of mutual funds and insurance products that earn relatively higher returns compared to fixed deposits in banks. Indeed, the participation of small retail investors in equity markets during the recent pandemic indicates that low returns on deposits may be inducing changes in the composition of savings, rather than any change in its quantum. By directing savings towards the equity market, access to savings by the corporate sector is likely to improve. Overall this remains an under-researched area. Apart from the studies by Kapoor and Ravi cited above, which explored a specific instance, there is hardly any empirical analysis of exactly how households' decision to purchase consumer durables, invest in residential housing, etc., is affected by the change in lending rates in India.

Lending rates affect the user cost of capital, which is an important determinant of investment decisions by firms.[9] However, several other factors (e.g. indirect taxes, import duties, etc.) also affect the cost of capital. Also, other than cost considerations, investment demand is influenced by demand conditions and expectations regarding the future. During the 2007–2008 global crisis, firms faced severe liquidity crunch as uncertainty loomed large and limits of traditional monetary policy, especially the interest channel came to the fore. In the Indian context, this was reflected, especially in the failure of monetary measures to address the prolonged slump in private business investments (Dastidar & Ahuja, 2019; Mallick & Agarwal, 2007; RBI, 2014) which has deepened further due to the COVID-19 pandemic. Indeed, unconventional policies (e.g. quantitative easing) and bold fiscal measures, tried and tested during the global financial crisis (Cecchetti et al., 2009; Walsh, 2009; Bean et al., 2010; Trichet, 2011; Yellen, 2011), are now becoming part of the 'new normal' policy response across the globe in response to economic crisis triggered by the Corona pandemic.

Other Channels of Transmission Among the other channels of monetary transmission, the asset price channel has been found to be relatively weak (Aleem, 2010), although there is some evidence to indicate it has strengthened in the post-LAF era (Sengupta, 2014; Khundrakpam & Jain, 2012). However, there is empirical evidence supporting the importance of the credit channel in India (Aleem, 2010; Khundrakpam & Jain, 2012; Sengupta, 2014).

---

senior citizen vs those where head is not senior citizen). They find that consumption patterns were similar prior to 2001, but differed significantly in 2005 and attribute this difference to the hike in deposit rates for senior citizens between 2001 and 2004.

[9]See Dastidar and Ahuja (2019) for a recent survey on the determinants of private corporate investments in India.

The credit channel of transmission appears to have important implications for consumption in the Indian context. Availability of credit contributed to increased household consumption in rural India, especially in the short run, in the 1970s and 1980s when significant expansion in rural bank branches took place, after the nationalization of banks in 1969 (Fulford, 2013).[10] More recently, banking and financial reforms over the 2000s decade seem to have alleviated the credit constraint facing households to a considerable extent. The share of personal loans in total bank credit surged from 13% in 2000–2001 to 23% in 2005–2006 and further to 28% by February 2020 (Nagaraj, 2013; Shetty, 2020). Indeed, borrowing by households for investment in housing is by far the most important component of personal loans. It accounted for over half of household borrowings in 2005–06 (Nagaraj, 2013); currently, housing loans have emerged as the single largest sector in terms of credit disbursed, accounting for 15% of total bank credit, compared to 11.3% for infrastructure (Shetty, 2020). In this context, macro-prudential policies may also affect household investments by changing the terms of credit. For instance, home loans surged in 2016, following the increase in loan-to-value (LTV) ratio in 2015.[11]

Traditionally, the banking system has also been an important source of credit to firms in the formal sector in India. Especially, in the pre-liberalization phase, the absence of vibrant equity and corporate debt markets rendered bank credit indispensable, especially for small and medium firms. Large firms could also rely on sizeable operating surpluses for financing investments. Despite substantial financial reforms in the new millennia, the corporate debt market in India has not taken off, and the equity market continues to serve relatively larger firms in the formal sector, leaving out a large body of small and medium enterprises, for whom bank credit is still the mainstay.

Trade liberalization has come a long way in India since the 1990s. The country experienced phenomenal export growth in the 2000s decade, prior to the global financial crisis and also in its immediate aftermath, as governments responded to the crisis with coordinated fiscal expansion. However, evidence indicates that the exchange rate channel, even though it does exist (Patra and Kapur, 2010), has been weak (Sengupta, 2014; Aleem, 2010; Khundrakpam & Jain, 2012; Mishra et al., 2016). The RBI's interventions for exchange rate stability (Aleem, 2010) combined with relatively low exchange rate elasticities of India's trade basket, no doubt, explain this finding. Studies indicate the importance of non-price factors (e.g. infrastructure) in holding back India's export performance, which explains why a real exchange rate depreciation in itself may not bring about an increase in exports (see Dastidar, 2015 for a survey). It is external demand, rather than price competitiveness, that explains much of India's phenomenal export growth between 2004 and 2007 (Nagaraj, 2013). India's export growth slumped since 2011–12, with little signs of picking up, despite

---

[10]Fulford (2013) also shows that credit availability may have adverse long-run effects by undermining savings and hence future income streams. A theoretical model is used along with empirical analysis based on NSSO data to study the dynamic effects of enhancing access to credit.

[11]After the RBI increased the loan-to-value (LTV) ratio to 90% for home loans of up to Rs. 30 lakhs or less (that fall under 'affordable' category in urban areas) in 2015, there was a surge in housing loans in the following year (RBI press release 2016–2017/1277).

substantial depreciation of the rupee since then. Indeed, exchange rate depreciation has been associated more with inflation than output growth in an oil-importing country like India (Bhattacharya et al., 2011; Kaur & Dastidar, 2019; Rangarajan & Arif, 1990).

In the Indian context, therefore, the literature indicates the relative importance of the interest rate and credit channels, while asset price and exchange rate channels seem to appear relatively ineffective in affecting aggregate output.

Impediments to Monetary Transmission Several factors limit the extent of monetary policy transmission to real economic activity (e.g. RBI, 2014; Mishra et al., 2016). Financial and credit market frictions impose severe constraints on the transmission mechanism (RBI, 2014). The economic structure in India, marked by the presence of a large informal sector, inhibits access, especially of smaller firms, to formal sources of credit. In the presence of credit market imperfections (e.g. high degree of information asymmetry, leading to large collateral requirements for loans) and the absence of well-developed corporate bond markets, borrowers face credit constraints. This essentially impairs the smooth intermediation needed to channelize household savings effectively for investments, holding back growth, and employment creation.

The impact of monetary policy on aggregate output is ultimately shaped by the responsiveness of investments (by households and firms) to changes in interest rates, in asset prices (via wealth effects) and to the availability of bank credit. Firms' cash flow situation and their market value relative to the cost of capital (i.e. Tobin's q) are also important drivers of business investments. Indeed, recent studies have highlighted the importance of business confidence (Anand & Tulin, 2014) and institutional reforms (Sen et al., 2014), rather than the cost of borrowing per se, for reviving business investments. The ongoing investment slowdown in India suggests that while the real interest rate may be important in the short run, uncertainty regarding the future can severely retard investment prospects in the medium run, leading to a prolonged slump (see e.g. Anand & Tulin, 2014; Dastidar & Ahuja, 2019). Expectation about the future is also an important determinant of the demand for housing, just as it for business investments. For any given cost of borrowing, higher expected growth in house prices and capital gains from house ownership effectively lowers the user cost of housing and raises housing demand (Himmelberg et al., 2005). Indeed house price expectations (e.g. future movement of house prices) seem to have driven the credit-house-price dynamics in India. Analysis of data on credit and house prices from Indian cities reveals causality running from house prices to credit growth and not the other way around (Arora et al., 2020).[12]

Overall, therefore, for monetary policy to effectively address consumption, private investments and job creation, the role of supporting institutions and of business and consumer confidence can hardly be overemphasized.

---

[12]Typically, expectations about future house price are based on the past trends. Using the past housing prices as proxy for house price expectations, Arora et al. (2020) show that real estate prices influence credit markets in Indian cities (Tier 1 as well as Tier 2 cities), with causality running from house price to credit. The result that housing prices are *causing* credit is indicative of the role of expectations in driving credit demand for housing.

Methodology and Data issues A challenge for deriving policy implications from this literature relates to the mixed evidence that emerges from it. Studies focusing on India are almost entirely empirical with results driven by choice of empirical strategy (e.g. technique as well as model specification used to evaluate Taylor rule), study period[13] and exact variables analysed. The techniques used range from OLS regression (Patra & Kapur, 2010; RBI, 2013) to time series models such as VAR (Aleem, 2010; RBI, 2013; Singh, 2011), SVAR (Khundrakpam & Jain, 2012), Cointegrated VAR (Singh & Kalirajan, 2007), VECM (Das, 2015), ARDL (Kaur and Dastidar, 2019), Bayesian estimation in a dynamic general equilibrium model (Anand et al, 2010) to mention a few. Moreover, the difference in choice of endogenous vis-à-vis exogenous variables in the class of VAR models creates further differences in results obtained.

The literature on the impact of monetary policy on inflation (discussed in Sect. 3 below) is also empirical in nature, covering different time periods and mainly involving the application of time series techniques. For instance, Alam and Alam (2016) use a bounds testing approach and Goyal and Pujari (2005) use SVAR, while Goyal, (2014) uses Granger causality tests, VECM and estimates demand and supply shocks using a SVAR framework. Chakraborty and Varma (2015) use an ARDL model, while Paul and Zaman (2015) use an ADL model in their study. Bhattacharya and Jain (2020) is a cross-country study, based on a panel of developed and developing economies over the period 2006–2016, using Panel VAR estimation. While both Anand et al. (2014) and Holtemoller and Mallick (2016)[14] use Bayesian estimation techniques in a dynamic general equilibrium, New Keynesian framework wherein results are affected by the choice of parameter values.

Therefore, the present chapter has bypassed any discussion on the magnitude of estimated coefficients, which differ widely and are not strictly comparable (owing to different variables and time periods covered in the study) and focused more instead on broad findings with respect to the underlying macroeconomic relationships under investigation. For a detailed discussion on estimation methods and results with respect to empirical evidence on monetary transmission, in the context of both developed and emerging market economies, see Bhattacharya et al. (2019).[15]

Efficient estimation using time series techniques relies heavily on the availability of high frequency, sufficiently long data series (e.g. at least 30 years for estimation of long-run effects). The need to control for lagged effects of variables can result in a significant loss in degrees of freedom. However, data may not always be available

[13]Even for studies that focus only on the post-1991 period, there is wide variation in the exact time period covered. For instance, the periods covered in some of the studies are as follows: Aleem (2010)—1996(Q4) to 2007(Q4); Das (2015)—March, 2002 to October, 2014; Kaur and Dastidar (2019)—May, 2001 to March, 2015; Kaur (2016)—1996 (Q1) to 2013 (Q3); Khundrakpam and Jain (2012)—1996–1997 (Q1) to 2011–2012 (Q1); RBI (2013)—2000–2001 to 2010–2011; Sengupta (2014)—1993–2012; Singh (2011)—March, 2001 to June, 2012; to mention a few.

[14]Holtemoller and Mallick (2016) also use SVAR model to show the impact of global food prices on food price and wholesale price inflation in India over the period 1996 (Q1) to 2013 (Q2).

[15]Bhattacharya et al. (2019) examine evidence on factors that weaken monetary transmission to output and inflation in the context of advanced and emerging economies in a meta-analysis framework.

on the most appropriate variable at the desired frequency. For instance, data on two crucial variables for studying monetary transmission, viz., GDP and gross fixed capital formation (GFCF), is available at quarterly (since 1997) and not monthly frequency. So, the Index of Industrial Production (IIP) is the most commonly used substitute measure of economic activity in empirical analyses based on monthly data. While it shows a high correlation with GFCF and GDP, the problem remains that it is ultimately a measure of outcomes based on investment decisions and real interest rates in the past.[16]

Further, use of nominal vis-à-vis real interest rates, call rates vis-à-vis repo rates to measure interest rates, GDP vis-à-vis IIP, to measure output, CPI vis-à-vis WPI to measure inflation, also contribute to differences in the results. Yet another problem relates to the recent change in estimation methodology for the latest GDP (Base year 2011–12) series, which has raised serious comparability issues with the past series (Base year 2004–05). 'The wide differences in the estimates under the two series pose major problems in the choice of data sets for examining the macro behaviour of the economy in recent years'. (Rakshit, 2016, p.81). In view of these underlying methodological differences, great care should be exercised while splicing the different series to create a single long time series.

4 Monetary Policy and Inflation

Concerns about inflation stem from the unequal impact it has on different strata in society. It reduces real wages and enhances inequality between wage and profit shares in national income. The poor are disproportionately affected, especially by food inflation, as food occupies a large share in their total expenditure, in line with Engel's law. Fall in real incomes impair further, the poor's limited capacity to save, enhancing vulnerability in the face of negative shocks. Inflation may also benefit the poor who are mostly net debtors, by eroding the real value of their debt, but this effect is not always captured in public perceptions of inflation. A fall in real wages may bring about an increase in employment (Ghura et al., 2002 & Romer and Romer, 1999), but episodes of high and volatile inflation create uncertainty and are detrimental to investments and hence medium-run prospects for output growth and employment. In general, the benefits of low, stable and positive rates of inflation

[16]The RBI regularly conducts various enterprise surveys on capacity utilization, inventories, etc. (e.g. OBICUS or Order Book, Inventory and Capacity Utilization Surveys), to capture investment plans, business confidence, etc. This data can also serve as proxy for investment plans of the private sector. The problem is that this data covers a limited sample with potential issues of inter-temporal comparability owing to changes in the underlying sample and so on. These may be among the reasons that such data is still not widely explored in the empirical literature.

are widely accepted. Indeed, the dangers of falling prices or deflation were clearly demonstrated during the 2008 global financial crisis.[17]

4.1 Inflation: A Few Conceptual Issues

Causes and Implications A clear idea about causal factors behind inflation in an open economy setting provides the necessary background for understanding the potential for monetary tools in controlling it. Broadly, these factors can be classified into those affecting price setting from the demand side and those from the cost and supply sides.

Excessive demand pressures can cause inflation, especially when matching increase in supply is not forthcoming either due to binding constraints or because all resources are fully employed. Inflation may be short-lived in the first case, especially when supply constraints are eased in the medium to longer term. When the economy is at full employment, demand expansion may result in a wage-price spiral and accelerating inflation until demand falls back in line with output. Indeed, the argument underlying the Phillips curve, a basic workhorse in macroeconomics for analysing the short-run inflation–unemployment tradeoff, is based on the links between labour and product market (wages and prices) outcomes, as shaped by the state of aggregate demand and overall market structure in the economy.

A rise in the price of key inputs such as fertilizer, energy (oil, power) and telecom services that affect transport and communication costs has a broad-based effect on costs of production and contributes to rise in the general price level. A rise in interest rates, the standard monetary response to control inflation, may itself contribute to inflationary pressures through a rise in the cost of credit (the cost channel of transmission). Also, public perception regarding the sources and duration of inflation shape inflationary expectations may themselves contribute to inflation in an economy.

Public policy can also play a crucial role, both on the demand and supply sides, as far as inflation is concerned. Expansionary fiscal policies in general and monetization of budget deficits, in particular, are typically held responsible for adding to inflationary pressures. Indeed, inflation itself feeds back into fiscal deficits by raising government expenditure to meet rising costs (for which government may borrow and incur further interest cost), even as it provides relief by eroding the real burden of public debt. On the supply side, public provision of infrastructure, both physical (e.g. roads and power) and financial (e.g. access to credit) govern the shape and substance of supply constraints, especially in emerging markets. For instance, farm support and food management policies of the government can play a crucial role in food inflation trends. Further, the policy response to inflation itself plays an important role in influencing inflationary expectations and inflation management.

[17] 'Deflationary' expectations led to prolonged periods of high real interest rates in a number of industrialized countries, jeopardizing prospects of recovery in business investments and pushing nominal interest rates into the negative zone!

In open economies, exchange rate depreciation can contribute to inflationary pressures by raising the cost of imported inputs, especially in oil-importing open economies. Most emerging countries today have adopted flexible exchange rates,[18] India being no exception. In such settings, large capital outflows can lead to sharp currency depreciation that can unleash inflationary pressures depending on the extent of pass-through to domestic prices.

However, evidence suggests that openness may also mitigate inflationary pressures (Romer, 1993). For instance, imports (e.g. food imports) can help meet domestic supply shortfalls, allow access to efficient and low-cost technologies and usher in price competition in the domestic market (lowering markups and prices charged by domestic firms). Further, capital account convertibility tends to reinforce fiscal discipline by imposing heavy costs on deviations[19] that can spill into the external sector and jeopardize currency stability (Obstfeld & Taylor, 2005). Many of these effects of openness on inflation may be observed only in the long run. However, exchange rate fluctuations and regulation of trade to address domestic production gaps may affect inflation even in the short run.

As far as food inflation is concerned, high food prices may be triggered by supply shocks (e.g. poor harvest due to adverse climatic conditions) or may be the result of institutional factors such as price manipulation and hoarding by traders and middlemen in the supply chain. Given the importance of food in the consumption basket of workers, a rise in food prices tends to have second-round impacts on prices via an increase in money wages. Key issues in this context relate to the pass-through effects of food inflation to the non-food or core sector through wage pressures and the likely cost effects on price setting by firms. Food price management is complex, calling for coordinated efforts in terms of government regulation of food procurement, farm support prices and food subsidies, along with monetary policy actions.

Controlling Inflation: The Role of Monetary Policy Inflation control lies at the heart of monetary policy for all inflation targeting economies. The theoretical underpinning of inflation targeting policies that stem from DSGE models stresses the importance of rule-bound, anticipated policy changes for inflationary expectations and for keeping inflation under control. A key question in framing optimal monetary policy is that should central banks target headline or core inflation? While headline inflation includes relatively volatile components of the aggregate price index (i.e. commodity (e.g. food, metals. etc.) and energy prices), core inflation comprises

[18]Periodic episodes of currency crises in Latin America in the 1990s and 2000s decades as well as the Asian crisis of 1997 have demonstrated the difficulties of managing fixed exchange rates with international capital mobility. Fiscal indiscipline and institutional weaknesses (e.g. weakly regulated financial and asset markets) have time and again jeopardized macroeconomic stability in emerging markets, especially in the face of volatile capital flows.

[19]E.g. Large fiscal deficits may lead to downgrading of credit ratings by international agencies like Fitch, Moodys, etc., that raises countries' borrowing costs in international markets.

mainly the prices of non-food components that are slow to change over time.[20] The theoretical premise indicates that targeting core inflation maximizes welfare only under complete financial markets (Aoki, 2001). Headline inflation (which includes food inflation) should be targeted when markets are incomplete (Anand & Prasad, 2010; Anand et al., 2015) and food constitutes a large share of expenditure (Catao & Chang, 2015; Pourroy et al., 2016), as is commonly observed in emerging economies.

In general, central banks respond to a rise in inflation by raising interest rates, an important tool for demand management, when they hold demand-side pressures responsible for inflation (Branson, 1979; Sikdar, 2006). This works by dampening aggregate demand (through the interest rate channel), although the interest rate hike may itself be inflationary (via the cost channel). Exchange rate management and adjusting liquidity and credit availability in the financial system are other measures used to maintain low and stable inflation in open economies. In this context, the composition of the trade basket and its overlap with the basket of goods whose prices are being targeted (e.g. CPI) introduces certain complications. Exchange rate fluctuations can have inflationary effects, as well as terms of trade effects on trade and current account deficits. All of these need to be factored while crafting a monetary response to inflation (Frankel, 2008).

The exact source of inflationary pressures, i.e. whether they originate in the commodities (e.g. food, energy) or in the core (non-food) sectors, has a bearing on central banks' response to deviations of inflation from target. Factors such as importance of food in the consumption basket, nature of the commodities market, the extent of financial development, etc.,[21] together govern the design and impact of monetary response to food inflation. After the global financial crisis, advanced economies seem to be using the policy rate to stabilize the output gap, whereas, in the emerging economies, stabilization of headline inflation, especially food inflation, seems to be a central concern (Bhattacharya & Jain, 2020).

Food inflation can lead to second-round spillover effects and raise prices across the non-food sectors, leading to the persistence of inflationary pressures. The resulting effect on core inflation may be significant, especially in developing nations, where food occupies a large share in consumption baskets of the bulk of the population. Persistent inflation, originating in food price shocks, indicates the presence of strong second-round reactions in terms of an increase in wage demand that calls for monetary intervention (Anand et al., 2014; IMF, 2015). This calls for a calibrated response from the central bank. In case food supply shocks are likely to die out soon, a contractionary monetary policy response may worsen the situation by leading to contractions of supply in non-food sectors (through the cost channel) and adding to output variability (Beddies, 1999). However, ignoring persistent food inflation can disrupt policy design in emerging markets like India where high and volatile

[20] Since commodity markets clear relatively quickly, this shows up in greater price fluctuations, compared to imperfectly competitive goods markets with sticky prices, that respond to cost changes only with lags.

[21] E.g. The presence of under-regulated commodity exchanges and futures markets may contribute to speculation and volatility in commodity prices.

inflation can have spillover effects on non-food commodities posing a stiff challenge for macro-management (Walsh, 2011).

Recent empirical evidence from developed and developing economies indicates that monetary tightening in response to food inflation may have a destabilizing impact in the following way (Bhattacharya & Jain, 2020). One-time monetary contraction, in response to food inflation, has demand, as well as cost effects. In emerging economies, weak financial institutions impede interest rate transmission, so that demand-side effects tend to be weak. In such cases, the cost effects may stoke further inflationary pressures in the non-food sectors by raising the cost of capital and prices. The substitution of expensive capital by relatively cheaper labour in production processes may lead to a rise in labour demand and wages. In turn, this can raise costs and prices of labour-intensive goods like food and further feeds into inflation. In developed economies, where interest rate transmission is stronger, sustained increase in interest rates has a dampening effect on aggregate demand; however, the cost effects can contribute to inflationary pressures.

However, monetary policy tightening can also reduce food inflation by enhancing supply, as storage costs or the costs of carrying inventories increase when real interest rates are high (Frankel, 2008).[22] Further, change in real interest rates may also trigger substitution between commodity-based financial instruments and government securities. Prices in the futures markets, that indicate whether or not commodity shocks are likely to persist,[23] influence the magnitude of such effects.

4.2 *Inflation: The Indian Experience*

Key Drivers of Inflation Studies on inflation for developing economies like India show that it cannot be explained by any single theory of inflation, be it monetarist, structuralist or Keynesian; rather a combination of factors must be used to understand this phenomenon (see e.g. Bhattacharya, 1984).

Just as excessive money supply- and demand-side factors have been found to fuel inflation (Alam & Alam, 2016; Bhattacharya & Lodh, 1990; Brahmananda & Najraj, 2002; Das 2003; Patnaik, 2010, etc.), the importance of supply-side factors has also been noted in the context of India (Balakrishna, 1991; Goyal & Pujari, 2004; Dholakia, 1990; Ramachandran, 2004; Kashik, 2011; Paul, 2009; Goyal, 2014; Chakraborty & Varma, 2015). A comparison of India and Bangladesh finds monetary factors to be the most important cause of inflation in both countries over the period 1970–2010 (Paul & Zaman, 2013).

[22]Frankel's (2008) arguments are in context of advanced economies like the USA and a set of emerging economies from Latin America, where he observes fall in inflation, in response to rise in policy rates. However, his finding for Mexico is the opposite, where commodity prices increase following a rise in real interest rates.

[23]E.g. High price of commodities in the futures markets signals persistence of high commodity prices in times to come (Frankel, 2008).

Inflationary expectations have also been a causal factor behind inflationary episodes in the Indian context (Pahlavani & Rahimi, 2009; Patra & Ray, 2010). High levels of inflation, leading to high inflationary expectations in the future, can create a mechanism for the persistence of inflation. The importance of the central bank's role in creating a stable anchor for expectations comes to the fore against this background.

Demand-side factors affecting inflation in the Indian context have shown a strong link with fiscal expansion. In the 1970s, especially monetization of budget deficits had become the norm and there is even evidence of a deficit-inflation spiral, with government expenditure more responsive to inflation than revenue (Rangarajan & Arif, 1990; RBI, 2005). The importance of fiscal deficit as a causal factor behind inflation (Dash, 2016; Khundrakpam & Pattanaik, 2010) suggests that inflation management in India should be seen as much as a fiscal responsibility as a monetary one.

On the supply side, the spike in international oil prices, higher import prices resulting from the depreciation of the rupee, rise in the price of key inputs such as fertilizers, coal and tariff on power and telecom services have all contributed to inflation in India both in the pre- and post-reform periods (Alam et al., 2016; Ummat, 1992; Shnkar, 1992; Ghoshal, 1993; Arunachalam & Sankaranarayanan, 1998). Through the 1990s and 2000s decades, greater openness to trade and capital flows have enhanced exchange rate fluctuations which have contributed significantly to inflationary pressures (Pahlavani & Rahimi, 2009). However, it has also been noted that supply-side factors tend to have mainly transitory effects on inflation (Srinivasan et al., 2006).

Time and again, rise in the price of petroleum products has unleashed inflationary pressures, as borne out during the infamous 'oil shocks' in the 1970s and 1980s and the Gulf crisis in the early 1990s. Oil prices also drove inflation during the growth phase of 2004–2014 (other than in the crisis period of 2007–2009, when food prices played a relatively important role (Dash, 2016; Malhotra & Krishna, 2015). The asymmetry here is that while domestic oil price typically responds to the rise in international prices, it can remain unchanged or even rise while international prices are falling. Most recently, this was observed during the ongoing Corona pandemic when global oil prices crashed (even hitting the negative zone for a while)[24] without affecting domestic prices. Indeed, domestic prices have steadily risen, as earnings from the levy on petroleum have assumed greater importance, with other sources of government revenue drying up as economic activity came to a standstill during the recent lockdown (Agarwal, 2020).

Food Inflation Food inflation matters in India as it is a key component in wage setting and has an important role in shaping inflationary expectations. For instance, as RBI's inflation expectation survey of households (December, 2012) shows as much as 95% of the respondents related the general price index to food prices, as against other product groups. This follows from the high share of expenditure incurred by average

[24]On 20 April 2020, the price of oil (West Texas Intermediate (WTI) benchmark oil price index) became negative (−\$37.63) as economic activity came to a standstill and demand for oil crashed due to the global lockdown (Nawaz, 2020).

Indian households on food items (45.1% according to NSSO 68th Round, 2011–12) and highly persistent inflation shocks.

Food and beverages have a weight of nearly forty-six per cent in India's CPI, and the importance of food prices in driving inflation in India has been widely noted (Sengupta, 1991; Sinha, 1998; Sethuraman, 2005; Pattnaik & Samantaraya, 2006; Chakravarthy, 2007; Balakrishna, 2007; Pant, 2007; Sharma, 2007; Rajwade, 2007; Tuteja, 2008; Chand, 2010). The importance of addressing the supply side, structural issues has been emphasized, especially in the context of India's move to adopt inflation targeting, wherein monetary policy would be playing a central role in controlling food inflation (Mohan, 2008). The inflation episode around 2007 has been attributed to an upsurge in food prices and used to make a strong case for addressing structural issues in Indian agriculture and improving the government's food management policies (Mohan, 2008; Balakrishnan, 2007; Chakravarthy, 2007; Chand 2010; Tuteja 2008; and Kumar et al. 2010). An interesting feature of inflation during this period is that it was driven more by prices of processed, rather than of primary food products (Rajwade, 2007). However, the delayed policy response has also been held partly responsible for this inflationary episode, and ultimately, a rise in farm sector productivity is seen as the chief long-term solution to this problem (Tuteja, 2008). Increasing food imports, modernization and entry of modern domestic and foreign retail for enhancing productivity to control the food prices have also been advocated in this context (Kumar et al., 2010).

With economic growth and improvements in standards of living, there has been a substitution of cheaper cereal items by relatively more expensive vegetables, fruits, milk and eggs in the Indian food basket. The gap between demand and supply of these items has contributed to a persistent rise in prices (Mohanty, 2014).

The minimum support prices (MSP) in agriculture have been one of the factors contributing to an increase in food prices (Kumar et al., n.d). These are set by the government, often on the basis of political priorities rather than the economic criterion, given the prevalence of vote-bank politics in a democracy like India. With greater international trade in agricultural goods, especially in the post-reform period, the influence of global prices in the domestic market is inevitable. However, the link between the two has not always been straightforward—this is borne out by evidence from across developed and developing countries (Bhattacharya and Jain, 2020).[25] There is mixed evidence from India. While there is empirical evidence indicating pass-through from global to domestic food prices, other factors, such as rainfall and domestic supply, are also quite important in the Indian context (Holtemoller & Mallick, 2016).[26] For instance, when world food inflation dropped sharply in the latter half of 2008, in India, it actually rose by 12–15% (Kumar et al., 2010).

Role of the RBI That RBI has an important role in demand management and inflation control in the presence of supply constraints, has been well acknowledged (Acharya,

[25]While global food prices rose sharply in 2016, individual country experience with food inflation over the same period showed wide variation (see Bhattacharya and Jain, 2020 for details).

[26]Holtemoller and Mallick (2016) find that global prices were important in affecting food inflation during the years 1999/2000, 2005, 2008 and 2010.

2010; Joshi, 2012). Indeed, better monetary management in the post-reform era has contributed to improved inflation control by the RBI (Pattnaik & Samantaraya, 2006; RBI, 2005). In particular, monetary reforms under the LAF reduced fiscal pressures, imparted greater autonomy to the RBI and contributed to better inflation management than in the past (Bhusnurmath, 2008; Rangarajan, 2006). However, the RBI's interest rate policy has also been held responsible for contributing to inflation by enhancing the cost of credit (Joshi, 2012).

The importance of food inflation has been duly acknowledged in policy circles. 'If food inflation is high, as is typically the case in many low-income countries including India, then we would be underestimating inflationary pressure on a systematic basis. That would mislead policy prescriptions'. (D.Subbarao, cited in Anand et al, 2014). The Urjit Patel Committee report (2014) also recognized the role of headline (food and fuel) inflation in contributing to inflationary expectations and dynamics as against core (non-food and non-fuel) inflation.

The RBI officially shifted to inflation targeting in 2016 and chose headline CPI (that includes food prices) as the most feasible and appropriate measure of inflation for the conduct of monetary policy. Commitment to an explicit inflation target can play a critical role; by providing a firm anchor for inflationary expectations, it can prevent transient supply shocks from having second-round effects that can raise costs and prices in the rest of the economy. According to former RBI Governor, D. Subbarao, '…the direct role of monetary policy in combating food price pressures is limited, but in the face of sustained high food inflation, monetary action may still be warranted to anchor inflation expectations'. (cited in Mohanty, 2014).

The ineffectiveness of monetary policy in controlling inflation originating in food and oil prices has been acknowledged in the popular press (Aiyar & Anklesaria, 2008) and in policy discussions (Rajwade, 2007). However, rigorous studies on the effectiveness of monetary policy in controlling food inflation in India are quite sparse (Anand et al., 2014; Holtemoller & Mallick, 2016). Food shocks have been found to be persistent, with core inflation catching up with and feeding into headline inflation quickly, indicating strong second-round effects of food on non-food prices (Anand et al., 2014). In view of this, it has been strongly suggested that monetary policy should respond to food price shocks. Indeed, monetary tightening has been found effective in controlling food inflation, indicating the importance of demand pressures behind such inflation (Anand et al., 2014). However, it is also found that monetary tightening in response to food price shocks does have a negative impact on the real sector (Holtemoller and Mallick, 2016). In contrast, recent empirical evidence indicates that in India, unlike in many other nations, the policy rate responded negatively to food inflation over the period 2006–2016, indicative of an accommodating monetary stance (Bhattacharya & Jain, 2020).

As far as nutritional security is concerned, controlling prices of fruits, pulses, vegetables, dairy and poultry products are critical. After all, access to affordable sources of protein can be an important agent of nutritional transformation in society, for which supply management and farm sector policies have a far more important role to play. However, monetary policy does have an indirect role via easing credit constraints on the supply side, especially targeting enterprises active in these sectors across rural India.

Using monetary policy to control inflation may unleash contractionary effects on the core sector, with negative consequences for output and employment. However, a positive impact on employment may also ensue owing to the substitution of capital by labour. Overall, this remains an area with ample scope for further research to inform the policy debate on this issue.

5 Sustainable Development, COVID-19 and Role of Monetary Policy

The ongoing COVID-19 pandemic presents perhaps the biggest challenge ever to achieving the SDGs with respect to mitigating poverty, inequality and ensuring food and nutrition security. The massive disruptions in global production, supply chains, trade and tourism caused by the pandemic are creating extreme volatility in financial markets and severely affecting global commodity prices. Close and complex inter-linkages among economies, sectors and individuals in a globalized world are having a cascading effect, magnifying the stress in financial economic conditions. Economists have warned of deep economic depression due to lockdown imposed the world over to combat the pandemic and due to second-round effects via collapse of global trade networks.

5.1 Key Policy Issues

The entire world (with the lone exception of China, where data as of July 2020 shows growth revival has been stronger than expected)[27] today is reeling under large-scale multiplier effects of Keynesian supply shocks, that seem to be triggering changes in aggregate demand which appear larger than the shocks themselves (Guerrieri et al., 2020). Aggregate demand is being affected by the supply shocks as workers in the affected sectors are losing income and reducing consumption. The negative demand effects are large, especially when workers face credit constraints and have high consumption propensities. The extent of the resultant fall in demand depends on the type of market, where impact tends to be maximum when markets are incomplete. For the economy to stabilize, workers in unaffected sectors need to compensate by increasing their demand for other goods. But this is useful only in the presence of a high degree of substitution across sectors, which may be quite unlikely. As such aggregate demand is contracting more than supply, so that employment in

[27]Quarterly growth of the Chinese economy reported in July, 2020 was just over 3%, exceeding the 2% recovery that was expected in the post-COVID scenario (Mc Donald, 2020).

initially unaffected sectors may also fall, enhancing the size of the negative impact and ushering in overall recession in the economy.

Fiscal policy seems to be the obvious choice for an immediate policy response to arrest the fall in aggregate demand and help revive economic activity (Baldwin & Mauro, 2020; Gourinchas, 2020; Krugman, 2020; Posen, 2020). Indeed, Modern Monetary Theorists (Kelton, 2020) argue running large budgetary deficits should not be a concern at a time like this when unemployment is high and monetization of the deficit is unlikely to cause inflation. However, it has also been pointed out that there may be sharp limits to the effectiveness of fiscal expansion in the current situation (Guerrieri et al., 2020).[28] Monetary policy is being expected to play a supportive role, via money-financed fiscal interventions or unrepayable funding by the central bank of the additional fiscal transfers (Benassy-Quere et al. 2020; Gali, 2020a, b; and Gourinchas, 2020). This is a kind of 'helicopter money', to be used only in cases of exceptional emergencies such as the present one.

Other than this, the role of monetary policy lies in increasing the optimal and efficient use of credit, avoiding any tightening of policy and preventing bankruptcies. Indeed, at present, monetary policy must be unconventional if needed, to prevent deflationary expectations, and maintain easy liquidity in the economy, preempting any tendency for the real interest rate to rise. That is, a deflation trap is to be avoided at any cost. Banks should give sufficient relaxations in the redemption of loans and capital requirements with special efforts from public sector banks to maintain adequate liquidity in the system in the interest of supporting investment activities (Odendahl & Springford, 2020).

Monetary policy, therefore, has an important role in flattening the recession curve by ensuring easy and sufficient liquidity in the economy, so that people have money to spend even if they are unemployed. Three important elements of monetary policy in the present situation are: 'First, safeguarding liquidity conditions in the banking system through a series of favourably priced long-term refinancing operations (LTROs); second, protecting the continued flow of credit to the real economy through a fundamental recalibration of the targeted longer-term refinancing operations (TLTROs); and third, via an increase in the asset purchase programme, preventing that financing conditions for the economy tighten in a pro-cyclical way'. (Phillip Lane, 2020; p. 141)

---

[28]The operation of the Keynesian multiplier may be impaired during the pandemic as marginal propensity to consume (MPC) may be unusually low. Further, the second and subsequent rounds of the multiplier may be severely limited in the presence of large-scale job losses, especially if these are concentrated in sectors where MPC is relatively high. Those losing jobs may receive transfer payments, but spending out of such transfers would not be coming back as income to the unemployed, limiting the effectiveness of the multiplier.

5.2 The Indian Experience

In India, monetary policy has been entrusted with a central role in the task of economic revival, supported by a slew of fiscal, mainly tax relief, measures. The RBI has taken some special measures (see Appendix for details) to combat the severity of a potential recession looming large in the horizon. Its recent Statement on Developmental and Regulatory Policies spells out several measures to address financial stress caused by COVID-19 (RBI Press Release, 2019–20). These include: (i) maintaining adequate liquidity to enable financial markets and institutions to function normally despite severe dislocations caused by the pandemic; (ii) improving access to bank credit on easier terms, especially to the affected groups; (iii) extending a moratorium on loan repayments and easing access to working capital to reduce financial distress; and (iv) strengthening financial markets in the face of high volatility and uncertainty brought on by the global pandemic.

As the Indian government announced total lockdown of the economy (barring essential services) in March 2020, the Monetary Policy Committee (MPC) in its meeting on 27 March 27 2020 reduced the policy rate under the LAF by 75 basis points[29] and announced its decision to remain committed to an accommodative stance. Monetary policy was to try and mitigate the impact of COVID-19 on the economy, focusing on reviving growth, while ensuring inflation remained within the target. Essentially, it communicated its willingness to 'Act fast and do whatever it takes' (Baldwin & Mauro, 2020). The RBI announced the second set of relief measures for ensuring adequate liquidity on 22 May 2020, aimed at incentivizing bank credit flows, easing financial stress and enabling smooth functioning of capital markets. An attempt to ensure easy and adequate provision of credit to all the stakeholders, especially to the most affected MSME sector, lies at the heart of these measures (see Appendix).

Can monetary policy revive aggregate demand at the current conjuncture? There is evidence of a rise in household savings, with rampant uncertainty marking the jobs' scenario amid the ongoing slowdown intensified, by the lockdown. Any turnaround in the housing sector which has been going through a prolonged slowdown seems unlikely in the near future. Further, with construction activity at a standstill, even as the lockdown eases, it is expected that households will shift from physical to financial assets, and house price expectations and housing demand are likely to remain subdued (RBI, 2020). However, a pick-up in spending on personal vehicles (especially in the second-hand market), in view of the changed circumstances with respect to public transport in post-COVID times is evident. Overall, this appears to leave monetary policy with relatively little room for manoeuvre in reviving household spending.

The entire might, especially of the local level government machinery, has been used to contain and prevent the spread of the pandemic as much as possible and to directly provide access to food and prevent hunger. However, there has been an

[29]The repo rate was reduced from 5.15 to 4.40% from with immediate effect. The marginal standing facility (MSF) rate and bank rate was reduced to 4.65% from 5.40%, and the reverse repo rate under LAF was reduced by 90 basis points to 4.0%.

overall failure to control food inflation in the open market, where prices of vegetables and fruits have soared. This is likely to have jeopardized nutrition security, especially among lower-income groups and informal workers, who may technically be above the poverty line but have lost jobs and suffered massive losses in regular income flows. Within such households, the most vulnerable, especially women, children and the elderly, are likely to bear the brunt of this crisis, whose full impact will only be visible over time. In this context, it is worth pointing out that the virtual collapse of the hospitality services sector (restaurant, hotels, etc.) during the lockdown has resulted in a glut in supply in certain food sectors (e.g. milk). This calls for imaginative use of public initiatives to channelize such surpluses to areas of need to address hunger in these challenging times.

India has used fiscal policy to respond directly to the public health emergency and to maintain food and nutrition security among the poorest of the poor (e.g. landless labour and casual workers in the informal sector), who have been frontline warriors in the economic pandemic wreaked by COVID-19 and the consequent lockdown. However, in India, by and large, the demand generating potential of fiscal policy has remained unexploited, especially when compared with developed countries like the UK and the USA. These nations made substantial direct income transfers to the private sector, especially to mitigate losses faced by small private enterprises. In India, while employment guarantee schemes like the MGNREGA are running full steam and some direct transfers have been made directly to poor women[30], the size of the fiscal stimulus at 3.5% of GDP is among the lowest in the G 20 group of nations.[31]

6 Concluding Remarks

The literature review carried out in this paper shows that inadequate financial development is a key factor underlying relatively weak monetary transmission in India, especially via the asset prices channel. Even though India has made impressive strides with respect to financial liberalization, it still has a long way to go on this front in terms of improving market quality and reducing adverse selection and moral hazard in financial markets. Emergence of a vibrant corporate debt market, for instance, can certainly contribute to the revival of private investments in India, *inter alia* by easing access to and cost of credit for firms and providing a direct link between savings and investment.

In India, today, the banking sector still plays a crucial role in channelizing savings for investments, so the importance of the bank lending channel remains

[30]Rs. 500 per month is being transferred to the bank accounts women holding Jan Dhan Accounts (meant for those below poverty line(BPL)) for three months.

[31]The fiscal stimulus in other large emerging nations stands at 4.4% for Indonesia, 4.9% for Argentina and 11% for Brazil (https://www.statista.com/statistics/1107572/covid-19-value-g20-stimulus-packages-share-gdp/).

paramount. Efforts being made by the central bank towards pass-through of policy to lending rates, ensuring ease of access to credit, re-capitalization and restructuring of public sector banks heavily burdened with non-performing assets (NPAs), are all very welcome steps likely to strengthen monetary transmission. However, the success of the best-laid plans lies one hundred per cent in their implementation. Procedural simplifications, especially aimed at reaching out to small businesses and entrepreneurs via secure, mobile-based digital means, may well hold the key to success in this context. Moreover, the literature also indicates that immense benefits can be reaped through institutional reforms that cut 'invisible costs' by reducing corruption, delays in decision-making processes and boosting business confidence.

As far as food inflation is concerned, the RBI definitely has a role in keeping it under control with a timely, adequate and well thought-out response that reflects a clear understanding of the complexity of the phenomenon. However, the ultimate responsibility for keeping food prices affordable, especially the price of nutrient-rich fruits, vegetables and dairy products, lies at the door of specific public policies that govern supply responses in the farm sector. So far as investments, output growth and employment generation are concerned, monetary policy can play a far more active role than it has done so far.

The Corona pandemic has unleashed corporate restructuring in India as never before. India must seize this opportunity to incentivize the adoption of green technologies across the board by making imaginative use of credit policies. After all, raging wildfires in the Arctic Circle (in Siberia), in the summer of 2020, are an urgent reminder that time for action on climate change is in the here and now.

Appendix

Details of measures adopted by the RBI to deal with the economic situation due to COVID-19 on May 22, 2020

- RBI announced a new Targeted Long-Term Repo Operation (TLTRO 2.0) of Rs 50,000 crore (in several tranches, and further possibility of expansion if needed) for mid- and small-sized nonbank financial companies (NBFCs) and microfinance institutions (MFIs) which have been more severely impacted by the disruptions of pandemic due to COVID-19.
- The RBI Governor, Shaktikanta Das announced a reduction in the repo rate by 40 basis points, from 4.4 to 4% and reverse repo rate to 3.35%, which would help in releasing surplus funds for providing higher credit for investment in the productive sectors of the economy.
- A special refinance facility of Rs 50,000 crore for National Bank for Agriculture and Rural Development (Rs 25,000 crore), the Small Industries Development Bank of India (Rs 15,000 crore) and the National Housing Bank (Rs 10,000 crore) to meet sectoral credit needs since they are facing difficulties in raising finances from the market.

- Ways and Means Advances (WMAs)[32] limit of states and union territories has been increased by 60% over and above the limit as on March 31, 2020, in order to provide greater comfort to states to deal with the present crisis.
- A major relaxation has been given in the asset classifications norm, wherein the moratorium period will be excluded while considering the 90-day NPA norm for those accounts for which lending institutions decide to grant moratorium or deferment and which were standard as on March 1, 2020. The NBFCs are thereby allowed to grant relaxed NPA classification to their borrowers and; the banks will need to maintain additional provisioning of 10% on standstill accounts.
- An extension has been given for the implementation of a resolution plan for stressed assets (or likely NPAs) by 90 days. Under this, now the banks need not maintain additional provisioning of 20%, which they did earlier within 210 days of such default. LCR requirement was brought down from 100 to 80% with immediate effect.
- In order to enable banks to save on capital in the present uncertain times, the RBI has decided that scheduled commercial banks and cooperative banks shall not make any further dividend pay-outs from profits pertaining to FY 2019–20. This may be reviewed based on the financial position of banks at the end of the second quarter of the financial year 2019–20.
- The **liquidity coverage ratio**[33] for scheduled commercial banks has been brought down from 100 to 80% in two phases.
- NBFCs' loans to delayed commercial real estate projects can be extended by a year without restructuring. Additionally, these loans to be given similar benefits as given by scheduled commercial banks.

References

Acharya, S. (2010). Macroeconomic performance and policies, 2000–2008. In S. Acharya, R. Mohan (Eds.), *India's economy, performance and challenges: Essays in honour of Montek Singh Ahluwalia* (pp. 39–81) Module 3. OUP New-Delhi.

Adolfson, M. (2001). Export price responses to exogenous exchange rate movements. *Economics Letters, 71*(1), 91–96.

Agarwal, N. (2020). Petrol, diesel price increased all over India, Mint, 7 June, 2020. https://www.livemint.com/news/india/petrol-diesel-price-increased-all-over-india-for-first-time-in-80-days-11591506701429.html. Accessed on 20th July, 2020.

Agrawal, P., Sahoo, P., & Dash, R. K. (2010). Savings behaviour in India: Co-integration and causality evidence. *The Singapore Economic Review, 55*, 273–295.

[32] **Ways and means advances** (**WMA**) are temporary advances (maximum expiry of three months) by the RBI to both the Central and State governments to meet temporary mismatches/shortfall in revenue over expenditure.

[33] The liquidity coverage ratio, introduced as part of Basel III reforms on Banking supervision, requires banks to hold enough high-quality liquid assets such as short-term government debt (which can be sold off) to meet short-term debt obligations.

Aiyar, S., & Anklesaria, S. (2008, April 16). India disproves Friedman on inflation. *Economic Times*. https://economictimes.indiatimes.com/swaminathan-s-a-aiyar/india-disproves-friedman-on-inflation/articleshow/2956991.cms

Alam, Q., & Alam, S. (2016). The determinants of inflation in India: The Bounds test analysis. *International Journal of Economics and Financial Issues, 6*(2), 544–550.

Aleem, A. (2010). Transmission mechanism of monetary policy in India. *Journal of Asian Economics, 21*(2), 186–197.

Anand, R., Ding, D., & Tulin, V. (2014). *Food inflation in India: The role for monetary policy*. IMF Working Paper No. 178. International Monetary Fund, Washington, D.C.

Anand, R., Peiris, S., Saxegaard, M. (2010). *An estimated model with macrofinancial linkages for India*. IMF Working Paper 21. International Monetary Fund, Washington, D.C.

Anand, R., & Prasad, E. S. (2010) *Optimal price indices for targeting inflation under incomplete markets*. Working Paper 16290. National Bureau of Economic Research

Anand, R., Prasad, E. S., & Zhang, B. (2015). What measure of inflation should a developing country central bank target? *Journal of Monetary Economics, 74,* 102–116.

Anand, R., & Tulin, V. (2014). *Disentangling India's investment slowdown*. IMF Working Paper 47. International Monetary Fund, Washington, D.C.

Aoki, K. (2001). Optimal monetary policy changes to relative price changes. *Journal of Monetary Economics, 48*(1), 55–80.

Arora, P. M., Dastidar, A. G., & Das, M. (2020). Inter-linkage between credit and housing prices in India: Some preliminary findings. In M. Datta, R. Mahajan, & M. Bose (Eds.), *Business, economics and sustainable development: The emerging issues* (pp. 291–308). New Delhi: Bloomsbury.

Arunachalam, P., & Sankaranarayanan, K. C. (1998). Liberalization and inflation in India. *Yojana, 42*(11), 7–9.

Athukorala, P. C., & Sen, K. (2004). The determinants of private saving in India. *World Development, 32*(3), 491–503.

Balakrishna, P. (1991). *Pricing and inflation in India*. New Delhi: Oxford University Press.

Balakrishnan, P. (2007). Growth and inflation. *Yojana, 51,* 8–10.

Baldwin, R., & Mauro, B. W. D. (Eds.). (2020). *Mitigating the covid economic crisis: Act fast and do whatever it takes*. London, Centre for Economic and Policy Research: CEPR Press.

Banerjee, R., & Bhattacharya, S. (2008). The RBI's monetary policy reaction function: Does monetary policy in India follow an inflation targeting rule?. In *Annual Conference on Money & Finance*. IGIDR. Mumbai, January 4

Barth, M. J., & Ramey, V. A. (2001) The cost channel of monetary transmission. In *NBER macroeconomics annual 2001* (Vol 16, pp. 199–256), 2002. National Bureau of Economic Research Inc.

Bean, C., Paustian, M., Penalver, A., & Taylor, T. (2010). *Monetary policy after fall*. Paper presented at Jackson Hole Symposium Wyoming, 28 August

Beddies, C. (1999). Monetary policy and public finances: Inflation targets in a new perspective. *IMF Economic Review, 46,* 293–314. https://doi.org/10.2307/3867645.

Benassy-Quere, A., Marimon, A. R., Pisani-Ferry, J., Reichlin, L., Schoenmaker, D., Mauro, B. W. (2020). COVID-19: Europe needs a catastrophe relief. *VoxEU*. Org, 11 March

Berananke, B., & Gertler, M. (1995). Inside the black box: The credit channel of monetary transmission. *Journal of Economic Perspectives, 9,* 27–48.

Bernanke, B. S., & Blinder, A. S. (1992). The federal funds rate and the channels of monetary transmission. *American Economic Review, 82,* 901–921.

Bernanke, B. S., & Blinder, A. S. (1988). Credit, money, and aggregate demand. *American Economic Review Papers and Proceedings, 78,* 435–439.

Bhattacharya, B. B. (1984). *Public expenditure, inflation and growth: Macroeconometric analysis for India*. New Delhi: Oxford University Press.

Bhattacharya, B. B., & Lodh, M. (1990). Inflation in India: An analytical survey. *Artha Vijnana, 32*(1), 25–63.

Bhattacharya, R., Patnaik, I., Shah, A. (2011). *Monetary policy transmission in an emerging market setting*. IMF Working Paper 5, Washington D.C.

Bhattacharya, R., Tripathi, S., & Chowdhury, Roy, S. (2019). *Financial structure, institutional quality and monetary policy transmission: A meta-analysis*. NIPFP Working Paper No. 274, 18-July-2019.

Bhattacharya, R., & Jain, R. (2020). Can monetary policy stabilise food inflation? Evidence from advanced and emerging economies. *Journal of economic modelling, 89*, 122–141.

Bhusnurmath, M. (2008). Murphy's Law for Central Banks. Economic Times, February 4. https://economictimes.indiatimes.com/blogs/Myth-n-Reality/murphy-s-law-for-central-banks/

Blanchard, O., & Gali, J. (2005). Real wage rigidities and the New Keynesian Model. *Journal of Money, Banking and Credit, 39*(1), 35–65.

Brahmananda, P., & Najraj, G. (2002). Inflation and growth in the world: Some simple empirics, 1970-99. *Macroeconomics and monetary policy: Issues for a reforming economy* (pp. 43–66). New Delhi: Oxford University Press.

Branson, W. H. (1979). *Macroeconomic theory and policy*. HarperCollin Publishers.

Carlin, W., & Soskice, D. (2015). *Macroeconomics: Institutions, instability and the financial system*. Oxford: Oxford University Press.

Catao, L. A., & Chang, R. (2015) World food prices and monetary policy. *Journal of Monetary Economics, 75*(C), 69–88

Cecchetti, S. G., Kohler, M., & Upper, C. (2009). *Financial crises and economic activity*. NBER Papers 15379, National Bureau of Economic Research, Massachusetts

Chakraborty, L., & Varma, K. O. (2015). *Efficacy of new monetary framework and determining inflation in India: An empirical analysis of financially deregulated regime*. NIPFP Working Paper No. 153, National Institute of Public Finance and Policy, New Delhi

Chakravarthy, S. (2007). Our fight against inflation. *Yojana, 51*, 47–48.

Chand, R. (2010). Understanding the nature and causes of food inflation. *Economic and Political Weekly, 45*(9), 10–13.

Chand, S. K., & Singh, K. (2006). How applicable is the inflation targeting framework for India? The India Policy Forum. *National Council of Applied Economic Research, 2*(1), 123–181.

Chowdhury, I., Hoffmann, M., & Schabert, A. (2006). Inflation dynamics and cost channel of monetary transmission. *European Economic Review, 50*, 995–1016.

Christiano, L. J., & Eichenbaum, M. (1992). *Liquidity effects and the monetary transmission mechanism*. NBER Working Paper No., 3974. National Bureau of Economic Research, Massachusetts

Dale, S., & Haldane, A. G. (1995). Interest rates and the channels of monetary transmission: Some sectoral estimates. *European Economic Review, 39*(9), 1611–1626.

Das, S. (2003). Modeling money, price and output in India: A vector autoregressive and moving average approach. *Applied Economics, 35*(10), 1219–1225.

Das, S. (2015). *Monetary policy in India: Transmission to bank interest rates*. IMF Working Paper No., 129. International Monetary Fund, Washington, D.C.

Das, S. (2020). Seven ages of India's monetary policy. Speech delivered at St. Stephen's College, University of Delhi on January 24, 2020. Available via Reserve Bank of India—Speeches. https://www.rbi.org.in/scripts/BS_SpeechesView.aspx?Id=1092. Accessed 3 July, 2020.

Dash, M. (2016). Impact of macroeconomic factors on inflation: An assessment on Indian economy by using vector auto-regressive modelling. *Journal of Decision Sciences Applications, 1*(1), 21–28.

Dastidar, A. G. (2015). India's experience with export-led growth. In J. Ghosh (Ed.), *India and the world economy. ICSSR research survey in economics* (pp. 21–64). New Delhi: Oxford University Press.

Dastidar, A. G., & Ahuja, R. (2019). A perspective on the slowdown in private corporate investments in India. In S. Bandyopadhyay & M. Dutta (Eds.), *Opportunities and challenges in development: Essays for Sarmila Banerjee* (pp. 31–50). Singapore: Springer Nature.

Dholakia, R. H. (1990). Extended Phillips curve for the Indian economy. *Indian Economic Journal, 38*(1), 69–78.

Dua, P. (2020). Monetary policy framework in India. *Indian Economic Review, 55,* 117–154.

Edwards, F., & Mishkin, F. S. (1995) *The decline of traditional banking: implications for financial stability and regulatory policy*. NBER Working Paper No. 4993, National Bureau of Economic Research, Massachusetts

Epstein, G. (2003). *Alternatives to inflation targeting monetary policy for stable and egalitarian growth: A brief research summary*. PERI Working Paper 62, Political Economy Research Institute, University of Massachusetts Amherst

Favero, C. A., Giavazzi, F., & Flabbi, L. (1999). *The transmission mechanism of monetary policy in Europe: Evidence from banks balance sheets*. NBER Working Paper No. 7231, National Bureau of Economic Research, Massachusetts

Fiore, D. (1998). *The transmission of monetary policy* in Israel IMF Working Paper No. 114, International Monetary Fund, Washington, D.C.

Frankel, J. A. (2008). The effect of monetary policy on real commodity prices. In *NBER chapters, asset prices and monetary policy* (pp. 291–333), National Bureau of Economic Research, Inc.

Fulford, S. L. (2013). The effects of financial development in the short and long run: Theory and evidence from India. *Journal of Development Economics, 104,* 56–72.

Gali, J. (2020a) Helicopter money: This time is now. In R. Baldwin, B. Mauro (Eds.), *Mitigating the covid economic crisis: Act fast and do whatever it takes* (pp. 57–62). London,, Center for Economic and Policy Research: CEPR Press

Gali, J., & Monacelli, T. (2005). *Monetary policy and exchange rate volatility in a small open economy review of economic studies, 72,* 707–734.

Gali, J. (2020b). The effects of a money-financed fiscal stimulus. *Journal of Monetary Economics*. https://doi.org/10.1016/j.jmoneco.2019.08.002.

Gaotti, E., & Secchi, A. (2006). Journal of Money. *Credit and Banking, 38*(8), 2013–2037.

Gerlash, S., & Smets, F. (1995). *The monetary transmission mechanism: Evidence from the G7 countries*. CEPR Discussion Paper No. 1219, Centre for Economic and Policy Research

Ghoshal, M. K. (1993). Inflation: Review and outlook. *Yojana, 36*(24), 4–5.

Ghura, D., Leite, C. A., Tsangarides, C. (2002). *Is growth enough? Macroeconomic policy and poverty reduction*. IMF Working Paper 118, International Monetary Fund, Washington, D.C.

Gourinchas, P.-O. (2020). Flattening the pandemic and recession curves. In R. Baldwin, B. Mauro (Eds.), *Mitigating the COVID economic crisis: Act fast and do whatever it takes* (pp. 31–40). London, Centre for Economic and Policy Research: CEPR Press.

Goyal, A. (2014). Understanding high inflation trend in India. *South Asian Journal of Macroeconomics and Public Finance, 4*(1), 1–44.

Goyal, A., & Pujari, A. K. (2005). Identifying long run supply curve in India. *Journal of Quantitative Economics, 3*(2), 1–15.

Guerrieri, V., Lorenzoni, G., Straub, L., & Werning, I. (2020). Macroeconomic Implications of COVID-19: Can negative supply shocks cause demand shortages?. *SSRN Electronic Journal* https://doi.org/10.2139/ssrn.3570096

Henzel, S., Hlsewig, O., Mayer, E., & Wollmershuser, T. (2009). The price puzzle revisited: Can the cost channel explain a rise in inflation after a monetary policy shock? *Journal of Macroeconomics, 31,* 268–289.

Himmelberg, C., Mayer, C., & Sinai, T. (2005). Assessing high house prices: Bubbles, fundamentals and misperceptions. *Journal of Economic Perspectives, 19*(4), 67–92.

Hofmann, B., & Bogdanova, B. (2012). *Taylor rules and monetary policy: A global "Great Deviation*. Switzerland: BIS Quarterly Review. Bank for International Settlements.

Holtemoller, O., & Mallick, S. (2016). Global food prices and monetary policy in an emerging market economy: The case of India. *Journal of Asian Economics, 46,* 56–70.

Hu, Y. (2006). The choice of inflation targeting—An empirical investigation. *International Journal of Economics and Economic Policy Springer, 3*(1), 27–42.

IMF. (2015). *Evolving monetary policy frameworks in low-income and other developing countries*. IMF Policy Paper. https://www.imf.org/external/np/pp/eng/2015/102315.pdf

Inoue, I., & Hamori, S. (2009). An empirical analysis of money demand function in India. *Economic Bulletin, 29*(2), 1225–1246.

Jardak, T., & Wrobel, E. (2009). The monetary transmission mechanism in Tunisia: Recent developments. *The Journal of Developing Areas, 48*(1), 145–164.

Jha, R. (2008). Inflation targeting in India: Issues and prospects. *International Review of Applied Economics, 22*(2), 259–270.

Joshi, V. K. (2012). Impact of monetary policy of India with special reference to CRR, repo and reverse repo in curbing inflation and econometric study. *Management Insight, 8*(2), 1–12.

Kelton, S. (2020). *The deficit myth: modern monetary theory and the birth of the people's economy*. Hachette UK.

Kanan, R. (1999). Inflation targeting: Issues and relevance for India. *Economic and Political Weekly, 41*(34), 115–122.

Kapoor, M., & Ravi, S. (2009). The Effect of Interest Rate on Household Consumption: Evidence from a Natural Experiment in India. *Available at SSRN 1346813.*

Kapoor, M., & Ravi, S. (2010). Elasticity of intertemporal substitution in consumption: Empirical evidence from a natural experiment. *Available at SSRN 1673140.*

Kaur, K. (2016). Monetary policy behaviour in India. *Journal of Business Thought, 6*(April 2015–March 2016), 44–56

Kaur, K., & Dastidar, A. G. (2019). Monetary policy transmission in India: Interest rate puzzle. *IUP Journal of Applied Economics, 18*(3), 37–58.

Kashik, B. K. (2011). Understanding inflation and controlling it. *Economic and Political Weekly, 46*(41), 50–64.

Katkhate, D. (2006). Inflation targeting: Much ado about something. *Economic and Political Weekly, 41*(49), 5031–5033.

Khundrakpam, J. K., Pattanaik, S. (2010). *Global crisis, fiscal response and medium-term risks to inflation in India*. RBI Occasional Papers 31(2): 1–29, Reserve Bank of India, Mumbai

Khundrakpam, J. K., Jain, R. (2012). *Monetary policy transmission in India: A peep inside the black box*. RBI Working Paper Series 11/2012, Reserve Bank of India, Mumbai

Krugman, P. (2020). The case for permanent stimulus. In R. Baldwin & B. Mauro (Eds.), *Mitigating the COVID economic crisis: Act fast and do whatever it takes* (pp. 213–219). London: CEPR Press.

Kumail, A. R. S., Bushra, N., & Mirza, N. (2012). Inflation targeting as a plausible monetary framework for India. *Research Journal of Recent Sciences, 1*(12), 74–78.

Kumar, R., Vashisht, P., & Kalita, G. (2010). Food inflation: Contingent and structural factors. *Economic and Political Weekly, 45*(10), 16–19.

Kumar, R., Krishna, G. D., Bhardwaj, S. (n.d) IFC is it a good framework for monetary policy of India?. Centre for Policy Research www.cprindia.org. Accessed 5 July, 2020

Lane, P. (2020). The monetary policy package: An analytical framework. In R. Baldwin, B. Mauro (Eds.), *Mitigating the COVID economic crisis: Act fast and do whatever it takes*. CEPR Press, London, pp. 139–144, Centre for Economic and Policy Research

Loayza, N., & Shankar, R. (2000). Private saving in India. *The World Bank Economic Review, 14*(3), 571–594.

Malhotra, A., & Krishna, S. (2015). The effect of crude oil prices on inflation and interest rates in India. *Evidence from DCC-GARCH Model*. https://doi.org/10.2139/ssrn.2472558.

Mallick, H., & Agarwal, S. (2007). Impact of real interest rates on real output growth in India: A long-run analysis in a liberalized financial regime. *The Singapore Economic Review, 52*(2), 215–231.

Mc Donald, J. (2020). *China's economy rebounds*. Time 16 July, 2020.

Mishkin, F. S. (1995). Symposium on the Monetary transmission mechanism. *Journal of Economic Perspectives, 9*(4), 3–10.

Mishra, A., & Mishra, V. (2009). *Pre-conditions for inflation targeting in an emerging economy—The case of India.* Development Research Unit Working Paper Series 08–09. Monash University
Mishra, P., Montiel, P., & Sengupta, R. (2016). *Monetary transmission in developing countries: Evidence from India.* IMF Working Paper No.167, International Monetary Fund, Washington, D.C.
Mohan, R. (2008). The role of fiscal and monetary policy in sustaining growth with stability in India. *Asian Economic Policy Review, 3*(2), 209–236.
Mohanty, D. (2012). *Evidence on interest rate channel of monetary policy transmission in India.* RBI Working Paper No. 6, Reserve Bank of India, Mumbai
Mohanty, D. (2014). Why is recent food inflation in India so persistent?. Annual Lalit Doshi Memorial Lecture, Xavier's Chapter, delivered at the St. Xavier's College, Mumbai on 13th January 2014. Available via Reserve Bank of India Speeches. https://www.rbi.org.in/scripts/BS_ViewBulletin.aspx?Id=14731#f3. Accessed 3 July, 2020.
Mohanty, M. S., Klau, M. (2004). *Monetary policy rules in emerging market economies: Issues and evidence.* BIS Working Papers 149, Bank for International Settlements, Switzerland
Mojon, B., Peersman, G. (2001). *A VAR description of the effects of monetary policy in the individual countries of the Euro area*, ECB Working Paper No. 92, European Central Bank, Germany
Nagaraj, R. (2013). India's Dream Run, 2003–08: Understanding the boom and its aftermath. *Economic and Political Weekly, 48,* 39–51.
Nawaz, S. (2020). Making history: Coronavirus and negative oil prices. *Global risk insights.* May 29, 2020 (https://globalriskinsights.com/2020/05/making-history-coronavirus-and-negative-oil-prices/)
Nelson, E. (2002). Direct effects of base money on aggregate demand: Theory and evidence. *Journal of Monetary Economics, 49*(4), 687–708.
Norris, E. D., & Floerkemeir, H. (2006). *Transmission mechanism of monetary policy in Armenia: Evidence from VAR analysis.* IMF Working Paper 248, International Monetary Fund, Washington, D.C.
Obstfeld, M., & Taylor, A. M. (2005). *Global capital markets: integration, crisis, and growth.* Cambridge University Press.
Obstfeld, M., & Rogoff, K. (1995). Mirage of fixed exchange rates. NBER Working Paper 5191, Naional Bureau of Economic Research, Massachusetts.
Odendahl, C., & Springford, J. (2020). Bold policies needed to counter with coronavirus recession. In R. Baldwin & B. Mauro (Eds.), *Mitigating the COVID economic crisis: Act fast and do whatever it takes* (pp. 145–150). London: CEPR Press.
OstaEraghi, A. (2015). The effectiveness of monetary policy in India: An ARDL analysis of Cointegration. *Indian Journal of Applied Research, 5*(11), 14–17.
Pahlavani, M., & Rahimi, M. (2009). Sources of inflation in Iran: An application of the ARDL approach. *International Journal of Applied Economics and Quantitative Studies, 6*(1), 61–76.
Pant, D. K. (2007). Inflation, growth and poverty. *Yojana, 51,* 11–14.
Patnaik, A. (2010). Study of inflation in India: A Cointegrated VAR approach. *Journal of Quantitative Economics, 8*(1), 118–129.
Patra, M. D., & Kapur, M. (2010). A monetary policy model for India. *Macroeconomics and finance in emerging market economies, 5*(1), 18–41.
Patra, M. D., Ray, P. (2010). *Inflationary expectations and monetary policy in India: An empirical exploration.* IMF Working Paper No. 84, International Monetary Fund, Washington, D.C.
Pattnaik, R. K., & Samantaraya, A. (2006). Indian experience of inflation—A review of the evolving process. *Economic and Political weekly, 41*(4), 349–357.
Paul, B. P. (2009). In search of the Phillips curve for India. *Journal of Asian Economics, 20*(4), 479–488.
Paul, B., & Zaman, H. (2015). When and why does Bangladesh's inflation differ from Indian's? *Macroeconomics and Finance in Emerging Market Economies, 8*(1–2), 45–66.

Posen, A. (2020). Containing the economic nationalist virus through global coordination. In R. Baldwin & B. Mauro (Eds.), *Mitigating the COVID economic crisis: Act fast and do whatever it takes* (pp. 203–212). London: CEPR Press.

Pourroy, M., Carton, B., & Coulibaly, D. (2016). Food prices and inflation targeting in emerging economies. *International Economics, 146,* 108–140.

Rajan, R. (2020). Dr Raghuram's Rajan prescription on how to stimulate the economy. BFSI News, Economic Times, May 9. https://economictimes.indiatimes.com/https://economictimes.indiatimes.com/news/economy/policy/raghuram-rajan-explains-how-best-to-stimulate-the-economy/articleshow/75640636.cms?utm_source=contentofinterest&utm_medium=text&utm_campaign=cppst

Raj, J., Khundrakpam, J. K., & Das, D. (2011). *An empirical analysis of monetary and fiscal policy interaction in India.* RBI Working Paper No. 15, Reserve Bank of India, Mumbai

Rajwade, A. V. (2007). Inflation and monetary policy. *Yojana, 51,* 17–19.

Rakshit, M. (2016). India's post-crisis macroeconomic slowdown: Some perspectives. Money & Finance, ICRA Bulletin, 49–84, April.

Ramachandran, M. (2004). Do broad money, output and prices count in India? *Journal of Policy Modeling, 26*(8–9), 982–1001.

Ramaswami, R., & Slok, T. (1998). The real effects of monetary policy in the European Union: What are the differences? *Economics Review, 45*(2), 374–396.

Ramey, V. (1993). How important is the credit channel in the transmission of monetary policy? *Carnegie-Rochester Conference Series on Public Policy, 39,* 1–45.

Rangarajan, C., & Arif, R. (1990). Money output and prices—A macro econometric model. *Economic and Political Weekly, 25*(16), 837–852.

Ranjan, R., Jain, R., & Dhal, S. C. (2007). India's potential economic growth: Measurement issues and policy implications. *Economic and Political Weekly, 42*(17), 1563–1572.

Ray, P. (2013). *Monetary policy.* New Delhi: Oxford University Press.

RBI. (2005). *Report on Currency and Finance.* Mumbai: Reserve Bank of India.

RBI. (2013). *Real interest rate impact on investment and growth—What the empirical evidence for India suggests.* Reserve Bank of India, Mumbai: Report on Currency and Finance.

RBI. (2014). *Report of the expert committee to revise and strengthen the monetary policy framework.* Mumbai: Reserve Bank of India.

RBI. (2020). Quarterly Estimates of Households' Financial Assets and Liabilities. RBI Bulletin, June, 2020 https://www.rbi.org.in/Scripts/BS_ViewBulletin.aspx?Id=18994

RBI Press Release. (2019–20). Press Release by Yogesh Dayal, Chief General Manager, Department of Communication, Central Office, RBI. Press Release: 2019–2020/2130. https://rbidocs.rbi.org.in/rdocs/PressRelease/PDFs/PR21302E204AFFBB614305B56DD6B843A520DB.PDF

Reinhart, C. M., & Sbrancia, M. B. (2011). *The liquidation of government debt.* NBER Working Paper 16893, March

Reserve Bank of India. (2020, April 9). COVID 19 to accentuate growth slowdown, impact on inflation ambiguous. *Economic Times.*

Romer, C. D., & Romer, D. H. (1990). New evidence on the monetary transmission mechanism. *Brookings Papers on Economic Activity, 21*(1), 149–213.

Romer, C., & Romer, D. (1999). Monetary policy and the well-being of the poor. *Federal Reserve Bank of Kansas City Economic Review. 1st Quarter*, 21–49.

Romer, D. (1993). Openness and inflation: Theory and evidence. *The Quarterly Journal of Economics, 108*(4), 869–903.

Sen, K., Kar, S., & Sahu, J. (2014). *The political economy of economic growth in India 1993–2013.* ESID Working Paper No.44. Manchester, UK: University of Manchester. www.effective-states.org

Sengupta, K. (1991). Procurement prices and inflation. *Yojana, 35*(18), 10–14.

Sengupta, N. (2014). Changes in transmission channels of monetary policy in India. *Economic and Political Weekly, 49*(49), 62–71.

Sethuraman, S. (2005). Effective inflation management. *Yojana, 49,* 54–55.

Shnkar, S. (1992). Bringing inflation under control. *Yojana, 36*(8), 27–28.
Sharma, D. (2007). Speculation holds the key. *Yojana, 51,* 15–16.
Shetty, M. (2020). Personal Loans are now 28% of total bank credit, Times of India (April 6, 2020) https://timesofindia.indiatimes.com/business/india-business/personal-loans-are-now-28-of-total-bank-credit/articleshow/74999627.cms
Sikdar, S. (2006). *Principles of macroeconomics.* New Delhi: Oxford University Press.
Sikdar, S. (2013). *Capital flows and exchange rate management.* New Delhi: Oxford University Press.
Singh, K. (2006). Inflation targeting: International experience and prospects for India. *Economic and Political Weekly, 41*(27), 2958–2961.
Singh, B. (2011). How Asymmetric is the Monetary Policy Transmission to Financial Markets in India?. *RBI Occasional Papers, 32*(2)
Singh, K., & Kalirajan, K. (2006). Monetary policy in India: Objectives, reaction and policy effectiveness. *Review of Applied Economics, 2*(2), 181–199.
Sinha, S. (1998). Are budget deficits inflationary? *Yojana, 42*(7), 8–10.
Smets, F., & Wouters, R. (2002). *An estimated dynamic stochastic general equilibrium model of the Euro Area.* ECB Working Paper 171, European Central Bank, Germany
Srinivasan, N., Mahambare, V., & Ramachandran, M. (2006). Modelling inflation in India: A critique of the structural approach. *Journal of Quantitative Economics, 4*(2), 45–59.
Taylor, J. (1993). Discretion versus policy rules in practice. *Carnegie-Rochester Conference Series on Public Policy, 39,* 195–214.
Taylor, J. B. (1995). The monetary transmission mechanism: An empirical framework. *Journal of Economic Perspectives American Economic Association, 9*(4), 11–26.
Taylor, J. B. (2000). *The monetary transmission mechanism and the evaluation of monetary policy rules.* Central Bank of Chile Working Paper No. 87. Santiago, Chile.
Trichet, J. C. (2011). *Introductory statement to the press conference.* European Central Bank, Frankfurt, October6.
Tuteja, U. (2008). Protect poor from food inflation. Economic Times, December 31. https://m.economictimes.com/protect-poor-from-food-inflation/articleshow/3915846.cms
Ummat, R. C. (1992). An agenda for containing inflation. *Kurukshetra, 40*(7), 9–10.
Virmani, V. (2004). *Operationalising taylor-type rules for the indian economy: Issues and some results (1992Q3 2001Q4).* IIMA Working Paper 2004–07-04, Indian Institute of Management, Ahmedabad
Walsh, C. E. (2009). Using monetary policy to stabilize economic activity. In *Jackson Hole symposium, Federal Reserve Bank of Kansas City.*
Walsh, J. P. (2011). *Reconsidering the role of food prices in inflation.* IMF Working Paper No. 71
Yellen, J. L. (2011). *Unconventional monetary policy and central bank communication.* Speech at the University of Chicago Booth School of Business U.S. Monetary Policy Forum. New York. February 25.

The Energy Scenario: Dilemmas and Opportunities

The Genesis of Electricity Reform in India and the UK, its Repercussions and the Way forward

Somit Dasgupta

1 The First Phase of Reforms

The Indian power sector had reached the absolute dead end by the 1980s. The yearly commercial losses of the State Electricity Boards (SEBs) without subsidy had crossed Rs. 3000 crore.[1] The sector was facing peak and energy shortages in various parts of the country, and severe financial burden was imposed on the state governments because of the performance of the SEBs.[2] The distribution infrastructure had become outdated and badly needed upgradation for which no funds were available. The utilities were overstaffed with poor efficiency levels, and retail tariffs were stagnant. The consumers suffered by way of load shedding coupled with poor quality of power supply.

This paper is partly based on the Ph.D. thesis of the author which was prepared under the guidance of Prof. Ramprasad Sengupta, Professor Emeritus of Economics, JNU. The author would like to express his sincere gratitude to Prof. Sengupta who was a constant source of inspiration to him. It was the guidance and encouragement of Prof. Sengupta that helped him in completing his thesis. The author has immensely gained from the wide domain knowledge of Prof. Sengupta.

S. Dasgupta (✉)
Indian Council for Research on International Economic Relations (ICRIER), Delhi, India
e-mail: somitdg@gmail.com

[1] This is equivalent to about US$ 400 million on the basis of today's exchange rate of Rs 75 to US$1.
[2] The peak deficit in the 1990s was about 10%, and energy deficit was about 7%.

P. Dasgupta et al. (eds.), *Sustainable Development Insights from India*,
India Studies in Business and Economics,
https://doi.org/10.1007/978-981-33-4830-1_7

1.1 Amendment of Electricity Laws

However, nothing really happened till 1991 when the existing electricity laws were amended to provide for private participation in generation. Specifically, the Electricity Laws (Amendment) Act of 1991 was enacted to encourage the entry of privately owned generators.[3] The change in policy coincided with the fact that India was facing its worst ever balance-of-payments crisis and was on the verge of defaulting which would have reduced India's bond rating in international credit markets.[4] Further amendments were carried out in 1998 when the transmission sector was also opened for private investments subject to the approval of the central transmission utility (CTU).[5] It was the government's viewpoint that if additional generation capacity could be created with the assistance of the private sector, the malaise could be rectified. In order to encourage private sector participation, several other policy measures were also undertaken. The private investors were offered a guaranteed 16% return in equity with a full five-year tax holiday. Sovereign guarantees and escrow benefits were also offered in case there were defaults on part of the SEBs. By 1995, there were about 189 offers to increase capacity by over 75 GW involving a total investment of over US $ 100 billion (Dubash and Rajan 2001). Eight projects were brought on the 'fast-track' route where government approvals were quickly expedited.[6] However, very soon the investors realised the tiring nature of having to work through the India bureaucracy. Escrow could not be granted to all projects as there clearly was a limit, given the revenue stream of the SEBs.[7] In fact, some of the banks like the State Bank of India, which gave overdraft facilities to the SEBs, refused to lift its lien on the receivables of the SEBs. The IPPs faced all kinds of problems, right from securing coal contracts to getting wagons from the railways for movement of their coal (Dubash and Rajan 2001). The failure of this policy to attract private investments was severely criticised domestically (Pillai and Krishanmurthy 1997). The private investors also realised that by providing incentives for additional capacity addition, the basic problem that is the bankruptcy of the SEBS does not get addressed. In fact, the problems would multiply as power from the new plants, if they do come up ultimately, would be a lot more expensive than the existing plants of the SEBs. (Purakayastha 1993). Reddy and d'Sa (1995) have stated that the energy cost

---

[3]This was followed up by a high-level delegation led by the Cabinet Secretary to the USA, Europe and Japan for seeking foreign investments in the Indian power sector.

[4]Apart from changing the policy for seeking investments in the power sector, other measures initiated during this period include measures to free currency and capital markets, reduce government control on banks, cut back on licensing requirements for industry, etc.

[5]The Powergrid Corporation of India (PGCIL) was the designated CTU, and it is felt that the PGCIL did not really allow private entities to come in fearing loss of its own monopoly position (Rao 2002).

[6]The eight projects were Dabhol (740+1440 MW), Bhadravati (1072 MW), Jegurupadu (235 MW), Godavari (208 MW), Vishakapatnam (1040 MW), Mangalore (1000 MW), Ib Valley (420 MW) and Neyveli (250 MW).

[7]To give an example, in Madhya Pradesh, the SEB had signed PPAs aggregating to 6500 MW, whereas the 'escrowable capacity' was fixed at 2561 MW by the financial institutions (D'sa, Murthy and Reddy, 1999).

from these projects frequently turned out to be one-and-a-half to two times more than that of comparable NTPC and SEB projects.[8] The high tariff was because of assured high PLF, high return on equity, high capital cost of plants, high variable costs due to management fee, testing fee, insurance charges, etc. (D'Sa et al. 1999).

1.2 Tweaking the Role of the CEA

Though it was the Ministry of Power which was taking the lead role in the policy formulation for attracting private capital for new projects, similar enthusiasm did not emanate from the other Ministries like the Finance Ministry who were apprehensive that these concessions may actually lead to net outflow of resources rather than inflow (Dubash 2002). The Finance Ministry was of the view that while they would raise resources in the domestic market, the profits would be remitted abroad. Even the Ministry of Environment and Forests and the Central Electricity Authority (CEA) were not happy with the way some of the technical and environmental clearance for smaller projects was handled. In fact, the role of the CEA has been progressively eroded since the mandatory requirement of the techno-economic clearance for power projects was slowly done away with. In 1995, the Government of India made TEC mandatory only for projects exceeding the cost of Rs. 1000 crores. This was enhanced to Rs.5000 crore in 1999.[9]Rumblings were also felt in NTPC since the government's policy of bending backwards was creating an uneven playing field. What was equally frustrating was the government was giving away sites to independent power producers which were originally identified for public sector units. Further, the absence of any competitive bidding gave rise to suspicion of corruption. Environmentalists and social activists were also alarmed seeing the haste and secrecy with which MOUs were being signed (Dubash and Rajan 2001). After 1995 however, the central government enforced competitive bidding for acquiring new capacity by way of IPPs.

1.3 Common Minimum National Action Plan for Power

In the meantime, some kind of political consensus was taking shape regarding reforms in the power sector. It began in 1991 when a committee was set up for the establishment of a common minimum agricultural tariff. The matter gained momentum when in 1996, the chief ministers conference proposed that agriculture tariffs should be at least 50 paise per unit which should be increased to at least 50 per cent of the average cost of supply within a period of 3 years. It is another matter, however,

---

[8]Countries like Indonesia, Pakistan and the Philippines are other examples where tariff from IPPs were relatively high leading to social unrest (Rao 2002).

[9]Today the stipulation is that only the hydro projects above Rs 1000 crore need to get a techno-economic clearance from the CEA mainly because it has interstate issues.

that no state implemented it. It may be pertinent to add that the Indian agricultural community in fact was prepared to pay higher tariffs in exchange for a better quality of power (Reddy 2000). The small farmers, in any case, maintained that low agricultural tariffs only helped the big farmers who had access to power-driven irrigation facilities. (Sant and Dixit 1996). There is one study (Ahluwalia 2000) which states that the agricultural community was, in fact, capable of paying higher tariffs and gain by the incremental productivity.

2 The Second Phase of Reforms

2.1 The Electricity Regulatory Commissions Act 1998

While Orissa was the first state to enact their own reforms act, it was followed by other states like Haryana (1997), Andhra Pradesh (1998), Uttar Pradesh (1999), Karnataka (1999), Rajasthan (1999), Delhi (2000), Madhya Pradesh (2000) and Gujarat (2003).[10] Each of these states, after passing their reforms act, unbundled their SEBs into separate entities of generation, transmission and distribution. The only difference was in the case of Orissa and Delhi which went a step further and privatised their distribution sector as well. In the meantime, around the mid-1990s, the Government of India too had come to realise that the distribution sector will have to be addressed first, and if the problems in the distribution sector can be addressed, investments in the generation sector will automatically flow. The Government of India therefore passed an Ordinance which later culminated as the Electricity Regulatory Commissions Act 1998. It was similar to the Orissa Reforms Act, and it paved the way for setting up of the Central Electricity Regulatory Commission. The states could also rely on this Act to set up their own state commissions or enact their own legislations for this purpose.[11] The functions of the CERC and the SERCs were clearly demarcated. While the CERC was responsible for all centrally owned stations and other stations having an interstate role, the SERCs were responsible for stations within their own state only. The primary intention for setting up of regulatory commissions was to ensure that tariffs were determined according to economic principles and that the entire process was free from any political interference. The role of the government was only that of a facilitator and catalyst which would lay down broad principles of policy.

The enactment of the Electricity Regulatory Commissions Act 1998 was only a partial step towards reforms. The Government of India had been mulling over a comprehensive reform act which would repeal all other existing electricity laws. The first draft of the bill was made in 2000 though there were some other steps taken by

[10]Some of these states also availed of loans from multilateral development banks, such as, Andhra Pradesh, Haryana, Uttar Pradesh and Rajasthan.

[11]Maharashtra, Punjab, Tamil Nadu and Delhi are some of the states which have set up their regulatory commissions under the Central Act.

the government during this time period to improve the functioning of the distribution sector.[12]

2.2 *The Electricity Act 2003*

The Electricity Act 2003 (EA 2003) came into being in June 2003. This Act repealed all the existing electricity laws, such as, the Indian Electricity Act 1910, the Electricity Supply Act 1948, etc., but saved the various reform Acts of some of the states which were already in operation.[13]

The primary objective of the EA 2003 was been to promote competition in order to enable the consumers to have the best possible price and quality of supply. In order to have competition, one needs a large number of sellers and buyers, and this is exactly what the EA 2003 had attempted through its various provisions. Before speaking of various provisions to promote competition, one of the most crucial (and debatable) statute needs to be mentioned, i.e. restructuring of the existing SEBs in a time-bound manner. The EA 2003 mentioned that all SEBs have to be unbundled into separate entities of generation, transmission and distribution (Sections 131 and 172). The model to be adopted would be similar to the 'World Bank' model which had been followed by Orissa to begin with and thereafter emulated by some other states. This type of model is also called the 'the single buyer mode'. This directive of the EA 2003 had been criticised in many quarters where the opinion has been that restructuring need not be necessary and that vertical utilities have also done well in some cases in India and abroad. In order to enhance generation, licensing was done away with completely except that techno-economic clearance would be required for hydro projects (Sections 7 and 8). Captive generation was promoted, and in fact, the definition for captive has been kept very wide, making it easier for the industry to opt for captive power plants (Section 9). Open access in distribution, to be introduced in a phased manner, had been recognised wherein a bulk consumer could access power from any other source provided certain technical constraints were met (Section 42). The EA 2003 also recognised the existence of two or more distribution licensees in the same geographical area, with the proviso that each will have its own set of wires (Section 14). This, however, was a debatable concept given the monopolistic nature of the wires business and the need for duplicating network infrastructure. On the issue of pricing, the provisions of the Sixth Schedule of the Electricity Supply Act 1948 had been done away with, and the job of price determination has been handed over to the regulatory commissions. The constitution of the state regulatory commissions was mandatory (Section 82). Power trading was recognised as a distinct activity with the safeguard that regulatory commissions were authorised to fix ceilings on trading margins, if necessary (Sections 12, 79 and 86). For the benefit of consumers,

[12]The first draft of the bill was prepared by the NCAER on behalf of the Ministry of Power.

[13]The states were Orissa, Haryana, Andhra Pradesh, Uttar Pradesh, Karnataka, Rajasthan, Delhi, Madhya Pradesh and Gujarat.

certain institutions like the consumers redressal forum and their appellate body, the Ombudsman, had been envisaged (Section 42). There were other safeguards as far as the consumer is concerned with special emphasis on performance standards (Sections 57 to 59). At the same time, in order to plug revenue leaks, 100% metering was made compulsory (Section 55) and provisions relating to theft of energy had been made very stringent (Sections 135–150).

Ever since the enactment of the EA 2003, there has been no major amendments except for some minor amendments carried out in 2007. This is in contrast with the case in UK where major changes were carried out at regular intervals.[14] The first major change which was tried in India in 2014 with the introduction of the concept of 'carriage and content'.[15] This concept basically means that in a given a geographical area, there would be only one owner of the distribution wires and there shall be several retailers who would compete against one another. This concept, however, could not be introduced because of stiff opposition from the states. The government has now come forward with another draft amendment bill where the concept of 'carriage and content' has been dropped.[16] Why the concept of 'carriage and content' is not considered appropriate in the Indian milieu is dealt with later on in this essay.

Today, the structure of the power sector is that in all states, there are state generators, the state transmission company and finally, the distribution companies which may range from two to four depending upon the size of the state. All the distribution utilities are public sector companies except in the case of Delhi and Odisha where they are private utilities. There are a few other private utilities functioning in certain parts of the country, such as in Mumbai, Kolkata, Greater Noida (Uttar Pradesh), Ahmedabad and Surat. In addition, we also have the central sector generating companies like the NTPC which usually supply power to more than one state and further, the independent power producers (IPPs) who are spread all over the country.[17] There are some variations across states, for example, in some states the transmission company purchases power on behalf of the distribution companies (discoms), but in most instances, the discoms do it directly from the generators since the PPAs of the erstwhile SEB have been redistributed amongst the discoms.

[14]Just to give an instance, in UK, just after passing the act in 1989, retail competition was introduced for big consumers in 1990, followed for medium consumers in 1994 and for all consumers in 1998. The wholesale market (called the Pool) was replaced by NETA in 2001, and this was replaced by BETTA in 2005. In between 1989 and 2005, several other measures were taken which clearly points to a keen regulatory oversight.

[15]This appeared in the Electricity (Amendment) Bill 2014. This bill was sent to the select committee for scrutiny which had submitted a report but nothing happened thereafter. It is said that the states had objected to various provisions of the bill, especially on the 'carriage and content' issue. The concept of 'carriage and content' which was the central subject of the bill has been dealt with later on this essay. The government in its budget speech for FY22 again spoke of having more than one discom in an area but details were not disclosed.

[16]Draft Electricity Act (Amendment Bill) 2020.

[17]There is a sizeable number of IPPs in India today and their share in capacity is as high as 47% today.

3 Restructuring of the Power Sector in Other Countries

The electricity industry in most countries is vertically integrated or linked by a common state ownership with the mandate to supply electricity to a well-defined geographical area. Along with this industry structure, there was usually some form of regulation to curb any monopolistic malpractice (Surrey 1996). In India, the electricity sector was initiated in the private sector in the early twentieth century but was slowly taken over by the government barring a few private utilities which exist even today. While India undertook reforms beginning from the early 1990s, there were various other countries who had already taken a proactive stand on reforms right from late 1970s. Notable among them are Brazil, Argentina, Chile in Latin America, the UK, some specific states in the USA, the Nordic countries, some of the ASEAN countries, etc. The reason for undertaking reforms, however, varied across countries and the organisational structure of the power sector, both before and after reforms were country specific. In the Latin American countries, reforms were initiated to raise resources for the Treasury. In the UK, reforms were undertaken for a different cause altogether, i.e to break the power of the trade unions and, simultaneously, raise resources for the Treasury. In the USA, reforms were undertaken since electricity tariff was high in some of the states, especially those states which did not have access to hydro resources. It may be also added that while the productivity of the power sector was poor in Latin American countries before reforms, the same cannot be said in respect of the power sector, both in the UK and USA. Further, while in the USA, the power sector was primarily in private hands before the reform movement, it was exactly the opposite in the case of UK. The crux of the argument is that there is no standardised notion of what the sector looked like in each of the countries which undertook reforms and that the position was completely country specific. Besides, any restructuring program that is carried out does not take place in a vacuum as it has to be in sync with the historical and local context, including political priorities (Dubash and Singh 2005). Moreover, choice of the market design depends upon the industry's current state. Significant changes should not be done too frequently as it hampers the growth of investments (Green 2005). Further, privatisation need not necessarily mean reforms (Thomas 2005). At the end of the day, while all countries seek a reliable, competent and efficient market, the mode of achieving the same has varied across countries (Dubash and Singh 2005). The reforms undertaken in UK are being described in detail in the following paragraphs.

3.1 Reforms in the UK

Before the power sector was privatised in UK, several other sectors were privatised which included the telecom (1984), gas (1986) and water (1989). The electricity sector privatisation, however, was considered to be the most complex where the assets were valued at 42 billion pounds in the 1980s. One primary aim of the privatisation programme in UK was to break the power of the trade unions. In addition, the government aimed at generating revenues through the privatisation process and also ensure widening of ownership.[18] The service of the industry as such was reliable and comparable to other European countries (Thomas 2005). Newbury (2004) was, however, of the view that the structure of the electrical supply industry was rigid, bureaucratic and inefficient. Supplies were at risk due to strike threats and fuel crisis. When the privatisation programme was launched in the UK, the country was in deep recession. Before privatisation, the electricity sector in the UK consisted of vertical, integrated structures. There was a two-part tariff (for both generation and transmission) to cover for capacity and energy charge. There were separate charges for peak hour capacity usage also.

3.1.1 Unbundling of the Utilities

There were six main elements to the British privatisation program (Thomas 2005) which were as follows:

(i) Creation of a wholesale spot market as the main price setting arena.
(ii) Creation of retail competition where consumers can choose their own electricity supplier.
(iii) Corporate separation between generation and retail supply.
(iv) Distribution of incentive regulation to set the prices to monopoly activities
(v) Sale of publicly owned assets to private investors.

The government passed the Electricity Act 1989 whereby the Central Electricity Generating Board (CEGB) with its 74 power stations and the national grid was restructured into four separate organisations.[19] There were two power generating companies, one transmission company called the NGC and a distribution network consisting of 12 regional electricity companies (RECs). The government, as part of the restructuring programme, split the CEGB into two generators, namely National Power (40 GW) and Power Gen (30 GW). A public-owned nuclear generating station called Nuclear Electricity (8 GW) was also created. The government actually wanted to privatise the nuclear generating stations also but realised later that they were not attractive to investors (Thomas 2005). The Electricity Act 1989 also created the post of Director General of Electricity Supply (DGES) to regulate the natural wires business of the NGC and the RECs and to set price caps, to be reviewed periodically every four to five years (Newbury 2004).

---

[18]Between 1947 and 1990, different governments followed different policies in respect of the power sector. The Labour Government in 1970s forced the electricity industry to curtail prices to control inflation, whereas in 1980s, the Conservative Government raised prices to reduce public borrowings (from the website of the Department of Energy, USA).

[19]The CEGB was established by the Electricity Act 1957. In 1983, the government had also passed the Electricity Act 1983 which was designed to encourage the growth of independent power producers. This act required the CEGB to purchase electricity from the private producers at avoided cost, something similar to PURPA, 1978 of USA.

3.1.2 Separation of Distribution and Retail

The RECs had to make an accounting separation of distribution and retail. The regulator was concerned with the cross-subsidy between retail and distribution because a significant portion of the staff and systems was common. The regulator, therefore, required legal separation of the business. Distribution business is the business of wires, i.e. the one who owns the wires, whereas retail business would be the business of buying/selling the power using these wires which do not belong to the retailer. The distribution side of the RECs business was to be regulated through RPI-X form of regulation. While RPI was the retail price index in Britain, X was the efficiency factor, a positive number to be decided by the regulator. Thus, RPI-X would mean that the real price should progressively come down.[20] RPI-X is not applied to the competitive segment of the industry where prices are expected to be decided by market forces. In late 1995, there was an eruption of mergers and acquisitions which saw a revival of the vertically integrated structure of the power sector. Thomas (2005) has mentioned that integration has lent an advantage since it gives a sure market to the generators. The fact that there are certain advantages of an integrated utility can also be gauged by the fact that, in Brazil, there was insufficient investment in generation which led the government to allow reintegration. In an unbundled structure, it is not just the generation investment which is adversely affected. The same can be said about investments in transmission. Earlier transmission investments were of integrated type and a mismatch can develop, post-restructuring (Joskow 1997).

3.1.3 Introduction of Retail Competition

Retail competition in the UK was introduced in stages. From Vesting Day, i.e. 1 April 1990, consumers with a demand greater than 1 MW (about 50,000 in number) could choose their own supplier. This limit was reduced to 100 KW in April 1994 (favouring another 50,000 customers), and by 1998, this facility was extended to small consumers also (about 23 million). This, according to Hunt and Shutteworth (1996), is the final step towards a complete electricity market. As a backup for those consumers who do not wish to choose a supplier, the local REC was obliged to offer supply to all consumers with demand less than 10 MW on a regulated, published tariff (Thomas 1996).

[20]The X factor varied across segments of the industry with transmission companies assigned an initial value of zero. For the 12 RECs, the X value ranged from zero to 2.5. There has been criticism from certain quarters that the X factor has been favourable to the industry, allowing them to have excessive profits.

3.1.4 Creation of a Power Pool

One of the main components of the British privatisation programme was the creation of a wholesale market by way of a power pool.[21] It was supply-side bidding only where all generating stations had to quote a price for its output. The NGC would stack up the offers and determine the market clearing price given the level of demand that it had estimated. The NGC also functioned as the ancillary service provider, the settlement system administrator and the Pool funds administrator. It is important to consider that there was no bidding from the demand side. It was thus a central dispatch system and all plants who had offered a bid below the market clearing price were directed to dispatch their schedule.

There were certain inherent problems in the functioning of the Pool. It was felt that the two main generating companies, i.e. National Power and the Power Gen were acting as a duopoly, and this was leading to a higher market clearing price than what could be dictated by market conditions. Green and Newbery (1992) feel that the scope of the exercise of market power has been seriously underestimated by the government, perhaps led by the notion that the Bertrand model is necessarily competitive, even in concentrated markets.[22] The government tried to solve this problem by further subdividing the two main generating companies. The two generating companies were compelled by the regulator to sell off 6 GW of their plant capacity to bring an element of competition.

3.1.5 Contract for Differences (CfDs)

While the market clearing price was determined on a daily basis on the basis of day-ahead bidding, there were price fluctuations and the wholesale price was considered to be quite volatile. In order to bring in an element of certainty, the distribution companies made bilateral agreements with generators called contract for differences (CfD). Any difference between the contract price and the Pool price was settled bilaterally between the generator and the distribution company. It may be added that more than 90% of the electricity in the system was under the CfD and less than 10% was being determined through the market, i.e. the Pool. Before the Pool came into operation, it was thought that price competition would quickly cause Pool prices to fall to short-run marginal costs. However, it turned out that mean annual Pool price rose by 40% (nominal) in the first four years of its operation, and remained well above the marginal costs upto and including 2000/01. Spot markets attract a lot of attention due to the frequently changing price and any company that relies on it and

[21]For several reasons, the rate of return regulation was rejected in the UK, partly because it required detailed industry data which would in turn require a large bureaucratic structure (from the website of the Department of Energy USA).

[22]The Bertrand duopoly model examines price competition among firms that produce differentiated but highly substitutable products. Each firm's quantity demanded is a function of not only the price it charges but also the price charged by its rival.

takes a lot of risks. Most companies prefer to have long-term contracts, not lasting decades but for a couple of years (Green 2005).

3.1.6 The New Electricity Trading Arrangement (NETA)

In October 1998, the government published a White Paper, accepting the recommendations of the regulator to replace the Pool with the New Electricity Trading Arrangements (NETA). NETA was finally introduced in March 2001 after developing and testing a new software. Thomas (2005) estimates that the cost of developing the system and running it for the first five years was around GBP 770 million. As mentioned earlier, the Pool had certain inherent problems like gaming being undertaken by the generating firms and also the fact that very high capacity payments were being made. There were other problems with the Pool system, for example, bids in the Pool were 'non-firm', i.e. the generators were not penalised if they failed to follow the schedule (Green 1999). Just before the introduction of NETA, Pool prices began to fall towards the end of 1999–2000 though retail prices did not. Pool price is the price at which bulk consumers buy, whereas retail prices are what they charge from the ultimate consumer. By the time NETA had completed its first year of operation, large industrial consumers were paying 15% less in nominal terms compared to 1990–91. Green (2005) is of the view that prices were low in the initial years of NETA because of divestitures by the major generators. Under NETA, generators and consumers had bilateral tie-ups for long-term power purchase and only a balancing mechanism was operated by the NGC for balancing the demand for power from technical considerations. It was thus a decentralised dispatch. The NGC was only involved in balancing the grid and had no role to play in the price being offered or accepted. Each generator and consumer had to inform the NGC its likely schedule called the Initial Physical Notification (IPN) for the following day. IPN is the initial requirement conveyed to the grid operator, i.e. how many megawatts of electricity is required for the following day for each hour. This would be a tentative estimate, and it could be altered while conveying the Final Physical Notification (FPN) till one hour before the actual schedule, called 'gate closure'. FPN is the final schedule conveyed to the NGC for the appointed hour, called gate closure. Any change in the final output vis-à-vis the final notification was balanced by the NGC. The entities were either required to pay or be paid for any imbalance in the system. If the entities needed more power, then they had to pay the system buy price (SBP) or if they had to sell, they were paid the system sell price (SSP). The SBP was always more than the SSP. This was not a zero-sum game and any profit or loss on this account was shared by the players operating in the system. To facilitate day-ahead and longer-term trading, two rival market operators (APX and UKPX) began operating screen-based exchange market where bids and offers could be anonymously posted. It may be added that a very small proportion of power flowing in the system was through the balancing mechanism and that almost all the power was through bilateral contracts. The replacement of the Pool with NETA was criticised by Newbury (1998) and Shuttleworth (1999) since they felt that it has been introduced without commissioning any detailed analysis. In 2005, further changes were made to NETA by including Scotland too in the power market, and the new structure was called the British Electricity Trading and Transmission Arrangement (BETTA). It is said that Scotland produced 70% more electricity than what it required and by including Scottish generators in the market, there will be a further downward pressure on prices.

3.1.7 The Gainers in UK's Restructuring Program

Who has been the gainer from the restructuring of the British power sector? Many economists have analysed this issue and some of the major findings are elaborated upon. Newbury and Pollitt (1997) have found substantial efficiency gains from privatisation and restructuring in the UK They have estimated an overall net benefit of GBP 6 billion and a 7.5% reduction in prices driven by a decrease in labour and operating costs. The authors, however, add that these gains have been unevenly distributed. While the new private utilities, whose share prices have tripled since floatation, have gained disproportionately, the government has gained moderately but consumers are paying more than what they would have under public ownership. De Oliveira (2004) is of the opinion that fuel suppliers and employees of the utilities were the big losers from reforms, while directors, management and shareholders were the big gainers.

Thomas (2005), however, doubts, whether the price gains can be attributed to competition and whether they are sustainable. Thomas adds that a large part of the reduction was actually obtained in the regulated sector, and further, it was the large consumers who actually gained. The other reasons for decrease in prices were because of lower coal and gas costs and because of the end of the government subsidy to nuclear plants. The fact that the drop in electricity rates was due to the decrease in the regulated sector and also because of the drop in nuclear power subsidy is also supported by Wright and Thomas (2001). In other words, competition was not the reason why there was a decrease in electricity rates. The authors further state that electricity prices were regressive in character and the prepayment rates (used largely by the poor consumer) were the highest. Green and McDaniel (1998) also subscribe to the view that the single largest cause for the decline in prices is because of decrease in fuel costs. It seems that though full retail was introduced by 1999, there were very few consumers who actually switched to a different supplier. The reason for this is high transaction costs. Green and McDaniel (1998), however, estimated that about 60% of over 1 MW consumers and about 40% of the 100 KW market actually changed their suppliers and all those who switched faced lower power bills. As far as the small consumers are concerned, it is debatable whether extending retail competition to them was worth the cost.

4 Difference Between Indian and UK Model

Now that one is familiar with the architecture of the reform program in India and the UK, one can study the similarities and differences between the two models. To begin with, both involved unbundling of vertical utilities into separate generation, transmission and distribution companies. The primary difference, however, is that in the case of India, a wholesale market was not created and competition in retail was also missing. In India, the distribution utilities had a defined geographical area where they had to serve and there was no other utility who could serve the same area. The EA 2003 does have a provision of another utility serving the same area but it has to lay down its own parallel network. Since the business of wires is a natural monopoly, it did not make much sense to have another utility in the same geographical area.[23] Competition in retail was also missing except that consumers with a load of 1 MW and above could access power from any source. However, to do that the consumer will have to pay for open access (OA), which would include a cross-subsidy surcharge and an additional surcharge to be determined by the regulatory commission concerned. The problem is that the regulatory commissions made these charges so stiff that it was uneconomical to go in for open access. So, in effect, the distribution utility had the monopoly to serve all consumers in the area. This is not to suggest that virtually there are no open access consumers. States having a sizeable share in industry do have open access consumers since the industrial tariff, which includes a cross-subsidy component, was exceedingly high compared to the cost of supply. The subject of open access by itself is huge with a lot of literature written on it but for the limited purpose of this essay, it would suffice to say that open access was successfully blocked by the regulatory commissions whose sympathy actually lay with the incumbent utility. In this context, it may also be added that there was no concept of open access charges in the UK.

In India, as opposed to wholesale markets, generation tariff continues to be determined by the regulatory commissions. The Tariff Policy, however, states that with the exception of hydro projects, all generation tariff beyond 2011 will be determined through a competitive bidding process, except in a few pre-defined situations. This means that the distribution utilities will float tenders and potential generators would give their bids. Since the process began only in 2011, even today, about 90% of generation has its tariff determined by the regulatory commissions on a cost-plus basis. There is a rumour that the EA 2003 did not allow for a wholesale market seeing what had happened in California in 2000 where generation tariffs went through the roof. However, there is no literature available on this issue.

When dealing with differences between India and the UK, one pertinent point is about the effectiveness of the regulatory bodies in both the countries. The British regulator, Office of Gas and Electricity Markets (OFGEM), is a very powerful body which is truly independent having access to large amount of resources in terms of both

[23] There is a case of Jamshedpur, Jharkhand, where the regulatory commission granted a license for parallel distribution.

finances and manpower.[24] The same cannot be said of the regulators in India. Most of the regulatory commissions in India have skeletal manpower whose capacity is also suspect. As a result, they suffer from 'regulatory capture'.[25] The independence of the Indian regulator is, perhaps, absent, and there are indications of constant bureaucratic interference especially when elections are around the corner. The manner in which regulators are selected is also a matter of concern, and there is a general apprehension that we are not selecting the best person for the job.

5 The Indian Experience

In an earlier paragraph, there was a brief overview of what had been the effect of the reform movement in the UK. Who were the gainers from the restructuring? Similarly, one needs to study who gained from the restructuring of the power sector in India. Did the restructuring at all help the distribution sector which was in the doldrums prior to the reform program? To answer the question whether the restructuring was helpful or not, one needs to answer some basic questions. The first question is whether the financial position of discoms is better today as compared to the situation prior to the restructuring process. Second, are the consumers better served today in terms of quality of power, lower outages, etc.? Has there been any improvement in the efficacy of the sector, post-restructuring? We shall answer each of these questions in the following paragraphs.

As far as financial performance is concerned, the discoms are in a much poorer state today than what they were in prior to restructuring. The Power Finance Corporation reports that the total losses (after tax) have reached about Rs. 39,600 crore (US$ 5.2 billion) by 2017–18.[26] Audited figures for discoms beyond 2017-18 are not available right now. The tariffs determined by the regulatory commissions are non-remunerative and do not cover the full cost of supply. The primary reason for this is that the governments have been exerting pressure on the commissions to keep retail tariff at the barest minimum. The revenue gap is being filled by deferred tariff decisions amounting to additional borrowing which is popularly known as 'regulatory assets'.[27] This means that the power sector is getting increasingly indebted to the banks, and there seems to be no avenue available as to how to either recover the

[24]Earlier OFGEM was known as the Office of Electricity Regulation (OFFER). OFGEM is said to have more than 750 employees working in the organisation which is many times over the combined manpower strength of the central and state regulatory commissions in India.

[25]This is a process where the regulated entity is better informed than the regulator, and hence, is in a position to influence the decisions of the regulator.

[26]On a per unit basis, while the average cost of supply was Rs. 5.60, the average revenue (inclusive of subsidy received) was Rs. 5.33. Thus, for every unit, there is a loss of Rs. 0.27.

[27]Creation of regulatory assets is strongly discouraged by the Tariff Policy unless there are extraordinary circumstances. The problem of regulatory assets is limited to about six to seven states only. The states/UTs are Uttar Pradesh, Rajasthan, Delhi, Tamil Nadu, Puducherry, Maharashtra and Chandigarh.

deferred costs or amortise these debts. In fact, these debts have become so huge that the banks today are not keen to finance the discoms any more, creating a massive liquidity problem for these utilities. The performance of the discoms also has not been praiseworthy since they have not been able to lower their commercial losses to any appreciable extent. Even today, the commercial losses are in excess of 22% on an average. At a granular level, it is seen that there were about 40 discoms whose loss levels were in excess of 15%, and out of this, 27 discoms had a loss level exceeding 20% and further, about 16 of them had losses in excess of 30%. There were 6 discoms whose loss levels were close to 40% or beyond![28] This is despite the fact that the discoms have been receiving financial assistance from the centre for upgradation of infrastructure and also for metering.[29] The fact remains that in the public-owned discoms, accountability is an issue, and there is a clear nexus between the field level staff of the discoms and the consumers. On a simple issue like metering, most of the agriculture sector is not metered, and it is generally reported that a large proportion of metres actually installed do not work at all.

As compared to the distribution sector, the generation sector and the transmission sector have performed well, post reforms. They have been earning their rate of return on the equity invested. However, over the last few years, the discoms have been unable to pay the generators due to their poor financial position.[30] This phenomenon has now started crippling the generation sector as well and they are facing cash-flow problems and in some cases, unable to service their debts. Unfortunately, generators have to pay for coal and railway freight upfront but getting paid by the discoms can get delayed by 6 months of more. The renewable generators suffer the most since their bargaining power vis-à-vis conventional generators is much lower. In order to stem this problem of mounting dues to generators, the government mandated the power will be supplied to only those discoms who open 'letters of credit' with banks so that payment to generators is assured.[31] It seems, by and large, this dictum of the government is being followed by all discoms.

---

[28]These commercial loss figures relate to 2017–18.

[29]There have been several schemes which have been implemented by the centre which began in the early 2000s. The first such scheme was the APDRP scheme which was later converted to what is now known as the Integrated Power Development Scheme (IPDS). The outlay for the IPDS was about Rs. 32,600 crores (US$ 4.3 billion) out of which budgetary support was around Rs. 25,300 crores (US$ 3.3 billion). The earlier scheme of APDRP had an outlay of about Rs 44,000 crore (US$ 5.8 billion). In both these schemes, funds are provided for upgradation of infrastructure and also for metering.

[30]According to the government portal 'praapti', as in May 2020, the discoms owed about Rs. 102,000 crores (US$ 13.6 billion) to the generators. Out of the total amount due, about 36% is payable to the central generating stations, about 21% to state generating stations, about 34% to the private generators and about 9% to renewable generators. The renewable generators are also primarily private generators. In order to help the discoms to pay the central generators, the government has started a new scheme under the aegis of 'Atmanirbhan Bharat' wherein the discoms will receive soft loans totalling to about Rs. 90,000 crores (US$ 12 billion). These loans will have state government guarantee.

[31]This has been under implementation since August 2019.

To sum up, the restructuring of the power sector has had little salutary effect on the finances of the distribution sector. In fact, the condition has deteriorated a lot more than what the situation was just prior to the enactment of the EA 2003. This brings us to the second issue of the quality of service. One of the duties of the regulatory commissions is to lay down performance standards which incidentally has been done by all commissions. However, there is no consistency across states since each regulatory commission has fixed its own standards in isolation.[32] Whether these standards laid down are followed or not varied across states depending upon how proactive the commission is. There is no doubt, however, that consumers today are better informed about the service they are expected to receive, for example, in how many days a new connection should be given, in how many hours an outage is supposed to be fixed, etc. Not only that, the consumers are also proactive during the hearings which take place at the time the tariff petitions are heard though their numbers are still small.[33]The biggest boon the consumers have had is the sudden spurt in generation capacity which took place during the last decade or so. This happened because the spot price of power in the power exchanges shot up to about Rs 10 per unit around 2010–11. This encouraged potential investors to set up additional capacity, mostly coal based. There was so much excitement that banks no longer waited for 'financial closure' or fuel linkage and extended loans to investors.[34] The growth in capacity was much higher than the growth in demand leading to the inevitable, i.e. surplus capacity lying idle.[35] Another reason for surplus capacity was lack of fuel linkage since coal supply has always been short compared to demand.[36] This spurt in generation capacity has led to a steep reduction in shortages, both peak and energy. However, there has been a simultaneous rise in the non-performing assets (NPAs) of banks and other financial institutions like the Power Finance Corporation and the Rural Electrification Corporation. The economic downturn during the last

---

[32]The CEA has been entrusted with the task of drafting a common performance standard which would be adhered by all discoms.

[33]In order to help the consumers understand the complex tariff petitions, some regulatory commissions have in the past appointed officers who would discuss the petitions with interested consumers. One such commission was the Delhi Electricity Regulatory Commission.

[34]This indiscriminate lending by commercial banks has led the way for creation of non-performing assets (NPAs). It is estimated that there were around 34 projects with an aggregate capacity of 40,000 MW who had been extended loans amounting to about Rs 2 lakh crore (US$ 26.6 billion). About seven to eight such projects have been revived by giving them fuel linkages which they did not have.

[35]While capacity in the last ten years grew at about 10% per year, the demand growth was only about 5% per year. The growth in the last two years, i.e. 2018–19 and 2019–20 was even lower due to the economic downturn and ever since the total lockdown from late March 2020, the growth was actually negative. The PLF of thermal power stations, due to all these reasons put together has been hovering at less than 50% during Marcj–May 2020. Part of the reason for low PLF is also on account of the coronavirus.

[36]To overcome the problem of coal linkage, the government introduced the scheme of 'Shakti' in May 2017 where coal is provided on the basis of auctions. The beneficiary plants are divided into various categories, such as those having valid PPAs, those not having PPAs, those which are owned by the government, etc.

three years or so also contributed to the growth in surplus capacity since the discoms facing demand shortages curtailed their scheduling.

Coming to the last point of efficiency in the sector, first let us revisit what happened in the UK. In UK, there have been divergent views expressed as mentioned in paragraph number 3.1.7. While some were of the view that there were efficiency improvements leading to lower prices, and there were others who felt that the reduction in prices was actually due to drop in fuel prices. Authors have also expressed the view that not everybody in society gained and that the gains were limited to a certain few like the directors, management and shareholders of the generation utilities. Some researchers had also expressed the view that the drop in prices was due to lowering of the regulated business rather than competition in retail. As far as India is concerned, we carried on with the cost-plus model of regulation, both at the generation and retail end. Given the strength of our regulatory institutions, we could not really expect a downward movement of real prices and that is exactly what happened. On the contrary, cost of generation continued to rise which ensured commensurate increase in the cost of supply also. Power purchase cost constitutes to about 80% of the cost of supply and any increase in this cost cannot really be offset somewhere else. Generation cost has been going up steadily on two counts, i.e. cost of coal and cost of railway freight. The Indian coal sector, in any case, is not really known for its efficiency, and all its inefficiencies are passed on to the power sector. When it comes to railway freight, coal is the main revenue earner, and the proceeds are used to subsidise passenger fares.[37] It may, however, be added that after introduction of tariff-based bidding in 2011, the market determined prices for generation were found to be much lower. Examples are of the Ultra Mega Power Plants (UMPP)[38] of Tata Mundra and of Sason and Krishnapatnam.[39] The Tata Mundra Plant, however, got into problems after the price of Indonesian coal went up substantially. There are not too many examples to quote since there has really been no bidding for fresh projects for the last several years since the discoms already have more power purchase agreements than what they need to meet their demand. Similar to generation, market determined prices for transmission are much lower than the cost-plus. Unlike generation, there are several cases of transmission projects which were bid out and most of them were cheaper than the regulated, cost-plus tariffs. Of course, there have been arguments that market determined prices may be lower but it is at the cost of quality of materials and design. In a nutshell, we can say that reforms in the power sector did not see any increase in efficiency because, primarily, we are still in the cost-plus regime.

---

[37] According to Brookings, India's fare to freight ratio is one of the lowest in the world at 0.24. The corresponding figures for Japan, Germany and China are 1.9, 1.5 and 1.2, respectively. Further, coal accounts for about 44% of the revenue earned through freight and about 60% of the coal used in power generation is transported through railways.

[38] UMPPs are large thermal plants of 4,000 MW which were entitled to certain tax benefits.

[39] The levelised tariff for the Tata Mundra Plant was Rs. 2.26 per unit, for Sason, it was Rs. 1.196 per unit and for Krishnaptnam, it was Rs. 2.33 per unit.

6 Way Forward

6.1 Privatisation of Distribution Utilities

It is quite evident that the restructuring of the power sector has not led us to a point that was envisaged. One had hoped that the restructuring would lead to a situation where the distribution sector would be financially healthy, would undertake regular upgradation of infrastructure, and where one would witness a progressive decline in the real cost of power. One should mention here that though the basic tenet of EA 2003 was promoting economy, efficiency and competition, the structure which emerged from the restructuring process was not conducive to competition. We did not create a wholesale market as done in the UK nor did we have retailers at the distribution end. We only unbundled our vertical SEBs and broke them down into separate companies dealing with generation, transmission and distribution. In the process, the entire burden of the sector fell on the distribution companies which emerged as inefficient and corrupt bodies with cultural legacies. So, despite restructuring, there was no change in the financial position of the distribution sector. A public sector discom is usually headed by a relatively young career bureaucrat who has no stakes in the organisation. In fact, he spends about two to three years in the organisation and moves on to some other organisation. There is no pressure on him to improve things since the apathy stems right from the government. Boards of these companies do not also have the optimum composition of functional and independent directors and, therefore, do not function autonomously. The discom chief is well aware that the state government is not too serious about reduction of commercial losses since that will disrupt their vote-bank politics. When it comes to determination of tariff, it is again vote-bank politics which forces the government to breathe down the necks of the regulatory commissions to ensure that there is no appreciable rise. It is because of these reasons that the discoms continue to be inefficient and loss-making bodies. Things, however, will change if the discoms are privatised. Privatised entities have accountability and immediate steps will be taken to lower commercial losses. True, the pressure on the regulatory commission will still be there not to raise tariffs but the privatised utilities are well-geared to handle such issues through litigation, while being able to implement efficiency gains. A public discom does not even dare to file a petition before the appellate authority. There are various instances when the public discom did not even file a tariff petition before the regulatory commission, forcing a situation where tariffs could not be raised.[40]

We have the case of privatisation in Delhi where the loss levels have been brought down from about 50% in 2002 to about 8% today. In fact, this loss level at a single digit figure has been there for at least the last seven to eight years. It is just not the loss levels but the quality of service which has seen a significant improvement.

[40]The situation had become so acute that the APTEL, in 2011, issued an order that the regulatory commissions should initiate suo-moto proceedings under Section 121 of EA 2003 in case tariff petitions are not filed by the discoms.

The privatised utilities in Delhi have been very active in pursuing matters in the courts also. Several tariff orders of the Delhi Electricity Regulatory Commission (DERC) have been contested in the Appellate Tribunal for Electricity (APTEL), and they have been successful in getting relief. While speaking about the success in Delhi, one needs to mention the case of Odisha also where privatisation has not been successful. There are reasons for this, and the fact is that the Delhi model that was adopted was different from that of Odisha. One of the main reasons for failure of the Odisha model was that the regulatory commission was rather strict in determining the loss levels which would be allowed in the tariff. The actual loss levels on the ground were much higher than what was allowed by the regulatory commission, which in turn implied that a major part of the expenditure remained uncovered, and this led to financial problems in the distribution companies. There were certain other problems like the overvaluation of assets to an unreasonable level which led to high tariffs, unrealistically high receivables, bogus billing, etc. As opposed to this, the Delhi model ensured that the sale price of the three utilities was just based on the business valuation method. Further, the opening loss levels were correctly assessed by the DERC to a reasonable degree. Also, the new private discoms were given a clean opening balance sheet and the unserviceable liabilities were placed in the books of the holding company, a government entity. Most importantly, however, the government provided a transition support to the tune of Rs 3450 crore (US$ 460 million) to help the newly created private discoms to tide over the losses in the initial years.

So, what is required is a good model for privatisation may be on the lines of the Delhi model but with transition support to enable the new entity to tide over the initial cash losses. It is not that the central government is not aware of the need for privatisation of the distribution segment to save the power sector from ruin. The central government has itself proposed privatisation of the distribution utilities in the union territories (which are under the control of the central government) while announcing its spate of measures under the aegis of 'Atmanirbhar Bharat'. However, privatisation of discoms takes time and can even take up to 2 years to become operational, but more importantly requires political consensus at the state level, electricity being on the Concurrent List of the Constitution.

6.2 *Role of Regulatory Bodies*

The Indian electricity regulators could never reach the stature of their counterparts in the UK. In UK, the regulatory institution is strong and has a lot of resources at their command. This is not to say that there was no criticism about the regulators.[41]

[41] To give a few examples, in the RPI-X regulation (mentioned in par 3.12), there were allegations that the value of X has been made favourable to the industry which allowed them to have excessive profits. Another criticism against the regulator was that the Pool was replaced by the NETA without any detailed analysis.

Several actions of the regulators were found to be flawed but they were definitely head and shoulders above the Indian regulators, especially at the state level. Part of the problem was on account of the constitutional provision in India. While there was a single regulator for the UK, in India, power being a concurrent subject and distribution being a function of the states, there is a separate regulatory commission in each state apart from a central regulator. Trivial as it may sound, the truth is that the state governments have to ensure a fair selection of regulators, keep the selection process above politics, maintain distance from the regulators and not interfere in their jurisdiction and create an environment where regulatory awards are implemented and not side stepped. The central government made an attempt to control the selection of regulators wherein a single composite committee was proposed for all regulators. This was mentioned in the draft Electricity Act (Amendment) Bill 2020 which was circulated, for comments in April 2020. As expected, the states have not found this to be favourable and have accused the central government of trying to interfere in the states' domain. What will be the final shape of the amendment bill, only time will tell.

6.3 Creation of Wholesale and Retail Markets

We finally come to the last recommendation that is creation of a wholesale and retail market in India, similar to what exists in the UK. However, let it be said upfront that this recommendation is for the future and cannot be implemented right away. The government made an attempt to introduce retail competition when it inserted the concept of 'content and carriage' in the Electricity Act (Amendment) Bill 2014. This provision never saw the light of day since it was forcefully opposed by the states. In the later amendment bill introduced in 2020, this clause of 'content and carriage' has been dropped altogether. This, however, is a step in the right direction, at least as of now, since 90% of the power generated is still linked to power purchase agreements (PPAs) where tariffs are determined on a cost-plus basis. Therefore, all retailers will face the same legacy costs of power purchase, and since power purchase accounts for about 80% of the cost of supply, there can be no competition and consumers will have nothing to differentiate from one retailer to another, unless and until retailers are given the freedom to source power and align their power procurement portfolio according to the market dynamics and changing consumer mix. In order to have an effective competition in retail, the existence of a wholesale market is imperative. This is only possible when we are able to dissolve the existing long-term PPAs and create deeper power markets allowing economic dispatch and flexible trades. This is a mammoth task which requires consultation pan India, and the cooperation of the state governments is required since they or their successor public discoms are the signatories to the PPAs.[42]

There is yet another reason why retail competition cannot be introduced right now and that is because of the existing cross-subsidies. A certain section of consumers, like the commercial and industrial sector, pays a tariff much higher than the cost of supply. This extra revenue is used to provide subsidised power to another class of consumers, such as agriculture and low end domestic, who pay below the cost of supply. If retail competition is to be introduced, management of this cross-subsidy program will become onerous unless the government steps in and provides more subsidy to the targeted consumers. All the state governments, put together, were already providing subsidy to the extent of Rs. 85,000 crore in 2017–18 (PFC 2017–18). Any further increase will put the state governments in severe financial pressure. It would be pertinent to add that in the UK, there was no concept of cross-subsidy, and therefore, introduction of retail competition could take place with ease. In 1990, retail competition was introduced for big consumers (1 MW and above), and in 1994, the limit was lowered to 100 KW. In 1998, all consumers, no matter how small, were given this privilege. Another major advantage that UK had when it comes to introduction of retail competition is that their commercial losses were very low. Therefore, they did not have to grapple with the problem of who is going to finance these losses, whether it shall be the retailers or the owner of the wires business.

6.4 Conclusion

In conclusion, it can be said that the Indian power sector restructuring exercise can at best be called 'work in progress' despite the fact that EA 2003 was enacted about 17 years ago. The restructuring exercise has not created markets, so competition which was one of the basic tenets of EA 2003 remains unfulfilled. Not only that, the regulatory commissions which are supposed to be the pillars in any reform exercise remain weak and stunted. Much of the blame for the plight of the regulatory commissions lies squarely at the doorsteps of the government. The government never wanted to create institutions of stature because they were apprehensive that they would lose control over the sector. Be that as it may, as things stand today, privatisation of distribution is the key and the only salvation available to us. Further, late as it may be, strengthening our regulatory institutions is something we cannot afford to delay any further. The final key, of course, is creation of markets, both and the generation and retail end. These markets will, however, have to be created simultaneously but this course of action should be pursued only after the power sector matures in India, and we get rid of the regime of cross-subsidies and also lower our commercial losses.

[42]The CERC had floated a consultation paper entitled 'Market-Based Economic Dispatch of Electricity' in December 2018 for creation of capacity markets by redesigning the day-ahead market in India.

References

Ahluwalia, S. (2000). Power sector reforms: A review of the process and an evaluation of the Outcomes', refereed paper for the NCAER-ADB supported project on economic reforms.

D'Sa, A., Murthy, K. V. N., & Reddy, A. K. N. (1999). Indian power sector liberalisation: An overview. *Economic and Political Weekly, 34*(20), 1427–1434.

De Oliveira, T. (2004). Regulatory performance analysis case study. *Energy Policy, 32,* 1261–1276.

Dubash, N. K. (2002). The changing global context of electricity reforms. In N. K. Dubash (Ed.), *Power politics*. Washington DC: World Resources Institute.

Dubash, N. K., & Singh, D. (2005). Of rocks and hard places. *Economic and Political Weekly, 40*(50), 5249–5259.

Dubash, N. K., & Rajan, S. C. (2001). Power politics-process of power sector reform in India. *Economic and Political Weekly, 36*(35), 3367–3390.

Green, R., & Newbery, D. M. (1992). Competition in the British electricity spot market. *Journal of Political Economy, 100*(5), 929–953.

Green, R., & McDaniel, T. (1998). Competition in electricity supply: Will 1998 be worth it? *Fiscal Studies, 19,* 273–293.

Green, R. (1999). Draining the pool: The reform in electricity trading in England and Wales. *Energy Policy, 29,* 515–525.

Green, R. (2005). Electricity and markets. *Oxford Review of Economic Policy, 21*(1), 67–87.

Hunt, S., & Shutteworth, G. (1996). *Competition and Choice in Electricity*. New York: Wiley.

Joskow, P. (1997). Restructuring, competition and regulatory reform in the US electricity industry. *Journal of Economic Perspectives, 11*(3), 119–138.

Newbury, D. M. (1998). The regulators review of the english electricity pool. *Utilities Policy, 7*(3), 129–141.

Newbury, D. M. (2004). *Issues and options for restructuring electricity supply industries*. Working Paper No. 0210, University of Cambridge.

Newbury, D. M., & Pollitt, M. G. (1997). The restructuring and privatisation of the CEGB-was it worth it. *Journal of Industrial Economics, 45*(3), 269–303.

Pillai, S. M. C., & Krishanmurthy, R. (1997). Problems and prospects of privatisation and regulation in India's power Sector. *Energy for Sustainable Development, 3*(6), 67–76.

Power Finance Corporation. (2017–18). Report on Performance of State Power Utilities.

Purakayastha, P. (1993). New power policy- bankrupting the power sector. *Economic and Political Weekly, 28*(15), 955–957.

Rao, S. L. (2002). The political economy of power. *Economic and Political Weekly, 37*(33), 3433–3444.

Reddy, A. K. N. (2000). *2000, June 15*. The Hindu: Paying for power.

Reddy, A. K. N., & D'Sa, A. (1995). The enron and other similar deals vs the new energy paradigm. *Economic and Political Weekly, 30*(24), 1441–1448.

Sant, G., & Dixit, S. (1996). Beneficiaries of irrigation pump subsidy and impact of tariff hike. *Economic and Political Weekly*, 3315–3322.

Shuttleworth, G. (1999): The electricity industry 1997–98, (Chapter 2). In *Regulatory review*.

Surrey, J. (Ed.). (1996). *The British electricity experiment*. London: Earthscan Publications Ltd.

Thomas, S. (1996). *The politicization of the british electricity experiment: Privatization, the record, the issues, the lessons*. London: Earthscans Publications Limited.

Thomas, S. (2005). British experience of electricity liberalisation—A model for India. *Economic and Political Weekly, 40*(50), 5260–5268.

Wright, P., & Thomas, S. (2001). Empirical reflections on the liberalisation of the UK electrical supply industry. *Economia delle Foti di Energia e dell Ambiente, 2,* 7–24.

Embeddedness of Economic Reforms in Regional Political Climate: A Case of Delayed Reforms in Bihar's Electricity Sector

Md Zakaria Siddiqui

1 Introduction

More often than not most experts and researchers have focused on national-level administrative and legal institutions proposed by the centre as the main determinant of changes in electricity sector. In hind sight it is obvious that not all states implemented the nationally proposed reform policies in the same spirit and speed. Some states have had very different approaches for their electricity sector and often resisted policies promoted by central government. However, some states differed significantly in the pace of implementation of national-level policies. One of the key states that stands out in resisting implementation of electricity sector reforms is Kerala. It did not go for outright unbundling of vertically integrated Kerala State Electricity Board on the basis of functional lines, i.e. generation, transmission and distribution. On the other hand, Bihar implemented such policies at a much later stage with its own tinkering. The main focus of this chapter is to highlight the importance of regional political climate of Bihar in implementation of electricity reforms.

Bihar has consistently ranked at the bottom for most social and economic indicators. So much so that the first two letters of "BIMARU" states represent Bihar to designate the usual suspects in the list of underdeveloped states of India. Bihar's development outcomes can only be compared to countries of Sub-Saharan Africa. Not surprisingly, Bihar ranks among the countries with the lowest per capita electricity consumption (311 units) in the World and is comparable to countries of Sub-Saharan Africa such as Ghana (341 units). Despite the state's leading role in initiating pro-democracy political movement during the 'emergency' of mid-1970s and being known for having a politically argumentative mass, governments have never been

Md. Z. Siddiqui (✉)
Gulati Institute of Finance and Taxation, Chavadimukku, Sreekaryam, Thiruvananthapuram, Kerala, India
e-mail: zak.siddiqui@gift.res.in

P. Dasgupta et al. (eds.), *Sustainable Development Insights from India*,
India Studies in Business and Economics,
https://doi.org/10.1007/978-981-33-4830-1_8

punished for lacking in accountability. Dismal performance of governments in provision of basic services like education, health and basic energy needs has hardly translated into the mainstream political discussions. Mundle et al. (2016) use composite index of several socio-economic indicators for interstate comparison ranking Bihar among the worst performers in the case of infrastructure, social service, and law and order delivery.

Since the anti-emergency movement popularly known as '*Sampoorn Kranti*' (complete revolution), there is considerable increase in participation of the socially stratified 'lower caste' politicians. Under the mentorship of Jayparakash Naryan, the leading figure of anti-emergency movement, several new politicians from the lower castes emerged, each one vouching to be the carrier of the legacy of 'complete revolution'. Lalu Prasad Yadav and Nitish Kumar are the most noticeable among them.

2 The Political Context

During the period of 1990s–2005, every Indian state barring Bihar went through historically unprecedented economic transformation. Bihar's economy was largely stagnant during this period. For instance, India's per capita national income grew at the rate of 4% annually in real terms while Bihar's per capita state net domestic product annual growth during the same period was merely 1.6%. Growth of per capita income in Bihar was higher in both and post-Lalu era—between 1980 and 1991 it grew at 2.1% and in post 2005 period, i.e. between 2005 and 2017, it grew by an annual average of 6.2%. Thus, Bihar's political history can essentially be seen in three epochs in which Lalu's period appears as central.

By the first half of 2000s, most states had implemented nationally proposed policies of electricity sector reforms, i.e. unbundling of vertically integrated electricity boards and inception of a state level independent quasi-judicial body for regulation of electricity industry. These bodies, are usually named as State Regulatory Commission, are expected to act at arm's length from the respective state governments. However, Bihar's electricity sector continued to operate under a monolithic electricity board mode without any regulator. Nevertheless, an additional change that shook the electricity sector was the bifurcation of the state into two regions, i.e. Bihar and Jharkhand. It caused a major erosion in the revenue base of the state's electricity board as most of the high tariff paying industrial consumers of electricity were situated in Jharkhand. Additionally, it lost access to cheap sources of power as most generating capacities with captive coal mining were also in the region that became Jharkhand.

Notwithstanding, the stagnant economy during the 15-year rule of Mr Yadav, the state experienced steep social and political mobility of *Dalits* and backward classes. The opposing dynamic of economic vis-à-vis sociopolitical changes in the state tempted Jeffery Witsoe to title his book as *Democracy Against Development* (Witsoe, 2013). Interactions with intelligentsia of Bihar during the field work reveal that many hold the view that political and social churning during Lalu's regime is fundamental to enhanced economic growth that can be seen in present-day Bihar. In a leading researcher's language, 'Lalu was enabler and Nitish is the provider. Obviously, the enabler is critically important'. Thus, Lalu's intervening period of 15 years can be seen as a significant rupture in the contemporary political history of the state. The most remarkable thing about Lalu's period is the progressive decline of poverty rate despite near zero economic growth. Between 1993 and 2005, the years of National Sample Survey on Consumption Expenditure that roughly coincide with Lalu's regime, the poverty ratio of Bihar (including Jharkhand) declined by 14% points (from 54.5 to 41.5%), compared to a less than 8% point decline nationally and a less than 2% point decline in Odisha.

2.1 Pre-Lalu Period

The period prior to 1990 represents upper caste dominated political landscape with no perceptible change in fate for the lower rungs of the society. Almost every institution of governance and media had negligible participation of lower caste or religious minorities in the state. Successive governments ruled the state without any sense of accountability or responsibility towards masses of people living under shackles of poverty. The budgetary resources including the transfers from the central government were routinely misappropriated by official–politician nexus with impunity. This mass scale organized loot of the state resources often allocated in the name of anti-poverty programmes was never reported as corruption by media. The best that media did to chastise the state for slow or no progress in social indicators and poverty alleviation was to term it as inefficiency of state machinery. High officials were never held accountable for not ensuring the appropriate use of tax-payers' money either by court or media. More than half of the state's population (54%) lived under poverty even after more than 40 years of independence as per 1993–94 survey conducted by NSS.

2.2 Lalu's Regime

Given the historical experience of near zero developmental achievement in the state, Lalu Yadav knew well that delivering development to his constituency of voters, i.e. lower castes and Muslims will not be possible through the bureaucracy. If anything, the bureaucracy had demonstrated extreme efficiency in siphoning off the money that came in the name of development expenditure. Instead, trying to turn around the bureaucracy which was dominated by upper castes, Lalu made deliberate attempts to follow the policy of 'incapacitating the state' by weakening state institutions and limiting public expenditure in order to prevent the flow of state resources to the upper castes. Lalu, in fact, provided a formidable counter-slogan to Indira Gandhi's famous '*Garibi Hatao*' ('Eradicate poverty') with '*Bhurabal hatao*" ('Remove upper castes' where upper castes include Bhumihars, Rajputs, Brahmins and Lalas or Kayasthas) and '*Vikas nahin Samman chahiye*' ('Not development, we want dignity').

Lalu sought to dislodge upper caste bureaucrats from influential positions (a) through frequent transfers, (b) by placing lower caste bureaucrats in influential positions by promoting or transferring them prematurely and (c) by avoiding new recruitments to fill vacant positions. Thus, weakening of institutions of governance was an unavoidable side effect in the process of curtailing the upper caste domination. Lalu likewise remained unfriendly to even corporate interests to weaken upper caste hegemony. For example, mining lease of Tata Industries was not extended (Kale & Mazaheri, 2014).

Given Lalu's tactic of 'state incapacity by design', Bihar's electricity sector also decelerated. Electrification made no progress during this 15-year period. In fact, percentage of household electrification declined to 10% in 2001 from 12% in 1991. Thanks to lawlessness that prevailed as a result of weakening of police forces in the state, theft of electricity, distribution wires and transformers became rampant.

2.3 Post-Lalu Period

After fifteen years out of power, the surviving upper castes forged a coalition with other disempowered castes whose interests Lalu had failed to address. A new party named Janata Dal United—representing the left-behind disempowered castes and led by Nitish Kumar—came into power with the help of the upper caste Bhartya Janata Party (BJP). Upper castes, in 2005, represented by BJP, for the first time in history of Bihar joined a government as secondary partner in power-sharing coalition.

Bihar's economic fate including electricity sector improved in post-2005 as Mr. Lalu lost the election to Mr. Nitish Kumar. In general, Bihar began to show signs of improved delivery of public services. Frequency of serious crimes also declined (Mukherji & Mukherji, 2012).

The political mobilization or empowerment of lower castes and poor masses during Lalu's period made it impossible for Kumar's government and bureaucracy to survive without addressing issues that masses faced. Kumar's government initially focused on reviving schools and building roads and bridges. However, not all crimes fell, as crime against women and Dalits rose with little state response (Gupta, 2010).

3 Changes in Electricity Sector Since 2005

Bihar's condition began to recoup from long slumber in governance after governor's rule was implemented due to indecisive election result in early 2005. Bihar Electricity Regulatory Commission (BERC) was established during the governor's rule in 2005. It issued its first tariff order for the financial year 2006–07. However, it took some

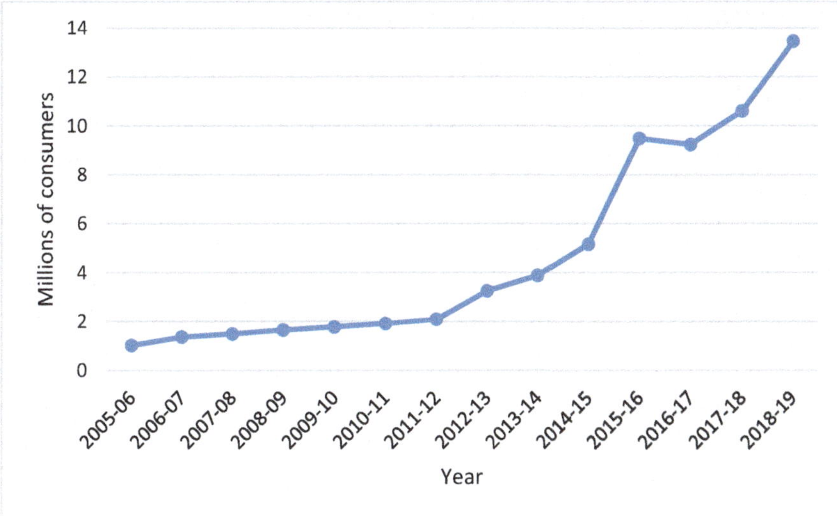

Fig. 1 Growth in number of domestic consumers 2005–06 to 2018–19. *Source* Various Tariff Orders of BERC

time for the sector as a whole to wake up. The standardized functional unbundling of Bihar State Electricity Board has not been done till 2012.

The government continued to neglect the electricity sector until widespread protests across the state were in full swing in 2011. Press reports from 2011 indicate that people agitated by blocking roads and destroying properties of electricity board throughout the state. For example, a group of more than 300 women laid siege to the BSEB General Manager's office in Bhagalpur during March 2011. This siege took a violent shape as people were enraged over the non-response of the authorities. The District Magistrate and Superintendent of Police narrowly escaped from being lynched by a mob. Such protests had become increasingly common in district towns across the state by the end of 2011. The severity of the crisis can be gauged from the fact that Bhagalpur was supplied only 1–7 MWs of electricity during March 2011 against a peak demand about 60 MW.

Owing to these protests, the Chief Minister made a commitment to fix the dismal performance in supply of and access to electricity in his Independence Day speech at Gandhi Maidan in Patna in 2012, failing which, he said, he will not seek re-election in forthcoming assembly election in 2015. Notably, BSEB was unbundled within less than two months.

3.1 Expansion of Network and Consumers

Figure 1 illustrates the rapid expansion of electrification in Bihar. The growth in domestic consumers since 2005–06 has been phenomenal. It went from one million in 2005–06 to more than 13 million in 2018–19. Major boost to new connections came in 2012. Village-level electrification was accomplished by November of 2018. Bihar continues to be a predominantly rural state. Even in 2011, about 89% of Bihar's 104 million population lived in rural areas (Census, 2011).

Despite improved access to electricity, as mentioned earlier, per capita consumption of electricity in Bihar is the lowest (311 units) among Indian states. Gujarat has the highest per capita electricity consumption among major Indian states at 2378 units nearly eight times that of Bihar. Even this low average is unevenly distributed across the rural–urban areas and districts within the state. For instance, district of Patna's per capita electricity consumption (about 800 units in 2019–20) is eight times higher than that of Araria. This low average consumption is despite the near universal electrification of households in the state. Such low consumption may follow from low-supply–low-demand dynamics. Given that power supply has remained highly unreliable for sufficiently long in the past, people have adapted to take power as state provided luxury, availability of which is as good as random except when political fates are to be decided. Life is organized around alternative sources of energy in which electricity is just one additional resource which should be utilized when available but life can go on uninterrupted even without it. For example, peak demand for power in Bihar was 6 Giga Watts (GW) in the month of August 2020 while for West Bengal which has very similar level of population, it was 8.5 GW. Similarly, Madhya Pradesh with very similar levels of economic development and significantly less population than Bihar had 10 GW peak demand for same month.

However, another serious dimension of energy deprivation which has significant impact on gender equity is access to clean cooking facilities. Bihar is still far from attaining the goal of universal access on this front. About 44% of rural household have access to some form of clean cooking facility as per National Sample Survey data collected during second half of 2018 (NSS 76th Round for Drinking Water, Sanitation, Hygiene and Housing Condition). The access to clean cooking in urban areas, however, is 91%. Again these averages mask the significant socio-economic gradation in prevalence of access to clean cooking. In relative scale, however, Bihar is significantly better in terms of making improvements in access to clean cooking. For example, in Odisha and West Bengal, 24% of the population have access to clean cooking in 2018. These access rates need careful interpretation as was highlighted earlier in case of electricity. Moreover, high rates of access in clean cooking facility do not necessarily translate into actual usage due to expensive refilling of the LPG bottles.

Rural Bihar can make immense economic and ecological gains by promoting innovative renewable energy industry. This may well be a major source for creating new jobs and entrepreneurship abilities for remote corners of the state. Such policies can potentially combat climate change and be pro-poor at the same time. Conventionally, poverty alleviation programmes are seen as having a trade-off with climate change (Bazilian et. al., 2011). However, accumulated learning from research indicates that there are synergies in policies for combating problems of human development, energy security and climate change (Haines et al., 2007; Biswas et al., 2001). However, political will for harnessing such synergies is absent. High-level officials often doubted the ability of state in harnessing renewable energy on account of high population density and intense use of land for agriculture.

Seeing low demand for new connections within electrified villages, Mr. Kumar announced electricity connection with zero upfront charges in November 2015 to every household to reach the goal of universal access by November 2017. Earlier only to below poverty line (BPL), households were eligible for free connection while non-BPL households had to pay Rs 1500 for connection.

3.2 *Adverse Effects of Bifurcation of Electricity Sector Assets*

A significant portion of erstwhile Bihar State Electricity Board's (BSEB) assets went to Jharkhand State Electricity Board in 2001 resulting division of state. Installed generating capacity Bihar reduced by 70%—from 2000 MW to less than 600. Bifurcation also impacted consumer mix of BSEB resulting in substantial loss of revenue paying industrial consumers. Proportion of industrial demand in the state reduced from 48 to 25%. A retired official with significant experience in power sector hinted that the loss of industrial consumers will have sustained adverse effect on financial prospect of electricity sector in Bihar. Loss of generation capacity may not be that significant as liberalized generation sub-sector is quite competitive now, leading to cheap availability of power for the state from third parties.

3.3 *Critical Role of the Holding Company After Unbundling*

Vertically integrated BSEB was unbundled on functional line in November 2012. The entire asset base of BSEB was divided into five companies, namely.

1	Bihar State Power (Holding) Co. Ltd. (BSPHCL)
2	Bihar State Power Generation Co. Ltd. (BSPGCL)
3	Bihar State Power Transmission Co. Ltd. (BSPTCL)
4	North Bihar Power Distribution Co. Ltd. (NBPDCL)
5	South Bihar Power Distribution Co. Ltd. (SBPDCL)

These five companies included one generation, one transmission and two distribution companies representing south and north Bihar. These companies were subsidiaries of the fifth company, i.e. Bihar State Power (Holding) Co. Ltd. All these de jure changes on paper hardly made any difference for a common man walking through the Bidyut Bhavan (literally meaning Electricity Building) in Patna as every organization pertaining to electricity sector including the BERC still operates from Bidyut Bhavan in Patna where BSEB was located. A remarkable difference in case of electricity sector unbundling in Bihar was the idea of a holding company. Having a parent or holding company meant that hierarchy needed to ensure coordination, sharing of capabilities and human resources across the companies remained intact despite the unbundling. Often same individuals were responsible for two Discoms at similar levels of hierarchy. For example, same person was serving as General Manager of Revenue in both Discoms. It was also common to see that individuals from different organization consulted each other for information or expert advice. For example, a senior Transco official dealt with power purchase planning at regular basis for two Discoms due to his experience of having worked with independent generators. The executive head of Bihar State Power (Holding) company has the authority to transfer employees across the organization. In many cases, contracts for other organizations are routed through Bihar State Power (Holding) company. Thus, separation of entities has increased the flow of information due to regulatory process but at the same time these companies could share their resources due to the presence of a glue, i.e. parent or holding company.

As a result of functional unbundling, Bihar's electricity sector like many other states potentially eliminated major shortcomings which were hallmark of the BESB era. Accounting and regulatory norms made it difficult for the sector to manipulate information regarding cost components and consumption data for which all state electricity boards are infamously remembered. However, one distinctive feature of Bihar's unbundling process was the idea of having a holding company. It helped the state in mitigating potential increase in transaction costs that usually arise when different organizations have to coordinate and cooperate within a value chain as is the case under post-unbundling scenario.

3.4 Surge in Demand for and Supply of Power

Notwithstanding the low peak demand which was highlighted earlier, power shortage was rampant till 2011. However, in post-2011, frequency of power shortage has reduced significantly both at capacity as well as at energy level. The cheap power available from short-term market or power exchange has enabled Bihar to purchase enough power. However, reliability of network particularly at distribution end is still a serious bottleneck in smooth delivery of power.

Figures 2 and 3 reveal that the state has experienced a significant surge in terms of peak capacity as well as total energy demand particularly since 2012. More importantly, there is an increased ability of the state in satisfying the fast-growing demand for power. Both figures show consistent decline in the amount of unmet demand with time and eventually to negligible levels. The increase in demand for power is

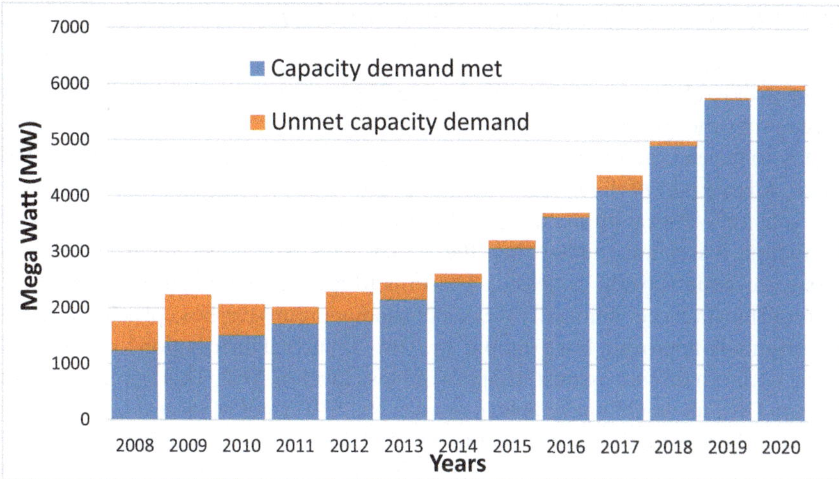

Fig. 2 Capacity demand (met + unmet) during April–August (MW). *Source* Calculated from Monthly Reports on Power Supply Position; https://www.cea.nic.in/monthlyarchive.html

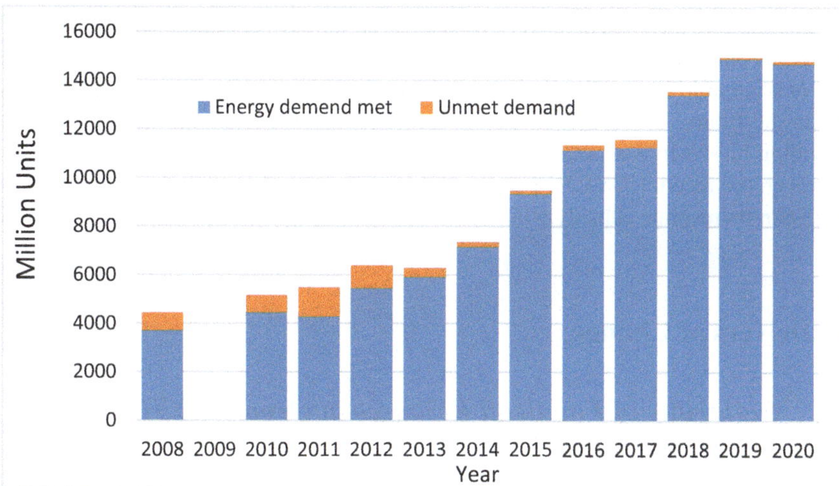

Fig. 3 Energy units demanded (met + unmet) during April–August (Million Units). *Source* Calculated from Monthly Reports archive on Power supply situation. https://www.cea.nic.in/monthlyarchive.html

primarily on account of growth of new domestic consumers since 2012 as result of fast paced electrification process as shown in Fig. 1. Despite the phenomenal growth for the demand for power in recent past, Bihar's electricity consumption continues to remain far below the global standard as has been highlighted earlier.

3.5 Subsidies to Retain Domestic Consumers

The growth in electricity consumption since 2012 was largely possible due to huge revenue subsidies from the state government. For example, in year 2014–15, revenue subsidy to the electricity sector—dubbed as 'resource gap grant'—totalled Rs. 2891 crores. A large part of these costs cannot be recovered through the BERC-approved tariff scheme—even if billing and collection efficiency is 100%—because approved distribution losses are smaller than the actual level. The government, through its massive revenue subsidy, is helping Discoms to recover more than these losses so that retail tariffs for economically weaker consumer groups can be kept at lower levels than originally approved. For example, in 2014–15, actual distribution loss was 38% for the northern discom against its approved loss level of 21%. This implied that the northern Discom would not be able to recover Rs. 519 crores of its cost because 17% of its distribution loss was not considered to be part of covered costs when BERC issued retail tariff. However, the government's subsidy to the northern Discom was more than enough to compensate for this revenue loss. In fact, the northern company received close to Rs. 700 crores in excess of its losses which allowed it to keep retail tariffs at lower levels than were specified by BERC.

During various interviews with high-level executives in power sector, it was evident that any increase in tariffs was seen as an unfeasible option because it might hinder the current momentum towards universalization of access to electricity. Once Discoms are able to establish their credibility of reliable supply of power, tariffs may rise in the future. Therefore, Discoms' initial focus on expanding the network and providing hassle-free experience to new consumers has nearly been accomplished. However, the recent COVID-19-induced economic crisis has forced the government to sustain its revenue subsidy which is to the tune of Rs. 3500 crores.

4 Drivers of Change

4.1 Availability of Financial Resource at Opportune Time

Bihar's electricity sector is fortunate enough to find necessary financial resources at an opportune moment when political class was compelled to address the sector. Interestingly, budgetary transfers from the central government under different heads complemented the needs of the sector appropriately. The power sector needed investment at three levels, i.e. expansion of rural distribution network, metering and reinforcement of urban distribution network and most importantly strengthening of the transmission network to support the increased demand for power due to new connections. Financial resources for the first two levels of investment came from central transfers under the Rajiv Gandhi Grameen Vidyutikaran Yojana (RGGVY) or its later avatar Deendayal Upadhyaya Gram Jyoti Yojana (DDUGJY) and the Accelerated Power Development Programme (APDP) and its later avatars such as Ujwal

DISCOM Assurance Yojana (UDAY). In other words, there was sufficient fund to expand and strengthen the distribution sector. Thus, it was not surprising to achieve massive growth number of consumers.

However, a significant expansion of distribution sector cannot sustain on its own. It needs complementary transmission capacity to evacuate sufficient amount of electricity from generating stations to serve the increased demand for power. However, there was no central sector budget for strengthening the transmission system. Several states in India face similar limitations. Many states achieved universal access to electricity in a fairly short period of time due to funds available under the programme but failed to make complementary investment in transmission network to serve the increased demand for power in a reliable manner. Additionally, Bihar traditionally struggled in spending even when financial resources were available. However, owing to the recent recruitment drive and the organizational restructuring of Discoms, the capacity to spend public resources has gone up significantly for at least the electricity sector. Incidentally, Bihar is a big beneficiary of the Backward Regions Grant Fund (BRGF). A large chunk of the BRGF fund was invested in transmission network which went a long way in supplementing availability and reliability of power in the state. Therefore, the recent success of electricity sector can largely be attributed to simultaneity in availability of investment funds in all sub-sectors of the industry.

Bihar's total entitlement for 12th five-year plan (2012–17) under the BRGF was Rs 12,000 crores. 70% of the entire BRGF money of Rs 8308.67 crores was earmarked for the electricity sector in Bihar. Even before the Fifth Plan period, the money available under Rashtriya Sam Vikas Yojana (RSVY) of the centre, a previous avatar of the BRGF scheme, was allocated to Bihar's electricity sector especially the transmission sub-sector.

Thus, due to the availability of the BRGF money at an opportune time, all subsectors could complement one another to improve the delivery of electricity services in Bihar. The cheap availability of power in short-term market also helped Discoms a great deal in procuring much-needed power especially after loss of installed capacity due to bifurcation of the state.

4.2 Organizational Changes

Availability of financial resources is just one part of the story. History of public sector procurement and human resource hiring in Bihar is marred with allegations of corruptions and legal disputes. Given the track record of the state, it was quite unlikely that such a massive spending programme will progress flawlessly. The cumbersome tendering process and limited availability of human resource was a major roadblock. These limitations could have turned the whole reform agenda into a fiasco. Restricted ability of public sector to spend money is a generic problem in the state. During first half 2014, two calls for competitive bidding of electrification project failed in attracting sufficient interest on account of restrictive eligibility conditions.

In a senior bureaucrat's view, it is best for an independent agency to execute the tendering process. This is because there is a genuine anxiety about corruption allegations among employees of the relevant organizations while handling the tendering process. This anxiety is based on fairly long history of legal disputes in public sector procurement processes in the state.

The leadership in Bihar State Power (Holding) company decided to change the rules of the game. As the first step, they were interested in discovering the reason behind lack of bidders' interest in rural electrification contracts. In an informal discussion, potential bidders revealed that certain provisions of eligibility criteria acted as entry barrier for them. Thus, these criteria were amended and necessary clearance of these amended provisions was sought from the funding agency, i.e. Rural Electrification Corporation. One of the prerequisites for technical eligibility that restricted many potential bidders from participating in the bidding process was experience of having dealt with at least 50% of BOQ (bill of quantities) of current bidding. This prerequisite was amended to include minimum work experience of the contractor in the relevant sector. Further, provisions for incentives and penalties were introduced to ensure execution of work in time-bound manner. To ensure transparency and to pre-empt legal disputes, bids were opened (both technical and financial) within three days of the closure of the call under the video surveillance. This allowed non-winners to see the details of the winning bids for their own satisfaction. The REC cooperated by releasing the money on time. Engineers of Discoms routinely inspected the progress of rural electrification for each contractor. It was a rare occasion for a tendering process to be accomplished without any legal dispute in Bihar.

Another perceptible change was in the area human resource management and augmentation. Engineers have traditionally managed the electricity sector. This is true for most states in India. In 2014 recruitment drive, however, a significant number of professionals without engineering backgrounds were brought in at high-level positions.

Graduate Aptitude Test in Engineering (GATE) score was used instead of organizing an in-house examination to recruit engineers. This was a smart move because it reduced the cost of hiring along with increased transparency. Again, it avoided much speculated legal haggling regarding legitimacy of examination process for which bureaucrats in Patna are infamous.

Additionally, the organizational hierarchy was restructured on functional lines. The organizational hierarchy in BSEB ran purely on the basis of years of experience without any regard to specialization in handling of any particular sub-sector. For example, an engineer who worked mostly in transmission sector could get posted in distribution sub-sector because his/her promotion deems him for a position that is available only in that sector.

The new organizational hierarchy now operates strictly along the well-identified functional lines, i.e. operation and maintenance, revenue and projects. In the pre-2014 period, considerable experience in functional lines were not seen as essential criteria for the purpose of filling up senior-level positions. As a result of this, fixing responsibilities on individuals became difficult. Further, in post-2014 era, with increased number of professionals due to new recruitments and clarity in roles and responsibilities of each staff member, sector's capacity to spend money on projects has increased manifold.

4.3 Rural Revenue Franchisees

The Rural Revenue Franchisees (RRF) model is a step away from the standardized national model formulated by Ministry of Power at the Centre. In Bihar, RRFs are compensated for each activity at predetermined rates while in other states, the standard practice is to compensate RRFs on the basis of overall collection efficiency. During 2016, RRFs earned Rs 4.50 for every additional metre reading, Rs 1.50 for every additional delivery of bill, and finally they earned 3% of every bill amount they could successfully collect. About 3,500 RRFs were operating to cover nearly 51 lakh rural consumers of the state during 2016. This minor change in rules of engagement for RRFs in Bihar turned it into a backbone of rural revenue collection. This may have been on account of the reduced revenue risk of RRFs in Bihar resulting from fixation of piece rate for each activity in the process of billing and collection. In most states, RRFs are either non-functional or dysfunctional.

4.4 Coordination Between Political and Executive Leadership

Top executives, leading the electricity sector since mid-2014, are award winning Indian Administrative Officers from Bihar cadre Mr Prataya Amrit and Mr R. Lakshmanan. They successfully demonstrated their abilities in improving bridges and road sector of Bihar before this. Transfer of these officers to the electricity sector revealed the seriousness of government's commitment to deal with the electricity sector before the assembly election in 2015. The government wanted to see similar improvements in the electricity sector as well.

These officials joined the electricity sector in mid-2014. They faced a strict time constraint, i.e. a little more than one years' time to turn things around. Mr Pratya Amrit admitted in his discussion that he had to deliver the expected outcome before the state elections which was due in November 2015. The first things he focused on were to improve delivery of electricity services in rural areas to fulfil the promise made by Nitish Kumar. Immediately after he took the charge of the sector, rural electrification contracts were awarded in speedy manner, details of which has already been discussed and 35,000 non-functional distribution transformers were replaced. Thankfully, momentum of reforms in electricity services did not die down with election victory of Nitish Kumar in November 2015. Thus, the political will to continue the reforms and concomitant support from bureaucracy has been a critical aspect of positive changes in Bihar's electricity sector.

5 Experiments with Distribution Franchising

Bihar experimented with three distribution franchisees (DF), namely in Muzaffarpur, Gaya and Bhagalpur. All the DFs were eventually abandoned by 2018. First distribution circle was under Northern region Discom (NBPDCL) while the remaining two are under Southern region Discom (SBPDCL). It is important to mention that experience with DFs in other parts of India was not very encouraging to start with. For example, operation of distribution franchises in cities of Madhya Pradesh, i.e., Ujjain, Gwalior, Sagar and Indore had already been suspended. Nagpur DF was also terminated. However, Maharashtra and Rajasthan have continued with DFs operating in some circles.

Under the standard model, DFs are not required to file for revenue requirements to the regulator because they operate under the licence of main distribution companies, i.e. they have same tariff as the Discom under whom they operate. The DF operates the distribution network and collects bills. It also has the authority to deal with stealing of electricity and pilferages. DF is expected to undertake capital expenditure (CAPEX) to create distribution assets in the distribution network but there is no stipulated amount.

The three franchisees in Bihar were contracted between end of 2013 and beginning of 2014. These franchisees were selected through competitive bidding floated by Bihar State Power (Holding) Company Ltd. The bidding process followed central Ministry of Power guidelines for appointing input urban franchise.

The experience of working with DFs was not different from experiences in other states. Discoms consistently failed in complying with regulatory requirements mandated under electricity Act 2003 pertaining to DFs operating under them. Discoms are required to produce details of capital expenditure by DFs and their asset creation plans to the regulator. However, Discoms failed to comply with this regulatory requirement because Discoms and DF could not mutually agree on CAPEX.

As per the information collected during visits, DFs did undertake capital expenditure but Discoms did not examine these CAPEX on time. According to a representative of a DF 'monitoring of Discom operated more like an auditing team rather than monitoring team'. Delayed inspection of CAPEX led to a number of issues that made it difficult for the Discom and DF to arrive at mutually agreed amount of CAPEX. For example, a transformer may have been implemented by DF but due to long gap between time of CAPEX and the inspection transformer may not be functional at the time of inspection either because it got stolen or became dysfunctional due to over loading. Delayed inspection also meant that monitoring cell was inspecting only a sample of all CAPEX undertaken by DF which obviously became a matter of controversy between the Discom and the DF. It was also found that availability of electricity in certain locations within a DF area was significantly lower particularly in neighbourhoods with poor records of socio-economic status. This was happening because DF deliberately avoided supplying 24X7 power in pockets with higher commercial and technical losses as these areas may not be as lucrative in terms of revenue.

Employees of DF, during discussions, did indicate towards such a strategy. On the contrary, Discoms have an incentive in supplying enough power to DF on priority basis because DFs for them act like a big consumer who is most likely to pay the bill. Another worth mentioning aspect is, DF areas were not receiving benefit in proportionate manner for which Discom was eligible. DFs were supposed to generate their own sources of finance for CAPEX. Upon further probing, with employees working in DF, it was revealed that DFs were not able to spend mandated amount for CAPEX as per DF agreement due to scarcity of staff and limited credibility in raising funds from the market. Thus, despite sufficient incentive for DFs to spend on CAPEX, they failed to do so due to their own limited capacity in human and financial resources. In summary, failure of DFs in most cases appears to be result of adverse selection.

6 Progress of Renewable Sources

Bureaucrats working in Bihar's energy sector at every level of hierarchy unanimously cited high population density and expensive land as major hurdle in tapping the renewable energy potential. Bihar Government has circulated a policy document 'policy for promotion of new and renewable energy sources 2017' envisioning expansion of renewable generation capacity in the state to 3433 MW. It is important to note that total grid connected renewable energy (RE) installed capacity was around 250 MW in 2017. So this is a highly ambitious target.

India's renewable energy potential is not evenly distributed across states of India. To motivate optimal utilization, available renewable potential across Indian States Central Electricity Regulatory Commission (CERC) instituted a market-based instrument, i.e., Renewable Energy Certificate (REC). This allows for separate trading of environmental attribute of energy produced from renewable sources. Thus, generators using renewable sources are free to sell their energy at general average cost/price of conventional power while the environmental attribute of renewable generation is converted into RECs which is equivalent to one kWh of energy from renewable sources. These RECs in turn can be traded in national-level energy exchange. Therefore, the utilities or Discoms operating in states with deficient renewable energy potential can buy these tradeable certificates from national exchange to fulfil their minimum renewable purchase obligation (RPO).

Price of REC's can vary between fixed floor and ceiling (forbearance) price by CERC. The 2022 target of 175 GW of renewable-based generation capacity was set by the Government of India in 2014—100 GW of solar and 60 GW of wind capacity. Though RPOs set by several state regulatory commissions remain way below the national target, Discoms have consistently failed in fulfilling them. Often small share of RECs on offer are sold at the floor price. For instance, in October 2016 less than 1% (19,000) of the total offered solar RECs (2.3 million) were traded. Trading of non-solar RECs has done little better. More than 2% (157,000) of total offered non-solar RECs (8.3 million) were traded. However, the situation has improved significantly since then with about 64% of the total solar RECs on offer (2.1 million) being traded

Table 1 RPO targets set by BERC for Discoms for different years

Year	Non-solar (%)	Solar (%)
2016–17	5	1.5
2017–19	5.5	2.25
2018–19	6	3.25
2019–20	6.75	4.75
2020–21	7.5	6.75
2021–22	9	8

Source various orders of BERC

in 2019. The corresponding number for non-solar RECs is 75% of the total on offer (6.2 million).

Enforcing RPOs was challenging initially because the penalty for non-compliance of any regulatory provision was only Rs one lakh which also applied to non-compliance of RPOs. For a Discom with turnover of Rs thousands of crores, a fine of Rs one lakh can hardly be a deterrent. Instead of complying with the RPO, Discoms preferred to pay the penalty. Finally, some SERCs including BERC changed the formula for penalty amount for non-compliance of RPO. It was calculated as product of quantum of non-compliance of RPO and to the forbearance (ceiling) price RECs (fixed by CERC). The penalty amount thus calculated was to go to dedicated RPO fund. BERC regulated that RPO fund can only be utilized for purchase of RECs or for providing evacuation facility for new renewable power projects in the state. The BERC has set the gradual increment in RPO target in the manner provided in Table 1.

Discoms in Bihar have been able to meet non-solar RPO with relative ease while they struggle to meet the RPO mandated from solar sources. In 2019, both Discoms achieved only one quarter of their total solar RPO target. In the latest tariff order, BERC has denied any further accumulation in solar RPO in case sufficient RECs are on offer at the national energy exchange. Given that only 64% of available solar RECs traded national energy exchange, Discoms in Bihar will have no option but to meet the solar RPOs through purchase of solar RECs in coming financial year.

Grid interactive rooftop solar panels are seen as yet another tool for promoting renewable energy in the state. However, it would require an upgradation in metering technology that can record withdrawls as well as injection of power to the grid from premises. Despite regulator's clear directive on this issue in 2016, not much has been achieved on this front by Discoms. The policy may well be the best-suited tool for promoting renewable energy in Bihar given the high population density and land prices.

7 Conclusion

The chapter demonstrates political context to delayed reforms in Bihar's electricity sector as a particular case. The purpose of this chapter is also to highlight that each state tinkered the national model of proposed reforms depending on their regional political context as has been demonstrated by Chatterjee (2017) and Dubash et el. (2018).

It is true that Lalu's period saw stagnation but it provided the much-needed empowerment to masses which was critical for establishing political accountability of the ruling elite. Although Lalu's ruling style of state incapacity by design punished the elite and the economy in general, it had a positive impact on poverty reduction and political empowerment of the poor. It would not be misplaced to concur that some of the gaps in the playing field between ruling elite and masses might have got levelled. Eruption of protests during 2011 and subsequent response by the government to bring perceptible change in electricity sector can be seen as a manifestation of empowerment of masses during Lalu's regime.

The impatience of people over dismal performance of electricity was a necessary condition for the initiation of reforms in the sector. However, its success critically depended on willingness of government to spend close of 70% of total BRGF money on electricity transmission network. Another factor that ensured that people were finally able to connect with grid was the policy of no upfront charges for connection. Rapid electrification of households in post-2012 period is in sharp contrast to dismal performance of electricity sector during pre-2005 era. The bureaucracy in Bihar is still largely dominated by upper castes. However, the new regulatory safeguards and lower caste mobilization have made it difficult for them to appropriate resources by way of corruption as was routine in pre-Lalu period.

The massive revenue subsidies have helped in addressing the lack of demand for new electricity connection. Policy wisdom is to sustain the subsidy till the demand stabilizes but get the infrastructure of billing and collection ready so that when charges are applied it can be effectively collected. Given the long history of very unreliable supply in the state, people have adapted to life where electricity is a luxury. Converting this compromise to a right to live with dignity is the real developmental challenge.

References

Biswas, K. W., Bryce, P., & Diesendorf, M. (2001). Model for empowering rural poor through renewable energy technologies in Bangladesh. *Environmental Science and Policy, 4,* 333–344.

Bazilian, M., Hobbs, B. F., Blyth, W., MacGill, I., & Howells, M. (2011). Interactions between energy security and climate change: A focus on developing countries. *Energy Policy, 39,* 3750–3756.

Haines, A., Smith, K. R., Anderson, D., Epstein, P. R., McMichael, A. J., Roberts, I., et al. (2007). Policies for accelerating access to clean energy, improving health, advancing development, and mitigating climate change. *The Lancet, 370*(9594), 1264–1281.

Mukherji, A., & Mukherji, A. (2012). *Bihar: What went wrong? And what changed?* Working Paper No. 12/107. National Institute of Public Finance, New Delhi.

Mundle, S., Chowdhury, S., & Sikdar, S. (2016). Governance performance of Indian states. *Economic and Political Weekly, 51*(36), 55–64.

Witsoe, J. (2013). *Democracy against development: Lower-caste politics and political modernity in postcolonial India*. University of Chicago Press.

Towards an Energy-Efficient Economy: Policy Measures by Government of India

Sangeeta Bansal and M. Rahul

1 Introduction

India, one of the largest and the fastest-growing economies of the world, is also the world's third-largest consumer of primary energy after China and the USA (BP, 2019). Between 2012–13 and 2019–20, India's GDP has grown at an average rate of 6.6% (Fig. 1). India's share in global energy consumption has reached 5.8% in 2018. With economic growth, the energy consumption is expected to increase manifold in future. The increase in energy consumption led to a 7% increase in carbon emissions in 2018, and India accounted for around 7% of global CO_2 emissions (BP, 2019). Energy plays a pivotal role in the social and economic development of the country and is necessary to meet the Sustainable Development Goals ranging from poverty alleviation to bridging the gender gap. Its increased consumption, however, has a deteriorating effect on the environment. Energy consumption leads to emissions such as nitrogen dioxide and sulphur dioxide causing air pollution and contributing to greenhouse gas emissions. Six out of the ten most polluted cities in the world are in India (IQ-Air, 2019). Saraswat and Bansal (2020) find that around 10 or 7 years of life expectancy would be gained if PM2.5 levels reached WHO standards or national standards, respectively.

Views are personal and do not represent those of the organisation that the author belongs to.

S. Bansal (✉)
Centre for International Trade and Development, School of International Studies, Jawaharlal Nehru University, New Delhi, India
e-mail: sangeeta.bansal7@gmail.com

M. Rahul
Indian Economic Service, Department of Economic Affairs, Ministry of Finance, New Delhi, India
e-mail: rahulmeco@gmail.com

P. Dasgupta et al. (eds.), *Sustainable Development Insights from India*,
India Studies in Business and Economics,
https://doi.org/10.1007/978-981-33-4830-1_9

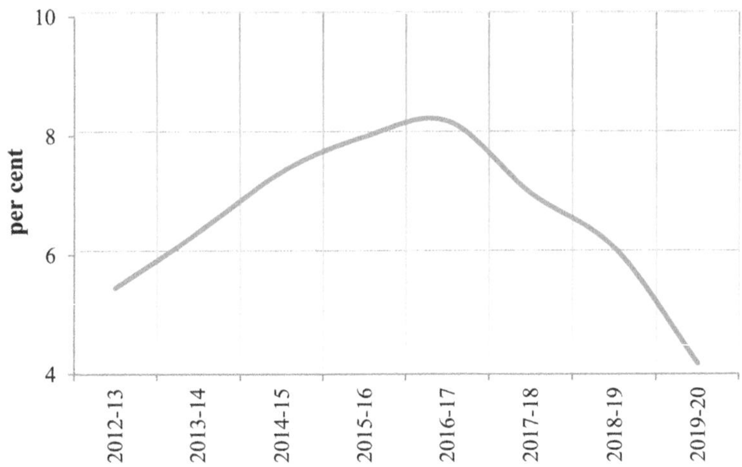

Fig. 1 India's annual GDP (at constant prices, 2011–12 series) growth rate. *Source* Ministry of Statistics and Programme Implementation, Government of India (MOSPI)

India's commitments at the United Nations on climate change require the country to reduce its emission intensity of GDP by 33–35% of its level in 2005 levels by 2030 (Government of India, 2015). One avenue that is likely to deliver significant gains in achieving the conflicting objectives of economic prosperity and protecting the environment is using energy more efficiently. Greater energy efficiency can lead to lower emissions resulting from energy production and use, deliver cost benefits and ensure energy security with minimum effect on the competitiveness of industries and the economy. Energy efficiency has been called "the first fuel" (IEA, 2020)—each unit of energy saved through its efficient usage is akin to a unit generated without the externalities that energy production entails.

Per capita primary energy consumption has been increasing in India over the years, as is expected for a fast developing economy, but its level remains far below that of the USA and China (Fig. 2). In 2018, USA's per capita primary energy consumption was around 12 times that of India. China's was around 4 times that of India's.

India's energy intensity has been continually falling (Fig. 3). Changing sectoral composition of the economy towards a larger share of the services sector and technological development has contributed to this decline. Energy efficiency in India, however, remains far below the potential and has substantial opportunities for improvement. Evaluating 25 of the top energy-consuming countries in the world across 36 different policy and performance metrics spread over four categories: buildings, industry, transportation, and overall national energy efficiency progress, International Energy Efficiency Scorecard find India's rank to be 15 (American Council for an Energy-Efficient Economy, 2018). Germany and Italy are tied for the first place. To realise this potential, the Government of India has adopted various policy measures that aim at greater energy efficiency in its industries and final products. In terms of the sectoral composition of India's final energy consumption, Industry

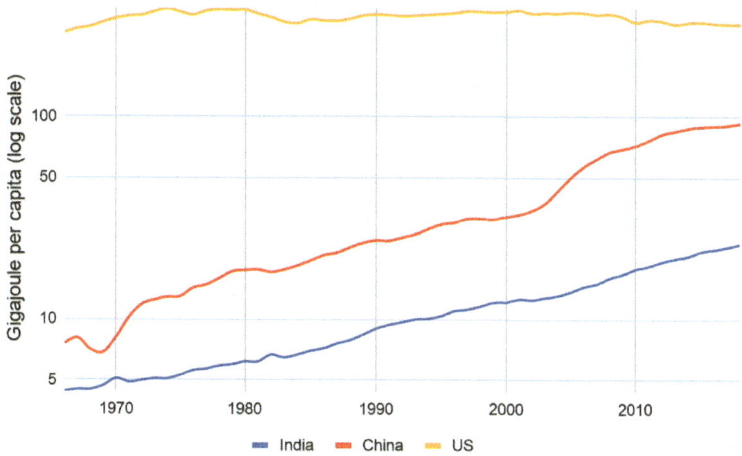

Fig. 2 Per capita primary energy consumption. *Source* BP (2019)

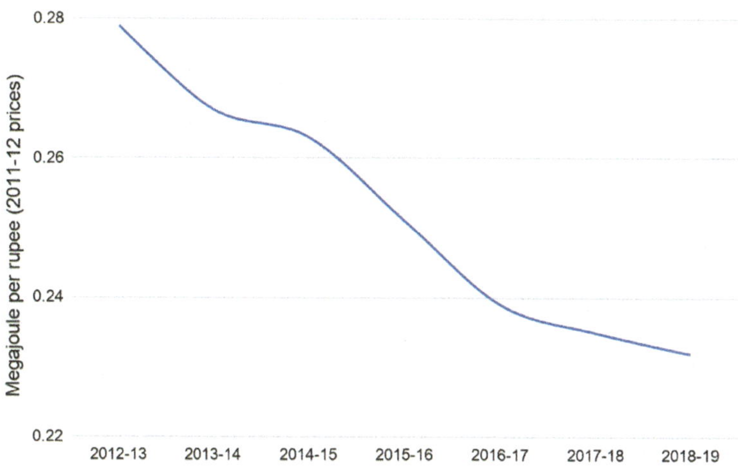

Fig. 3 India's energy intensity. *Source* MOSPI (2020)

accounts for around 56%, transport accounts for around 10%, and residential sector accounts for around 9% (Fig. 4). These three sectors continue to be the dominant users of energy and therefore hold the potential for major energy efficiency improvements. This chapter aims at studying the Government of India's energy efficiency policies and assesses their performance in terms of leading the economy towards a more energy-efficient India.

The rest of the chapter is organised as follows. The next section discusses the economics of energy efficiency and various policy instruments that can be used to enhance it. While Sect. 3 describes various policy instruments adopted by India, Sect. 4 evaluates their performance. Finally, Sect. 5 contains concluding remarks.

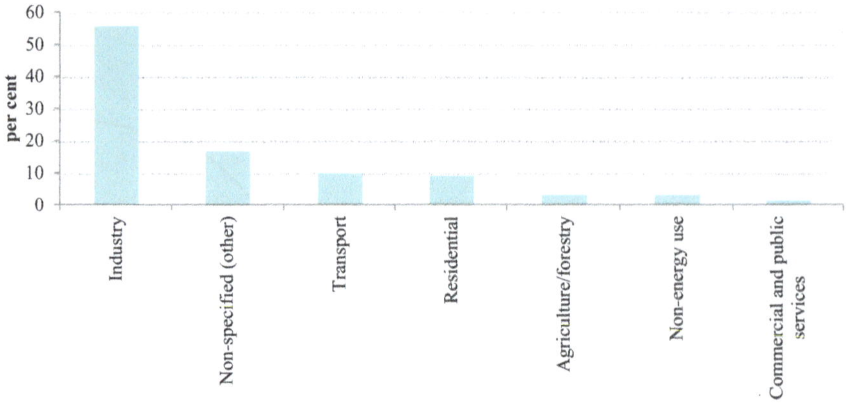

Fig. 4 Share of different sectors in India's final energy consumption in 2018–19. *Source* MOSPI (2020)

2 Economics of Energy Efficiency

At the outset, it may be useful to understand the difference between the concepts of energy efficiency and energy conservation. Energy efficiency refers to the amount of energy used in deriving a particular outcome. An increase in energy efficiency therefore would refer to a greater level of that outcome from the same level of energy input. The literature quantifies it with energy intensity. However, energy conservation, on the other hand, refers to a reduction in the total use of energy. Thus, energy conservation may result from energy efficiency but not necessarily so; overall energy use may increase along with an increase in energy efficiency (Gillingham et al., 2009).

All energy efficiency interventions are based on a premise that there is a socially optimal level of energy efficiency that is yet to be realised. This "energy efficiency gap" (Jaffe et al., 2004) could arise from a variety of reasons that prevent the market outcome to achieve a socially efficient outcome. There are two crucial steps in the path towards improving energy efficiency: energy-efficient technologies are developed, and the available technologies are widely adopted. Technological innovation is the linchpin of energy efficiency. The basic requirement for the adoption of energy-efficient technologies is that they are available. The private sector is not always forthcoming to invest in the development of new technologies owing to the large sunk costs in research and development (R&D), the uncertainty inherent in research and technology development, and relatively long gestation periods as well as the fact that the new products may not be competitive compared to the existing products. This calls for policy intervention in the form of incentivising investments in developing energy-efficient technologies. Provision of financial and technical support to firms and start-ups wishing to develop new energy-efficient technologies is a good starting point. Effective translation of research and development into a marketable product that can be commercialised is also important. Support for the marketing of innovative energy-efficient products would help its commercialisation. However, an important aspect for incentivising innovation is also the availability of an innovation-friendly intellectual property rights regime. Adequate protection needs to be accorded to innovators so that the costs incurred in the R&D process are rewarded through a temporary grant of the sole right to gain from the innovations. This would provide incentives for embarking upon a risky innovation process. An ideal intellectual property rights regime also has to strike a balance between protecting innovators for a reasonable amount of time while at the same time making the technical knowledge available to the public domain after considerable gains have been reaped by the innovators to foster competition.

Once these technologies are available, the next step is increasing their adoption. The diffusion of innovation is usually viewed as an S-shaped curve (Fig. 5). The objective of policy interventions is to shift the diffusion curve upwards so that the adoption of energy-efficient innovation takes place at a faster rate. Economists have a range of policy instruments in their arsenal for achieving this. It would be useful to categorise the potential economic instruments that can aid in achieving energy efficiency objectives into three:

(1) **Market mechanisms**

Coase theorem tells us that, with clearly assigned property rights and no transaction costs, an efficient solution can be achieved through a bargaining process between the economic agents. When there are a large number of agents and likely asymmetry of information, such a bargaining process may not be feasible. This is usually the case

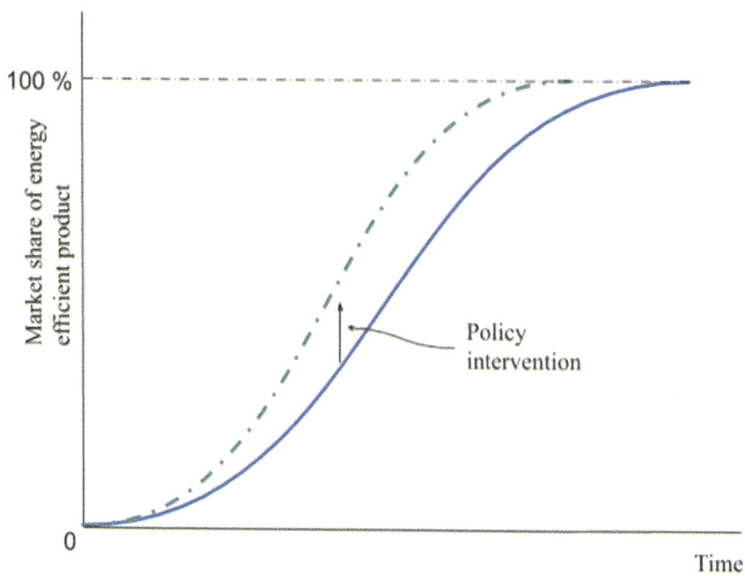

Fig. 5 Diffusion of energy-efficient innovation

in real life. In such a case, the optimal outcome is achieved through the creation of a market for the externality under question. One such market is the market for energy-saving certificates. An upper limit on the energy intensity for a group of economic agents is decided. This is allocated among economic agents, in the form of energy intensity permits. The agents who are able to achieve an energy intensity less than the allotted permits are allowed to trade them with the agents who are unable to achieve their target energy intensity. Trading between the agents ensures that the optimal level of emissions is achieved at the lowest cost. The advantage of such a mechanism is that it is technology agnostic and allows the economic agents involved to choose the best way to meet the targets.

(2) **Fiscal instruments**

Taxes

A key fiscal measure to promote energy efficiency is the imposition of taxes according to the polluter pays principle. A tax can be imposed on either the producer or the consumer and works by increasing the cost of doing a certain activity, thereby dissuading entities from doing more of that activity. In the context of energy use, an energy tax incentivises firms to save energy. The revenue generated from the tax can be channelled into activities that require explicit government support for promoting energy efficiency, for instance, for introducing technology advancement at the industry level.

Financing

A second fiscal instrument that can be deployed for energy efficiency is providing financial support. Governments can provide concessional loans or grants to fully or partially finance steps required to improve energy efficiency to industries. Financing can be provided for improvement of existing inefficient facilities, as well as new or existing facilities, where new technologies are being implemented which impose risks great enough to deter investors to undertake improvements. A key financial instrument in this regard is viability gap funding, which can help businesses meet the initial cost of introducing a new technology that will improve energy use. Financing as an instrument should be used ultimately to create an enabling economic environment capable of providing long-term financing and to establish a financing structure overtime where the necessary funding will come from private sources.

Green Public Procurement

Green public procurement is defined as the acquisition of goods or services by the public sector taking environmental aspects into account. As one of the largest purchasers, the public sector has substantial power to exert influence over the market. Public sector procurement can create a much-needed demand for products and services that foster energy efficiency. The practice of green public procurement can help encourage the market to produce and sell more energy-efficient products and services. This, in turn, can help the market to mature and foster innovation across the board.

(3) Other regulatory measures

Energy efficiency can be improved through the use of other regulatory measures such as setting norms and standards. Norms and standards are rules and targets set by public authorities specifying minimum levels that need to be met. These are supposed to encourage the use of energy-efficient technologies and are subsequently enforced by compliance procedures.

However, using standards to enhance energy efficiency can yield the desired results only if they are effectively implemented. If enforcement is poor, as is in many developing countries, such measures would end up increasing the cost of operation for businesses without energy efficiency gains. Another regulatory decision is how frequently these should be revised in the light of new technologies or information. On the one hand, it seems intuitive to tighten the standards as technologies improve; on the other hand, such a policy may create strategic incentives to delay innovations in anticipation of tighter standards (Bansal & Gangopadhyay, 2005). Committing to a standard, before the improvement actually takes place, provides the right incentive for a strategic firm to invest in R&D.

(4) Nudge/Behavioural instruments

The insights provided by behavioural economics and psychology are being increasingly used in various policy scenarios, and environmental policy can also borrow from them. Behavioural economics suggests that economic agents could be guided in their actions by perceptions of fairness, social norms and social status, and even by other idiosyncratic factors rather than pure rational decision-making as modelled in conventional economic theory. One instrument could be moral suasion. Repeated appeals could be made to economic agents to behave in a particular way. This has been conventionally used by Central Banks to affect desired behaviour among the commercial banks. Transparency could also be used as a potential instrument to affect behaviour of economic agents. Richard Thaler and Cass Sunstein have suggested disclosures as an environmental policy instrument. While there may not be any regulation requiring attaining of a particular physical target, mandatorily requiring economic agents to disclose the impact of their activities on the environment can have a positive impact on the activities of these agents. The success of such a scheme was due to the worst offenders being targeted by the media and environmental groups, providing a social nudge.

The policy interventions in the context of energy efficiency should be guided by efforts at removing barriers to the adoption of energy-efficient products and technologies. The literature has suggested a range of reasons that could result in the suboptimal adoption of energy-efficient innovation. This could be a result of, among others, environmental externalities, lack of adequate information or behavioural biases (Jaffe et al., 2004; Patrik et al., 2010; Howarth & Andersson, 1993; Gillingham et al., 2009). It is important to understand the sources of market inefficiency as the policy intervention that addresses a particular issue effectively could vary. Informational issues are one of the most prominent barriers to the adoption of energy-efficient technologies. First, uncertainty about the performance of energy-efficient products inhibits the adoption of more energy-efficient technologies (Patrik et al., 2010; Howarth & Andersson, 1993). The adoption of an energy-efficient technology by an agent also provides an opportunity for other agents to learn from the experience of early adopters. Thus, there involve positive externalities in the adoption of new technologies, and therefore, there would be under-provision of the same in the market due to non-internalisation of the same (Jaffe et al., 2004). The policy intervention could be in the form of subsidising new technologies so that more people experience it, and through positive externalities, this could result in a wider diffusion.

Another informational issue is that of asymmetry of information between different agents. It is likely to be the case that producers of products are more informed about the energy efficiency characteristics than the consumers of these products. This may lead to adverse selection resulting in the suboptimal choice of energy efficiency investment. Another form of principal–agent problem arises when the owner of a building or premises that has been provided on rent has to invest in energy efficiency equipment but the utility bills have to be paid by the tenants (Jaffe and Stavins, 1994; Jaffe et al., 2004; Sanstad & Howarth, 1994). This leads to underinvestment in energy efficiency measures. To address this barrier, energy efficiency standards for products could be specified, and labels that convey information on their energy efficiency could be provided.

Behavioural economics suggests that consumers are not rational in making their decisions and have cognitive biases. These include norms and values of energy efficiency, inertia and bounded rationality (Gillingham et al., 2009; Sanstad & Howarth, 1994; Patrik et al., 2010).

Another barrier to energy efficiency could be that households and small firms may be credit constrained and therefore unable to opt for the more energy-efficient options that have higher upfront costs (Hirst & Brown, 1990). Further, studies have found relatively high discount rates in the case of energy efficiency investments compared to interest rates in the rest of the economy (Hirst & Brown, 1990; Jaffe & Stavins, 1994).

All these barriers to energy efficiency are usually from the perspective of users of products that consume energy in their operation. However, a major concern is regarding the production of energy, especially, from fossil fuels. It is a process that involves considerable environmental externalities. Since the environmental costs from the production of energy are not internalised without regulatory intervention, the producer has no incentive to produce energy in a socially optimal manner. The result is that as long as the private gains from energy efficiency are not sufficient to induce the producer of energy to reach the socially optimal level, it would not do so. Taxes or emission trading mechanisms have the potential to nudge the producers of energy towards more energy-efficient means.

Thus, we have seen that, where the barrier to energy efficiency results from gaps in information, the policy interventions that are most likely to help are those that increase the level of information available with the consumer such as conducting information campaigns, labelling programmes and rating programmes (Hirst & Brown, 1990). Labelling and rating schemes are also likely to help in cases where bounded rationality makes it difficult to make informed decision-making. In the case of asymmetric information-induced inefficiencies, in addition to information enhancing policies, enforcement of standards and norms is useful in inducing optimal behaviour. Limited access to capital can be addressed through financial incentives for energy efficiency investments or tax credits. As we shall see in the following section, energy efficiency policy in India has leveraged almost all the above-mentioned policy options in encouraging energy efficiency in the country.

3 Energy Efficiency Policy in India

The institutional framework for energy efficiency in India is based on the Energy Conservation Act, 2001. Section 3 of the said Act paved the way for the creation of the Bureau of Energy Efficiency (BEE). The Act has fixed a gamut of functions for BEE ranging from recommending the norms for processes and energy consumption standards, norms for appliances, guidelines for energy conservation building codes, to the training of personnel and dissemination of information. The Act was amended in 2010.

A number of programmes have been initiated to address energy conservation by BEE. These schemes cover a wide range of sectors, namely households, buildings, electrical appliances, demand-side management in agriculture and municipalities, as well as micro, small and medium enterprises (MSMEs) and large industries (Fig. 6). In terms of the policy instruments discussed in the previous section, India

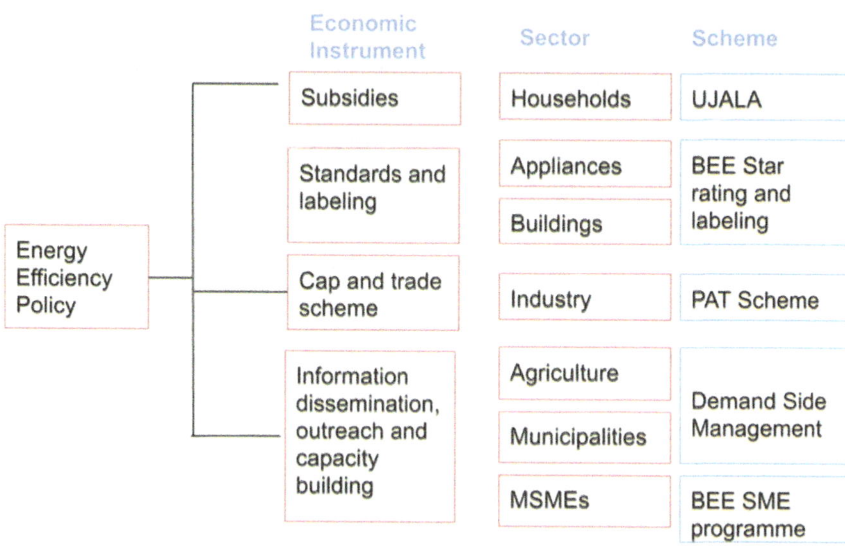

Fig. 6 Some selected energy efficiency schemes in India by type of economic instrument and sector

has attempted to use almost all major policy instruments including subsidies, standards and labelling, cap and trade scheme as well as information dissemination programmes. Below we give a brief description of the various schemes according to the different sectors they are implemented in:

3.1 Industry Sector

In the industrial sector, the major energy efficiency interventions are the **Perform, Achieve and Trade (PAT)** Scheme for large industry and the **BEE SME** (small and medium-scale enterprises) **Programme, the Global Environment Facility-United Nations Industrial Development Organisation-BEE (GEF-UNIDO-BEE) Programme, GEF-World Bank-BEE** Programmes for the Micro, Small and Medium Enterprises (MSME) sector (BEE, 2020).

PAT is essentially a cap and trade scheme in energy efficiency launched from 2012 onwards under **National Mission for Enhanced Energy Efficiency (NMEEE)**. PAT imposes energy consumption targets on firms (designated consumers) in energy-intensive industries. Designated consumers which are able to achieve energy savings greater than that mandated receive energy-saving certificates (ESCerts). Designated consumers who are unable to meet their targets are allowed to meet the shortfall through the purchase of ESCerts from those with a surplus. PAT cycle-I ended in 2015 with a saving of 8.67 million tonne of oil equivalent (MTOE). The second PAT cycle was launched with effect from April 2016 for the period 2016–17 to 2018–19. Under this, 89 new DCs were identified from existing sectors and 84 DCs from three new sectors, railways, refineries and electricity DISCOMs were included. Overall, a reduction of 8.869 million tonnes of oil equivalent from a total of 621 DCs was targeted in this cycle. PAT cycle-III was notified with effect from April 2017, PAT cycle-IV from 1 April 2018 and PAT cycle-V from April 2019. PAT scheme is now being implemented on a rolling cycle basis with the inclusion of new sectors/DCs every year (GoI, 2019; MoEFCC, 2018).

In the MSME sector, BEE SME programme was initiated to bridge the gap in the technological know-how of the SMEs by conducting technology demonstrations and imparting training programmes. Four industrial clusters are part of the BEE SME programme. These cover forging (Ludhiana), textile (Pali), food (Indore) and brick kilns (Varanasi) (BEE, 2020). In order to ensure finance for energy efficiency in MSME industrial clusters, BEE-WB-GEF programme was introduced with a grant agreement being signed in 2010. A revolving fund has also been created under this to provide concessional finance for energy efficiency projects in the sector. Another national project is being executed by BEE in collaboration with the UNIDO under GEF funding. Under this, a range of activities includes assessment of the current operational efficiency, technology identification, etc., to MSMEs for implementation of energy efficiency interventions in 12 MSME clusters covering brass, ceramics, dairy, foundry and hand tools.

With regard to financing instruments for energy efficiency, the **Energy Efficiency Financing Platform (EEFP)** aims at the creation of mechanisms that would help finance demand-side management programmes. Major activities under this have been related to outreach and training at financial and banking institutions (MoEFCC, 2018). **Framework for Energy-Efficient Economic Development (FEEED)** was intended to develop fiscal instruments for energy efficiency. Partial Risk Guarantee Fund for Energy Efficiency (PRGFEE) provides partial risk coverage to financial institutions for lending to energy efficiency enhancing investments (BEE, 2019; MoEFCC, 2018).

3.2 Domestic Appliances and Building Sectors

Market Transformation for Energy Efficiency (MTEE) Scheme aims at "accelerating the shift to energy-efficient appliances in designated sectors through innovative measures to make the products more affordable" (MoEFCC, 2018). Refrigerators, ceiling fans, air conditioners, water heaters and motors were identified as the priority products for initial standards and labelling development. One of the programmes under this scheme was the Bajat Lamp Yojana, later rechristened as the **Unnat Jyoti by Affordable LEDs for All (UJALA)** was launched in 2015 with the aim to provide LED bulbs to domestic consumers with a target to replace 770 million incandescent bulbs with LED bulbs by March 2019. As on 2 April 2020, 36,22,65,188 LEDs have been distributed under the scheme resulting in estimated savings of over ₹18 crore each year and energy savings of 47,046 million kWh per year (National UJALA Dashboard, 2020). Energy Efficiency Services Ltd. (EESL) is the implementing agency for the programme. LED bulbs are distributed at subsidised rates. Domestic consumers can procure LED lights at a low price, with the balance through easy instalments through their electricity bills. Another programme under MTEE is the Super-Efficient Equipment Programme (SEEP). SEEP was launched with the aim to subsidise the production of super-efficient fans to reduce energy consumption in Indian households.

Energy Conservation and Building Code (ECBC) was launched in 2007, and a new ECBC was launched in 2017 that goes beyond to encourage building energy consumption. ECBC 2017 is applicable to commercial buildings that have a connected load of 100 kW or greater or a contract demand of 120 kVA or greater (BEE, 2020). In order to measure energy efficiency, an index called energy performance index which is the ratio of annual energy consumption to the total built-up area excluding unconditioned basements is considered. Along with minimum energy efficiency requirements, the code also requires buildings to have a mandatory installation of renewable energy generation as well as passive design strategies such as daylight and shading. Buildings under the code have been classified into hospitality, educational, businesses, assembly, health care and shopping facilities (BEE, 2020). In the area of residential buildings, EcoNiwas Samhita 2018 was launched which prescribes minimum energy efficiency norms for residential buildings. An energy efficiency labelling scheme for residential buildings has also been proposed. Voluntary labelling of buildings in the form of Star Labels for commercial buildings was launched in 2009. Buildings are rated from 1 to 5 based on their actual energy performance, 5 being the best. A total of 261 buildings have been star rated. A star rating is valid for 5 years (BEE, 2020).

Standards and labelling for energy efficiency has been used in the area of electrical appliances since 2006 initially as voluntary labels for refrigerators and tube lights. Mandatory labels were introduced in 2009. Today, 24 appliances are covered under standards and labelling scheme, with 10 of these appliances requiring mandatory labelling. While standards prescribe minimum energy efficiency requirements for appliances, labelling involves attaching labels that provide information on the energy efficiency characteristics of the appliances. BEE has issued two types of labels. One is a comparative label that allows consumers to compare the energy efficiency of particular products in terms of star ratings. The other labelling is an endorsement labelling which indicates that the particular appliance is highly energy efficient in its category.

3.3 Municipal and Agricultural Sectors

Demand-side management programmes have been introduced with respect to Agriculture, Municipal/Urban Local Bodies, and Distribution Companies (DISCOMs). Irrigation constitutes a major share of electricity use in the agricultural sector, and therefore attempts have been made under DSM to generate awareness about energy-efficient pump sets (GoI, 2019; MoEFCC, 2018). BEE nationwide awareness programmes have been undertaken to address energy efficiency in water pumping, sewage pumping, street lighting and public buildings across urban local bodies (ULBs).

Municipal Energy Efficiency Programme (MEEP) aims to retrofit energy-efficient pumps in 500 Atal Mission for Rejuvenation and Urban Transformation (AMRUT) cities. Energy audit has been completed in more than 250 ULBs, and EESL will be conducting the upgradation of pumping systems in these cities. Conventional street lights are being replaced under the Street Light National Programme (SLNP) (BEE, 2020).

4 Impact of Energy Efficiency Programmes

As per Government of India estimates, the implementation of energy efficiency schemes in India has resulted in a total cost savings of around ₹53,000 crore in 2017–18 and reduced CO_2 emission by 108.28 million tonnes, mainly contributed by the schemes PAT, UJALA and standards and labelling (GoI, 2019). In 2018–19,

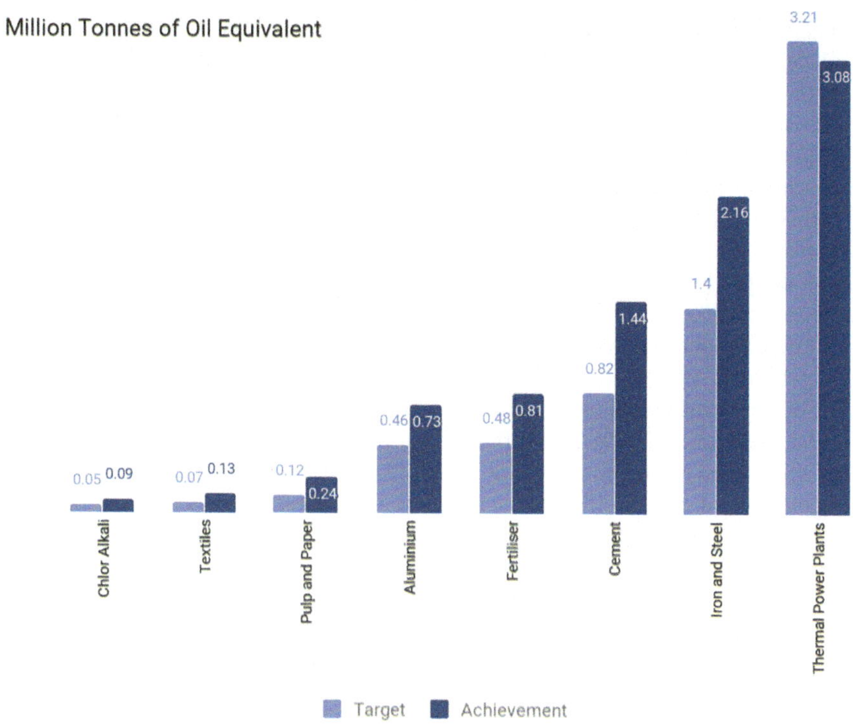

Fig. 7 Sector-wise total targets and achievements under PAT cycle-1. *Source* MoEFCC (2018)

the savings have been estimated at ₹89,122 crore, emission reductions of 151.74 $MTCO_2$. In the first cycle of PAT, from 2012 to 2015, 478 industrial units from aluminium, cement, chlor-alkali, fertiliser, iron and steel, paper and pulp, thermal power and textile sectors were included. Under the first cycle, 309 designated consumers exceeded their targets (BEE, 2020). The actual achievement in terms of total energy saved in each sector was above target in all sectors except thermal power plants where it was marginally less (Fig. 7) (MoEFCC, 2018).

Energy efficiency market-based instruments have been used in many other countries. European Union (EU) had issued energy efficiency directives[1] for member states to set national energy efficiency targets based on either primary or final energy consumption, primary or final energy savings, or energy intensity. It also directed the member states to establish an energy efficiency obligation scheme in order to achieve energy efficiency targets by 31 December 2020. The target was to be "at least equivalent to achieving new savings each year from 1 January 2014 to 31 December 2020 of 1.5% of the annual energy sales to final customers of all energy distributors or all retail energy sales companies by volume, averaged over the most recent three-year period prior to 1 January 2013". Around 15 EU member states have active

[1]EU Directive 2012/27/EU.

energy efficiency obligation schemes: Austria, Bulgaria, Croatia, Denmark, France, Greece, Ireland, Italy, Latvia, Luxembourg, Malta, Slovenia, Spain, Poland and the UK (Fawcett et al., 2019). In the UK, the Carbon Reduction Commitment Energy Efficiency Scheme (CRC) was introduced in 2010 to incentive energy efficiency for large energy users. Participants in this scheme were required to buy allowances for their carbon emissions (UK Govt., 2017). The scheme was run in two phases: from April 2010 till March 2014 and from 1 April 2014 till 31 March 2019. The scheme was decided to be closed after the 2018–19 compliance year. Energy-saving targets and trading in it in Italy were introduced in 2005 for electricity and gas distributors with at least 50,000 consumers (Stede, 2017). Only additional[2] energy savings are rewarded with energy-saving certificates. South Korea introduced Energy Efficiency Obligations in 1995 with the objective of incremental energy savings of 0.20% per year in comparison with total fuel consumption (IEA, 2017).

Oak and Bansal (2019) use a difference-in-differences estimation to show that the PAT scheme led to a fall in energy intensity of DCs in cement and fertiliser industries. A sector where energy efficiency schemes seem to have had a negligible impact is the paper and pulp industry (Oak & Bansal, 2019). A major criticism of the PAT scheme has been that the targets under the scheme have not been stringent enough, leading to the easy achievement of these targets and actually over-achievement by most sectors (Singh & Sharma, 2018; Haider et al., 2019; Sahoo et al., 2017). Sahoo et al. (2017), based on data envelopment analysis (DEA), and find that PAT targets for thermal power plants were less than the sector's potential. At full potential, they estimate that the sector could produce 4.7 million additional ESCerts. Based on stakeholder interviews, Bhandari and Shrimali (2018) find that PAT is not additional and major improvements in energy efficiency were on account of rising energy prices during the period. Haider et al. (2019), using DEA-based analysis, found that the Indian paper and pulp industry has the potential to reduce energy input along with all proportionately by 18%. Dasgupta and Roy (2017) find that while sectors like aluminium, cement and fertiliser are operating efficiently as per global standards, paper and pulp and iron and steel sectors are lagging behind. The unit-specific targets in the scheme take a lenient view of highly inefficient firms due to the unit-specific targets. Further, while setting the target, BEE does not take into account factors such as raw material composition and quality, internal consumption of products by the plant itself and in-house energy conversion (Singh & Sharma, 2018). Another criticism is that since the issuance of the ESCerts is after the verification of the energy savings, it does not allow trading during the cycle and therefore the generation of price signals for energy-efficient investments (Bhattacharya & Kapoor, 2012).

An important sector that has great potential for energy savings is the building sector. The adoption of ECBC 2017 is estimated to reduce energy use by 50% by 2030 and a savings of ₹ 35,000 crore and 250 million tonnes of CO_2 (BEE, 2020). Thirteen states have made ECBC mandatory for commercial buildings. As of 2018–19, 117 buildings, both constructed and under various stages of construction, were

[2]Additionality implies that only measures that would have not taken place in the absence of the policy are rewarded.

under the ECBC mandate (BEE, 2020). Twenty-two buildings out of these 117 have completed their constructions and have resulted in energy savings of 44.55 MU. In terms of star-rated buildings, between 2015–16 and 2018–19, 49 buildings have been star rated and have resulted in a total savings of 82.5 MU between 2015–16 and 2018–19 (BEE, 2020).

Based on an impact assessment of 13 appliances conducted by BEE that were covered under standards and labelling scheme, it was found that the total savings for appliances sold between 2015v16 and 2018–19 amounted to 55.7 MU in 2018–19. This led to an estimated reduction of 45.7 million tonnes of CO_2 during 2018–19. Under the UJALA scheme, a total of 347.4 million LED bulbs, 7.35 million LED tube lights and 2.22 million energy-efficient fans have been sold between 2015–16 and 2018–19. The programme is estimated to have led to energy savings of around 44,852 MU of energy (BEE, 2020). In the ULBs, more than 84 lakh LED street lights have been replaced between 2015–16 and 2018–19 under the SLNP. This has resulted in an estimated energy savings of 5647 MU and emission reductions of 4.6 million tonnes of CO_2 in 2018–19 (BEE, 2020).

With regard to labelling, Jain et al. (2018) using a discrete choice experiment showed that prior knowledge of label increased consumers' willingness to pay for energy-efficient air conditioners and refrigerators in India. The willingness to pay for five-star rating as compared to three-star rating air conditioners and refrigerators is Rs. 9060 and Rs. 6633, respectively. Chunekar (2014) compared the standard and labelling programme for refrigerators in India, with the USA, China and the European Union energy star programmes. The article found that the range of consumption levels in a particular star label is much wider in India as compared to other countries. In addition, India lags behind other countries on its consumption levels corresponding to the highest energy efficiency rating. Parikh and Parikh (2016) estimated savings between 52 and 145 billion kWh in 2030 from four household appliances—ACs, refrigerators, televisions and ceiling fans (10–27% reduction). The carbon emission reduction is estimated in the range of 42 megatons to 116 megatons in 2030 (30% reduction).

Grover et al. (2019) conduct a discrete choice experiment in New Delhi to assess consumers' willingness to pay for fuel-efficient cars. They use a novel approach to evaluate the effect of combining the labelling policy with a regulatory incentive. For the purpose, they incorporate the odd–even scheme that was recently implemented in Delhi in their experiment. According to the scheme, cars with an odd-numbered licence plate were allowed to run on odd dates and those with even numbers on even dates. They find that consumers in New Delhi are willing to pay more for fuel-efficient cars. Further, driving restrictions tied to a labelling system seem a promising policy to increase the uptake of fuel-efficient cars in New Delhi. They find an increase in respondents' stated willingness to pay (WTP) for the best efficiency label from 4.93 thousand US dollars to 7.48 thousand US dollars. They interpret the difference as regulatory costs—i.e. the extra 2.55 thousand US dollars represent the amount that respondents are willing to pay for an energy label that would exempt them from the driving restrictions.

5 Recommendations and Conclusions

Over the years, the Government of India has taken several policy measures to enhance energy efficiency of the economy; however, India still ranks low in terms of energy efficiency and there is potential for further gains. Some suggestions on energy efficiency policy are as follows:

- Consumer awareness is an important aspect in the success of government efforts. Lack of awareness about energy efficiency, products and instruments is a major impediment in the adoption of energy-efficient technologies. Consumer awareness campaigns and making information about the energy efficiency part of the school curriculum could go a long way. Sengupta (2017) using a survey of 250 households in Delhi showed that people are reluctant to shift to LEDs due to high prices and being habituated to incandescent lamps. The paper suggested that an effective campaign could bring social acceptance of energy-efficient lighting. Not taking into account consumers' responses can yield less than desirable results. A drawback of the SEEP scheme is that it does not take into account the consumers' behaviour and their purchasing propensity for super-efficient fans (Troja, 2016).
- Financial incentives are likely to have a positive impact on the adoption of energy-efficient appliances by households. These financial incentives could be in the form of low-interest loans or bringing down the cost of appliances through large-scale procurement by the government as was in the case of procurement of LED bulbs by BEE (Parikh & Parikh, 2016).
- It is important that the schemes are reviewed and evolved as per the changing landscape. Though BEE claims that the PAT scheme is highly effective, rigorous studies that quantify the additional gains in energy efficiency due to the scheme need to be conducted, and the results are used for the implementation of future phases of the scheme. Further targets should be set that yield the economically optimal energy efficiency improvements. Where standards are used as instruments, implementation and enforcement would yield desired results. There is a need for constant monitoring and updation of standards.
- With reference to energy efficiency trading, it is important to have a clear long-term target so that there is minimal policy uncertainty for stakeholders involved. This would encourage them to make concrete investments in energy efficiency improvements.
- Buildings hold great potential for future energy efficiency gains as India is on the path of urbanisation and economic growth (Mathur, 2019). It is important that energy efficiency standards are implemented for this sector in a comprehensive manner for both domestic and commercial constructions.
- Digital technologies can be leveraged to improve energy efficiency. The use of equipments such as smart metres can lead to better energy management and therefore reduce avoidable energy losses.
- Public procurement can have energy efficiency guidelines so that only goods and services that meet the minimum energy efficiency standards are procured by public authorities. This could give a fillip to energy-efficient products in the country.

Energy efficiency is a crucial component of India's overall climate strategy. It is an area that is perceived to deliver a win-win situation for all the stakeholders involved. Given the uncertainties governing the current global economy in the aftermath of COVID-19 and the resulting slowdown, it is yet to be seen how renewable energy investments would be impacted in the coming days. In such a scenario, energy efficiency measures could provide the much-needed impetus for climate mitigation actions in the coming times.

References

Adam B. Jaffe, Richard G. Newell, & Robert N. Stavins. (2004). Economics of energy efficiency. *Encyclopedia of Energy, 2.*

Adam B. Jaffe, & Robert N. Stavins. (1994). The energy efficiency gap: What does it mean? *Energy Policy, 22*(10), 804–810.

American Council for an Energy-Efficient Economy (2018). *The 2018 international energy efficiency scorecard.* https://www.aceee.org/sites/default/files/publications/researchreports/i1801.pdf.

Bansal, S., & Shubhashis, G. (2005). Incentives for technological development: BAT is BAD. *Environmental & Resource Economics, 30*(3), 345–367.

BEE. (2019). *Unlocking national energy efficiency potential (UNNATEE) strategy plan towards developing an energy efficient nation (2017–2031)* Bureau of Energy Efficiency, Ministry of Power, Govt. of India.

BEE. (2020). *A report on impact of energy efficiency measures for the year 2018–19.* Bureau of Energy Efficiency, Ministry of Power, Government of India.

Bhandari, D., & Shrimali, G. (2018). The perform, achieve and trade scheme in India: An effectiveness analysis. *Renewable and Sustainable Energy Reviews, 81,* 1286–1295.

Bhattacharya, T., & Kapoor, R. (2012). Energy saving instrument–ESCerts in India. *Renewable and Sustainable Energy Reviews, 16*(2), 1311–1316.

BP (2019). BP Statistical Review of World Energy. BP: London, UK.

Chunekar, A. (2014). Standards and labeling program for refrigerators: Comparing India with others. *Energy Policy, 65,* 626–630.

Dasgupta, S., & Roy, J. (2017). Analysing energy intensity trends and decoupling of growth from energy use in Indian manufacturing industries during 1973–1974 to 2011–2012. *Energy Efficiency, 10*(4), 925–943.

Fawcett, T., Rosenow, J., & Bertoldi, P. (2019). Energy efficiency obligation schemes: Their future in the EU. *Energy Efficiency, 12,* 57–71.

Gillingham, K., Newell, R. G., & Palmer, K. (2009). Energy efficiency economics and policy. *Annual Review of Resources and Economics, 1*(1), 597–620.

GoI. (2019). *Enabling inclusive growth through affordable, reliable and sustainable energy in economic survey 2018–19,* vol. I. Government of India.

GoI. (2015). *India's intended nationally determined contribution.* Government of India.

Grover, C., & Bansal, S., Martinez-Cruz, A. L. (2019). May a regulatory incentive increase WTP for cars with a fuel efficiency label? Estimating Regulatory Costs Through a Split-Sample DCE in New Delhi, India (June 24, 2019). Available at SSRN: https://ssrn.com/abstract=3408942 or http://dx.doi.org/10.2139/ssrn.3408942.

Haider, S., Danish, M. S., & Sharma, R. (2019). Assessing energy efficiency of Indian paper industry and influencing factors: A slack-based firm-level analysis. *Energy Economics, 81,* 454–464.

Hirst, E., & Brown, M. (1990). Closing the efficiency gap: Barriers to the efficient use of energy. *Resources, Conservation and Recycling, 3*(4), 267–281.

Howarth, R. B., & Andersson, B. (1993). Market barriers to energy efficiency. *Energy Economics, 15*(4), 262–272.

IEA. (2017). Energy efficiency obligation. international energy agency. Retrieved from https://www.iea.org/policies/792-energy-efficiency-obligation?country=Korea&jurisdiction=National&sector=Industry&status=In%20Force&topic=Energy%20Efficiency&type=Market-based%20instruments. Last accessed 26 May, 2020.

IEA. (2020). Energy efficiency indicators 2020. Paris: International Energy Agency. Retrieved from https://www.iea.org/report/energy-efficiency-indicators-2020.

IQ-Air. (2019). *World air quality report.* Url https://www.iqair.com/world-most-polluted-cities/world-air-quality-report-2019-en.pdf. Accessed May 30, 2020.

Jain, M., Rao, A. B., & Patwardhan, A. (2018). Appliance labeling and consumer heterogeneity: A discrete choice experiment in India. *Applied Energy, 226,* 213–224. https://doi.org/10.1016/j.apenergy.2018.05.089.

Mathur, A. (2019). Public costs and private benefits: The governance of energy efficiency in India. *Building Research and Information, 47*(1), 123–126.

MoEFCC. (2018). *India: Second biennial update report to the united nations framework convention on climate change.* Ministry of Environment, Forest and Climate Change, Government of India.

MOSPI. (2020). *Energy statistics 2020.* Government of India: Ministry of Statistics and Programme Implementation.

National UJALA Dashboard. (2020). http://www.ujala.gov.in/. Accessed on April 2, 2020.

Oak, H., & Bansal, S. (2019). Effect of Perform-Achieve-Trade Policy on Energy Efficiency of Indian Industries. *Available at SSRN 3412317.*

Parikh, K., & Parikh, J. (2016). Realizing potential savings of energy and emissions from efficient household appliances in India. *Energy Policy, 97,* 102–111.

Patrik, T., Jenny, P., & Patrik, R. (2010). Categorizing Barriers to energy efficiency: An interdisciplinary perspective. *Energy Efficiency*, 49–62.

Sahoo, N. R., Mohapatra, P. K., Sahoo, B. K., & Mahanty, B. (2017). Rationality of energy efficiency improvement targets under the PAT scheme in India—A case of thermal power plants. *Energy Economics, 66,* 279–289.

Sanstad, A. & Howarth, R. (1994). 'Normal' markets, market imperfections and energy efficiency. *Energy Policy, 22*(10), 811–818.

Saraswat, Y., & Bansal, S. (2020). *Health effects of sustained exposure to fine particulate matter: Evidence from India* (February 21, 2020). Available at SSRN: https://ssrn.com/abstract=3542183 or http://dx.doi.org/10.2139/ssrn.3542183.

Sengupta, S. (2017). Social acceptability of energy-efficient lighting. In *Sustainable Smart Cities in India* (pp. 275–294). Springer.

Singh, A., & Sharma, B. (2018). DEA based approach to set energy efficiency target under PAT framework: A case of Indian cement industry. *Central European Review of Economics and Management,* 2543–9472.

Stede, J. (2017). Bridging the industrial energy efficiency gap–Assessing the evidence from the Italian white certificate scheme. *Energy Policy, 104,* 112–123.

Troja, B. (2016). A quantitative and qualitative analysis of the super-efficient equipment program subsidy in India. *Energy Efficiency, 9*(6), 1385–1404.

UK Govt. (2017). *CRC Energy efficiency scheme.* United Kingdom Government. Retrieved from https://www.gov.uk/government/collections/crc-energy-efficiency-scheme. Last accessed 26 May, 2020.

Climbing Energy Ladder or Fuel Stacking in Indian Households: A Multinomial Logit Approach

Chetana Chaudhuri

1 Introduction

Access to affordable clean energy is one of the Sustainable Development Goals outlined by the UN (Goal 7). Lack of adequate and affordable energy services often leads the households to vicious cycle in which people who lack access to clean and modern energy are often trapped in a re-enforcing cycle of deprivation, lower income and unhealthy living conditions. Access to clean and modern forms of energy is essential to eradicate poverty, improve economic condition, generate employment opportunities and promote sustainable human development (Karekezi et al., 2012). Government of India has recognized this as a target of utmost priority due to its effect on poverty alleviation, health outcomes and environmental protection Chafe et al. (2014); MHFW Report of the Steering Committee on Air Pollution and Health Related Issues, 2015). Pradhan Mantri Ujjwala Yojana (PMUY) was launched in 2016 to safeguard the health of women and children and also to promote women empowerment through provision of LPG connections to the economically unprivileged families.

Exposure to biomass smoke has several health effects on children, which include low birth weight and neonatal deaths (Patel & Chauhan, 2020; Epstein et al., 2013). Smoke generated from combustion of fuel at household for cooking causes indoor pollution and has adverse effects on the health of household members, especially for women and children who are exposed to the smoke inside the house due to their socially determined roles (Saghir, 2004; Miller & Mobarak, 2013). Use of solid fuel is also linked to acute respiratory infections among children (Arlington et al., 2019; Patel et al., 2019). James et al. (2020), in their study, observed that two-thirds of women using biomass fuel for cooking were positively associated with self-reported

C. Chaudhuri (✉)
Public Health Foundation of India, Gurgaon, India
e-mail: chetana.chaudhuri2@gmail.com

P. Dasgupta et al. (eds.), *Sustainable Development Insights from India*,
India Studies in Business and Economics,
https://doi.org/10.1007/978-981-33-4830-1_10

health symptoms, which include ophthalmic, respiratory, cardiovascular and dermatological conditions and/or symptoms. Collection of fuelwood is generally done by women and children which affects their education and participation in workforce adversely (Hughes & Dunleavy, 2000). Over-collection of fuelwood causes environmental degradation and threatens environmental protection. In spite of all these harmful effects, fuelwood continues to be in use in developing countries, because it can be accessed easily without bearing any physical cost at all or at a very low cost vis-à-vis the costly clean fuels. In India, unclean fuels can also be chosen because clean fuels as an alternative are often unavailable in the specific region even if the household can afford it. The reason may further be the high cost of clean fuels and its cost of installation of associated stoves, which the household is unable to afford. But the data regarding this is very much limited for India. However, it is quite evident that households do not shift from one fuel to another in a very linear manner; i.e. there are many factors that determine the complete or partial switch of fuels, other than price of fuels or income of the household, which are considered to be the only factors behind fuel switching decision according to the 'energy ladder theory' (Leach 1975, 1992). Many households 'stack' multiple fuels, which negate all the positive effects of establishing a clean fuel connection in those households.

Many households in India rely on fuels of low quality like fuelwood, dung cake and kerosene for cooking. These fuels are used in traditional chullahs which are not energy efficient due to insufficient heat transfer and cause indoor pollution by releasing harmful gases like carbon monoxide, methane, nitrogen oxides, respirable particulate matter, etc. (Warwick & Doig, 2004). Clean fuels, on the contrary, are less polluting and are associated with better energy efficiency and convenience though with higher cost. In India, LPG for cooking is of the highest energy efficiency and convenience because the use and connection of natural gas are very limited.

There has been a major change in fuel choice in India over the last few years due to the change in lifestyle. Programmes have been launched to increase awareness, and government initiatives have been taken to encourage poor households to shift to clean fuels. LPG has been subsidized for many years, and steps have been taken by the government to improve access to LPG. But it is often seen that despite attaining connection of clean fuel sources, households are prone to use multiple fuels, effectively refuting the positive effect of clean fuels on indoor air quality. For efficient design of policy measures, analysis of the factors determining the actual choice of fuel or fuels is important. The situation is very much different in rural and urban areas. Availability of biomass at a very low direct cost is a major reason for choosing to use biomass in rural areas. But ideally it should shift to cleaner fuels if LPG connectivity is established in the household. The primary objective of the paper is to analyse the fuel stacking behaviour of rural and urban India for cooking purposes. The study tries to explore whether rural households are actually substituting biomass with clean fuels in this case. The study also aims to identify the factors that lead to simultaneous use of multiple fuels. In the urban sector, households have a wider set of choices of fuels, with easier accessibility caused by better connectivity and greater affordability. With different appliances and facilities, energy demand of urban households has increased many folds over the recent years. But the use of multiple fuels has been perceived in semi-urban and urban areas significantly. Different socio-economic parameters come into play in such fuel choices. The study also attempts to explore whether urban India behaves differently in adopting clean fuels. The present study analyses whether the households are actually switching from unclean to clean fuels or are practising stacking of multiple fuels and highlights the factors that influence their choice.

2 Conceptual Framework

In the context of residential energy consumption, the 'energy ladder' theory has been validated in many studies in the past (Baldwin, 1986; Leach & Mearns, 1988; Hosier & Dowd, 1988; Leach, 1992). The traditional energy ladder model proposes that with the increase in income and socio-economic status, the families are likely to abandon inefficient, less costly and polluting technologies, which are 'lower' in the energy ladder such as dung, fuel wood and charcoal in favour of technologies (stoves and fuels) which are higher in the 'energy ladder'. The main constraints on the transition are poor access to modern fuels and high cost of appliances for using them. The studies argued that households switch from more convenient energy forms with the increase in their disposable income. Some studies have confirmed the link between household income and fuel choice and emphasized that energy transition in rural households is largely driven by income (Hosier & Dowd 1987a, b; Davis 1998).

However, many studies oppose this idea and argue that there is no positive correlation between economic growth and modern fuel intake. Many studies have found that multiple fuels are used in many countries, especially in low-income or developing countries, across all income classes (Adamu et al., 2020; Leach, 1992; Choumert-Nkolo et al., 2019; Cheng & Urpelainen, 2014; Nansaior et al., 2011). Studies suggest that with economic growth and urbanization, total household energy use has increased in most of the developing countries but biomass continued to be an important component of the energy portfolio of the households, especially in rural areas. Though there has been a decline in the use of biomass for cooking, there is no sharp discontinuity in utilization of energy sources, as predicted by the energy ladder model.

According to some studies, fuel switching is often found not to be unidirectional in nature and people can even switch back to traditional biomass after adopting modern energy services (Herington & Malakar, 2016; Maconachie et al., 2009). Also, the appliances used in the household require different energy sources, leading to a diversified energy demand (Foley, 1995). Masera et al. (2000) opposed the view of energy ladder and criticized that the energy ladder theory is not able to explain the dynamics of fuel use of the households. According to his view, the transition from biomass to more advanced and less polluting fuels is not linear. In fact, the households follow a 'stacking procedure', which means that the traditional fuels are not always completely abandoned with the increase in socio-economic status or changed lifestyle, but they are used in conjunction with modern fuels. The study proposed an alternate 'multiple fuel' model of stove and fuel management based on the observed pattern of household accumulation of energy options using data from a four-year (1992–96) case study of a village in Mexico and from a large-scale survey from four states of Mexico. This model integrates four factors as essential in household decision making under conditions of resource scarcity or uncertainty, which are: economics of fuel and stove type and access conditions to fuels; technical characteristics of cook-stoves and cooking practices; cultural preferences; and health impacts.

Fuel stacking behaviour is observed in many studies (Uhunamure et al., 2017; Heltberg, 2005; Hiemstra-Van der Horst & Hovorka, 2008). Some studies identified that fuel price plays a crucial role in determining the choice of fuel (Hosier & Kipondya, 1993). According to Murphy (2001) and Masera et al. (2000), culture and traditions also restrain complete transition to modern fuels for those who often practise traditional methods of cooking. Availability and ease of use also play crucial role for the choice of fuel (Gupta & Köhlin, 2006). According to Rahut et al. (2014), several factors influence the choice of clean energy for cooking, apart from income, e.g. age, education and gender of the household head, access to electricity, location, etc.

Choice of fuel sources and the underlying factors have been discussed in the context of residential energy consumption in India in many studies. Viswanathan and Kumar (2005) discussed the pattern of cooking fuel use in India for the years 1983–2000 and determined the factors determining the particular choices. Ravindranath and Ramakrishna (1997) conducted a regional-level study in some parts of South India, determined the efficiency of eleven cooking devices and estimated the quantity of eight fuels required to cook a 'standard' meal in those fuel–device combinations through thermal efficiency and controlled cooking tests. The study also analyses the environmental implications of these different options and discusses the potential and barriers to these options. Pandey and Chaubal (2011) discussed different factors behind the choice of clean fuel use for cooking purposes. Joon et al. (2009) explored the role of income and other socio-economic characteristics in determining the choice of fuels through a survey conducted in rural Haryana, India. Reddy (2003) identified different technological options for comparing costs and energy-saving potential and rate of return for the residential consumers. Comparison of average total cost of energy, including capital costs of equipment and appliances used to avail energy services, would enable the residential sector to improve energy services and reduce CO_2 emissions through improvement in energy efficiency. An energy efficiency scenario analysis is done in this study showing that significant energy saving can be achieved through improvement in efficiency, which can increase energy security as well as benefit low-income households. Reddy (2004) discusses the interdependence of energy and poverty and impacts of household energy use on livelihood and gender issues. Pachauri and Jiang (2008) compare the household energy transitions in China and India through the analysis of both aggregate statistics and nationally representative household surveys. Ekholm et al. (2010) present a model with focus on cooking fuel choices and explore response strategies for energy poverty eradication in India. Alternate future scenarios are developed to explore the effect of different policy mechanisms such as fuel subsidies and micro-financing on the diffusion of modern and efficient energy sources in India. O'Neill et al. (2012), in their study, pointed out that urbanization, along with changes in consumption preference due to income growth, would be a major factor of determining the fuel choice. Gould et al. (2020) found the perception of the chief wage earner and female education to be strongly positively associated with LPG ownership for two states of India, Kerala and Rajasthan. Sharma et al. (2020) suggested that willingness to pay for LPG is much less than the market price in India. They opined that apart from income, distance for collection of clean fuel, taste of meal and season are important determining factors for the choice of household cooking fuel. Choudhuri and Desai (2020) pointed out that the use of clean fuel in the household is also determined by women's access to salaried work and control over household expenditure decisions.

Most countries have initiated campaign to encourage households to shift from indoor polluting fuels to energy-efficient clean or less polluting fuels in order to reduce adverse health, social and environmental impact. Household indoor pollution (HAP) has caused millions of premature deaths and loss of healthy life years globally (Chafe et al. 2014). Millions of cases of chronic bronchitis, tuberculosis, cataract among adult Indian women and stillbirths in India are associated with the household indoor air pollution generated from biomass used for cooking (Sehgal et al. 2014). But research (Modi et al. 2005) found that for the countries with more than 75% of population living below US$2 per capita income, non-biomass energy consumption is higher (in a scale of 50–400 kgoe per capita) as compared to countries with 40–75% population earning less than $2 per day. In spite of the inconveniences generated from biomass energy use, biomass is often found in Indian households as the primary fuel for cooking. A study by the World Bank found that inter-fuel substitution has taken a significant pace within urban households in Hyderabad, a city in India, in the last twenty years, and that is partly due to the government policies that encourage to subsidize household fuels. But the study also concludes that these subsidies, which were primarily aimed to assist the poor, are misused to the benefit of high-income households (ESMAP, 1999). Ravindra et al. (2019) conducted a case study in Punjab, India, and found that up to 2010–11, only 2% of the rural households shifted from solid biomass to cleaner fuels. Their study does not support the energy ladder hypothesis, and they found several socio-economic factors to play crucial roles in shaping the fuel choice. Hanna and Oliva (2015), using data from a field experiment in India, examined the effects of a transfer programme that provided rural poor households with greater levels of assets and cash and did not observe a shift to cleaner cooking fuels.

The paper attempts to explore the extent of biomass use along with other fuels for cooking in Indian households and the reasons behind such choice of fuel. Households in developing countries are found to use fuels of low quality. Such fuels are, in fact, characterized in microeconomics as 'inferior' goods. In the case of cooking in India, the fuel range is large, among which LPG is with the highest efficiency and cleanliness, followed by kerosene and biomass (firewood, agricultural waste, crop residue or dung cake) in traditional cook-stoves. Improved cook-stoves with higher efficiency and lower emissions have, however, been introduced to alleviate pollution externalities. They would obviously come in between kerosene and biomass.

The household decision to complete or partial energy transition is quite complex and multidimensional, which includes many different factors apart from income and assets of the household. There is a need to look beyond income as the prime driving force behind fuel switching (Van der Kroon et al., 2013). The decision-making regarding fuel switching depends on household characteristics, cultures and practices, external political and institutional context and the household's capability which includes income, women empowerment, etc. This study wants to capture the factors driving the decision of use of single or multiple fuels in a comprehensive and structured manner and identify policy priority areas for fuel switching behaviour. In this context, internal factors such as human capital, women participation in the work-force, household characteristics such as age, labour force participation and income and some external factors like access to fuels and price levels of fuels would play important roles in determining the fuel choice. Some studies have used multinomial logit model for analysis of fuel choice (Rao & Reddy 2007; Jumbe & Angelsen, 2011; Danlami et al., 2019; Liao et al., 2019). This study intends to utilize the model to explain the factors which influence the household to use multiple fuels or to practise stacking behaviour.

3 Methodology and Data Source

The study uses multinomial logit model to explore the fuel stacking behaviour in India for the rural and urban sectors separately. The multinomial logit model is applied in this study to identify the socio-economic determinants of the following fuel choices for cooking, namely only biomass, LPG and no biomass, kerosene and no biomass, biomass with other fuels. In multinomial logit model, all the logits for each dependent variable are estimated simultaneously, and the effect of explanatory variables and parameters of the model on the dependent variables are captured efficiently. In this model, log of the odds of outcomes is modelled as a linear combination of the explanatory variables and relative odds of one alternative being chosen over a second which should be independent of the existence of an un-chosen third alternative.

Multinomial logit model is an extension of logit model. Unlike the logit model, dependent variable in multinomial logit model has more than 2 categories, say, 'M' number of categories. One value of the dependent variable is designated as reference category. The probability of falling into other categories is compared to the probability of falling into the reference category.

Therefore, if the first category is the reference, then, for $m = 2, \ldots, M$,

$$\ln \frac{P(Y_{i=m})}{P(Y_{i=1})} = \alpha_m + \sum_{k=1}^{K} \beta_{mk} X_{ik} = Z_{mi}$$

Therefore, for $m = 2, \ldots M$,

$$P(Y_{i=m}) = \frac{\exp(Z_{mi})}{1 + \sum_{h=2}^{M} \exp(Z_{hi})}$$

And for the reference category,

$$P(Y_{i=1}) = \frac{1}{1 + \sum_{h=2}^{M} \exp(Z_{hi})}$$

The model assumes that stalking behaviour depends on household size, price of alternative fuels, socio-economic characteristics of the household, such as religion, age of the household head, educational attainment of the household head, occupational category of the household, expenditure decile group in which the household falls into, land cultivation by the household, gender of the household head and social group (caste) of the household. The study uses the latest published consumption expenditure data by NSSO for the year 2011–12 to capture the use of energy services in the household sector.

4 Results

4.1 Energy Profile of Household Sector

Energy services in households are required for a variety of purposes to meet the energy need of the household, such as lighting, heating, cooking and use in electrical appliances. Based on the purpose, household energy services include fuelwood, dung cake, agricultural residues, coal, charcoal, kerosene, liquefied petroleum gas (LPG) and electricity. This study is limited to the analysis of energy services for the purpose of cooking only and is concentrated on the energy services and associated cost that are relevant to cooking food for the household.

India is the second largest populous country in the world. With this huge population, energy needed for the domestic sector is quite large. While the increasing volume of population causes increase in the total demand for energy, the degree of urbanization and growth in income as a result of development cause shifts in the pattern of fuel consumption. With the considerable diversity in geographical and agroclimatic zones, the energy consumption pattern varies according to place and season. Firewood historically dominates cooking energy choice in almost all the states in rural India irrespective of the income level.

At the all-India level, the share of households using firewood as primary fuel for cooking (77% in 2011–12) varies from around 92% for the lowest expenditure class to around 46% in the highest expenditure class in the rural sector (Fig. 1). For the urban sector, LPG use has been increased by a significant amount in 2011–12 as compared to 1993–94. However, biomass use in urban sector is limited to low-income households in 2011–12 (Fig. 2).

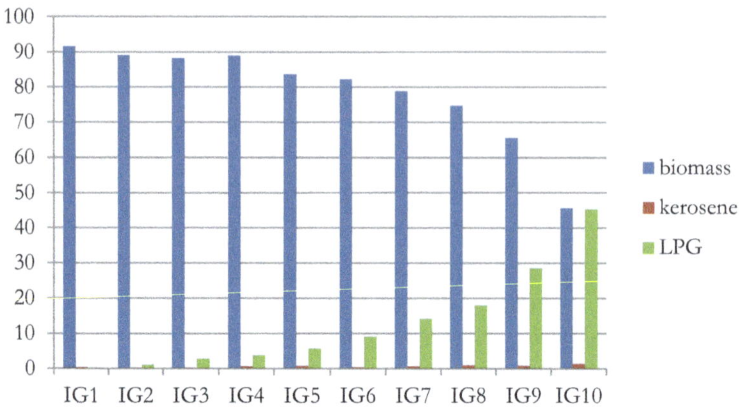

Fig. 1 Percentage of households depending on biomass, kerosene and LPG as their primary fuel for cooking in rural India across income classes (2011–12). *Source* NSSO 68th round, 2011–12

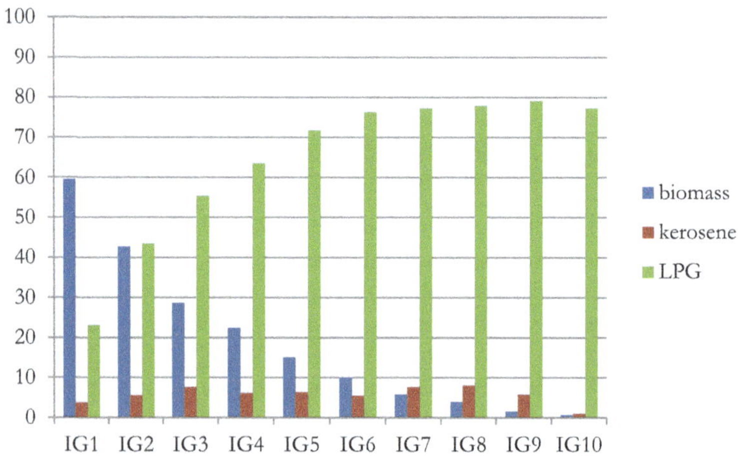

Fig. 2 Percentage of households depending on biomass, kerosene and LPG as their primary fuel for cooking in urban India across income classes (2011–12). *Source* NSSO 68th round, 2011–12

Though percentage of households depending on biomass as primary fuel for cooking has decreased significantly from 90% in 1993–94 to 77% in 2011–12 in rural sector, it is still much higher than the official head-count ratio of poverty (26%) (Fig. 3). Moreover, the per capita consumption of biomass is higher in higher-income households in the rural sector (Fig. 4). Average consumption of biomass was quite high in rural areas as compared to urban areas in 2011–12. In every income class in rural and urban India, average consumption of LPG is lower as compared to biomass (in calorific values of end-use energy) (Fig. 4). This is partially due to the fact that LPG can provide more useful heat value than firewood if we compare the same

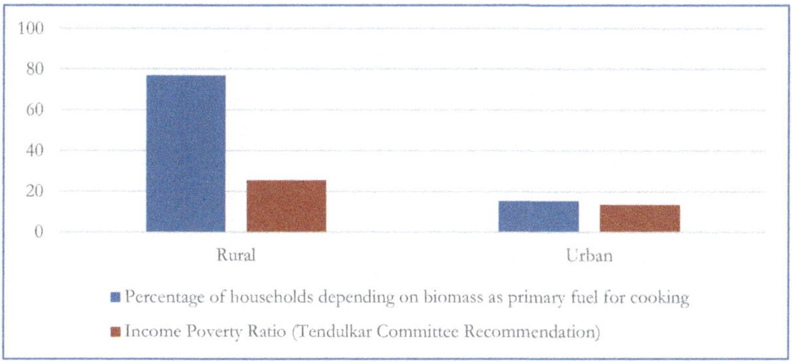

Fig. 3 Percentage of households depending on biomass as primary fuel for cooking and income poverty ratio (Tendulkar Committee Recommendation). *Source* Author's calculation and GOI documents

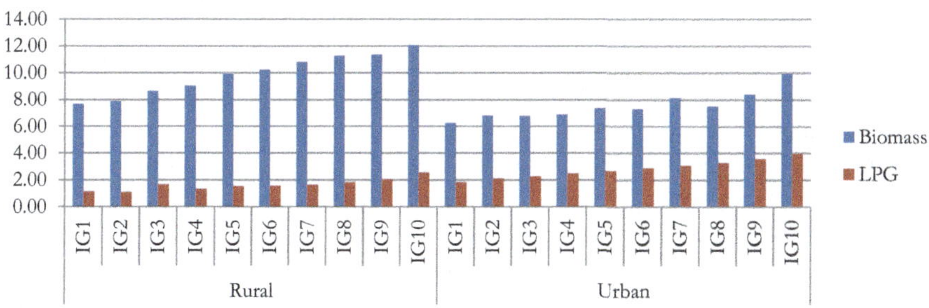

Fig. 4 Average consumption of cooking fuels in rural and urban households across income decile groups in 2011–12 (kgoe per month). *Source* NSSO 68th round, 2011–12

amount of end-use energy of the two sources. The data clearly indicates that the households who have LPG connectivity still use biomass in significant proportion of their cooking energy; the 'energy ladder model' is not essentially followed in India. On the contrary, with increases in income, households continue to use of unclean inefficient fuels and often increase their consumption due to income effect of higher real income. However, we have observed significant difference in the pattern of fuel use among the rural and urban sectors. Access to clean cooking energy sources in urban areas is generally driven by affordability, as cleaner fuels are sufficiently available. The issue of availability is a problem in rural areas, especially in far flung hilly areas. The penetration of cleaner fuels in urban areas has gained significant momentum.

The pattern of fuel use in cooking varies spatially as well. Figure 5 depicts the rural and urban scenarios in the major Indian states in 2011–12, which suggests that the reliance on traditional energies for cooking was quite high in rural areas in most of the states. In urban areas, people have shifted from the use of traditional fuels for cooking in majority of the states. However, biomass use in urban areas is high in Orissa, Chhattisgarh, Kerala, Madhya Pradesh, Uttar Pradesh, Tripura and Bihar

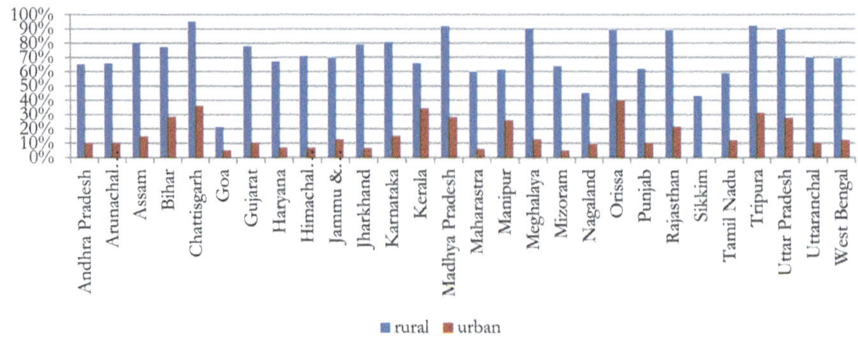

Fig. 5 Biomass distribution as primary fuel for cooking across the Indian states for rural and urban sector (2011–12). *Source* NSSO 68th round, 2011–12

among other states. But in rural areas, even in 2011–12, majority of households depend on biomass as their energy source for cooking in majority states and the degree of reliance is also quite high. Reliance on biomass as energy for cooking is comparatively lower in rural areas of Tamil Nadu, Punjab, Kerala and Andhra Pradesh among the large states.

In brief, a large section of the Indian population (around 162 million households according to Census 2011) relied on traditional energies to satisfy cooking energy needs in 2011. Rural areas are more dependent on traditional energies, and this is irrespective of the income levels of households and geographic location. Poor households in urban areas rely on traditional energies, while richer families tend to use cleaner fuels such as LPG and kerosene. Access to modern cooking fuel is severely limited in rural areas. As this is a common problem in most major states, major national policy initiatives are required to bring in changes in the cooking fuel use pattern. Transition to modern and clean cooking fuels can have significant implications for the supply side of the industry. High reliance on traditional energies has significant social costs including costs due to health effects on women and children. As rural households across all expenditure classes rely significantly on traditional energies for cooking, the issue of access to clean energies assumes greater importance, because affordability alone cannot explain such widespread reliance on polluting energies.

A more in-depth analysis shows that though biomass is largely used in rural areas as primary fuel, in majority of the cases, it is not used as the only fuel for cooking. NSSO data shows that households spend simultaneously on biomass, kerosene, LPG and other fuels. The use of more than one fuel is very common. Biomass, dung cake and crop residue can be obtained without incurring any cost in India, especially in rural areas. The study explored the distribution of energy services utilization in physical units and found out that only 3.75% of rural and 1.64% of urban households rely solely on biomass as a cooking fuel while biomass with other fuels is used in 85.44% of rural and 23.66% of urban households (Table 1).

Table 1 Utilization of multiple fuels for cooking in Indian households (%)

	Rural	Urban
Only biomass	3.76	1.64
LPG but no biomass	3.73	45.26
Kerosene but no biomass	5.84	21.63
Biomass with other fuels	85.44	23.66
Data unavailable	1.24	7.82

Source NSSO 68th round, 2011–12

5 Household Characteristics

Table 2 describes the sample household characteristics. All the households who reported primary fuels for cooking have been considered for the analysis. The average household size is 4.6 in rural areas, whereas the same is 4.1 in urban areas. Since LPG and kerosene prices vary largely across region, LPG and kerosene prices are estimated as the imputed average prices of fuel, whereas average prices (per kg for LPG and per litre for kerosene) are estimated for different income classes across states. Household characteristics also vary widely. Among the households, 84.42% are Hindu and 11.03% are Muslim in rural areas, whereas 80.42% are Hindu and 13.55% are Muslim in urban areas. In rural areas, the age of household head is on an average more than that in the urban areas. The share of household heads, whose age is below 35, is 25.42% in rural areas and 30.31% in urban areas. Around 38% people in rural areas are illiterate as compared to 15.35% in urban areas. Only 9% of people in rural areas have attained education at higher secondary level and above, while the share is 34.4% in urban areas. In both the areas, household head is generally a male member. In India, there is a large number of social groups, such as caste. 32.58% of the people in rural areas and 17.74% of them in urban areas fall into either Scheduled Caste or Scheduled Tribe category. Distribution according to occupational class shows that in rural areas, 34.42% are self-employed in agriculture, 21.44% are casual labour in agriculture, 13.11% are casual labour in non-agriculture and only 8.93% are regular wage/salary earners. In urban areas, 41.52% households are regular wage/salary earners and 34.42% are self-employed. It is clear that household characteristics vary widely across rural and urban region and so is the pattern of fuel choice, as discussed in the earlier section. We need to explore how these characteristics are influencing the fuel stacking behaviour of the household.

6 Factors Affecting the Fuel Stacking Behaviour of Households

In order to understand the factors determining the choice of fuels, a multinomial logit regression has been estimated to understand the fuel stacking behaviour of

Table 2 Sample household characteristics

Characteristics of the sampled households					
Rural (n = 59,695)			Urban (n = 41,963)		
Variables	Mean	Standard deviation	Variables	Mean	Standard deviation
Number of household members	4.6	2.2	Number of household members	4.1	2.2
LPG price	31.1	5.0	LPG price	29.4	1.2
Market price of kerosene	27.7	4.8	Market price of kerosene	32.3	5.8
Monthly per capita expenditure (Rs.)	1414.5	1168.8	Monthly per capita expenditure (Rs.)	2912.7	2756.0
Percentage of households (dummy variable)					
	No. (unweighted)	% (weighted)		No. (unweighted)	% (weighted)
Religion					
Hindu	45,603	84.42	Hindu	31,456	80.42
Muslim	7043	11.03	Muslim	6093	13.55
Christian	4294	2.19	Christian	2774	3.04
Others	2754	2.36	Others	1640	2.99
Age of household head					
Less than 35 years	12,976	25.42	Less than 35 years	10,209	30.31
35–50 years	25,335	41.42	35–50 years	17,391	39.66
More than 50 years	21,383	33.16	More than 50 years	14,363	30.03
Education of household head					
Not literate	17,247	39.08	Not literate	6496	15.35
Below primary	7454	13.57	Below primary	3505	8.36
Primary	8094	13.15	Primary	4359	10.77
Secondary	17,515	25.19	Secondary	13,161	31.11
Higher secondary	4349	4.86	Higher secondary	4981	11.59
Above higher secondary	5031	4.15	Above higher secondary	9458	22.81
Whether owned land					
Yes	20,280	37.76	Yes	22,788	52.76
No	39,414	62.24	No	19,175	47.24

(continued)

Table 2 (continued)

Characteristics of the sampled households					
Rural ($n = 59{,}695$)			Urban ($n = 41{,}963$)		
Variables	Mean	Standard deviation	Variables	Mean	Standard deviation
Gender of household head					
Male	53,249	87.92	Male	36,656	88.27
Female	6445	12.08	Female	5307	11.73
Social groups					
Scheduled Caste and Scheduled Tribe	20,194	32.58	Scheduled Caste and Scheduled Tribe	9129	17.74
OBC	23,757	44.19	OBC	16,156	40.62
Others	15,734	23.22	Others	16,673	41.64
Occupational class					
Self-employed in: agriculture	16,788	34.42	Self-employed	15,647	34.43
Non-agriculture	15,294	16.06	Regular wage/salary earning	16,364	41.52
Regular wage/salary earning	10,705	8.93	Casual labour	5385	12.53
Casual labour in agriculture	4889	21.44	Others	4552	11.52
Casual labour in non-agriculture	8758	13.11			
Others	3248	6.04			

Source NSSO 68th round, 2011–12

the household through analysing the association with wide range of exogenous variables representing the household's socio-economic characteristics for rural and urban sector separately. Multinomial logit estimates the determinants of household's choice between only biomass, LPG but no biomass, kerosene but no biomass and biomass with other fuels. Biomass with other fuels is the omitted variable for both rural and urban sectors. The model captures the fuel stacking behaviour of the households and explores factors that lead to the choice of biomass as a cooking fuel.

The multinomial logit model includes independent variables, namely the number of members in the household, price of LPG, price of open-market kerosene, religion, age of the head of the household, educational level of the head of the household, monthly per capita expenditure decile group, whether land is cultivated by the household or not, gender of the head of the household, social group and the occupational category of the household. The results of the multinomial logit model for the analysis of the determinants of use of multiple fuels as cooking fuel in the rural and urban Indian context are given in Table 3. The coefficients of almost all the factors have been found to be significant at the 1% level of significance.

Results suggest that for rural area, household size plays a major role in the practice of fuel stacking. It is found that, in rural areas, larger the household size, more probability is there that the household would choose biomass with other fuels, i.e. would stack fuels, rather than choosing the option of only biomass, or LPG or kerosene. For urban sector, on the other hand, with increase in number of household members, household is more likely to prefer LPG only over other options.

Higher LPG price and kerosene prices also encourage rural households to choose mix of fuels or kerosene. In urban sector, with an increase in LPG price, the likelihood of choosing the combination of biomass and other fuels increases.

The relative log odds of choosing 'only biomass' against 'biomass with other fuels' decrease by 0.345 with a movement from Hindu to Muslim. For the Christians, households are more likely to choose only biomass over biomass mixed with other fuels. In urban areas, a religion-wise analysis shows Muslims and Christians are more likely to choose other fuels or fuel mix over LPG only as compared to the Hindu population.

For older household heads, the likelihood of a household choosing biomass mixed with other fuels increases. Similarly, in urban areas too, with increase in age of the household head, probability of choosing LPG over biomass only increases in urban areas.

With higher education attained by the household head, it is more likely that the household chooses LPG only. It can be seen that for educational attainment of below primary and primary levels, as compared to 'not literate' household heads, the probability of choosing 'only biomass' increases as compared to biomass with combination of other fuels. This may be attributed to the income effect, which allows the household to acquire more quantity of unclean fuel, but the decision of switching to expensive clean fuel is not yet taken. On the contrary, even at educational attainment of below primary and primary levels, urban households are prone to choosing 'biomass with combination of other fuels' as compared to 'only biomass'. This may be caused by unavailability of biomass or easy availability of clean fuels. In urban areas, with more education attained by household head, they are prone to choose LPG over 'biomass only' or biomass mix with other fuels.

It is also seen that as income increases, households are more likely to choose LPG (with higher coefficients) over other options. With increase in income, there is a high probability of choosing LPG over any other fuel options in the urban sector.

The households possessing own land have a higher probability of choosing biomass along with other fuels, perhaps because of the abundant supply of crop residues. In urban areas, not owning land leads to choosing 'only biomass' option as compared to 'biomass with other fuels', since they are expected to have lower assets as compared to the households who own land.

A female household head is more likely to choose 'only biomass' over 'biomass with other fuels' in the rural sector. They also are less likely to choose LPG over

Table 3 Results of multinomial logit model on fuel stacking

Rural				Urban			
	Only biomass	LPG but no biomass	Kerosene but no biomass		Only biomass	LPG but no biomass	Kerosene but no biomass
Household size	−0.007***	−0.112***	−0.099***	Household size	−0.068***	0.053***	−0.05***
LPG price	−0.113***	−0.371***	0.005***	LPG price	−0.024***	−0.121***	−0.068***
Market price of kerosene	−0.131***	−0.021***	0.063***	Market price of kerosene	−0.076***	0.002***	0.01***
Religion (omitted: Hindu)				Religion (omitted: Hindu)			
Muslim	−0.345***	−0.229***	0.24***	Muslim	−0.405***	−0.427***	−0.164***
Christian	1.003***	−0.254***	−0.587***	Christian	−0.047***	−0.791***	−0.755***
Others	1.556***	1.022***	0.12***	Others	0.702***	0.534***	−0.042***
Age of household head (omitted: <=35 years)				Age of household head (omitted: <=35 years)			
35–50 years	−0.308***	−0.142***	−0.121***	35–50 years	−0.497***	−0.213***	−0.15***
More than 50 years	−0.511***	−0.216***	−0.174***	More than 50 years	−0.956***	−0.352***	−0.231***
Education of household head (omitted: not literate)				Education of household head (omitted: not literate)			
Below primary	0.229***	0.146***	−0.247***	Below primary	−0.036***	0.375***	0.35***
Primary	0.053***	0.476***	−0.064***	Primary	−0.055***	0.56***	0.562***
Secondary	−0.062***	1.003***	0.254***	Secondary	−0.495***	0.891***	0.705***
Higher secondary	−0.524***	1.434***	0.64***	Higher secondary	−0.845***	1.546***	1.022***
Above higher secondary	−0.575***	1.616***	0.855***	Above higher secondary	−2.3***	1.792***	1.01***
Monthly per capita expenditure decile groups (omitted: Decile 1)				Monthly per capita expenditure decile groups (omitted: Decile 1)			
Decile 2	−0.298***	3.241***	0.076***	Decile 2	0.096***	1.151***	0.43***
Decile 3	0.251***	3.052***	0.085***	Decile 3	0.229***	1.601***	0.763***
Decile 4	0.425***	4.021***	−0.007**	Decile 4	0.138***	1.979***	0.708***

(continued)

Table 3 (continued)

Rural				Urban			
	Only biomass	LPG but no biomass	Kerosene but no biomass		Only biomass	LPG but no biomass	Kerosene but no biomass
Decile 5	0.325***	3.716***	0.517***	Decile 5	−0.232***	2.324***	0.959***
Decile 6	0.445***	4.633***	0.135***	Decile 6	−0.112***	2.726***	1.114***
Decile 7	0.439***	4.797***	0.499***	Decile 7	−0.123***	3.202***	1.433***
Decile 8	0.367***	5.033***	0.402***	Decile 8	0.527***	3.478***	1.551***
Decile 9	0.841***	5.55***	0.628***	Decile 9	−0.779***	3.786***	1.464***
Decile 10	0.583***	6.158***	0.854***	Decile 10	0.293***	4.081***	0.989***
Whether owned land (omitted: yes)				Whether owned land (omitted: yes)			
No	−0.585***	−0.391***	−0.182***	No	0.12***	−0.231***	−0.032***
Gender of household head (omitted: male)				Gender of household head (omitted: male)			
Female	0.032***	−0.18***	−0.085***	Female	−0.307***	0.046***	−0.077***
Social groups: Scheduled Caste and Scheduled Tribe=1 (omitted), OBC = 2, others = 3)				Social groups: Scheduled Caste and Scheduled Tribe=1 (omitted), OBC = 2, others = 3)			
OBC	−0.073***	0.451***	0.194***	OBC	−0.366***	0.172***	−0.006***
Others	0.075***	0.863***	0.78***	Others	−0.221***	0.792***	0.57***
Occupational class: (omitted: self-employed in agriculture)				Occupational class: (omitted: self-employed)			
Self-employed in non-agriculture	−0.185***	1.353***	0.916***	Regular wage/salary earning	0.269***	0.546***	0.429***
Regular wage/salary earning	−0.102***	1.87***	0.952***	Casual labour	0.314***	−0.914***	−0.565***
Casual labour in agriculture	0.019***	−0.296***	0.393***	Others	0.444***	0.142***	0.004**
Casual labour in non-agriculture	0.163***	0.252***	−0.028***				

(continued)

Table 3 (continued)

Rural				Urban			
	Only biomass	LPG but no biomass	Kerosene but no biomass		Only biomass	LPG but no biomass	Kerosene but no biomass
Others	0.125***	1.277***	0.554***				
Constant	4.006***	2.23***	−5.239***	Constant	1.289***	0.457***	0.445***
Number of obs		56,824		Number of obs		39,360	
Pseudo R2		0.1617		Pseudo R2		0.2033	

**Significant at 5%, ***significant at 1% level
Source Author's estimation from NSSO 68th round, 2011–12

multiple fuels. In urban areas, female household heads are more likely to choose LPG only.

It is also observed that households belonging to OBC and other castes, as compared to Scheduled Caste or Scheduled Tribe households, are more likely to choose LPG and kerosene over biomass with other fuels. Like in the rural sector, households belonging to OBC and other castes in the urban sector are more likely to choose LPG and kerosene over biomass with other fuels.

For occupational class, the categories are differently defined for rural and urban sector. Since agriculture is a crucial sector in rural India, the occupational classification of household is: self-employed in agriculture, self-employed in non-agriculture, regular wage/salary earner, casual labour in agriculture, casual labour in non-agriculture and others. On the other hand, for urban sector, the classification is: self-employed, regular wage/salary earner, casual labour and others. As compared to self-employed in agriculture, households who are self-employed in non-agriculture are more likely to choose LPG over biomass or multiple fuels in the rural sector. This may be due to the unavailability of crop residue to the latter group of households. In rural areas, for casual labours in agriculture, it is more likely that the household would choose biomass with other fuels over LPG only. In the urban sector, regular wage/salary earners would prefer LPG only as compared to other fuel options, while for casual labour it is more likely that they would choose biomass only, kerosene only or biomass mix, respectively.

7 Conclusion

The study reinforces widespread use of biomass in the rural sector. Around 77% of rural households from all income classes were using biomass as their primary fuel for cooking in 2011–12. Even the average consumption of biomass increases with income in rural areas. This essentially shows that the energy ladder model is not followed in India. With increase in income, households are using larger amounts of biomass rather than shifting to fuels like LPG. Use of biomass is very high in rural areas in states like Chhattisgarh, Madhya Pradesh, Uttar Pradesh and Odisha among large states. The factors behind the practice of fuel stacking are further explored through a multinomial logit model. Results show that in rural areas, households' preference for biomass or stacking fuel can be influenced by age and gender of the head of the household, employment status, socio-economic status and the education level of the members of the household. Prices of alternative fuels can also encourage rural households to choose a mix of fuels. The households who own land have more probability of choosing biomass with other fuels, perhaps because of the abundant supply of crop residues. On the contrary, in urban areas, households are more likely to choose LPG only over other options with increase in household size, age and educational attainment of the household head and household income. Fuel stacking behaviour of rural areas is very much led by the availability of fuelwood, dung cake or crop residue, which they can avail without incurring any cost. In urban areas, unlike rural areas, households are more likely to follow the 'energy ladder' model, where the household shifts from unclean fuels to clean fuels with increase in income or living standard.

There has been a significant increase in the use of clean fuels for cooking like LPG in India in the past years, especially after the government started promoting clean fuels through programmes like Pradhan Mantri Ujjwala Yojana, and an estimated number of 284.6 lakh LPG connections were released in 2017–18. But fuelwood is still being used in Indian households. Ensuring that households continue to use LPG or other clean cooking fuels on a sustained basis is a difficult task to accomplish. National Family Health Survey also reported that 74% of households in rural India are using wood or animal dung or agricultural waste in 2015–16. Supply-side initiatives for adoption of LPG should be matched with demand-side management, under which households need to be aware of the harmful effects of pollutants generated from combustion of solid fuels. This requires overcoming gender, behavioural and cultural barriers, which often ignores the drudgery of women. Availability of clean fuels and their affordability should also be substantially increased so that people can have access to their preferred choice of fuel.

With huge burden of population, energy demand of the residential sector of India is already very huge. The government has taken several steps to increase access to efficient fuels. India historically had provided subsidy on LPG, which is often argued to be fiscally unsustainable. Policy measures are required to provide well-monitored and well-directed subsidy through far-reaching supply chains and viable models of distribution.

Biomass is considered to be a polluting fuel because of indoor pollution generated by it. But it is an environmentally sustainable fuel which can help us to combat the adverse effects of climate change in the long run since it is renewable in nature. Research is needed to utilize these resources in environmentally sustainable manner. Using fuels in an efficient manner can reduce the burden on the ecosystem, arrest land degradation and deter over-exploitation of resources. Biomass can even be used in pollution-less devices and technologies. Biomasses in improved chullahs, biomass briquettes and biogas are safer forms of the fuel. But these technologies could not spread widely in India due to high capital cost for installation, lack of necessary infrastructure and maintenance. Efforts are needed to be taken to make these programmes commercially viable and economically attractive.

Refined energy demand estimation requires extensive information related to energy use pattern to get insights into energy efficiency, income and price elasticities of energy demand, factors influencing the purchase of appliances, fuel switching, etc. National-, state- and/or local-level data need to be collected on regular basis in order to identify the factors that drive residential energy use and improve policy response to address these issues.

Use of biomass and poverty is often considered to be very much linked in developing countries. Poor people are more dependent on forests for their livelihood. The poor people are the most vulnerable to the adverse effects of climate change and also the most affected by the climate extremes. Policies should aim to utilize the rich natural resources that we already have in a sustainable way. To pursue the process of economic development in an environmentally sustainable manner, creation of additional ecological space is important to protect a large proportion of people in the developing world from a situation of abject poverty. Proper institutional arrangement is needed to provide poor people with their basic necessities of life without affecting ecological and social sustainability.

References

Adamu, M. B., Adamu, H., Ade, S. M., & Akeh, G. I. (2020). Household energy consumption in Nigeria: A review on the applicability of the energy ladder model. *Journal of Applied Sciences and Environmental Management, 24*(2), 237–244.

Arlington, L., Patel, A. B., Simmons, E., Kurhe, K., Prakash, A., Rao, S. R., et al. (2019). Duration of solid fuel cookstove use is associated with increased risk of acute lower respiratory infection among children under six months in rural central India. *PLoS ONE, 14*(10), e0224374.

Baldwin, S. F. (1986). Biomass stoves: Engineering design, development and dissemination, volunteers in technical assistance. *Center for Energy and Environmental Studies. Princeton University, Princeton NJ*.

Chafe, Z. A., Brauer, M., Klimont, Z., Van Dingenen, R., Mehta, S., Rao, S., Riahi, K., Dentener, F. & Smith, K. R. (2014). Household cooking with solid fuels contributes to ambient PM2. 5 air pollution and the burden of disease. *Environmental health perspectives, 122*(12), 1314–1320.

Cheng, C. Y., & Urpelainen, J. (2014). Fuel stacking in India: Changes in the cooking and lighting mix, 1987–2010. *Energy, 76*, 306–317.

Choudhuri, P., & Desai, S. (2020). Gender inequalities and household fuel choice in India. *Journal of Cleaner Production*, 121487.

Choumert-Nkolo, J., Motel, P. C., & Le Roux, L. (2019). Stacking up the ladder: A panel data analysis of Tanzanian household energy choices. *World Development, 115*, 222–235.

Danlami, A. H., Applanaidu, S. D., & Islam, R. (2019). Movement towards the adoption of non-traditional household lighting fuel energy in developing areas. *Biofuels, 10*(5), 623–633.

Davis, M. (1998). Rural household energy consumption: The effects of access to electricity—evidence from South Africa. *Energy policy, 26*(3), 207–217.

Ekholm, T., Krey, V., Pachauri, S., & Riahi, K. (2010). Determinants of household energy consumption in India. *Energy Policy, 38*(10), 5696–5707.

Epstein, M. B., Bates, M. N., Arora, N. K., Balakrishnan, K., Jack, D. W., & Smith, K. R. (2013). Household fuels, low birth weight, and neonatal death in India: The separate impacts of biomass, kerosene, and coal. *International Journal of Hygiene and Environmental Health, 216*(5), 523–532.

ESMAP. (1999). Household energy strategies for urban India, the case of Hyderabad. *Report of the Joint UNDP/World Bank Energy Sector Management Assistance Program and the Indstitute of Energy and Environmental Studies*, (214/99).

Foley, G. (1995). *Photovoltaic applications in rural areas of the developing world*. The World Bank.

Gould, C. F., Urpelainen, J., & Sais, J. H. (2020). The role of education and attitudes in cooking fuel choice: Evidence from two states in India. *Energy for Sustainable Development, 54*, 36–50.

Gupta, G., & Köhlin, G. (2006). Preferences for domestic fuel: Analysis with socio-economic factors and rankings in Kolkata, India. *Ecological Economics, 57*(1), 107–121.

Hanna, R., & Oliva, P. (2015). Moving up the energy ladder: The effect of an increase in economic well-being on the fuel consumption choices of the poor in India. *American Economic Review, 105*(5), 242–246.

Heltberg, R. (2005). Factors determining household fuel choice in Guatemala. *Environment and development economics, 10*(3), 337–361.

Herington, M. J., & Malakar, Y. (2016). Who is energy poor? Revisiting energy (in) security in the case of Nepal. *Energy Research and Social Science, 21*, 49–53.

Hiemstra-Van der Horst, G., & Hovorka, A. J. (2008). Reassessing the "energy ladder": Household energy use in Maun, Botswana. *Energy Policy, 36*(9), 3333–3344.

Hosier, R. H., & Dowd, J. (1987). Household fuel choice in Zimbabwe: An empirical test of the energy ladder hypothesis. *Resources and energy, 9*(4), 347–361.

Hosier, R. H., & Dowd, J. (1988). Household energy use in Zimbabwe: An analysis of consumption patterns and fuel choice. *Household energy use in Zimbabwe: An analysis of consumption patterns and fuel choice.* 83–109.

Hosier, R. H., & Kipondya, W. (1993). Urban household energy use in Tanzania: Prices, substitutes and poverty. *Energy Policy, 21*(5), 454–473.

Hughes, G., & Dunleavy, M. (2000). *Why do babies and young children die in India?*. The World Bank: The role of the household environment.

James, B. S., Shetty, R. S., Kamath, A., & Shetty, A. (2020). Household cooking fuel use and its health effects among rural women in southern India—A cross-sectional study. *PLoS ONE, 15*(4), e0231757.

Joon, V., Chandra, A., & Bhattacharya, M. (2009). Household energy consumption pattern and socio-cultural dimensions associated with it: A case study of rural Haryana, India. *Biomass and bioenergy, 33*(11), 1509–1512.

Jumbe, C. B., & Angelsen, A. (2011). Modeling choice of fuelwood source among rural households in Malawi: A multinomial probit analysis. *Energy Economics, 33*(5), 732–738.

Karekezi, S., McDade, S., Boardman, B., & Kimani, J. (2012). Energy, poverty, and development. In T. B. Johansson, N. Nakicenovic, A. Patwardhan, & L. Gomez-Echeverri (Eds.), *Global energy assessment—Toward a sustainable future* (pp. 151–190). Cambridge, United Kingdom and New York, NY, USA: Cambridge University Press.

Leach, G. (1992). The energy transition. *Energy Policy, 20*(2), 116–123.

Leach, G., & Mearns, R. (1988). *Beyond the fuelwood crisis: People, land and trees in Africa* (pp. 23–40). London: Earthscan.

Liao, H., Chen, T., Tang, X., & Wu, J. (2019). Fuel choices for cooking in China: Analysis based on multinomial logit model. *Journal of Cleaner Production, 225,* 104–111.

Maconachie, R., Tanko, A., & Zakariya, M. (2009). Descending the energy ladder? Oil price shocks and domestic fuel choices in Kano, Nigeria. *Land Use Policy, 26*(4), 1090–1099.

Masera, O. R., Saatkamp, B. D., & Kammen, D. M. (2000). From linear fuel switching to multiple cooking strategies: A critique and alternative to the energy ladder model. *World Development, 28*(12), 2083–2103.

Miller, G., & Mobarak, A. M. (2013). *Gender differences in preferences, intra-household externalities, and low demand for improved cookstoves* (No. w18964). National Bureau of Economic Research.

Modi, V., McDade, S., Lallement, D., & Saghir, J. (2005). Energy Services for the Millennium Development Goals. *Energy services for the millennium development goals.*

Murphy, J. T. (2001). Making the energy transition in rural East Africa: Is leapfrogging an alternative? *Technological Forecasting and Social Change, 68*(2), 173–193.

MHFW, N. (2015). Report of the steering committee on air pollution and health-related issues. *Ministry of Health and Family Welfare, Government of India, New Delhi.*

Nansaior, A., Patanothai, A., Rambo, A. T., & Simaraks, S. (2011). Climbing the energy ladder or diversifying energy sources? The continuing importance of household use of biomass energy in urbanizing communities in Northeast Thailand. *Biomass and Bioenergy, 35*(10), 4180–4188.

O'Neill, B. C., Ren, X., Jiang, L., & Dalton, M. (2012). The effect of urbanization on energy use in India and China in the iPETS model. *Energy Economics, 34,* S339–S345.

Pachauri, S., & Jiang, L. (2008). The household energy transition in India and China. *Energy policy, 36*(11), 4022–4035.

Pandey, V. L., & Chaubal, A. (2011). Comprehending household cooking energy choice in rural India. *Biomass and Bioenergy, 35*(11), 4724–4731.

Patel, R., & Chauhan, S. (2020). Risk of low birth weight and exposure to type of cooking fuel in India. *International Journal of Pregnancy & Child Birth for MedCrave Group, 6*(1), 8–11.

Patel, S. K., Patel, S., & Kumar, A. (2019). Effects of cooking fuel sources on the respiratory health of children: Evidence from the Annual Health Survey, Uttar Pradesh, India. *Public health, 169,* 59–68.

Rahut, D. B., Das, S., De Groote, H., & Behera, B. (2014). Determinants of household energy use in Bhutan. *Energy, 69,* 661–672.

Rao, M. N., & Reddy, B. S. (2007). Variations in energy use by Indian households: An analysis of micro level data. *Energy, 32*(2), 143–153.

Ravindra, K., Kaur-Sidhu, M., Mor, S., & John, S. (2019). Trend in household energy consumption pattern in India: A case study on the influence of socio-cultural factors for the choice of clean fuel use. *Journal of Cleaner Production, 213,* 1024–1034.

Ravindranath, N. H., & Ramakrishna, J. (1997). Energy options for cooking in India. *Energy policy, 25*(1), 63–75.

Reddy, B. S. (2003). Overcoming the energy efficiency gap in India's household sector. *Energy Policy, 31*(11), 1117–1127.

Reddy, B. S. (2004). Economic and social dimensions of household energy use: A case study of India, In Ortega, E. & Ulgiati, S. (editors): Proceedings of IV Biennial International Workshop "Advances in Energy Studies". Unicamp, Campinas, SP, Brazil. June 16–19, 469–477.

Saghir, J. (2004). Energy and poverty: Myths, links, and policy issues. Energy Sector Notes. Energy and Mining Sector Board, 4. *World Bank, Washington, DC.*

Sehgal, M., Rizwan, S. A., & Krishnan, A. (2014). Disease burden due to biomass cooking-fuel-related household air pollution among women in India. *Global Health Action, 7*(1), 25326.

Sharma, D., Ravindra, K., Kaur, M., Prinja, S., & Mor, S. (2020). Cost evaluation of different household fuels and identification of the barriers for the choice of clean cooking fuels in India. *Sustainable Cities and Society, 52,* 101825.

Uhunamure, S. E., Nethengwe, N. S., & Musyoki, A. (2017). Driving forces for fuelwood use in households in the Thulamela municipality, South Africa. *Journal of Energy in Southern Africa, 28*(1), 25–34.

Van der Kroon, B., Brouwer, R., & Van Beukering, P. J. (2013). The energy ladder: Theoretical myth or empirical truth? Results from a meta-analysis. *Renewable and Sustainable Energy Reviews, 20,* 504–513.

Viswanathan, B., & Kumar, K. S. K. (2005). Cooking fuel use patterns in India: 1983–2000. *Energy Policy, 33*(8), 1021–1036.

Warwick, H., & Doig, A. (2004). *Smoke–The killer in the kitchen.* London: ITDG.

Understanding Energy Use in Indian Agricultural Production System in Post-WTO Period

Manoj Bhatt and Surya Bhushan

1 Introduction

In the context of Indian agriculture, the recent decade of the 2000s, especially post-reform and WTO[1], has been unprecedented on two counts—firstly, the sector recorded 3.8% annual growth in value added since 2004–05 which is highest since 1950–51, and secondly, for the first time in the history of Indian agriculture that the absolute number of cultivators and agricultural labourers has started falling. However, the issue of maintaining food security and sustaining growth has become more difficult now than in the past. With decline in the quality of land and water, agriculture faces intense problems in maintaining sustainability of production (Bhushan 2014).

The structural changes in terms of composition of output–input mix have been observed in Indian agriculture. On the output side, there are increasing trends in diversification towards high-value crops, with strong output expansion of livestock, horticulture, fisheries and poultry sectors, and on the input side, there is substantial increase in the use of modern inputs and farm mechanization. The average farm power availability has propelled to 2.02 kW/ha in 2013–14 from about 0.30 kW/ha

This paper is a completely revised and improved version of an earlier draft presented by the authors at a conference at Indian Institute of Foreign Trade, New Delhi, on 11–12 December 2014.

M. Bhatt (✉)
Department of Economics, University of Jammu, Jammu, India
e-mail: manojbhatt@gmail.com

S. Bhushan
Development Management Institute (DMI), Udyog Bhawan, Patna, Bihar, India
e-mail: surya.bhushan@gmail.com

[1]There exists a sizable body of the literature on the politics of economic reforms in India initiated in the early 1990s (Bardhan, 1999, 2001, 2003, 2005; Jenkins, 1999; Varshney, 1999; Corbridge & Harriss, 2000; Mooij 2005).

P. Dasgupta et al. (eds.), *Sustainable Development Insights from India*,
India Studies in Business and Economics,
https://doi.org/10.1007/978-981-33-4830-1_11

in 1960–61, an increase of almost seven times (Singh et al., 2014). The major reason for this transformation is attributed to the changes in power use composition for the agriculture from mobile sources (constitutes human and draught animals) to stationary sources (constitutes machine use) in the recent times. In 1970–71, the mobile sources contributed 60% to the total energy use in agriculture, while electricity and fossil energy together provided 40% energy. However, in a span of three and a half decades, the share of these energy inputs in agriculture has undergone a significant change—the contribution of electricity and fossil energy together has gone up to 86% and that of mobile sources has come down to 14% (Jha et al., 2012). They also found that for any target growth of agricultural gross domestic product (GDP), growth in energy use should be more than two times the agricultural GDP growth. This shows that the additional need of farm power is being met through mechanical and electrical sources of power. These developments have significant implications for energy use in agriculture.

However even after this, Indian agriculture operates at a very low level of energy ladder using traditional or non-commercial fuels like animal labour or human labour. Owing to the energy poverty that the sector faces as well as due to political reasons, most of the states provide free or highly subsidized electricity to the agriculture sector. Yet in recent years, the electricity consumption in agriculture sector has come under much criticism (Swain, 2006; Badiani, 2010). Most argue that the free power policy only helps large landed farmers and is solely done for political reasons but lack economic logic (Gulati & Narayanan, 2000, 2003; Howes & Murgai, 2003); some others argue that free or near free electricity has led to inefficient usage of it in agriculture sector and does not provide any incentive to farmers to improve their efficiency (Swain et al. 2012). Many have even linked free power argument to ground water depletion (Badiani, 2010).

This paper is an attempt to clarify major trends of energy use in production and productivity of food grain in Indian agricultural landscape. Using panel data on the value of food grain output of 10 major producing states, we seek to estimate the growth differences and to understand how energy use affects agricultural growth. The panel data approach is applied to Commission for Agricultural Costs and Prices (CACP) annual data of inputs and outputs for the period 2000–2010 for food grain, for which the most comprehensive temporal data available. The rest of this paper is organized as follows: Sect. 2 presents energy use pattern in Indian agriculture. Section 3 discusses the data and methodology used in the study. The data and their sources are described in this section. Section 4 infers the results and implications for the study, and Sect. 5 presents the summary and conclusions.

2 Energy Use in Indian Agriculture

Indian agriculture has undergone some profound structural transformations since last six decades. Structural metamorphosis, especially in terms of composition and

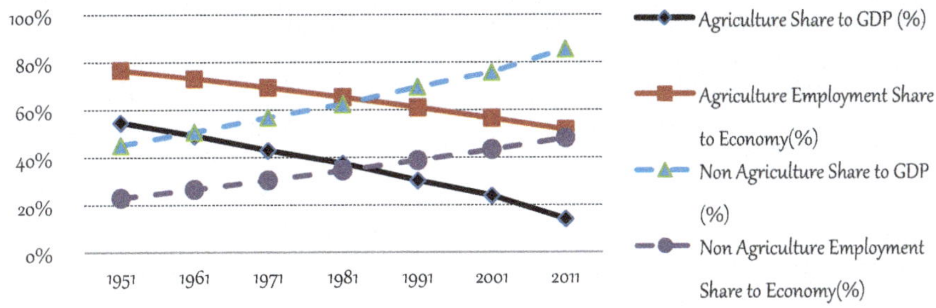

Fig. 1 Structural transformation of Indian economy (1951–2011). *Source* Compiled from Agricultural Statistics at a Glance (2011), Central Statistics Office, New Delhi, and Registrar General of India

means of production, is a significant feature in the process of economic growth and development of an economy (Fig. 1).

As shown in Fig. 1, the pace of structural transformation has been sluggish with slacking decline in the share of labour in agriculture relative to the decline in the share of agriculture in aggregate GDP of the Indian economy (Bosworth et al., 2008; Binswanger-Mkhize and Hans, 2013). India's tryst with transformation has also been characterized as 'stunted' (Binswanger-Mkhize and Hans, 2013) due to the existing labour moving primarily into the rural non-farm and informal sector and becoming increasingly 'casualized' (Lanjouw & Murgai, 2009). This atypical demographic transition places a heavy tax on rural well-being and prosperity. Clearly, as Fig. 1 suggests, India is still far away from a 'turning point', the point at which the inter-sectoral labour productivities start to converge, in its structural transformation (Binswanger-Mkhize and Hans, 2013). Recently during the decades of the 2000s, there has been a perceptible change in the agricultural wage growth trend, which had been substantially low otherwise (Binswanger-Mkhize and Hans, 2013). This may be due to the adoption of right-based employment guarantee policy like the Mahatma Gandhi National Rural Employment Guarantee Act (MGNREGA) and increase in rural minimum wages subsequently. Gulati et al. (2013) noted a V-shaped behaviour in real farm wages, during the 2000s. Annually, it drops by 1.8% during 2000–01 to 2006–07, and then rapidly rising by 6.8% during 2007-08 to 2011–12. Rising real wages have potential implications for employment both on and off the farm, as they are likely to induce greater mechanization on the farm and more capital intensity off the farm. The structure of energy consumption in Indian agriculture may reveal much better picture on this.

The energy inputs in Indian agricultural production can be classified into two parts: one direct use of machinery, electricity consumption, human and animal labour, and second indirect use of fertilizers and other chemicals.

The total energy use in Indian agriculture has increased more than 5 and half times in almost three decades between 1970 and 2009, while the increase in food grain productivity has been just above 2 times for the same period (Table 1). Further, during these periods, the contribution of animal energy dropped significantly from

Table 1 Temporal distribution of farm power sources in Indian agriculture

Year	Food grain yield (T/Ha)	Farm power (Kw/Ha)	Source-wise (%)					
			Agricultural workers	Draught animals	Tractors	Power tillers	Diesel engines	Electric motors
1971–72	0.872	0.35	10.64	52.86	8.45	0.11	17.16	10.79
1981–82	1.023	0.63	9.2	33.55	18.46	0.11	22.85	15.82
1991–92	1.294	0.92	7.22	20.5	26.14	0.16	21.14	24.84
2001–02	1.723	1.35	5.7	11.76	36.77	0.36	19.1	26.31
2005–06	1.715	1.66	5.39	9.97	38.45	0.44	20.09	25.66
2009–10	1.92	1.72	5.12	8.55	41.67	0.52	19.01	25.13

Source Singh et al. (2011), State of Indian Agriculture (2012)

43.9 to 5.8% and human energy from 36.7 to 7.9%, and the commercial energy has increased significantly during the period (electricity from 0.19 to 38.1%, diesel from 2.4 to 18.3% and fertilizer from 16.4 to 29.7%). This reflects the increasing use of commercial energy in the Indian agriculture. The table also shows a high correlation between farm power availability and increased food grain productivity.

3 Data and Methodology

The primary source of input and output data is the various reports of CACP collected under the *Comprehensive Scheme for Studying Cost of Cultivation of Principal Crops* by the CACP, Directorate of Economics and Statistics, Ministry of Agriculture (various volumes) for the period 2000–2010. The detailed features of our data set are described in Bhushan (2014). The value of output and input costs used in the study is made at constant prices by corresponding input and output index. All the data are in quantity per hectare. The dependent variable is value of output of agriculture, and independent variables are direct energy use as human labour, draft animal labour, machine; for indirect energy use, we have taken chemical fertilizer use in food grain production. We have used electricity consumption (in million kWh) in agricultural sector from the Central Electricity Authority (CEA) as one of explanatory variables.

Table 2 reports the descriptive statistics of the major variables used in estimating the panel data of food grain from 2000 to 2010 for the major food grain-producing states in terms of area and output in alphabetical order, Andhra Pradesh (AP), Assam, Bihar, Haryana, Karnataka, Madhya Pradesh (MP), Orissa, Punjab, Uttar Pradesh (UP) and West Bengal (WB). West Bengal (WB), Punjab and Haryana have highest mean output. However, when it comes to usage of modern inputs, Karnataka, Haryana and Andhra Pradesh (AP) lead in use of chemical fertilizer and Punjab, Haryana and Andhra Pradesh lead in usage of machine labour. The presence of traditional inputs

Table 2 Summary of mean of output and inputs per hectare (2000–2010)

States	Metric	Value of output	Human labour	Draft animal	Machine labour	Chemical fertilizers	Electricity consumption
AP	Mean	62,040	2865	220	688	668	1871
	CV (%)	22	16	40	29	12	23
Assam	Mean	52,007	1772	691	84	50	12
	CV (%)	17	11	5	63	18	27
Bihar	Mean	23,702	1502	188	298	264	113
	CV (%)	12	10	29	11	12	21
Haryana	Mean	50,846	2333	21	694	677	1511
	CV (%)	15	15	23	6	19	23
Karnataka	Mean	41,868	2652	531	669	882	1317
	CV (%)	10	16	23	14	13	14
MP	Mean	18,956	1130	438	173	187	358
	CV (%)	18	16	25	35	17	11
Orissa	Mean	33,552	2040	587	131	313	32
	CV (%)	18	11	14	20	16	10
Punjab	Mean	48,964	1500	22	898	617	1179
	CV (%)	13	17	40	10	15	31
UP	Mean	38,319	1679	186	447	433	291
	CV (%)	14	10	15	17	8	16
WB	Mean	68,523	2901	600	215	426	158
	CV (%)	14	12	32	21	9	25

CV Coefficient of variation

used in food grain production, like animal labour, is higher in Assam, West Bengal and Orissa.

Of all the energy inputs, the human labour seems to be major inputs in food grain production. Conceptually, as noted by other scholars (e.g. Raghavan, 2008) labour use, which is a function of labour intensity in cultivation, i.e. the relative level of application of human labour to machine labour, is generally negative, as human labour is displaced by machine labour. Further, the hours of human labour applied in cultivation depend on the extent of draught labour use, which are positively correlated as more and more use of draught labour would necessitate the requirement of more and more human farm labour. The low level of animal labour entails the increasing mechanization in agricultural production. The tractors and other farm machines, it seems, have increasingly replaced animal labour for preparing land, planting and threshing.[2]However, our analysis figures out that even when animal labour is on a

[2]Bhalla and Singh (2010) observed a declining trend in interstate disparity in the use of modern inputs over 1962–65 to 2003-06. The coefficient of variations among states declined from 398 to 152 for tractors used, from 733 to 62 for number of tube wells, from 531 to 118 for fertilizer

decline human labour has increased in nearly all the states irrespective of their level of mechanization which is quite contrary to what Bhalla and Singh (2010) suggest.

In order to eliminate partly short-term fluctuations in the agricultural outputs due to heavy dependence on weather, we use three-year weighted and centred moving averages for all the variables. This may be enough to capture the short-term cyclical variations.

Methodological Underpinnings

We have tested a panel data across the states under the scope of current study for the latest decade of 2000–2010. One obvious advantage of the panel data approach is that it can be helpful for the 'correction of the bias generated by omitted variables and heterogeneity in the classical cross-sectional regression' (Islam, 1995). Panel data, in fact, allow for technological differences across regions (or at least the unobservable and unmeasurable part of these differences), by modelling the regional specific effect.

We construct our empirical regression as log–log model for the longitudinal data as follows:

$$\begin{aligned} Ln\mathrm{Y}_{it}^{\mathrm{All}} &= \alpha_i + \beta_{\mathrm{HL}} Ln\mathrm{HL}_{it} + \beta_{\mathrm{AL}} Ln\mathrm{AL}_{it} + \beta_{\mathrm{ML}} Ln\mathrm{ML}_{it} \\ &\quad + \beta_{\mathrm{CL}} Ln\mathrm{CL}_{it} + \beta_{\mathrm{IEL}} Ln\mathrm{EL}_{it} + \varepsilon_{it} \ldots \end{aligned} \tag{1}$$

where the left-hand variable is value of output in agriculture, Y_{it}, in state i and time t. The regressors are $\log(\mathrm{HL})_{it}$ (log of human labour in state i in time t), $\log(\mathrm{AL})_{\mathrm{i}}$ (log of draft animal labour use in state i in time t), $\log(\mathrm{ML})_{it}$ (log of machine labour in state i in time t), $\log(\mathrm{CL})_{it}$ (log of chemical fertilizer use in state i in time t), $\log(\mathrm{EL})_{\mathrm{it}}$ (log of electricity consumption in agriculture in state i in time t) and ε_{it} (the error term).

β's represent input elasticities that are assumed to be the same for all states and factors that affect state-specific regression coefficients.

α_i represents parameters that are time invariant and account for any state-specific effect not included in the regression equation.

As discussed in Arbia et al. (2005), two different interpretations may be given to the parameters α_i; i.e. two different models may be distinguished according to this interpretation. Equation 1 is a fixed-effect (FE) panel data model in case of α_i assumed to be fixed parameters, else if the α_i's are assumed to be random, it is random effect (RE). Generally, fixed-effect model is more appropriate when the regression analysis is limited to a precise set of individuals (regions), while random effect is a more appropriate specification if we are drawing a certain number of individuals randomly from a larger population.[3]

---

consumption, and from 251 to 88 for irrigation intensity during these periods. They further raised the question of long-run sustainability to maintain the agricultural growth through increasingly higher use of costly and heavily subsidized inputs that not only lead to soil and environmental degradation but also putting pressure on political economy.

[3]For details on econometric methodology, see Baltagi (2013, Chap. 2) and Wooldridge (2013, Chap. 14) for good overviews of fixed-effect and random-effect models. STATA has been used to

4 Econometric Results

Regression results reported in Tables 3 and 4 provide estimation results on the role played by the energy inputs in the production of food grains across Indian states. Before discussing result, some statistical features need to be emphasized as highlighted by Démurger (2001) such as the need for several tests for choosing the correct specification between random and fixed-effect models, such as the Hausman test which indicates that a fixed-effect model is preferred to a random-effect model (Table 5). To check the robustness of our results (following Mody and Srinivasan, 1998), the random-effect model provides a composite picture, as it combines the within and between perspectives, while the use of different panel data techniques allows for the extraction of the maximum information from the data and to test the robustness of the estimates. Moreover, the use of a random-effect model allows us

Table 3 Panel data model results (fixed effects)

Fixed-effect (within) regression						
R-sq:	Within	0.7702	Obs per group		Min	11
	Between	0.1236			Avg	11
	Overall	0.1973			Max	11
			$F(6,94)$		Prob > F	
corr(u_i, Xb)		−0.1352	63.67		0	
Model estimates						
Value of output	Estimates	Std. err.	t-value	$P > \|t\|$	[95% conf. interval]	
Intercept	8.641558	0.530715	16.28	0	7.587955	9.69516
Human labour	0.487241	0.071652	6.8	0	0.344993	0.629488
Draft animals	−0.09132	0.033411	−2.73	0.007	−0.15765	−0.02499
Machine labour	0.268123	0.035444	7.56	0	0.197758	0.338488
Chemical fertilizer	−0.58965	0.062976	−9.36	0	−0.71467	−0.46462
Electricity consumption	0.089566	0.034881	2.57	0.012	0.020318	0.158814
sigma_u	0.411038	s.d. of residuals within groups *ui*				
sigma_e	0.079588	s.d. of residuals (overall error term) *ei*				
Rho	0.963863	([(sigma_*u*)^2/{(sigma_*u*)^2 + (sigma_*e*)^2}}intra-class correlation				
F test that all u_i = 0						
F(9, 94)	152.74	Prob > F	0.0000			

estimate this model. There is considerable debate regarding the choice between the FE and RE models (Griliches, 1984).

Table 4 Panel data model results (random effects)

Random-effect GLS regression						
R-sq	Within	0.7697		Obs per group:	Min	11
	Between	0.1518			Avg	11
	Overall	0.2245			Max	11
				Wald chi2(6)	Prob > chi2	
corr(*u_i*, *X*)	0 (assumed)			321.35	0	
Model estimates						
Value of output	Estimates	Std. err.	*t*-value	$P > \|t\|$	[95% conf. interval]	
Intercept	8.577562	0.520971	16.46	0	7.556476	9.598647
Human labour	0.501276	0.068987	7.27	0	0.366064	0.636488
Draft animals	−0.09971	0.032219	−3.09	0.002	−0.16286	−0.03657
Machine labour	0.266071	0.035119	7.58	0	0.197239	0.334903
Chemical fertilizer	−0.57728	0.057088	−10.11	0	−0.68917	−0.46539
Electricity consumption	0.082544	0.030855	2.68	0.007	0.022068	0.143019
sigma_u	0.420409	s.d. of residuals within groups *ui*				
sigma_e	0.079588	s.d. of residuals (overall error term) *ei*				
Rho	0.965401	([(sigma_*u*)^2/{(sigma_*u*)^2 + (sigma_*e*)^2}}intra-class correlation				

Table 5 Hausman test (fixed effect vs. random effects)

Hausman test	Fixed (*b*)	Random (*B*)	Difference (*b* − *B*)	sqrt(diag(*V_b* − *V_B*))
Human labour	0.487241	0.501276	−0.01404	0.01936
Draft animals	−0.09132	−0.09971	0.008396	0.008847
Machine labour	0.268123	0.266071	0.002052	0.004787
Chemical fertilizer	−0.58965	−0.57728	−0.01236	0.02659
Electricity consumption	0.089566	0.082544	0.007022	0.016268
b = consistent under Ho and Ha				
B = inconsistent under Ha, efficient under Ho				
Test: Ho: difference in coefficients not systematic				
chi2(6) = (*b* − *B*)′[(*V_b* − *V_B*)^(−1)](*b* − i) = 3.69			Prob > chi2 = 0.5961	

to test explanatory variables that are likely to be affected by economic development and consequently to be inversely correlated to growth (Démurger, 2001).

The F test indicates that the coefficients in the model are different than zero. Further, 'rho', the intra-class correlation, shows 98% of the variance is due to differences across states.

We use Hausman specification test to decide between a random-effect and fixed-effect model (Hausman, 1978).[4]

The panel data results show the existence of considerable degree of dynamism in recent years in food grain production systems across Indian states. The regional dimension of food grain production systems depicts an interesting picture of interstate disparity in productivity. Barua and Das (1996) investigated the determinants of the persistence of regional inequality, using maximum entropy method, and find that differences in agriculture and infrastructure are the largest sources of inequality among the various regions of India. The statistically positive response of human labour, machine labour and electricity consumption indicates the importance of these inputs in food grain production. The estimated coefficient of chemical fertilizer use is negative suggests that the low fertilizer use states tend to grow faster than the higher fertilizer use states, other things equal. The negative response of chemical fertilizer signals the presence of diminishing returns to soil fertility for high yield states. We already witnessed this across high yield states, like Punjab, Haryana and Andhra Pradesh. Sidhu and Byerlee (1992) reported high fertilizer use, exceeding the recommended dose, in some of the major developed districts of Punjab, such as Ludhiana, and already showing a sign of diminishing returns to fertilizer use. However, at the same time we also observed a substantially high return to marginal response of chemical fertilizer for states like Assam, Bihar and Orissa. The negative response of draft animals to agricultural output shows the declining importance of this input in favour of mechanization in production systems.

Table 6 suggests that the intensities of each type of energy usage have shown more or less a downward trend in all the states barring machine labour. The electricity sales

[4]The Hausman test helps in detecting violation of the random-effect modelling assumption that the explanatory variables are orthogonal to the unit effects. In case of no correlation between the independent variable(s) and the unit effects, then estimates of β in the fixed-effect model $\left(\hat{\beta}_{FE}\right)$ should be similar to estimates of β in the random-effect model $\left(\hat{\beta}_{RE}\right)$ (for instance, as in Haspolat, 2015; Clark & Linzer, 2015). The Hausman test statistic H is a measure of the difference between the two estimates:

$$H = \left(\hat{\beta}_{RE} - \hat{\beta}_{FE}\right)' \left[Var\left(\hat{\beta}_{FE}\right) - Var\left(\hat{\beta}_{RE}\right)\right]^{-1} \left(\hat{\beta}_{RE} - \hat{\beta}_{FE}\right)$$

Under the null hypothesis of orthogonality, H is distributed chi-square with degrees of freedom equal to the number of regressors in the model. A finding that $p < 0{:}05$ is taken as evidence that the two models are different enough to reject the null hypothesis, and hence to reject the random-effect model in favour of the fixed-effect model.

Table 6 Intensities of various energy inputs

	AP	Assam	Bihar	Haryana	Karnataka	MP	Orissa	Punjab	UP	WB
AL intensity										
1990–91	0.1977	0.2895	0.3167	0.0578	0.3919	0.3615	0.3530	0.0121	0.1862	0.2481
1995–96	0.1163	0.2869	0.1901	0.0211	0.2483	0.3825	0.2695	0.0037	0.0842	0.1691
2000–01	0.0881	0.2469	0.0791	0.0034	0.2775	0.3170	0.3365	0.0023	0.0486	0.1714
2005–06	0.0344	0.2414	0.0449	0.0042	0.1191	0.1502	0.1806	0.0019	0.0531	0.1115
2009–10	0.0278	0.2069	0.0486	0.0025	0.1630	0.1521	0.2007	0.0039	0.0313	0.0709
HL intensity										
1990–91	1.2348	0.7322	0.9066	0.5612	1.5548	0.6899	1.0618	0.2923	0.6041	0.9067
1995–96	1.1872	0.8537	0.6659	0.5347	1.4047	0.7880	1.0829	0.2719	0.5532	0.8611
2000–01	0.7649	0.6615	0.5328	0.3749	1.2547	0.6588	1.0372	0.1873	0.4257	0.6363
2005–06	0.4987	0.5515	0.4264	0.2836	0.6346	0.4077	0.6163	0.1462	0.3492	0.5016
2009–10	0.7257	0.5739	0.5544	0.4336	1.0110	0.5600	0.8459	0.2369	0.3892	0.6746
ML intensity										
1990–91	0.2239	0.0098	0.0567	0.1020	0.1246	0.0374	0.0158	0.1465	0.1427	0.0349
1995–96	0.1889	0.0151	0.0563	0.1476	0.2267	0.0716	0.0251	0.1331	0.0835	0.0401
2000–01	0.1415	0.0212	0.0883	0.0994	0.2648	0.0475	0.0447	0.1207	0.1251	0.0389
2005–06	0.1275	0.0158	0.1123	0.1039	0.2001	0.0772	0.0456	0.0901	0.0791	0.0330
2009–10	0.2170	0.0547	0.1162	0.0964	0.2900	0.1109	0.0571	0.1101	0.1133	0.0585
EL intensity										
1990–91	0.5831	0.0092	0.1368	0.3525	0.6011	0.1866	0.0325	0.2859	0.2216	0.0479
1995–96	0.8058	0.0116	0.1088	0.3566	0.8739	0.4914	0.0459	0.3023	0.2370	0.0957
2000–01	0.7827	0.0114	0.0928	0.3717	0.9133	0.3414	0.0349	0.1713	0.1190	0.0570
2005–06	0.6011	0.0056	0.0649	0.4743	0.8843	0.3585	0.0213	0.3240	0.1440	0.0598
2009–10	1.0934	0.0074	0.0678	0.6034	1.0208	0.2762	0.0200	0.3924	0.1524	0.0954
CL intensity										
1990–91	0.4087	0.0105	0.1498	0.1962	0.4833	0.1656	0.1752	0.1740	0.1424	0.1477
1995–96	0.3552	0.0061	0.1626	0.1893	0.5245	0.1888	0.1788	0.1269	0.1397	0.1285
2000–01	0.1941	0.0203	0.0932	0.1307	0.4265	0.1085	0.1784	0.0892	0.1064	0.0963
2005–06	0.1307	0.0145	0.0891	0.0911	0.2909	0.0646	0.0960	0.0640	0.0909	0.0719
2009–10	0.1244	0.0171	0.0706	0.0759	0.2459	0.0915	0.0923	0.0642	0.1023	0.0876
Electricity sales to agriculture to total sales of electricity in the state										
1990–91	0.4179	0.0182	0.2040	0.4481	0.3631	0.1873	0.0382	0.4254	0.3995	0.2209
1995–96	0.4962	0.0248	0.1239	0.4675	0.4632	0.3648	0.0686	0.3729	0.3672	0.2639
2000–01	0.4334	0.0213	0.1351	0.4512	0.4008	0.2650	0.0322	0.2847	0.2043	0.2920
2005–06	0.3572	0.0109	0.2868	0.4180	0.3408	0.3324	0.0221	0.3015	0.1756	0.2945
2009–10	0.3154	0.0098	0.1309	0.4029	0.3421	0.2681	0.0122	0.3346	0.1764	0.2637

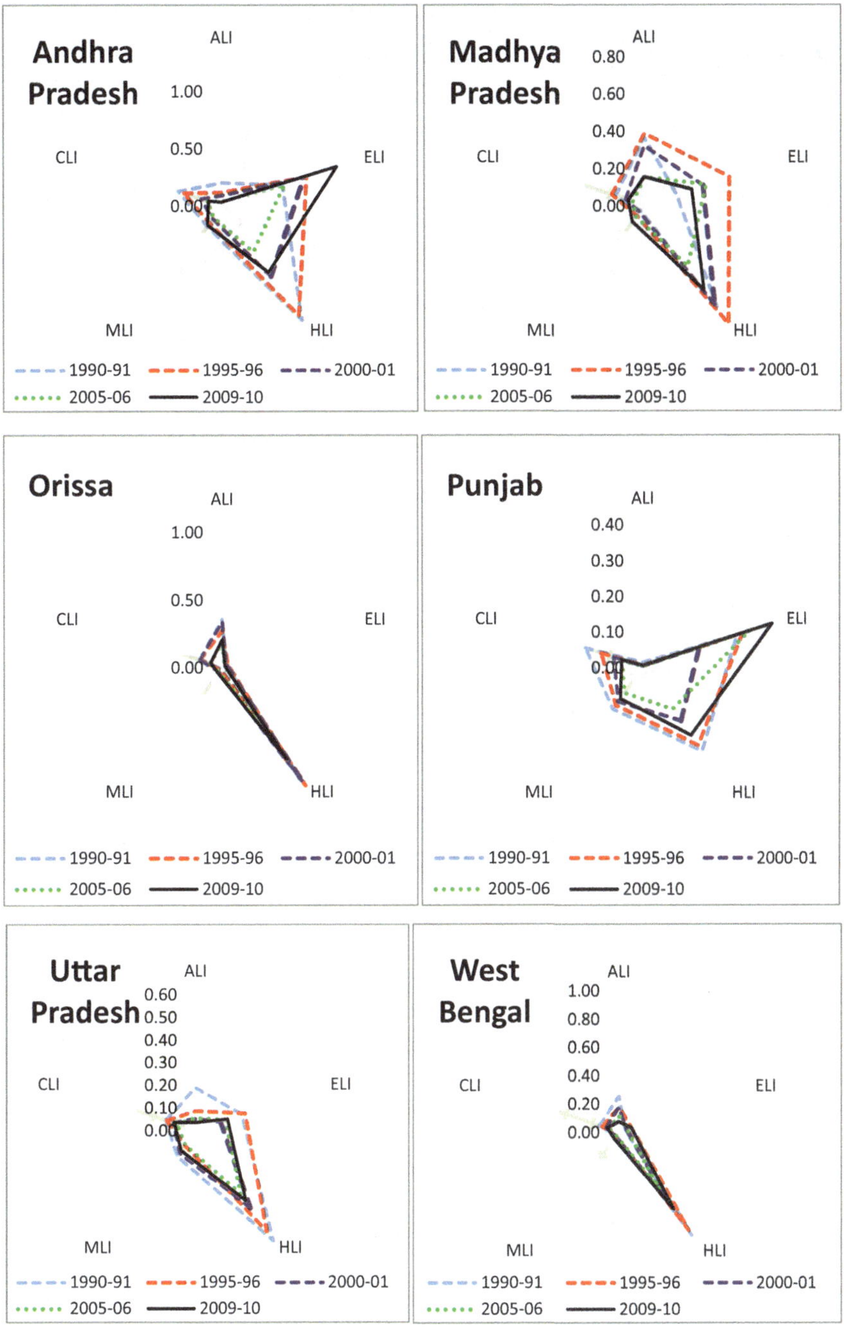

Fig. 2 Intensities of various energy inputs in each state

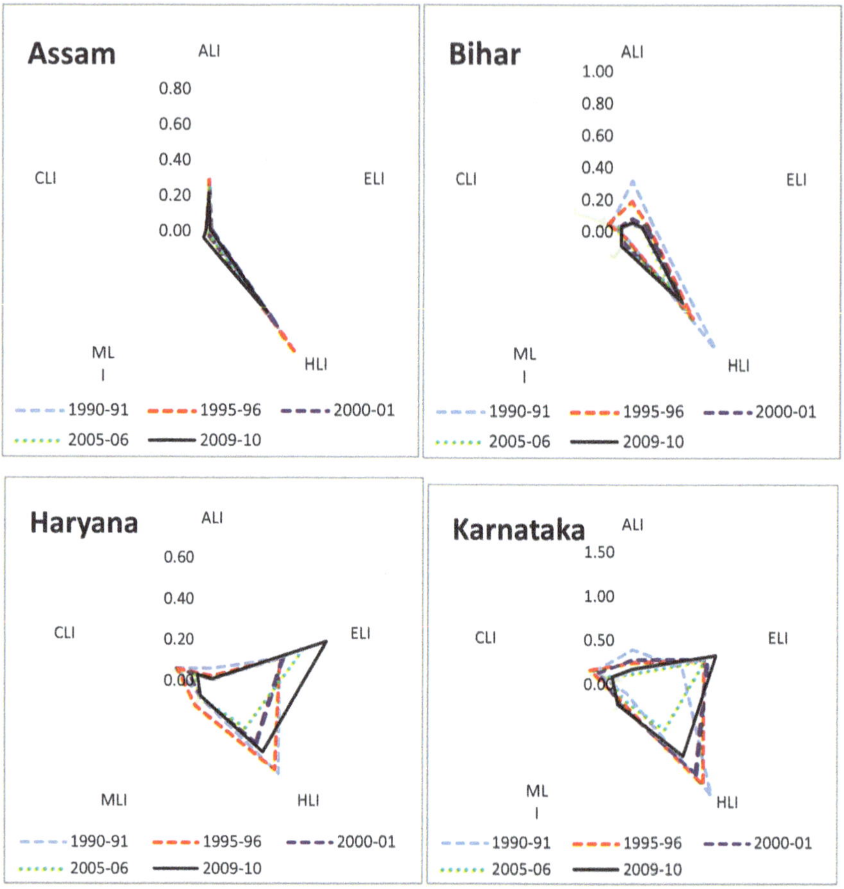

Fig. 2 (continued)

to agriculture as a share of total sale of electricity in the state show a positive trend only in case of West Bengal. Figure 2 shows the pictorial depiction of the same results it clearly portrays that most of the states have become energy efficient over time barring Punjab, Haryana and Andhra Pradesh.

5 Concluding Remarks

The analysis presented in this paper is the most up-to-date depiction of agricultural dynamism in terms of energy use in the post-WTO India.

The composition of energy use in Indian agriculture has changed significantly with a shift from animal and mobile power to static (Singh et al., 2014). The current trends in Indian agriculture, as the panel data results reveal in the study, reveal that its energy requirement will increase in years to come. However, with this energy intensity of food grain production decreased in last ten years for most fuel types which depicts that the sector is becoming energy efficient. Nonetheless, there is further need of introducing technological change involving energy-efficient farm machinery, electricity and human labour. Managing growing demand for energy in agriculture has become major concern for our policymakers. The policy implications of the study warrant actions on two fronts, one on efficient utilization of the available energy resources to partially address the supply constraints, and second, creating an enabling environment for the promotion of alternative renewable sources of energy involving technologies.

References

Agricultural Statistics at a Glance. (2011). Central Statistics Office, New Delhi, and Registrar General of India (various issues).

Arbia, G., Basile, R., & Piras, G. (2005). *Using spatial panel data in modelling regional growth and convergence (September 2005).* ISAE Working Paper No. 55, Available at SSRN: https://ssrn.com/abstract=936321.

Badiani, R., & Jessoe, K.K. (2010). *Electricity subsidies, elections, groundwater extraction and industrial growth in India.* Available at: http://mitsloan.mit.edu/neudc/papers/paper_194.pdf.

Baltagi, B. H. (2013). *Econometric Analysis of Panel Data.* 5th ed. Chichester: John Wiley and Sons.

Bardhan, Pranab. (1999). *The political economy of development in India.* New Delhi: Oxford University Press.

Bardhan, P. (2001). Sharing the spoils: Group equity, development, and democracy, in Atul Kohli (ed.) *The success of India's democracy.* Cambridge, U.K: Cambridge University Press.

Bardhan, P. (2003). The politics of economic reform in India. In *Poverty: Agrarian structure and political economy in India.* New Delhi: Oxford University Press.

Bardhan, P. (2005). The nature of opposition to economic reforms in India. *Economic and Political Weekly, XL*(48), 4995–4998.

Barua, Alokesh, & Das, S. K. (1996). Regional disparity, economic growth and liberalization: A study of the Indian economy. *Journal of Development Studies, 32*(3), 364–390.

Bhalla & Singh. (2010). *Final report on planning commission project growth of Indian agriculture: A district level study,* March accessed at http://planningcommission.nic.in/reports/sereport/ser/ser_gia2604.pdf.

Bhushan, S. (2014). *Agricultural productivity and environmental impacts in India: A parametric and non-parametric analysis.* Ph.D. Thesis submitted to Jawaharlal Nehru University, New Delhi.

Binswanger-Mkhize, & Hans, P. (2013). The stunted structural transformation of the Indian economy: Agriculture, manufacturing and the rural non-farm sector. *Economic & Political Weekly, Review of Rural Affairs; Supplement June 29, XLVIII*; 26 and 27, 5–13.

Bosworth, B., & Susan M. C. (2008). Accounting for growth: Comparing China and India. *Journal of Economic Perspectives, 22*(1), Winter, 45–66.

CACP. (Various Issues): *Comprehensive Scheme for the study of Cost of Cultivation of Principal Crops in India*, Commission For Agricultural Costs And Prices, Department of Agriculture & Cooperation, Ministry of Agriculture, Government of India, New Delhi.

Clark, T. S., & Linzer, D. A. (2015). Should I use fixed or random effects. *Political Science Research and Methods, 3*(2), 399–408.

Corbridge, S., & Harriss, J. (2000). *Reinventing India: Liberalization, Hindu nationalism and popular democracy*. Cambridge: Polity Press.

Démurger, S. (2001). Infrastructure development and economic growth: An explanation for regional disparities in China? *Journal of Comparative Economics, 29*(1), 95–117.

Griliches, Z. (1984). Data problems in econometrics. In Z. Griliches & M. Intriligator (Eds.), *Handbook of econometrics* (Vol. 3). North-Holland: Amsterdam.

Gulati, A., & Narayanan, S. (2000). Demystifying fertiliser and power subsidies in India. *Economic and Political Weekly, 35,* 784–794.

Gulati, A., & Narayanan, S. (2003). *The subsidy syndrome in Indian agriculture*. New Dehli: Oxford University Press.

Gulati, A., Surbhi J., & Nidhi S. (2013). *Rising farm wages in India: The 'pull' and 'push' factors*. Discussion Paper No. 5, April, Commission for Agricultural Costs and Prices; New Delhi, Government of India. Accessed on 15 November 2013 http://cacp.dacnet.nic.in/Farm_Wages_in_Rural_I ndia.pdf.

Haspolat, F. B. (2015). Analysis of Moody's sovereign credit ratings: Criticisms towards rating agencies are still valid? *Procedia Economics and Finance, 30,* 283–293.

Hausman, J. A. (1978). Specification tests in econometrics. *Econometrica, 46,* 1251–1271.

Howes, S., & Murgai, R. (2003). Karnataka: Incidence of agricultural power subsidies—An estimate. *Economic and Political Weekly, 38,* 1533–1535.

Islam, N. (1995). Growth empirics: A panel data approach. *Quarterly Journal of Economics, 4,* 1127–1170.

Jenkins, R. (1999). *Democratic politics and economic reforms in India*. Cambridge, U.K.: Cambridge University Press.

Jha, G. K., Suresh, P., & Alka, S. (2012). Changing energy-use pattern and the demand projection for indian agriculture. *Agricultural Economics Research Review, 25*(1), January–June, 61–68.

Lanjouw. P, & Murgai, R. (2009). Poverty decline, agricultural wages, and non-farm employment in India: 1983–2004. Policy Research Working Paper, No. 4858. World Bank, Washington, DC.

Mody, A., & Srinivasan, K. (1998). Japanese and U.S. firms as foreign investors: Do they march to the same tune? *Canadian Journal of Economics, 31*(4), 778–799.

Mooij, J. (2005). Introduction. In J. Mooij (ed.), *The politics of economic reforms in India*. New Delhi: Sage.

Raghavan, M. (2008). Changing pattern of input use and cost of cultivation. *Economic and Political Weekly, 43,* 123–129.

Sidhu, D. S. & Byerlee, D. (1992). *Technical change and wheat productivity in the Indian Punjab in the post-green revolution period*. CIMMYT Economics Working Paper 92–02. Mexico, D.F.: CIMMYT.

Singh, S. P., Singh, R. S., & Singh, Surendra. (2011). Sale trend of tractors and farm power availability in India. *Agricultural Engineering Today, 35*(2), 25–35.

Singh, Surendra, Singh, R., & Singh, S. (2014). Farm power availability on Indian farms. *Agricultural Engineering Today, 38*(4), 44–52.

Swain, A. K. (2006). *Political economy of public policy making in the Indian electricity sector: A study of Orissa and AndhraPradesh*. M. Phil.: Jawaharlal Nehru University.

Swain, A., &Olivier C. (2012). *In pursuit of energy efficiency in India's agriculture: Fighting 'free power' or working with it*? Working Paper 126, Agence Française de Dévelopement.

Varshney, A. (1999). Mass politics or elite politics? India's economic reforms in comparative perspective. In J. D. Sachs, A. Varshney, & N. Bajpaj (Eds.), *India in an era of economic reforms.* New Delhi: Oxford University Press.
Wooldridge, J. M. (2013). *Introductory econometrics: A modern approach (5th ed.).* Mason, OH: South-Western, Cengage Learning.

COVID-19 and the Big Oil Price Crash: Exploring the Anatomy

Kaushik Ranjan Bandyopadhyay

1 The Backdrop

In December 2016, at the OPEC ministerial meeting in Vienna, 24 ministers participated from OPEC and Non-OPEC oil exporting countries, and came out with a 'Declaration of Cooperation' (DoC) (OPEC Secretariat, 2017) to achieve oil market stability in the interest of all oil producers and consumers. The declaration was signed to arrest a rapidly tumbling crude oil price. In 2018, the crude price crossed the $70 a barrel mark as sanctions were imposed by USA on Iran and Venezuela, both of whom are major oil producers (EPW Engage, 2019). Since the beginning of 2020, however, the crude oil prices have fallen drastically due to the lethal double blow of collapse of DoC in the beginning of March due to defection of Russia to go for production cut (see Fig. 1) coupled with economic contraction caused by the outbreak of the novel coronavirus disease (COVID-19) arising from Wuhan in China.

In the quest for retaining market share due to substantial demand drop because of pandemic, Saudi Arabia wanted to go for production cut but Russia refused to comply with the same for the fear of losing its own market share which led to suspension of DoC. The Saudis retaliated and decided to pump crude at will. Eventually a price war got waged and led to a protracted disequilibrium in the crude oil market. Soon after the price of two crude benchmarks Brent and WTI tumbled to more than 50% over two weeks in March 2020. Daily Brent plummeted to $24.9/barrel (b) on March 18 from $51.9/b on March 2, while at the same time WTI fell to $20.4/b from $46.8/b over the same period. The market observed some extremely volatile price movements. Historical highs have also been recorded by OVX and VIX, the two benchmark

K. R. Bandyopadhyay (✉)
Indian Institute of Management, Lucknow, India
e-mail: krban@iiml.ac.in

P. Dasgupta et al. (eds.), *Sustainable Development Insights from India*,
India Studies in Business and Economics,
https://doi.org/10.1007/978-981-33-4830-1_12

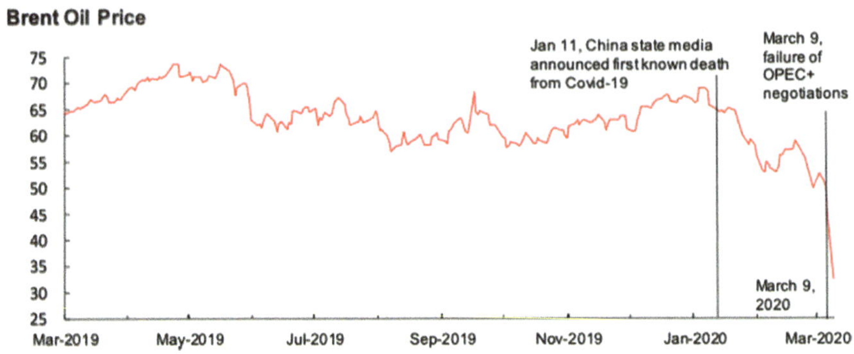

Fig. 1 Trajectory of brent crude prices from March 2019 to March 2020 *Source* adopted from Arezki & Fan (2020); the primary data is sourced from Bloomberg LP

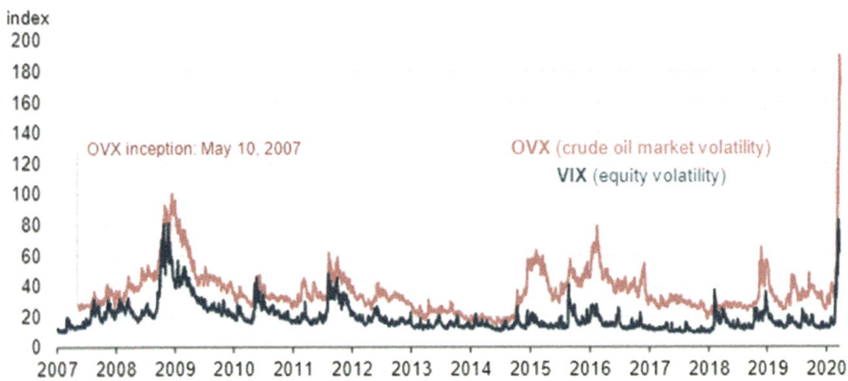

Fig. 2 Implied volatility measures (Jan 2007 to March 2020). *Source* EIA (2020)

measures of implied volatility in crude oil markets and S&P 500[1] respectively. As reported by Department of Energy, USA, the VIX index reached 82.7 on March 16, a notch higher than any point during the financial crisis of 2008–09, and on March 20, OVX reached 190, the highest value since its inception in May 2007 (see Fig. 2 for the variation in implied volatility measures).

Although Saudi Arabia and Russia eventually returned to the negotiating table in the month of April with pressure from USA and with mediation of G20, the damage had already been done by then. The 23 oil exporting countries decided to withhold

[1]Implied volatility measures an asset's expected range of near-term price changes. OVX measures the implied volatility of oil prices and is calculated using movements in the prices of financial options for WTI, the light, sweet crude oil priced at Cushing, Oklahoma. VIX measures the implied volatility of the Standard and Poor's (S&P) 500—a stock market index of 500 large companies listed in the United States. Crude oil volatility is typically higher than the S&P 500's volatility, generally because OVX represents changes in one commodity and VIX represents changes across a diverse group of 500 companies (see EIA, 2020).

Fig. 3 The sub-zero crude slide on black Monday (April 20). *Source* EIA (2020a)

collectively 9.7 million barrels a day of oil from global markets starting May 1 to the end of June (Said & Faucon, 2020a, b). Most of the experts and analysts, however, contended that the market is flooded with so much of surplus that the negotiated curtailment, albeit robust, would fail to offset the steep 30% drop in global fuel demand, with extended lockdowns, continued travel bans, insignificant vehicle usage and huge curb on economic activity (French & Moise, 2020). The final nail was put on the coffin after WTI crude oil futures plunged below zero for the first time on 20th April and made it a Black Monday. The price of a barrel of West Texas Intermediate crude to be delivered in May, which closed at $18.27 a barrel on 17th April, went to the sub-zero level and registered a historically low price of up to—$40 a barrel on 20th April (see Fig. 3) (Grubb, 2020). Spot prices also fell below zero, and panicky oil producers and traders dumped a large volume of futures contracts. That effectively implies that sellers literally have to pay the buyers to take barrels off their hands.

The volatile oil markets that resulted therefrom continued to threaten to bankrupt energy companies across the world, with shale coming out as the worst casualty; caused huge job losses and also battered the financial institutions that have been backing these industries. Furthermore, the coupling of unprecedented demand and supply shocks have tested the oil market and its storage capacity to the limits and eventually converted the oil crisis to a storage crisis. To understand all these issues and the imbalances that had been building in the system more deeply, it is crucial to look at the anatomy of the oil market more carefully as the impact of COVID-19 was unfolding (Fattouh et al., 2020). I intend to take this up in the next few sections.

2 Oil Market Dynamics in a Pandemic Struck World and Its Fallouts

2.1 Price War: A Miscalculated Masterstroke

Some experts and believers of mean field game theory[2] views the price war launched by Saudi Arabia in March after Russia's defection from the DoC as a 'game theory masterstroke' but unfortunately it was miscalculated and played at a wrong time when the bout of pandemic and the containment measures implemented globally has sucked out the effective demand for crude and precipitated a disaster for the industry globally with inherent fallouts on other associated sectors and the economies. The effective demand for crude comes from the end-use of petroleum products like petrol or gasoline, diesel, aviation turbine fuel etc. The demand for these products evaporated as flights got grounded, passenger travel came to a standstill, and lockdowns got implemented globally.

It may not be appropriate to gauge the behaviour of bigger oil producers based on just one situation or a one-off event but it is important to understand if there has really been any observed change in their behaviour in the more recent years and the factors pertaining therewith. Geopolitical challenges have always been a disruptive factor when it comes to dealing with Middle East and North African countries. But there are number of structural or deeper global policy related factors that have exacerbated the recent increase in volatility in demand for oil. Some of these major factors are –(1) the uncertainty in the pace of energy transition as more stringent climate or environment related regulations started coming in place; (2) environmental, social and governance (ESG) issues are increasingly getting internalised in mainstream investment decision-making (Eccles, 2020) and the risks of stranded assets looms large[3]; (3) stakeholder interests starts getting more prominence and influence the decisions in the board rooms of corporation (Paine, 2014). It is quite obvious that due to the compound effect of all these factors, investments in fossil fuel industry have been showing a jittery trend causing the volatility.

Given this increased volatility in oil demand, the big low-cost producers like Saudi Arabia and Russia, with the intent of optimising their oil revenues, has to keep on juggling between their conflicting price and market-share aspirations. In order to serve these interests in the best possible manner, they often tend to choose the path of monetising their reserves as quickly as possible, produce more and offer more

---

[2]The behavioural psyche of the dominant producer within OPEC like Saudi Arabia who waged a price war could find explanations with the recent advances in game theoretic approach to model behaviour of oil producers. The recent advances known as mean field game theory has been advocated and applied by French mathematicians Pierre-Louis Lions, Jean Michel Lasry and Olivier Gu´eant in their recent paper focusing on oil production (Lions et al., 2020).

[3]Stranded assets are "assets that have suffered from unanticipated or premature write-downs, devaluations, or conversion to liabilities" (for more details on different perspectives on stranded assets see Caldecott 2017).

discounts to squeeze out relatively high-cost producers.[4] This is exactly what seems to have happened in the current situation when both Saudis and Russians decided to pump more oil, brought down the price, and eventually roiled the high cost shale producers of USA.

Russia defied from the production cuts, proposed by the Saudis, as its market share concerns were much different than those of the Saudis and other major oil exporters. Russia's exports are usually confined to a few discrete markets, with most of its shipments cruising to Europe and a smaller percentage is transmitted by pipeline to China (Jaffe, 2020). Hence, the immediate impact of pandemic would not only be felt on Russia's chief export outlets, but it would also make Russia more vulnerable to competition from other suppliers seeking to sell in Europe, including the U.S. shale exporters. Saudi Arabia, on the other hand, has a better and bigger network of global customers including useful oil storage arrangements that enhance its operational flexibility. Russia's defection from the deal was also reportedly stoked by U.S. sanctions on completing Nord Stream 2 gas pipeline in the Baltic Sea and sanction on Rosneft because of trading Venezuela's crude.

With Saudi Arabia also adopting a strategy of pumping oil at will and continuing to increase supplies, post Russia's non-compliance, situation invariably turned out to be worse in the pandemic-stricken world already grappling with excess supply of oil. Collection of oil revenues plummeted, making any attempts towards economic diversification within oil producing economies difficult, created challenges for upstream investments and made it difficult to raise or sustain their production capacity (Halff, 2020). Thus, managing producer-producer relations turned out to be critical. Saudis and Russians eventually decided to come back to the negotiating table. The pressure from USA threatening to impose a tariff on Saudi and Russian crude exports to USA in absence of a deal and mediation of other G20 members made the deal happen. However, the demand shock arising from containment measures pertaining to COVID-19 had more than offset the promised cut and the crude price slid to a historic low on 20th April, when the futures contract of the US benchmark crude Western Texas Intermediate (WTI) for May delivery plunged into the negative territory for the first time. An explanation for this historic crash has been given in the following sub-section.

Although Saudis and Russians eventually were forced to return to the negotiating table and play the balancing role and stick to the negotiated output cut, there is absolutely no second thought that the cut did not in reality serve the interests of the producers in the best possible manner. Furthermore, how much does the production eventually drop at a given price depends on a host of companies taking decisions to prune supply and is also contingent upon interplay of multiple factors. These factors include: respecting fiduciary duties to shareholders; meeting executive compensation targets; covenants with creditors; hedging obligations; and above all, movements

[4] I have argued earlier that it is not correct to think that Saudi Arabia, the dominant producer within OPEC always act as a residual swing producer and respond to the call or the amount of oil demanded from it (after accounting for NOPEC production and inventory adjustment), unless doing so serves its interests in the best possible manner (see Bandyopadhyay, 2008).

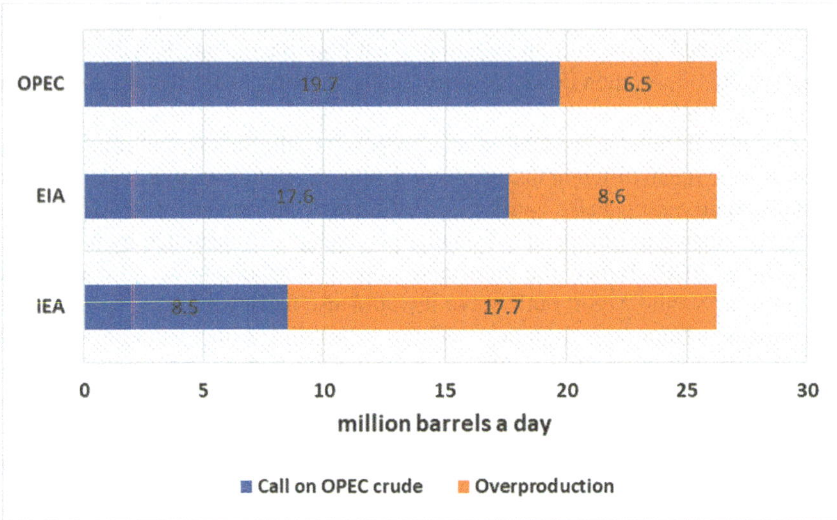

Fig. 4 Call on OPEC and predicted overproduction by IEA, EIA and OPEC *Source* Based on Short Term Oil Market Reports of IEA, EIA and OPEC pertaining to April 2020

in prices (Brower, 2020). In other words, the actual production restriction eventually enforced by a falling price would in more likelihood be an outcome of market rationing supply, and may not necessarily be concomitant with the collective action of OPEC plus cartel. In other words, even though a full compliance eventually plays out or if the big producers actually go for deeper cuts than proposed, still there would be no guarantee or room for complacency that oil market would balance unless one really gets a clearer picture on how fast the world is moving on the trajectory of recovery from the pandemic, which has rightly been dubbed as a black swan and that continued to lead the oil market into a tailspin causing announcements of more force majeure, continued filing of insolvency and repeated shutdowns in the oil and gas sector.

As an illustration, Fig. 4 juxtaposes the call on OPEC[5] and overproduction in the second quarter as predicted by three key agencies IEA, DOE and OPEC in the month of April 2020. Figure shows that OPEC over-production in the second quarter had been predicted to lie anywhere between 6.5 million and 17.7 million barrels a day a lion's share of which was invariably expected to go into storage.

Although the production restriction through an OPEC plus deal did calm the turbulence in the oil market afterwards, but the calming process was only temporary and was battered time and again. There is no second thought that time was not really

[5]International Energy Agency (IEA) and Energy Information Administration, Department of Energy, USA (EIA) tend to assume the existence of an equilibrium price path. After calculating the world oil demand and non-OPEC output, the latter is subtracted from the former after allowing for stock adjustment. This gives the oil demanded from OPEC (often referred to as "call on OPEC"). For more details see Bandyopadhyay (2008).

ripe for such a hostile quest for market share for both Saudis and Russians at the first go that has exacerbated unneeded excesses, tested storage capacity to its limits, and made the entire oil and gas sector bleed worldwide. This also created challenges for the weaker OPEC producers in terms of expenditure cuts and made even the Saudis and Russians vulnerable economically by stressing their budgets as the entire world is grappling with the lethal double bout of health and financial crisis and as the protracted global recession hardly showed any immediate sign of respite.

2.2 *Bruising America's Hype on Shale and Energy Dominance*

The U.S. turned out to be the world's largest oil producer in 2019, overtaking Saudi Arabia and is primarily attributable to explosion of shale fracking (Champion, 2020). The report brought by Energy Information Administration (EIA), DoE in April 2020, however, hinted clearly to the fact that US might soon lose that position as the largest exporter and would start importing more oil than it produces, with production expected to drop by some 500,000 barrels per day in 2020, despite the renegotiated agreement that has been reached between OPEC and Non-OPEC members (EIA, 2020b).

Although U.S. shale industry had a wild run over the last decade from 2010 onwards and continued to register record production levels, but their 'growth-at-all-costs' business model was clearly unsound and led them to deeper financial trouble (Denning, 2020). In fact, what Paul Stevens talked about in an interesting Chatham House Report way back in September 2010 (Stevens, 2010), when shale was just on its way to ride the boom actually turned out to be true as shale returned to bust at the beginning of 2020. The report also had caste serious doubts over the industry confidence in the 'revolution', on grounds of environmental concerns, high depletion rates and questioned the replicability of the same elsewhere. The biggest worry that Prof. Stevens had raised was about investor uncertainty that could reduce investment in future gas supplies. The scenario of investment in shale plays indicates that although initially investors have preferred the lure of shale development risk to that of conventional exploration risk as it appeared as a good bet to them but eventually the hopes got reversed. The faster returns that came initially was largely triggered by high initial production rates for wells. Trading off the risk of exploration of dry holes with shale development at large scale may have seemed a good bet then but has eventually proved otherwise.

Opponents of fracking also highlighted problems faced by the communities because of nearby fracking activities, including contamination of groundwater, air pollution and negative health consequences, and increase in the number of earthquakes in drilling areas. Climate concerns about methane leakage from well sites, pipelines, and processing facilities, as well as from burning fossil fuels, in general, also play a big role in calls for a fracking ban (CFR, 2020). Concerns have been reportedly raised especially with respect to water stress and associated business risks for fracking in water deficient regions in a WRI report (Reig, 2014) and concerns for risks to air quality and water quality through contamination has been brought out by General Accounting Office Report on Shale Development (GAO, 2012). Incidentally, the Democratic Party's presumptive 2020 presidential nominee, former Vice President Joe Biden, also promised to stop issuing permits for new oil and gas drilling on federal lands and waters. But he stopped short of supporting a full ban on fracking in the United States (CFR, 2020).

Fracking is complex and a highly cost intensive activity in the US. There is also a wide variation across the wells in terms of performances and yields. Given the high degree of variability, the more expensive wells that do not perform well can compound losses. A typical expectation from an investment in shale fracking is a 10% return on capital (Michot, 2020). This is based on the assumptions that companies can re-invest out of returns net of investor obligations (interest on debt and dividends). However, for that to happen, the shale producers need a total cost structure (capex plus opex plus total return) that pays back annual capex as well as ongoing booked finding and development expenses and does not exceed commodity price. However, that has not been met in 2018 and 2019, when costs remained marginally below the trading price of the benchmark light sweet crude, West Texas Intermediate (Michot, 2020).

After a decade of ups and downs, 2019 turned out to be the crucial year as investors began to shy away from investing in the shale industry triggered by falling yield and paltry returns. The challenge is exacerbated by mainstreaming of Environmental, Social and Governance (ESG) issues in investing decision with signs of more divestment in the fossil fuel sector in the offing and the rise of conscious capitalism (Mackey and Sisodia, 2013). Changes in decision making have undergone a sea change in boardrooms, as socially conscious investors and shareholders increasingly demand to know whether company profits are coming at the expense of other stakeholders namely environment, workers' well-being, health and safety issues or the overall health of society (Paine, 2014). Drillers have already started to face high-level scrutiny on the impact of fracking on climate change that influenced the investment decision-making at big banks. Major U.S. lenders started to prepare to become operators of oil and gas fields across the country for the first time in a generation to avoid losses on loans to energy companies on the fear that they would soon go bankrupt. JPMorgan Chase & Co, Wells Fargo & Co, Bank of America Corp, and Citigroup Inc are each in the process of setting up independent companies to own oil and gas assets (French et al., 2020). With crude price on an unabated rout and downslide, maintaining a breakeven for the shale producers turned out to be an insurmountable challenge (Adams-Heard & Crowley, 2020).

As reported on April 09, even US shale giant like Occidental had been looking for the U.S. government to "provide liquidity to the energy industry through this period of unprecedented demand destruction and unsustainable pricing until normal economic conditions return," according to the letter linked in an April 7 email and reported by

Bloomberg News.[6] Moody's also downgraded Occidental Petroleum's credit rating to junk (Adams-Heard & Crowley, 2020a). Whiting Petroleum, a notable exploration and production company also filed for bankruptcy protection on April 1 (Eaton & Scurria, 2020). Callon Petroleum Company and Chesapeake Energy operating in the Permian basin also reportedly hired restructuring advisors. Furthermore, Shale driller Unit Corp., based in Oklahoma, also planned to file for bankruptcy in the wake of collapsing crude prices (Gladstone et al., 2020). The shale industry countered a lot of challenges plagued by leveraged balance sheets and dwindling shareholder returns over the past decade.

A more recent estimate made by Morgan Stanley indicates that the industry needs $51 per barrel just to fund their capex budgets this year, let alone pay off debt or send money to shareholders.[7] Another estimate from University of Chicago indicates profitable drilling and fracking a new need something in the neighbourhood of $40 per barrel (Bornstein, 2020a). Yet another estimate by the U.S. Federal Reserve Bank of Dallas indicates that exploration and production firms need an average West Texas Intermediate (WTI) price of $30 a barrel to cover operating expenses for existing wells and $49 a barrel to profitably drill a new well (Federal Reserve Bank of Dallas, 2020). With WTI now creating history by reaching a negative value of up to -$40 a barrel for the expiring basket of WTI crude futures for May delivery, there was no second thought that only a generous bailout from the Government could actually save the industry. As revenue plummeted and assets deteriorated in value, some companies expressed their inability to repay their debts (French & Moise, 2020). Going by the record of Haynes and Boone's over the entire five-year period ending August 31, 2020, 244 producers have filed for bankruptcy involving more than $172 billion in aggregate debt with over $50 billion so far in 2020. Of these filings, as many as 36 U.S. oil and natural gas companies filed for bankruptcy in 2020 itself till end August as the industry continues to grapple with depressed prices for the commodities (Haynes & Boone, 2020).

In fine, the oil crash triggered by the double blow has literally turned the much-hyped America's energy independence dream riding on shale industry to bubble. According to David Victor, the co-chair of the Brooking's initiative on Energy and Climate Change, the shale rocks laden with oil and gas may not go away completely, it is only that 'the pecking order in the patch will change'. He seems to go along with the Darwinian principle and believes that the bigger and more financially solvent players who have better control over financial risks will survive the storm and define the new normal for the industry (Victor, 2020). Amy Jaffe from the Council of Foreign Relations, however, strongly contends that U.S. shale is uniquely resilient "as the pressure for production comes from the artificial means of hydraulic fracturing which can be turned off and on easily" (Jaffe, 2020a). He further underscored that whenever

[6] https://oilprice.com/Latest-Energy-News/World-News/Shale-Giant-Calls-For-Federal-Help-As-Oil-Prices-Fail-To-Bounce-Back.html for more details (accessed on 2 September 2020).

[7] https://oilprice.com/Energy/Energy-General/The-Great-US-Shale-Decline-Has-Already-Begun.html.

the capital, equipment, and workers are there to produce it, it can be restored quickly in a matter of days or months.

With the Black Swan not expected to provide respite very soon, it remains to be seen how the situation really pans out and the cloud starts progressively receding as lockdowns get gradually lifted worldwide. Despite the high hopes expressed by the likes of Amy Jaffe, the shale patch, however, continued to look vulnerable beginning with Whiting Petroleum, the first company to file for Chap. 11 bankruptcy (Eaton & Scurria, 2020). Even the prominent ones like Noble Energy (NBL), Halliburton (HAL), Marathon Oil (MRO) and Occidental (OXY) ended up losing more than 66% of their market cap in just a few short months. Even majors such as Exxon (XOM) have lost as much as 40% of their value (Kern, 2020).

2.3 Deep Contango, Black Monday and Storage Crisis

In a world that was at a standstill with the pandemic starting to rule the roost; with the hostile quest for market share of Saudis and Russians that added to the excesses of crude that nobody wanted; and with large importers like China on a staggered recovery (Meidan, 2020), a huge storage crisis loomed large with hardly any places left to store oil. Refineries, storage facilities, pipelines and even ocean tankers filled up rapidly since billions of people around the world started getting confined in their homes to contain the spread of COVID-19 (Said & Faucon, 2020a, 2020b). Furthermore, refineries expressed unwillingness to refine crude oil into gasoline (petrol), diesel and other products because of progressive stalling of commuting and grounding of flights, and international trade registered a sharp decline. Oil was already getting stored on floating barges as land-based storages were getting over-stressed leading to higher costs.

Going by the jargon of commodity market trading, the rout of the pandemic and other factors made the market flip from backwardation to a contango structure in a forward curve (Kaminska, 2020). A contango structure usually shows up in a commodity market when the price of commodities in futures contracts exceeds the cash price of same commodities in the spot market.[8] The reverse situation is known as backwardation. Contango provides traders the opportunity to buy oil at a cheaper price now and then sell it off at the futures market at a higher price at some agreed point of time in the future. However, when it comes to crude oil, the profitability in trading depends largely on whether the cost of storing oil is lower than the profit generated by the trade attributed to the contango. If the cost is lower, the contango tends to encourage hoarding. In an oversupplied market, a supplier whose stocks are building because of a dip in demand needs to discount his product to encourage

[8] In addition to futures contracts, another way for market participants to invest in crude oil is through the buying and selling of options contracts. Options allow for investment exposure with limited potential for losses and provide an insurance-like instrument against adverse commodity price movements. See https://www.eia.gov/finance/markets/crudeoil/financial_markets.php (accessed 28 August 2020).

someone who doesn't really need to buy to actually make him do so. The inducement to the discretionary buyer is reflected in the spot price trading at a discount to the forward. If the surplus supply persists, prices will continue to slide further, and the contango steepens further creating more distress in the market. And this is where the market reached in April 2020.

Going down the memory lane in 2008 the economy was a similar victim of a massive oil demand destruction and the contango was so deep that the spare capacity for all on-the-ground storage facilities got completely exhausted. However, the profit that could be derived out of trading in crude futures was more than adequate to pay for the cost of buying charter tankers for storing oil offshore and still end up with a handsome amount in hand. But this time the situation turned out to be starkly different as there was a serious crisis of physical storage capacity to park the excess global oil supply. As reported by Reuters, the increased demand for storage had placed significant upward pressure on land storage costs worldwide and also raised the rate of crude oil maritime shipping, which is usually considered as an alternative to on-shore storage (Kumar & Hiller, 2020). The supply demand imbalance in the face of lockdown announcements worldwide deepened the contango[9]as inventories continued to build and traders increasingly started resorting to floating storage. The excess supply from OPEC producers further caused a substantial increase in Very Large Crude Carriers (VLCC) rates as the producers especially Saudi Arabia started sending oil to USA. Chartering costs for VLCC had more than doubled since February (IEA, 2020). Serious concerns arose with respect to storing different qualities of crude oil at many sites as special tanks were required for some products.[10] The storage concerns continued to put pressure on front prices and the shape of the forward curve in the next few months till the pandemic curve flattens.

An extreme manifestation of the stressed market situation triggered by the storage challenges was observed when the price of May 2020 WTI crude contract went to sub-zero level reaching a historical nadir of—$40 a barrel. This essentially implies that anyone who is trying to sell a barrel of crude would have to end up paying a buyer to offload it. This is because, WTI futures contracts that need buyers to take possession of oil in May were expiring on April 21, but because of market flooding with surplus oil coupled with lack of effective demand, nobody really wanted oil as there was a severe crunch of space to store it. This led to steep price slide to sub-zero level on April 20, a day before the expiry of the contract.

However, there is also a need to provide a quick clarification that albeit the sub-zero price is a manifestation of severe storage crisis, it is purely related to storage capacity in Cushing, a landlocked terminal, located in Oklahoma, USA and only pertains to the 2020 WTI Crude futures contract for May delivery. As on April 21, contracts for June delivery were still trading for about $22 a barrel, albeit down by 16% for the day. The positive pricing of other crude oil benchmarks with the Brent contract for June 2020 delivery closing at $19.33/b on April 21; positive prices for

[9]The contango gets deepened when the near-term futures prices are way lower than longer-dated ones.

[10]https://www.iea.org/reports/oil-market-report-April-2020.

other longer-dated WTI prices, and positive spot prices for other U.S. crude oils reinforced the fact that the slide was predominantly triggered by the stress created due to timing of the May 2020 contract expiration of WTI crude futures plus the storage concerns (IEA, 2020).

To be more precise, one needs to be actually thorough with the terms and conditions contained in the settlement procedures[11] of the May 2020 WTI crude contract to gauge the real reason behind the recent crude slide. On expiration, the holder of a WTI contract had two options to meet the contract's physical delivery requirement. A contract holder could settle the position by entering into an Exchange for Physical (EFP) contract with a counterparty which involves transfer of the contract in exchange for cash or other futures contracts with later expiration dates. Alternately, settlement could occur if a contract holder takes physical delivery of the crude oil. As per the contract's specifications, delivery of the physical crude oil volumes must occur at a pipeline or storage facility in Cushing. Furthermore, the delivery should also occur within a specific time, which is currently set no earlier than the first calendar day of the contract month and no later than the month's last calendar day.[12]

Under normal circumstances in Cushing, buyers can easily have the oil transferred into a storage facility or pipeline that they own or lease or can transfer ownership of the crude oil elsewhere in the pipeline and storage system after taking due consent of the sellers. However, COVID-19 have precipitated an extraordinary situation. As a result of complete drying up of demand, the piling surplus of imported oil plus domestically-produced crude oil volumes had to go straight into storage. Thus, on 17th April i.e. just three days before the Black Monday, 76% of Cushing's storage capacity was already full. Figure 5 shows the steep rise that happened in 2020.

Although there was still some unfilled physical storage space available, some of those had already been leased out or otherwise committed, thus restricting the uncommitted storage availability. Given the high demand for storage, anybody who intends to store oil would have to shell out a much higher rate to storage operators to make headway through the uncommitted storage space.

The unavailability of uncommitted storage or exorbitant storage cost coupled with deepened contango since early March 2020, as explained before, made it really challenging for some market participants to take physical delivery. However, if they continue to own the contract when trading stops, they'll be required to take that delivery at higher prices, failing which there could be serious consequences.[13]

[11]For more details see: https://www.cmegroup.com/trading/energy/crude-oil/light-sweet-crude_quotes_settlements_futures.html (accessed on August 23, 2020).

[12]The explanation and illustration draws largely on the information and details contained in https://www.eia.gov/petroleum/weekly/includes/analysis_print.php (accessed on August 20, 2020).

[13]In case of a failure to accept physical delivery the specific costs that an owner of crude future has to incur depends on the specific contractual arrangements entered into by the contract holder and the Futures Commission Merchant (FCM)—the entity responsible for executing the buying and selling of futures contracts on behalf of a client. The possible costs may involve a combination of direct monetary penalties, reputational consequences, the liquidation of the collateral deposited by the client in the margin account with the FCM, the revocation of trading privileges,

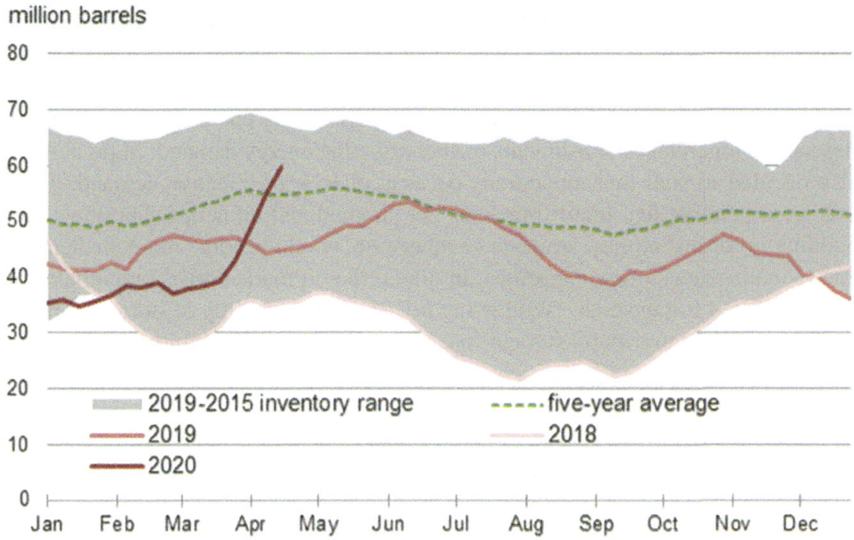

Fig. 5 Cushing commercial crude oil inventories *Source* EIA (2020a)

This essentially implied that they had to settle the May 2020 WTI contract financially by selling the contract to another market participant even if that amounts to selling at rock bottom prices or even negative prices to other traders to exit their contracts and avoid physical settlement. The extreme market environment that resulted therefrom made several participants sell their contract at negative prices. In other words, this is equivalent to paying the other party to take possession of the contract before expiration. This is also in line with the traders' sentiments who usually buy oil futures contracts as a way of betting on price movements, without any intention of taking physical delivery of barrels. However, the worst was still not over for the oil price. Unlike financial assets bonds and stocks, commodities are usually considered as spot assets and must clear the supply and demand. The rising glut of oil made global storage capacity (onshore plus offshore) gradually reach its limits and created more volatility. Oil tanks had either been filled up or booked out by traders, while the amount of crude and fuel stored on vessels at sea surged. The seaborne crude had reported stocks at 175 m barrels, up from 100 m in late March (Sheppard et al., 2020)

Since WTI crude futures for May delivery traded negative in May 20, more than 40% of the June contract was reportedly liquidated with a fear of another disastrous slide of crude future prices futures contract of WTI crude for June delivery. Holdings of the July contract had been stable, while those on September futures jumped by almost 20% (Raimonde, 2020). With nowhere to store the oil, supply had no other

and the costs of any legal settlements resulting from the breach of contractual obligations. (see-7/200422/includes/analysis_print.php (accessed on 05 September 2020).

option but to be shut-in down in-line with the expected demand losses and the drastic output cuts globally.

Energy companies worldwide also started receiving force majeure notices from customers as the persistent lockdown made it increasingly challenging to run factories and commercial establishments further affecting energy demand. Many refiners also decided to stall their operations because of lack of effective demand. There was an impending fear that if pipelines get jammed and refineries shut down then building up of inventories, strategic or otherwise, would become more challenging due to inadequate storage capacities. In effect, the oil market crisis precipitated an unprecedented storage crisis. With rising prices and profitability of storage, it rather made more sense to own oil storage space than to own a crude futures contract.

3 Conclusion

The IMF's chief economist Gita Gopinath pointed out - "Given the fact that COVID-19 has precipitated a crisis like no other, and there is substantial uncertainty about its impact on people's lives and livelihoods, a lot actually depends on the epidemiology of the virus, the effectiveness of containment measures, and the development of therapeutics and vaccines, all of which are hard to predict at this moment" (Gopinath, 2020).

In our economics textbook we get to learn about pathological cases of demand and supply. We now have a live example of a pathological glut and went through all the noises and chaos that it created. On one hand demand for oil literally had a free fall as people were not buying petroleum fuels like gasoline or petrol or jet fuels despite lower prices for these products. This was driven by the minimum essential travel demand that existed coupled with grounded flights. Furthermore, in the new normal that people started to get acclimatised to, the chance of oil demand reviving to its pre-pandemic level soon appeared rather bleak. Probing on the supply side, the oil supply continued as it is very costly to shut down a producing well. In fact, for many producers, it almost turned out to be an all or nothing choice—shutting down is not an easy option and not practical. This is especially true for high-pressure, high-temperature wells that are harder to cap and halting production from them is more permanent and expensive and may lead to irreversible losses. Thus, in the bigger interest of the medium to long term allowing them to operate is the only way to go ahead (Wharton School of Business, 2020). Therefore, the only option that remained was to keep pumping even at a rock bottom price. Consequently, all unneeded oil went into reserve, strategic or otherwise, till the time such space existed for storing beyond which shutting in by refineries and capping of wells eventually becomes inevitable.

By destroying the effective derived demand, the pandemic has also altered the market dynamics for fuels and led to a deep slide in the crude prices globally roiling all crude benchmarks and WTI futures contract slid to a negative zone for the first time in history. Although other benchmarks like Brent or Dubai crude did not slide that low, but with global oil slosh and storage crisis their prices were also hovering at a rock bottom level. The turn of events rattled the trust on a crude benchmark like WTI. The betting behaviour of the traders in the commodity futures market continued to rule the roost and drove the price to an unhealthy zone irrespective of where the fundamentals lie. Albeit triggered by a contango structure betting in a dangerously inelastic oil market coupled with a severe storage crisis created a huge disconnect with the very foundation and fundamentals of oil and gas economics, which is obviously a matter of concern.

The entire crisis also blatantly exposed the vulnerabilities of American energy dominance that has been riding on shale for a decade. What one could expect at the most is a leaner shale industry with stronger players who could manage to sail through the crisis with or without a stimulus package from the government. The sudden drop for shale from the cliff is also a great lesson for other shale players worldwide in terms of generating consciousness about the hollowness and shaky foundation on which the US shale revolution was based, although it made USA one of the largest exporters at the end of 2019 surpassing the Saudis and the Russians. In fact, the shale industry could manage to sail through the last decade only because of the reasonably high oil and gas price that could help them to reach their breakeven easily but the situation does not appear to remain favourable any more. The era of free riding on the high oil price is almost over. Sooner the industry come to terms with this reality, the better it is for its business strategy and future course of action.

The untimely and undesirable brawl for market share and price war between Saudis and Russians might appear to be a strategic move but there is hardly any doubt that it eventually turned out to be a miscalculated blunder. The compound effect of the pandemic and price war rattled the economics of oil and gas industry in an unprecedented manner. Breaking-out of competition is not new in the world oil market and we have observed that consecutively in 1985, 1999, 2008 and 2014. In most of these cases, however, it took quite some time before some coordinated OPEC agreement started having some real effect in the oil market (Bornstein, 2020a). This time the big producers proposed to cut daily output in a span of one month. Be it under pressure of US or G20; be it due to a steeply cratering demand that made fulfilment of their own aspirations challenging; be it due to their own plus other weaker producers' finances being under severe stress; this time OPEC plus could actually agree to deeper cuts to balance the market. However, the continued drop in consumption does not seem to provide any respite so soon in the changing normal and turmoil in the oil markets shall continue to rule the roost for the financial year 2020–21.

Leaving aside the more specific fallouts, there is hardly any second thought that with an energy sector that has been bruised by a historically steepest slide in crude prices, it is very unlikely for the earlier "normal" to return. Given the critical role that oil plays in driving the global economy and in terms of providing an important source of revenue for the government; providing an important avenue for investments by pension funds or hedge funds, everything will now have to adjust to this 'new normal' irrespective of the plights and challenges that may arise therefrom. As noted in a recent research paper to guide the policymakers that came out in April

27, Altman notes, "the linchpin for a strategy to move out of lockdown seemingly rests on increased testing and contact tracing, possible return-to-work permits based on immune status, repurposed or new therapeutics" (Altman, 2020). Assuming the policymakers follow all these carefully while going for a staggered lifting of lockdown across the world and people progressively resumes travel, a lot will still depend on how behaviour of commuters changes for short distance travel or for long haul in a post-COVID world and with a second wave of infection that may still loom large.[14] Given that we are now getting acclimatised with remote working, telecommuting and videoconferencing; people would think twice before travelling and even the organisations would carry out cost-benefit analysis to examine whether the need for physical travel could actually be reduced in the post-COVID world. That may inherently reduce the demand from one of the biggest contributors for oil demand, transport sector. The requirement of cooling and heating offices shall also reduce concomitantly. In other words, the volatility and the roller coaster ride in oil sector is only expected to continue further.

References

Adams-Heard, R., & Crowley, K. (2020, March 10). 'Shale's new reality: Almost all wells drilled now lose money. *Bloomberg*. Available at https://www.bloomberg.com/news/articles/2020-03-09/shale-s-new-reality-almost-all-wells-drilled-now-lose-money?sref=TuZHMJro. (Accessed on 03 September, 2020).

Adams-Heard, R., & Crowley, K. (2020a, April 9). Occidental seeking federal lifeline for U.S. oil industry. *BNN Bloomberg*. Available at https://www.bnnbloomberg.ca/occidental-seeking-federal-lifeline-for-u-s-oil-industry-1.1419703. (Accessed 03 September, 2020).

Altmann, D. M., Douek, D. C., & Boyton, R. J. (2020, April 27). What policy makers need to know about COVID-19 protective immunity. *The Lancet*. Available at https://doi.org/10.1016/S0140-6736(20)30985-5. (Accessed September 2, 2020).

Arezki, R., & Fan, R. Y. (2020). Oil price wars in a time of COVID-19. Available at https://voxeu.org/article/oil-price-wars-time-covid-19. (Accessed 13 August, 2020).

Bandyopadhyay, K. R. (2008, November 15). OPEC's price-making power. *Economic and Political Weekly 43*(46). Available at https://www.epw.in/journal/2008/46/commentary/opecs-price-making-power.html. (Accessed 22 Aug, 2020).

Bornstein, S. (2020a, April 6). The policy and politics of the COVID-19 oil market crash'. Berkeley: Energy Institute Blog, Hass School of Business, University of California. Available at https://energyathaas.wordpress.com/2020/04/06/the-policy-and-politics-of-the-covid-19-oil-market-crash/. (Accessed 04 September, 2020).

[14]The second wave of infection could actually be more deadly as evinced by the experience of Spanish Flu, see https://www.miamiherald.com/news/coronavirus/article242371006.html (accessed on September 2, 2020). For an illustration of impact of second wave of infection please see: https://www.wsj.com/articles/why-a-second-wave-could-be-even-worse-for-sports-11587117600 (accessed on September 2, 2020). Also see an excellent commentary that came out in The Guardian on the lessons that we can apply for the current pandemic from Spanish Flu https://www.theguardian.com/commentisfree/2020/apr/29/us-responses-1918-flu-pandemic-offer-stark-lessons-coronavirus-now (accessed on September 2, 2020).

Bornstein, S. (2020, March 16). Oil market impacts of COVID-19" energy institute blog, Hass School of Business, UC Berkeley. https://energyathaas.wordpress.com/2020/03/16/oil-market-impacts-of-covid-19/.

Brower, D. (2020). Why the record OPEC cut is no match for coronavirus hit to demand?' *Financial Times,* April 15. Available at https://www.ft.com/content/2a91fd26-c337-427f-8b24-9f53bc321bb2. (Accessed 24 August, 2020).

Caldecott, B. (2017). Introduction to special issue: Stranded assets and the environment. *Journal of Sustainable Finance and Investment* 7(1). Available at https://www.tandfonline.com/doi/full/10.1080/20430795.2016.1266748. (Accessed 19 August, 2020).

Champion, M. (2020, March 10). *The changing winners and losers from oil's historic plunge.* Bloomberg. Available at https://www.bloomberg.com/news/articles/2020-03-10/the-changing-winners-and-losers-from-oil-s-historic-plunge. (Accessed 19 August, 2020).

Council for Foreign Relations. (2020, April 15). FAQ: A shale new deal . Available at https://www.cfr.org/blog/faq-shale-new-deal. (Accessed 30 August, 2020).

Denning, L. (2020, March 17). Trump's energy dominance dream submits to reality. *BloombergQuint.* Available at https://www.bloombergquint.com/gadfly/shale-bailout-would-expose-emptiness-of-energy-independence. (Accessed 20 August ,2020).

Eaton, C., & Scurria, A. (2020, April). Whiting petroleum becomes first major shale bankruptcy as oil prices drop. *Wall Street Journal.* Available at https://www.wsj.com/articles/u-s-shale-driller-whiting-petroleum-to-file-for-bankruptcy-11585746800. (Accessed 04 September, 2020).

Eccles, R. (2020). Why it's time to finally worry about ESG. HBR Idea Cast, Episode 683. Available at https://hbr.org/podcast/2019/05/why-its-time-to-finally-worry-about-esg. (Accessed 22 August, 2020).

Energy Information Administration. (2020, March 27). Oil market volatility is at all time high. USA: Department of Energy. Available at https://www.eia.gov/todayinenergy/detail.php?id=43275. (Accessed 11 August, 2020).

Energy Information Administration. (2020a, April 22). WTI crude oil futures prices fell below zero because of low liquidity and limited available storage. USA: Department of Energy. Available at https://www.eia.gov/petroleum/weekly/archive/2020/200422/includes/analysis_print.php. (Accessed on 23 August, 2020).

Energy Information Administration. (2020b, April). Short Term Energy Outlook. Available at https://www.eia.gov/outlooks/steo/archives/apr20.pdf?utm_source=newsletter&utm_medium=email&utm_campaign=newsletter_axiosgenerate&stream=top. (Accessed on 24 August, 2020).

EPW Engage. (2019, December 11). *Reckoning oil's worth: The OPEC, brent index and how we calculate global oil prices.* Available at https://www.epw.in/engage/article/reckoning-oils-worth-opec-brent-index-and-how-we-calculate-oil-prices. (Accessed 30 September, 2020).

Fattouh, B., & Imsirovic, A. (2020, April). *Shocks and differentials: How are oil markets coping*? Oxford Energy Comment. Available at https://www.oxfordenergy.org/wpcms/wp-content/uploads/2020/04/Shocks-and-Differentials-how-are-oil-markets-coping.pdf?v=c86ee0d9d7ed. (Accessed 20 August, 2020).

Federal Reserve Bank of Dallas. (2020, March 25). *Energy Survey,* First Quarter. Available at https://www.dallasfed.org/research/surveys/des/2020/2001.aspx#tab-questions. (Accessed 04 September, 2020).

Foss, M. M. (2020, March 19). U.S. shale goes viral. *Forbes.* Available at https://www.forbes.com/sites/thebakersinstitute/2020/03/19/us-shale-goes-viral/#1b88be165a88. (Accessed 01 September, 2020).

French, D., & Moise, I. (2020, April 10). U.S. banks prepare to seize energy assets as shale boom goes bust. Money News, Reuters. Available at https://in.reuters.com/article/usa-banks-energy-assets-exclusive-idINKCN21S05V. (Accessed 17 August, 2020).

Gladstone, A., & Biswas, S. (2020, April 21). Shale driller unit corp. Prepares for bankruptcy filing. *Bloomberg.* Available at https://www.wsj.com/articles/shale-driller-unit-corp-prepares-for-bankruptcy-filing-11587497829?cx_testId=3&cx_testVariant=cx_2&cx_artPos=3#cxrecs_s. (Accessed 04 September, 2020).

Gopinath, G. (2020, April 14). The great lockdown: Worst economic downturn since the great depression. IMF Blog. Available at https://blogs.imf.org/2020/04/14/the-great-lockdown-worst-economic-downturn-since-the-great-depression/. (Accessed August 19, 2020).

Government Accountability Office. (2012, September). Information on shale resources, development, and environmental and public health risks', GAO-12-732, A report to congressional requesters. Available at https://www.gao.gov/assets/650/647791.pdf. (Accessed 31 August, 2020).

Grubb, M. (2020, April 16). Why oil prices will never recover?' *Asia Times*. Available at https://asiatimes.com/2020/04/after-the-storm-why-oil-will-never-recover/. (Accessed 18 August, 2020).

Halff, A. (2020, April 1). Saudi-Russia oil war is a game theory masterstroke. *Financial Times*. Available at https://www.ft.com/content/1da60fa2-3d63-439e-abd4-1391a2047972. (Accessed 20 August, 2020).

Haynes & Boone, LLP. (2020, August 31). Oil patch bankruptcy monitor. Available at https://www.haynesboone.com/-/media/files/energy_bankruptcy_reports/oil_patch_bankruptcy_monitor.ashx?la=en&hash=D2114D98614039A2D2D5A43A61146B13387AA3AE. (Accessed 05 September, 2020).

International Energy Agency .(2020). Oil market report. April, IEA, Paris. Available at https://www.iea.org/reports/oil-market-report-April-2020. (Accessed September 03, 2020).

Jaffe, A. (2020, March 10). Why current Saudi-Russia oil price war is not Déjà Vu'. Council on Foreign Relations. Available at https://www.cfr.org/blog/why-current-saudi-russia-oil-price-war-not-deja-vu. (Accessed 23 August, 2020).

Jaffe, A. (2020a). Oil ground zero: Running out of storage', April 6, Council on Foreign Relations. Available at https://www.cfr.org/blog/oil-ground-zero-running-out-storage. (Accessed 04 September, 2020).

Kaminska, I. (2020).Oil's big storage problem. *Financial Times* Alphaville. Available at https://ftalphaville.ft.com/2020/03/19/1584620541000/Oil-s-big-storage-problem/. (Accessed on September 05, 2020).

Kern, M. (2020). Oil prices crash 24% as storage fears mount. Available at https://oilprice.com/Energy/Oil-Prices/Oil-Prices-Crash-24-As-Storage-Fears-Mount.html. (Accessed 05 September, 2020).

Kumar, D. K. & Hiller, J. (2020, April). A hunt for any storage space turns urgent as oil glut grows. Reuters. Available at https://www.reuters.com/article/us-global-oil-storage-fracking/a-hunt-for-any-storage-space-turns-urgent-as-oil-glut-grows-idUSKBN2230I3. (Accessed on September 04, 2020).

Lions, P. –L., Lasry, J.-M., & Gu´eant, O. (2020). A mean field game approach to oil production. Available at http://www.wec-france.org/DocumentsPDF/RECHERCHE/57_Rapportfinal(inenglish).pdf. (Accessed 21 August, 2020).

Mackey, J., & Sisodia R. (2013, January 14). Conscious capitalism is not an oxymoron. *Harvard Business Review*. Available at https://hbr.org/2013/01/cultivating-a-higher-conscious. (Accessed 02 September, 2020).

Meidan, M. (2020, April). China's rocky road to recovery. *Oxford Energy Comment*. Available at https://www.oxfordenergy.org/wpcms/wp-content/uploads/2020/04/Chinas-rocky-road-to-recovery.pdf. (Accessed 03 September, 2020).

OPEC Secretariat. (2017). *Declaration of Cooperation*, Available at https://www.opec.org/opec_web/en/publications/4580.htm. (Accessed 02 August, 2020).

Paine, L. S (2014, July-August) Sustainability in the board room. *Harvard Business Review*. Available at https://hbr.org/2014/07/sustainability-in-the-boardroom. (Accessed 20 August, 2020).

Raimonde, O. (2020, April 29). Oil falls after major index bails out of june wti contract. Available at https://www.bloomberg.com/news/articles/2020-04-27/oil-hangs-on-near-13-as-etf-selloff-exacerbates-glut-concerns?sref=TuZHMJro. (Accessed September 03, 2020).

Reig, P., Luo, T., & Proctor, J. N. (2014). Global shale gas development: Water availability and business risks. Report, World Resources Institute. Available at https://files.wri.org/s3fs-public/wri14_report_shalegas.pdf. (Accessed 30 August, 2020).

Said, S., & Faucon, B. (2020, April 20). Saudis consider cutting oil output ahead of schedule as price crashes. *The Wall Street Journal.* Available at https://www.wsj.com/articles/saudis-consider-cutting-oil-output-ahead-of-schedule-as-price-crashes-11587416271. (Accessed on 16 Aug, 2020).

Said, S., & Faucon, B. (2020, April). Saudis consider cutting oil output ahead of schedule as price crashes. *The Wall Street Journal.* Available at https://www.wsj.com/articles/saudis-consider-cutting-oil-output-ahead-of-schedule-as-price-crashes-11587416271?emailToken=afb56be3993d6f6ace1b421e8ca7d669QcERX4A8S/A1KoQkeXAcxIOeAapgcs0ykFta3PK4G9aMUN7XmBsW6lOhVHONtj0zRVUcF3BCOcezPXW3e1wgdk21eTPfDlU + Swy7DUXGrQoljyobCZpueuTLf9JuMEQGD9Ac4k7WiTyS0O40 + aRAQ%3D%3D&reflink = article_copyURL_share. (Accessed 31st August, 2020).

Sheppard, D., Gross, A., & Hale, T. (2020, April). US oil prices swing as coronavirus fuels storage fears. *Financial Times.* Available at https://www.ft.com/content/3eb1910e-cda0-4d10-a7e8-4ad0e48b3275. (Accessed September 02, 2020).

Stevens, P. (2010). In *The 'Shale gas revolution': Hype and reality.* A Chatham House Report, 1 September. Available at https://www.chathamhouse.org/sites/default/files/public/Research/Energy%2C%20Environment%20and%20Development/r_0910stevens.pdf. (Accessed 29 August, 2020).

Victor, D. G. (2020, April 3). *Forecasting energy futures amid the coronavirus outbreak.* USA: Brookings Institution. Available at https://www.brookings.edu/blog/order-from-chaos/2020/04/03/forecasting-energy-futures-amid-the-coronavirus-outbreak/. (Accessed 06 September, 2020).

Wharton School of Business .(2020, April 28). Oil price shock: What it means for producers and consumers, Knowledge@Wharton, University of Pennsylvania. Available at https://knowledge.wharton.upenn.edu/article/oil-price-shock-means-producers-consumers/?utm_source=kw_newsletter&utm_medium=email&utm_campaign=2020-04-28.

Sustainability Cross-Cuts: Developmental Aspects

Recourse to the Circular Economy: The Path Ahead

Robin Singhal

1 Introduction

The twenty-first century is expected to be marked by the risks emerging from the current economic paradigm that has been guided by the proposition that the availability of natural resources is *endless* and their increasing withdrawal from nature for greater prosperity and human well-being is *unproblematic*. There has been a lack of appreciation of *planetary boundaries* for resource availability and explicit attention to the harmful impacts for nature—both as a source of matter and energy and as a sink for disposal of wastes. This has led to the concerns for *safe operating space* assuming gradually the central focus in the discourse of economic decision-making, thereby posing challenges for the neoclassical paradigm. Consequently, it is imperative to undertake measures for addressing environmental and resource-related risks for promising a *sustainable economy* in the times ahead. Unless there are concerted efforts to decouple economic growth from resource use and its impacts on the environment, the realisation of Sustainable Development Goals (SDGs) would remain elusive (WEF, 2019).

The advancements in science and technology have raised our understanding regarding the *levels* and *types* of unsustainability to a greater degree. However, despite several attempts, the world is facing formidable challenges in laying down a path to move towards a sustainable economy. One plausible explanation for this is based on a growing realisation that "sustainability is a systems problem" wherein economics, technological progress and public policy have a critical role to influence the variables (such as *stocks*, *rates* and *trade-offs*) that are fundamental to envisage such a transition. Both natural and human systems are dynamic ones that undergo transition and

R. Singhal (✉)
School of Liberal Studies, Dr. B.R. Ambedkar University Delhi, Lothian Road, Kashmere Gate, Delhi, India
e-mail: rbnsinghal@gmail.com

P. Dasgupta et al. (eds.), *Sustainable Development Insights from India*,
India Studies in Business and Economics,
https://doi.org/10.1007/978-981-33-4830-1_13

evolution over time and space. Much to the dismay, the unsustainability characterising the inter-linkages of human and natural systems continues unabated. Moreover, the emergent behaviour[1] of these systems tends to confound attempts aiming for their transition to sustainable pathways (Graedel and van der Voet, 2010).

Undoubtedly, several supply-side factors inclusive of physical parameters are crucial in the sustainability discourse. However, the demand-side factors have a critical role to play in determining how long-term sustainability would unfold. Such demand for resources is in turn influenced by the choices of economic agents—producers and consumers, whose behaviours are largely governed by the framework of institutions in which they operate. It is projected that, if the current consumption patterns continue to persist, the global demand for primary material use would touch a level of 186 billion tonnes by the year 2050. This is an alarming trend since it implies a more than doubling of the global material use in just about one-third of the twenty-first century estimated at 90 billion tonnes in 2017, which stood at a level of just 7 billion tonnes at the turn of the twentieth century (WEF, 2019).

Globally, the concept of circular economy (CE) is being put forth as an effective means to foster the preservation of natural resource base and its optimum utilisation, thereby minimising negative environmental externalities and ensuring decoupling of economic growth from environmental degradation. In this context, this chapter provides a review of the conceptual foundations of the CE as was first proposed by Pearce and Turner, and analyses the scope and methodological framework of CE in terms of its inter-linkages with other fields such as industrial ecology and ecological economics (see Sect. 2). It further provides an overview of the recent initiatives of the Government of India towards the adoption of CE in the Sect. 3. Finally, it puts forth an economic perspective towards CE and highlights some potential hindrances in its mainstreaming from the economic methodology point of view in the realm of neoclassical economic paradigm (see Sect. 4). The concluding observations are discussed in the Sect. 5.

2 Linear Versus Closed System

The neoclassical paradigm has attempted to integrate environmental problems with the broader set of economic issues under the subject of *environmental economics* and the issues regarding the exploitation or harvest of natural resources based on the economic principles along with some sustainability considerations under the subject of *resource economics*. However, its focus has been to explore the inter-linkages between the human economy and the natural environment which are assumed as being *linear*.

As a linear system, the human system is considered to be largely an independent system wherein the act of production and consumption is performed without an

[1]It refers to the one "in which even a detailed knowledge of one level of a system is insufficient to predict behaviour at a different level" (pg. 4, Graedel and van der Voet, 2010).

explicit appreciation of its inter-linkages with the natural environment. Consequently, its implications for the natural environment in terms of the inflow of matter and energy on the one hand and the outflow of wastes, on the other, remain out of the purview. The material needs of an ever-expanding human system, wherein the scale of economic activities has been growing at a rapid pace facilitated by factors such as technological advancements, globally integrated markets for goods and services and desire for the attainment of a higher standard of living for a growing population base, are considered to be the genesis of several environmental problems. In this backdrop, there arises a need to revisit such a linear system as it tends to ignore the various economic functions performed by the natural systems which are—(a) "to provide resource inputs to the productive system"; (b) "to take wastes and to convert them back into harmless or ecologically useful products"; and (c) "a direct source of utility in the form of aesthetic enjoyment and spiritual comfort" (Pearce & Turner, 1990).[2]

2.1 Dimensions of the Circular Economy

Based primarily on the work of Kenneth Boulding and Nicholas Georgescu-Roegen that had its foundations in the laws of thermodynamics and their application to economic systems, Pearce and Turner attempted integration of these three economic functions performed by the natural environment into the realm of human systems. This involved: (a) considering economy as a *closed* system wherein the economic system is not only subject to the limits or boundaries set by the natural systems, but their interactions are circular rather than being characterised by linear inter-linkages; and (b) conforming the functioning of the economic system, subject to entropy law, to a *sustainable* system wherein wastes generated get recycled. The lack of emphasis on recycling waste originating from human systems is in sharp contrast to the natural systems that have an inherent tendency of re-utilising its waste to the maximum extent; for instance, waste generated by one species is put to use for its usefulness by another species before ultimately getting absorbed given the assimilative capacity of the natural environment. These considerations led them to envision the economic system as being closed and circular for it to be a sustainable system, against being a linear and an open one. Such an economic system is what they referred to as the *circular economy*.

Further, they argued that there is nothing inherent to the functioning of economies as such that can ensure their consistency with the natural environments linked to them and to ensure that they both "coexist in equilibrium". The fundamentals to realise the CE lie in relating "the scale and configuration of an economy to the set

[2]Broadly speaking, these "can be considered as components of one general function of natural environments—the function of life support" (Pearce & Turner, 1990). According to the Millennium Ecosystem Assessment, the ecosystem services are broadly classified as provisioning, regulating, cultural and support services (Costanza et al., 2014).

of environment–economy interrelationships underlying that economy". According to them, the key objective should be to sustain an economy, and the act of sustaining involves "making it last, to keep it in being and make it endure". One can thus argue that a sustainable economy is the one that adheres to the framework of CE which in turn requires the adoption of the closed and circular system. There is no denying the fact that the ultimate purpose of a functioning economy is to create utility, but for it to be a sustainable one, there is a need to organise it as a closed and circular system, which undoubtedly would have implications for "what can be done by way of achieving that utility". Consequently, in terms of organising the economy while being subjected to the laws of thermodynamics, it becomes crucial that concerted efforts are made to deal with the aspects that are critical to the circular economy such as managing *stocks* of resources, their *rates* of harvest or exploitation, *trade-offs* in terms of continued use of a resource in an economic system vis-à-vis its ultimate disposal as wastes to the natural environment and implications for nature's assimilative capacity.

2.2 Circular Economy and Its Inter-linkages

In recent times, as the emphasis on the concept of CE has gained momentum owing to the unsustainability concerns (Ghisellini et al., 2016), there has been renewed interest in the research on its historical evolution (Winans et al., 2017; Murray et al., 2017) and conceptual inter-linkages with some of the important concepts such as *industrial ecology* (IE), *ecological economics* (EE), *sustainability* (Geissdoerfer et al., 2017), *sustainable development* (SD) (Korhonen et al., 2018; Millar et al., 2019) and *bio-economy* (Giampietro, 2019). However, the concept of CE is intrinsically linked to the field of IE and EE.

Industrial Ecology and Circular Economy: Robert U. Ayres is credited for introducing the concept of *industrial metabolism* that refers to "the whole integrated collection of physical processes that convert raw materials, energy and labour into finished output and wastes in a steady-state situation" (Ayers, 1994; Manderson & Considine, 2018). Ayers' adoption of the word—*metabolism*—given its biological interpretations, in the context of the economic system allowed him to highlight the distinguishing features among biological organisms and industrial systems. He underscored that the living organisms tend to reproduce themselves and are highly specialised ones with their behaviour undergoing evolution only over a longer time frame. Further, the life cycle of nutrients in the natural environment, for instance, hydrological cycle, carbon cycle, nitrogen cycle, etc., is a closed one (Ayers, 1994).

Such observations about the natural systems are in sharp contrast to the firms or industries in the economic system. Most importantly, these production systems are an open one, not geared towards keeping their materials cycle to be closed. Note that a system qualifies to be a closed one "if there are no external sources or sinks" and a closed system in turn "becomes a closed cycle if the system is also in steady state that is if the stocks in each compartment are constant and unchanging at least on the average". In other words, a sustainable industrial economy is the one which goes beyond the consideration of resource availability (i.e. stock considerations) and addresses concerns for recovery, recycle and reuse of materials (i.e. flow considerations) through tracing their flow from source to sink as wastes (Ayers, 1994).

Developing on the foundations laid down in terms of the concept of industrial metabolism, the industrial ecology (IE) has evolved as an interdisciplinary field following the principles of systems thinking and underscoring the need for exploiting the interdependencies among units as well as industries, also referred to as industrial symbiosis, towards efficient secondary resource management in production systems (Saavedra et al., 2018; Bruel et al., 2019). It attempts to integrate environmental issues in the industrial ecosystem for their transformation to environmentally compatible ones. IE thus envisions industrial systems to be developed as being an analogue to natural ecological systems, wherein firms/industries move towards a closed-loop system and wastes are considered as commodities of value that are meant to be recovered, recycled and reused in the complex interconnected networks of firms/industries. It thus emphasises that unit processes and industries shall be treated as interactive systems instead of being considered as isolated components (Richards et al., 1994; Bruel et al., 2019).

It is important to note here that the literature dealing with the set of issues in the domain of IE tends to focus primarily on technical issues. The orientation towards economics and policy issues is lacking. The bibliometric analysis reveals that in the literature on CE and IE, the economic and environmental dimensions are resorted to in terms of linkages but the critical third dimension of sustainable development (SD), i.e. social sustainability, remains lacking (Saavedra et al., 2018). Undoubtedly, IE has an important role to play in facilitating the implementation of CE. The IE tools such as material flow analysis, life cycle assessment and eco-design are useful for capturing the direct and indirect environmental impacts on account of industrial processes and the associated material and energy flows. The integration of such information into policy formulation and adoption of instruments can enhance the degree of policy effectiveness with respect to the outcomes achieved through public intervention. However, given the choice of tools and techniques of IE, the nature of assessments carried out either remains predominantly descriptive or is aimed at conducting accounting exercises for material and energy flows across the value chain or intervening stages of manufacturing semi-finished or final products. Hence, there is an urgent need to bring together the economic principles and foundations of IE in an integrated manner to develop an analytical framework facilitating the transformation of industrial systems into a sustainable one, thereby enabling the transition to CE (Manderson & Considine, 2018).

Ecological Economics and Circular Economy: Ecological economics (EE) sets out a trans-disciplinary agenda to overcome the disciplinary boundaries in addressing issues regarding the allocation of resources, their distribution among different members of the society and the scale of economic activities which have a bearing on the flow of matter and energy into the human systems. The neoclassical economics framework does deal with the allocation and distribution issues, but in particular, it is the recognition of the scale of economic activities and its implications for the life-support system on the planet earth that makes EE a distinct field from it. The subject of *environmental economics* under the realm of the neoclassical economics, as an attempt to address the issues of externalities arising from the process of production and consumption, recommends the use of policy instruments towards attaining the socially optimal level of pollution following the notion of *weak sustainability* (i.e. the notion of sustainability which allows for the substitution between man-made capital, human capital and natural capital). In contrast, EE follows the notion of *strong sustainability* which not only rules out the possibility of substitution between these different forms of capital but also among the different forms of natural capital. Also, it underscores the need to preserve the critical forms of natural capital as an essential prerequisite for keeping intact the *regulating* and *supporting* services of the ecosystem besides the *provisioning* and *cultural* services and thereby sustaining the process of life itself. It thus criticises the neoclassical perspective regarding the inter-linkages between the natural environment and the human economy which envisions them as being two independent systems (Costanza et al., 2014). It rather advocates that the human systems are only a sub-system of the natural ecosystem or biosphere, subject to the laws of thermodynamics, and their expansions shall be sought while adhering to the notion of *diversity, stability and resilience* of ecosystem (Hussen, 2013).

EE adopts a system thinking perspective for integrating socio-economic systems with the ecological systems and thus considers system analysis to constitute "a more natural scientific base and worldview for the inherently integrative trans-discipline of ecological economics than classical, reductionist science". For such an analytical framework, the definition of system boundaries and the spatial scale of an ecosystem to be analysed become vital. Therefore, to develop a comprehensive understanding of the interacting systems, it is considered crucial to study "the similarities and differences among different kinds of systems at different scales and resolutions" (Costanza et al., 2014).

Similarly, though CE has its roots in the system thinking, it is important to emphasise the relevance of the issue of scale (such as micro-, meso- and macro-level) in (a) formulating plans and programmes for its mainstreaming and (b) developing strategies given the different approaches such as top-down and bottom-up adopted towards its implementation. This necessitates further research to identify the challenges in its successful implementation at the different levels while securing participation from businesses, government and the society at large (Ghisellini et al., 2016).

3 Mainstreaming Circular Economy in India

The impetus for the current emphasis on resource efficiency (RE) and considerations of CE development in India came from the Indo-German bilateral cooperation that led to a project—"Resource Efficiency and Sustainable Management of Secondary Raw

Material". This project got funding from the German Federal Ministry of the Environment, Nature Conservation and Nuclear Safety under its International Climate Initiative (IKI) and has been implemented jointly by the Deutsche Gesellschaft für Internationale Zusammenarbeit (GIZ) GmbH and the Indian Ministry of Environment, Forest and Climate Change (MoEFCC). The deliberations among the project partners led to the establishment of the Indian Resource Panel (InRP) in the year 2015 as an advisory body under the MoEFCC. This panel comprised ten[3] members ensuring wider institutional collaborations and was entrusted with the role "(a) to assess the existing policies about resource efficiency and secondary resource management, (b) to integrate such considerations in the flagship policies and programmes of the government and (c) to carry out a baseline assessment of the policy landscape in India to identify the gaps as well as potential synergies to inform the future policy direction/public interventions" (Becker et al., 2019).

3.1 Recent RE/CE Initiatives in India

The InRP published a policy brief entitled "Recommendations for an Indian Resource Efficiency Programme (IREP)" in April 2017 to serve as a guiding document for the policymakers to devise resource-efficient strategies in the country. This document published by GIZ was developed by the InRP in collaboration with several organisations which assisted it either in the capacity of being a consultant such as Adelphi Research Gemeinnützige GmbH (Adelphi) or as knowledge partners such as Institut für Energie-und Umweltforschung Heidelberg GmbH (IFEU), The Energy and Resources Institute (TERI), Development Alternatives (DA), VDI Zentrum Ressourceneffizienz GmbH (VDI ZRE). It outlined the broad contours of a resource efficiency programme for India given the development needs of the country and its projected material demand trajectories for the future. It laid down ten major action points for developing such strategies based on the two guiding principles—a) maximising the value creation from the natural resource base for human well-being and b) minimising costs from the exploitation of natural resources for society as a whole. It also underscored the imperativeness of formulating suitable policy measures following the life cycle approach, and through identifying key industrial and strategic sectors (also referred to as hotspot sectors), materials and encouraging multi-stakeholder participation (InRP, 2017).

On 2 June 2018, the Ministry of Environment, Forest and Climate Change (MoEFCC) signed a Memorandum of Understanding (MoU) with TERI for setting up the Resource Efficiency (RE) Cell at the ministry. The objective behind this initiative has been to establish an institutional framework that could serve as a

[3]The members were Mr. Vishwanath N. Anand, Dr. Prodipto Ghosh, Dr. Tishyarakshit Chatterjee and Mr. Rajen Habib Khwaja (former officials from the MoEFCC); Dr. Ajay Mathur (Bureau of Energy Efficiency); Dr. Ashok Khosla (Development Alternatives); Ms. Seema Arora (Confederation of Indian Industry); Mr. Ravi Agarwal (Toxics Link); Dr. Prasad Modak (Environmental Management Centre); and Ms. Sunita Narain (Centre for Science and Environment).

platform for mainstreaming concerns related to RE in the formulation of public policy and the pursuit of suitable policy goals and targets in the country. The RE Cell was also assigned the task of enabling the formulation of the RE policy in the country while adopting a system-based thinking approach and facilitating the coordination among various ministries and public/private agencies (PIB, 2018). Further, the MoEFCC reconstituted the RE Cell in October 2018 and also the InRP into an advisory committee—Resource Efficiency Steering Committee (RESC) to the Cell in November 2018 (TERI, 2019).

The MoEFCC also signed a Joint Declaration of Intent (JDI) on 2 June 2018 with the European Union (EU) for the implementation of the European Union's Resource Efficiency Initiative (EU-REI) project in India. This project aimed at facilitating the promotion of RE considerations and had a three and a half years duration ending in July 2020. Under this project, some of the key sectors identified were electric vehicles (mobility), solar photovoltaics mobility (renewable energy), building and construction, e-waste and plastic packaging for which sectoral-level assessments have been carried with support from the consortium partners such as GIZ, TERI, Adelphi and the Confederation of Indian Industry (CII) in September 2018 (EU-REI, 2018a, b, c, d). Besides, the National Institution for Transforming India (NITI) Aayog has also released sectoral-level assessment for different sectors such as aluminium, steel, electrical and electronic equipment, construction and demolition during January 2019, in association with the concerned ministries such as the Ministry of Mines, Ministry of Steel, Ministry of Electronics and Information Technology, and Ministry of Housing and Urban Affairs, respectively (NITI Aayog, 2019a, b, c, d).

In this backdrop, TERI submitted a "Reference Report for National Resource Efficiency Policy for India" to the MoEFCC on 12 April 2019 wherein the sectoral studies as conducted under the EU-REI project and by the NITI Aayog formed the basis of drawing strategies for mainstreaming RE in the seven sectors, namely automobile, plastic packaging, construction and demolition, e-waste, steel, solar photovoltaic and aluminium. It adopted an integrated RE approach and followed the principle of 6Rs—reduce, reuse, recycle, redesign, remanufacture and refurbish in making recommendations towards the development of a policy framework for the promotion of RE. The report underscored the need for adoption of the life cycle approach in public policymaking for ensuring sustainable production and consumption in the country. Further, it is emphasised that the scope of the recommendations remained limited to the non-energy abiotic material resources at this juncture (TERI, 2019).

3.2 *National Resource Efficiency Policy and the Overarching Framework for RE/CE in India*

In India, the Draft National Resource Efficiency Policy 2019 (hereafter, NREP 2019) was released on 23 July 2019 by the MoEFCC in the public domain inviting comments and suggestions. This policy has been prepared by the MoEFCC after incorporating inputs from the RESC in consultation with multi-stakeholders both within and outside the government (MoEFCC, 2019).

The guiding principles of this policy are sustainability considerations and optimum resource use, attaining material security, innovations in business models and creating employment opportunities during the envisaged transition of the economy to the one practising RE and adopting the CE framework. To develop an enabling institutional and regulatory framework towards facilitating the process of transition, it proposes (a) the setting up of National Resource Efficiency Authority (NREA), under the aegis of the MoEFCC, to mainstream resource-efficient strategies and the promotion of crucial dimensions of the CE, and (b) constituting an inter-ministerial advisory board—National Resource Efficiency Advisory Board (NREAB) to ensure collaborative efforts among the several stakeholders. It remains noteworthy that the scope of NREP 2019 covers both biotic and abiotic resources "across all the life cycle stages of any sector". However, the action plan laid down in the policy document initially for the three years from 2019 to 2022 relates to the abiotic resources across the seven hotspot sectors, namely aluminium, automobiles including electric vehicles, buildings, construction, chemicals (plastics), solar photovoltaics and steel. It also provides for a comprehensive review of the policy after ten years to examine the need for any changes in the rules as well as the institutional structure (MoEFCC, 2019).

Further, the NITI Aayog in collaboration with the EU Delegation to India published a status paper entitled "Resource Efficiency and Circular Economy: Current Status and Way Forward" in January 2019. It outlined an overarching framework for the Indian economy identifying six broad pillars: (i) policies, (ii) programmes and mainstreaming, (iii) regulations, (iv) dynamic recycling industry, (v) research and development (R&D) and technology development, and (vi) capacity development, outreach and monitoring (see Appendix I for further details). Initiatives under these heads are deemed necessary for the adoption of CE as it goes beyond just managing wastes and aims at promoting the sustainability of resource use throughout their life cycles (NITI Aayog, 2019e).

4 An Economic Perspective on Circular Economy

Broadly speaking, a successful transition from a linear to a circular economy would entail making concerted efforts towards a range of enabling technical, economic and social factors (see Box 1). Also, there arises an urgent need for collaborative efforts among all stakeholders such as governments, businesses, researchers, civil society and citizens towards realising a fundamental shift in the socio-economic system (Ghisellini et al., 2016).

Box 1 Enabling Factors of a circular economy

1.	Eco-design	• Products designed for a longer life, enabling upgrading, reuse, refurbishment and remanufacture • Product design based on the sustainable and minimal use of resources and enabling high-quality recycling of materials at the end of a product's life • Substitution of hazardous substances in products and processes, enabling cleaner material cycles
2.	Repair, refurbishment and remanufacture	• Repair, refurbishment and remanufacture given priority, enabling reuse of products and components
3.	Recycling	• High-quality recycling of as much waste as possible, avoiding down-cycling (converting waste materials or products into new materials or products of lesser quality) • Use of recycled materials as secondary raw materials • Well-functioning markets for secondary raw materials • Avoidance of mixing and contaminating materials • Cascading use of materials where high-quality recycling is not possible
4.	Economic incentives and finance	• Shifting taxes from labour to natural resources and pollution • Phasing out environmentally harmful subsidies • The internalisation of environmental costs • Deposit systems • Extended producer responsibility • Finance mechanisms supporting circular economy approaches
5.	Business models	• Focus on offering product-service systems rather than product ownership • Collaborative consumption • Collaboration and transparency along the value chain • Industrial symbiosis (collaboration between companies whereby the wastes or by-products of one become a resource for another)

(continued)

(continued)

6.	Eco-innovation	• Technological innovation • Social innovation • Organisational innovation
7.	Governance, skills and knowledge	• Awareness-raising about changing lifestyles and priorities in consumption patterns • Participation, stakeholder interaction and exchange of experience • Education • Data, monitoring and indicators

Source Adopted from EEA 2016

In this context, it is worth emphasising that the key considerations from an economist's point of view are—*efficiency* and *equity*. The neoclassical school of thought which emphasises the market mechanism in the realisation of these two objectives relies primarily on the functioning of the invisible hand in achieving equilibrium. This equilibrium is perceived to be influenced by the changing market conditions as reflected by any adjustment in the market forces of demand and supply and is expected to result in a new equilibrium after the due adjustment process which accounts for the shortage/surplus conditions as the case may be. The equilibrium achieved is considered desirable as it is in itself a manifestation of a *social order* which under the market mechanism gets realised despite the free spirit of economic agents.

However, the absence of the crucial prerequisites such as atomistic economic agents, perfect information and zero transaction costs in real-world situations tends to limit the significance of market mechanism in ensuring allocative efficiency. The public intervention is sought after not only for overcoming such imperfections of markets on a case-to-case basis for the efficient provision of private goods but also for dealing with the situation of externalities and efficient provision of public goods, wherein the market fails in achieving the desired optimal outcomes. Further, despite the claims regarding the distribution neutrality of the markets, the world has witnessed ever-increasing concentration of wealth and income in the hands of a few, raising serious doubts regarding the gains from higher economic growth to trickle down in the absence of public intervention. Despite the widespread recognition of such limitations of the market mechanism, there have been arguments in favour of designing suitable policy interventions to correct for the market's inadequacies, thereby achieving the much-desired objective of social order while permitting the freedom of choice to the economic agents (Nayak, 2020). In other words, it is claimed that the social order can still be reinforced through appropriate public interventions.

It is noteworthy here that there is increasing evidence that the optimality achieved through market mechanism could still be a cause of concern in itself. For instance, it could well be the case that the optimal level of pollution/wastes achieved far exceeds the assimilative capacity of nature, thus leading to unabated environmental degradation. Further, the optimal scale of economic activities could still be beyond the carrying capacity of the ecosystem and can thereby threaten the earth's life-support system (Hussen, 2013). This can potentially unfold into a *higher degree of disorder* (owing to the climate crisis, nature crisis, pollution and waste crisis) which would not only fundamentally disturb the social order effected through the market mechanism in the first place but would also, in turn, undermine its significance as an institution ensuring the social order itself (i.e. the key role it is envisioned to perform). The reason being that the market mechanism as an institution fundamentally deals with the situations in and around the set of scarcity issues (i.e. achieving allocative efficiency) and at best can be manoeuvred for realising equity considerations through designing suitable public interventions which may or may not interfere with the decision-making of economic agents. However, there arises a need for assessing the adequacy of market mechanism for (a) addressing emergencies arising from such crises that threaten the very survival of life on planet earth (for instance, the prevailing unprecedented crises due to the COVID-19 pandemic), (b) coping with concerns for sustainability arising from the increasing intensity and frequency of extreme weather events (such as cyclones and droughts), (c) facilitating decision-making in situations of uncertainty and (d) dealing with the irreversibility of environmental changes in the wake of an alarming growth in human footprints on nature in the recent times. Such events do expose the vulnerability of the human systems and end up introducing a higher degree of disorder in the socio-economic systems to be managed.

Thus, it may not be incorrect to argue that any attempt to re-establish order in the socio-economic systems under such challenging situations would entail revisiting the social relations as effected through the market mechanism. For instance, the disorder that emerges, on account of the inconsistencies of the market outcomes vis-à-vis ecological considerations driven by the law of thermodynamics, would necessitate reorienting the social relations suitable for ensuring coordination/cooperation of actions towards the promotion of social good. Therefore, if the objective is to ensure sustainability as a social good, it is felt necessary that there should be responsible and "sustainable consumption and production patterns" in the society (i.e. SDG-12). However, the challenge in realising this is aptly put forward by Joseph E. Stiglitz (hereafter, Stiglitz) in the following words.

> In recent decades, economists have focussed on the need for collective action. Society is better off if or when its acts collectively – through the provision of public goods, proscribing activities that give rise to negative externalities, and encouraging those that give rise to positive externalities. There can be Pareto improvements. But the most important arena for collective action is *the establishment of the rules of the game*, enabling a market economy to function, enforcing contracts, and preventing the abuse of power, whether within an institution or within society. (Pg. 20–21, Stiglitz, 2017)

In the above backdrop, it is important to focus on the recent initiatives in the domain of business model innovations under the purview of implementing CE. This is considered to be one of the key enabling factors in the transition to the CE framework in the long term while having the potential to contribute towards sustainable consumption and production (i.e. SDG-12) in the near or medium term through facilitating RE. Such innovative business models have been broadly categorised into (a) service-*and function-based models* such as product-oriented services, user-oriented services and result-oriented devices, (b) *collaborative consumption*-based models involving sharing, swapping, trading or leasing of products and other assets (such as land or time) and (c) *waste-as-a-resource* business models emphasising exploitation of cross-sectoral and cross-cycle links in the flow of resources such as industrial symbiosis. It is emphasised that these innovative models are characterised by disruptive changes in the socio-economic system that can have positive effects for the society as a whole. However, this process of transition would involve trade-offs as there are potential negative effects for the traditional business models as well as stakeholders in the associated value chains, adverse implications for financial institutions, fiscal policy and regulatory framework from an economic point of view. In this backdrop, it is argued that there arises a need for concerted efforts towards providing adaptive financial mechanisms and innovative policy frameworks to strengthen the positive vis-à-vis negative outcomes during such a transition (EEA, 2016). In other words, this calls for *rewriting the rules* in the broadest sense.

In a democratic set-up, *the establishment of the rules of the game* is to be administered by the government, i.e. the elected representatives, who *in principle* are expected to conform to the mandate of the electorates.[4] Thus, it is the *prevailing* social preferences that tend to inform the determination of such rules which, in turn, implies that society ultimately serves as the governing institution towards their formulation. The adequacy of both these institutions in executing their responsibilities in contemporary times is best put forth by Stiglitz in the following words:

> Thus, the system of checks and balances has (so far) prevented one branch of the government dominating over another; but it has not prevented powerful groups from capturing the entire government, or to put it more mildly, from exercising disproportionate influence, of a kind inconsistent with democratic values. This failure can be traced to the failure of a broader set of checks and balances – within our society. (Pg. 24, Stiglitz, 2017)
>
> But in a deeper sense, in terms of the functioning of society and the political system as a whole, there is an absence of checks and balances—no way, short of a wholesale recommitment to an agenda of greater equality, of preventing those at the top from continuing their aggrandizement of power; no way to prevent the concentration of economic and political power; no way to ensure a democracy even in the market place of ideas. (Pg. 27, Stiglitz, 2017)

Hence, any move towards mainstreaming the CE would then have to necessarily overcome the following potential hindrances[5]:

---

[4] How widely such mandates reflect (or capture) the social preferences remains subject to the choice of the voting rule and the pursuit of democratic values and culture in the society as a whole. Such a discussion remains beyond the scope of this study.

[5] This is not to imply them as being an exhaustive list of such hindrances (or barriers). For instance, Kirchherr et al. (2018) identify a different set of barriers in the implementation of CE for the European Union and classify them as being cultural, market-related, regulatory and technological in nature.

(a) The inadequacy of the notion of Pareto efficiency in guiding such a transition, given the wide disparities in the socio-economic indicators of human well-being and the skewed distribution of resources across different sections of society. More importantly, any move which would necessarily end up making someone better off at the expense of someone else during the process of transition would be considered untenable following the notion of Pareto efficiency and as Charles D. Kolstad puts it

> If the Pareto criterion is used to make societal decision, then decisions may tend to be biased towards the status quo. If society is only willing to take steps that improve on the status quo for everyone, then implicitly, there is the assumption that the status quo is acceptable. (Pg. 49, Kolstad, 2012)

(b) At the more fundamental level, this would necessitate modelling the behaviour of individual economic agents embedded in the realm of social conduct, i.e. behaving in a socially responsible manner, as against just being reduced to "self-interested, own regarding pursuers of utility maximisation—'Max-U'—defined only over their own private outcomes". According to Smith and Wilson, this amounts to revisiting the

> …neoclassical tradition that swung too far in displacing, rather than more modestly supplementing, Smith's classical systems-oriented thinking. The new equilibrium concepts were defined too narrowly over outcomes, a substitution that seemed superior in the context of institution-free general equilibrium market analysis and the partial-partial equilibrium analysis of game theory. At some point even the human being was dropped as the subject of our general inquiry as a social science. (Pg. xvi, Smith & Wilson, 2019)

Further, they argue that one of the fundamental weaknesses of the neoclassical tradition of utility is its inappropriateness of the understanding of the contextualisation of "one's own interest" in Adam Smith's body of work (especially concerning The Theory of Moral Sentiments and An Inquiry into the Nature and Causes of the Wealth of Nations) and is certainly not at par with the modern interpretation of "self-interest" which runs counter to its original interpretation in principle. Hence, the decision-making of individual economic agents being reduced to their self-interest behaviour under the neoclassical tradition has introduced an anomaly in the understanding of Adam Smith's perspective.

> Thus, if the modern economist espouses naked self-interest as the foundation for economic decision-making, she does so incompatibly with the founder of the discipline and more generally with the genius of the Scottish Enlightenment. There are moral rules, just rules, that govern our conduct in impersonal markets (Pg. 5, Smith & Wilson 2019).

> For Smith there is no unresolved observed contradiction between people pursuing their own interest, say in money, and choosing actions that are other-regarding. One's own interest includes living harmoniously and ethically with others, and choosing socially fit actions. (Pg. 11, Smith & Wilson, 2019)

Consequently, according to them, there has been misplaced emphasis on just the *outcomes* of actions and lack of appreciation of their *origin*, a crucial aspect about their social context, as understood and emphasised by Adam Smith.

> Max-U had served well-enough the observational demands of decision in market supply and demand experiments under perfect enforcement of property, but not in the interactive world of personal social exchange. That world required a plethora of new experiments designed to understand why the postulated mapping from action to outcome to utility was so sensitive to the particular context. However, none of the new efforts to improve understanding were guided by *a comprehensive theory of human sociability as had been provided in Sentiments wherein individual actions are signals of rule-governed relational conduct, where context matters because it gives meaning to outcomes*. (Pg. 159, Smith & Wilson, 2019)

(c) The need for emphasising long-term perspective versus short-term gains towards mainstreaming systemic-level changes for addressing the sustainability concerns while adopting the framework of CE. As Nitin Desai aptly puts it in the following words

> Is environmental protection a hindrance for profit-seeking businesses? Not if these businesses have a long-term vision of their viability…The real pressure for diluting environmental scrutiny comes from hit-and-run businesses that are looking for quick profits rather than long-term sustainability (Desai, 2020).

Besides addressing the above forces resisting the change towards the CE, another crucial aspect relates to the need for its standardisation, given the variety of approaches followed towards its implementation—top-down, bottom-up, etc. It is expected that concerted efforts in this regard would be crucial in eliminating the vagueness in its implementation strategies and to facilitate comparison in terms of achievements by developing a threshold in terms of "frameworks, guidance, supporting tools and requirements for the implementation of activities of all involved organisations". Recognising such a need, the International Standard Organisation (ISO) has constituted a technical committee (ISO/TC 323) under the chairmanship of Mrs. Catharine Chevauche in 2019. This committee is administering the development of four standards focussing on the crucial areas related to the CE—(a) framework and principles for implementation (ISO/WD 59004), (b) guidelines on business models and value chains (ISO/WD 59010), (c) measuring circularity framework (ISO/WD 59020) and (d) performance-based approach—analysis of case studies (ISO/CD TR 59031) (Naden, 2019).

5 Concluding Remarks

Going forward, there is an urgent need to move beyond the techno-centric and business-oriented understanding of CE to a framework that attempts to integrate with the socio-economic realities and development priorities of the developing economies. The implementation of CE envisages profound shifts in the production structures and consumption patterns during the process of transition from the linear economy to the circular one. However, the elected governments in these economies, despite their attempts to implement strategies focussing on CE, are most likely to uphold the developmental priorities towards promising inclusive development and improving well-being crucial for social cohesion. This is not to imply that the adoption of the CE framework is contrary to the process of economic growth and development. The trade-offs involved in the intervening transition phase won't present a win-win situation in the near-or medium-term. Thus, it is expected that in the times to come the mainstreaming of the CE in the development discourse for realising long-term sustainability would remain contingent upon social acceptance towards traversing the path of transition through suitable public policy interventions and an enabling business environment. Has the increased frequency of extreme weather events in recent years and above all the unprecedented prevailing situation owing to the COVID-19 pandemic brought the society to such a *juncture* remains to be validated in the times ahead. But certainly, the resilience of human systems that has been tested by the prevailing circumstances has undoubtedly brought us as a society to the *crossroads* wherein the time to act is *now*.

Appendix I: RE Framework in India

The key thrust areas and the set of initiatives that are considered crucial for promoting RE in India are as follows:

I. *Policies*
• Formulate a national policy on RE for all types of resources (biotic and abiotic) addressing various life cycle stages and key stakeholders • Formulate a national policy on Sustainable Public Procurement (SPP) to minimise consumption of resources, reduce waste generation and GHG emissions, as well as contribute to innovation in materials and technology in the space of RE • Strengthen existing sectoral policies and programmes of Ministry of Mines by incorporating RE principles • Formulate a national policy for end-of-life-vehicles (ELVs) • Formulate a Waste to Resource Management Directive based on existing waste and hazardous substance management rules/regulations following a life cycle approach targeting relevant stakeholders and focussing on RE

(continued)

(continued)

II. *Programmes and Mainstreaming*
• Mainstream RE initiatives by leveraging existing flagship programmes and schemes like Swachh Bharat Abhiyan, Smart Cities, Make in India, Startup India, Digital India and others • Industry may leverage Corporate Social Responsibility (CSR), Corporate Environmental Responsibility (CER) and Extended Producer Responsibility (EPR) for RE initiatives • Build on the National Chemical Management Plan being drafted by Ministry of Environment, Forest and Climate Change (MoEF&CC) to develop a strategy, framework and guidelines for the safe and circular management of chemicals • Leverage the national clean energy and environment fund to finance infrastructure, clean technologies and related RE initiatives
III. *Regulations*
• Establish a national coordinating body—Bureau of Resource Efficiency (BRE) between various ministries to identify, implement and achieve national RE goals • Establish state-level coordinating bodies to identify, implement and achieve state-level RE goals • Large and resource-intensive industries and bulk waste generation may be mandated to file the Resource Use and Efficiency Statement • Establish and mandate a "Consent to Close" requirement for medium and large industries in the "RED" category to ensure that waste streams are responsibly managed and recycled before closure • Rationalise tax regime on critical virgin raw materials to make secondary raw material price competitive
IV. *Setting up a Dynamic Recycling Industry*
• Promote the establishment of Material Recovery Facilities (MRFs) with the allocation of land in urban areas and industrial estates • Facilitate urban local bodies (ULBs) to undertake urban mining and create secure landfills. • Facilitate the establishment of Producer Responsibility Organisation (PRO) for waste recycling and for engagement with the informal sector • Facilitate innovation to enhance resource recovery and improve working conditions by integrating the informal sector into the waste value chain • Establish a remanufacturing council or association to catalyse the growth of the remanufacturing industry • Establish and manage platforms for waste exchange by expanding the SBM portal
V. *R&D and Technology Development*
• Support R&D to develop scalable technologies for RE • Create and manage knowledge platforms that facilitate open innovation, provide access to experts and engage academia to support the transition towards RE • Leverage technologies like artificial intelligence (AI), robotics, block chain, etc., for the recycling industry

(continued)

(continued)

VI. *Capacity Development, Outreach and Monitoring*
• Facilitate creation of accredited laboratories that could conduct testing (especially for recycled products) as well as provide advisory services • Provide capacity development support on RE for ministries/departments at the national and state levels • Develop and promote programmes and certifications for informal sector skill development in RE • Develop and launch citizen awareness programmes on RE • Foster intergovernmental collaboration and knowledge exchange with the G20, RE dialogue and other bodies like International Resource Panel and other national and international forums • Develop monitoring and outcome indicators for tracking progress on RE • Establish and mandate the certification for operators managing waste-to-resource recycling centres to ensure safe, efficient and net positive operations

Source GOI, 2019

References

Ayres, R. U. (1994). Industrial metabolism: Theory and policy. In: B. R. Allenby & D. J. Richard (Eds.), *The greening of industrial ecosystems*, Washington, DC: National Academic Press.

Becker, U., Fernandes, T., Arora, R., Banerjee, A., & Saluja, M.S. (2019). The Indian resource panel: A mechanism to promote resource efficiency policy throughout the Indian economy. In *Waste management and resource efficiency* (pp. 275–285). Singapore: Springer.

Bruel, A., Kronenberg, J., Troussier, N., & Guillaume, B. (2019). Linking industrial ecology and ecological economics: A theoretical and empirical foundation for the circular economy. *Journal of Industrial Ecology, 23*(1), 12–21.

Costanza, R., Cumberland, J. H., Daly, H., Goodland, R., Norgaard, R. B., Kubiszewski, I., & Franco, C. (2014). In: *An introduction to ecological economics*. CRC Press.

Desai, N. (2020, July 13). Nature in peril. *Business Standard*. Available via https://www.business-standard.com/article/opinion/nature-in-peril-120071301511_1.html. Accessed on 13th July 2020.

EEA. (2016). *Circular economy in Europe: Developing the knowledge base*. European Environment Agency.

EU-REI. (2018a). Towards resource efficiency electric vehicle sector in India. European Union's Resource Efficiency Initiative (EU-REI) Project, New Delhi: Deutsche Gesellschaft für Internationale Zusammenarbeit (GIZ) GmbH.

EU-REI. (2018b). Greening the solar PV value chain. European Union's Resource Efficiency Initiative (EU-REI) Project, New Delhi: Deutsche Gesellschaft für Internationale Zusammenarbeit (GIZ) GmbH.

EU-REI. (2018c). Fostering resource efficiency in the India building and construction sector. European Union's Resource Efficiency Initiative (EU-REI) Project, New Delhi: Deutsche Gesellschaft für Internationale Zusammenarbeit (GIZ) GmbH.

EU-REI. (2018d). Enhancing resource efficiency through extended producer responsibility—sector study on plastic packaging and E-Waste management in India. European Union's Resource Efficiency Initiative (EU-REI) Project, New Delhi: Deutsche Gesellschaft für Internationale Zusammenarbeit (GIZ) GmbH.

Geissdoerfer, M., Savaget, P., Bocken, N. M., & Hultink, E. J. (2017). The circular economy–A new sustainability paradigm? *Journal of Cleaner Production, 143*, 757–768.

Ghisellini, P., Cialani, C., & Ulgiati, S. (2016). A review on circular economy: The expected transition to a balanced interplay of environmental and economic systems. *Journal of Cleaner Production, 114,* 11–32.

Giampietro, M. (2019). On the circular bioeconomy and decoupling: Implications for sustainable growth. *Ecological Economics, 162,* 143–156.

GOI. (2019). *Economic survey 2018-19* (Vol. II). New Delhi: Government of India.

Graedel, T. E., & van der Voet, E. (Eds.). (2010). *Linkages of sustainability.* Cambridge, MA, USA: MIT Press.

Hussen, A. (2013). *Principles of environmental economics and sustainability: An integrated economic and ecological approach* (3rd ed.). New York: Routledge.

InRP. (2017). Recommendations for an indian resource efficiency programme: A guiding document for policy makers by the indian resource panel, New Delhi. Available via http://re.urban-industrial.in/live/hrdpmp/hrdpmaster/igep/content/e64918/e64922/e67075/e67084/DMS_GIZ_IREP_PolicyBrief.pdf. Accessed on 13th April 2020.

Kirchherr, J., Piscicelli, L., Bour, R., Kostense-Smit, E., Muller, J., Huibrechtse-Truijens, A., et al. (2018). Barriers to the circular economy: Evidence from the European union (EU). *Ecological Economics, 150,* 264–272.

Kolstad, C. (2012). *Intermediate environmental economics.* South Asia Edition: Oxford University Press.

Korhonen, J., Honkasalo, A., & Seppälä, J. (2018). Circular economy: The concept and its limitations. *Ecological Economics, 143,* 37–46.

Manderson, E. J., & Considine, T. J. (2018). An economic perspective on industrial ecology. *Review of Environmental Economics and Policy, 12*(2), 304–323.

Millar, N., McLaughlin, E., & Börger, T. (2019). The circular economy: Swings and roundabouts? *Ecological Economics, 158,* 11–19.

MoEFCC. (2019). Draft national resource efficiency policy 2019. Ministry of Environment, Forest and Climate Change, New Delhi: Government of India.

Murray, A., Skene, K., & Haynes, K. (2017). The circular economy: An interdisciplinary exploration of the concept and application in a global context. *Journal of Business Ethics, 140*(3), 369–380.

Naden, C. (2019). *Connecting the dots in a circular economy: A new ISO technical committee just formed.* Accessed 16 June 2020. <https://www.iso.org/news/ref2402.html>.

Nayak, P. B. (2020). Present crises of capitalism and its reforms. *Economic and Political Weekly, 55*(17), 42–48.

NITI Aayog. (2019a). *Strategy on resource efficiency in aluminium sector.* New Delhi: National Institution for Transforming India, Government of India.

NITI Aayog. (2019b). *Strategy on resource efficiency in steel sector.* New Delhi: National Institution for Transforming India, Government of India.

NITI Aayog. (2019c). *Strategy on resource efficiency in electrical and electronic equipment sector.* New Delhi: National Institution for Transforming India, Government of India.

NITI Aayog. (2019d). *Strategy on resource efficiency in construction and demolition sector.* New Delhi: National Institution for Transforming India, Government of India.

NITI Aayog. (2019e). *Resource efficiency and circular economy-current status and way forward.* New Delhi: National Institution for Transforming India, Government of India.

Pearce, D. W. & Turner, R. K. (1990). In: *Economics of natural resources and the environment.* JHU Press.

PIB. (2018). Environment Ministry, TERI Sign MOU to Set up a Resource Efficiency Cell; Launch Initiatives to Reduce, Reuse and recycle Plastic Waste, Press Information Bureau, Available via https://pib.gov.in/PressReleasePage.aspx?PRID=1534176. Accessed on 13th April 2020.

Richards, D. J., Allenby, B. R., & Frosch, R. A. (1994). The greening of industrial ecosystems: Overview and perspective. In B. R. Allenby & D. J. Richard (Eds.), *The greening of industrial ecosystems*, Washington, DC: National Academic Press.

Saavedra, Y. M., Iritani, D. R., Pavan, A. L., & Ometto, A. R. (2018). Theoretical contribution of industrial ecology to circular economy. *Journal of Cleaner Production, 170,* 1514–1522.

Smith, V. L., & Wilson, B. J. (2019). In *Humanomics: Moral sentiments and the wealth of nations for the twenty-first century*. Cambridge University Press.

Stiglitz, J. E. (2017). Markets, States and institutions. In A. Mishra & T. Ray (Eds.), *Markets, governance and institutions in the process of economic development: A festschrift in honour of Kaushik Basu*. Oxford: Oxford University Press.

TERI. (2019). *Reference report for national resource efficiency policy for india, prepared for ministry of environment forests and climate change (MoEFCC)*. New Delhi: Government of India, The Energy and Resources Institute.

WEF. (2019). *The next frontier: Natural resource targets—Shaping a competitive circular economy within planetary boundaries*. White Paper: World Economic Forum.

Winans, K., Kendall, A., & Deng, H. (2017). The history and current applications of the circular economy concept. *Renewable and Sustainable Energy Reviews, 68*, 825–833.

Ambient Air Pollution and Respiratory Illness: A Study in Opencast Coal Mining Region of Odisha

Indrani Roy Chowdhury, Anusree Paul, and Tapaswini Nayak

1 Introduction

The adverse impact of air pollution to environment and economy is alarming in terms of health externalities. Several research findings have advocated that longer exposure to air pollution (PM_{10}) leads to high morbidity, increased respiratory illness, asthma, high blood pressure, reduced lung functions and heart diseases (Gupta, 2008; Pope et al., 1995; Chowdhury & Imran, 2010). According to the *State of Global Air 2019* report by the Health Effects Institute (HEI), mortality due to air pollution is ranked 5th among all reported causes of death (which rank just below smoking). It is evident that more people die from air pollution-related disease than from road traffic injuries or malaria. The report by Greenpeace Southeast Asia and the Centre for Research on Energy and Clean Air (2020) have estimated the global economic costs of air pollution to be $2.9 trillion, which is approximately 3.3% of the world's GDP. The report further claims 4.5 million deaths due to $PM_{2.5}$ pollution, 1.8 billion days of work loss, 4 million new cases of child asthma and 2 million preterm births. According to the report, disability from chronic diseases cost the world's economy $200 billion in 2018, with sick leave and preterm births costing $100 billion and $90 billion, respectively.

I. Roy Chowdhury (✉)
Centre for Studies in Regional Development, School of Social Sciences, Jawaharlal Nehru University, New Delhi, India
e-mail: indraniroychowdhury01@gmail.com

A. Paul
BML Munjal University, Gurgaon, Haryana, India
e-mail: paul.anusree12@gmail.com

T. Nayak
Department of Economics, Prananatha Autonomous College, Khordha, Odisha, India
e-mail: tapaswininayak82@gmail.com

P. Dasgupta et al. (eds.), *Sustainable Development Insights from India*,
India Studies in Business and Economics,
https://doi.org/10.1007/978-981-33-4830-1_14

According to that report, the estimated costs of ambient air pollution alone accounts for 5.4% of India's GDP, in 2018. However, it is to be noted that the economic cost is underestimated, as pollution hazards in many mining infested remote corners of India, left unaccounted in the estimation. These health problems are highly associated with economic costs, which include treatment costs of the diseases and productive days lost (Ostro, 1994).

India is endowed with the fifth largest reserve of coal in the world and holds the second position globally in terms of production of coal (after China) in 2018. Coal is treated as the cheapest source of energy and serves as a critical input for energy and infrastructure generation. The share of coal in India's total energy requirements is around 55% (MoM, 2013). Since the nationalization act of coal mines in 1973, the Coal India Limited (CIL) enjoyed a monopoly right in the extraction of coal, till very recently in India.

The paper attempts to analyse the impact of respiratory illness due to ambient air pollution in the open coal mining in Odisha. In India, open cast coal mining is most dominant mining practice. While underground mining is unsafe for various occupational hazards, open cast mining, which extends to a large tract of exposed surface, is more hazardous, in terms of air pollution, water pollution, soil degradation, etc. (Ghosh & Majee, 2001; Ghose & Banerjee, 1995; Pathak et al., 2007; Hendryx 2015). All the mining process from drilling, blasting, sizing, loading unloading to transportation, movement of vehicles, etc., are the major sources of toxic emissions like total suspended particulate (TSP) matter and inhalable particulate matter (PM_{10}, $PM_{2.5}$) (Chadwik et al., 1987; Nair & Sinha, 1987; Ghose, 1989). Further, air pollution often gets aggravated by rampant mine fires. Given that developing countries suffer from a combination of poor state capacity, weak institutions, laxer environmental regulations, unorganized civil societies and poverty, (Dasgupta et al., 2002), lack of sophisticated abatement technology, widespread pollution from rampant mining have severe health impact of population in the proximity of the mining location (Brunekreef & Holgate, 2002; Hendryx & Ahern; 2008; Hendryx & Zullig, 2009). The impact of open cast coal mining is devastating and irreversible in terms of erosion of the natural resource base, forest cover, water shades, biodiversity, etc. (Ericson et al., 2008).

Mining threatens the sustainability of local livelihood displaces people from their ancestral homesteads and disturbs the social cohesion (Downing, 2002; Auty, 2006; Mishra, 2002). The loss of access and degradation of common property resources have a serious impact livestock and agricultural yield along with nutritional intake of the local community. In Indian context, there exist a number of studies which have thrown light on the share of coal mining in pollution (Birley 1995, Mishra 2014; Mishra, 2012 and Mukhopadhayay & Kadekodi, 2011), etc. Studies by Hendryx & Ahern (2008); Hendryx & Zullig (2009) have highlighted the dangerous impact of coal mining on human health in terms of chest infections, allergies and asthma because of air pollution. In addition, there are other morbidities like waterborne diseases or hookworm infections.

India experiences a steep increase in coal extraction in the recent years, to cater the growing demand for electricity generation.[1] Coal extraction offers an attractive option for states, which are endowed with rich reserves, to jack up its employment, growth, revenue, foreign exchange earnings, etc. However, there is a huge asymmetry in the distribution of benefits and the costs (Bush, 2008). The ecological and health externalities are being confined to the people in the proximity of the mining region, whereas the benefit is being enjoyed by the country as a whole. Further, the benefits in terms of electricity generation, enhanced economic activities are mostly tangible in nature; the major share of the costs in terms of adverse environmental externalities in human life and livelihood is mostly intangible and therefore difficult to capture (in the presence of many non-marketable categories of welfare loss).

Pricing of coal fails to reflect the social costs, which exceeds the costs of extraction and transportation, by several folds. The internalization of environmental and health externalities remains a deferred priority at the policy level and is mostly treated as isolated regional phenomena. These social costs are often remained overshadowed by poverty and political alienation of the local community. This is particularly a serious issue, owing to the fact that vast tracts of mining resources in India are mostly located in the remote forested region inhabited by mostly tribal people.

For an economically backward state like Odisha, mining sector has offered huge potential to expand economic activities through various backward and forward linkages, but the trade-off in terms of environmental degradation and health shocks has been grossly underreported. So, it is critically important to estimate the health impact of air pollution in the opencast coal mining region of Odisha. Given this backdrop, the objective of the present paper is to test empirically the health burden of the people living in the proximity to open cast coal mining areas in Orissa. As cited in many of the literature (Stephens & Ahern, 2001), we analyse the incidence of respiratory illness (RI) as health outcome caused by ambient air pollution.

The rest of the paper is organized as follows: Sect. 2 presents the survey design, data and the tools of analysis. The following Sect. 3 enumerates the socio-economic and health status of the treatment and control groups and discusses the findings of the regression analysis. Finally, Sect. 4 presents some concluding remarks.

2 Odisha—The Study Area

In a mineral-rich state like Odisha, the coal sector plays a vital role in the overall development of the state, through its various backward and forward linkages. The state holds a significant position in terms of various mineral reserves and production in the country (Murthy & Rao, 2006). During 2017–18, Odisha was the leader in mineral production (contributed to 34.3% of total mineral production in the country) followed by Rajasthan, Chhattisgarh, Karnataka, Madhya Pradesh and Jharkhand (see Fig. 1).

[1]According to India's National Electricity Plan (2018), a massive coal-based electricity generation capacity is planned during 2017–2022.

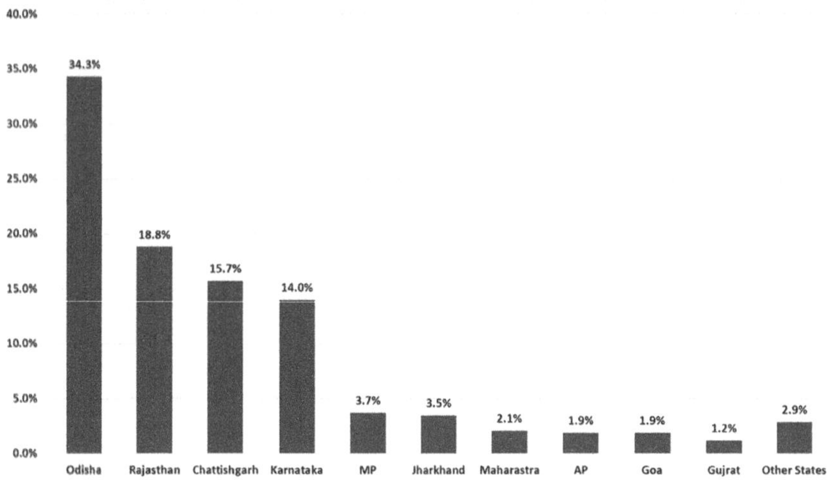

Fig. 1 Percentage share of the value of mineral production by major states, 2017–18, *Source* Odisha Economic Survey, 2018–19

In terms of coal reserves, the state is just after Jharkhand. In 2017–18, it was estimated that 25% (77.29 billion tons) of India's coal reserves are in Odisha. According to Odisha Economic Survey (2018–19), the mining and quarrying sector contributed nearly 10.79% of Gross State Value Added (GSVA), and its estimated growth rate is 4.3%. In terms of employment generation, the largest number of workers are employed in the coal sector, followed by iron ore, chromite and manganese (see Fig. 2). The Odisha Economic Survey has reported that mining revenue receipt is steadily increasing over the past decade in the state, and the state has been the attractive destination of foreign direct investment.

The two Gondwana coalfields of the state (namely Talcher coalfield and Ib River coalfield) are managed by Mahanadi Coalfields Limited (MCL), which is a subsidiary of Coal India. Our study area, Angul–Talcher region, is located in the Brahmani River Basin, with 1,813 km^2 of coal-containing area (under MCL), and is one of the major industrial zones in Odisha and India (CMPDI, 2005). Talcher coal field is having the highest geological reserve (51.163 billion tonnes), whereas Ib River coalfield has the third highest geological reserve (26.122 billion tonnes) in the country.[2]

In spite of its huge economic importance, coal extraction is a dirty activity and is responsible for severe environmental hazards. Chaulya (2004) has pointed out that the annual average total suspended particulate (TSP) concentration in Ib Valley coalfield area of Orissa exceeded the respective standards set in the National Ambient Air Quality Standard (NAAQS) protocol in major part of the residential and industrial areas. Data of Central Pollution Control Board (CPCB) reveals that the RSPM (PM_{10}) and $PM_{2.5}$ always exceed the respective NAAQS protocol in MCL areas of Talcher,

[2]https://mahanadicoal.nic.in.

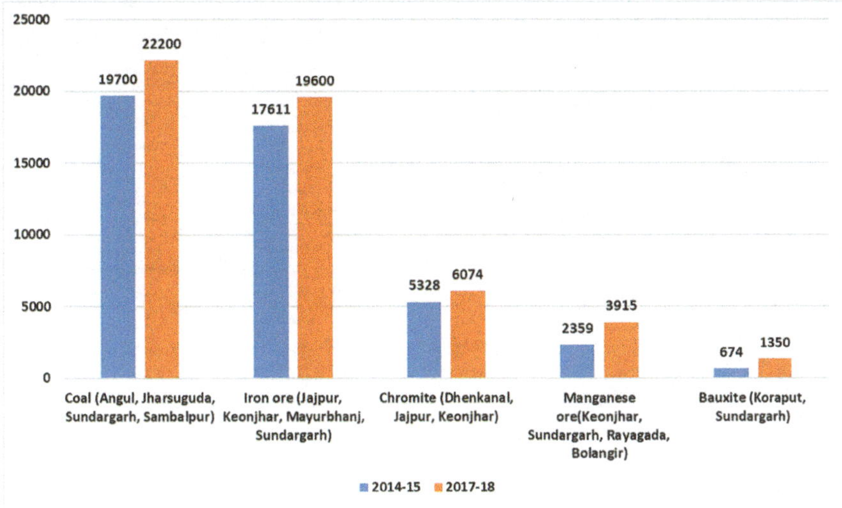

Fig. 2 Number of workers directly employed in major mineral activities, *Source* Odisha Economic Survey, 2018–19

Table 1 National ambient air quality standard (NAAQS) *(residential/industrial)*

Pollution level	RSPM (PM_{10}) (Mg/m^3)	$PM_{2.5}$ (Mg/m^3)
Low	0–30	0–20
Moderate	30–60	20–40
High	60–90	40–60
Critical	> 90	> 60

Source State Pollution Control Board, Bhubaneswar

district of Odisha. The standard air quality or the PM_{10} level criterion is 0–30 Mg/m^3, and $PM_{2.5}$ level criterion is 0–25 Mg/m^3 (see Table 1).

In 2018, the range of average PM_{10} lies between 81 and 162 Mg/m^3, and for average $PM_{2.5}$, it is 30–73 Mg/m^3.[3]

The social environment, natural vegetation and crops in the Angul–Talcher belt of Odisha have been severely affected by the establishment of Mahanadi Coalfields Limited (MCL) and National Thermal Power Corporation (NTPC). Although MCL is carrying out CSR activities, it is always far from adequate (Mishra, 2014). Forest degradation is highly prevalent, and seed germination has been severely affected in this belt. Further, the mines of MCL and NTPC draw about 25 crores litres of water per day and release thousands of gallons of waste water to the Brahmani River, containing substances like ash, oil, heavy metals, grease, fluorides, phosphorous, ammonia, urea and sulphuric acid. Fluoride pollution is quite significant in this belt. The incidences of incurable skin infections, lumps of dead skin and white spots all

[3] Authors' collection from CPCB, Odisha.

Fig. 3 Location map of Talcher coalfield, *Source* MCL, 2017

over the body are reported (Murty et al., 2006). While there may be many long-term health impacts of open cast mining, we have narrowed down to it by focusing only short-term health consequences.

2.1 Area of Study and Sample Design

The present study is based on a primary survey in the Angul–Talcher coal field region of Odisha. Talcher coalfield is endowed with highest geological reserve of coal (51.163 billion tonnes) in the country and covers an area of about 1800 km^2 (Fig. 3). The area is constituted of south-eastern part of the Lower Gondwana basins within Mahanadi Valley. Major part of the coalfield falls in the Angul district.[4] It has eight opencast and three underground coal mines, namely Jagannath area, Bharatpur area, Lingaraj area, Hingula area and Talcher area. The coalfields are managed by Mahanadi Coalfields Limited (MCL), a subsidiary of Coal India Limited (CIL).

We collected the baseline information through a pilot survey along with a few focus group discussions, through a random selection of two villages and households in the MCL area during the end of May 2018. The final questionnaire was designed on the basis of the information gathered from the pilot survey. Following Saha et al. 2011 and Mishra 2015, we hypothesized that closer is the proximity of the villages

[4]Besides, a small part of the coalfield in the west lies in Sambalpur district and in the north lies in Deogarh district, whereas another small part lying to the east of the Brahmani River falls in Dhenkanal district.

to the open cast coal mines, and higher is the load of ambient air pollution. Based on that, we selected the six treatment villages and three control villages. Following Gupta 2008 & Adhikari 2012, the survey was conducted through two-stage stratified sampling procedure. In first stage, from Talcher block (in the MCL area), we selected six treatment villages (namely Badasinghara, Kalamchui, Kandhal, Langijuda, Narharipur and Saluda), which are located at a distance of 0.2–3 km, from the mining areas of Bhubaneswari, Bharatpur, Hingula and Lingraj OCPs, respectively. We selected three non-mining villages (namely Amana, Bauligada and Narachandrapur), which are located in 15–21 km distance from the MCL mining area (Table 2).

To capture the seasonality of ambient air pollution and its potential impact on health outcomes, we conducted longitudinal household survey, at three points of time (in the pre-monsoon, post-monsoon and winter season)—during the period of June 2018 to January 2019. The information of RI episodes was collected on the basis of self-reported morbidity of the respondents, with one-month recall period.

In the second stage, in order to make our sampling well representative, we followed stratified random sampling to include different social categories, in the selection of households, from each village. In order to capture information on socio-economic demographic profile along with RI episodes, we selected 97 sample households (which includes 16–17 households from each village) from all the six treatment villages. Similarly, following similar stratified random sampling, 50 sample households were selected from the three control villages. Thus, our pooled sample consisted of 147 households from both treatment and control villages. We have a sample size of 393 individuals in the treatment and 201 individuals in the control villages, with an average household size of four (in both the treatment and control). We interviewed the same 147 households over three points of time, through a structured questionnaire, to capture the seasonality. Thus, we have 594 individuals in our pooled panel for each period (with an overall sample size of 1782).

Table 2 List of villages in the treatment and control groups

	Village	Opencast mine	Distance (KM)
Treatment group	Badasinghara	Bharatpur	2.0
	Kalamchui	Lingraj	0.5
	Kandhal	Lingraj	1.0
	Langijuda	Lingraj	0.2
	Narharipur	Bhubaneswari	0.5
	Saluda	Hingula	3.0
Control group	Amana	Non-mining village	15.0
	Bauligada	Non-mining village	22.0
	Narachandrapur	Non-mining village	16.0

Source Field Survey

The selection of variables which are assumed to have potential impact on respiratory illness of individuals is mostly drawn from the literature. The list of variables is provided in Table 3.

Health factors:

An epidemiological link is well established between respiratory illness (RI) and exposure to particulate matters in the existing environmental health literature (Hendryx & Ahern, 2008; Brunekreef & Holgate, 2002; Hedlund et al., 2006; Ross & Murray, 2004). After consulting the doctors from the Nehru Satabdi Central Hospital in Talcher and Sub-Divisional Hospital in Mundapara, we compiled the most commonly reported episodes of illness in the mining neighbourhood under the variable of respiratory illness (RI), which is the key health outcome variable in this study. Thus, from the list of respiratory disorders from the hospital record, the compiled list includes mild moderate and acute syndromes of bronchial asthma, cough with mucus and sputum production, respiratory allergy to dust, allergic cough, running nose, headache, flu, chest tightness and acute bronchitis. We considered the listed symptoms rather the disease for our survey.

The *incidence of RI* is the self-reported binary response to any listed respiratory disorders, within a recall period of one month, in our sample. The *severity of RI* is the self-reported degree of severity of RI measured in an ordinal scale (mild, moderate and severe). We collated the cost of treatment due to reported RI episodes, which include doctor consultation fee, costs of medicines, diagnostics, cost of hospitalization and travel costs incurred by the household, and attributed it to the variable *health expenditure*. Further, we have also collected information related to the exposure to *chronic disease* in the last one year, as we assume that suffering from any *chronic disease* reflects a poor health stock and makes an individual more vulnerable towards RI. So, the respondents were asked to provide information whether they are suffering from any chronic diseases like asthma, jaundice, hepatitis, diabetes, hypertension/heart diseases, tuberculosis, cancer, kidney malfunctions, severe anaemia/sickle cell anaemia, arthritis/joint pain, nerve disorder and stomach disorder.

Again, addiction to smoking is assumed to aggravate the incidence of RI. Hence, we collected the data on *smoking habits* of an individual and is recorded as a binary response variable. We have also asked for the *overall health status* of individual by asking them to rank their status (1 = Excellent, 2 = Good, 3 = Average, 4 = Poor, 5 = Very Poor).

Accessibility to healthcare facilities also affects the incidence and health expenditure of RI. We have taken *distance to nearest hospital* as an indicator of the accessibility to healthcare facilities, as a proxy to common mitigating activities of RI. The common mitigating activities of the villagers are reported to be seeking treatment to the Sub-Divisional Hospital (60% of the respondents); colliery hospitals (30% of the respondents); private doctors (30% of the respondents); homeopathy, ayurveda and other (10% of the respondents).

Table 3 Factors and variables

Factors	Variable	Descriptions
Health factors for respiratory illness (*RI*)	*ri_inc*	Dummy variable captures the episodes of respiratory illness (RI), equal to 1 if the individual is suffering from RI, 0 otherwise
	ri_severity	Dummy variable captures the episodes of RI severity, takes the value 1 if the severe, 0 otherwise
	cost_ri	Cost incurred in last one month due to RI episodes (in rupees)
	chronic	Chronic disease self-reported with one-year recall period, dummy takes the value 1 if yes, 0 otherwise
	hlth_status	Dummy of self-reported overall health status, it takes the value 1 if health status is average to excellent, 0 otherwise
	smoking	Smoking habits dummy takes the value 1 if yes
	hospital	Distance to nearest hospital in kilometres
Pollution externality	*coal_mine*	Distance of the village from nearest mine in kilometres
	seasonality	Time dummy
Socio-economic factors	*age*	Age in years
	gender	Gender dummy, if male, it takes the value 1 and 0 for females
	GEN	Caste dummy, if General, it takes the value 1, 0 otherwise
	SC	Caste dummy, if SC, it takes the value 1
	ST	Caste dummy, if ST, it takes the value 1
	OBC	Caste dummy, if OBC, it takes the value 1
	education	Number of years of education
	wrk_mine	Dummy, if working in mining, it takes the value 1, 0 otherwise
	mnthPCI	Monthly per capita income in rupees
	trmt	Dummy variable takes the value 1 if the individual belongs to treatment group of villages, 0 otherwise

Socio-economic factors:

Gender and *age* composition of household are two important determinants of health outcomes which are assumed to affect the health cost. As children and older adults are more vulnerable segments of the population due to the severity of ambient pollution load, we considered *age* and *gender* as the two other predictor variables. Due to the fact that women's participation is restricted in the Indian coal mining sector

(Noronha, 2005), mining sector work is male-dominated. Male population who are involved in the mine or mine-related activities is more exposed to pollution and is expected to have direct impact on health as compared to women. While that is more subject to occupational hazard and thus needs to be controlled for understanding the probability of RI episodes due to the various covariates. Further, we considered the *occupational pattern,* to capture the heterogeneity of the effect of health hazards, due to the nature of the job like mining, non-mining and non-working individuals. Under occupational patterns, we have considered five categories, viz. mining, non-mining worker, students, homemakers and unemployed. For our analysis, we have consolidated the last three categories as non-working/ dependent population (Table 3).

Education as a predictor variable is considered as the education level helps to process information and creates awareness, which may induce averting and mitigating behaviour due to adverse pollution.

Household monthly income is an indicator of the household's location in the socio-economic gradient. If somebody belongs to higher income category, he/she is supposed to be better educated, endowed with better health stock and better access to health care and higher propensity to spend on health.

Pollution externality factors:

In order to understand the impact of the air pollution on the RI episodes, we have taken the distance from the mine as a proxy to the intensity of ambient air pollution. Finally, we have considered time dummies as a proxy of seasonality. Given the concentration of PM_{10} and $PM_{2.5}$ differ significantly during the various seasons (see Table 4), we capture the seasonality of disease episodes, by collecting self-reported RI episodes in three points of time, with one-month recall period. The air pollution level increases in winter as compared to the season just before and after the monsoon. Therefore, we assume that seasonality is expected to have significant effect on the episodes of RI.

Table 4 Ambient air pollution load (PM_{10} and ($PM_{2.5}$) in Mahanadi Coal Field Area during 2018

Months	(in mg/m^3)	
	PM_{10}	$PM_{2.5}$
January	155	73
June	121	35
October	83	50

Source SPCB, Bhubaneswar

3 Tools of Analysis—Econometric Model

The environmental health outcome, i.e. self-reported episodes of *RI* (*ri_inc*), is binary in nature. Hence, to examine the covariates of episodes of respiratory illness (RI_{ijt}), we formulate the following panel probit model:

$$\Pr(\mathrm{RI}_{ijt}|x'_{ijt}) = G\left[\gamma_t + \mu_j + x'_{ijt}\beta + \varepsilon_{ijt}\right],$$
$$t = 1, 2, 3 \tag{1}$$

where x'_{ijt} consists of 2 sets of variables, viz. X_{ijt} and Z_{ijt}. X_{ijt} is the vector of socio-economic and demographic indicators, viz. gender, age, education, caste and per-capita household income of *i*th individual in *j*th village and $t\mathrm{th}period.Z_{ijt}$ is the vector of controls related to health of *i*th individual in *j*th village. It includes distance from the mine (*coal_mine*) as a proxy for the intensity of air pollution, chronic illness, smoking habits, overall health status and proximity to healthcare facilities and a treatment dummy (*trmt*). γ_t is the time-specific intercept, which captures the seasonality and ε_{ijt} is idiosyncratic error term. It is assumed that $\varepsilon_{ijt} \sim N(0, 1)$. Finally, μ_j controls for village-level heterogeneity.

Further, to supplement this analysis, we run the panel tobit model (truncated or censored regression models) by hypothesizing that RI-related health expenditure depends on socio-economic and demographic variables, smoking habits, health stock, including healthcare accessibility. The model is truncated if the observations outside a specified range are lost and censored if one can at least observe the exogenous variables, where the expected errors are not supposed to be equal to zero. Since ordinary least squares (OLS) assumes a normal and homoscedastic distribution of the disturbance term and the dependent variable (Maddala, 1983; Amemiya, 1984), therefore, estimation with an OLS regression of health cost of RI would lead to a biased parameter estimate. The standard tobit model can be defined as follows for observation *i*:

$$y^*_{ijt} = x^*_{ijt}\beta + \epsilon_{ijt} = y_{ijt} = x'_{ijt}\beta + \mu_j + \gamma_t + \varepsilon_{ijt},$$
$$y_{ijt} = 0\begin{cases} \text{if } y^*_{ijt} \leq 0 \\ \quad y^*_{ijt}, \quad \text{if} \quad y^*_{ijt} > 0 \end{cases} \tag{2}$$

where y_{ijt} is observed dependent variable (RI-related health expenditure), 0 is the lower limit, y^*_{ijt} is a latent variable. $i = 1, 2, \ldots, N$ representing individuals, $j = 1, 2, \ldots, 9$ representing the sampled villages in the treatment and control, $t = 1, 2, 3$ indicates the period, x_{ijt} is a vector of explanatory variables, $\beta_i s$ are parameters to be estimated. γ_t is the time effect, controls for seasonality. The time-invariant village-specific effect is captured by μ_j, and ε_{ijt} is the random error term.

We have controlled for all the socio-economic variables including education, gender, age, caste, per-capita income and working in mine, whereas smoking habits and severity of respiratory illness (RI), chronic disease, overall health status and proximity to healthcare facilities are the health components and health infrastructure-related factors. The proximity to the coal mine and the treatment dummy is the two predictor variables of interest corresponding to the objective of our study.

4 Results and Analysis

Socio-economic and health status of treatment and control group

In Table 7, we have reported the descriptive statistics of RI-related indicators (mentioned in Table 2) for both treatment and control groups. Survey captured that respondents in the treatment villages reported 42% of RI episodes with 36% reported severity in RI, over the entire survey period. In the control villages, respondents reported 7% of RI episodes with 4% reported severity in RI, over the three periods (see Table 7).

In treatment villages, 79% of children in 0–5 years of age group, and 82% of children in 6–12 years of age group have reported RI episodes in the peak season. But out of them, only 37–39% have incurred health cost. In control group, 6% of children (aged between 0 to 5 years) and 14% of children in 6–12 years of age group have reported RI episodes, during the peak season. Further, we have also seen relatively high percentage of RI episodes in old age group (61–90 years) both in treatment (77%) and control (20%) villages. The RI-related health expenditure is also relatively high for this group than the other age group respondents. Fourty-seven % of the respondents of 61–90 age group in treatment villages and 13% in the control villages have spent on RI-related health mitigation (see Table 5).

We further categorized the households' self-reported RI episodes and health expenditure on the basis of their per-capita income. We have taken five inter-quintile

Table 5 Age group-wise RI episodes and health cost in the peak season

Age-gr (years)	*ri_inc*		*cost_ri_binary*	
	Treatment (%)	Control (%)	Treatment (%)	Control (%)
0–5	79	6	37	0
6–12	82	14	39	10
13–17	48	9	19	9
18–30	31	0	15	0
31–60	45	11	26	2
61–90	77	20	47	13

Source Authors' calculation from survey data

Table 6 Self-reported RI episodes and health expenditure across income quintiles

Income groups	*ri_inc*		*cost_ri_binary*	
	Treatment (%)	Control (%)	Treatment (%)	Control (%)
1	49	4	25	1.4
2	55	14	27	8.5
3	55	12	29	0
4	42	0	26	0
5	42	0	23	0

Source Authors' calculation from survey data

Table 7 Education level, RI incidence and health cost

Edu_level	*ri_inc*		*cost_ri_binary*	
	Treatment (%)	Control (%)	Treatment (%)	Control (%)
1	56	12	29	5
2	57	4	32	0.5
3	39	7	22	0.5
4	23	0	12	0

Source Authors' calculation from survey data

categories of household per capita income[5] and found that in the treatment group, 42–55% of respondents of all income category have reported RI and 23–29% of them have incurred RI-related health cost. The distribution of self-reported morbidity of RI episodes is approximately even across the five per-capita income quintiles. This indicates all-pervading nature of ambient air pollution in the treatment villages. In the control villages, overall, lesser percentage of respondents have reported RI episodes and incurred much lesser health expenditure. People of the control group in the Fourth and Fifth quintiles did not report any RI incidence, and hence, have not incurred any health cost. Fourteen % of respondents of income category 2 (Rs.1375–2000) have reported RI and out of which 8.5% have incurred cost (see Table 6).

Again, we have considered education level as a proxy to awareness level and categorized the years of education into four, from less than primary to graduation and above.[6] The mean years of education in treatment is 6 years and in control is 5 years (see Table 8). Our survey reveals that both in treatment and control, 56–57% respondents with 0–9 years of education (Category 1 and Category 2) have reported relatively lower RI incidence. In control, 4–12% of them have reported RI. As education level increases, awareness level also increases. In our sample, we find in control no one with graduation and above (12–18 years of education—category

[5]Household per capita income categories: Rs (300–1333 = 1, 1375 -2000 = 2, 2200–3000 = 3, 3333–5000 = 4 and 5333–50,000 = 5).

[6]1 = 0–5 years (primary); 2 = 6-10 years (secondary); 3 = 11-12 years (higher secondary); 4 = 13-18 years (graduation and above).

Table 8 Descriptive statistics of major RI-related indicators of treatment and control villages

Variable	Treatment				Control			
	Mean	Std. Dev	Min	Max	Mean	Std. Dev	Min	Max
ri_inc	0.42	0.49	0	1	0.07	0.26	0	1
ri_severity	0.36	0.48	0	1	0.04	0.20	0	1
ln(coal_mine)	−0.19	0.92	−1.61	1.10	2.80	0.15	2.71	3.04
ln(cost_ri + 1)	1.17	2.13	0	6.50	0.14	0.80	0	6.40
ln_mnthPCI	8.15	0.96	6.06	10.82	7.42	0.53	5.70	8.87
education	6.31	5.19	0	18	4.83	4.38	0	15
work_mine	0.26	0.44	0	1	0.11	0.32	0	1
Observation	1,179				603			

Source Author's calculations

4) have reported RI and incurred cost. In treatment village, this percentage is also relatively less among all categories. Twenty-three % have reported RI, and 12% of them have incurred health cost. (see Table 7). Higher education categories (4 and 5) have reported lesser RI episodes in both the treatment and control villages.

Regarding the variable addressing pollution externality (*coal_mine*), the average distance for the control villages is 18.6 km from its closest open cast mine of the Talcher region, whereas the treatment villages are located on an average 1.2 km vicinity to its nearest mine.

To understand the co-morbidity, we collected data on chronic disease information. In the treatment and control groups, it is 34 and 21% of individuals, respectively, who have reported their chronic disease, whereas the percentage of healthy people are much higher (87%) in control over treatment (60%). Regarding the smoking habits, 15.5% of adult individuals in treatment and 11% of adult individuals in control have reported it. Distance to hospital is considered as a proxy of accessibility for mitigating activities of RI. The average distance to a nearest hospital in treatment is 14.5 km, and in control it is 11.6 km.

Coming to the socio-economic profile of the sample, in the treatment village, 61.6% of working population are engaged in mining sector and 38.4% in non-mining sector, whereas in the control village, only 3% of working population are engaged in mining and 97% are working in non-mining sectors. As higher percentage of working population in the treatment group is working in MCL compared to control group, the mean monthly per-capita income of household is higher in the treatment group (Rs. 5899.0) as compare to the control group (Rs. 1938.3). This information reflects the trade-off between the income and quality of life in the mining region. Mining extraction has ensured income generating activities but at the cost of higher environmental and health risks.

The inhabitants of both the category of villages are all Hindus. The caste distribution of our sample reveals that 45% (27%) of households belong to general caste in control (treatment) group, whereas in the treatment group proportion of STs are comparatively higher (34%) than the other three categories. Thus, the treatment group sample reflects a fair representation of all four social categories (see Table 3). The male–female ratio is 53: 47 in treatment group and 50:50 in control group. The average age of our sample population is 34 years having average years of education equal to 6.

Regression Results

We run the regression based on the two models described in the methodology section for a pooled sample of 1782 individuals (incorporating all in the treatment and control groups), by taking the explanatory variables mentioned in Table 2, in Table 9, columns 1–2 are the probit regression results, considering RI incidence *(ri_inc)* as the dependent variable (Eq. 1). In column 1, we have taken covariates as explained in Table 3. In column 2, we have added one more interactive term to capture the differential impact of the health cost air pollution *(coal_mine*trmt)* on treatment villages over control.

In columns 3 and 4, we reported the estimation results of tobit regression (Eq. 2) where RI incidence (*ri_inc*) and RI severity(*ri_severity*) are considered as exogeneous covariates that affect health expenditure of individuals. As *ri_inc* and *ri_severity* highly correlated,[7] we run separate regressions (columns 3 and 4) to avoid possible multicollinearity. In all specifications, we have controlled for seasonality and village-level heterogeneity.

In the probit models, we have taken *distance to mine (ln(coal_mine))* and treatment dummy *(trmt),* as main predictor variables of our interest. Both the covariates serve as a proxy for the concentration of ambient air pollution. The coefficients are found to be statistically significant, with their signs matching to our hypothesis (negative sign for the former and positive sign for the later). It indicates that higher distance from the source of air pollution reduces the probability of RI incidence (column 1). The negative coefficient of the interactive term *coal_mine* trmt* (in column 2) indicates further higher incidence of RI in treatment villages over control villages. Significant and positive treatment (at 0.10% level, Column 1) dummy indicates higher probability of RI incidence in treatment villages over control villages.

Coming to the health factors of individuals, it is found that people who are having smoking habits have a higher probability of RI incidence. These coefficients are significant at 1% level. Overall health status, i.e. whether the person possesses sound health or not, significantly reduces the probability of having respiratory illness. The history of chronic diseases increases the probability of respiratory illness.

The socio-economic variables, such as, age, years of education (proxy for awareness) and work type, are significant in explaining the probability of incidence of RI of individuals. The coefficients of social categories STs and SCs are significant at 0.05% level reflecting higher likelihood of RI incidence as compared to the general category. Mine workers have higher probability of RI incidence over other categories in the area. This covariate is incorporated to control the episodes of occupational hazards

[7] The correlation between RI incidence and RI severity have come out 0.83 for treatment group and 0.77 for control group.

Table 9 Results of probit and tobit models

Variables	Probit results		Tobit results	
	(1)	(2)	(3)	(4)
	Dep Var. *ri_inc*		Dep Var. *ln(cost_ri + 1)*	
ri_severity				**9.459*****
				(0.384)
ri_inc			**13.04****	
			(6.015)	
ln(coal_mine)	**−0.232*****	**−0.174*****	0.181	0.141
	(0.0717)	(0.0637)	(0.338)	(0.307)
*ln(coal_mine)*trmt*		**-0.0968***		
		(0.0549)		
chronic	**0.564*****	**0.562*****	**1.409*****	**1.117*****
	(0.0822)	(0.0887)	(0.341)	(0.416)
hlth_status	**−0.193****	**−0.192*****	**−1.038*****	**−1.143*****
	(0.0811)	(0.0743)	(0.396)	(0.351)
smoking	**0.362*****	**0.364*****	0.274	**0.567¥**
	(0.127)	(0.113)	(0.454)	(0.437)
ln(hospital)	−0.871	−1.055	**10.47***	**15.42****
	(1.425)	(1.274)	(6.038)	(6.493)
wrk_mine	**0.193***	**0.193***	**−0.853¥**	−0.360
	(0.102)	(0.118)	(0.541)	(0.460)
age	**−0.0479*****	**−0.0480*****	**0.0295****	**0.0374*****
	(0.00569)	(0.00680)	(0.0117)	(0.00961)
age^2	**0.00069*****	**0.00069*****		
	(7.63e^{-05})	(8.26e^{-05})		
education	**−0.0357*****	**−0.0356*****	**−0.118****	**−0.159*****
	(0.00951)	(0.00927)	(0.0483)	(0.0465)
ST	**0.323****	**0.328****	−0.036	−0.225
	(0.132)	(0.157)	(0.742)	(0.566)
SC	**0.218****	**0.218***	0.428	0.322
	(0.104)	(0.127)	(0.655)	(0.544)
OBC	**0.176¥**	0.171	0.908	**0.834***
	(0.132)	(0.154)	(0.766)	(0.504)
gender	−0.0820	−0.0819	**1.042****	0.543
	(0.0793)	(0.0855)	(0.476)	(0.466)
ln(mnthPCI)	0.0590	0.0580	0.106	0.109
	(0.0544)	(0.0552)	(0.212)	(0.277)

(continued)

Table 9 (continued)

trmt	**0.647***	**0.852¥**	**0.250***	**0.254¥**
	(1.053)	(0.536)	(0.080)	(0.985)
Constant	1.304	1.580	**−41.49*****	**−47.58*****
	(3.084)	(2.727)	(15.20)	(14.65)
var(e. ln(cost_ri + 1))			**14.67*****	**14.12*****
			(0.846)	(1.325)
Time effect (seasonality)	*Yes*	*Yes*	*Yes*	*Yes*
Village effect	*Yes*	*Yes*	*Yes*	*Yes*
Wald chi2	738.35	496.27	196.48	2676.30
Prob > chi2	0.00	0.00	0.00	0.00
Pseudo R square	0.2475	0.2484	0.3414	0.3322
Log likelihood	−823.2232	−822.19592	−1012.417	−1026.7048
Observations	1.782	1.782	1.782	1.782

Bootstrapped standard errors in parentheses.
N B: General category (Gen) is the reference category for the covariates -SC, ST and OBC, representing social categories.
***$p < 0.01$, **$p < 0.05$, *$p < 0.1$, ¥$p < 0.2$

due to mining-related job. Further, the positive coefficient of age^2 indicates a convex relation between age and incidence of RI. The marginal values tell us that dy/dx is −0.0196 < 0 and d^2y/dx^2 is 0.00026 > 0. Further, for the whole sample, the estimated threshold age (A^T), is 37.6 years and the mean age ($\bar{A}$) is 33.5 years. Hence, in the feasible range, $A^T > \bar{A}$ indicating respiratory illness falls as age increases. Per capita household income *(ln(mnthPCI))* does not have any impact on the probability of RI incidence.

To check the robustness of the above results, we have run logistic regressions by taking RI incidence as dependent variables. The estimates are found robust. We have omitted those results for brevity.

We have taken full set of time dummies and village dummies to control for seasonality and village-level heterogeneity. In both specifications, village dummies have come statistically significant at 5% level, which ensures village heterogeneity in RI episodes as well as RI-related health care expenditure.

Coming to the tobit regression results of Eqs. (2), in columns 3 and 4, results reveal that all health-related factors are significant determinants of health expenditures of individuals. RI incidence (column 3) and RI severity (column 4) positively affect heath expenditure of individuals. History of chronic diseases of individuals increases the health expenditure, whereas overall good health status reduces the RI-related health expenditure. Higher is the proximity to healthcare facilities, more is the probability of incurring RI health expenditure by the individuals. The source of air pollution (distance to mine) does not impact the health costs. However, significant treatment dummy indicates treatment villagers spend more on health mitigation than the control villagers.

Among the socio-economic factors, per-capita income and social caste do not have any impact on RI-related health expenditure. Male are more probable to incur RI-related health expenditure as compared to female (significant at 0.05% level). The probability of RI-related health expenditure increases with age and decreases with years of education (which is a proxy for awareness of air pollution).

5 Concluding Remarks

Coal is the cheapest source of energy and thus the economic importance of coal is critical for an emerging economy like India. Coal is one of the dirtiest industries, and coal extraction is hazardous with environmental externalities and adverse health impacts. Although the benefit of coal is enjoyed by the entire nation, the environmental and health risks are highly confined to the mining neighbourhood. The social costs are often remained overshadowed due to the poverty and political alienation of the local community.

In this study, we try to examine whether the high concentration of ambient air pollution affects the respiratory illness (RI) and hence triggers the health mitigating cost of the inhabitants, who reside in the close proximity of open cast coal mining in the MCL area of Angul–Tacher coal field region of Odisha. Our results suggest that the probability of self-reported RI episodes is negatively affected by the distance to mine and is positively affected by the treatment dummy, when we control for village fixed effects, seasonality and a bunch of socio-economic, health and demographic determinants. The statistical significance of these two predictor variables (which serve as proxy for the concentration of ambient air pollution) confirm our hypothesis. High ambient air pollution load triggers the vulnerabilities of RI risks in the mining neighbourhood. Among the control variables, age, education level, overall health, chronic disease, social categories (STs and SCs), smoking habit are the significant determinants of RI episodes. Moreover, the RI-related health expenditure incurred is significantly determined by the incidence (and severity) of respiratory illness, proximity to healthcare facilities, overall health status, after controlling for the village fixed effects, seasonality and a bunch of socio-economic and demographic determinants.

The voracious appetite for energy to achieve a breakthrough from the vicious cycle of subsistence, dominates the Indian policy front and obscures the critical social costs associated with rampant coal extraction. This is more pronounced in the face of laxer environmental regulations, weak institutions and disorganized civil society, which a developing country like India is broadly characterized with. So, the poor people bear the social costs of environmental and health risks. The internalization of such costs remains a deferred priority at the policy level and are mostly treated as isolated regional phenomena. This is particularly a serious issue, owing to the fact that vast tracts of mining resources in India are mostly located in the remote forested region inhabited by mostly marginalized tribal people. Pricing of coal fails to reflect the costs, which exceeds the costs of extraction and transportation, by several folds. Thus, the study tries to draw policy attention to look beyond the obvious positive economic impacts of mining and recommends appropriate design of comprehensive compensation package to partially internalize the social costs of health and well-being of the local community in the mining neighbourhood.

Acknowledgements We would also like to acknowledge the research assistance from Paroma Roy Chowdhury of Ashoka University.

Declaration of Funding We would like to acknowledge the funding from the UGC/ UPE II grant from Jawaharlal Nehru University (JNU), New Delhi, India for conducting the field work and supporting the research assistance.

Authors' Contribution I. Roy Chowdhury was involved in conceptualizing the research, designing the survey, participating in data collection, designing the methodology and data analysis, interpreting the results and writing the paper.
A. Paul participated in the systematisation, statistical processing, data analysis, interpreting the results and writing the paper.
T. Nayak actively participated as a local anchor during the entire survey and participated in the data collection.

Declaration of Conflict of Interests All the authors declare no conflict of interest.

References

Adhikari, N. (2012). In *Measuring the health benefits from reducing air pollution in kathmandu valley*. Working Paper no. WP 69–12, Kathmandu: South Asian Network for Development and Environmental Economics.

Auty, R. (2006). Mining enclave to economic catalyst: Large mineral projects in developing countries. *Brown Journal of World Affairs, 13*(1), 135–146.

Amemiya, T. (1984). Tobit models: A survey. *Journal of Econometrics, 24*, 3–61.

Birley, M. H. (1995). The health impact assessment of development project. London: HMSO brookshire and randall (1978).

Brunekreef, B., & Holgate, S. T. (2002). Air pollution and health. *The Lancet, 360*(9341), 1233–1242.

Bush, R. (2008). Scrambling to the bottom? Mining, resources and underdevelopment. *Review of African Political Economy, 35*(117), 361–366.

Chadwik, M. J., Highton, N. H., & Lindman, V. (1987). *Environmental Impacts of coal mining and utilization*. England: Pergamon Press.

Chaulya, S. K. (2004). Assesment and management of air quality for an opencast coal mining area. *Journal of Environmental Management*, 1–14.

Chaudhary, T., & Imran, M. (2010). *Morbidity costs of vehicular air pollution: Examining Dhaka City in Bangladesh*. Kathmandu: South Asian Network for Development and Environmental Economics.

CMPDI. (2005). *EIA and EMP for open cast mine (Jagannath and Ananta) of Mahanadi coal limited* (Vol. II). Bhubaneswar: CMPDI.

Dasgupta, S., Laplante, B., Wang, H., & Wheeler, D. (2002). Confronting the environmental Kuznets curve. *Journal of Economic Perspectives, 16*(1), 147–168.

Downing, T. E. (2002). Avoiding new poverty: Mining-induced displacement and resettlement. In *Mining, minerals and sustainable development series*, no. 58, London: International Institute for Environment and Development. commdev.org/ files/1376_file_Avoiding_New_Poverty.pdf. (Accessed online January 2010).

Ericson, B., Hanrahan, D., & Kong, V. (2008) *The World's worst pollution problems: Top ten of the toxic twenty*. New York: Blacksmith Institute. (Accessed online January 2010): /www.blacksmithinstitute.org/top10/10worst2.pdfS.

Farrow, A., Miller, K.A. & Myllyvirta, L. (2020). Toxic air: The price of fossil fuels. *Seoul: Greenpeace Southeast Asia*. (February 2020).

Ghose, M. K., & Banerjee, S. K. (1995). Status of air pollution caused by coal washery projects in India. *Environmental Monetary and Assessment, 38*, 97–105.

Ghose, M. K. (1989). Pollution due to air borne dust particles in coal mining its monitoring and abatement measure. *Mine Tech, 10*(1), 91–95.

Ghose, M. K., & Majee, S. R. (2001). Air pollution caused by opencast mining and its abatement measures in India. *Journal of Environmental Management, 63*(2), 193–202.

Government of Odisha. (2018). Economic Survey 2018–19. Available at https://pc.odisha.gov.in/Download/Economic_Survey_2018-19.pdf

Gupta, U. (2008). Valuation of urban air pollution: A case study of Kanpur City in India. *Environmental and Resource Economics, 41*(3), 315–326.

Health Effects Institute (HEI). (2019). Global Air 2019. *Special report Boston HEI*, ISSN 2578 6873

Hedlund, U., Jarvholm, B., & Lundback, B. (2006). Persistence of respiratory symptoms in ex-underground iron ore miners. *Occupational Medicine, 56*(6), 380–385.

Hendryx, M. (2015). The public health impacts of surface coal mining. *The Extractive Industries and Society, 2*(4), 820–826.

Hendryx, M., & Ahern, M. M. (2008). Relations between health indicators and residential proximity to coal mining in West Virginia. *American Journal of Public Health., 98*(4), 669–671.

Hendryx, M., & Zullig, K. J. (2009). Higher coronary heart disease and heart attack morbidity in Appalachian coal mining regions. *Preventive Medicine, 49*(5), 355–359.

Maddala, G. S. (1983). *Limited dependent and qualitative variables in econometrics*. Cambridge: UK, Cambridge University Press.

Mishra, S. (2002). Development, displacement and rehabilitation of tribal people: A case study of Orissa. *Journal of Social Sciences, 6*(3)

Mishra, S. K. (2015). putting value to human health in coal mining region of India. *Journal of Health Management, 17*(3), 339–355.

Mishra, P. P., & Mishra, S. K. (2014). Coal mining and local livelihoods. *Economic and Political Weekly, 49*(08), 25–26.

Mishra, S. K. (2012). Coal mining externalities: A study in Basundhara Coalfield, India. New Delhi: Project submitted to Indian Council of Social Science Research (ICSSR).

Ministry of Mines. (2013). Government of India. National Mineral Scenario. https://mines.nic.in/writereaddata/UploadFile/National_Mineral_Scenario.pdf. Published 2013.

Mukhopadhayay, P., & Kadekodi, G. K. (2011). Missing the woods for the Ore: Goa's development Myopia. *Economic and Political Weekly, 46*(46), 61–67.

Murthy, A. A., & Rao, G. (2006). *Status paper on mining leases in Orissa*. Bhubaneswar: Vasundhara, Conversation and Livelihood Team.

Nair, P. K, Sinha, J. K. (1987, August). Dust control at deep hole drilling for open pit mines and development of a dust arrestor. *Journal of Mines, Metals and Fuels*

Noronha, L., Subramanya, N. (2005, January 1–7) Assessing quality of life in a mining region. *Economic and Political Weekly (EPW), 40*(1), 72–78 (7 pages).

Ostro, B. (1994). *Estimating the health effects of air pollutants*. Policy, Research working paper; No. WPS 130. Washington, D.C. : WorldBank Group. https://documents.worldbank.org/curated/en/355391468752348015/Estimating-the-health-effects-of-air-pollutants-a-method-with-an-application-to-Jakarta

Pathak, G., Avishek, K., Gorai, A. K. (2007). Environmental and social impacts of coal mining and its management practices in India. In *First International Conference on Managing the Social and Environmental Consequences of Coal Mining in India* , pp. 19–21. New Delhi: Organized by Australian National University.

Pope, C. A., III., Bates, D. V., & Raienne, M. E. (1995). Health effects of particulate air pollution: Time for reassessment. *Environmental Health Prospective, 103*(5), 472–480.

Ross, M. H., & Murray, J. (2004). Occupational respiratory disease in mining. *Occupational Medicine, 54*(5), 304–310.

Saha, S., Pattanayak, S. K., Sills, E. O., & Singha, A. K. (2011). Under-mining health: Environmental justice and mining in India. *Health and Place, 17*(1), 140–148.

Stephens, C., Ahern, M. (2001). Worker and community health impacts related to mining operations internationally: A rapid review of the literature. In: *Mining, Minerals and Sustainable Development Series*, no. 25, London: International Institute for Environment and Development. /www.iied.org/pubs/pdfs/G01051.pdfS. (Accessed Online July 2008).

Rice Production Systems and Drought Resilience in India

K. S. Kavi Kumar

1 Introduction

Hydro-climatic events such as drought, flood and cyclones tend to be responsible for much of agricultural output losses and to some extent income and livelihood loss across vulnerable communities. Several crops which are important for ensuring food security and sustaining livelihood are vulnerable to such disasters. While weather-induced natural disasters (in particular drought conditions) have had significant influence all along on agriculture world over, the potential change in the Earth's climate and its likely influence on the intensity and frequency of hydro-climatic events have further enhanced the policy relevance of such events. Though the climate change impact literature has traditionally focussed on the effects of gradual changes in climate on climate-sensitive sectors such as agriculture, there is growing interest among academicians and policy analysts to enhance the scope of climate change impacts and understand the resilience of agriculture to hydro-climatic events like drought. Such understanding, particularly in developing countries where the climate change impacts are expected to be more adverse compared to the developed countries (Mendelsohn et al., 2006), will provide crucial insights about the factors that facilitated enhancing the adaptive capacity of farming systems.

Agriculture has always been a key sector in India—in early times due to its handsome contribution to the gross domestic product (GDP) and provision of livelihood for a large percentage of the workforce and in more recent times as a provider of employment to more than 50% of the workforce. As per the Economic Survey 2017–18, the share of agriculture in GDP was only 18% (Government of India [GoI], 2018). This structural inconsistency points to a large and growing difference in inter-sectoral relative productivities. Indian agriculture is also characterized by

K. S. Kavi Kumar (✉)
Madras School of Economics, Chennai, India
e-mail: kavi@mse.ac.in

P. Dasgupta et al. (eds.), *Sustainable Development Insights from India*,
India Studies in Business and Economics,
https://doi.org/10.1007/978-981-33-4830-1_15

an increasing number of small and marginal farmers due to contraction of cultivable land area over time and a resultant decline in the average size of landholding. Despite the large-scale expansion of irrigation infrastructure since independence, about half of India's cropped area is still dependent upon the monsoon, which is likely to be increasingly characterized by the uncertainty associated with climate change.

Starting in the mid-nineties, a large number of studies have looked at various issues associated with climate change impacts on Indian agriculture. These studies vary not only in terms of the geographic coverage, methodology used and treatment of adaptation but also in terms of assessing impacts due to potential changes in climate or analysing the sensitivity of Indian agriculture to observed weather/climate variability. Based on observed changes in temperature and rainfall over the past several decades, several studies have highlighted the impact of changing climate on some of the crucial cereal crops such as rice and wheat. Pattanayak and Kavi Kumar (2014) argue that the average rice yield would have been 8.4% higher, and had the pre-1960 climatic conditions prevailed over the period 1969–2007. Further their estimates suggest that observed changes in climate have resulted in an average annual production loss of 4.4 million tons per year. Gupta et al. (2016), on the other hand, estimate that the wheat yields in India were lowered by about 5.2% due to changes in climatic conditions over the period 1981–2009. Studies also suggest adverse economic implications due to expected changes in climate with about 8–12% loss in total agricultural net revenue following a 2 °C rise in temperature and 7% increase in precipitation (Kavi Kumar & Parikh, 2001; Sanghi & Mendelsohn, 2008). The literature further highlighted that climate change impacts will have significant distributional effects with poorer farmers getting more adversely affected than better off farmers (Gupta et al., 2017; Jacoby et al., 2014).

As mentioned above, while the literature on climate change impacts traditionally focussed on the effects of changes in primary stressors such as temperature and rainfall on agricultural outcomes, the focus in the recent past has also been on assessing the influence of derived stressors such as drought. It is against this backdrop the present study aims to explore the trends and geographic patterns associated with drought conditions in India and assess the influence of drought on agricultural productivity. Given its importance in the dietary intake of an average household in India and in providing livelihoods to millions of farmers, the study focusses on rice crop for the analysis. The analysis is based on a comprehensive district-level data assembled from various sources including ICRISAT and IMD. The data set comprises over 300 districts spread across 20 states of India and 50 years (1966–2015). The results suggest that while rice, in general, has become resilient to drought conditions in India, there is greater confidence about the resilience of rice yield towards low and moderate droughts. Though the overall result is similar to that reported earlier (Birthal et al., 2015), the results from this study based on a different empirical strategy than one adopted by Birthal et al. (2015) provide more robust estimates.

The rest of the paper is organized as follows: the rest of this section provides a brief review of the literature assessing linkages between drought and agriculture in India. Section 2 describes the data set used, characterizes drought, and discusses trends and patterns of drought in India. The next section describes the empirical model used and discusses the model estimates. Section 4 provides concluding observations.

Drought and Indian Agriculture: Brief Literature Review

Several studies have analysed the linkages between drought and agriculture in India. At the aggregate level, Gadgil and Gadgil (2006) have analysed the impact of the inter-annual variation of the summer rainfall on the GDP using data over five decades. Notwithstanding the decline in the contribution of agriculture to GDP over time in India, they estimate that severe drought lowered annual GDP by around 2–5% during 1951–2003. In another study, Pandey et al. (2007) analysed drought in three Eastern Indian states (Jharkhand, Chhattisgarh and Odisha) and showed that household income reduced by 24–58% in drought years compared to normal years. The drop in household income is shown to contribute towards an increase in poverty headcount ratio in these states (12–33%). This study also found that households adopted several strategies to cope with the loss in income caused by droughts, and these include cutting down expenditure on non-essential items (clothing, social functions, etc.) as well as essential items (food and health). The study also showed that more than 50% of the farming households have undertaken extreme measures such as curtailing the education of children which could have long-term welfare implications.

In addition to the above-mentioned direct effects of drought, several studies have also analysed the indirect effects of drought in India. Jayachandran (2006) examined the impacts of productivity changes caused by rainfall shocks on rural wages and argued that wage is more responsive to fluctuations in productivity in areas with fewer banks or higher migration costs. Sarsons (2015) analysed the three-way linkage between rainfall shocks, income and conflicts. The study shows that in districts downstream of dams in India, income is insensitive to rainfall shocks and thus argues that rainfall could be a poor instrument for rioting in India. However, the study estimates that a positive rainfall shock lowers the probability of conflict by 2.9% per year in India. Using data on test scores and schooling from rural India, Shah and Steinberg (2017) showed that positive rainfall shocks increase wages by 2% and decrease math test scores by 2–5% of a standard deviation, school attendance by 2 percentage points and probability that a child is enrolled in school by 1 percentage point. They argue that during periods of higher rainfall children drop out of school to engage in productive work which has a long-lasting impact on human capital formation. Parida et al. (2018) study the effect of extreme weather events, mainly drought and flood, on farmer suicides in 17 Indian states and show that drought has significantly raised the incidence of farmer suicides across Indian states although flood has almost no direct impact on the occurrence of farmer suicides. They observe that the states of Karnataka, Maharashtra, Kerala, Andhra Pradesh and Madhya Pradesh which have seen the highest incidence of farmer suicides also feature among the states with the highest percentage of drought-prone area.

In direct relevance to the present study, Birthal et al. (2015) and Fontes et al. (2020) analyse the influence of drought on rice cultivation in India and its resilience. Birthal et al. (2015) analysed the influence of drought—a major constraint to sustainable improvements of agricultural productivity, on the rainfed rice ecosystem. More specifically, the authors examine whether the frequency, severity and spread of droughts in India have had any influence on rice production in the country. The authors argue that nearly one-third of the area under rice cultivation in India is affected by droughts that are of moderate intensity and that the frequency of such moderate intensity droughts has increased in recent years. However, based on the analysis of nearly 200 districts over the period 1969–2005, they show that drought-induced losses in rice yields have reduced owing to improvements in farmer-adaptive capacity attributable primarily to the expansion of irrigation facilities and increased availability of improved varieties for rainfed production systems. Fontes et al. (2020) classify droughts into Type 1 and Type 2 categories based on above and below average cooling degree days, respectively. Using district-level data of India over the period 1966–2009, the authors argue that it is important to account for both types of droughts for accurate estimation of drought impact on rice yield. They further argue that irrigation is a more appropriate adaptation strategy for addressing Type 2 droughts than Type 1 droughts.

2 Drought in India: Definition, Trends and Patterns

2.1 Drought in Terms of Rainfall Anomaly

Rainfall anomaly suggests the extent to which actual rainfall in a particular year differs from its long-term average at any given location. Usually, rainfall anomalies are used for declaration of drought in a given region. For the purpose of discussion here, the district-level data from the Southern state of Tamil Nadu over the period 2004–2014 is used.

Below normal rainfall (rainfall shortage) trends over the period 2004–2014 suggest that in 9 out of the 11 years, at least one district in the state has witnessed below normal rainfall. During the period 2004–2008, there were 45 instances of rainfall shortage across districts compared to 98 instances of rain shortfall during the period 2009–2014, indicating an increasing trend in the number of districts experiencing a shortage in rainfall. A comparison of the average shortfall in rain between the same two periods also suggests an increase from 8.8% during the 2004–2008 to 14.14% during the 2009–2014.

District-wise analysis of rainfall shortage over the period 2004 and 2014 reveals almost all districts have shown an increase in the exposure to rainfall shortage during 2009 and 2014 compared to 2004 and 2008. This suggests the increasing frequency of low rainfall events in Tamil Nadu which closely corresponded with the drought declaration across districts in the state.

Comparison of rainfall shortages during 2008–09 and 2013–14 across agriculturally important districts suggests that some of the districts which are major contributors to total foodgrain (or rice) production in the state also faced a significant shortage in rainfall during 2008–09 and 2013–14 (see Fig. 1). Thanjavur, Thiruvarur, Cuddalore,

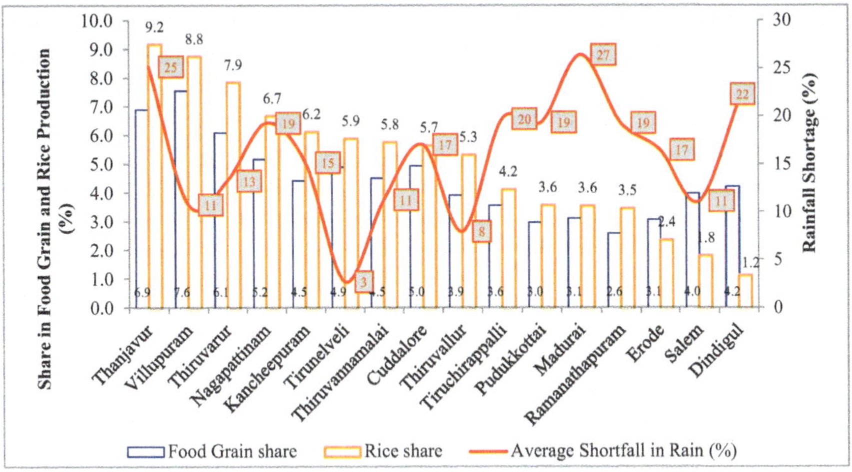

Fig. 1 District-wise average rainfall shortage, food grain and rice production share in Tamil Nadu: 2008–09 to 2013–14. *Source* SoETN (2017)

Madurai and Nagapattinam are particularly vulnerable to the rainfall anomaly, given their large contributions to agricultural production.

2.2 Drought Index

Although drought is usually associated with a lack of adequate rainfall, in reality temperature also contributes significantly to drought conditions in a region. Thus, rainfall and temperature anomalies (compared to their long-term mean value of a region) contribute towards drought definition of a region. The intensity of the hotness (dryness) can be measured as the degree to which temperature (rainfall) departs from the normal. The higher (lower) the temperature (rainfall) deviates above (below) the historical mean value, the larger will be the value of the drought index. A simultaneous occurrence of high temperatures and sparse rainfall is characterized as drought. The index comprises the two most important causes of crop damage—excess heat and lack of moisture and hence is more appropriate for assessing the impacts of extreme events on agriculture. Originally proposed by Yu and Babcock (2010), this index has been widely used in the literature. Both Birthal et al. (2015) and Fontes et al. (2020) broadly follow similar characterization of drought in their analyses.

Following Yu and Babcock (2010), drought index is defined as the product of a measure of rainfall deficit and hotness:

$$\mathrm{DI}_{it} = -[\max(0, \mathrm{MTD}_{it}) * \min(0, \mathrm{TRD}_{it})]. \tag{1}$$

where MTD and TRD are standardized deviations of mean temperature and total rainfall from their long-term mean values during the growing season. The drought index (DI) attains zero value whenever either temperature is below average or the rainfall is above average indicating 'no drought' conditions. DI defines 'drought' only when an area suffers both low rainfall and high temperature.

Since drought is better understood in terms of its severity, based on the distribution of the drought index, the severity of a drought is categorized into low drought, moderate drought and severe drought categories.

2.3 Trends and Patterns

The analysis reported in this paper is based on district-level data sourced from ICRISAT. The data set consists of 308 districts spread over 20 major states of India over the period 1966–2015. The weather data is sourced from IMD to supplement the ICRISAT data. The weather data corresponding to the *kharif* growing season (i.e. June, July, August and September) is used for assessing the average temperature and total rainfall variables relevant to the drought index calculation. For the purpose of analysis, the data is divided into five regions—East (comprising the districts from the states of Odisha, Bihar, Jharkhand, West Bengal and Assam), South (comprising the districts from the states of Andhra Pradesh, Telangana, Tamil Nadu, Karnataka and Kerala), West (comprising the districts from the states of Gujarat and Rajasthan), North (comprising the districts from the states of Uttar Pradesh, Uttarakhand, Punjab, Haryana and Himachal Pradesh) and Central (comprising the districts from the states of Maharashtra, Madhya Pradesh and Chattisgarh).

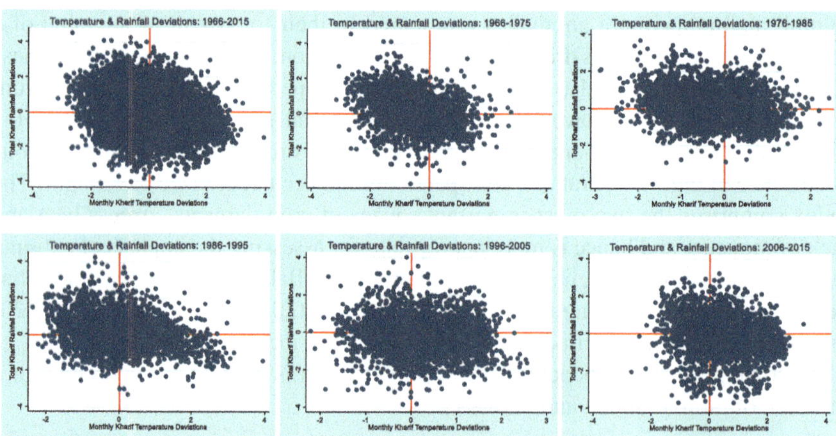

Fig. 2 Scatter plot of temperature and rainfall deviations—1966–2015

Figure 2 shows the scatter plot of temperature and rainfall deviations over the entire period of analysis (1966–2015) and for different decades (i.e. 1966–1975; 1976–1985; 1986–1995; 1996–2005 and 2006–2015). In each scatter plot, the points in the fourth quadrant represent the drought conditions as they correspond to excess heat and lack of moisture. It may be noted that some studies (Fontes et al., 2020) have identified the points in the third quadrant also to represent drought conditions (referred to as 'Type 2' drought) characterized by moisture deficit alone. However, the analysis in this study is based on the drought conditions characterized by both excess heat and lack of moisture. As could be seen from Fig. 2, the incidence of drought has increased over time with the most recent decades reporting more instances of excess temperature and rainfall deficit compared to the long-term mean values. The drought categories also correspondingly show a similar trend over the decades, with the occurrence of severe droughts increasing over time (see Fig. 3).

To get a sense of the influence of drought on rice yield, for each district–year combination in the data set, the yield deviations from its long-term trend are plotted against the drought index. The yield deviations are estimated using the Hodrick–Prescott filter. Figure 4 shows the scatter plot of the yield deviations and drought index at the all-India level as well as five sub-regions of India. While there is a clear negative correlation between the yield deviations and the drought index across all regions, the extent of the influence of drought on rice yield is different in different regions. The Northern and Southern Indian regions exhibit a relatively less adverse effect of drought on rice yield compared to the Eastern, Western and Central India.

Among other things, irrigation could help in ameliorating the adverse effects of drought on crop yield. To see the role of irrigation in the context of rice yield, the rice yield deviations and drought index are regressed on the share of irrigated area under

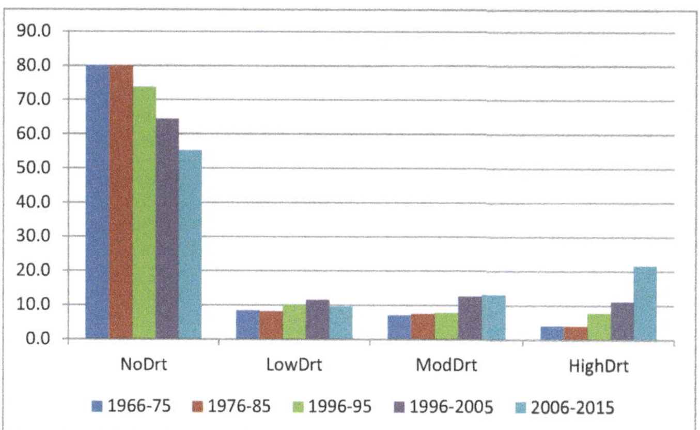

Note: 'NoDrt' – No drought; 'LowDrt' – Low drought; 'ModDrt' – Moderate drought; 'HighDrt' – Severe drought

Fig. 3 Drought categories—temporal variation. *Note* 'NoDrt'—No drought; 'LowDrt'—Low drought; 'ModDrt'—Moderate drought; 'HighDrt'—Severe drought

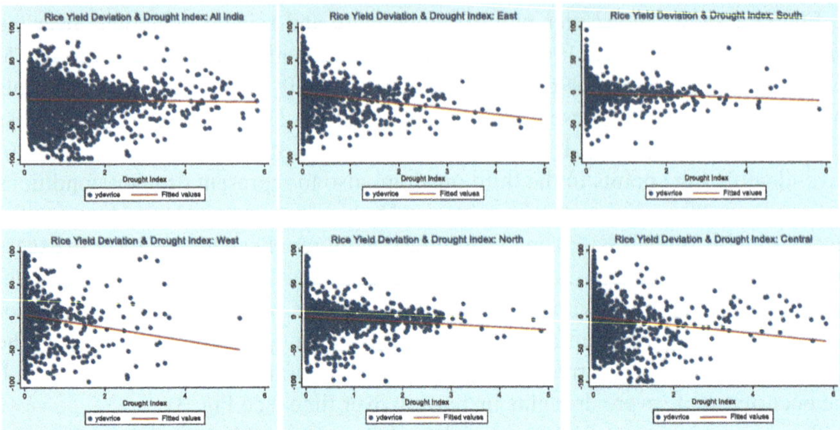

Fig. 4 Relationship between rice yield deviations and drought index—India and sub-regions

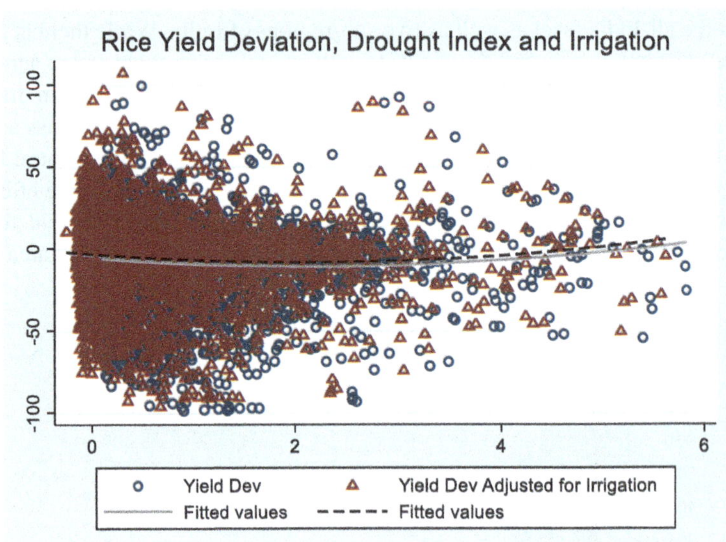

Fig. 5 Relationship between rice yield deviations and drought index—role of Irrigation

rice cultivation and the residuals are plotted against each other. Figure 5 shows the scatter plot of rice yield deviations and drought index after accounting for irrigation. As expected the irrigation does moderate the adverse effects of drought on rice yield with the black-dashed line lying always above the grey solid line. However, the extent of moderation effected by irrigation varies with the severity of the drought.

3 Impact of Drought on Rice Yield—Empirical Estimation

The main hypothesis of the paper is to assess whether rice yield has become resilient to drought conditions in India. For this purpose, two different empirical models are specified and estimations are carried out using the district-level data set described and used in the previous section. The first empirical specification (Model 1, given in Eq. 2) closely follows the model proposed and used by Birthal et al. (2015).

$$\begin{aligned}\ln(Y_{it}) = \mathrm{DCT}_i &+ \sum \phi_i[\mathrm{DCT}_i * T] + \beta_1\mathrm{DI}_{it} + \beta_2(\mathrm{DI}_{it} * \mathrm{DI}_{it}) \\ &+ \beta_3(\mathrm{DI}_{it} * T) + \beta_4(\mathrm{DI}_{it} * \mathrm{DI}_{it} * T)_{it} + \beta_5\mathrm{IRR}_{it} \\ &+ \beta_6(\mathrm{DI}_{it} * \mathrm{IRR}_{it}) + \beta_7(\mathrm{DI}_{it} * \mathrm{DI}_{it} * \mathrm{IRR}_{it}) \\ &+ \beta_8(\mathrm{DI}_{it} * \mathrm{IRR}_{it} * T) + \beta_9(\mathrm{DI}_{it} * \mathrm{DI}_{it} * \mathrm{IRR}_{it} * T) + \varepsilon_{it} \qquad (2)\end{aligned}$$

where Y is the rice yield; DI is the drought index; T is time trend; *IRR* is the share of rice area under irrigation; DCT_i represents district fixed effects; i and t subscripts represent district and year, respectively. Significant and positive β_3 (and also β_4) suggests that rice production has become less vulnerable to drought over time.

Since the drought index, DI used in the above specification is an index, it makes the interpretations of the estimated coefficients difficult. Hence, an alternative model is specified (Model 2, given in Eq. 3) where different drought categories are used along with their interaction with the time trend as independent variables to explain the variability in rice yield.

$$\ln(Y_{it}) = \mathrm{DCT}_i + \sum \phi_i\mathrm{DRTG}_i + \sum \delta_i\mathrm{DRTG}_i * T + \gamma\mathrm{IRR} + \varepsilon_{it} \qquad (3)$$

where Y is the rice yield; *DRTG* is the drought category (low, moderate and severe); T is time trend; *IRR* is the share of rice area under irrigation; DCT_i represents district fixed effects; i and t subscripts represent district and year, respectively. The coefficient vector δ represents the instantaneous growth rate of yield under no drought and different drought conditions. Significant and positive δ coefficients and their relative magnitudes provide information about the resilience of rice yield over time. If δ coefficient associated with the severe drought category is higher than that associated with moderate, low and no drought categories, then it can be inferred that rice crop has become resilient to drought over the study period.

3.1 Model Estimations

Table 1 reports the estimated coefficients of Model 1. Estimates based on two different specifications are reported—one involving only linear terms of drought index and another with both linear and quadratic terms of drought index. Both the specifications

Table 1 Drought index and rice yield relationship: model estimates

Variables	Specification-1	Specification-2
Drought index (DI)	−0.545*** (0.061)	−1.210*** (0.112)
Irrigation (IRR)	0.086*** (0.027)	0.090*** (0.028)
DI * trend	0.012*** (0.001)	0.025*** (0.003)
DI*IRR	0.386*** (0.079)	0.980*** (0.132)
DI * IRR * trend	−0.009*** (0.002)	−0.021*** (0.003)
DI-square		0.329*** (0.044)
DI-square * trend		−0.007*** (0.001)
DI-square * IRR		−0.287*** (0.049)
DI-square * IRR * trend		0.006*** (0.001
No. of observations	14,246	14,246
R-square	0.7759	0.7823
District fixed effects	Yes	Yes
Year fixed effects	Yes	Yes

Note Robust standard errors are in parentheses, *** $p< 0.01$, ** $p< 0.05$, * $p < 0.1$

follow panel fixed effects estimation procedure and report the estimated coefficients with robust standard errors. While the Model 1 is similar to that reported in Birthal et al. (2015), the estimated coefficients are robust and follow expected sign—in particular as per the first specification shown in column 2 of Table 1.

The estimates reported in column 2 of Table 1 suggest that as expected the coefficient of drought index is negative indicating that drought conditions have adverse effects on rice yield, whereas the extent of irrigation enhances rice yield as indicated by the positive and significant coefficient of variable *IRR*. The positive and significant coefficient of the interaction between drought index and time trend indicates that rice yield has become less susceptible to drought over time, validating the main hypothesis of the study. The coefficient of the interaction between drought index and irrigation is significant and positive, suggesting that irrigation moderates the adverse effects of drought on rice yield. However, the extent of moderation provided by irrigation on the adverse impacts of drought on rice yield has declined over time as indicated by the significant and negative coefficient on the interaction term between drought index, irrigation and time trend. The inclusion of the quadratic term of drought index in the model specification (Specification-2, column 3 of Table 1), however, does not

Table 2 Drought categories and rice yield relationship: model estimates

	All India	Eastern India	Southern India	Western India	Northern India	Central India
Low Drgt	−0.207*** (0.024)	−0.188*** (0.057)	−0.044*** (0.040)	−0.520*** (0.085)	−0.144*** (0.044)	−0.297*** (0.048)
Mod Drgt	−0.322*** (0.028)	−0.170*** (0.053)	0.017*** (0.041)	−0.456*** (0.087)	−0.281*** (0.060)	−0.569*** (0.060)
Sev Drgt	−0.576*** (0.061)	−0.181*** (0.071)	−0.150*** (0.058)	−1.062*** (0.150)	−0.344*** (0.104)	−1.494*** (0.191)
No Drgt * trnd	0.016*** (0.000)	0.019*** (0.001)	0.019*** (0.000)	0.017*** (0.001)	0.019*** (0.001)	0.008*** (0.001)
Low Drgt *trnd	0.020*** (0.001)	0.022*** (0.002)	0.019*** (0.001)	0.028*** (0.003)	0.021*** (0.001)	0.016*** (0.002)
Mod Drgt* trnd	0.023*** (0.001)	0.023*** (0.001)	0.017*** (0.001)	0.026*** (0.002)	0.024*** (0.002)	0.020*** (0.002)
Sev Drgt * trnd	0.027*** (0.001)	0.020*** (0.002)	0.021*** (0.001)	0.040*** (0.004)	0.025*** (0.002)	0.041*** (0.005)
Irrigation	0.213*** (0.046)	−0.076 (0.051)	−0.073*** (0.024)	0.142*** (0.036)	0.298*** (0.033)	0.162* (0.094)
No. of observations	14,246	2666	2096	2430	3868	2986
R-square	0.741	0.634	0.772	0.561	0.776	0.608
District FE	Yes	Yes	Yes	Yes	Yes	Yes

Note Robust standard errors are in parentheses, *** $p< 0.01$, ** $p< 0.05$, * $p < 0.1$

provide expected sign to the coefficients. Thus, based on the results reported here, the impacts of severe drought conditions on yield are inconsistent. Further as mentioned above, the interpretations are difficult with the drought index and hence alternative specification provided in Eq. (3) is used for further analysis.

Table 2 reports the estimated coefficients of Model 2. The results pertaining to the all-India specification and five regional specifications are reported in Table 2. All the estimations are based on panel fixed effects estimation procedure, and the table reports the robust standard errors along with the estimated coefficients. At all-India level (column 2 in Table 2), the coefficients of drought dummies and irrigation variable are of the expected sign. Severe drought conditions are more harmful to rice yield than moderate and low drought conditions, as do are moderate drought conditions compared to low drought. Since the dependent variable is in log terms, the coefficient of the interaction term between drought characterization and time trend provides an estimate of the instantaneous growth of the yield. The positive and significant coefficient associated with these interaction terms suggests an increase in the yield of rice crop subjected to different drought conditions. A higher value of the coefficient attached to the interaction term between severe drought category and time trend compared to that between no/low/moderate drought category and time trend indicates a convergence of yield affected by severe drought towards the yield

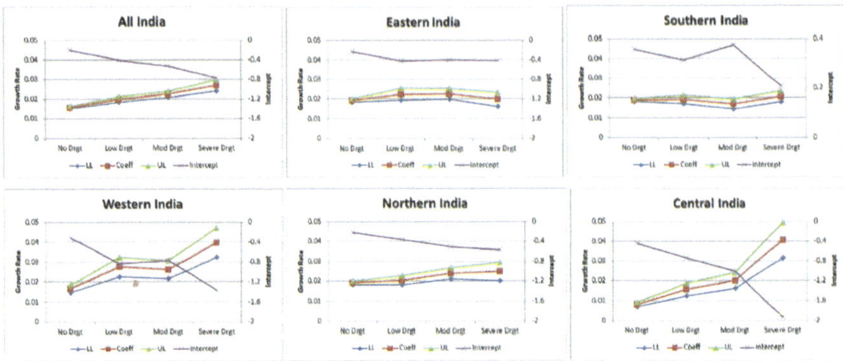

Fig. 6 Effect of different drought categories on rice yield: all india and sub-regions

affected by either no, low or moderate drought. The regional level estimates by and large follow a similar pattern reported for all-India.

Figure 6 shows the all-India and regional results in graphical form. In each graph, the left vertical axis represents the growth rate, and the right vertical axis depicts the intercept term. As can be seen from the downward sloping line in the all-India graph at the top left corner of Fig. 6, low, moderate and severe drought conditions are progressively more harmful to the rice yield. The upward sloping lines capture the estimated growth rates of rice yield along with the corresponding confidence interval under no, low, moderate and severe drought conditions. Progressively, higher growth rates of rice yield under different drought conditions highlight that rice has become resilient to drought in India over the study period of 1966–2015. However, widening confidence interval for the growth estimates associated with severe drought conditions suggests that there is greater confidence about the resilience of rice yield towards low and moderate droughts compared to severe drought conditions. The figure also highlights the varying nature of resilience of rice production systems to drought conditions across different regions of India. The Northern, Central and Western regions of India shape the overall resilience of rice to drought conditions in India.

4 Conclusions

Hydro-climatic events such as drought tend to be responsible for much of agricultural output losses and to some extent income and livelihood loss across vulnerable communities in India. Several crops which are important from ensuring food security and sustaining livelihood are vulnerable to drought. Using rice as a representative crop, this study assessed the impact of drought on rice production systems in India. Based on a comprehensive district-level data set spanning over five decades, the study explored whether rice has become resilient to drought in India. The study also probed the extent of influence irrigation had in ameliorating the adverse impacts of drought on rice yield. The findings based on multiple empirical strategies suggest that rice crop has indeed become resilient to drought in India. The results also suggest significant regional disparities in the resilience of rice yield to different drought conditions. Irrigation did play an important role in making rice crop less vulnerable to drought. However, irrigation is more effective in easing the adverse effects of low and moderate drought on rice yield than those imposed by severe drought. For addressing severe drought conditions, there is a need for augmenting farm management strategies with the use of drought-tolerant rice cultivars.

The Government of India has taken several measures to enhance the resilience of agriculture to drought. These include policies/programs to expand irrigation, use of better technology and development of drought-resistant cultivars, etc. However, a wide gap exists in terms of implementation of various programs including those aimed at drought management. Regarding technology uptake by the Indian farmers, Palanisami et al. (2015) observe that the farm-level adoption rate of water management technologies developed by the research centres is only 22%, and more than three-fourths of the water-related farm practices followed by the farmers are based on local and traditional wisdom. Despite resilience exhibited by some of the important crops such as rice to climate extremes like drought, the losses may increase substantially under climate change as constraints on further expansion of irrigation become more and more binding. Corroborating this, Zaveri and Lobell (2019) in their study on wheat yields in India over the past forty years argue that yield gains from irrigation expansion have slowed in recent years. In the context of the findings of the present study, this highlights the need for understanding the behavioural and institutional factors constraining the technology adoption at the farm level.

Acknowledgements The author would like to thank Prof. Brinda Viswanathan and Dr. Anubhab Pattanayak for their valuable inputs. An earlier version of this paper was presented at the Tenth INSEE Biennial Conference held at CESS, Hyderabad, during 6–8 November, 2019. The author gratefully acknowledges the VDSA-ICRISAT team for providing access to the Meso level apportioned database and Ms. Madhumitha for the preparation of the data set used for the study.

References

Birthal, P. S., Negi, D. S., Khan, T., & Agarwal, S. (2015). Is Indian Agriculture becoming Resilient to Droughts? Evidence from Rice Production Systems. *Food Policy, 56*, 1–12.

Fontes, F., Gorst, A., & Palmer, C. (2020). Does Choice of Drought Index Influence Estimates of Drought Induced Rice Losses in India? *Environment and Development Economics*. https://doi.org/10.1017/S1355770X2000011X.

Gadgil, S., & Gadgil, S. (2006). The Indian Monsoon, GDP and Agriculture. *Economic and Political Weekly, 41*(47), 4887–4895.

Government of India (, GoI, &). (2018). *Economic Survey of India*. New Delhi: Ministry of Finance.

Gupta, E., Ramaswami, B., & Somanathan, E. (2017). *Climate change, food prices, and poverty in India*. Discussion Papers in Economics 17-01, Indian Statistical Institute, New Delhi.

Gupta, R., Somanathan, E., & Dey, S. (2016). Global warming and local air pollution have reduced wheat yields in India. *Climatic Change, 140*(3). https://doi.org/10.1007/s10584-016-1878-8
Jacoby, H., M. Rabassa, and E. Skoufias (2014), "Distributional Implications of Climate Change in India", *American Journal of Agricultural Economics*, 1–22. https://doi.org/10.1093/ajae/aau084
Jayachandran, S. (2006). Selling labor low: Wage responses to productivity shocks in developing countries. *Journal of Political Economy, 114*(3). https://doi.org/10.1086/503579
Kavi Kumar, K. S., & Parikh, J. (2001). Indian agriculture and climate sensitivity. *Global Environmental Change, 11*(2), 147–154.
Palanisami, K., Suresh Kumar, D., Malik, R. P. S., Raman, S., Kar, G., & Mohan, K. (2015). Managing water management research: Analysis of four decades of research and outreach programmes in India. *Economic & Political Weekly, L*(26&27), 33–43.
Pandey, S., Bhandari, H., & Hardy, B. (2007). *Economic Costs of Drought and Rice Farmer's Coping Mechanisms: A Cross-country Comparative Analysis from Asia.* Manila: International Rice Research Institute.
Parida, Y., Dash, D. P., Bhardwaj, P., & Chowdhury, J. R. (2018). Effects of Drought and Flood on Farmer Suicides in Indian States: An Empirical Analysis. *Economics of Disasters and Climate Change, 2*(2), 159–180.
Pattanayak, A., & Kavi Kumar, K. S. (2014). Weather sensitivity of rice yield: Evidence from India. *Climate Change Economics, 5*(04). https://doi.org/10.1142/S2010007814500110.
Sanghi, A., & Mendelsohn, R. (2008). The Impacts of Global Warming on Farmers in Brazil and India. *Global Environmental Change, 18*(4), 655–665.
Sarsons, H. (2015). Rainfall and Conflict: A Cautionary Tale. *Journal of Development Economics, 115,* 62–72.
Shah, M. and B. M. Steinberg (2017), "Drought of Opportunities: Contemporaneous and Long-term Impacts of Rainfall Shocks on Human Capital", *Journal of Political Economy*, 125(2). https://doi.org/10.1086/690828.
SoETN. (2017). *State of Environment Report for Tamil Nadu.* Chennai: ENVIS Centre, Department of Environment, Government of Tamil Nadu.
Yu, T., & Babcock, B. A. (2010). Are US Corn and Soybeans Becoming More Drought Tolerant? *American Journal of Agricultural Economics, 92*(5), 1310–1323.
Zaveri, E., & Lobell, D. B. (2019). The Role of Irrigation in Changing Wheat Yields and Heat Sensitivity in India. *Nature Communications, 10,* 4144. https://doi.org/10.1038/s41467-019-12183-9.

Water Disputes in the Cauvery and the Teesta Basins: Conflictual Federalism, Food Security, and Reductionist Hydrology

Nilanjan Ghosh and Sayanangshu Modak

1 Introduction

Water governance is a complex problem! This is primarily because water is a 'fugitive' resource crossing boundaries. While in geostrategic studies, transboundary waters are being delineated as those crossing international boundaries, the recent definitions encompass 'transboundariness' of waters as one crossing boundaries of any form (from the international level to the most micro-level of the society) including the sectoral boundaries (Beach et al., 2000; Ghosh, 2015). This expanded scope definitely entails interstate waters within a nation. In fact, the most recent form of transboundary water conflicts occurs between the economic sector and the ecosystem sector, as human interventions over flow regimes for meeting short-term economic needs result in substantial losses for downstream ecosystem. Despite the imminent rationale and the longstanding recognition that river basins are the ideal natural units for planning and management of surface water resources (Lloyd et al., 1963), there has been an equally widespread trend and poignant history of fragmenting the basins for governance based on jurisdictions that were human-centric (Howe, 2009) and solely focussed on the reductionist view of water as a stock of resource (Bandyopadhyay, 2006).

The very frequent interstate as well as centre-state water dispute within India can be attributed to the fragmented nature of governance due to the federal structure of the democracy. India has twenty-five major river basins and 103 sub-basins, many of which are spread across more than one state and come under the jurisdictional purview of each riparian state as enshrined under the federal distribution of powers in the

N. Ghosh (✉) · S. Modak
Observer Research Foundation, Kolkata, India
e-mail: nilanjanghosh@orfonline.org

S. Modak
e-mail: sayanangshu@orfonline.org

P. Dasgupta et al. (eds.), *Sustainable Development Insights from India*,
India Studies in Business and Economics,
https://doi.org/10.1007/978-981-33-4830-1_16

Indian constitution (Choudhry et al., 2016). As argued by Ghosh and Bandyopadhyay (2009), the very fragmented nature of governance of an inherently cohesive and connected water system is responsible for the emergence of the conflicts over water use, rather than being induced by mere physical scarcity of the resource. The vestation of power over water use at the state levels has resulted in intense political contestations based on the conflicting perception of property rights over transboundary waters (Ghosh et al., 2018).

This chapter looks at the two cases of water conflicts of varying nature—the conflict over the Cauvery waters at the subnational level and the transnational Teesta water conundrum with Bangladesh being the lower riparian where federal politics also plays a role. In fact, the Teesta case also brings to the fore the problems that the basin ecosystem encounters due to unbridled economic ambitions. The paper identifies three policy-driven factors which are have not merely influenced but have shaped these disputes—the federal distribution of power in the Indian constitution concerning water governance resulting in a fragmented governance, a reductionist delineation of food security by incentivising the production of water-intensive crops and finally, the lack of an integrated ecosystems approach that considers the nexus of land, water and food production.

This paper is divided into five sections. Section 2 talks about the constitutional provisions of interstate water governance and how conflictual federalism can evolve from here. Section 3 brings to the fore how the federal structure has been responsible for the water conflicts over Cauvery and Teesta. Section 4 highlights that the wrong delineation of food security in India through promotion of water-intensive crops is responsible for water conflicts especially during dry months. Section 5 throws light on the lack of integrated approach in water governance in India accentuating the conflicts. The concluding Sect. 6 summarises the arguments presented and recommends in favour of a paradigm shift in water governance and policy making in India from a reductionist approach to a holistic approach.

2 Constitutional Framework of Interstate Water Governance and Conflictual Federalism

On 31 July 2019, Lok Sabha cleared an amendment to the decades-old Interstate River Water Disputes Act, 1956. This amendment sought to speed up the process of dispute resolution by delineating a time frame for completing the process of adjudication and subsequent referral. Furthermore, it empowers the central government to form a Disputes Resolution Committee (DRC) for effectively operationalising the provision of a negotiated settlement before the dispute gets referred to an Inter-State River Water Disputes Tribunal. The tribunals themselves are set to get a massive facelift in terms of making them a permanent feature in the judicial landscape of the country with multiple benches in different parts of India. Moreover, the bill also envisages establishing a greater degree of adherence to the award of the tribunal by making it final and binding on the parties involved in the dispute while necessitating the central government to make schemes to give effect to the decisions (PRS Legislative Research, 2019). This amendment reflects everything that is lacking in the process of adjudication and dispute resolution, but before that, it is important to understand why interstate water disputes arise in the first place.

Federalism is a fundamental and unamendable tenet of the nation (Kulshrestha, 2018; Goel, 2019). In the given federal setup, the legislative powers concerning water are distributed between the centre and the states in a manner that is expected to secure optimum utilisation of the precious resource while balancing the interests of the states. Schedule VII of the Indian Constitution creates a distinction between the use of water within a state and the purpose of regulating interstate waters. It bestows power on the Union Parliament to formulate laws and mechanisms for regulating interstate rivers (Entry 56 of List I—Union List) while allowing the states to decide on the use of water for various purposes like water supply, irrigation and canals, drainage and embankments, water storage and water power (Entry 17 of List II—State List), subject to the provisions of Entry 56 of List I.

The traditional justification for this arrangement has been the rationale that interstate rivers are not confined by political or administrative boundaries, and therefore, no state can claim an exclusive right and deprive other states their just share. However, it is important to note that unlike the explicit mention in the Union List for 'interstate water', the State List does not specify 'intra-state' and simply uses the expression 'water'. Therefore, effectively, the states have full power to legislate on all matters mentioned in Entry 17 of List II even if the source of the river or that of its tributaries, or a part of the river system is located in another state. This power can only be ousted if the Parliament enacts a law in the larger public interest to override the indiscriminate use of interstate water. The Sarkaria Commission had noticed that even for such legislation, the Parliament has to comply with the precedent condition of declaring the extent to which its involvement to regulate and develop the interstate river is in the public interest. Moreover, the Union Parliament can only do as much as declaring its intent without any competency to enforce it since the Entry 17 of the State List comprehends within its scope even interstate rivers because of the lack of clarity as discussed earlier (Sarkaria Commission, 1988).

As a result, the Union Government has largely steered clear of being proactive and instilling a basin-wide approach and instead has largely relied on the exigent formula of dispute resolution. Chokkakula (2019) explains by highlighting the lack of a reliable policy mechanism for interstate collaboration with the policy ecosystem being tuned to respond to exigency-driven contingent responses. He cites the example of two acts which were created in the same year—the Interstate (River) Water Disputes Act, 1956, and the River Boards Act, 1956. While the former has been invoked numerous times and has been amended at least a dozen times, the latter which empowers the centre to create boards to enable interstate cooperation has remained untouched. So much so that the river boards which have been created so far—Upper Yamuna River Board, Betwa River Board, Brahmaputra Board, etc.— have been done by alternative and ad-hoc channels without invoking this act (Chokkakula, 2019). The discussions point to the existing ambiguity in the constitutional framework with regard to interstate river water governance and the prevalent policy ecosystem hardly instils the confidence of states cooperating amongst themselves, as the Union Government stays away from exercising its constitutional role of regulating interstate waters. This can be termed as 'conflictual federalism of interstate water' which impede the adoption of an Integrated River Basin Management (IRBM) approach as the primer for river basin governance in India (Ghosh, 2016).

3 Conflictual Federalism: Common Origins, Different Implications

The federal dynamics of transboundary water governance play out at two levels. One which is predominantly subnational such as the Cauvery water dispute while the other is over an international watercourse for which the Union Government of India is yet to reach a water-sharing agreement with a co-riparian, such as the Teesta impasse with Bangladesh, due to the centre-state disagreement between the Union and the state of Weste Bengal (as also with Sikkim). Both these cases illustrate the inadequacy of a federal mechanism for reaching a negotiated agreement either between the riparian states (Cauvery) or between the Union Government and a state (Teesta) leading to hostile hydropolitics.

3.1 The Cauvery Conflict

The Cauvery, with its origins in the Tala Cauvery on the eastern aspect of the Western Ghats mountains, comprises of an area of 81,155 km^2. The basin is shared by Tamil Nadu (54.05%), Karnataka (42.23%), Kerala (3.5%) and Karaikkal region of Pondicherry (0.18%). Physiographically, the basin can be divided into three parts—the uplands in the Western Ghats, the plateau region of Mysore and finally, the deltaic region of Tamil Nadu and Pondicherry. The basin receives rainfall from both the seasonal winds—the south-west (SW) monsoon (June to September) and the north-east (NE) monsoon (November to January). However, the intensity and distribution of the rainfall are highly uneven over space and time. While the SW monsoon generates heavy rainfall in the uplands, thereby contributing to the flow in the headwaters of the system, there is a sharp decline in precipitation in the lower parts of the basin comprising of the state of Tamil Nadu and Pondicherry. These parts receive the bulk of the precipitation from the NE monsoon, whose effects are limited to the delta (Cauvery Water Disputes Tribunal, 2007). The disproportionate distribution of precipitation has a bearing on the emergence of the conflict as will be discussed later (Fig. 1).

The Cauvery water dispute is firmly embedded in the historical development of water resources and irrigation facilities in the states of Karnataka and Tamil Nadu

Fig. 1 River Basin Atlas - National Remote Sensing Centre. *Source* https://www.nrsc.gov.in/sites/default/files/pdf/RiverBasinAtlas/05.Cauvery%20Basin.pdf

(Table 1). Historically, downstream Tamil Nadu had been using the bulk of the waters of the Cauvery to irrigate the paddy fields in the delta. The state always emphasised that this should be remembered and the prescriptive rights of the downstream users in the state must be protected. Therefore, it goes back to the agreement of 1924 which allowed Karnataka to develop its irrigation coverage to a limit which did not jeopardise the longstanding downstream use of water for irrigation in Tamil Nadu (Iyer, 2003). This is closely aligned to an extreme principle of property right which assumes historical use of water, despite being located in the downstream, as the basis for conferring the primary right to those users—the doctrine of History. This doctrine is in direct conflict with the Harmon doctrine adopted by Karnatakathat bestows the primary right to the user who owns the source of the water (if water drops on my roof, it is mine). Karnataka holds the view that delayed development of irrigation in the state cannot be a reason for it to forego its right to make full use of the water of the Cauvery for agriculture and other purposes when there are a clear scarcity and inadequacy of water. It also cites various other reasons such as the history of wrongful imposition by a relatively superior British authority which ruled Madras back in the day, and that the parties to the agreement—Madras Presidency and the princely state of Mysore—did not exist after independence to fulfil the requirements from a legal perspective. However, another hydrometeorological argument forwarded by Karnataka points out the fact that Tamil Nadu enjoys spells of rainfall from both SW monsoon as well as NE monsoon (as discussed before) while Karnataka has to stay contented with only spells from NE monsoon. The state considers this to be inherently unfair while it has to share 64% of the drought-prone area in the basin (Anand, 2004).

Table 1 Phases of irrigation development and evolution of hydropolitics between Karnataka and Tamil Nadu

Phases	Status of irrigation development	
	State of Mysore/Karnataka	Madras Presidency/Tamil Nadu
Phase 1: before 1892	The state of Mysore was traditionally attuned to dryland agriculture (growing millets). The traditional mode of irrigation was through tanks with channels to divert water From the middle of the nineteenth century, Mysore started expanding their irrigated area, much to the discomfort of engineers in the Madras Presidency. By the end of 1890s, proposals were being exchanged by the two states	Aided by ruling dynasties such as the Cholas, Tamil Nadu had a rich history of irrigation development and agricultural expansion (paddy) that based itself on the delivery of NE monsoon From the 1850s onward, Madras Presidency under the British government started the use of sluice gates, allowing for regulation of flow and further agricultural expansion, thereby increasing the dependency on assured supplies from up stream Mysore
Genesis of conflicting water needs for Kuruvai paddy (Tamil Nadu), Kharif paddy (Karnataka, exacerbated by delayed or weak arrival of SW Monsoon. The signing of the agreement of 1892		
Phase 2: 1892–1934	By, 1910 Mysore had already floated the idea of Krishnarajasagar (KRS) dam. This Kannambadi project was to happen in two stages and Mysore urged for the immediate clearance of the first stage and retaining the option to initiate the second stage	Madras gave its consent to the first phase while objecting to the second one on the pleas that it would affect the existing irrigation in the Cauvery delta. Madras had also put forward its own plan to construct the Mettur dam which did not receive an approval from government of India
Two successive arbitrations failed to resolve the impasse until the agreement of 1924, forged by the Secretary of State. It mandated Mysore to construct KRS but follow 'rules of regulation' as annexed. Mettur dam construction was cleared		
Phase 3: 1934–1974	With independence in 1947, the princely state of Coorg merged with Karnataka. Irrigation coverage increased manifold, from 121,457 ha in 1930 to 178,138 ha in 1971 through the construction of small reservoirs, anicuts and channels from the tributaries	Malabar region of erstwhile Madras broke away and joined the new state of Kerala. Meanwhile, Tamil Nadu registered a much more rapid and significant expansion in irrigation to the tune of 259,109 ha from the pre-Mettur figures, augmented through the Mettur dam the first and second five-year plans

(continued)

Table 1 (continued)

Phases	Status of irrigation development	
	State of Mysore/Karnataka	Madras Presidency/Tamil Nadu
The conflict had continued to deepen in the previous phase with Mysore seemingly stifled by the agreement of 1924. In 1974, the agreement fell due to lack of 'reassessment' and 'renewal' according to Tamil Nadu while it 'expired' for leaders in Karnataka		
Phase 4: 1974–1990	Karnataka gave up any adherence to the previous scheme of regulation of water from KRS, and instead brought to fruition several projects—Suvarnavathy (1973), Hemavathy (1978), Varuna canal (1979), Yagachi (1983), Nallur Amanikere (1987) and Teetha (1987). The share of Karnataka in total utilisation of Cauvery waters increased from 27.6% (1970–80) to 42.2% (1980–90)	Tamil Nadu continued to develop many small schemes in sub-tributaries in dry areas of Dharmapuri, Salem, Periyar, Dindigul and Thiruchirapally districts. However, the diversion of water inflow above Mettur continued to rattle it as an attempt to forge an agreement in 1976 by the Additional Secretary of Ministry of Irrigation and Power failed. The state formally made a formal request for adjudication in 1986
The Cauvery Water Tribunal (CWT) was finally set up on 2nd June 1990 after two decades of failed negotiations		

Source Ghosh et al. (2018)

The divergent views of property rights became evident when the agreement of 1924 lapsed after 50 years and Karnataka started enforcing its position in phase 4 of the conflict. It must be noted that the 70s also witnessed an attempt by the Government of India to forge an agreement by employing a fact-finding committee and proposing the parties (Tamil Nadu, Karnataka and Kerala) to manage their water demand. It was suggested that the saved water could then be redistributed after the savings had accrued for a period of 15 years (Gebert, 1983). Moreover, the forward-looking agreement also suggested the setting up of an inter-state authority for the Cauvery basin. This attempt at reaching a negotiated agreement arbitrated by the Union Government can be identified as closely aligned to the Hobbesian doctrine of dispute resolution by arriving at a mutually agreeable definition of property right for all parties. These negotiations failed to bridge the gap in the way the main parties to the conflict—Karnataka and Tamil Nadu perceived property rights over the Cauvery waters. Therefore, to a large extent, the origin of the conflict should not be traced merely to conflict over water use, but also to conflict over definition of property rights in a federal regime that bestows water use rights definition to the states themselves. Here lies the contention of 'conflictual federalism'.

According to Upadhyay (2002), frequent resort to court mediation reflected the growing politicisation of the issue with increased reliance on speedier judicial orders than taking the relatively slower recourse of forums for participatory discussion to redress grievances. This can be further corroborated by the fact that the emergence of the 'hardline' narrative in the states could have been electorally crucial for the states. According to evidence from electoral data unearthed by Anand (2004), the share of the members to the respective state assemblies from the Cauvery district constituencies in the state ruling coalitions increased significantly over time. The gamut of the crisis thus created, found the perfect leeway for hostile expression as there was an inherent lack of incentive for the states to denounce their hardline positions for a basin-wide approach to integrated development. This gave shape to the conflictual relations between two basin states with the centre's role being largely reduced despite the constitutional mandate for the regulation of interstate rivers.

(a) **The Teesta impasse**

The Teesta originates as the ChhomboChhu from the KhangchungChho glacial lake, which is located amidst the high mountains of the Eastern Himalaya in the Sikkim state of India. The river gets its name after the confluence of Lachen Chu (whose headwater is the ChhomboChhu) and the Lachung Chu at Chungthang in Sikkim. Teesta takes a turbulent course through mountainous terrain before finally emerging from the mountains at Sevoke and draining into the alluvial plains of North Bengal. The rapid descent of the river in the mountains and the perenniality of flow in the river makes it an ideal contender for hydropower development. In the plains of North Bengal, the Teesta is joined by a few more tributaries like Neora, Leesh, Geesh, etc. as it makes its way through Jalpiguri district of West Bengal. The river enters Bangladesh in Dimlaupzila of Nilphamari district and traverses another 121 km to finally meet the Jamuna (Brahmaputra) at TeestamukhGhat in Rangpur district (Stokes, 2013). The bulk of the basin (59%) is located at an altitude of 3000 m and above, while only meagre area (6%) is located at an altitude of 1000 m or below (Goyal & Goswami, 2018) (Fig. 2).

Agriculture has remained the mainstay of the people in the basin with paddy being the most important crop. It is a common practice in both the countries to grow paddy in three seasons—*aus* (autumn rice), *aman* (winter rice) and *boro* (summer rice). Both the countries have developed their irrigation capacity to facilitate the expansion of agriculture with India initiating the Teesta Barrage Project (of which Gazaldoba is a part) in 1976 and Bangladesh constructing the Dalia barrage in 1990 (Strategic Foresight Group 2013). Despite the expansion of agriculture, the hydrometeorological realities of the basin continue to enforce significant constraints which have dictated the form of this conflict. The mean annual rainfall is 3279.9 mm and the annual potential evapotranspiration is to the tune of 1085.0 mm, signifying that the basin is well endowed with moisture and water. However, when one considers the temporal skewness of this distribution, with the bulk of the rainfall being concentrated in the monsoon season (80.2%) (Ranade et al., 2007), the crisis gets contextualised better.

The estimated mean annual flow of the Teesta is 60 BCM with a high degree of variation between the wet period of monsoon (June to September) and the lean period (October to April/May) when the volume of flow drops to 500 MCM per month (Strategic Foresight Group, 2013). According to Mondal and Serajul Islam (2017),

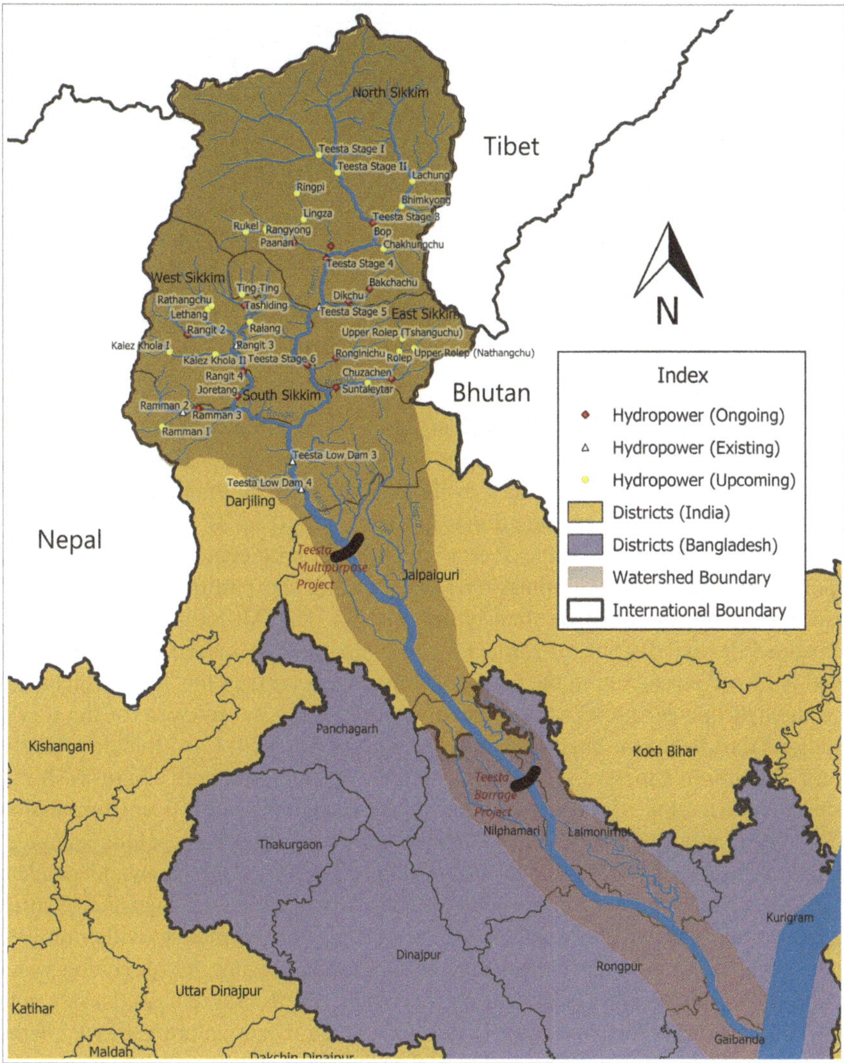

Fig. 2 Dams in the Teesta Basin (for representative purpose only). *Source* Prepared by authors; based on Rahaman and Mamun (2020)

the regulation of river flow through the irrigation barrage at Gazaldoba by India from 1987 has been instrumental in scripting Bangladesh's misfortune as a downstream riparian. Within the period 1999–2006, the minimum monthly discharge at Kaunia station for the months between December and April never exceeded 100 m^3/s. The lowest flow during this period was recorded on 15 February 2005 and it was only 5.47 m^3/s. This is the bone of contention between the two countries as Bangladesh continues to point out that India has been diverting water through the Gazaldoba

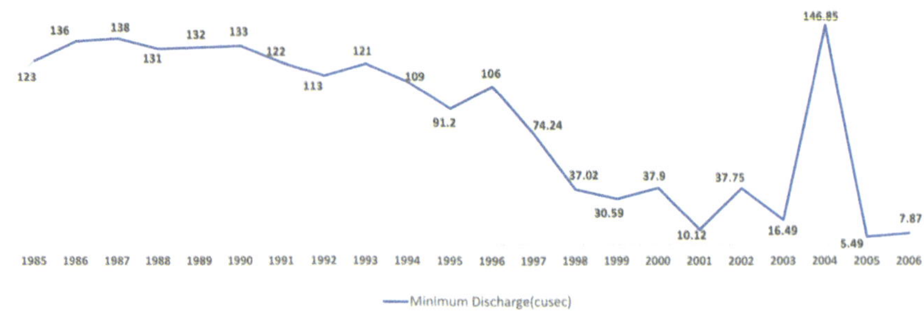

Fig. 3 Minimum discharge in Teesta at Kaunia, Bangladesh. *Source* Mondal and Islam (2017), based on data from Bangladesh Water Development Board (BWDB)

basin and the Teesta Mahananda link canal to irrigate agricultural fields outside the Teesta basin and for urban water supply, leaving little water for Bangladesh during the lean period. Further, it also accuses India of releasing all the floodwaters during the rainy season, thereby causing floods in Bangladesh (Fig. 3).

The very first mention of the Teesta in a political arrangement was made in the report of the Boundary Commission (1950) during the partition of the country, marking the beginning of the first phase of talks. The All-India Muslim League demanded the two districts of Darjeeling and Jalpaiguri and asked it to be incorporated in East Pakistan citing the reason that they were parts of the Teesta catchment and the hydropower projects over the river could serve the interests of the newly proposed East Pakistan. This was subsequently refused by Sir Cyril Radcliffe (Partition Commission Papers, 1950). Throughout the 50s and 60s, both countries shared data and information. The next mention can be traced to the Joint River Commission (JRC) negotiations that started in 1972 with a primary focus on reaching an agreement over the sharing of the Ganga waters between India and the newly independent Bangladesh, Teesta playing a second fiddle. The two countries still managed to stitch together a two-year ad-hoc arrangement in 1983 that allowed India to withdraw 39% while Bangladesh could withdraw 36% of the waters leaving the remaining water unallocated (Salman and Uprety, 2003). Thereafter, the Teesta remained a side note in the discussions as the two countries developed their irrigation infrastructure in the Teesta basin without securing a deal over the sharing of waters.

The second phase begins after Ganga Water-Sharing Treaty had been signed in 1996 and cleared off the table. The focus shifted to the Teesta and a Joint Committee of experts was formed in 1997, which conducted a series of meetings till 2004 with little progress towards a water-sharing agreement (Stokes, 2013). In its 36th meeting, the JRC observed, 'the lean season flows in [the] Teesta will not meet the needs of both the countries and hence any sharing formula for the lean season flows should be based on shared sacrifices' (Indian Archive, 2011). The Union Government of India has shown a certain degree of keenness to arrive at a common ground. A joint communique was issued on the occasion of the Prime Minister of Bangladesh—Sheikh Hasina's visit to New Delhi in January 2010, which stated that the talks on the sharing of Teesta waters should conclude expeditiously to alleviate the sufferings of the people on both sides during the season of lean flows (MEA, 2010). A draft agreement was also exchanged between the two sides and the stage was set for the signing of a treaty during Indian Prime Minister Manmohan Singh's visit to Dhaka in the September of 2011. However, the deal could not be signed as the West Bengal government led by Mamata Banerjee dissented to the strategic water-sharing agreement (Swami, 2011) which proposed allocating 50% of the water of the river to Bangladesh (Stokes, 2013). In the subsequent years, the bilateral discussions between the two riparian nations have to remain intractable despite progress made on other fronts like settling the Land Boundary Agreement in 2015, when West Bengal CM even joined the Indian Prime Minister in Dhaka for the exchange of ratified papers. The more recent stance of the state government has been to claim that the river has only one sixteenth of the total water requirement of dry season *boro* paddy in the two countries. Instead, West Bengal has suggested that the Union Government may consider other rivers like the Torsa, Jakdhaka or Raidhak for water sharing with Bangladesh (Basu, 2017). This has resulted in a state of dispute between the centre and the state. While the centre shows its intentions to get into a water-sharing agreement with Bangladesh, West Bengal, has stuck to the position that there is not adequate water in the Teesta to be shared (Basu, 2017). There is a generic feeling that a large part of Bangladesh–India geopolitical relations is also contingent upon the sharing of the Teesta waters (Ghosh, 2019), which now clearly presents itself as a classic case of two-level game in water negotiations (see Richards & Singh, 1997).

The Teesta stalemate unveils another dimension of conflictual federal relation manifested as a direct consequence of the ambiguity that has prevailed in enforcing the constitutional mandate of regulating waters crossing state boundaries. The government of West Bengal is well within its rights to make decisions regarding the use of the water. However, as pointed out by Ghosh (2019), what has been missing is an institutional approach that could have enabled an integrated mechanism to water governance at the basin level. Therefore, water diversion from the river has continued in an unregulated manner as has been the increased assertion of the state government in dictating the terms of engagement. The position of West Bengal indicates a stand that is aligned to the Harmon doctrine of a property right as it looks to secure water availability for its people leaving the river dry and bereft of flow. It also highlights how divergent views of the union and state government have resulted in a transboundary crisis that remains to be resolved despite the active role of JRC.

4 Flawed Food Policy

The peculiar and conflictual interplay of actors in the federal setup of India gets further compounded by an incorrect delineation of policies for ensuring food security. This leads to choosing economic instruments like a minimum support price (MSP) from the government that incentivises the cultivation of water-intensive cropping like paddy over the indigenous, water-efficient crops of the region such as millets. This has been found to increase the competing demands for water over a long period, thereby further aggravating the conflict. In the case of Cauvery and Teesta, the introduction of dry season paddy and its expansion has been instrumental in reducing the flow endowment while creating a reliance on irrigation and fuelling demand for water.

As explained earlier in the section on Cauvery, the conflict becomes imminent if the arrival of the SW monsoon gets delayed, leading to a convergence in demand for the limited supply of water in the Cauvery. The Kuruvai paddy of Tami Nadu is sown during June and is largely dependent on irrigation from the Cauvery waters. However, this period also coincides with the irrigation schedule for the summer paddy in Karnataka, the cultivation of which is a rather a recent phenomenon. A look at the trend of expansion in agriculture reveals that mainly the part of the basin in Karnataka experienced an increase in gross sown area between 1980 and 1990, which subsequently declined in the late 90s and 2000s. The change in the decadal means of the acreage was also found to be significant in the 90s as compared to the 80s, at five per cent levels of significance. This substantiates the observation made earlier that Karnataka assumed the lapse of the agreement of 1924 as an opportunity to bolster its capacity to harness the waters of the Cauvery for agricultural expansion (Ghosh and Bandyopadhyay, 2009). The availability of additional water through irrigation in the 1990s resulted in an increased acreage of paddy between 1991–1992 and 1997–1998. According to data compiled by Ghosh et al. (2018) from various government sources, the acreage of paddy grew by 10% while the other water-efficient crops like jowar (25%), bajra (58%) and ragi (6%) all registered a decline. Moreover, it must be noted that by 1991–1992, paddy had already become the primary crops of the Cauvery Basin, comprising of 45% of the total acreage while ragi being the distant second with an acreage of 26%. This gap has only widened ever since for the next two decades.

It is evident from the discussion above that the acreage of paddy increased manifold in Karnataka (Table 2) which in turn drove the expansion of paddy in the Cauvery basin. Summer paddy quickly emerged as an important dry season crop in the state at the expense of millets and this became a prime contender for a share of the crucial supply of water, thereby reducing the supply of water for an equally crucial Kuruvai paddy crop in downstream Tamil Nadu. Ghosh and Bandyopadhyay (2009) point out two economic factors that fuelled this change in the choice of crop and the expansion of irrigated paddy. The first is a minimum support price (MSP) regime of the government that incentivised the production of paddy over ragi. This can be established by understanding the change in the mean price ratio (the price of ragi divided by that of paddy). Before 1981–82, the ratio was poised at one which thereafter continued to increase until 1996–97 when it stood at 1.22580 before dipping. Moreover, the public distribution system further promoted the sale of rice at a much lower price than any other crop, thereby creating a strong and stable market demand for rice. The second factor relates to a diminishing real cost of irrigation despite attempts to revise it in the late 1980s, which was only met by vociferous protests from farmers.

Table 2 Season-wise paddy acreage in Karnataka (1980–81 to 2013–14)

Year (time period)	Average area under Kharif Paddy (000 ha)	Average area under Rabi Paddy (000 ha)	Average area under Summer Paddy (000 ha)
1980–81 to 85–86	261.78	0.64	33.39
1986–87 to 90–91	255.03	6.14	46.22
1991–92 to 95–96	280.55	6.79	65.83
1996–97 to 98–99	287.81	6.78	68.87
1999–2000 to 2002–03	251.86	4.82	42.26
2003–04 to 2005–06	278.86	1.49	50.39
2006–07 to 2009–10	282.90	4.59	55.98
2010–11 to 2013–14	246.79	1.54	23.58

Source Ghosh et al. (2018)

Therefore, the cost of irrigation in the basin has remained low and inconsequential creating strong barriers for the demand management of irrigation waters (Fig. 4).

In the case of the Teesta, the discontentment in neighbouring Bangladesh and the reluctance of India to share the waters of the Teesta also has an economic reason at its root. Bangladesh constructed the Dalia Barrage on the Teesta in August 1990 and started its operations in 1993. Acclaimed as the country's largest irrigation project, water from the Dalia barrage had enabled around 16,000 acres of land to be brought under High Yielding Variety (HYV) of *boro* paddy cultivation. Covering seven districts of northern Bangladesh, the project had a target of expanding the irrigation coverage to 540,000 hectares along with flood control (Islam, 2016). Meanwhile, India had also completed the construction of the Gazaldoba barrage by 1990 and was drawing water from the river through two canals on either side of the river (Noolkar-Oak, 2017). The Culturable Command Area (CCA) envisaged in this project is 342,000 hectares, and it would also provide drinking water to the tune of 4.98 million cum to the burgeoning city of Siliguri in Jalpaiguri district (Government of West Bengal, 2010). Table 3 highlights the progress made in the first sub-stage of Phase-1 as of March 2010.

However, the ambitions of the two countries concerning the water diversion plans are not just in conflict with each other, but also appear to be untenable in the long run. Rudra (2017) points out that minimum flow in the Teesta dwindles to less than 200 cumecs during February which is insufficient either to operationalise Gazaldoba, which is designed to withdraw 520 cumecs or Duani barrage that is supposed to

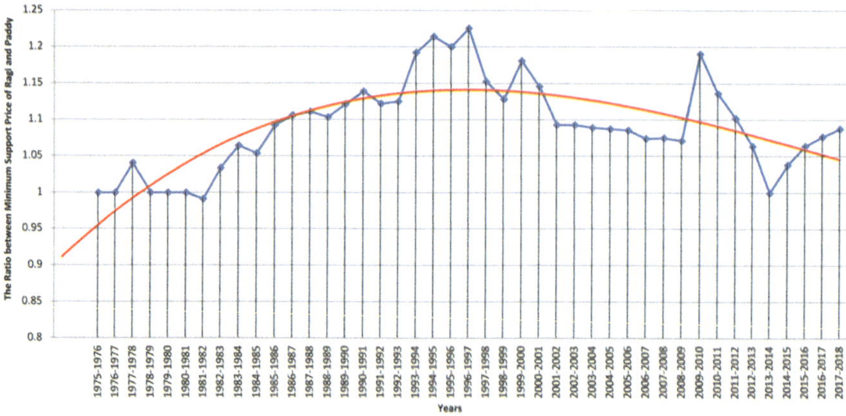

Fig. 4 Ratio between minimum support price of paddy and ragi (1975–76 to 2017–18). *Source* Ghosh et al. (2018)

withdraw 283 cumecs in their full capacity. Moreover, neither of the two has been designed to store water during the monsoons which can then be put to use in the dry season. Islam (2016) has also noted that the marginal productivity (in terms of agricultural products) of the targeted land area of Dalia project drops successively with a drop in the flow rate with the lower limit being 4000 cusecs, below which the system cannot operate. It is also worthwhile to ponder what would require all the water for irrigation. It is here that the focus shifts to the *boro* variety of paddy, which emerged as the most popular variety of agricultural produce in West Bengal (Ray and Ghosh, 2007).

The *boro* crop can grow only through irrigation and the crop is noteworthy for its higher productivity. Therefore, it was introduced as part of the Green Revolution and helped to enable accelerated agricultural growth in West Bengal through improvement in productivity of rain-fed *aman* and rapid uptake of *boro* and a dramatic increase in its acreage (Saha and Swaminathan, 1994). The expansion of *boro* cultivation acreage is also closely linked with the expansion in canal networks and/or the proliferation of tube wells. Ray and Ghosh (2007) have identified two phases in the change in the annual rate of growth of *boro* yield—1965 to 1990 and 1990 to 2000 (Table 4).

Based on the above data, a tailored analysis of six districts that are fed by the Teesta water draws an interesting picture. All the districts in the Teesta basin in West Bengal, more glaringly Coochbehar and Jalpaiguri, registered a phenomenal growth rate in the area under *boro* paddy in the second phase. This can be partly attributed to the expansion of canal networks and the steady diversion of water from the Teesta.

Table 3 Teesta irrigation project status

Unit-II, Main canals with its branches						
Description			Total project	Ccompleted part (Dec'09)	Balance part (after Dec'09)	Locations of the command
			Length (km)	Length (km)	Length (km)	Districts
Left Bank Canal	TJMC	Main canal	30.31	20.521	9.789	Jalpaiguri, Coochbehar
		Branch canal	491.43	9.11	482.32	
	TMLC	Main canal	25.75	25.75	0.00	Jalpaiguri, Coochbehar
		Branch canal	332.27	215.7	116.57	
Right Bank Canals	MMC	Main canal	32.22	32.22	0.00	Darjeeling, N-Dinajpur
		Branch canal	303.29	69.29	234.00	
	DNMC	Main canal	80.2	26.695	53.505	N-Dinajpur
		Branch canal	768.93	33.81	735.12	
	NTMC	Main canal	42.20	0.00	42.20	N-Dinajpur, D-Dinajpur, Malda
		Branch canal	385.56	0.00	385.56	
Total			2492.16	423.096	2059.83	

Teesta Mahananda Link Canal (TMLC), Mahananda Main Canal (MMC), Dauk Nagar Main Canal (DNMC), Teesta Jaldhaka Main Canal (TJMC), Nagar-Tangaon Main Canal. (NTMC)

Source Government of West Bengal (2010)

Therefore, the need to become self-reliant in food grains has created an entire policy ecosystem which has led to the increased expansion of a water-intensive crop and the subsequent use of water in an unsustainable manner.

5 Lack of Integrated Approach

South Asian water governance is generally based on a reductionist approach, rather than promoting holism (Ghosh, 2015). At the very outset, the federal structure that promotes property and user rights being defined by the states themselves is symptomatic of the fragmented approach of water governance. The global practice has now

Table 4 Segregation of kinked exponential growth rates of boro paddy in West Bengal and selected districts, 1965–84 and 1985–2002

Districts	1965–1984			1985–2002		
	Output	Area	Yield	Output	Area	Yield
Malda	7.14	3.8 (53.22)	3.34 (46.77)	7.16	6.58 (91.89)	0.58 (8.10)
Coochbehar	8.09	3.5 (43.26)	4.59 (56.73)	25.03	25.48 (101.79)	−0.45 (1.79)
Dinajpur	14.12	11.76 (83.28)	2.36 (16.71)	14.86	14.21 (95.62)	0.65 (4.37)
Jalpaiguri	7.08	1.14 (16.10)	5.94 (83.89)	25.67	26.79 (104.36)	−1.12 (4.36)
Darjeeling	8.46	5.09 (60.16)	3.37 (39.83)	−0.87	0.38 (43.67)	−0.49 (56.32)
West Bengal (average)	14.02	12.06 (86.09)	1.95 (13.90)	5.47	5.19 (94.88)	0.28 (5.11)

Note Figures in the parentheses are percentage changes. *Source* Ray and Ghosh (2007)

moved to an Integrated River Basin Governance, whose tenets have been discussed by Ghosh and Bandyopadhyay (2019) and Ghosh (2020), where the basin ecosystem being the unit of governance. This new paradigm that essentially attempts to promote Integrated Water Resources Management at a basin scale can be summarised in the following forms.

1. Water is an integral component of the global eco-hydrological cycle and not merely an economic resource that can be stocked for human use only. Rather, there are ecosystemic requirements of water that have huge implications for the long-term ecosystem services.
2. Water and food need not have a positive linear relation. Rather newer water management norms, and heterodox economic thinking in water governance propagates that ever-increasing supply of water is not a prerequisute for promoting food security.
3. There is a need for classifying and prioritising the various types of demands for water, including those of the ecosystems. This is the fundamental tenet of the integrated approach.
4. The 'Neo-Malthusian' thinking of addressing 'scarcity' of water through supply augmentation plans needs to be replaced by demand management of water thereby helping the process of keeping water instream.
5. Rather than a reductionist and fragmented assessment, there remains the need for a more holistic and integrated assessment of the water development projects keeping in view the ecosystem processes, functions and services of water. With ecological economics being the pivotal discipline for such assessments, a new transdisciplinary framework for assessment needs to be adopted.

6. A trandisciplinary knowledge base needs to be developed acknowledging the dynamic interactivity of the various economic, ecological, social and cultural forces. This will require combining fluvial geomorphology, engineering, hydrology, hydrogeology, ecological sciences, tectonic sciences, ecological economics, law, international relations, political sciences, sociology, social anthropology, humanities and culture, and institutional theory so as to emerge with the appropriate institutional mechanisms for basin-level governance.
7. Holism in water governance needs to be promoted by comprehending the basin ecosystem as the unit of governance.
8. The flow regime should be understood as an equilibrium emerging from the dynamic interactivity of water-energy-biodiversity-sediments (WEBS). Any deviation from the equilibrium can create perturbation in the basin ecosystem (Bandyopadhyay, 2019).
9. Appropriate insitutional mechanisms for integrated basin governance needs to be designed carefully taking into consideration the multiplicity of the problems of water governance.
10. There is a need for shifting to a new globally accepted state-of-the-art definition of 'environmental flows' replacing the presently followed definition entailing barely percentage of total flow.

If one takes the cases of the Cauvery and the Teesta, this fragmented approach becomes extremely apparent. In fact, one may easily note that the above norms are completely vitiated. As far as the Cauvery case is concerned, there has been unbridled supply development especially in the upper reaches of the basin, with much concern to the delta ecosystem. This has not only caused flow regime changes in the downstream, but has also proved detrimental for a shrinking delta under conditions of sea-level rise (Ghosh et al., 2018). The fragmented governance has been noted in various other contexts in the Cauvery basin (Anand, 2004; Janakarajan, 2006). In 2007, the Cauvery Water Tribunal setup in 1990 gave its final award. The Tribunal's Award is a clear exhibition of the inherent reductionism often referred to as 'arithmetic hydrology' (Ghosh et al., 2018). The Tribunal arrived at a sum total of allocable water at 740 TMC, considering on 50% dependability of flows based on past precedence of estimates (Ghosh and Bandyopadhyay, 2018). The award reserved the 'quantity … for environmental protection' and 'quantity determined for inevitable escapages to the sea' as 10 TMC Ft and 4 TMC Ft, respectively. These numbers seem to be based on ad-hoc arrangements and arbitrary thinking not being supported by any scientific assessment, given that their origins have not been revealed in the award document.

They are merely 'arithmetic hydrological' solutions merely looking at economic use of water and treating it as a stock of resource to be stored and used for human convenience without any recognition of the impacts on the basin ecosystem.

The award completely ignored the impacts of climate change projections on the changing precipitation in South Asia that affects the seasonality and quantity of the Cauvery basin flows (Gosain et al., 2006). The sustainability of the proposed schedule recommending for greater releases during the period of July–September remains questionable, given the possibility of greater variability in the precipitation pattern.

Even the Tribunal does not bring groundwater within the ambit of allocation, despite extensively discussing about groundwater as an additional resource in Volume III of the *Report of the Cauvery Water Disputes Tribunal* discusses. As rightly Thakkar (2007) points out, '… Tamil Nadu, being the lower riparian, has significant availability of groundwater, while Karnataka and Kerala, being the upper riparian, have relatively little of it. … To allow unrestricted groundwater use and not to include groundwater in calculating water availability … is unscientific'.

The order has not really helped the process of setting up any statute or precedence of allocation that may be replicated in other disputes. Importantly, it has failed to create any mechanism to reward water use efficiency. Given the increasing propensity of water use in the basin especially for irrigated paddy, the Tribunal is expected to recommend some mechanism for improving the efficiency—for instance, through water pricing. Unfortunately, the award seems to be going the other way round.

However, subsequent controversies with the award brought the Supreme Court to intervene. In the Judgement of February 2018, departing from the existing view of water being state subject, the Supreme Court observed that water of the Cauvery river is a 'national asset and no single state could claim ownership over it' (Ghosh, et al., 2018; Mittal and Poovanna, 2018). This verdict, acknowledging the diversity and multidimensionality of water use, sets a benchmark in Indian water governance being a departure from archaic reductionist thinking. However, the present verdict does not have the cause of the ecosystem in its scope. For a more holistic water governance approach, it is important that 'environmental flows' literature is brought in the debate from the perspective that there is hardly a stakeholder who speaks for the ecosystem in contested claims for shared waters. Therefore, it remains on ecological scientists to advocate the cause of the ecosystems for life in the basin (Ghosh, 2018).

Even if the cause of the ecosystem remained missing, the Supreme Court verdict also directed GoI to set up of the Cauvery Management Board (CMB) in line with the Final Order of the Cauvery Water Tribunal, within 40 days of passage of the order. The centre pleaded for more time, and finally on 1 June 2018, the Cauvery Water Management Authority (CWMA) was constituted.

As can be noted from the tenets of promoting an integrated and holistic governance approach at the basin scale, the need for a basin-level organisation like CMB can never be overemphasised. River basin organisations (RBOs) can take a basin-scale perspective to governing flow regimes, though as institutions their success rates, in practice, have been variable. Yet, there is no denying that almost all the best practices imbibed in the RBOs have three characteristics in common: (a) there is an institutional acknowledgement of multidimensionality of water use and basin ecosystem; (b) there is a team constituted from various governmental agencies, academia, NGOs and civil society with both disciplinary competence and interdisciplinary understanding of critical issues and challenges of the respective basin; (c) a bottom-up governance structure and participatory approach is being followed.

The design of the CMB, as stated in the CWDT Award of 2007, misses out on all the elements. According to the award, the fulltime chairman should be an irrigation engineer of the rank of chief engineer, while the two members CMB needs to be made from the subject of engineering and agronomy, nominated from the respective ministries, namely water resources and agriculture. The representatives of the Central Government and the riparian states, and the secretary of the board are proposed to be irrigation engineers in different capacities. Such mono-track and mono-disciplinary board composition, confined to engineers and agronomists even in the Cauvery Water Regulation Committee (a committee to be constituted by the board), gives the perception as if this complex imbroglio can be resolved only by traditional engineering and agricultural solutions. This goes clearly against with ongoing global best practices and knowledge frontiers of integrated basin governance acknowledging the multidimensionality of the basin ecosystem in terms of its socio-economic, political and ecological criticality (Bandyopadhyay, 2009). It is not that such perspectives are new in India. The significance of such multidisciplinary perspectives in water governance in India finds copious mentions in two important reports published in 2016 from the Ministry of Water Resources, Government of India, namely *Draft National Water Framework Bill 2016*, and *A Twenty-first Century Institutional Architecture for India's Water Reforms*. Both were prepared under the chairmanship of Dr. Mihir Shah, but kept under carpet ever since.

At the same time, the very conceptualisation of the CMB in terms of its institutional structure makes its governance approach largely top-down, thereby making it exclusionary. This is clearly in contravention with global thinking of an integrated approach to the governance of river basins that recognises the multidimensionality of water in terms of its social, political and ecological importance. Such reductionist perspective of 'arithmetic hydrology' has aggravated the Cauvery conflict to the extent that exists today. It needs to include a great many more stakeholders at various levels including those for the ecosystems so as to follow a bottom-up approach, as can be witnessed in the case of the Mekong River Commission. The opportunity of creating a new RBO may be better used with a widening of the composition as argued above.

Even in the case of the Teesta, such reductionist engineering and 'arithmetic hydrological' thinking is quite prominent. Lack of an integrated approach to governance and sole reliance on the reductionist engineering paradigm that only considers marginal economic benefits with a myopic vision, the water resource development in the Teesta basin continues to follow a pathway that is socially and ecologically unsustainable by all means. The ramifications of such large-scale alterations in various stretches of the river and its tributaries are beginning to impact the local ecology and society in varied ways. This becomes apparent when one looks at the series of hydrpower projects on the basin. Most of these projects are in the upper reaches of the basin in the state of Sikkim (Basu, 2017).

With a total hydropower potential of 5352.7 MW (EPDS, 2020), the state of Sikkim is almost entirely located within the Teesta basin and is a frontrunner for hydropower development. A total of 47 hydropower projects are proposed in the mountainous parts of the basin spread over the states of Sikkim and West Bengal. As reported, 15 projects are in different stages of construction and are stated to be completed by 2022 (Rahaman and Mamun, 2020). In the rush to harness the hydropower potential and export the only resource that is available at scale, the regions fragile ecology and the dependence of the community on the resource is jeopardised. The construction of dams, the transfer of water through tunnels and the altered flow regime disrupt the longitudinal connectivity and habitat conditions for the freshwater biodiversity. There is water diversion from Gajaladoba through the Teesta Mahananda irrigation canal to meet the urban water needs of the growing urban centres of Siliguri and Jalpaiguri. The problem gets aggravated with the increasing acreage of irrigated paddy due to the movement of terms of trade towards paddy.

Lately, when the issue of Bangladesh–India water sharing recurred, the West Bengal CM took the position that the overall flow in Teesta in West Bengal has declined. As per an excerpt from a recent internal report on the Teesta prepared by an Expert Committee of West Bengal Government, as published in an article in thethirdpole.net on 14 April 2017, the water flow is '*one sixteenth of total water requirement in [the] two countries*'. (see Basu, 2017). This is in the context of boro paddy.

While such measurements have not been left for scrutiny and review, the mystery that arises is with increasing irrigated paddy acreage with a declining stream flow over years. It seems that neither West Bengal, nor Bangladesh has an idea that the mystery of disappearing water in the summer months needs to be traced back to the inorganic process of killing the river by as many as 30 hydropower projects (most of which are in Sikkim) in the stretch of the Teesta (operating and planned). Though hydropower is claimed to be 'non-consumptive' use of water being operational as 'run-of-river', during the phases of low flows the water needs to be stored in the 'pondages' upstream of these projects. Our own field observation reveals that due to the low flow at least 12–15 h of storage daily is required, before the turbines could function. With successive projects being at very short distances from each other, this substantially fragments the river, dries up the downstream, and proves detrimental for the biodiversity and critical ecosystem services like water provisioning and fisheries. At the same time, Bangladesh asserts that more than 4.45 million metric tons of rice production have been lost since 2006–07 due to massive irrigation failure due to the water diversion (Arfanuzzaman and Ahmad, 2015). The extraction of groundwater in northwest Bangladesh has also risen due to the three folds in dry season *boro* cultivation during 1981–2014 leading to widespread water insecurity in the region (Dey et al., 2017). This is a classic example of how myopic economics dominates over long-run sustainability concerns!

Chakrabarty and Homechaudhuri (2014) applied the predictions of the *River Continuum Concept* to chart out the zonation pattern based on fish species assemblage and their ecological attributes along the longitudinal stretch of Teesta in West Bengal. Their study of fish guild structure points out that the ichthyological diversity is maximum in the middle stretch (Gajoldoba, Domohoni) out of the total 142 km long stretch of the river from Rishi Khola to Haldibari that was studied. The diversity declines both upstream and downstream from the middle stretch. This richness in fish diversity is primarily attributed to optimal habitat and environment conditions in the middle stretch that allowed for large fish biomass, species diversity and community composition. With hydropower development and other anthropogenic pressures altering the quality and timing of flow as well as trapping sediments behind the concrete walls of dams, these conditions may change irreversibly.

The entire gamut of hydrological obscurantism also extends to viewing the waters of the Teesta as a stock of resource that needs to be diverted for 'productive purposes' of irrigation water supply. It also needs to be kept in mind that the irrigation infrastructure that has already been developed in West Bengal and Bangladesh is primarily focussed at facilitating the cultivation of dry season *boro* paddy. This invariably leads to a tussle between the two riparian nations during the lean period of flow over a highly critical stock of resource. Despite the writing on the wall for an immediate need of water demand management through a shift to water-efficient cropping, the situation has only provided fuel to regionalist sentiments with West Bengal claiming too little water to be shared and Bangladesh pointing at regional food insecurity in Bangladesh due to India's unilateral water withdrawal. Finally, global warming and climate change may impact the precipitation distribution in the basin at a scale which is both spatial and temporal. This will create its own share of contingencies and any project being developed in any part of the basin must take into account such possibilities. The lack of foresight regarding the impacts of changed precipitation pattern and flow regime in the planning and implementation of projects could further jeopardise the future hydro-relation between the two neighbours.

The Teesta case also brings to the fore the importance of 'free-flowing' rivers (Grill et al., 2019). It is generally difficult to delineate a free-flowing river, but the working definition goes as a river system that is largely unaffected by human interventions in its flow and connectivity. This entails a flow regime with water, silt and other natural materials sustaining the basin ecosystem in its natural form. This idea resonates well with the WEBS concept as stated earlier (Bandyopadhyay, 2019). The water-energy-biodiversity-sediment (WEBS) perspective of rivers is an important step towards developing a holistic basin governance perspective that includes combining the social and cultural aspects with ecological and engineering perspectives. This holism is missing in the governance of the Teesta basin. Neither there have been any attempts to develop any institutional mechanism for the purpose.

6 Concluding Remarks

The objective of this paper was to highlight that water disputes in India or as such in South Asia are results of three forces, namely the conflictual federalism (with water use being made a state subject), a wrong delineation of food security that completely misses out on the broader socio-ecosystemic implications, and lack of an integrated river basin approach to water governance. If one looks at all the three forces deeply, they all point to one umbrella factor: lack of a holistic approach. Here, we use the term 'holism' in order to indicate the theory that propagates that parts of the 'whole' are interconnected with each other in a way that that they cannot exist independently of the whole: the whole therefore needs to be understood as greater than the sum of the parts. This is exactly the case with governing river basins. The cases of Cauvery and Teesta adequately expose the lack of 'holism', and clearly reveal the fragmented nature of water governance.

With water use rights falling in the ambit of the federal states, water management falls under two different regimes, which leads to a fragmented governance approach much in contrast to holism. The case of Cauvery shows the conflict between two states on the basis of conflict over definitions of property rights. In the case of the Teesta, the conflict has taken the shape of a disputed situation not merely between two nations, but between the Union Government and the state of West Bengal. Whereas the Union Government shows intentions to get into an agreement with Bangladesh, it simply cannot bypass the state's concerns. On the other hand, hydropower projects in Sikkim have fragmented the river, leading to substantial drying out of the lean season flows.

On the other hand, a reductionist delineation of the food security is also responsible for the conflicts between the states and nations. Food security had traditionally been viewed from the perspective of producing water-guzzling paddy and wheat. While it started with the Green Revolution in the late 1960s, the introduction of minimum support price (MSP) mechanism in the late 1970s, governmental procurement policies through the Food Corporation of India (FCI) and state procurement agencies, and extensive development of irrgation potential acted together to make rice and wheat the crop of preference across the nation (Ghosh, 2019). With the MSP acting like a hedging instrument 'put option' with governmental procurement taking place, the farmers found that if the prices fall below the MSP, there is an option of selling their product at the MSP, which now becomes the 'floor price' for rice and wheat. This cushion against falling prices led to a ready market even under conditions of overproduction. Over time, MSP emerged as the price-setter in the markets. As shown earlier, the Commission for Agricultural Costs and Prices (CACP) increased the MSP of rice and wheat at faster rates than less water-consuming millets thereby affecting the market prices.

Finally comes the concern of reductionist engineering ways of looking at water. This is essentially the colonial tradition that south Asia still bears. This pradigm owes its origin in India to the establishment of Thompson Engineering College at Roorkee (now IIT Roorkee) during the British era that to train Indian engineers in the European knowledge of water engineering. The Sarada Barrage, flood control mechanisms of the Kosi, and the Upper Ganges Canal to divert water from the Ganges at Hardwar near Roorkee are all classic embodiments of this colonial engineering thinking. However, the British engineers could hardly understand and appreciate the Indian rivers, as the notion of 'summer monsoon' had been missing in their river management paradigm. Therefore, there was hardly a concept of 'drought' (or lean season flow) and 'floods' (peak flow) in their paradigm of 'arithmetic hydrology', where abundance or scarcity is defined only in per capita terms. Rather, the monthly hydrographs of most European rivers were almost horizontal lines with small undulations, with nominal seasonal changes that can be traced to variations in the precipitation regimes. Therefore, regular annual occurrences of monsoonal floods in the Ganges or the Cauvery floodplains were thought of as aberrations. Therefore, multipurpose projects that entailed irrigation benefits, flood control mechanisms and hydel projects were heralded at as harbingers of economic development. These projects were completely oblivious of the long-term implications on the ecosystem structures, processes, functions and eventually the ecosystem services which play an important role in livelihoods. The colonial hangover still continues in the water technocracy in India (Ghosh, 2020).

The need of the hour is a paradigm change from the reductionist approach to a holistic approach. These can be summarised in the following ways. First, ecosystems concerns need to be integrated in the long-term food security concerns of the society. This will entail an integrated resource governance approach taking into considertation the intextricable dynamics of land–water ecosystems at the basin level. Second, there is an urgent need to develop institutional mechanisms at the basin scale. Water being made into a state subject has fragmented water governance within the nation and has led to the phenomenon of 'conflictual federalism'. Third, IWRM needs to be taken up as the doctrine governing water at the basin scale. This will require appropriate institutional arrangements in the form of a transboundary river basin organisation with a transdisciplinary knowledge base, as has been stated earlier. Fourth, proper economic instruments like promotion of competing crops through support pricing and cost-recovery pricing of irrigation water is of utmost need in a scenario where agricultural water and energy use are highly subsidised and are subjected to reprehensible wastage.

References

Anand, P. B. (2004). *Water and identity: An analysis of the Cauvery River water dispute.* https://bradscholars.brad.ac.uk/bitstream/10454/2893/1/Paper3 Anand Water and Identity.pdf.

Arfanuzzaman, Md., & Ahmad, Q. K. (2015). Assessing the regional food insecurity in Bangladesh due to irrigation water shortage in the Teesta catchment area. *Water Policy, 18*(2), 304–317. https://doi.org/10.2166/wp.2015.072.

Bandyopadhyay, J. (2006). Criteria for a holistic framework for water systems management in India. In *Integrated water resources management. Global theory, emerging practice and local needs* (pp. 145–71). SAGE Publications Pvt. Ltd. https://www.cabdirect.org/abstracts/20073119034.html.

Bandyopadhyay, J. (2019). Towards a synergy-based approach to river basin governance. *Observer Reserach Foundation, 308.* https://www.orfonline.org/research/towards-a-synergy-based-approach-to-river-basin-governance-54786/

Basu, J. (2017). Teesta has one-sixteenth of water needed. *The Third Pole.* April 14, 2017. https://www.thethirdpole.net/2017/04/14/teesta-has-one-sixteenth-of-water-needed/

Beach, H. L., Hammer, J., Hewitt, J.J., Kaufman, E., Kurki, A., Oppenheimer, J. A., & Wolf, A.T. (2000). *Transboundary freshwater dispute resolution: Theory, practice, and annotated references.* New York: United Nations University Press.

Cauvery Water Disputes Tribunal. (2007). The report of the Cauvery water disputes tribunal with the decision: 5 Volumes. New Delhi.

Chakrabarty, M., & Homechaudhuri, S. (2014). Fish guild structure along a longitudinally-determined ecological zonation of Teesta, an Eastern Himalayan River in West Bengal, India. *Arxius de Miscel·lània Zoològica, 11* (0 SE-Articles). https://doi.org/10.32800/amz.2013.11.0196

Chokkakula, S. (2019). Interstate river water governance: shift focus from conflict resolution to enabling cooperation. *Centre for Policy Research.* June 13, 2019. https://www.cprindia.org/news/interstate-river-water-governance-shift-focus-conflict-resolution-enabling-cooperation

Choudhry, S., Khosla, M., Mehta, P. B., & Salve, H. (2016). *Inter-state river water disputes*. Oxford University Press. https://doi.org/10.1093/law/9780198704898.003.0028

Commission, Sarkaria. (1988). *Chapter XVII: Inter-State River Water Disputes*. https://interstatecouncil.nic.in/wp-content/uploads/2015/06/CHAPTERXVII.pdf

Council and Cooperation: International Cooperation—Water Resources—Sectors: National Portal of India. (2011). February 17, 2011. https://archive.india.gov.in/sectors/water_resources/index.php?id=6

Dey, N. C., Saha, R., Parvez, M., Bala, S. K., Saiful Islam, A. K. M., Paul, J. K., & Hossain, M. (2017). Sustainability of groundwater use for irrigation of dry-season crops in Northwest Bangladesh. *Groundwater for Sustainable Development, 4*, 66–77. https://doi.org/10.1016/j.gsd.2017.02.001

EPDS. (2020). Status of ongoing and/or completed schemes. *Energy & Power Department, Government of Sikkim*. https://power.sikkim.gov.in/status-of-ongoing-andor-completed-schemes/

Gebert, R. I. (1983). *The Cauvery River dispute: hydrological politics in Indian Federalism*. https://open.library.ubc.ca/collections/831/items/1.0095680

Ghosh, N. (2015). Challenges to environmental security in the context of India-Bangladesh trans-boundary water relations, *Decision* (Springer), *42*(2), 211–28. Special Issue on Managing Critical Resources: Food, Energy and Water.

Ghosh, N. (2016). Sustaining the liquid mosaic. *Economic and Political Weekly*. https://www.epw.in/journal/2016/52/water-governance/sustaining-liquid-mosaic.html

Ghosh, N. (2019, November 25). Why India has not been able to resolve the Teesta stalemate. *Observer Research Foundation*. https://www.orfonline.org/research/why-india-has-not-been-able-to-resolve-the-teesta-stalemate-58093/

Ghosh, N. (2020). Water wars over paradigms. *Observer Research Foundation*. https://www.orfonline.org/expert-speak/water-wars-over-paradigms-66120/

Ghosh, N., & Bandyopadhyay, J. (2009). A scarcity value based explanation of trans-boundary water disputes: The case of the Cauvery River Basin in India. *Water Policy, 11*(2), 141–167.

Ghosh, N., & Bandyopadhyay, J. (2018). Water needs a multi-disciplinary approach, Hindu Business Line, May 5. https://www.thehindubusinessline.com/opinion/water-needs-a-multi-disciplinary-approach/article23775668.ece

Ghosh, N., & Bandyopadhyay, J. (2019). Governance of the Brahmaputra Sub-basin: Exploring the Enabling Conditions, in Choudhury, E. and S. Islam (Eds) Complexity of Transboundary Water Conflicts: *Enabling Conditions for Negotiating Contingent Resolutions*. London: Anthem Press.

Ghosh, N., Bandyopadhyay, J., & Thakur, J. (2018). *Conflict over Cauvery waters: Imperatives for innovative policy options*. New Delhi: Observer Research Foundation.

Goel, S. (2019). S.R. Bommai vs. Union of India. *Law Times Journal*. October 2, 2019. https://lawtimesjournal.in/s-r-bommai-vs-union-of-india/

Government of West Bengal. (2010). Information on the present status of Teesta Barrage Project with respect to formulation of packages for execution under national project. https://eservices.wb.gov.in/portal/documents/10180/0/Programmes+of+the+state+government+for+the+welfare+of+unorganized+workers.../dc2fbfd8-0a04-4fd6-af76-9f89a236711f;jsessionid=mJzQD8ygoeQwe3UKr9c2TXTM?version=1.0

Goyal, M. K., & Goswami, U. P. (2018). Teesta River and its ecosystem BT. In D. S. Singh (Eds.), *The Indian rivers: Scientific and socio-economic aspects* (pp. 537–551). Springer. https://doi.org/10.1007/978-981-10-2984-4_37

Group, Strategic Foresight. (2013). *Rivers of peace: Restructuring India Bangladesh relations*. Strategic Foresight Group. https://www.files.ethz.ch/isn/172871/22345riversofpeace-website.pdf.

Howe, C. (2009). The return to the river basin: The increasing costs of 'jurisdictional externalities.' *Journal of Contemporary Water Research & Education, 131*(1), 26–32. https://doi.org/10.1111/j.1936-704x.2005.mp131001005.x.

Islam, Md. (2016). *Water use and poverty reduction* (Vol. 8). Springer. https://doi.org/10.1007/978-4-431-55172-0

Iyer, R. R. (2003). *Water: Perspectives, Issues, Concerns*. SAGE Publications India.
Joint Communiqué Issued on the Occasion of the Visit to India of Her Excellency Sheikh Hasina, Prime Minister of Bangladesh. (2010). Media Centre, Ministry of External Affairs. January 12, 2010. https://mea.gov.in/bilateral-documents.htm?dtl/3452/Joint+Communiqu+issued+on+the+occasion+of+the+visit+to+India+of+Her+Excellency+Sheikh+Hasina+Prime+Minister+of+Bangladesh
Kulshrestha, R. (2018). *Kuldip Nayar v. Union of India and Ors.—Case summary*. September 14, 2018. https://lawtimesjournal.in/kuldip-nayar-v-union-of-india-and-ors-case-summary/.
Lloyd, E. H., Maass, A., Hufschmidt, M. M., Dorfman, R., Thomas Jr, H. A., Marglin, S. A., & Fair, G. M. (1963). Design of water-resource systems; New techniques for relating economic objectives, engineering analysis, and government planning. *Journal of the Royal Statistical Society. Series A (General)*. https://doi.org/10.2307/2982245.
Mondal, Md. S. H., & Serajul Islam, Md. (2017). Chronological trends in maximum and minimum water flows of the Teesta River, Bangladesh, and its implications. *Jamba (Potchefstroom, South Africa), 9*(1), 373. https://doi.org/10.4102/jamba.v9i1.373
Noolkar-Oak, G. (2017). *Geopolitics of water conflicts in the Teesta River Basin*. https://gaurinoolkar.files.wordpress.com/2017/12/teesta-conflicts_gno.pdf.
PRS Legislative Research. (2019). The Inter-State River Water Disputes (Amendment) Bill, 2019. *PRSIndia*. July 26, 2019. https://www.prsindia.org/billtrack/inter-state-river-water-disputes-amendment-bill-2019
Rahaman, M. M., & Al-Mamun, A. (2020). Hydropower development along Teesta River Basin: Opportunities for cooperation. *Water Policy*. https://doi.org/10.2166/wp.2020.136.
Ranade, A., Singh, H., Sontakke, N. A. (2007). *Characteristics of hydrological wet season over different river basins of India*. RR-119. Indian Institute of Tropical Meteorology. https://doi.org/10.13140/RG.2.1.2034.9603
Ray, S., & Ghosh, D. (2007). Modern agriculture and the ecologically handicapped: Fading glory of Boro Paddy cultivation in West Bengal. *Economic and Political Weekly, 42*(26), 2534–2542. https://www.jstor.org/stable/4419758
Boundary Commission. (1950). *Reports of the members and awards of the Chairman of the Boundary Commissions*. Alipore.
Richards, A., & Singh, N. (1997). Two level negotiations in bargaining over water. In T. Parthasarathy, B. Dutta, J. A. M. Potters, T. E. S. Raghavan, D. Ray, & A. Sen (Eds.), *Game theoretical applications to economics and operations research*. Theory and Decision Library (Series C: Game Theory, Mathematical Programming and Operations Research) (Vol. 18). Springer.
Rudra, K. (2017). Sharing water across Indo-Bangladesh border. In T. D. S. Bandyopadhyay, A. Torre, & P. Casaca (Eds.), *Regional cooperation in South Asia* (pp. 189–207). Springer.
Saha, A., & Swaminathan, M. (1994). Agricultural growth in West Bengal in the 1980s—a disaggregation by districts and crops. *Economic and Political Weekly, 29*(13), A2–A11. https://www.epw.in/journal/1994/13/review-agriculture-review-issues-specials/agricultural-growth-west-bengal-1980s
Salman, S. M. A., & Uprety, K. (20030. *Conflict and cooperation on South Asia's international rivers*. In R. V. Van Puymbroeck (Ed.), *Law, justice, and development*. The World Bank. https://doi.org/10.1596/978-0-8213-5352-3
Stokes, D. (2013). *Political economy analysis of the Teesta River Basin*. Asia Foundation.
Swami, P. (2011). Manmohan says Mamata assented to Teesta Deal. *The Hindu*. September 8, 2011. https://www.thehindu.com/news/national/manmohan-says-mamata-assented-to-teesta-deal/article2433343.ece
Upadhyay, V. (2002). Cauvery, courts and some larger questions. *Economic and Political Weekly*. https://www.epw.in/journal/2002/35/commentary/cauvery-courts-and-some-larger-questions.html

Renewable Energy in India: What It Means for the Economy and Jobs

Meeta Keswani Mehra, Saptarshi Mukherjee, Gaurav Bhattacharya, and Sk. Md. Azharuddin

1 Background

Energy is an important input for spurring economic growth and development in that both fossil energy (FE) and renewable energy (RE) have strong interlinkages with crucial factors that characterize the macroeconomy, demographic profile, employment and energy economy of an emerging market economy such as India. Until 2017–2018, India recorded among the highest economic growth rates in the world, with an annual gross domestic product (GDP) growth of around 7–8%. However, in the second half of 2019, India began to experience a phase of economic slowdown attributed to the sluggish growth of industrial production, mainly, capital goods and electricity generation (Economic Times, 2020). In the last three quarters of the financial year (FY) 2019–20, the growth rate (at 2011–12 prices) witnessed a steady

The present study builds on the authors' earlier work as a four-report series published by the Climate Policy Initiative (CPI), New Delhi (Mehra et al. 2018). The authors are grateful to CPI for supporting this earlier work.

M. K. Mehra (✉)
Centre for International Trade & Development (CITD), School of International Studies (SIS), Jawaharlal Nehru University (JNU), New Delhi, India
e-mail: meetakm@jnu.ac.in

S. Mukherjee
Department of Humanities and Social Science (H&SS), Indian Institute of Technology - Delhi, New Delhi, India
e-mail: saptarshi@hss.iitd.ac.in

G. Bhattacharya · Sk. Md. Azharuddin
CITD, SIS, JNU, New Delhi, India
e-mail: gauravbh.eco@gmail.com

Sk. Md. Azharuddin
e-mail: azharlowa@gmail.com

P. Dasgupta et al. (eds.), *Sustainable Development Insights from India*,
India Studies in Business and Economics,
https://doi.org/10.1007/978-981-33-4830-1_17

decline from 4.3% in Q2 to 3% in Q4 (MoSPI, 2020). Moreover, it was during the last quarter of FY20 when the Indian economy reeled under an unanticipated shock with the outbreak of COVID-19 and the subsequent nationwide lockdown announced by the government. Therefore, as the nation grapples with the pandemic, the target of around 8% growth per annum during 2018–2023 (NITI Aayog, 2018) necessitates significant policy initiatives to fillip faster growth for the next 40 years. Under these extenuating circumstances, India's energy needs cannot be overlooked (MoSPI, 2017). India's economic growth has been estimated to have reduced to 4.2% in FY 2019–20 (ending in March 2020). Further, aggregate GDP is predictable to grow smaller by about 3.2–4.5% during the FY 2020–21, when the impact of COVID-19 will be felt the most. It is perceived that since stringent measures have been adopted to contain the spread of the virus, it will heavily curtail economic activity, resulting in an economic contraction in the short to medium term (IMF, 2020; World Bank, 2020). Notwithstanding the immediate impact of COVID-19, India aims to strive for a higher economic growth path in the medium to long run.[1] In fact, the government policy think-tank, National Institution for Transforming India (NITI) Aayog, is optimistic that the economy is going to revive after the containment of the disease, as the effects of stabilization policies like the fiscal stimulus amounting to 10% of GDP and the repo rate cuts are realized (Economic Times, 11 June 2020). Energy being a vital input to the production and consumption processes of an economy, it is relevant that its steady supply to each of the sectors is guaranteed for an inclusive, sustainable and clean overall economic growth.

There are several policy imperatives that deem it necessary to propel the Indian economy on a sustainable long-run growth path. At present, India accounts for around 18% of the world population; however, its share in global energy consumption is a mere 6%. Even as India's energy consumption almost doubled between the years 2000 and 2015, its per capita energy demand continued to be low, at around one-third of the world average, and much below the levels exhibited by the United States of America (USA) and the European Union (EU). However, the government is actively working towards strengthening distribution and access to modern and reliable energy sources through programmes such as the Integrated Power Development Scheme (IPDS), the Restructured Accelerated Power Development and Reforms Programme, the Saubhagya Scheme and the Deen Dayal Upadhyaya Gram Jyoti Yojana (DDUGJY). The year 2018 marked the achievement of 100% rural electrification, and there has been a subsequent decline in the estimated population without access to electricity from 240 million in 2015 to 100 million in 2018 (IEA/IEO, 2020).

In the longer run, India's energy consumption is slated to rise rapidly. According to India's Energy Outlook, 2015, brought out by the International Energy Agency, some of these trends are quite incredible (IEA/IEO, 2015). India's total energy demand is

[1]In one such statement, the World Bank Chief Economist for South Asia, Hans Timmer seems to suggest that, in the short run, India ought to start planning for a growth rebound, involving creation of new job opportunities, particularly at the local levels, coupled with the financial programs to avert bankruptcies, especially of the small- and medium-sized enterprises. In the longer run, one needs to perceive this as an opportunity for course correction and progressing the Indian economy on a sustainable growth path, both fiscally and socially (ET, 13 April 2020).

expected to be risen by the year 2040 on account of the size of its economic output that would enlarge to more than five times its prevailing level in terms of aggregate GDP, and a population growth rate that would make it the most populous country. Accordingly, IEO/ IEA (2015) envisages India's aggregate energy consumption to more than double by 2040, with a tremendous rise in the offtake of coal, oil and natural gas, often registering it as among the top energy consumption growth countries of the world.

In particular, the power sector will continue to be pivotal to India's future energy economy. The installed power capacity is expected to rise from around 380 gigawatts (GW) today to over 1000 GW in 2040 (Ministry of Power, 2020). Even as coal-fired generation would continue to play a key role (mostly at higher thermal efficiency levels), the rapid growth in RE, steered by solar and wind power, together with the increases in nuclear capacity would imply that these energy supply sources would account for over half of the new capacity additions between now and 2040 (IEA/IEO, 2015). However, these projections are sensitive to shocks created by the pandemic as worldwide energy demand has shrunk amidst dipping oil prices. While the government's efforts to revive the economy through various stimulus packages would mitigate the looming current economic uncertainty, the outcomes are likely to be discernible only in the medium to long term.

In the present scenario, two relevant questions with regard to the implications for energy demand emerge: one pertaining to concerns of energy security and another relating to environmental sustainability. The pandemic itself testifies the growing vulnerability of nations and re-establishes the contentious free-trade debate. As most nations openly censure China with its alleged role in the spread of the virus, the gradual move towards anti-globalization is perceptible. Measures to reduce import dependence and to seek relatively secure sources of goods and services in the world market would largely influence the growth trajectory of India. With substantial energy import dependence and sizeable potential for growth in per capita consumption as well as energy access for larger sections of population, India encounters the challenge of placating its energy security concerns.

Specifically, India's net energy import dependence has increased risen from around 31% in 2000 to 47% in 2015, and, recently to 49% in 2019, with little change in the diversity of supply sources (IEA Statistics; MoSPI, 2020). India has also set an ambitious target to set the share of natural gas in the energy mix to 30% in 2030 from 6% today. Despite the government's intensive efforts to diversify the sources of energy supply, the International Energy Agency estimations point out that the country's import dependency for oil (which was 80% in 2018) is likely to increase significantly in the coming decades. The IEA projections under the New Policy Scenario of India's Energy Outlook, 2015, show that India is likely to occupy the centre stage of the global energy landscape, with its share at around a quarter of the incremental global energy use up to the year 2040, which exceeds the levels for any other country, and amounts to the largest additional rise in both coal and oil consumption (IEA/IEO, 2015). Notwithstanding these trends, it is important to note that India is also expected to emerge as a key RE producer, with the second-largest solar market in the world.

India's increasing reliance on imported energy—especially oil and petroleum products—would have overwhelming implications for India's energy security, with overall energy import reliance likely to rise to 90% in 2040 (amounting to around 9.3 million barrels/ day in 2040) from 80% in 2018 (IEO/IEA, 2015). Thus, the adoption of appropriate policies helps enhance indigenous production as well as switch to alternative and sustainable sources of energy, such as solar and wind, is imminent. The government's intensive efforts to diversify the sources of energy supply and to reduce import dependence have been reflected in the adoption of major upstream reforms like Hydrocarbon Exploration and Licensing Policy (HELP), increased investment in overseas oil fields in the Middle East and Africa, expansion of stockholding capacities and reforms in the natural gas market (IEA/IEO, 2020).

In the absence of stricter environmental regulation aimed at controlling energy-related emissions of gases, dust and fumes from the power generation, industry and transport sectors as well as biomass and stubble burning, India's air pollution problems have been menacing. The reliance on conventional sources of energy (namely, coal, petroleum and natural gas) has posed a threat to environmental sustainability, at both local and global levels. The burning of fossil fuels and traditional biomass fuels releases carbon dioxide (CO_2), particulate matter (PM), nitrogen oxides (NO_x) and sulphur oxides (SO_x), all of which contribute to outdoor and indoor air pollution, global warming and climate change. India contributed 2238 million tons of CO_2 emissions in the year 2014, which is much higher than the 2000 level of 1032 million tons (World Bank, WDI). Projections by the World Resources Institute suggest that the level of emissions is going to rise significantly to 5271 million tons of CO_2 emissions in the year 2030 under the baseline inclusive growth (BIG) scenario (World Resources Institute, 2016). As countries negotiate to strike a cooperative mechanism in compliance with the Paris Agreement, the voluntary pledges of individual nations to lower greenhouse gas emissions may translate into a conceding on growth and development targets given the existing trade-offs. As for local pollution, the average annual exposure to particulate matter 2.5 ($PM_{2.5}$) ambient air pollution concentration in India in 2017 stood at 90.9 $\mu g/m^3$, which was found to be much higher than the world average of 45.5 $\mu g/ m^3$, and way above the mean levels for high-income industrialized countries of 14.7 $\mu g/ m^3$ (World Bank, WDI).

It is in this milieu that India's ambitious resolve to achieve its RE targets over the next 5 years or so gains eminence. India has been striving to attain the target of 175 GW of RE capacity by 2022, which includes 100 GW of solar and 60 GW of wind energy. In the longer run, it has resolved to achieve an ambitious target of 450 GW of renewable energy by 2030 (Economic Times, 31 Jan 2020). Higher RE dissemination could not just help feed into energy demands resulting from a rebounding economy in the medium to short run, and it would also help create job opportunities in local or regional settings. At the micro-level, a way to mitigate the economic and humanitarian shocks faced by India, especially by the rural poor and the informal (often self-employed) workers migrating back from cities and towns to rural areas, to earn a living and gain access to health care, is to examine rigorously the role that RE could play in providing alternative employment opportunities. From a more macroeconomic perspective, RE deployment has interactions with key variables that include GDP, demography, fiscal stimulus, energy imports, and energy access (rural electrification and access to clean fuels), all of which are facing stressful dynamics arising out of a slowing down of India's economic growth and made worse by the COVID-19 pandemic (ET, April 13, 2020). Resultantly, energy projections for the future serve as a guiding factor for the prevailing and proposed policy focus.

In light of all of the above, it is important to carry out a rigorous analysis to find answers to the following set of questions: (i) what are the key quantitative linkages between macroeconomic variables (such as GDP, population, employment, fiscal deficit, energy imports, energy access and return on capital) and RE growth in India? (ii) what will these relationship(s) imply for alternative paths for RE capacity development in India, both over medium- and long- time periods? (iii) what would be the predictions of RE generation in future? (iv) what will RE diffusion mean for creation of employment opportunities or jobs in the RE sector?

To answer the above questions, the paper delves into macroeconometric time-series methods to capture the potential role of RE in India, with special emphasis on the linkages that it may have with key macroeconomic variables, such as GDP, population, fiscal deficit, call money rate, energy imports and population's access to energy. The analyses include tests of stationarity, Granger causality tests and estimating a long-run co-integrating relationship using the auto regressive distributed lag (ARDL) model for the estimation and future projection of RE potential under alternative assumptions on macroeconomic variables used as drivers of RE. Further, the contribution of RE to job creation is assessed in this study by utilizing the normative estimates of NRDC-CEEW data (CEEW & NRDC, 2015, 2017) and mapping these onto RE projections from our macroeconometric exercise.

In energy economics, a motley of techniques has been used in order to project future energy scenarios, viz., optimization models like the Market Allocation model (MARKAL) (Seebregts et al., 2002; The National Energy Map, TERI, 2006), AIM/end-use model (Akashi et al., 2014), TIMES (Koljonen et al., 2012); dynamic simulation models including the Global-Macroeconometric Energy-Economy-Environment model (E3ME) and the Long-range Energy Alternatives Planning system (LEAP) (Dagoumas & Barker, 2010; Roinioti et al., 2012); computable general equilibrium (CGE) model (Proenca & Aubyn, 2013); and time-series modelling (Tiwari, 2011). Optimization models like MARKAL, AIM and TIMES employ linear programming techniques. While MARKAL takes into account the entire life cycle of an energy resource, starting with the point of their extraction to the their end-use, in choosing the optimum activity levels of processes that satisfy the constraints, such as primary energy availability, access to certain technology, emissions standards, at minimum cost, AIM and TIMES are advanced versions of MARKAL with new sets of features. In contrast, simulation models like E3ME, LEAP and CGE capture interlinkages and interdependencies between different parts of the economic and energy systems through feedback effects. CGE modelling has been one of the most powerful approaches to develop energy projections including Nong and Simshauser (2020) who use a GTAP-E-Power Model, a global CGE structure that utilizes comparative statics and to encompass details of electricity generation from different technologies. They derive the change in the output of the energy sectors using RE like wind power in India to be 408 in the baseline case, and this increases to 3941 under the scenario with a substantial push on input factor-augmenting technologies over the time span of 40 years from 2011 to 2050. With the expansion in RE systems in electricity generation, there is a concomitant fall in the percentage change in electricity output generated from FE; the percentage change being 474 and 69, respectively. A recent study by Laha et al. (2020) on energy demand for electricity generation develops a future RE scenario for the year 2030 with zero energy imports and exports and finds that the maximum share of RE in electricity generation would be around 32.7%, with an installed capacity of 80 GW of solar PV, 165 GW of wind and 15 GW of biogas. The corresponding projections by the International Renewable Energy Agency (IRENA) and The Energy and Resources Institute (TERI) stood at 31.3% and 37.8%, respectively. Chabadiya et al. (2020) use a simple logistic curve to simulate RE deployment in India under two scenarios, namely the realistic maximum and the theoretical maximum, and find that the solar power will attain saturation level in the year 2035, followed by bioenergy in 2040 and wind power in 2045.

The existing literature on time-series macroeconometrics modelling that aims to examine a time-based dependence structure between energy demand and/ or supply and macroeconomic drivers such as economic growth, employment, trade balance and emissions has provided mixed results as far as the time-dependent associations are concerned. Often, the disparate and equivocal conclusions are a result of varied methodologies used by these studies, for different groups of countries, different reference periods and utilizing diverse datasets. Most cross-country studies have relied on a structural vector autoregressive (SVAR) model or a vector error correction model (VECM) or a panel estimation (Silva et al., 2011; Onafowora & Owoye, 2015; Sasana & Ghozali, 2017). These examine the long-term association between RE consumption and economic growth. Furthermore, the aspect of employment generation from RE has been addressed by Wei et. al. (2010) and Lehr et. al. (2012), which suggests that the use of non-fossil fuel technologies generates more jobs than fossil fuel-based technologies. Studies on energy projections based on time-series estimation models have been quite sparse and unexplored to date.

The present analysis contributes to the existing literature on the long-run association between RE deployment and major macroeconomic variables, even as it takes into account the short- to medium-term economic implications of COVID-19 along with capturing the overall energy transitions in India. We take into account the inevitable short-run contraction in the RE markets in the country driven by the massive disruption in supply chains, labour supply shocks and policy changes resulting from tariff barriers to imports of solar PV panels and other RE equipment from China amidst the pandemic as well as the growing border tensions between India and China. Notwithstanding the sudden break in the energy transition path, it is expected that the market for RE will recover in the long run.

The key findings of this research were

- The ARDL model estimation pointed towards an equilibrium long-run co-integrating relationship between RE and select macroeconomic variables alluded to above. The long-run level of GDP, call money rate and ratio of renewable energy to fossil energy tariffs were found to be positively associated with RE diffusion, while variables such as the fiscal deficit, net energy imports, population access to electricity, population level and unemployment displayed a negative relationship with it.
- The growth of RE was found to be the maximum under the optimistic scenario, attaining a value of over 13.69 million tons of oil equivalent (MTOE) in 2022, 40 MTOE in 2032 and 104.48 MTOE in 2042. The analogous capacity levels for RE were estimated to be 105.34 GW in 2022, 285.87 GW in 2032 and a whopping 693.55 GW in 2042. The share of energy generated by RE in aggregate primary energy supply (TPES) (in MTOE) was found to rise from the prevailing less than 1–1.23% in 2022, 2.54% in 2032 and 5.18% in 2042.
- The growth under the business-as-usual case was not too far than in the optimistic one the initial years, but the gap tended to enlarge over time. RE generation was estimated slightly lower at 12.89 MTOE in 2022, 36.88 MTOE in 2032 and 91.88 MTOE in 2042. This would entail RE capacity of 104.84 GW, 270.96 GW and 609.88 GW in the respective years. Moreover, these implied relatively lower shares of RE to TPES (in MTOE) of 1.18% in 2022, 2.41% in 2032 and 4.58% in 2042.
- Under the pessimistic case, the growth of RE was found to be more sluggish, both in terms of energy supplied and RE capacity installed, as compared to BAU and OPT. It reached an energy supply level of 11.87 MTOE in 2022, 27.67 MTOE in 2032 and merely 50.90 MTOE in 2042. The associated capacity installed was estimated to be 102.34 GW, 209.32 GW and 337.88 GW in 2022, 2032 and 2042, respectively. Commensurately, it was estimated that the share of RE to TPES will be much lower at 0.92% in 2022, 1.60% in 2032 and 2.31% in 2042.
- Notably, relative to the *initial* official targets of *RE* capacity of 175 GW by 2022 projected by the government, our estimations show that these would be achieved with some delay. This finding conforms to the apprehensions voiced in this regard, given the available policy framework moving away from feed-in-tariffs to auction-based purchases, lack of grid infrastructure and evacuation constraints (LiveMint, 28 Dec 2017). More recently, the strain in India–China relations, and the consequent barriers to the imports of RE equipment from China, could also result in somewhat sluggish RE diffusion in the short- to medium-time frames. Specifically, we got that the official target is likely to be achieved during 2027–28 under the business-as-usual, a bit earlier, in 2026–27 under the optimistic case, and a lot later, in 2028–29 in the pessimistic scenario. Some of these outcomes could change as more recent data are incorporated in the analyses.
- More recently, the government of India has revised its RE capacity target to 227 GW by 2022, which according to our estimation will presumably be realized by

2029–30 under both—business-as-usual and optimistic scenarios—and by 2033–34 under the pessimistic case.

- The incremental jobs in the RE sector by the year 2022 would amount to 375 thousand, 379 thousand and 355 thousand in the business-as-usual, optimistic and pessimistic cases. In 2032, the cumulative jobs would expectedly rise to 1695 thousand, 1814 thousand and 1205 thousand, respectively, under the three scenarios. In 2042, the cumulative job creation levels would rise to 4390 thousand, 5055 thousand and 2227 thousand respectively, in the three alternative cases of business-as-usual, optimistic and pessimistic ones, respectively.
- Notwithstanding the delays in the achievement of RE targets, in addition to enhancing energy and environmental security, RE could offer significant employment co-benefits to the macroeconomy of India. This is especially relevant as India embarks on economic recovery in a post-COVID-19 phase.

The remaining sections of this paper are structured as follows. Section 2 provides a discussion of the specific methods and models that are used for quantifying the relationship between RE and key macroeconomic variables, lays out the results and provides a discussion on these in terms of its key implications. Section 3 lays down the assumptions for forecasting RE diffusion in the medium and long runs under alternative macroeconomic, policy and demographic scenarios for India, as well as discusses the results of this forecasting exercise. Section 4 utilizes the estimates of Sects. 2 and 3 to forecast the job creation potential for RE in India, based on normative data. Finally, Sect. 5 summarizes the important takeaways from this research and concludes.

2 RE Growth and Its Macroeconomic Linkages in India

2.1 Methods and Models

Select macroeconometric time-series estimation methods have been used to establish the long-run equilibrium relationship between RE supply/ generation and other macroeconomic variables, namely, economic output, rate of unemployment, budgetary deficits, net energy imports, population size, call money rate and relative RE-FE tariffs for India. The aim was to ascertain the long-run co-movement of variables. To begin with, unit-root tests were carried out to check whether the time-series variables are stationary (non-stationary), that is, whether a shift in time causes a change in the shape of the distribution of the variable or not.[2] For our analysis, the unit-root test utilized was the modified Dickey–Fuller test (also known as the DF-GLS test) as suggested by Elliott et al. (1996). Further, Granger causality tests

[2]Stationarity implies the basic properties of the distribution, such as the mean, variance and covariance, remaining constant over time. The innovative work for deriving unit-root test in time series was done by Dickey and Fuller (Fuller, 1976; Dickey & Fuller, 1979).

were attempted.[3] Granger causality tests carried out for any pair of variables showed the manner in which the causality between them would work. These were useful in estimating the underlying relationships that helped to set up the macroeconometric model. Finally, an ARDL model was estimated for establishing the temporal relationship between RE and the macro variables listed earlier. The ARDL model typically derives the quantitative relationship between (economic) variables in a single-equation time-series setting.[4] ARDL method was introduced by Pesaran et al. (2001) in order to incorporate a mix of stationary or integrated of order zero, i.e. I(0), and non-stationary, integrated of order 1, i.e. I(1), time-series variables in the same estimation. In case all the variables are stationary (i.e. I(0)), then OLS is appropriate, and if all are non-stationary (i.e. I(1)), then it has been advised to use the vector error correction (VECM) model (Johansen, 1988, 1991). This estimated ARDL equation helped us predict RE generation and associated RE capacity in the future.

2.2 Dataset

The data used in this study were annual statistics for the 27-year period, spanning 1990–2016.

The macroeconomic variables considered were: gross domestic product (constant prices) (GDP_CONS), population (POP), unemployment rate ($UNEMP$), gross fiscal deficit (FIS_DEF), call money rates ($CALL\_RATE$), renewable energy generation (comprising solar, wind and biomass only) (RE), total primary energy supply ($TPES$), net energy imports (NET_EN_IMP), annual energy outlay of the government (EN_OUT), population with access to electricity ($POP\_ACCESS\_PERCENT$) and RE-FE tariff ratio ($RE\_TO\_FE\_TARIFF$).

The data on GDP_CONS, POP, $POP\_ACCESS\_PERCENT$ and $UNEMP$ were extracted from the World Bank data, specifically, from the World Development Indicators (various issues). The time series on $CALL\_RATE$ and FIS_DEF was obtained from the Reserve Bank of India database. Next, the dataset on RE, $TPES$ and NET_EN_IMP was derived from the country-level energy balance tables of the International Energy Agency (online database). The time series on EN_OUT was from the Economic Survey (various issues) brought out by the Ministry of Finance, Government of India. Finally, the series on the ratio $RE\_TO\_FE\_TARIFFS$ was worked out from the data published by the Central Electricity Regulatory Commission (CERC's annual reports, various issues).

The units of measurement of these variables as well as the detailed data sources are provided in Table 1.

---

[3]Granger causality is a statistical concept of causality that is based on the prediction of a time series by using prior values of another time series.

[4]ARDL models are standard least squares regressions that include lags of both the dependent variable and explanatory variables as regressors (Greene, 2008).

For select and variables, the data were missing. These missing data have been imputed by using the method of interpolation.

2.3 Results

2.3.1 Unit-Root Test Results

The specific test used in this research to investigate the presence of unit root in the variables was DF-GLS method. The modified Dickey–Fuller t-test was carried out.[5]

Table 1 Variables names, codes, units of measurement and data sources

Variable	Code used	Unit	Source
Gross domestic product	*GDP_CONS*	Billion INR (constant 2011–12 prices)	World Bank[a]
Population	*POP*	Billions	World Bank[b]
Unemployment rate	*UNEMP*	Percent	World Bank[c]
Gross fiscal deficit	*FIS_DEF*	Billion INR (current prices)	Handbook of Statistics on the Indian Economy, Reserve Bank of India[d]
Call money rate	*CALL_RATE*	Percent	Database on Indian Economy, Reserve Bank of India[e]
Renewable energy (solar, wind, biogas)	*RE*	Million tons of oil equivalent (MTOE)	Country Statistics, International Energy Agency[f]
Total primary energy supply	*TPES*	MTOE	Statistics, International Energy Agency[g]
Net energy imports	*NET_EN_IMP*	MTOE	Statistics, International Energy Agency[h]
Energy outlay of government	*EN_OUT*	Billion INR at current prices	Handbook of Statistics on the Indian Economy, Reserve Bank of India[i]

(continued)

[5]Basically, this test is an expanded version of the Augmented Dickey–Fuller test, where the time series are transformed through generalized least squares (GLS) regression before doing the test.

Table 1 (continued)

Variable	Code used	Unit	Source
Percent of population with access to electricity	*POP_ACCESS_PERCENT*	Percent	World Bank[j]
Relative RE-FE tariffs	*RE_TO_FE_TARIFF*	Unit free ratio	Annual Reports, Central Electricity Regulatory Commission[k]

[a]World Bank, World Development Indicators (WDI). https://data.worldbank.org/data-catalog/world-development-indicators; downloaded 10 Sept 2017.
[b]Ibid.
[c]Ibid.
[d]Reserve Bank of India, Handbook of Statistics on Indian Economy. https://www.rbi.org.in/Scripts/AnnualPublications.aspx?head=Handbook%20of%20Statistics%20on%20Indian%20Economy; downloaded 1 Oct 2017
[e]Reserve Bank of India, Database on Indian Economy. https://dbie.rbi.org.in/DBIE/dbie.rbi?site=home; downloaded 1 Oct 2017
[f]International Energy Agency (IEA) Statistics. https://www.iea.org/statistics/statisticssearch/report/?country=INDIA&product=balances&year; downloaded 10 Sept 2017
[g]Ibid.
[h]Ibid.
[i]Ibid.
[j]Ibid.
[k]Central Electricity Authority (2016). https://www.cea.nic.in/reports/monthly/installedcapacity/2016/installed_capacity-03.pdf; downloaded 23 Aug 2017

Studies by Elliott et al. (1996), and some later research, have shown that this test has a significantly higher power over the earlier variants the augmented Dickey-Fuller test.

The main results of the DF-GLS test for all the variables considered for our analysis are tabulated in Table 2.

The results in Table 2 show that the variables GDP_CONS, FIS_DEF, RE, $TPES\_$, NET_EN_IMP and ratio of $RE\_to\_FE\_TARIFF$ are non-stationary, i.e. integrated of order one or I(1). The remaining variables such as POP, $CALL\_RATE$, $UNEMP$, EN_OUT and $POP\_ACCESS\_PERCENT$ were found to be stationary, namely, integrated of order zero or I(0).

2.3.2 Granger Causality Test Results

Two tables (Tables 3 and 4) display the results of the Granger causality tests for different variables with alternative lag structures.

As can be seen in Table 4, RE was found to Granger cause $CALL\_RATE$, while FIS_DEF and RE display a two-way causality. Further, GDP_CONS Granger causes RE, RE Granger causes NET_EN_IMP, and there is a two-way causality between RE and $RE\_TO\_FE\_TARIFF$, RE and POP and RE

Table 2 Results of DF-GLS unit-root stationarity test

Variable	Order of integration found
GDP_CONS	I(1)
POP	I(0)
UNEMP	I(0)
FIS_DEF	I(1)
CALL_RATE	I(0)
RE	I(1)
TPES	I(1)
NET_EN_IMP	I(1)
EN_OUT	I(0)
POP_ACCESS_PERCENT	I(0)
RE_TO_FE_TARIFF	I(1)

Source Authors' calculations

Table 3 Results of the Granger causality tests

Granger causality from $X \rightarrow Y$	Number of lags	Level of significance corresponding to these alternative lags
$D\_RE \rightarrow CALL\_RATE$	5	10%
$D\_FIS\_DEF \rightarrow D\_RE$	2, 3	5%, 5%
$D\_RE \rightarrow$ D_FIS_DEF	5	5%
$D\_GDP\_CONS \rightarrow D\_RE$	2, 3, 4	5%, 5%, 5%
$D\_RE \rightarrow D\_NET\_EN\_IMP$	2, 3, 4	5%, 5%, 5%
$D\_RE\_TO\_FE\_TARIFF \rightarrow D\_RE$	5, 6, 7	10%, 5%, 5%
$D\_RE \rightarrow D\_RE\_TO\_FE\_TARIFF$	7	5%
$POP \rightarrow D\_RE$	2, 3	5%, 10%
$D\_RE \rightarrow POP$	3, 4	10%, 5%
$POP\_ACCESS\_PERCENT \rightarrow D\_RE$	2, 3, 4	5%, 5%, 5%
$D\_RE \rightarrow POP\_ACCESS\_PERCENT$	2, 4	5%, 5%
$D\_RE \rightarrow UNEMP$	2, 4, 5, 6	10%, 10%, 10%, 5%

Source Authors' calculations

and $POP\_ACCESS\_PERCENT$. Finally, RE Granger causes $UNEMP$. These causalities helped in explaining later the relationships that were derived from the co-integration ARDL equation.

Table 4 Direction of relation between key variables

Direction of the causality relationship	Cases
Unidirectional from RE to others	*RE →CALL_RATE*
	RE →FISCAL_DEFICIT
	RE →NET_ENERGY_IMPORTS
	RE → UNEMPLOYMENT_RATE
Unidirectional towards RE from others	*RE ←GDP*
Bidirectional causality	*RE ↔FISCAL_DEFICIT*
	RE ↔RE_TO_FE_TARIFF
	RE ↔POPULATION
	RE ↔ POPULATION_ACCESS_PERCENTAGE

Source Authors' estimations

2.3.3 ARDL Model Estimates and Interpretation

The Johansen co-integration test results pointed to the fact that the variables are co-integrated. The VECM estimation results were not found to be acceptable as the error correction term was non-converging. Furthermore, the VECM procedure was unable to combine I(0) and I(1) variables. So, we relied upon an ARDL model estimation, especially in view of the unit-root test results that showed that some of the variables mentioned in were I(0), while some other important ones were I(1) (see Table 2 for these details). Several combinations of variables were assessed that could potentially drive the dissemination of RE in India. Also, different lag structures were tested to estimate most accurate ARDL model.

The following long-run equilibrium co-integrating ARDL relationship was found among the specified variables:

$$\begin{aligned}\mathrm{RE} = {} & 9.2186 + 0.0017CALL\_RATE - 0.00004FIS\_DEF \\ & + 0.00013GDP\_CONS - 0.0017NET\_EN\_IMP - 11.6036POP \\ & - 0.005474POP\_ACCESS\_PERCENT \\ & + 0.05937RE\_TO\_FETARIFF - 0.1475UNEMP. \end{aligned} \tag{1}$$

Further, the coefficient estimated for the previous period error correction term [ECM(-1)] was found to be negative and significant and also lying-in range −1 and 0. Specifically, this was found to be −0.46, which indicated that any short-run deviation in the last period was corrected for in the next period by almost 46%, implying convergence in values over time.

The equilibrium co-integrating long-run relationship in Eq. (1) implied that, in the long run, GDP_CONS, $CALL\_RATE$ and $RE\_TO\_FE\_TARIFF$ are positively associated with the RE diffusion, while variables such as FIS_DEF, NET_EN_IMP, POP, $POP\_ACCESS\_PERCENT$ and $UNEMP$ have a negative relationship with RE dissemination in India.

Table 5 ARDL bound test results

Calculated F-statistics	Df	10% Critical value		5% Critical value		1% Critical value	
		Lower bound	Upper bound	Lower bound	Upper bound	Lower bound	Upper bound
5.47	8	1.85	2.85	2.11	3.15	2.62	3.77

Source Authors' estimations

The results of the bound test for above estimations are reported in Table 5.

As can be seen from Table 5, the calculated F-statistics was found to be higher than both the lower bound critical values and as well as the upper bound critical values at all the levels of significance. Thus, the null hypothesis of the non-existence of no long-run relationship among the variables is rejected.

In intuitive terms, the results in Eq. (1) can be explained as follows.

RE generation (RE) is positively associated with $CALL\_RATE$, as the coefficient of $CALL\_RATE$ in the right-hand side of Eq. (1) is estimated as 0.0017. In general, a higher $CALL\_RATE$ constitutes either the cost of capital (that may dampen investment in RE) or a return on capital investment (that encourages investment in RE equipment). From a macroeconomic perspective, for the period being analysed, the latter effect would have outweighed the former, implying that RE and $CALL\_RATE$ have been found to move together.

Further, according to Eq. (1), the coefficient of the budgetary deficit variable FIS_DEF is found to be negative, at −0.00004, implying that RE generation (or RE) moves counter-cyclically with FIS_DEF. Note that, ARDL captures the co-movement of the macro variables. Here, in the aggregate, a higher FIS_DEF is primarily indicative of higher fiscal support to FE generation. Moreover, RE prices are now derived from reverse-price auction bids by the private companies in this sector. This has reduced the dependence on feed-in-tariffs, and the associated reliance on subsidies or other forms of fiscal support. Consequently, a higher level of RE penetration could move concomitantly with a lower fiscal deficit on account of a relatively contracting share of FE generation. The direction of this relationship might undergo a change as more recent data become available on RE diffusion or else the support policies provide for higher fiscal support.

RE generation (that is, RE) is also found to be positively linked to GDP_CONS. The coefficient estimated for GDP_CONS in Eq. (1) is 0.00013, which could be interpreted as higher incomes inducing a higher willingness to pay for RE or a higher demand for RE, entailing this positive relationship. This could also take to mean that RE is a normal good, implying cleaner energy is demanded more at higher incomes at the macro-level.

RE is found to have been negatively correlated with reduced the NET_EN_IMP, which is as one would expect. This derived from the sign of the coefficient of $NET - EN\_IMP$ being −0.0017. On average, a higher RE generation translates into lower energy imports, which in India, which are mainly

FE imports of hydrocarbon and coal. Thus, RE substitutes for FE in the aggregate, implying a countering relationship between these two variables over time.

Interestingly, with both aggregate POP and $POP\_ACCESS\_PERCENT$, RE generation (RE) is found to have a negative correlation for the time period being analysed. The respective numerical coefficients are found to be -11.6036 and -0.005474. Seemingly, a bigger population size or a larger access of the population to power supply places a heavier demand on the economy in terms of demand for energy. Given the limited time-series dataset (for 27 years only) and India's excessive dependence on FE in a large measure so far, the estimation shows that both—higher POP and $POP\_ACCESS\_PERCENT$—tend to inhibit RE penetration—or that these move in opposite directions over time. The direction of this link is likely to undergo a change as more RE diffusion occurs, especially in remote geographical locations.

A positively signed coefficient of 0.05937 for $RE\_TO\_FETARIFF$ points to the fact that RE and relative RE to FE tariffs are linked positively. This is straightforward, as a higher $RE\_TO\_FETARIFF$ implies a more lucrative tariff for RE, implying a larger diffusion level for it.

The coefficient of $UNEMP$ in the right-hand side of Eq. (1) is found to be -0.1475. That is, RE generation (RE) is estimated to move negatively, or countercyclically, with aggregate $UNEMP$ rate in India. A higher RE diffusion is typically associated with lower unemployment rate, at the economy-wide level, pointing towards significant job creation potential in the RE sector.

On the whole, the study finds that RE diffusion in India is positively related to GDP_CONS, $CALL\_RATE$ and $RE\_TO\_FE\_TARIFF$ and negatively with FIS_DEF, NET_EN_IMP, POP, $POP\_ACCESS\_PERCENT$ and $UNEMP$. These relationships carry important policy messages. For example, a higher economic growth rate, a higher return on investment and more remunerative RE tariff would incentivize RE growth. Alternatively, a higher budgetary support (by running larger fiscal deficit) and energy imports will tend to dampen RE diffusion and vice versa. Likewise, for India, a case can be made for the fact that a higher level of population or a higher energy access of the population would generally translate into greater reliance on FE rather than RE. This last effect can be offset or even inverted as more stable, cheaper and technologically advanced RE supply options are discovered and deployed.

Next, by utilizing the ARDL Eq. (1), three alternative features, namely, business-as-usual (BAU), pessimistic and optimistic are charted out for RE penetration in India's energy economy. These both—RE generation and associated RE capacity—are done for the years 2020–2042, for each of the three cases. Among these alternative scenarios, it is the pessimistic case that captures most accurately the present-day reality of the impact of COVID-19 pandemic on macroeconomic aggregates and government policies, both in the short- to medium-time frames.

In what ensues, a discussion on the assumptions made to characterize these three scenarios, and the forecasted values of RE (both generation and capacity) into the future are presented.

3 Forecasting of RE Generation and Associated Capacities in India Under Alternative Scenarios

By relying on the estimated long-run co-integrating relationship for the temporal behaviour of the concerned variables using the ARDL model, as defined in Eq. (1), three different scenarios, namely, BAU, pessimistic and optimistic were articulated.

The three scenarios have been constructed by linking these to the alternate official trends or policy targets that would have consequences for trends in key macro variables for the Indian economy going forward. This is based on a detailed reading of the official documents and other policy papers towards judicious construction of these alternative futuristic cases. The ARDL equation can be further relied upon for creating additional configuration of assumptions to derive more scenarios and carry out the sensitivity analysis with respect to RE growth and job creation potential; the latter are discussed in the next section.

BAU depicts the business-as-usual scenario for RE penetration, which hypothesizes a continuation of the older trends and policies, with no significant discontinuities. The optimistic scenario (OPT) subsumes the movement of the key driving variables being such that these encourage a higher growth of RE as compared to the BAU. Alternatively, the pessimistic scenario (PES) defines a case where all the main driving macroeconomic variables move in a fashion in the future so that they dampen RE diffusion. It is this last case that replicates the prevailing economic situation of slower economic growth and higher unemployment rates as is being faced by the Indian economy (at least in the short to medium term) due to the recent lockdown on account of the COVID pandemic. The OPT and PES cases imply important policy and structural changes, which are not modelled explicitly but rather driven through changes in the macroeconomic variables.

In the next section, the assumptions made about the path of the key macro variables that drive these three different scenarios are presented and discussed.

3.1 Assumptions Underlying Alternative RE Forecasts

3.1.1 Call Rate

The call money rate ($CALL\_RATE$) was taken to be the same across all the three cases, resting on the premise of an independent central bank that basis its decisions on the economic fundamentals and monetary policy of the country, and has no association with any policy framework for promoting RE. The average weighted monthly call money rate of the Reserve Bank of India (RBI) for most of the months in 2019 was found to be around 6%. At the beginning of 2020, RBI announced a 75 basis points (bps) reduction in the repo rate, following RBI's COVID-19 measures (Economic Times, 30 Mar 2020). To incorporate this reduction in the repo rate in our model, we have taken into account the call money rate for the year 2020 to be

Table 6 Forecasted values of call money rate for the BAU, optimistic and pessimistic scenarios (percent)

Year	Call rate
2020	5.2
2021–24	5.8
2025–29	5.6
2030–34	5.5
2035–42	5

5.2%, which is a reduction of 80 bps from the previous year. Furthermore, we have assumed that the call rate will be 5.8% from the next year onwards till 2024 as the economy begins to recover from the COVID-19 shock. Over the longer time period, the call money rate is assumed to fall slowly and become constant at around 5% for the remaining years up to 2042. The specific assumptions are listed in Table 6.

3.1.2 Gross Fiscal Deficit (as a Percentage of GDP)

As regards gross fiscal deficit percentage (*FIS_DEF*), the baseline (BAU) scenario was described based on the figures suggested by the NITI Aayog report titled, "Three Year Action Agenda, 2017–18 to 2019–20" (NITI Aayog, 2017). Under the optimistic scenario, *FIS_DEF* was assumed to plummet at a slower rate than in the case of the BAU, assuming an increase in the public expenditure for developmental infrastructure and others. Contrasting with this, the pessimistic scenario is characterized by a fall in *FIS_DEF* at a rate higher than in the case of the optimistic scenario as well as the BAU. As a measure to tackle COVID-19, the central government of India has announced a Rs 20 lakh crore[6] package on 12 May 2020 to stimulate the economy. This stimulus package is put at around 10% of GDP. The entire package of Rs 20 lakh crore had been criticized on several grounds as having a smaller direct impact (The Hindu BusinessLine: 19 May 2020; The Wire: 17 May 2020). Specifically, it is being claimed that a mere 1–2% of GDP would be directed as the net stimulus package for the economy to mitigate the impact of COVID-19. In light of these arguments, the *FIS_DEF* as a percentage of GDP for 2020 was assumed to be 5.2%, 5.5% and 4.8% under the BAU, optimistic and pessimistic scenarios, respectively. For other years, the specific values postulated are provided in Table 7.

3.1.3 GDP Growth Rate

Business-as-Usual

In the year 2020, the GDP (*GDP_CONS*) growth rate declined significantly on account of a weaker growth experience of the previous year and the economic shock

[6] 1 lakh = 10^5 and 1 crore = 10^7.

Table 7 Forecasted values of gross fiscal deficit under different scenarios (percent)

Year	BAU	Optimistic	Pessimistic
2020	5.20	5.50	4.80
2021–24	3.30	3.45	3.20
2025–29	3.20	3.30	3.10
2030–34	3.00	3.20	3.00
2035–42	3.00	3.00	2.90

Table 8 Forecasted values of annual GDP growth rate under different scenarios (percent)

Year	BAU	Optimistic	Pessimistic
2020	−3	−1.5	−3.5
2021–24	7.5	8	6.5
2025–29	8	8.2	6
2030–34	8	8.5	5.5
2035–39	8.2	8.8	5
2040–42	8.5	9	5

of COVID-19. Following the forecast of the World Bank,[7] we have assumed that the growth rate for the year 2020 under the BAU scenario would be (-)3% (a negative growth experience). However, the Indian economy would witness a faster recovery or rebound in the following years, such that during 2021–2024, the growth rate has been assumed to rise to 7.5% per annum, followed by an even higher rate of 8% annually for the next ten years. For 2035–2039, the annual GDP growth rate was assumed at 8.2%. Further, from 2040 onwards, it was assumed to be around 8.5% (see Table 8 for this).

Optimistic

Under this scenario, the annual GDP growth rate in constant prices (*GDP_CONS*) was assumed to accelerate faster in comparison with the other two scenarios. In 2020, despite the COVID-19 shock, GDP would shrink by a smaller amount, registering a (negative) growth rate of (−)1.5%, and from 2021 onwards, GDP would recover and grow at a rate of 8% per annum up until 2024, and then by 8.2% annually till 2029. From 2030 onward, the annual growth rate was assumed to be around 8.5% followed by an even higher 8.8% annual rate for 2035–2039. These can be found in Table 8.

Pessimistic

The pessimistic scenario is portrayed by a slowing down of the annual GDP growth rate (*GDP_CONS*) from 6.5% in 2021–24 to 5% in 2035–2042, again with the

[7]The Indian economy is assumed to contract by 3.2% according to Global Economic Prospects, June 2020, a World Bank group's flagship report. Following this we have assumed a 3% contraction in the Indian economy for our analysis.

Table 9 Future values of share of NET_EN_IMP in TPES under different scenarios (as fraction)

Year	BAU	Optimistic	Pessimistic
2020–24	0.450	0.430	0.470
2025–29	0.420	0.400	0.440
2030–34	0.419	0.399	0.439
2035–39	0.415	0.395	0.435
2040–42	0.412	0.392	0.432

significant exception for the year 2020 where (a negative) GDP growth rate was assumed to be at (-)3.5% due to COVID-19. This follows the commonly available estimates of growth in this year. The trend of these growth rates is tabulated in Table 8.

3.1.4 Net Energy Imports (as a Percentage of Total Primary Energy Supply)

The BAU scenario assumptions for net energy imports share (*NET_EN_IMP* to *TPES* ratio) are derived from the projections made by the India Energy Outlook, World Energy Outlook Special Report, 2015. The NITI Aayog's report on "Draft National Energy Policy (2017)" predicts *NET_EN_IMP*'s share in *TPES* to be around 36–55% (which include imports of non-commercial energy as well). In addition, the "Report on Energy Efficiency and Energy Mix in the Indian Energy System (2030), Using India Energy Security Scenarios, 2047" (2015) also presupposes it to be around 45–59.3% under the optimistic scenario. Since we have excluded non-commercial energy from our analysis, the ratio of *NET_EN_IMP* to *TPES* was assumed to be slightly lower than the above-mentioned levels. For the pessimistic scenario, we have made a 2-percentage point addition to the BAU figures. More details can be found in Table 9.

3.1.5 Population

The aggregate population (*POP*) of India in the year 2016 was estimated at 1.32 billion. From the year 2020 onward, population (*POP*) increases are predicted at five-yearly intervals as shown in Table 10. Accordingly, the average population level for 2020–24 was put at 1.353 billion, and similarly for the later years, on each five-yearly basis. Furthermore, the level of population was assumed to remain unchanged across all the three scenarios.

Table 10 Forecasted levels of population for BAU, optimistic and pessimistic scenarios (billions)

Year	Population
2020–24	1.353
2025–29	1.37
2030–34	1.39
2035–39	1.4
2040–42	1.45

Table 11 Forecasted values of population with access to electricity for BAU, optimistic and pessimistic scenarios (percent)

Year	Population percentage with access to electricity
2020	85
2021	85.009
2022	85.011
2023	85.013
2024	85.015
2025–42	100

3.1.6 Share of Population with Access to Electricity

As per the Pradhan Mantri Sahaj Bijli Har Ghar Yojana ('Saubhagya') and Deen Dayal Upadhyaya Gram Jyoti Yojana (DDUGJY), it has been planned that by the end of the year 2018, every family in rural and urban India would have been fully electrified. But, the analysis of the data seems to suggest that, in 2016, only 82% of the population had access to electricity in India. Even though, through DDUGJY, almost all the villages in India are now electrified, making electricity available for 24 × 7 h as well as its last-mile supply remains a challenge for the government (LiveMint, 29 Dec 2019). Thus, it would be somewhat optimistic to assume that full electrification of the country with complete access by the end of 2018 was accomplished. We have, thus, moderated this level by assuming a slower (though steady) rise in the fraction of the population with access to electricity (*POP_ACCESS_PERCENT*), such that according to our assumptions, the country would get fully electrified (with last-mile connectivity) only by the year 2025. The anticipated s population share with access to electricity has been taken as the same across the three scenarios (Table 11).

3.1.7 RE Versus FE Tariffs

The report of the Expert Group on 175 GW RE by 2022 (2015) by NITI Aayog has projected that the price of RE to conventional coal-based thermal power price would be equalized by 2031–32. Beyond this time point, RE prices would in fact fall below the coal-fired power prices. Since this target seems to be rather ambitious, we have assumed more realistic numbers under each of our three scenarios. We expect that the ratio of these prices (*RE_TO_FE_TARIFF*) would reach 1:1 the quickest in the

Table 12 Forecasted values of RE versus FE tariff under different scenarios (ratio)

Year	BAU	Optimistic	Pessimistic
2020	1.2399685	1.2828201	1.1256978
2021	1.2056873	1.2592517	1.0628489
2022	1.1714061	1.2356834	1
2023	1.1371249	1.2121151	1
2024	1.1028437	1.1885467	1
2025	1.0685624	1.1649784	1
2026	1.0342812	1.14141	1
2027	1	1.1178417	1
2028	1	1.0942734	1
2029	1	1.070705	1
2030	1	1.0471367	1
2031	1	1.0235683	1
2032–42	1	1	1

pessimistic scenario, followed by the BAU case and the optimistic scenario. This is plausible as we consider these prices to be supply-side tariffs. Since relative prices change based on the regulatory regime, which occurs with a time lag, the numbers unavailable for a few intermittent years have been worked out by interpolation. For the specific values, see Table 12.

3.1.8 Unemployment Rate

Business-as-usual

Due to the COVID-19 pandemic shock to the labour market in the year 2020, it has been assumed that under BAU, the unemployment rate (*UNEMP*) would increase to an average of 8%.[8] From the year 2021, the unemployment rate would be moderated to 7.2%, which was assumed to fall further to 6.8% during 2022–2024. Then onwards, it has been assumed that the unemployment rate would change only every four to five years. The specific assumptions on unemployment rates under BAU are shown in Table 13.

[8]During January 2020 and February 2020, the unemployment rate in India was 7.2% and 7.7%, respectively (CMIE), even though during March, April, May and June, unemployment is expected to rise sharply but may decrease in the later part of the year as the economy is expected to have a strong recovery later (India's economy will see strong recovery next year- S&P, RT, 15 June 2020, https://www.rt.com/business/491827-india-economy-strong-recovery/), accessed 20 Jun 2020. Thus, unemployment for the entire year is assumed to be 8% under BAU.

Table 13 Forecasted values of unemployment rate under different scenarios (percent)

Year	BAU	Optimistic	Pessimistic
2020	8	6.8	9.5
2021	7.2	6.4	8.5
2022–24	6.8	6.3	8
2025–29	6.5	6	7.5
2030–34	6	5.7	7
2035–39	5.7	5.3	6.5
2040–42	5.5	5	6

Optimistic

In case of the optimistic scenario, for the year 2020, the unemployment rate was taken to be 6.8%, and for 2021, it was assumed to be 6.4%. But, for the subsequent years (that is, post 2021), it was assumed that *UNEMP* will decrease and will fall at a faster rate as compared to the BAU scenario. Like in BAU, in the optimistic scenario as well, it has been taken that *UNEMP* will change every four to five years, whose details are provided in Table 13.

Pessimistic

In the year 2020 and 2021, under the pessimistic scenario, the unemployment rates have been assumed to be the highest, at around 9.5% and 8.5%, respectively. Later, from the year 2022 to 2024, *UNEMP* has been assumed to fall. For the other years starting from 2025, unemployment rate would change every four to five years. More details are compiled in Table 13.

3.2 RE Energy and Capacity Forecasts Under Alternative Scenarios

RE forecasts have been made using the estimated co-integration ARDL equation in (1) and by imputing assumed future values of the variables in the right-hand side of the equation as laid out in the discussion of the last subsection. As for the specific projections, the following results were derived.

As shown in Table 14, the growth of *RE* was found to be the highest under the optimistic (OPT) scenario, reaching a value of over 13.69 MTOE in 2022, 40 MTOE in 2032 and 104.48 MTOE in 2042. The corresponding capacity levels for *RE* were found to be 105.34 GW in 2022, 285.87 GW in 2032 and a whopping 693.55 GW in 2042. For this, we have used initial average capacity utilization factors for RE be in the range of 15–16% and slowly rising to 20% in the future years. The estimates for the year 2040 and 2041 were derived to be 581.98 GW and 635.58 GW, respectively,

Table 14 RE (Solar, wind and biogas) energy and capacity forecasts under alternative scenarios

Year	BAU case		Optimistic case		Pessimistic case	
	RE forecast in BAU (in MTOE)	RE capacity BAU (in GW)	RE forecast in OPT (in MTOE)	RE capacity OPT (in GW)	RE forecast in PES (in MTOE)	RE capacity PES (in GW)
2020	9.78	81.17	10.40	81.21	9.17	81.13
2021	11.36	93.30	12.05	93.45	10.55	92.17
2022	**12.89**	**104.84**	**13.69**	**105.34**	**11.87**	**102.34**
2023	14.48	116.57	15.44	117.94	13.20	112.35
2024	16.19	129.03	17.33	131.43	14.62	122.83
2025	17.99	141.93	19.28	145.08	15.89	131.76
2026	20.12	157.06	21.55	161.00	17.37	142.14
2027	**22.41**	**173.22**	**24.01**	**178.08**	**18.94**	**152.96**
2028	24.89	190.47	26.68	196.41	20.60	164.24
2029	27.58	208.87	29.57	216.07	22.37	176.01
2030	**30.35**	**227.54**	**32.64**	**236.77**	**23.94**	**185.91**
2031	33.49	248.54	36.17	260.42	25.75	197.40
2032	**36.88**	**270.96**	**40.00**	**285.87**	**27.67**	**209.32**
2033	40.55	294.90	44.16	313.27	29.69	221.70
2034	44.51	320.46	48.67	342.76	31.83	234.56
2035	48.84	348.08	53.74	375.67	33.85	246.27
2036	53.59	378.09	59.27	411.28	36.00	258.51
2037	58.74	410.20	65.29	449.72	38.26	271.15
2038	64.31	444.56	71.84	491.20	40.64	284.23
2039	70.34	481.33	78.97	535.99	43.13	297.76
2040	**76.56**	**518.64**	**86.39**	**581.98**	**45.25**	**308.36**
2041	83.90	562.65	95.04	635.58	48.01	322.88
2042	**91.88**	**609.88**	**104.48**	**693.55**	**50.90**	**337.88**

Source Authors' calculations
Bold refer to the RE capacity forecasts for years that serve as milestones with regard to the goals of the government of India on RE generation

which were found to be closer to the estimates by NITI Aayog under Vision 2040.[9] The share of energy supplied by *RE* to *TPES* was found to rise from the prevailing less than 1–1.23% in 2022, 2.54% in 2032 and 5.18% in 2042.

In comparison, the growth of *RE* under the BAU was estimated to be closer to OPT in the early years, but the gap tends to widen over the longer period of time. It was estimated at lower levels of 12.89 MTOE in 2022, 36.88 MTOE in 2032 and 91.88

[9]Draft National Energy Policy, NITI Aayog, GOI (Version as on 27.06.2017). It says that "by 2040 a likely capacity (for renewables) of 597–710 GW is expected to be achieved", page 41, Chapter 6, Sect. 6.1.

MTOE in 2042. These amounted to capacity requirements of 104.84 GW, 270.96 GW and 609.88 GW in the respective years, based on the same plant utilization factor levels as in OPT. Moreover, these amounted to the shares of *RE* to TPES (both measured in MTOE) of 1.18% in 2022, 2.41% in 2032 and 4.58% in 2042.

Finally, under the pessimistic (PES) outlook, the growth of RE was found to be much slower, both in terms of RE energy supplied and associated required capacity to be installed, as compared to BAU and OPT. It reached an energy generation level of 11.87 MTOE in 2022, 27.67 MTOE in 2032 and merely 50.90 MTOE in 2042. The associated capacity needed to be installed, assuming the same levels of plant capacity utilization factors, would be 102.34 GW, 209.32 GW and 337.88 GW in 2022, 2032 and 2042, respectively. Accordingly, it was estimated that the share of *RE* to *TPES* will be 0.92% in 2022, 1.6% in 2032 and 2.31% in 2042.

The following three graphs capture these trends over time (see Figs. 1, 2 and 3).

Notably, in comparison with the earlier announced official goal of RE capacity of 175 GW by 2022, and the later revised capacity of 227 GW projected by the government, our estimations have shown that these are likely to be achieved with a delay. This ties in with the recent forebodings expressed about the prevailing policy regime for encouraging RE development now moving away from feed-in-tariffs to auction-based purchases as well as lack of grid infrastructure and evacuation constraints (LiveMint, 28 Dec 2017). More recently, tensions between India and China have led to some concerns about the rise in tariff barriers on imports of RE equipment from China, which would potentially further slowdown RE diffusion. Specifically, our estimations have shown that the initial government targets of 175 GW would likely be achieved only by 2027–28 under the BAU, a bit earlier, in 2026–27 in case of the OPT, and much later, in 2028–29 in the PES scenario. The Government of India revised its targeted RE capacity to a more ambitious level of 227 GW by 2022. According to our estimations, these capacities would presumably be realized only by 2029–30, both under BAU and optimistic scenarios, whereas the same are likely

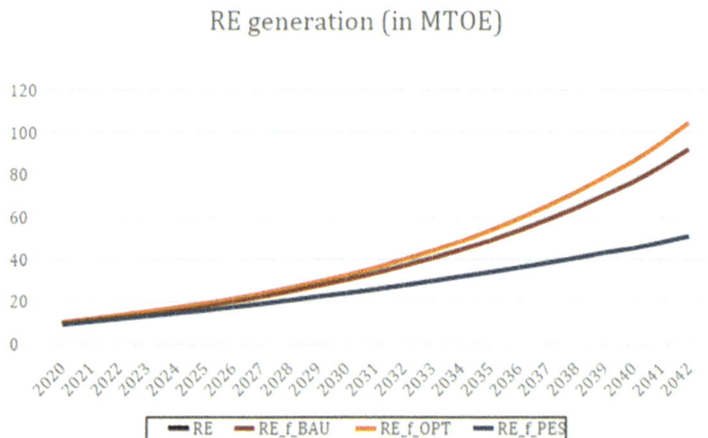

Fig. 1 RE generation forecasts under the three scenarios. *Source* Based on authors' calculations

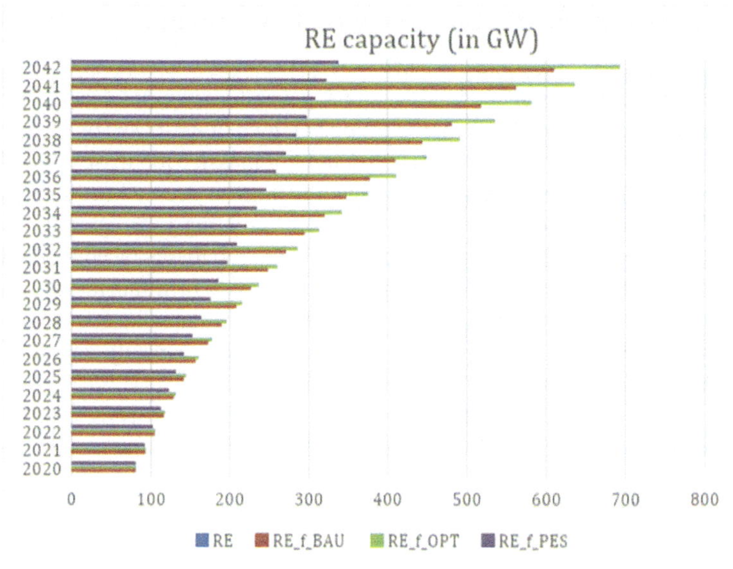

Fig. 2 RE capacity forecasts under the three scenarios. *Source* Based on authors' calculations

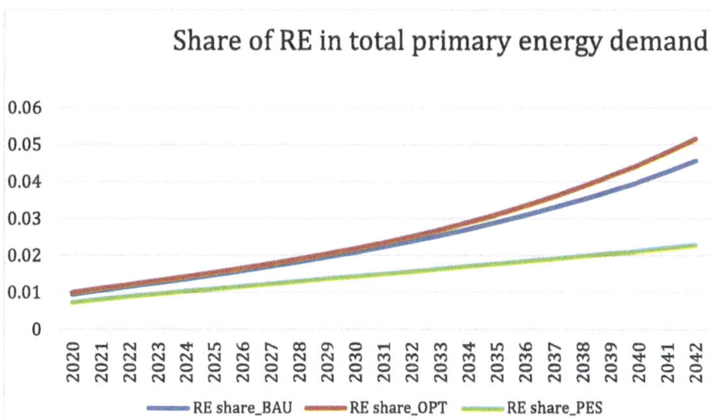

Fig. 3 Share of RE in total primary energy supply under the three cases. *Source* Authors' calculations

to be achieved by 2033–34 under the pessimistic scenario. Thus, the revised official forecasts have been found to be a bit too bold, and plausibly, likely to be achieved somewhat later in time, depending on how the macroeconomic scenarios, policy execution and technical (grid-related) constraints unfold over time. Much, of course, depends on how the RE technology evolves to deal with issues of intermittency and storage and extent of supportive policies for faster RE diffusion.

4 Future RE Capacity and Job Creation Potential

As India endeavours to augment the share of RE generation in its total primary energy supply, an important thought is the job creation potential of RE-based power capacity. This aspect gains even greater importance in light of massive job losses faced by the workforce in India consequent upon the recent lockdown deemed necessary due to the COVID-19 pandemic. Additional avenues for creating jobs, such as those in the RE sector, could be a way forward to mitigate the job losses faced by the Indian labour force, especially in the rural and informal sectors. In fact, Jain and Patwardhan (2013), who also studied the employment impacts of RE, state that RE technologies create a higher number of jobs per unit of installed power capacity and per unit of power generated than conventional FE technologies.

While not attempting to do any comparisons with FE, our analysis in this section aims to estimate the direct employment generation from the incremental RE capacity that would be installed, as those worked out in Sect. 3.

This section lays out the methodology and estimates the number of jobs created due to diffusion of solar (distinctly for ground-mounted and rooftop solar PV) and wind power projects in India. For working out the shares of solar PV and wind, we had assumed the proportions of incremental capacities and jobs created per unit capacity to be similar to CEEW and NRDC (2017) (refer to Table 15). According to CEEW and NRDC (2017), the levels of the job years comprise those for the purpose of business development, design and pre-construction, actual construction and project commissioning and operations and maintenance. The specific values used are also compiled in Table 15.

By relying on these values and utilizing the assumption that the shares across different RE technologies would not change over the time frame of forecasting, we obtained the following direct jobs generation potential for India (see Tables 16, 17 and 18 for these estimates). The additional jobs by 2022 would be around 375 thousand, 379 thousand and 355 thousand in case of BAU, OPT and PES scenarios, respectively. In 2032, the cumulative additional green jobs are expected to increase to 1695 thousand, 1814 thousand and 1205 thousand, respectively, under the three cases. Further into the future, in 2042, the cumulative job creation levels would mount to 4390 thousand, 5055 thousand and 2227 thousand respectively, in the case of BAU, OPT and PES, respectively.

It is important to emphasize that the specific variable pertaining to unemployment considered for estimating the ARDL equation (in Sect. 3) is the *rate* of unemployment in the economy (denoted by UNEMP). Despite our efforts, we could not access

Table 15 Assumptions used for solar and wind capacity shares and job years by type of technology

RE technology	Shares in total capacity	Job years/MW
Ground-mounted solar PV	0.375	3.45
Rooftop solar PV	0.25	24.72
Wind	0.375	1.27

Source CEEW and NRDC (2017)

Table 16 Incremental and cumulative job creation under BAU scenario ('000 jobs)

BAU				
Year	Incremental jobs in ground-mounted solar	Incremental jobs in rooftop solar	Incremental jobs in wind	Cumulative jobs (solar + wind)
2022	61	291	22	375
2032	215	1027	79	1695
2042	438	2095	161	4390

Source Authors' calculations

Table 17 Incremental and cumulative job creation under optimistic scenario ('000 jobs)

OPT				
Year	Incremental jobs in ground-mounted solar	Incremental jobs in rooftop solar	Incremental jobs in wind	Cumulative jobs (solar + wind)
2022	62	294	23	379
2032	234	1116	86	1814
2042	527	2519	194	5055

Source Authors' calculations

Table 18 Incremental and cumulative job creation under pessimistic scenario ('000 jobs)

PES				
Year	Incremental jobs in ground-mounted solar	Incremental jobs in rooftop solar	Incremental jobs in wind	Cumulative jobs (solar + wind)
2022	58	276	21	355
2032	138	661	51	1205
2042	166	795	61	2227

Source Authors' calculations

data on a consistent time series on the *level* of unemployment, or the number of unemployed people, for India for the 27-years period which our analysis spans. Thus, we could not estimate the aggregate macro-level (net) job creating potential of RE. Nevertheless, the results presented here will be useful for policymakers in estimating the employment potential of RE generation, subject to the proviso that these numbers *may not* necessarily be incremental. For the latter, a more elaborate, economy-wide general equilibrium analysis is deemed necessary, which was outside the scope of this study.

5 Conclusion and Key Takeaways

India's energy consumption and supply are expected to rise substantially in coming decades. According to India's Energy Outlook, 2015, brought out by the International Energy Agency, some of these future trends are quite overwhelming (IEA/IEO, 2015). India's aggregate energy demand is expected to rise by 2040, on account of the sheer size of its economic output (GDP), which is likely to expand to more than five times its prevailing level and population growth that would make it the most populous country in the world. Accordingly, IEO/ IEA, 2015, predicts that India's aggregate energy consumption would more than double by 2040, implying that this would be among the highest energy consumption growth experienced by any country across the globe.

The growing demand for energy has raised two key concerns: those pertaining to environmental sustainability and energy security. Absent stringent regulation to control and mitigate energy-related emissions of gases, dust and fumes from the power sector, industry and transport, India's air pollution problems loom large, especially in urban and industrial towns and cities. The tremendous dependence on imports of conventional energy like coal, oil, natural gas has posed a grave threat to India's energy security. With the substantial potential for growth in consumption per person as well as the emphasis on providing greater energy access, India faces the challenge of placating its energy security concerns. Consequently, adoption of customized policies aimed at enhancing indigenous production as well as encouraging the use of cleaner, sustainable and decentralized sources of energy, such as solar and wind, is impending. Apparently, the recent policy push towards RE and indigenous production of energy substantiates an optimistic scenario for the future of India's energy economy.

The Government of India has ramped up the ambitious plan of achieving 175 GW of RE by 2022 to approximately 227 GW, of which the break-up proposed across technologies is: 113 GW of solar, 67 GW of wind, 10 GW of biomass, 6 GW of small hydro and 31 GW of floating solar and offshore wind.

RE (as much as FE) tends to have a strong interface with the key factors that describe the macroeconomy, demographics and the energy economy of India. Accordingly, the scope of this research was charted out. In the aggregate, this research aimed to quantify the relationships between macroeconomic and demographic variables (namely, GDP, population, employment, fiscal deficit, energy imports, energy access, return on capital and so on) with RE deployment in the Indian context. Using macroeconometrics and time-series methods, these relationships were captured under alternative cases of RE diffusion (linked to the key macroeconomic and demographic variables), in the short-, medium- and long-run time frames. These comprised of tests of stationarity, Granger causality tests and co-integration using an ARDL model framework. Based on these relationships, forecasts of RE generation and associated capacity requirements were worked out for three different scenarios (business-as-usual, optimistic and pessimistic). The research also ascertained the impact of RE diffusion on the incremental job generation in the RE sector, using prescriptive data on job creation per unit of capacity installed in the solar and wind sectors.

The key results and takeaways from our analysis were as follows.

The ARDL model equation derived an equilibrium co-integrating long-run relationship between *RE* and important macroeconomic variables. The long-run levels of *GDP_CONS, CALL_RATE* and *RE_TO_FE_TARIFF* were found to have a positive association with the diffusion of *RE*, while variables such as *FIS_DEF, NET_EN_IMP, POP, POP_ACCESS_PERCENT* and *UNEMP* displayed a negative link with RE in India. Intuitively, we have the following takeaways.

RE generation was found to be positively linked to *CALL_RATE*. In general, a higher *CALL_RATE* could be perceived either as the cost of capital (that may inhibit investment in RE) or a return on capital investment (that boosts investment in RE technologies). At the macro-level for the years being considered, the latter effect seemed to be more important than the former, implying that *RE* and *CALL_RATE* moved pro-cyclically. *RE* generation was found to move inversely with *FIS_DEF*. That is, a higher *FIS_DEF* pointed towards higher financial support to *FE* generation. A higher level of *RE* diffusion was, thus, commensurate with a lower fiscal deficit on account of a lower share of FE generation.

As expected, *RE* generation was also found to be positively related to *GDP_CONS*, implying positive income effects on the demand for *RE*. Further, *RE* displayed a negative relationship with *NET_EN_IMP*. Thus, RE could be a strong substitute for *FE* in the aggregate, implying a mutually offsetting movement between the two.

Interestingly, with aggregate *POP* and *POP_ACCESS_PERCENT*, *RE* generation displayed a negative correlation or counter cyclicality. Intuitively, a larger population size or higher access of the population to power supply tends to place a heavier demand for energy. Given the limited time-series dataset (for 27 years only) and India's excessive dependence on *FE* so far, the estimation seems to point out that both—higher population or population's access to electricity—were inclined towards lowering RE penetration. We reckon that the direction of this link would change as more RE diffusion happens.

RE and *RE_TO FE_TARIFF* moved together in a direct fashion. This was due to the fact that a higher *RE_TO_FE_TARIFF* implied a more lucrative tariff for *RE*-based technologies, entailing its higher diffusion. Further, *RE* generation was found to move counter-cyclically with aggregate *UNEMP* rate. A higher RE diffusion is generally believed to have a larger employment potential at the economy-wide level.

Utilizing the ARDL equation in (1), three different scenarios, namely business-as-usual (BAU), pessimistic and optimistic, were postulated for forecasting different levels of *RE* diffusion in India's energy economy. The forecasts of RE generation and associated *RE* capacity were made for the years 2020–2042, for each of the three scenarios.

The growth of *RE* was found to be the sharpest under the optimistic (OPT) scenario reaching a level of over 13.69 MTOE in 2022, 40 MTOE in 2032 and 104.48 MTOE in 2042. The corresponding capacity levels for *RE* technologies were found to be of the order of 105.34 GW in 2022, 285.87 GW in 2032 and a whopping 693.55 GW in 2042. The estimate for the year 2040 was 510 GW, which is closer to those put out by the NITI Aayog. Commensurate with these numbers, the share of energy supplied by *RE* in aggregate *TPES* was found to rise from the existing around 1% to 1.23% in 2022, 2.54% in 2032 and 5.18% in 2042. The predictions for BAU were found to be nearer to those in OPT in the early years, but the gap tended to widen over the longer run. RE generation was estimated slightly lower at 12.89 MTOE in 2022, 36.88 MTOE in 2032 and 91.88 MTOE in 2042. This amounted to a required capacity of 104.84 GW, 270.96 GW and 609.88 GW in these respective years. Moreover, these translated into a share of *RE* to *TPES* of 1.18% in 2022, 2.41% in 2032 and 4.58% in 2042. For the pessimistic (PES) case, the growth of *RE* was substantially sluggish, both in terms of energy supplied and capacity installations, as compared to BAU and OPT. It reached an energy supply level of 11.87 MTOE in 2022, 27.67 MTOE in 2032 and merely 50.90 MTOE in 2042. The associated capacity installation levels were estimated at 102.34 GW, 209.32 GW and 337.88 GW in 2022, 2032 and 2042, respectively. Accordingly, the share of *RE* to *TPES* was lower at 0.92% in 2022, 1.60% in 2032 and 2.31% in 2042.

Notably, relative to the *initial* official targets of *RE* capacity of 175 GW by 2022 projected by the government, our estimations show that these are likely to be achieved later in time. This could be ascribed change in the policy support that has moved away from feed-in-tariffs to auction-based purchases, lack of grid infrastructure and evacuation constraints (LiveMint, 28 Dec 2017) and, more recently, the strained India–China relations and the consequent impact on imports of RE equipment. Specifically, we get that the target is likely to be achieved during 2027–28 under the BAU, a bit earlier, in 2026–27 under the OPT case, and a lot later, in 2028–29 in the PES scenario. More recently, the government of India has revised its RE capacity target to 227 GW by 2022, which according to our estimation will presumably be realized by 2029–30 under both—the BAU and the optimistic scenario—and by 2033–34 under the pessimistic case.

Using these RE capacity addition requirements, assuming that the shares across different RE technologies (solar, wind and others) remain stable over the years of forecasting, and relying on select norms of job creation for the individual technologies, we obtained the following direct additional job creation potential for India. It was found that the incremental jobs by 2022 would be about 375 thousand, 379 thousand and 355 thousand in BAU, OPT and PES scenarios, respectively. In 2032, the cumulative additional jobs were expected to rise to 1695 thousand, 1814 thousand and 1205 thousand, respectively, under the three cases. In 2042, the cumulative job creation levels would rise to 4390 thousand, 5055 thousand and 2227 thousand respectively, in the case of BAU, OPT and PES.

Furthermore, the results of our research have important policy implications. The study pointed out that key macroeconomic factors are links with RE penetration in India. RE diffusion was found to have a positive association with *GDP_CONS*, *CALL_RATE* and *RE_TO_FE_TARIFF* and a negative one with *FIS_DEF, NET_EN_IMP, POP*, *POP_ACCESS_PERCENT* and *UNEMP*. These carry significant messages, such as a higher economic growth rate, a higher return on investment, and a more remunerative RE tariff would stimulate RE technology growth. Alternatively, higher subsidies to FE and greater reliance on energy imports will inhibit RE diffusion. Similarly, for India, a case can be made for the fact that a higher population level or higher energy access could translate into greater reliance on *FE* rather than *RE*. Thus, for a clear switch to RE, a greater technological and policy push would be needed.

The study would be useful to policymakers in estimating the employment potential in general and green jobs in particular associated with RE generation. This is, of course, subject to the proviso that these numbers may not necessarily be incremental. To come up with the additional job creation potential of RE, a more extensive, economy-wide general equilibrium analysis may be required. Nevertheless, given that employment generation is high on the priority of the government, any quantified estimates of potential employment opportunities in the RE sector constitute useful co-benefits for policy formulation.

References

Central Electricity Authority. (2016). Monthly Report. New Delhi. https://www.cea.nic.in/reports/monthly/installedcapacity/2016/installed_capacity-03.pdf. Accessed August 23, 2017.

Chabhadiya, K., Ranjan Srivastava, R., & Pathak, P. (2020). Growth projections against set-target of renewable energy and resultant impact on emissions reduction in India. *Environmental Engineering Research, 26*(2), 200083.

CEEW and NRDC. (2015). *Clean energy powers local job growth in India*. https://shaktifoundation.in/wp-content/uploads/2014/02/NRDC-CEEW-Report-India-CleanEnergyJobs-Feb-20151.pdf. Accessed August 23, 2018.

CEEW and NRDC. (2017). *Greening India's workforce: Gearing up for expansion of solar and wind power in India*. https://ceew.in/pdf/CEEW%20NRDC%20%20Greening%20India's%20Workforce%20report%2020Jun17.pdf. Accessed August 23, 2018.

Central Electricity Authority (2016). https://www.cea.nic.in/reports/monthly/installedcapacity/2016/installed_capacity-03.pdf. Accessed August 23, 2017.

CMIE, Unemployment rate in India. https://unemploymentinindia.cmie.com/. Accessed 30 Jun 2020.

Dickey, D. A., & Fuller, W. A. (1979). Distribution of the estimators for autoregressive time series with a unit root. *Journal of the American Statistical Association, 74*(366a), 427–431.

Elliott, G., Rothenberg, T. J., & Stock, J. H. (1996). Efficient tests for an autoregressive unit root. *Econometrica, 64*, 813–836.

ETBFSI. (2020). Indian banks cut interest rates following RBI COVID-19 measures. ET 30 Mar 2020. https://bfsi.economictimes.indiatimes.com/news/banking/indian-banks-cut-interest-rates-following-rbi-covid-19-measures/74896358. Accessed June 10, 2020.

Fuller Wayne, A. (1976). *Introduction to statistical time series*. New York: Wiley.

Government of India. (2017). Draft National Energy Policy (Version as on 27.06.2017). NITI Aayog, New Delhi.

Government of India. (2018). *Strategy for New India @75*. New Delhi: NITI Aayog.

Government of India. (2020a). *Energy statistics 2020*. New Delhi: Ministry of Statistics and Programme Implementation, National Statistics Office.

Government of India. (2020b). Monthly report April 2020. New Delhi: Central Electricity Authority, Ministry of Power.

Government of India (2020c) Press note on provisional estimates of annual national income 2019–2020 and Quarterly Estimates of Gross Domestic Product for the Fourth Quarter (Q4) of 2019–2020. Ministry of Statistics and Programme Implementation, New Delhi.

Greene, W. H. (2008). *Econometric analysis*. NJ: Prentice-Hall.
IEA/IEO, International Energy Agency. (2020). *India 2020 energy policy review*. France: IEA Country Report.
International Energy Agency (IEA) Statistics. https://www.iea.org/statistics/statisticssearch/report/?country=INDIA&product=balances&year. Accessed September 10, 2017.
Jain, M., & Patwardhan, A. (2013). Employment outcomes of renewable energy technologies: Implications of policies in India. *Economic & Political Weekly, 16*, 84–89.
Johansen, S. (1988). Statistical analysis of cointegration vectors. *Journal of Economic Dynamics and Control, 12*, 231–254.
Johansen, S. (1991). Estimation and hypothesis testing of cointegration vectors in Gaussian vector autoregressive models. *Econometrica, 59*, 1551–1580.
Laha, P., Chakraborty, B., & Østergaard, P. A. (2020). Electricity system scenario development of India with import independence in 2030. *Renewable Energy, 151*, 627–639.
Lehr, U., Lutz, C., & Edler, D. (2012). Green jobs? Economic impacts of renewable energy in Germany. *Energy Policy, 47*, 358–364.
Mehra, M. K., Mukherjee, S., Bhattacharya, G., & Md. Azharuddin, Sk. (2018). *An assessment of india's energy choices: What it means for the economy, jobs, and energy security, A four-report series on an assessment of India's energy choices, climate policy initiative, New Delhi*. https://www.climatepolicyinitiative.org/wp-content/uploads/2018/05/What-it-Means-for-the-Economy-Jobs-and-Energy-Security_Technical-Report-1.pdf. Accessed October 20, 2020.
Nong, D., & Simshauser, P. (2020). On energy and climate change policies: The impact of baseline projections. *Applied Energy, 269*, 115062.
Onafowora, O. A., & Owoye, O. (2015). Structural Vector Auto regression analysis of the dynamic effects of shocks in renewable electricity generation on economic output and carbon dioxide emissions: China, India and Japan. *International Journal of Energy Economics and Policy, 5*(4), 1022–1032.
Pesaran, M. H., Shin, Y., & Smith, R. J. (2001). Bounds testing approaches to the analysis of level relationships. *Journal of Applied Econometrics, 16*(3), 289–326.
Press Trust of India. (2020). India growth to revive after containment of COVID-19: Niti Aayog vice-chairman. *The Economic Times*, E-paper 11 June 2020. https://www.deccanherald.com/business/india-growth-to-revive-after-containment-of-covid-19-niti-aayog-vice-chairman-848450.html. Accessed June 17, 2020.
Radhika, M. (2020). Why the ₹20-lakh crore stimulus adds up to just ₹2-lakh crore direct impact. *The Hindu BusinessLine*, 19 May 2020. https://www.thehindubusinessline.com/portfolio/news-analysis/why-the-20-lakh-crore-stimulus-adds-up-to-just-2-lakh-crore-direct-impact/article31620474.ece. Accessed June 20, 2020.
Reserve Bank of India, Database on Indian Economy. https://dbie.rbi.org.in/DBIE/dbie.rbi?site=home. Accessed October 1, 2017.
Reserve Bank of India, Handbook of Statistics on Indian Economy. https://www.rbi.org.in/Scripts/AnnualPublications.aspx?head=Handbook%20of%20Statistics%20on%20Indian%20Economy. Accessed October 1, 2017.
RT Question More. (2020). India's economy will see strong recovery next year- S&P. RT 15 Jun 2020. https://www.rt.com/business/491827-india-economy-strong-recovery/. Accessed on June 20, 2020.
Sasana, H., & Ghozali, I. (2017). The impact of fossil and renewable energy consumption on the economic growth in Brazil, Russia, India, China and South Africa. *International Journal of Energy Economics and Policy, 7*(3), 194–200.
Sree Ram, R. (2017). Renewable energy future hinges on policy execution. *LiveMint*, December 28, 2017. https://www.livemint.com/Money/vd9N429itd0KUjcFb7NxoM/Renewable-energy-future-hinges-on-policy-execution.html. Accessed 26 May 2020.
Silva, S., Soares, I., & Pinho, C. (2012). The impact of renewable energy sources on economic growth and CO_2 emissions—VAR approach. *European Research Studies, 15*(4), 133–144.

Smith, N. (2020). How to get India out of this frustrating and complex recession. *The Economic Times*, E-paper 25 February, 2020. https://economictimes.indiatimes.com/news/economy/policy/how-to-get-india-out-of-this-frustrating-and-complex-recession/articleshow/74294487.cms?utm_source=contentofinterest&utm_medium=text&utm_campaign=cppst. Accessed June 17, 2020.

The Wire Analysis. (2020). Modi's Rs 20 lakh crore package will likely have fiscal cost of less than Rs 2.5 lakh crore. *The Wire*, May 17, 2020. https://thewire.in/economy/modi-rs-20-lakh-crore-package-actual-spend. Accessed June 30, 2020.

Unemployment rate in India, CMIE. https://unemploymentinindia.cmie.com/. Accessed July 5, 2020.

Utpal, B. (2019). All villages electrified, but last-mile supply a challenge. *LiveMint*. 29 Dec 2019.https://www.livemint.com/industry/energy/all-villages-electrified-but-last-mile-supply-a-challenge-11577642738875.html. Accessed May 26, 2020.

Wei, M., Patadia, S., & Kammen, D. M. (2010). Putting renewables and energy efficiency to work: How many jobs can the clean energy industry generate in the US? *Energy Policy, 38*(2), 919–931.

World Bank. (2020). Global economic prospects, June 2020. Washington DC: World Bank. https://openknowledge.worldbank.org/handle/10986/33748. Accessed July 1, 2020.

World Bank, World Development Indicators (WDI). https://data.worldbank.org/data-catalog/world-development-indicators. Accessed September 10, 2017.

World Resources Institute. (2016). CAIT—Emissions Projections. USA.

Externality Empirics: Knowledge and Practice

Embracing Natural Resource Accounting in India: Some Reflections

Shalini Saksena

1 Introduction

As the world's largest democracy, India struggles to achieve sustainable development in the face of growing consumerism and environmental decline. It is riddled with environmental concerns such as rising air and water pollution, falling groundwater tables, growing water scarcity, poor waste management, land degradation and loss of biodiversity and forests coupled with energy security issues and uncertain long-run economic effects of climate change and asset losses due to possible sea level rise. Given the size of the country, national level policies on environment and climate are bound to have global consequences.

Recent global initiatives such as the 2030 Agenda for Sustainable Development, the post-2020 biodiversity agenda and international climate policy are testimonies of growing realisation that economic growth is pushing ecosystems towards their critical limits as the rising levels of production and consumption exceed Earth's ecological budget. World's resources are being drawn at rates faster than their restoration, and wastes and pollutants are being released at rates faster than the Earth's absorption capacity. Human's current use of Earth's biological resources is nearly 70% more than what it can regenerate, i.e. the equivalent of 1.7 planets worth of Earth's resources and ecological services (WWF, 2018). Economic growth measured in terms of growth in gross domestic product (GDP) fails to reflect the significant externalities in the form of environmental degradation. There is growing realisation in the global community of the imperativeness of undertaking prompt and effective measures to offset resource depletion and environmental degradation in order to sustain long-term growth within the natural limits set by the availability of natural resources and

S. Saksena (✉)
Department of Economics, Delhi College of Arts & Commerce, University of Delhi, New Delhi, India
e-mail: ssaksena@dcac.du.ac.in

P. Dasgupta et al. (eds.), *Sustainable Development Insights from India*,
India Studies in Business and Economics,
https://doi.org/10.1007/978-981-33-4830-1_18

environmental services. It also underscores the need to look beyond macroeconomic indicators of economic growth such as GDP or GDP per capita as measures of a country's sustainable development.

The conventional approach to the preparation of national accounts in most countries is primarily based on the System of National Accounts (SNA). Over the years, SNA's accounting framework and methodology have been comprehensively updated in view of the evolving economic interactions and appearance of new economic phenomena in the world. However, the conceptual basis of the SNA is the neoclassical market theory, and it focuses on key indicators that are based mostly on short-run Keynesian macro models, not on any long-run growth theory or models. Against this backdrop, this paper discusses the limited scope and coverage of national accounts based on SNA which render them inadequate for obtaining information on the various determinants the growth process and sustainability of development.

The understanding of an operational notion of sustainable development in terms of non-declining per capita (comprehensive) wealth, adjusted for distribution (Arrow et al., 2013; Polasky et al., 2015; Mumford, 2016) has significant and radical implications for the way national accounts are prepared and interpreted in countries (Dasgupta, 2013). It is well understood that the widespread adoption of a system of natural resource accounting that integrates information on environment-economy interactions is needed to aid sustainability analyses. In this regard, concerted international efforts by agencies such as the UNEP, UNSD and World Bank have led to the development of an environmental accounting framework called the System of Integrated Economic and Environmental Accounting (SEEA). Initiatives at revising the SEEA framework and accounting methodology have been underway for more than two decades, and the 2012 SEEA Central Framework (SEEA CF) is the latest version. It is envisaged that as an international standard, the SEEA CF can serve as an ideal international statistical framework which can support critical global initiatives such the monitoring of SDG indicators (Pirmana et al., 2019; UNCEEA, 2016), the post-2020 biodiversity agenda and international climate policy.[1] In this context, this paper attempts to highlight the latest standardised methodological framework available for countries to mainstream implementation of SEEA.

Operationalising the sustainable development agenda calls for wider adoption of SEEA across countries. All countries are urged to implement the SEEA CF within their national statistical systems by adopting a flexible and modular approach to its implementation, keeping in mind the availability of data, statistical capacity and specific policy context of countries. In view of the emerging consensus in the international community on mainstreaming of the SEEA, this paper attempts to contextualise the experiences and recent initiatives in India with regard to its implementation. The rest of the paper is organised as follows: Sect. 2 of this paper highlights the limitations of the SNA and the derived macroeconomic aggregates in capturing the rate of economic growth which can be sustained over the long term, thus highlighting the need to adopt the SEEA. Section 3 of the paper describes in some detail

[1] https://seea.un.org/content/seea-and-global-policy#:~:text=and%20Global%20Policy-,The%20SEEA%20and%20Global%20Policy,Sustainable%20Development%20Goals%20(SDGs).

the conceptual framework of the SEEA as well as the scope and coverage of its various accounts and tables which countries can construct in order to mainstream its implementation. Section 4 presents India's narrative with respect to environmental accounting and valuation, focusing on the recent surge in government initiatives towards mainstreaming of SEEA implementation. Section 5 presents some concluding remarks.

2 The Need to Look Beyond GDP and Other SNA-Based Macroeconomic Indicators of Growth

Economic growth continues to remain a fundamental policy objective in almost all societies. Based on the classical theory of value suggested by Adam Smith and developed by David Ricardo, whereby economic values are created by the use of factors of production, economic growth is defined in terms of growth in gross domestic product (GDP). Such is the importance of GDP in the macroeconomic lexicon that in most contexts, economic growth is explicitly or implicitly understood as an increase in GDP. However, while GDP serves as an appropriate index for evaluating economic performance, it cannot serve as an indicator of sustainable economic growth. There have been several instances of countries which have experienced periods of significant growth in per capita GDP even as they have depleted their productive base, resulting in a decline in per capita wealth. Growth achieved by liquidating stocks of natural capital is clearly not sustainable. Sustainable economic growth and development calls for an increase in economic activity without reducing the ability of the economy and ecosystems to assist the same level of economic activity in future as well. This requires a decoupling of economic growth from resource consumption and environmental degradation wherein growth in GDP is achieved without a concurrent increase in the rate of resource input use (International Resource Panel, UNEP 2011), implying improvements in resource efficiency in consumption and production. While GDP serves its role well as a measure of all economic activities, it conveys little about resource use efficiency and in fact, camouflages the extent of environmental depletion and degradation that accompany the achieved level of economic activities. Hence, efforts to achieve a decoupling of growth and consumption of environmental resources must focus on alternative measures of economic progress (Malmaeus, 2016).

National accounts of most countries are based on the System of National Accounts (SNA) which lays out the framework for aggregating and estimating the macroeconomic variables of a country's national accounts. While the SNA framework has been updated comprehensively over the years, its conceptual basis remains the neoclassical market theory, and hence, SNA accounts focus on key indicators that are based mostly on short-run Keynesian macro models and not on any long-run growth theory or models. In the context of environmental considerations, conventional national accounts based on the SNA do not explicitly account for the contributions made by natural capital since they do not include the full economic value of environmental assets or their contribution as important environmental inputs. Environmental inputs, like free gifts of nature, are implicitly valued at zero prices. Their depletion as well as degradation is not accounted for. Moreover, all receipts from sale of natural resources are treated as current income available for consumption. Such income[2] obtained from liquidating the natural capital base of a country is clearly unsustainable.

It is important to note that natural resources display both the flow and stock dimensions of reproducible man-made capital. Hence, not only should their depletion and/or degradation be accounted for in the net domestic product (Hartwick, 1990), their values should also be a part of a comprehensive measure of national wealth (Hartwick, 1995). The difference in the treatment of produced capital and natural capital in the conventional economic accounts based on SNA can typically be traced under four categories (Sengupta & Saksena, 2007):

i. The entry for additions to stock of natural resources parallel to the entry for additions to stock of man-made capital structures and equipment is missing.
ii. No explicit entry exists for the contribution of natural resources to current production measured in terms of GDP, while there are specific entries for value addition by produced capital. Although it must be noted that some of the contribution of natural capital gets reflected in national accounts in terms of royalties, rents and changes in value of land.
iii. While depreciation of produced capital is accounted for to arrive at net domestic product, no such adjustment is made for the extent of depletion of the stocks of natural resources.
iv. Values of stocks of natural resources and stocks of reserves-inventories are excluded from national balance sheets of countries which prepare them, thus underestimating their national wealth.

Several studies have proposed the estimation of a more comprehensive measure of wealth of a country (Arrow et al., 2013; Polasky et al., 2015; Mumford, 2016) by including explicitly the value of natural capital assets along with measures of produced and human capital. Economic growth needs to be assessed in terms of growth in per capita wealth, defined as the social worth of an economy's productive base comprising the entire set of capital assets (Dasgupta, 2013). The World Bank (Lange et al., 2018) report traces economic progress and sustainability of 141 countries over the years 1995 and 2014, based on estimates of total wealth comprising of natural capital (such as land, forests and minerals), human capital (earnings over a person's lifetime), man-made/produced capital (buildings, infrastructure, etc.) and net foreign assets. It finds several examples of low-income countries, with a dominant share of natural capital in their total wealth in 1995, move up to the middle-income category, attributable primarily to the judicious investment of earnings derived from the use of natural capital into other forms of capital, particularly investment into

---

[2]Where '*income*' based on Hicksian notion of sustainable income is defined as "...a man's income (is defined) as the maximum value which he can consume during a week and still expect to be as well off at the end of the week as he was in the beginning." (Hicks, 1946).

enhancing the regenerative capacity of renewable natural capital, building up of physical infrastructure and human capital (health and education). The fact that the value of natural capital for the high income countries is found to be three times that of the low-income countries, it cannot be denied that rapid growth can be achieved and sustained without running down overall stocks of natural capital. Countries need to leverage and not liquidate natural capital in order to achieve sustainable growth. However, unless national accounts explicitly include the contribution of natural resources as critical inputs and include them in measures of a country's national wealth, it will not be possible to assess whether economic growth is being achieved by leveraging or liquidating the country's natural capital base.

Ignoring the contribution of natural resource inputs also creates problems in productivity analysis. When the estimation of production functions includes only estimates of land, labour and capital and excludes measures of natural resources as inputs (which are significant in some sectors), productivity growth may be overestimated in countries where growth relies heavily on depletion of natural capital. Likewise, productivity growth may be underestimated in countries which invest significantly into more efficient use of natural resources (OECD, 2016), thus giving a misleading idea of growth prospects, resulting in less-than-optimal state budgeting decisions.

Proponents of sustainable development recommend adoption of a system of natural resource accounting to prepare a set of aggregate national data that links and highlights the interaction between the environment and the economy, with the objective of integrating macroeconomic and environmental policy to ensure better long-term management of natural resources. The SEEA lays out the statistical framework and methodological basis for the construction of satellite as well as integrated accounts, to supplement and/or adjust the SNA-based aggregates for environmental costs, contribution and benefits. While the *integrated accounts* change the calculation of GDP and other key national aggregates to obtain estimates of environmentally adjusted aggregates, *satellite accounts* (of which physical asset accounts are one example) are only linked to the SNA as supplements, providing useful environmental data without threatening the consistency of the information in SNA accounts. The following section discusses the conceptual framework and scope of the latest version of the SEEA, i.e. SEEA Central Framework, 2012.

3 The SEEA Central Framework

The adoption of the 2030 Agenda for Sustainable Development has been a landmark initiative, providing for a shared global vision towards sustainable development for all. The implementation and monitoring needs of the Sustainable Development Goals (SDGs) critically rely on the capacity of countries to produce core economic statistics and administrative data to inform policy making, monitor the progress and ensure accountability. Strengthening the capacity to provide structured, complete and coherent information in an integrated manner is essential to promote evidence-based decision making for the benefit of the most vulnerable groups in any country.

Policies for sustainable development need to adopt an integrated approach based on an information system encompassing the social, economic and environmental components of sustainability, their interconnections and trade-offs. Information on the environmental component of sustainable development is mostly collected for specific purposes, often to guide setting of certain standards or regulations, or to estimate an indicator. Such ad hoc collection of environmental information, based on competing theories and concepts, only presents an unclear picture, often not up to the measurement challenge.

Proposed by the United Nations and developed through extensive intergovernmental process, SEEA provides a multi-purpose conceptual framework for understanding the economy–environment interactions, particularly of the impact of economic activity on environmental assets. The SEEA Central Framework (SEEA CF) was adopted by the UNSD as the first international statistical standard for environmental-economic accounting in 2012. Keeping in mind its multidisciplinary scope, the SEEA CF is designed such that it remains coherent with and complementary to other international standards, recommendations and classifications, including the 2008 SNA, the Balance of Payments and International Investment Position, the International Standard Industrial Classification of All Economic Activities (ISIC), the Central Product Classification (CPC) and the Framework for the Development of Environment Statistics (UN, 2014).

The SEEA CF utilises the same concepts, definitions, structures, classifications, accounting rules and principles as adopted in the SNA. It adopts a *systems approach* to the organisation of environmental and economic information into tables and accounts in an integrated and coherent manner, which can be further used to derive important aggregates and indicators designed specifically to provide information about the effectiveness and efficiency of environmental and economic policies at regional, national and international levels (UN, 2017). It aids the assessment of trends in the use and availability of various natural resources, determination of the extent of discharges and emissions to the environment arising from economic activity and as assessment of the amount of economic activity undertaken for environmental purposes.

Effective integration of environmental-economic data can take different forms such as (i) presentation of information using common format and classifications, (ii) presentation of descriptive statistics and indicators on pressure, state and response, (iii) construction of analytical models for environmental-economic analysis. Such integrated information helps in identifying the socio-economic drivers, pressures, impacts and responses that affect the environment. It aids productivity analysis and helps attain greater precision for environmental regulations and natural resource management strategies. For example, in case of energy resources, energy supply and use tables can be constructed both in physical and monetary terms which provide information on, *inter alia*, energy dependency, industry reliance on particular sources of energy, profile of energy products supplied and used, etc. These help in formulating evidence-based policies on energy for more efficient means of meeting the needs of the economy.

The scope of the information in the SEEA CF includes a broad spectrum of environmental and economic issues, representing a melding of perspectives from various disciplines such as economics, statistics, hydrology, energy, forestry, fisheries and environmental sciences. While remaining within the System of National Accounts (SNA) asset boundary, the SEEA CF lays out rules for valuation of land as well as renewable and non-renewable natural resources. Valuation of assets and flows related to land and natural resources that go beyond the values already included in the SNA is not included in the SEEA CF. Different modules dealing with specific natural resources and SEEA applications have been released from time to time, which include: SEEA Experimental Ecosystem Accounting in 2013, SEEA Applications and Extensions in 2017, Revised SEEA Ecosystem Accounting, SEEA Water and SEEA Energy in 2019 and a module on SEEA Agriculture, Forestry and Fisheries which is on its way.

SEEA essentially includes the compilation of three main accounts: *Physical flow accounts, Stock/Asset accounts and Functional accounts.* The SEEA physical flow accounts comprise of various supply and use tables that depict the physical flows of materials and energy that take place (i) from the environment to the economy (such as natural input flows of water, mineral and timber), (ii) within the economy (such as product flows which add to the stock of fixed capital) and (iii) from the economy to the environment (including residual flows such as air and water pollution and solid waste). The flows of natural inputs from the environment to the economy result in changes in the stock of environmental assets[3] in a country. These are captured in *the SEEA asset accounts* for environmental assets such as minerals, forests, land and ecosystems in both physical and monetary terms. In the SEEA framework, environmental assets are considered as individual components of the environment which serve as natural inputs and provide material benefits from their direct use in all economic activities. Examples of such individual environmental resources include timber resources, mineral and energy resources, land and water resources. Non-material benefits from indirect use of such resources, such as benefits from ecosystem services (e.g. carbon sequestration), forest tourism, water purification etc., are not the focus of SEEA CF.[4] *Functional accounts* in SEEA CF are those that explicitly identify economic activities that already exist in the SNA and are related to environmental activities. These include activities aimed to reducing or eliminating pressures on the environment (like environmental protection expenditure), those that are undertaken to make more efficient use of natural resources, environmental taxes and subsidies and a range of other payments and transactions related to the environment.

[3]SEEA CF 2012 defines environmental assets as "the naturally occurring living and non-living components of the Earth, together constituting the biophysical environment, which may provide benefits to humanity".

[4]Non-material benefits from ecosystem services include regulating services (such as carbon sequestration) and cultural services (such as forest tourism). SEEA Experimental Ecosystem Accounting focuses on the ability of the ecosystems to generate the same range, quantity and quality of ecosystem services which get degraded due to excessive economic and human activities. Such ecosystem accounting includes recording the capacity of the living components of an ecosystem and their interaction with the non-living environment in generating flows of ecosystem services.

Important aggregates and indicators related to resource use and environmental intensity, contribution of environmental assets to overall economic growth, share of environmental expenditure in total government expenditure, share of environmental taxes in total tax revenue, depletion-adjusted value added of mining industries, etc., can be derived from the accounting structure of the SEEA CF. Aggregates such as total air emissions, extent of deforestation and depletion of exhaustible resources are directly embedded in SEEA CF accounts. Some indicators can be calculated as ratios of variables from different SEEA CF accounts, while others can be derived by simple linking of data in SEEA CF with that in SNA or other national accounts such as the census. *SEEA Applications and Extensions* (UN, 2017)[5] is a document that lays out the methodology of constructing various indicators and the kinds of analyses that can be carried out using such indicators. For example, depletion of mineral resources in the SEEA CF is defined as a measure of physical change in the stock of the resources brought about by their extraction. A comparison of the rate of extraction with new discoveries can be used to assess the asset lives of different minerals. The ratio of reserves to extraction level of exhaustive resources is indicative of the sustainability of resource supply. A comparison of extraction level with total resource use/supply in the economy (production to total supply ratio) can be used as an index of self-sufficiency.

As an international standard, SEEA CF can serve as a potential monitoring tool for more than 50 indicators of the 232 potential SDG indicators, covering 10 out of the 17 SDGs (UNCEEA, 2016). Countries are urged to align their accounting practices by adopting and implementing the SEEA CF incrementally. The proposition is not to compile every table and account for all environmental assets and themes. Countries must focus on comprehensively accounting for their environmental-economic structure, given the most important aspects of their environment and on providing information on issues of global concern, based on a common measurement framework. As more and more countries adopt the SEEA CF, greater international statistical comparability will be possible which will help provide policy-relevant information at international levels. India has long adopted the spirit of the SEEA in principle, and recent government initiatives that are underway to facilitate the mainstreaming of its implementation are particularly noteworthy. The following section reflects upon such efforts in India aimed towards implementation of the SEEA.

4 Environmental Accounting in India

India's experience with natural resource accounting (NRA) initiatives has been sporadic and piecemeal, although these efforts have gathered momentum in the recent years. NRA involves substantive interdisciplinary research efforts specific to the country and its ecosystem. In India, several research initiatives, not necessarily driven by the requirements of SEEA implementation, have taken place in the

[5]See the document online at https://unstats.un.org/unsd/envaccounting/seeaRev/ae_final_en.pdf.

area of environmental impact analysis and valuation of environmental benefits and damages (Parikh & Parikh, 1997; Chopra & Kadekodi, 1997; Chopra et al. 2001; Sankar, 2004; Kadekodi, 2004; Murty & Kumar, 2004; Sengupta & Mandal 2005). They provide useful results for developing both the methodology and estimates of the concerned measures for SEEA implementation in India. Amongst the earliest studies focusing on the construction of asset accounts and adjustments in macroeconomic aggregates along the lines of the SEEA, Parikh et al. (1993) is notable in developing an NRA framework for India for the compilation of physical accounts for soil, air, water, forests, biodiversity and a number of non-renewable resources. TERI (1999) undertook the first pilot study on NRA to value the extent of depletion of iron-ore reserves in Goa and estimate depletion-adjusted state domestic product from mining which were found to be lower than the conventional SNA estimates by 8–10% over the concerned period. Works of Murty (2003) in developing physical and monetary accounts of water and air pollutants, Haripriya (1998, 2000, 2003) in developing accounts for forest resources and eight monographs of the Green Indian States Trust (GIST) over the years 2005–2007, served as building blocks for the ultimate construct of integrated environmental and economic accounting in India.

There have also been comprehensive studies on estimating the contribution of natural capital in India's overall economic growth. An OECD (2016) study on economic productivity analysis, where 14 subsoil resources are included as natural capital inputs into the production process, finds that most of the economic growth in India has been achieved on account of increase in the combined use of labour, produced capital and natural capital. The contribution of multifactor productivity gains to overall growth, after adjusting for environmental degradation and depletion of natural capital, is relatively smaller.

A World Bank study covering a period of two decades (1995–2014) by Lange et al. (2018) estimates comprehensive wealth of 114 countries covering produced capital, 19 types of natural capital, net foreign assets and human capital. In case of India, the report finds a shift away from an asset portfolio dominated by agricultural land and forests (renewable natural capital) to a more diverse one now, with a dominant share of human capital, infrastructure and produced capital. Share of produced capital (28%) is found to be only slightly larger than that of natural capital (26%) in 2014.

The study by Agarwal & Sawhney (2020) is amongst the most recent ones that account for the share of natural capital in overall wealth estimates and their contribution to overall growth in the country. They construct comprehensive wealth and investment estimates for the country over the period 1975–2013. Their measure of national wealth includes produced capital, natural capital and human capital. They also estimate investment adjusted for environmental damages because of carbon emissions and particulate emissions. The estimates of comprehensive wealth reveal a change in the composition of wealth in the country, from a predominance of natural capital to a dominance of human and produced capital over the concerned period. India's growth is thus found to have been weakly sustainable, assuming perfect substitutability between different forms of capital assets, although the authors expectedly raise doubts about such an assumption. Loss of natural forests and associated biodiversity cannot really be compensated for by an increase in other forms of capital. They also find deterioration in the quality of natural capital due to rising emissions.

Several government initiatives have been undertaken with regard to facilitating natural resource accounting in the country. The Ministry of Statistics and Programme Implementation (MoSPI) is mandated with the preparation and publication of national accounts in India. It has published 16 issues of the Compendium of Environment since 1997 until 2017 based on the United Nations Framework for Development of Environment Statistics (FDES) 1984. It initiated several NRA projects between 2006 and 2008[6] and followed it up with the setting up of an expert group in 2011 to revise and firm up a functional accounting system for constructing green national accounts in India based on SEEA by the year 2015. The group submitted its report in 2013 (Dasgupta et al., 2013) and recommended evaluation of economic progress on the basis of a comprehensive notion of wealth which includes reproducible capital, human capital and natural capital. It recommended compilation of asset accounts and supply-use tables as envisaged in SEEA CF. The report extensively covered techniques of calculating the social value of the change in comprehensive stocks of assets per capita using the shadow prices of resources. Although the target of preparing green national accounts of 2015 was not achieved, several government initiatives were undertaken in line with the recommendations of the expert group resulting in the publication of 'Statistics related to Climate Change' in 2013 and 2015 by the Central Statistics Office (CSO). This report and the compendium were later replaced by the publication called 'EnviStats India' since 2018. EnviStats India 2018 (CSO, 2018, 2018a) provides data, in physical terms, on the stock position of four natural resources in India, namely land, forest, mineral and water across the States in India. EnviStats India 2019 (CSO, 2019) broadened the scope of environmental accounts to also capture quality characteristics. It presents physical accounts based on the quality characteristics such as soil nutrient index and water quality accounts in respect of surface, ground and sea water. It also includes compilation of state-wise values of cropland ecosystem services and nature-based tourism.

EnviStats India 2018—Supplement on Environmental Accounts (CSO, 2018a) needs special mention here since it is the only document which states categorically that its compilation is driven primarily by requirements of SEEA implementation in the country. It presents abridged versions of physical asset accounts of land cover, minerals, water and forests. Although no time series data are compiled (for instance, data on mineral resources are presented for the years 2005, 2010 and 2015) and only stock positions of these resources are presented (and no flow accounts are constructed), the data from these accounts along with estimates of government revenue from resource extraction have been used to arrive at some measure of the value of natural capital and its growth rate in the country. The report, without divulging details on exact calculations, states the following:

> "The average growth rate of GSDP during 2005–15 for almost all the States is around 7–8%. So the growth in natural capital, if any, is almost insignificant and the economic development

[6]See the reports at http://mospi.nic.in/publication/natural-resource-accounting-project.

> seems to be happening at the cost of environment. Therefore, the States may not be able to sustain the rate of development for long." (CSO, 2018a, Page x).

Clearly, efforts are on to not just prepare satellite accounts, but also undertake construction of integrated accounts at some stage in order to arrive at natural capital depletion-adjusted value addition by different sectors. Another important recent government initiative is the formation of the Government Accounting Standards Advisory Board (GASAB) with the mandate of preparing a roadmap for implementation of NRA and identifying the issues and challenges. The concept note prepared under this mandate (GASAB, 2020) proposes the implementation process of NRA through short, medium and long-term goals (see Table 1). It specifically suggests formats for constructing asset accounts for mineral and energy resources, water

Table 1 Goals of implementation of NRA in India

Highlights	Years covered	Challenges to address
Short-term goals		
• Preparation of asset accounts on mineral and energy resources in States • Initiation and preparation of disclosure statement on revenues and expenditure related to NRA	2019–20 to 2021–22	• Mandating the reporting requirements by private sector regarding the use of resources, water and release of effluents/residuals • Identifying the authority to manage and monitor online information from private sector
Mid-term goals		
• Preparation of national asset accounts on mineral and energy resources • Preparation of asset accounts in respect of other three resources namely water, land and forest resources • Preparation of supply and use tables in physical and monetary terms showing flow of natural resource inputs, products and residuals	2022–23 to 2024–25	• Periodicity of the asset accounts of water, land and forest resources to be decided • Mapping the periodicity of data management with the requirement of asset accounts • Decision on the agency which would prepare the asset accounts in respect of the resources at national level
Long-term goals		
• Preparation of the economic accounts highlighting depletion-adjusted economic aggregates; and • Preparation of functional accounts recording transactions and other information about economic activities undertaken for environmental purposes	2025–26 onwards	--

Source GASAB (2020)

resources, land resources and forestry and wildlife resources. It also proposes to bring the private players within the ambit of NRA framework by proposing specific reporting requirements with regard to resource use and management of residuals or effluents.

India is at an early stage of commencing annual environmental accounting of its resources. It may be noted that the national accounts in India have only flow accounts of production, income and expenditure. Accounts of economic assets including non-produced economic assets like land, subsoil minerals, fossil fuel reserves, etc., are not constructed periodically (GASAB, 2020). Even though it is well understood that continuous generation of asset accounts at regular intervals is the essence of NRA, efforts until now have been sporadic. EnviStats-2018 presents accounts of subsoil assets with their stock position and extraction levels given only for some time points. Annual series are not presented. These accounts of non-renewables are constructed through collection of data from the source agencies, and such accounts can be easily updated and published every year to present a continuous time series on stock positions and extraction levels.

While the government and associated ministries remain fully committed to construct physical use and supply tables and asset accounts for different resources along SEEA guidelines, lack of sufficient micro level data on natural capital and the complexity of the exercise pose hindrances.

> "It is undenying that at present, a consolidated database on availability and physical extraction/use of natural resources, revenue generated therefrom, expenditure incurred on extraction and mitigation of environmental degradation is not available in the States as well at the national level. Such a database will be immensely helpful for having a broad idea of the revenue generating resources, costs involved and their sustainability for the future generations." (GASAB, 2020).

In 2019, the government embarked on conducting the first ever National Environment Survey (NES), which is a planned over the next five years to ascertain the status of environment beginning with district level information on geography, farmland, wildlife, pattern of emissions and other indicators of environmental health.[7] The objective is to eventually calculate every state's 'green' GDP. An exercise at such a disaggregated level will also aid policy making particularly with respect to decisions on appropriate compensation with respect to climate mitigation and land acquisition. Clearly, several government initiatives are underway to firm up the framework, identify and tackle the challenges, decide on short, medium and long-term goals of undertaking NRA. These initiatives may have been sporadic, but by no means meagre for a populous country like India. EU funded Green Economy Coalition (GEC) which tracks and benchmarks the transitioning of countries to being greener, guided by the ecological limits, within their local and national contexts, recognises the governmental efforts in this direction (see Table A1 in the Appendix).

[7] See http://iictenvis.nic.in/ViewMajorActivity.aspx?Id=2758&Year=2019

5 Conclusion: A Green Economy Response

The global economy finds itself in unchartered water as the ongoing pandemic has exposed the inherent mutual dependency of human and ecosystem health. More importantly, it has laid bare the fact that the current global economic system is totally unprepared for a damaging crisis like the COVID-19 pandemic. The Earth overshoot day this year has been delayed by more than three weeks, representing a decline in humanity's ecological footprint by 9% (https://www.footprintnetwork.org/2020/) mainly on account of lockdowns across countries in the world. Although this sudden contraction due to the pandemic is a far cry from the kind of structural changes needed to achieve economic and social wellbeing while maintaining ecological balance, it has also highlighted the possibilities of global communities acting swiftly to work collaboratively towards solving a problem bigger than that faced by any one country. As governments in different countries announce economic recovery packages in order to reinvigorate their economies, it becomes extremely critical to ensure that such packages do not focus only on immediate short-term coping mechanisms. They must also have a long-term vision to steer the economies towards becoming more resilient by following a 'greener' and a more inclusive path of development where they are better integrated with nature.

In India, voices have been raised against the dilution of the Environment Impact Assessment notification 2020 as the dangers of rising industrial emissions, industrial accidents, loss of forests and biodiversity, etc., loom large. "The need to focus on environmental factors has become more evident. As a basis for that, putting necessary environmental laws and regulations in place and effective implementation is the need of the hour to make the national policy strategy to follow a 'green' and sustainable path." (Dr. Satabdi Datta, Manager, Policy and Planning, Development Alternatives).[8] In the current context, the need to integrate environmental concerns in our accounting systems cannot be emphasised any further. The Indian narrative with respect to the mainstreaming of SEEA implementation shows that the intent is well in place albeit a lot of ground still needs to be covered.

Acknowledgements I would like to take this opportunity to express my gratitude to my supervisor, Prof. Ramprasad Sengupta, who introduced me to the topic of Sustainable Natural Resource Accounting. His guidance and support, all through my Ph.D. research, and the rich learning experiences while co-authoring two academic papers with him, shall always remain invaluable.

Appendix

See Table A1.

[8]See https://www.greeneconomycoalition.org/news-analysis/indias-environmental-laws-and-covid-19.

Table A1 India's green economy tracker: policy scores

Policy	Analysis	Policy description	Score
National green economy plan	The three year action agenda (2017–20), together with a mid-term 7-year strategy and long-term 15-year vision, is India's macroeconomic plan. It aspires for sustainable and balanced growth and recognises the importance of decarbonisation largely through efficiency gains and mass deployment of renewable energy, but envisions continued use of coal and does not set a net-zero goal. Climate action tracker identifies India's climate policy trajectory as being potentially "2 °C Compatible", assuming targets are met	Implement a national green economy plan to coordinate green policies towards a sustainable and inclusive net-zero carbon economy by 2050	Score: 4 Up-to-date green economy plan with clear commitments, but partially lacking in detail, or ambition
SDG and NRA business strategy	Proposal to include the private sector in overall framework of NRA (GASAB, 2020), requiring them to report resource use and management of effluents/residuals. No specific requirements for businesses to report on SDG goals, but the 2013 Companies Act mandates all firms to invest in Corporate Social Responsibility (CSR) initiatives, and the Reserve Bank of India has established sustainable development reporting guidelines for commercial banks	Promote a national strategy that rewards businesses and organisations who are taking action to achieve the UN Sustainable Development Goals and aid NRA	Score 2 Limited national initiatives promoting private sector involvement with SDG implementation

(continued)

Table A1 (continued)

Policy	Analysis	Policy description	Score
Wealth accounting	First country in the world to publish natural wealth accounts, tracking plants, animals, water and other natural capitals since 2010, and the Central Statistics Office has published detailed accounts covering land, water, air and minerals since 2018. Has partnered with UN-SEEA and the CBD for Natural Capital Accounting and Valuation of Ecosystem Services (NCAVES)	Mandate development of a comprehensive national wealth framework that takes all types of capitals—human, social, natural, financial/physical—into account	Score 4 Work underway to combine existing capital accounts into statistically comprehensive national wealth accounts
Green sectoral policy plan	No overall intersectoral body for green policy at the sectoral level. The 12th Five Year Plan (2012–17) called for the establishment of new inter-ministerial institutions to resolve issues around air quality, waste, water and forestry sectors, but these have not yet been implemented	Commission an independent, cross-sector body to develop and coordinate green economy policy across key sectors; including agri-food, energy, transport, buildings, waste, etc.	Score 2 Weak sectoral sustainability policies covering few key sectors; no coordination
Carbon budgeting	No carbon budget in place; main decarbonisation goal is to reduce the emissions intensity of its GDP by 35% by 2030, although current plans to continue building coal power capacity undermine this	Commit to legally binding carbon budgets that are consistent with India's Nationally Determined Contribution and meet the Paris Agreement's 1.5 °C ambition	Score 2 Carbon budgeting under discussion but no clear pathway to implementation

(continued)

Table A1 (continued)

Policy	Analysis	Policy description	Score
Clean Energy Policy	Ambitious targets recently strengthened to 228 GW of renewables by 2022 and 40% clean electricity capacity by 2030; supported by massive public investments in renewables, energy efficiency and electrification; heavy reliance on hydro-power; national energy strategy continues to include new subsidised coal	Adopt ambitious medium and long-term targets for share of renewable energy in final consumption, and commit to a corresponding clean energy investment plan	Score 4 Solid RE target; funding and support scheme in place, but with further ambition needed
Natural capital accounts	The Green Accounting for Indian States Project (GAIST), created in 2004, publishes accounts on state-level sustainability and holistic economic measures beyond GDP. Central Statistics Office started publishing accounts covering land, water, air and minerals in 2018. CSO has issued supplement on Environment Accounts in September 2018 wherein the physical stock of four natural resources across India have been enumerated. Subsequently, CSO has also brought out the EnviStat-2019 based on the quality characteristics namely soil nutrient index and water quality accounts	Produce comprehensive natural capital accounts that distinguish between value of nature to communities, the economy and the global environment	Score 4 Natural capital strategy in place; with comprehensive accounts under development, some initial accounts available

(continued)

Table A1 (continued)

Policy	Analysis	Policy description	Score
Nature-based fiscal reforms	Some environmental fiscal policies already in place, largely managed through taxes. A tax on coal—known as the "Clean Energy Cess"—channels revenue from coal consumption into the National Clean Energy Fund. No clear funds set aside for natural capital management and restoration	Replace fiscal and monetary policies that damage nature with sustainable conservation and restoration policies, supported by a ring-fenced natural capital budget	Score 4 Some environmental taxation and spending policies in place supporting environmental restoration, covering certain sectors

Notes The Green Economy Coalition has identified key policies that are crucial to the transition to green and fair economies; for each policy, the tracker uses a 5-point scale to score how ambitious it might be in supporting a green economy. A score of "5" reflects high ambition, while a "1" represents minimal ambition. The scoring criterion is based on the ambition of the most recent policies, pledges, targets and legislation that are relevant to the policy

Source Adapted from https://greeneconomytracker.org/country/india#ref-1 (last accessed on 1st September 2020)

References

Agarwal, P., & Sawhney, A. (2020). Sustainability and comprehensive wealth accounting: The case of India. In *Environment, development and sustainability: A multidisciplinary approach to the theory and practice of sustainable development*, pp. 1–25.

Arrow, K. J., Dasgupta, P., Goulder, L. H., Mumford, K. J., & Oleson, K. (2013). Sustainability and the measurement of wealth: Further reflections. *Environment and Development Economics, 18*(4), 504–516.

Chopra, K., & Kadekodi, G. (1997). *Natural resource accounting in yamuna basin: Accounting for forest resources (monograph).* New Delhi: Institute of Economic Growth.

Chopra, K., Bhattacharya, B. B., & Kumar, P. (2001). *Contribution of forestry sector to gross domestic product in India' draft*. Institute of Economic Growth, New Delhi: Project sponsored by the Ministry of Environment and Forests, Government of India.

CSO. (2018). *EnviStats India 2018*. New Delhi: Central Statistics Office, Ministry of Statistics and Programme Implementation. Government of India.

CSO, (2018a). *EnviStats India 2018: Supplement on environmental accounts*. New Delhi: Central Statistics Office, Ministry of Statistics and Programme Implementation. Government of India.

CSO. (2019). *EnviStats India 2019: Volume-II environment accounts*. New Delhi: Central Statistics Office, Ministry of Statistics and Programme Implementation. Government of India.

Dasgupta, P. (2013). The nature of economic development and the economic development of nature. *Economic and Political Weekly, 48*(51), 38–51.

Dasgupta, P., Anant, T. C. A., Basu, K., Chopra, K., Desai, N., Gundimeda, H.,… & Shyamsundar, P. (2013). *Green national accounts in India: A framework*. Report by an expert group Convened.

GASAB. (2020). *Concept paper on natural resource accounting in India–An initiative of GASAB*. New Delhi: Government Accounting Standards Advisory Board Secretariat.

Haripriya, G. S. (2003). Carbon budget of the Indian forest ecosystem. *Climatic Change, 56,* 291–319.

Haripriya, G. S. (1998). Forest resource accounting for the state of Maharashtra in India. *Development Policy Review, 16*(2), 131–151.

Haripriya, G. S. (2000). Integrating forest resources into the system of national accounts in Maharashtra. *Environment and Development Economics, 5,* 143–156.

Hartwick, J. M. (1990). Natural resources, national accounting and economic depreciation. *Journal of Public Economics, 43*(3), 291–304.

Hartwick, J. M. (1995). Constant consumption paths in open economies with exhaustible resources. *Review of International Economics, 3*(3), 275–283.

Hicks, J. R. (1946). *Value and capital*. Oxford: Oxford University Press.

International Resource Panel, UNEP. (2011). *Decoupling natural resource use and environmental impacts from economic growth*. United Nations Environment Programme. Sustainable Consumption, Production Branch/Earthprint.

Kadekodi, G. (Ed.). (2004). *Environmental economics in practice*. New Delhi: Oxford University Press.

Lange, G. M., Wodon, Q., & Carey, K. (Eds.). (2018). *The changing wealth of nations 2018: Building a sustainable future*. The World Bank.

Malmaeus, J. M. (2016). Economic values and resource use. *Sustainability, 8*(5), 490.

Mumford, K. J. (2016). Prosperity, sustainability and the measurement of wealth. *Asia and The Pacific Policy Studies, 3*(2), 226–234.

Murty, M. N., & Kumar, S. (2004). *Environmental and economic accounting for industry*. New Delhi: Oxford University Press.

Murty, M. N. (2003). *Measuring environmentally corrected net national product: Case studies of industrial water pollution and urban air pollution in India*. Delhi: Mimeo, Institute of Economic Growth.

OECD. (2016). *Greening productivity measurement*. Environmentally Adjusted Multifactor Productivity Growth, Policy Perspectives.

Parikh, K. S., & Parikh, J. (1997). *Accounting and valuation of the environment: Vol 1: A premier for developing countries* (Vol 2). Case Studies from ESCAP region, New York:United Nations.

Parikh, K. S., Parikh, J. K., Sharma, V. K., & Painuly, J. P. (1993). *'Natural resource accounting-A framework for India.* Indira Gandhi Institute of Development Research, Report prepared for the Ministry of Environment and Forests, Government of India.

Pirmana, V., Alisjahbana, A. S., Hoekstra, R., & Tukker, A. (2019). Implementation barriers for a system of environmental-economic accounting in developing countries and its implications for monitoring sustainable development goals. *Sustainability, 11*(22), 6417.

Polasky, S., Bryant, B., Hawthorne, P., Johnson, J., Keeler, B., & Pennington, D. (2015). Inclusive wealth as a metric of sustainable development. *Annual Review of Environment and Resources, 40,* 445–466.

Sankar, U. (2004). Pollution Control in Tanneries. In G. Kadekodi (Ed.), *Environmental economics in practice.* New Delhi: Oxford University Press.

Sengupta, R., & Mandal, S. (2005). *Health Damage cost of automotive air pollution: Cost benefit analysis of fuel quality upgradation for indian cities.* New Delhi: National Institute of Public Finance and Policy, Working Paper no. 37.

Sengupta, R., & Saksena, S. (2007). Macroeconomics and sustainable accounting of resources and income. *India Macroeconomic Annual*, 39–103.

TERI. (1999). Pilot project on natural resource accounting in Goa (Phase I), prepared for Directorate of Planning and Statistics, Goa: Tata Energy Research Institute Project Report No. 99RD61.

UN. (2014). Bureau of the Committee of Experts on Environmental-Economic Accounting (2014). *System of environmental-economic accounting 2012: Central framework.* United Nations Publications.

UN. (2017). In *System of environmental economic accounting 2012–Applications and extensions.* United Nations, New York.

UNCEEA. (2016, June 22–24). *Broad-Brush analysis of SEEA relevant SDG indicators.* New York: United Nations Committee of Experts on Environmental-Economic Accounting.

WWF. (2018). In *Living Planet Report—2018: Aiming Higher* M. Grooten & R. E. A. Almond Grooten (Eds.), Gland, Switzerland: WWF.

Environment and People: Reflections on Perception, Education and Behaviour

Anindita Roy Saha and Nawin Kumar Tiwary

1 Introduction

Environmental policy-making based on neoclassical economic theory may not always be sufficient in achieving the desired outcomes. Studies have shown that social psychology and behavioural economics can play a cardinal role in policy design which can effectively address environmental issues (Cornforth, 2009). Behavioural economics will integrate inputs from social and cognitive psychology to identify and predict people's economic choices (Samson, 2014). An effective environmental policy should make people aware of their habits that are not pro-environmental and should provide alternatives with incentives for environmentally conscious attitude and behaviour. Changing human behaviour is crucial for dealing with many environmental problems, such as pollution, climate change, biodiversity loss and so on. This change may be brought in by incorporating social norms, competitions, group dynamics and other key insights from behavioural economics. Group cooperation can lead to better community outcomes and build a sense of community belonging. The collective identity can lead to a cooperative search for solutions in the realm of public problems, such as those related to the environment. For sustainable resource use and responsible consumer behaviour, there is a definite need for cost-effective and mass scalable behavioural solutions (Frederiks et al., 2015; Garcia-Sierra et al., 2015). It is also worth noting that sometimes economic incentives for environmental services may not be effective as per the expectation. Intrinsic motivation can take

A. R. Saha
Department of Economics, Indraprastha College for Women, University of Delhi, Delhi, India
e-mail: aroysaha@hotmail.com

N. K. Tiwary (✉)
Department of Environmental Studies, Indraprastha College for Women, University of Delhi, Delhi, India
e-mail: tiwarynawin@gmail.com

P. Dasgupta et al. (eds.), *Sustainable Development Insights from India*,
India Studies in Business and Economics,
https://doi.org/10.1007/978-981-33-4830-1_19

a lead in such situations (Lapeyre et al., 2015). In fact, policy nudges that account for the influence of cognitive factors can help overcome barriers and shift choices in socially desirable directions (Valatin et al., 2016).

Individuals not only optimize self-interest, but they also act as members of the civil society that is connected through common interests and collective action. Environmental concerns are perhaps the most connected among all other choices that human beings have to make today. Community awareness is central to solving environmental problems, and the correct behaviour of the group leads to the greatest welfare. Since the ultimate stakeholders in collective outcomes are the members of the community, the success of any environmental policy depends ultimately on the stakeholders' response. Environmentally inclined and trained individuals can contribute to creating a more conscious community that can practise the targeted policies and move towards the desired goals. Economic experience has shown that individuals do not always act on selfish motives but care about fairness and collective benefit in many economic settings (Kesternich et al., 2017). Community awareness and collective behaviour build the foundation for environmental protection, risk management and resilience to the sustainable path. Awareness and education, both individual and collective, can lead to pro-active behaviour that can be central to reviving the damages on ecology, environment and natural resources caused by various anthropogenic activities. The pro-environmental behaviour of individuals, such as a lowered carbon footprint, may not have noticeable changes at a micro-level in the short run. However, small steps of individual members may lead to large, aggregate and long-term benefits for the community and bring in significant societal changes. Science, state and society can play a coordinated role in influencing people's decisions for sustainable choices. Some of these may be currently relevant while some may look diffuse at present and will be needed in future. The role of knowledge and training is crucial to guide individuals in making rational choices in a world bounded by a lack of information. Sometimes, it is also observed that self-reported knowledge and values are not effectively translated into observable behaviour in case of many environmental issues (Frederiks et al., 2015). The human tendency of information avoidance may hinder the process of optimal environmental choices and must be overcome by pro-active policies of sensitization, awareness generation and preparedness. Several agencies other than the state, such as family, educational institutions, media and so on can act as the information base and thereby influence people's perception, consciousness and response to stakes.

2 Environmental Consciousness and Community Response

Environmental consciousness may be described as an extensive and multifaceted psychological construct that reflects an individual's awareness and perception of the environment. An ecologically sensitive individual is one who engages in an extensive range of pro-environmental behaviours based on certain values and attitudes. Thus, environmental consciousness corresponds to what can be considered as the attitudinal aspect of pro-environmental behaviour (Sánchez & Lafuente, 2010). Environmental consciousness functions on the key endogenous factors that influence environmental behaviour. However, certain studies have shown that pro-environmental behaviour may also be influenced by other non-attitudinal exogenous or situational factors. Pro-environmental practices may enhance the level of satisfaction of an individual and his close association with the environment.

Environmentalism encompasses questions about values or beliefs and generally witnesses the relationship between human beings and the environment. Environmental consciousness is an outcome of specific psychological parameters or constructs related to an individual's inclination to participate in pro-environmental behaviour (Schultz & Zelezny, 1999). It deals with the level of endorsement of pro-environmental behaviour (Van Liere & Dunlap, 1981; Dunlap et al., 2000; Dunlap & Liere, 2008). The moral dimension of pro-environmental behaviour has been operationalized by determining the level of personal obligation (Schwartz, 1977). This also reflects the degree to which a person assumes responsibility for environmental problems and considers that it is essential to take action independent of what others do. People's awareness along with the willingness to create any impact in society towards pro-environmental action can bring in an overall societal change.

Examining environmental consciousness requires four attitudinal aspects of human behaviour to be studied in conjunction. These include the act of endorsement of pro-environmental values and the awareness about environmental conditions, called affective dimension; the level of information or specific knowledge, called the cognitive dimension; individual response towards particular environmental action, namely the dispositional dimension and the engagement or involvement in pro-environmental behaviours, namely the active dimension. The pro-environmental behaviour of an individual can be strengthened by general beliefs, certain attitudinal instincts and sensitivity that may be enriched by information, knowledge and training.

2.1 Environmental Education for Pro-Environmental Behaviour

In the real-world characterized by bounded rationality, there are limitations in people's decisions due to their limited thinking capability and lack of information, time and skills. Knowledge and education can play significant roles in facilitating rational decision making for individuals and community groups. Education for sustainable development encompasses a new version of education that aims to empower people to assume responsibility for creating and enjoying a sustainable future. It further empowers people to make informed choices for environmental integrity, economic viability and a just society.

The role of environmental education is to create new patterns of behaviour of individuals, groups and societies towards the environment (Hungerford & Volk, 1990).

The present-day environmental crisis calls for an urgent need to prepare suitable strategies for environmental education among people for saving the natural resources and the planet Earth (Jickling, 2003). Though environmental knowledge may not directly lead to pro-environmental behaviour, it can inspire emotional involvement leading to a pro-environmental consciousness and meaningful action (Kollmuss & Agyeman, 2010). Several studies have explicitly outlined the importance of environmental education at different levels in the formal curriculum in developing a pro-environmental behaviour among its target recipients. Environmental education can provide an important platform for merging values and behaviour with learnt theories and actual practices. The introduction of environmental education can not only enhance the discipline-specific environmental knowledge of students but also facilitate the development of environmental thinking for sustainable development (Charatsari & Lioutas, 2017).

The idea of environmental education dates back to 1968 at the UNESCO Biosphere Reserve Conference held in Paris. This was followed by the Stockholm Conference (1972) where the International Environmental Education Program (IEEP) was created. The objective was to have a coordinated and planned programme for research, learning and educating people for environmental activities and initiatives for sustainable development. International environmental education got a further boost through the Belgrade Charter (1975), Tbilisi Declaration (1977), Brundtland Commission (1987) and later through a series of environmental summits. The attempt to sensitize and educate people about the environment is an ongoing journey in the world reeling under climate emergency.

Since the environmental crisis is largely one of maladaptive behaviour, it is necessary to shift the attitudes and behaviours of people. A combination of several factors leads to the formation of environmentally responsible behaviour. Several agencies contribute to the creation of environmental knowledge, awareness and motivation for such behaviour. The major institutions in this respect are educational institutions, family and public forums such as media, non-governmental agencies and civil society organisations. Schools and colleges can provide the institutional structure for curriculum-based education and activities. Teachers may act as powerful motivators. However, family is the primary unit where the training in lifestyle and values is initiated. It is remarkable to note that even before students are admitted to higher education, they have exposure to various forms of sustainability value sets (Shephard et al., 2009). Communication channels can also have a strong impact on people, thereby influencing their perception, consciousness and resultant behaviour. A community prepared through proper education and training is expected to show greater resilience towards the environmental crises.

2.2 *Preparedness for Environmental Disasters*

Developing countries are more vulnerable to climate change, natural disasters and human tragedy due to the lack of necessary resources and the knowledge about mitigation technologies to face these challenges. The inadequacy in education and training lies in the core of the lack of awareness and preparedness for disasters. The need for skill formation and capacity building for efficient disaster management is paramount.

Disaster preparedness is an extension of environmental education. Knowledge about various safety and mitigatory measures is a pre-requisite for a community's resistance and resilience to disasters. Proper training in disaster management can help people combat disaster and reduce its impact. This may be achieved through a well-designed initiative to educate people at every level to get aware and be prepared to handle disasters, especially in areas that are prone to disasters. The need for disaster risk preparedness has gained tremendous importance in recent times with the increasing number of calamities all over the world.

Natural disasters occur from the natural processes of the earth. A natural disaster can be endo-dynamic or exo-dynamic depending on whether the hazards are arising from within the earth or are originating from outside the earth (Sarvothaman & Kumar, 2013). The former includes earthquakes, volcanic eruption, landslide, tsunami, etc., and the latter includes cyclones, floods, forest fires, etc. Besides the natural ones, there can be anthropogenic disasters for which humans are responsible, such as accidents on road and travel, industrial tragedy, the collapse of structures due to poor quality of construction and so on. Since these have causes rooted in the way society functions and economic activities take place, there must be proper developmental policy planning to handle such events. On the other hand, natural disasters are the ones for which the community needs to be made aware and prepared to combat and reduce the risks. This is where environmental education and training can help build a resilient community.

Disaster risk reduction rests on eight strategies of disaster education. These include knowledge dissemination, educational needs assessment, educational planning, educational approaches, educational content, educational tools, involved organizations and educational learning barriers and challenges (Aghaei et al., 2018). Properly implemented disaster education programs help reduce people's vulnerability to disasters and people have been observed to respond well to such programs (Torani et al., 2019). Children as resources need to be cultivated and mobilized for preparedness, response, recovery and resilience towards disasters (Pfefferbaum et al., 2018). Although children are at the maximum negative risk of natural disasters because of their physical vulnerability to illness, injury and death (Peek, 2008), they are the ones where community preparedness should begin from.

The role of schools can be pivotal in disaster preparedness and risk reduction. It has been observed that the inclusion of disaster issues in the teaching curriculum can prepare the children against disasters in a better way. It is not a hard task to transfer knowledge about disaster through necessary disaster education programmes (Adiyoso & Kanegae, 2013). The participation of students can produce an effective and promising output in disaster management (Ronan et al., 2010). Teachers, parents and leaders can have a great influence on children. Teachers, in particular, can educate children effectively about how to face stress in the everyday world and situations of disasters by using their explanatory style, mind set and hardiness.

They are more likely to be successful in enhancing the resilience of children and young people (Brown, 2015). Studies have also shown that participation in disaster mitigation and management yields numerous potential benefits for children. This may enhance their personal development as well as interpersonal relationships. This helps in organizing community activities through improved social connections and networks which are crucial for disaster preparedness and the development of leaders for the future (Pfefferbaum et al., 2018).

2.3 Environmental Communication for Sensitization

Information is a crucial factor behind the development of people's perception and awareness about environmental protection. While there may be several agencies to sensitize people, media is one of the most impactful instruments because people in developing countries pose faith in what comes in print and what comes as a picture. The role of mass media coverage of any environmental issue is important to bring public consensus and support in favour of the proposed solutions and their effective implementation. People rely on different forms of media, such as print and electronic, to gather theoretical information and recent advances about local and global environmental issues. Therefore, the role of media in influencing people and increasing their commitment to environmental issues becomes very critical.

While children gain knowledge about the environment from textbooks used in schools, they also rely largely on what is available in the mass media platforms. Family, educational institutions and media may thus be considered to be the three main pillars of environmental education and sensitisation. It has been observed that children identify parents, teachers, newspapers and television as complementary sources of information and training. Media is often used as a promotional tool by governments and organizations to induce environmental actions among pro-active individuals (Lowe & Morrison, 1984; Huang, 2016). Several government programmes launched through newspapers and televisions have seen successful implementation due to its huge readership and deep penetration into the remote parts of countries across various socio-economic classes. Governments depend on communication and mass media for disseminating information, setting an agenda for development and dispersal of innovations. On the other hand, media provides important checks and balances to the power of the government. Media gives voice to democracy and acts as an informative bridge between the government and the public. It is supposed to play a crucial role in society by providing unbiased information, acting as a watchdog group against the government and through moral conditioning of the masses. Media, properly utilised, can be an influential agent in guiding people towards pro-environmental behaviour.

However, consistently adhering to journalistic norms can impede the coverage of anthropogenic environmental issues (Boykoff & Boykoff, 2007). Sometimes, corporate firms and institutions with negative environmental legitimacy can use media for changing perceptions regarding their environmental stand (Rupley et al., 2012).

There is a need for media and communications research on environmental issues and controversies in order to reconnect with the traditional sociological concerns about power and inequality in the public sphere (Hansen, 2011). The role of Indian media is equally challenging because the economic development of a fast-growing country can often come in direct conflicts with several binding emission targets and resource use restrictions (Billett, 2010). The media must be careful and unbiased in reporting the scientific evaluation of the issue at hand.

3 Cross-Cutting Environmental Consciousness in India

In view of the central role of the community in attaining environmental goals, it may be pertinent to study the current status of environmental awareness and training of the people of India that is expected to induce pro-environmental behaviour. This section investigates some cases of how education, preparedness and communication have worked in this direction in some select urban areas in India. While environmental education is a mandate from the Supreme Court of India, disaster preparedness is not yet a part of the regular curriculum. The complementary role of the media as an agent of environmental sensitisation may also be put under scrutiny. Three studies carried out in the National Capital Territory (NCT) of Delhi are presented here to provide an insight into the perception, education and connectedness of the members of the civil society through curriculum, training and information.

3.1 Environmental Education: A Case Study in University

Nature occupied a prominent place in ancient Indian scriptures and literature. Conservation of the environment, preservation of the five basic elements and protection of wildlife can be traced back in the records of history. The national education policy and curricula were developed after independence. The constitutional amendment of 1962 included protection and improvement of the natural environment in the fundamental duties. A scheme of environmental orientation to secondary education was introduced in 1988, preceded by the Environment, Education, Awareness and Training (EEAT) programme of the Government of India. Environmental education was made compulsory in formal education in schools through a judgement of the Supreme Court of India in 2003. It took more than ten years to bring in such courses at the levels of higher education all over India. A compulsory course on Environmental Science (EVS) was introduced for students across all disciplines during the first year of their undergraduate programme at the University of Delhi in 2014.

A study was conducted at several colleges of the University of Delhi with an aim to examine the effectiveness of the newly introduced compulsory EVS course that was intended to create a change in the environmental behaviour of the students (Choudhary et al., 2019). The study was designed to analyse the knowledge, sensitivity and attitude of the students towards the environment and the key environmental issues. It also searched for possible behavioural changes among them after completing the compulsory EVS curriculum (Choudhary, 2017). Students in the second year were taken as a sample to evaluate the retention of knowledge and development of consciousness expected out of the compulsory environmental education. In order to have a comprehensive idea about the attitudes of all stakeholders, the viewpoint of the teachers of EVS was also taken into consideration. A questionnaire-based survey was used to collect information from students belonging to different disciplines in different colleges. Simultaneously, teachers were interviewed in the respective colleges.

The first and foremost objective of any educational programme is to impart knowledge that students will retain and apply in appropriate situations. The study revealed some interesting outcomes related to the retention of knowledge from the classroom teaching of the compulsory EVS course. Based on their responses to the questions designed to test their knowledge, students were assigned scores in the range of 0–25. Around 65% of the students scored below 10 and only a small number of students could score above 16. Surprisingly, none of them could score in the highest bracket of 20–25 (Fig. 1). A major reason for this could be their diverse streams of study at the previous levels in school. Results also varied according to the different disciplines they were currently enrolled in, namely science, commerce and humanities. Students with a background in science at the senior secondary level have been found to be generally more informed about various environmental issues and challenges in comparison to those without a background in science. The above result indicates that the current syllabus and pedagogy of the compulsory EVS course is neither adequate

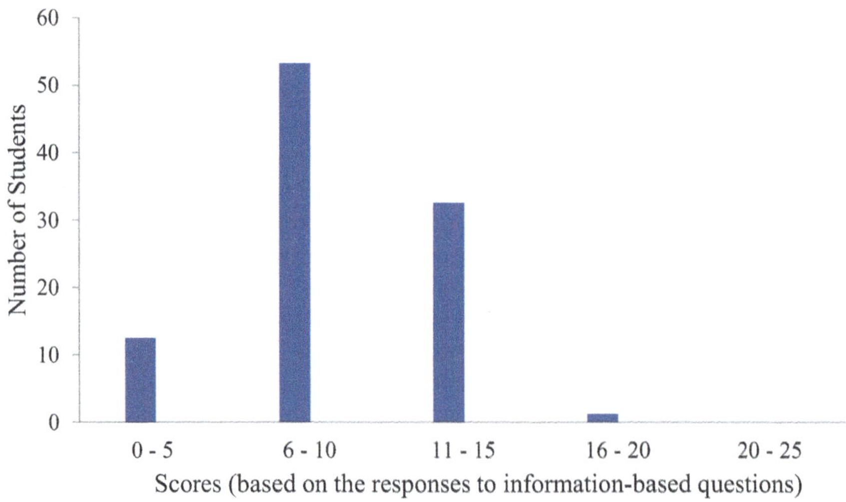

Fig. 1 Knowledge retained by students (in scores out of 25) after studying EVS course

nor inclusive for students of diverse courses and backgrounds. The poor knowledge across the board points to an overall deficiency in the curriculum.

Students are the leaders for tomorrow. Their perception of responsibility in matters related to environmental protection will chart the future path for civil society. The students considered their personal responsibility of environmental conservation to be greater than those of industries, governments and environmental action groups. It is encouraging that the young students of urban India are willing to own the task of maintaining a healthy environment for all. In this journey, they want to have other agents, such as media, family and teachers along with them. Media seems to have the greatest impact in sensitizing them (Fig. 2). Furthermore, media has brought to them the information about the significant role of the non-governmental organisations in leading environmental actions along with the effective generation of information and knowledge base that is necessary for environmental conservation. Family and teachers play a significant and somewhat equal role in spreading awareness among children. On the contrary, textbooks have a minimum contribution to make when it comes to creating consciousness about contemporary environmental issues. Hands-on training and exposure to practical problems make greater impact in environmental education. Students have revealed the lowest preference for textbook curriculum as an instrument of sensitisation beyond being a mere source of knowledge.

The study further investigated how the students perceive the relative importance of various environmental challenges, such as pollution, deforestation, resource depletion, waste management, overpopulation, climate change and so on. They considered overpopulation to be the most severe environmental problem of the twenty-first century, followed by climate change, air pollution and water scarcity (Fig. 3). It was interesting to note that the students considered deforestation, water pollution, resource depletion and waste management as relatively less important when compared to the more popular problems like overpopulation and climate change. The understanding of the macro—and micro-environmental issues as parts of a whole is

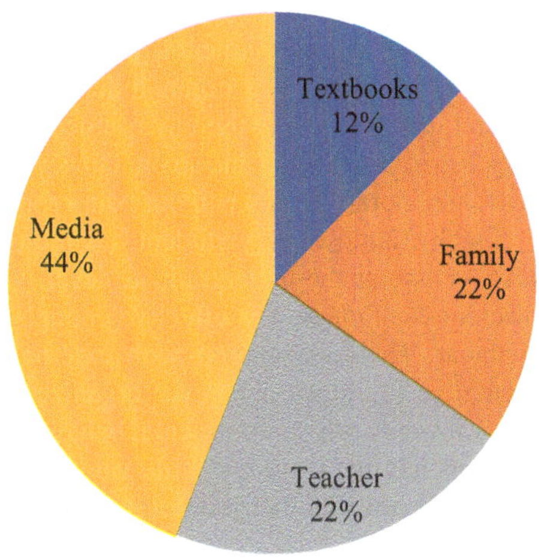

Fig. 2 Students' perception about various instruments of environmental awareness

Fig. 3 Students' perception about the importance of various environmental issues

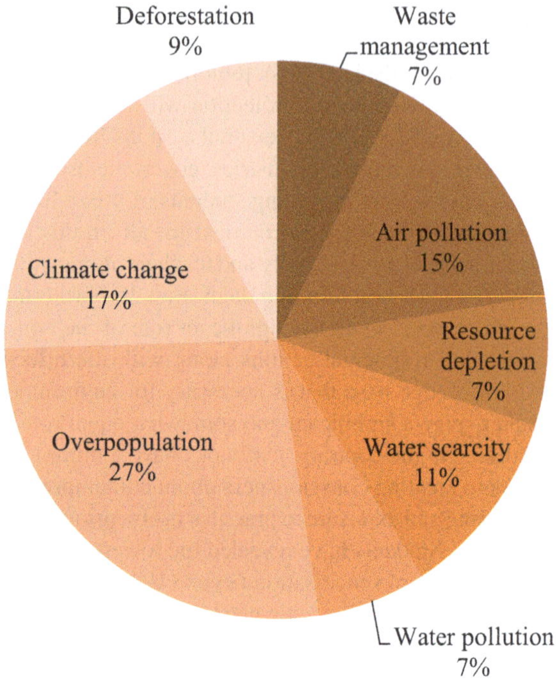

important to comprehend the extent and dimensions of the bigger picture of the environmental crisis. Unless they are initiated towards comprehensive thinking about environmental problems, it may be difficult to create a brigade of environmentally conscious youth geared to lead a community.

Students were also asked about their opinion on the relative roles of classroom teaching and extra-curricular activities in generating interest in environmental issues. They assigned almost equal weights to formal education and other activities. Active participation in environmental projects, academic seminars and conferences are attractive to them. The urban Indian youth is enthusiastic about celebrating the special days related to the environment, such as Earth Day, Wetland Day, Ozone Day, Environment Day and so on. However, the latter may be a behaviour influenced by contemporary trends without being rooted in any conscious perception.

Finally, almost every student has the opinion that the current pedagogy of the EVS course at the undergraduate level is not effective in creating environmental awareness although it is effective enough in imparting knowledge about the environment. Their association with external agencies and involvement in environmental programmes, wherever organized, have actually driven them more effectively towards pro-environmental behaviour than the curriculum. Almost 80% of the students felt that there was little value addition through this EVS course over what they had learned in their school in terms of both education and awareness. Students revealed eagerness to go for field trips for greater understanding and hands-on experience. However, more than half of the students have not been taken for any field trip during this course. A common consensus among students was that the current form of compulsory environmental education has been more theoretical. A true education in the environment can be imparted only when practical teaching complements the classroom.

The other major stakeholders in the process of education are the teachers. The survey was extended to study their perception about the effectiveness of the existing pedagogy and tools used for disseminating environmental education. Similar to the students, teachers attached the greatest importance to media in spreading awareness among people regarding environmental issues (Fig. 4). They consider families to be a powerful institution too. Textbooks and regular curricula are less impactful than participation in environmental activities, both on the ground as well as in academic seminars and conferences. The dependence on other sources and agencies for imparting education shows some kind of a limitation in their roles that the teachers perceive. A redesigning of the curriculum and rethinking of the pedagogy can help attract the students and encourage pro-environmental behaviour.

The need for linking classroom teaching with real-life environmental issues as a part of projects on awareness and education has long been identified (Goyal & Gupta, 2014). Problems originating from real-life situations are important for environmental education. Students can be encouraged more about the environment if they are exposed to the challenges faced and observed around them. The teachers agreed that the curriculum is loaded with theories, focusing on the concepts of sustainable development, ecological challenges and so on. Students seem to be more inquisitive about real-life problems, such as resource scarcity, pollution, global warming. The teachers felt that the involvement in activities outside the classrooms has succeeded more in generating interest in the young minds. Their sensitivity towards trees, plants and wildlife has been fostered through events like tree census, bird walk, butterfly

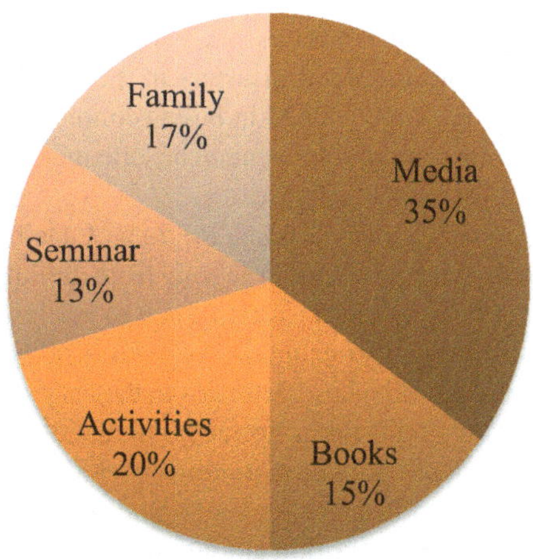

Fig. 4 Teachers' perception about various instruments of environmental awareness

count and so on, wherever organized. The majority of the teachers felt that there is an observable change in the behaviour of the students. However, the effectiveness of the compulsory classroom education cannot be credited as the prime reason for this. Unfortunately, all teachers did not seem to be excited about teaching this course too. Dedication on the part of the educator and blending of classroom lessons with practical components are what seem to be the two major lacunae that need immediate attention. A combined involvement of the mentors and mentees can make environmental education holistic. Bringing in behavioural change in the community will remain unattainable unless there is a convergence of interest among all stakeholders. The collective efforts of all involved parties is the key to the success of environmental education (Chawla & Cushing, 2007).

Successful implementation of environmental education requires a proper administrative setup for the development of curriculum and curricular materials, training, research, monitoring and evaluation (Shimray, 2016). In a fast-changing world with new types of environmental challenges arising every day, the policymakers of environmental education must make active efforts to ensure that the curriculum and syllabus are sustainable and remains relevant over a period of time.

3.2 Disaster Risk Preparedness Among Youth: A Case Study in Schools

India is among the top countries that most frequently faced natural disasters during the last two decades. The climatic condition and geographical location make India vulnerable to disasters. Almost 60% of the landmass of India lies in the areas prone to earthquakes ranging from mid to high intensity. The Himalayan belt, especially the region covering Northern and North-Eastern India, is very active and experience frequent earthquakes. India is home to a large number of rivers whose conditions cause floods and drought frequently. In India, 75% of the rainfall causes a heavy discharge of water and 12% of India's landmass is prone to flood. The country experienced several disasters in the last 30 years which have killed a large number of people and resulted in huge economic losses (Kumar et al., 2011). India has also become vulnerable to nuclear, chemical and biological accidents in the course of developmental activities.

The National Capital Region of Delhi has a multitude of environmental and ecological problems, ranging from pollution to disaster risk. Delhi is vulnerable to several natural disasters, such as earthquakes, fire and floods due to geographical as well as socio-economic reasons. The greatest risk of natural disasters in Delhi is one of earthquakes. Delhi lies in the very sensitive seismic zone 4 with a large number of active fault lines. So far 20 potential fault lines around the region of Delhi have been identified within a radius of 300 km. Delhi's seismicity is associated with the Delhi-Haridwar Ridge geological structure (Iyengar & Ghosh, 2004). Delhi occupies the third position among the five most earthquake-prone cities in India. Around

6.5% of the residential houses in Delhi have a high risk of getting damaged and 85.5% of houses are likely to suffer moderate damage in case of an earthquake with the shaking intensity of 8 (Ministry of Urban Development,1997). The flooding of Yamuna is an annual feature causing major disruption to people living in the flood-plains in particular and residents of the city in general. Apart from the geological factors, the high density of the population is another major concern. With a large population of 11,034,555 (Census of India, 2011) and a small area of 1484 km^2, the risk of disaster is very high in several parts of Delhi. There is a significantly large number of unauthorized colonies and settlements in various locations that add to the worries. Fire becomes an uncontrollable disaster that generates from such dense living conditions, both in residential settlements and in the factory areas. There is also a fast increase in the number of infrastructure projects, such as metro rail, road bridges, underpasses, flyovers, that do not always follow environmental compliance. All these factors have made the national capital city vulnerable to various kinds of natural and man-made calamities.

The immediate goal of community response to the risk of disasters should be preparedness. Disaster training is a life skill that can build the long-term resilience of communities. Although people practise several short-term measures to handle calamities and the government has standardized systems of disaster management, a well-planned policy of sustainable preparedness must be available with the communities as a knowledge for life. Capacity building in disaster preparedness must start from schools, homes and civil societies. Teachers, parents and leaders can create long-lasting impacts on young minds by training the children today and building the leaders for tomorrow. The current case study examines the status of disaster risk awareness and preparedness of school-going children in some selected schools of Delhi.

A survey was conducted in select schools of the National Capital Territory run by the Government of Delhi. The students of classes six to ten were asked a set of questions meant to assess their knowledge and skill to face disasters that were expected to have been attained through curriculum design, implementation and skill development programs (Singh, 2019). The main objective of the study was to trace a possible time path of knowledge and preparedness of the students as they grow up through the phases of secondary education. The respondents were asked questions related to basic knowledge about natural and man-made disasters, such as earthquakes, floods, fire. The respondents were asked questions related to basic knowledge about natural and man-made disasters, such as earthquake, flood and fire, covering their definition, types, causes, measures and so on. The respondents also answered questions on mitigation techniques, helpline numbers and other possible responses in case of such calamities.

The study showed that the basic knowledge about disasters did not increase directly with the increase in the academic class for most of the students. Forty-four % of the students in class six had adequate knowledge about different types of disasters like earthquake, fire and flood. The share increased significantly to 56% in class seven and 68% in class eight. However, the percentage share of correct answers started to fall after the peak in class eight, namely 57% in class nine and

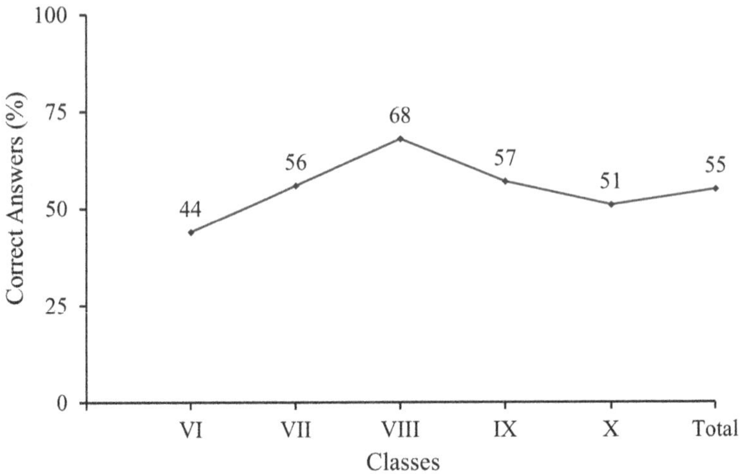

Fig. 5 Knowledge of students about disasters

51% in class ten (Fig. 5). The downward trend in knowledge retention is alarming from the viewpoint of capacity building. This may be traced in the casual attitude of the students as they grow up. This may also be due to the academic pressure for school-leaving examinations in the formal education system in India. Co-curricular education getting deprioritized is a major concern because disaster education must be imparted simultaneously if a society is to be made aware and equipped to handle disasters.

Students were further assessed on the level of their preparedness to face fire, flood, earthquake and other disasters. The preparedness for fire hazards was satisfactory (Fig. 6). Maximum number of students knew the helpline number of the fire brigade although very few of them knew about the general disaster management helpline. While most of the respondents knew about the fire brigade, not even half of them were aware of the 'stop, drop and roll' technique that is the immediate necessary action even before the arrival of the fire tender. They also lack specific knowledge about mitigation techniques for the different types of fire, such as fire from natural causes, electricity, LPG cylinder and so on. All schools have installed fire extinguishers under government directives. However, on being asked at a personal level, students admitted that they do not know the use of fire extinguishers. The other technique of 'drop, cover and hold' to be used as safety against earthquake was also unknown to the majority of the respondents. The students lack any clear idea about the real risks and intensity of disasters in general and earthquakes in particular. The low level of awareness and preparedness for earthquakes is a matter of concern in a city like Delhi that is so prone to earthquakes.

There was a progression in the awareness about helpline numbers related to disasters, particularly fire, with higher levels of formal education. With increasing age and education, gathering information from external sources becomes easier. On the

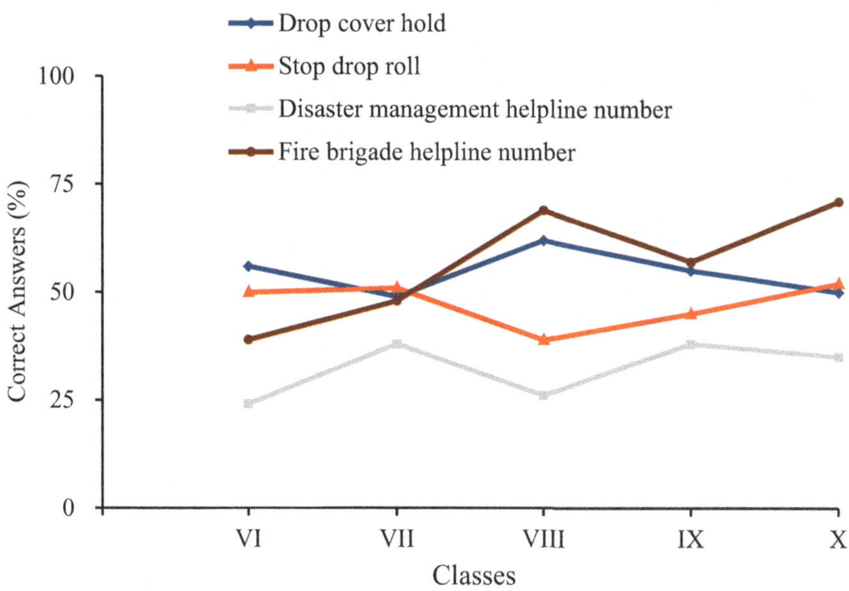

Fig. 6 Awareness about mitigation techniques related to disasters

contrary, their basic skills of immediate actions have not improved with time. The class-wise patterns and fluctuations in indicators of preparedness have evened out over time in cases of basic skills. The overall status of preparedness remains somewhat the same across classes and is less than satisfactory. Considering the basic knowledge and specific management skills of the students in the sample, it may be said that the disaster education in Delhi is far less than adequate. To build a disaster-resilient society, the national capital of India has to go a long way.

The poor state of awareness and preparedness for disasters calls for scrutiny of the school curricula, pedagogy and teaching practices. Two indicators were used in this regard, namely textbooks as a source of knowledge and mock drills and/or hands-on training in schools. It was surprising that the students, in general, have responded in the affirmative regarding the identification of textbooks as the basic source of knowledge. They have also stated that mock drills were conducted in schools. However, it did not turn out to be very effective as the students performed poorly on both awareness and preparedness indicators. While theoretical knowledge is imparted in the class, there is not enough understanding among the students about the real-time response to disasters.

Although not designed initially in the survey objectives, an interesting pattern was observed in the gender distribution among the students in the indicators of disaster risk awareness and preparedness. Female students showed greater awareness in basic knowledge about floods and disasters in general (Fig. 7). Although the male students were more aware about earthquake and fire, a larger number of girls knew about the basic techniques of 'stop drop roll' and 'drop cover hold'. Both boys and girls know

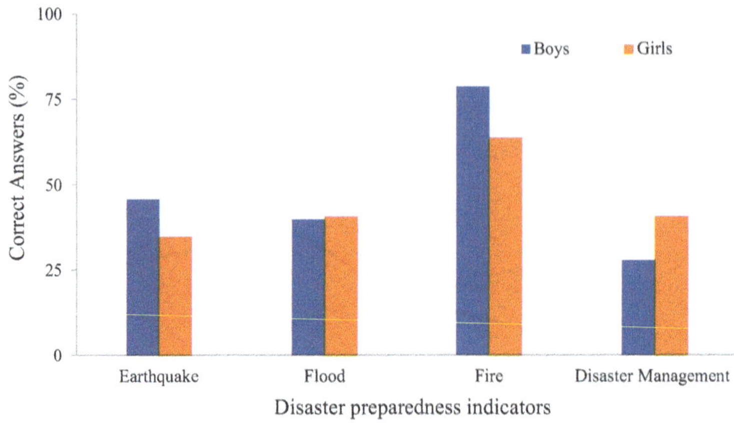

Fig. 7 Gender-wise distribution of disaster awareness and preparedness

less about earthquakes and floods than fire. This may be the result of their greater exposure to frequent fires in the dense urban settlements. On the whole, girls have revealed somewhat higher levels of awareness as well as knowledge about mitigation techniques. This may be an important input in designing policies for disaster training and team building. Girls may be used in larger numbers and in leading positions in building the task force for disaster management.

The management bodies of the schools were also surveyed as the other group of stakeholders involved in designing and implementing policies. Their attitude and efficiency reflect in the education and training outcomes of the students. It was found that most schools lack the necessary infrastructure and logistical support to handle disasters. Electrical wiring and fittings were not regularly replaced. The fire extinguishers were mostly non-functional although their number was large. Schools kept the mandatory sand buckets although the students are not well-versed with the use. The mandatory disaster management kits were available in the schools. Mock drills, visit by the medical and disaster rescue teams were part of the school activity calendar. However, these do not seem to have trickled down to the target group, namely students. The school managements were regular with sending relief in cases of disasters elsewhere and seemed to be complacent with such an indirect role.

To sum up, the study reveals major deficiencies in the existing school curriculum regarding the generation of knowledge and development of necessary skills for disaster management. The level of knowledge and basic skills among school children was found to be less than satisfactory. Urgent attention needs to be paid in designing textbooks, developing pedagogy and imparting skills among children in order to build a capacity to cope with disasters. The results suggest an immediate and mandatory education for disaster management as part of the regular school curricula to ensure safe living.

3.3 Environmental Communication: A Case Study in Media

The development of community consciousness in India seems to have been far behind the desired level. Formal education systems have not been successful in creating a community of students that is conscious, aware and trained duly in matters related to the environment. While there have been attempts through academic curricula, the onus of sensitisation also remains significantly with the family, media and similar institutions. The final case study focuses on the role played by the media in igniting pro-environmental behaviour among people. It attempts to examine how far the Indian print media has been successful as an influencer of environmental consciousness by giving due coverage to environmental issues in recent years (Dwivedi, 2019).

The Constitution of India guarantees freedom of speech and expression under Article 19 (a) which formed the basis of free media. The modern-day media can be broadly classified into print media (newspapers and magazines), broadcast media (television and radio) and Internet (social media, blogs, websites and other channels). Media has played an important role in bringing environmental issues to the fore and thereby raising environmental awareness among masses. Magazines like *Down to Earth* have helped in bringing Indian environmental issues to the general public. *Dainik Bhaskar*, a Hindi newspaper started '*Jal Bachao Abhiyan*' among its readers in different states and had a great impact. For over a decade, *Dainik Bhaskar* organizes '*Jal Satyagrah*' during April and May to raise awareness and appeals to individuals to 'save water'. The campaign motivates people to take a pledge and encourages them to save 15% of daily water usage. There are other influential mediums of broadcasting information. Channels like *Discovery*, *Animal Planet* and *National Geographic* on television and programmes like '*Ye Kahan aa Gaye Hum*' on radio have helped in increasing awareness about the environment among people. However, more and more people are now relying on the internet for news and information instead of traditional sources like print and broadcast media. Social Media websites like Twitter, Facebook, Instagram are popular among people as it gives voices to millions of people which was otherwise impossible a few years ago. Many successful social media campaigns have emerged recently. For example, the *Ice Bucket Challenge* raised awareness regarding Alzheimer's disease and the *MeToo* movement against sexual harassment of women. Similarly, environmental consciousness can be propagated by the successful use of these modern forms of media.

Climate change, global warming, depleting ice cover, particulate matter emissions, sustainable development are some of the buzzwords in media these days. The environmental problems, which threaten not only the present-day existence but also the future of humanity and life on earth, are brought to people's attention by the media. Mass media can play a vital role in creating peoples' awareness about the environment and conservation of natural resources. It can help mobilize people to take necessary actions for promoting environmental quality and preserving ecological balance. As communication contributes to dialogue and social actions, it helps create people's awareness about the environment just as it does for any other social issue.

The current case study is based on the scrutiny of selected newspapers in terms of the reporting on environmental issues in national dailies in vernacular (Hindi) and English languages. The newspapers with the highest readership are representative of the extent of reach to the common mass who are the greatest stakeholders. Based on the IRS 2019 (Indian Readership Survey 2019) for the National Capital Region of Delhi, *Hindustan Times* had the highest readership among the English dailies while *Navbharat Times* had the largest readership among the Hindi dailies. Hence, these two newspapers were selected to collect data on articles on environmental issues published over a representative period of one year, namely May 2018 to April 2019. The three major categories of environmental news chosen for the study were air quality and pollution, solid waste management, water pollution and sanitation. These are identified as representative of daily environmental threats in the urban ecosystems.

The study showed a seasonal pattern in the reporting of items. The news articles related to air pollution were published in large numbers during October, November and December in both English and Hindi newspapers (Fig. 8). The highest number of articles related to air pollution appeared in November. This is usually the period when air pollution in Delhi is at the peak due to temperature inversion, stubble burning and cracker burning during Diwali. However, news articles relating to air quality appeared throughout the year in the English daily, though far less in importance than the early winter months. Coverage in the Hindi newspaper is comparatively less throughout the year. This may be attributed to the elitist readership associated with English and the urban inclination of the entire pollution discourse. The major section of readers of Hindi newspapers are the poorer people with greater exposure to hazardous indoor air quality in various forms, ranging from polluting cooking fuel to suffocating factory environments. Since poor air quality is a part of their life, ambient air pollution does not add much to their existing consciousness about health risks. The awareness about ambient air pollution draws more attention of those otherwise enjoying cleaner environments.

On the contrary, the coverage of issues related to water was more dominant in the Hindi newspaper. This gained even greater significance during the monsoon months of July and August. Issues related to water aggravate during the rainy season because of the poor drainage system of the city and old water pipelines. The older parts of the city that inhabit more of the Hindi-speaking population face these problems more than the developed parts of New Delhi. The clear divide between the people of Delhi distributed over the old and new areas correlate directly with both the linguistic divide and the priority of pollution variables like air and water. This points to a deficiency in the overall coverage of the larger pollution picture across the class of readers.

Solid waste management as a topic of news coverage has shown a similar pattern of elitism in reporting. The English-speaking people typically reside in areas better managed in terms of civic amenities. Therefore, the English newspapers covered comparatively fewer news items on waste. The poorer section of the population, residing mostly in areas with poorer civic infrastructure is the target reader of the Hindi newspapers. The greater inclusion of waste management problems in the Hindi

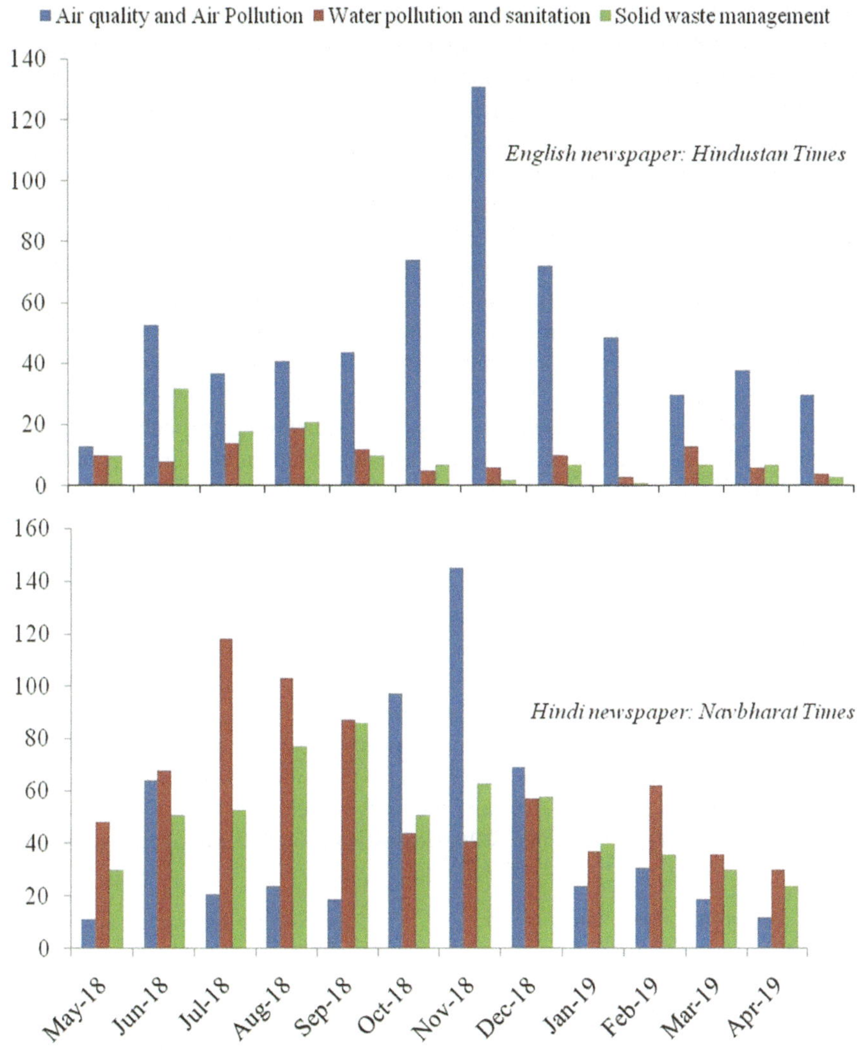

Fig. 8 Number of news articles on different types of pollution published in English and Hindi dailies

dailies may thus be explained by this simple difference in the social character of communities.

The gravity of any news article can easily be estimated by the position assigned to it. In the case of newspapers, it may be with reference to the page where the particular news article appears. Any news which is in a prime position on the front page catches the eye of the reader immediately. Stories on the editorial page tend to assign greater importance to an issue while the news in the city or metro section remains more or less local. News published in the national section is the ones designated with national importance. The second objective of the study was to scrutinize the location of environmental information in these alternative places, thereby trying to gauge the significance environmental information receives.

The English daily covered the environmental issues throughout the study period in all four sections, viz. Front Page, Metro, National and Editorial. However, most of the coverage was in the metro Sect. (78.5%). Only 13.7% of the news was printed on the first page and a mere 3.5% got a place in the editorial section. A mere 4.3% of the news articles in the national section refer to environmental issues, thereby showing the limited significance assigned to the capital's environmental problems in the national context. Similarly, the majority of the news coverage (86.6%) in the Hindi daily was published in the metro/city section and 13.2% of news articles on the front page (Fig. 9). Environmental news did not figure in editorial and national sections at all in the Hindi newspaper. There is an overall trend of confining environmental news to a local level. While this may be adequate in generating awareness among the people directly concerned, it fails to spread awareness among the larger population. The clear deficit in publishing environmental news in the prime locations, except for the crucial months, shows a lower priority assigned to environmental information in India.

The importance assigned to a particular type of news may be judged by the area devoted to it in the newspaper. It has already been found that environmental news as a whole has not gained much importance in the Indian dailies. That same pattern may be observed in the shares of areas dedicated to environmental information vis-à-vis other news in the newspapers. Further scrutiny may be made to check the relative significance of air, water and waste as components of the pollution matrix. Air quality and pollution seem to be of comparatively greater significance in both English and Hindi newspapers (0.65–0.76% of the total area, respectively). On the other hand, the shares of news related to water pollution possess merely 0.1 and 0.5% in the two

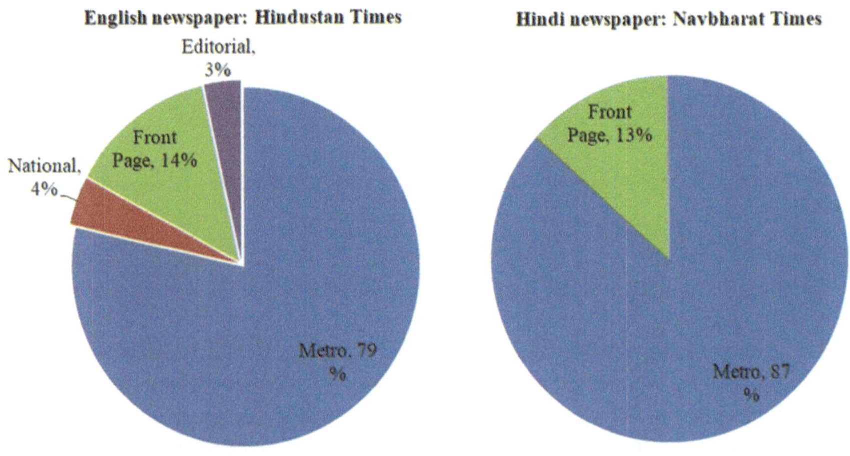

Fig. 9 Section-wise coverage of news in English and Hindi dailies

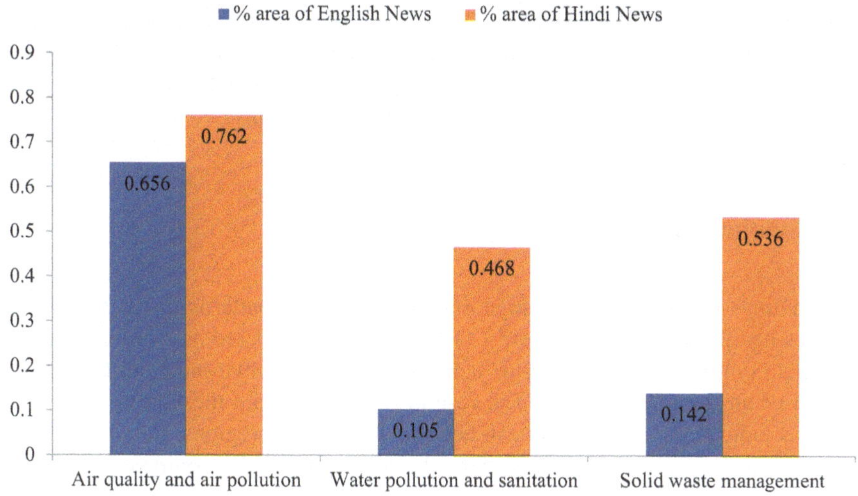

Fig. 10 Shares of news related to pollution in English and Hindi dailies

newspapers, respectively. The corresponding shares of issues related to waste are somewhat similar to the latter (Fig. 10). However, it may be noted that all shares are abysmally low.

The print media in the national capital seems to have assigned much lower priority to environmental information than required. News items shoot up with sporadic episodes of environmental threats, such as smog, flood and so on. There is no regular trend in reporting the continuous degradation and damage that is happening in the environment of Delhi in particular and elsewhere in general. The air quality of Delhi is unhealthy during most of the year and the river Yamuna is polluted even after a large sum of money has been spent on the cleaning projects. Solid waste mountains are encircling Delhi. Yet consistent reporting on these issues is majorly absent. Moreover, there are hardly any follow-ups of the sensational pollution stories. The real environmental crisis calls for a lot more than merely event-based and spot-based journalism.

Environmental journalism is a complex issue. It connects economy, history, geography and politics along with science and technology. Hence, in the absence of expert involvement in presenting the information, it becomes difficult for readers to understand these interconnected issues, especially in the case of the readers of the Hindi newspapers. Media has the potential to play a prominent role in breaking the silence when it comes to environmental problems and in creating an atmosphere that encourages discussions, community participation and behavioural change. Media's efforts to sensitize the public on environmental issues and in leading the struggle against the cause of the environment are very crucial. There are many parameters on which our editors and journalists can improve while covering stories related to the environment. Recruitment of experts on the environment in media houses will help lift the layers from the complex stories so that the common man can understand them easily. It is also important to note that reporting should not be based on criticism only. Media is an agency that can influence people by providing optimistic solutions. Positive stories can help in fostering confidence among people and help them motivate further to solve environmental problems by pro-environmental action.

4 Concluding Remarks

The findings of the above investigations reveal certain patterns in the way India handles her environmental concerns. Delhi may be considered as representative of the urban culture of the country as it faces most of the environmental challenges typical of an urban ecosystem. The results emanating from these studies may be taken as indicative of issues that can be extended to other regions. Lessons may be learnt from these smaller investigations in understanding environmental issues of greater significance and in looking for suitable solutions.

The observations point at an overall inadequacy in the current state of environmental education, preparedness of students, commitment of teachers and involvement of public agencies in the goal of creating an eco-resilient civil society. Compulsory environmental education, both at school and in higher education, has not been able to meet the objective of community sensitisation. The regular curricula have failed to attract the youth towards pro-environmental behaviour despite imparting basic knowledge in the classroom. In a situation where the youth is ready to take up initiatives for sustainable living, the leaders and policymakers must guide them in the right direction.

The regular school curriculum in India does not incorporate co-curricular education in disaster risk preparedness. Although there are mandatory drills, inspections and combatting equipment, the level of knowledge and extent of skill among the children is insufficient to handle real-life situations. There is an immediate need to impart disaster training to the children if the long-term goal of building a resilient society is to be met.

While the stipulated curriculum on the environment is expected to play the role of the educator, there needs to be additional sources of sensitisation to bring in behavioural change. These include community outreach programmes, media involvement and so on. With universal involvement, greater focus and proper implementation of the environmental education policy, generations of students can be produced with heightened environmental consciousness and pro-environmental behaviour.

The role of Indian media has also been limited in sensitizing the members of civil society. Insufficient coverage of environmental news, the bias in reporting and lack of consistent focus on environmental journalism have resulted from the lower priority assigned to environmental issues. The power of media must be directed towards building a society concerned and committed to the environmental cause. Recruitment of experts on the environment in various media houses will help in bringing the right analysis behind any complex environmental issue to a larger audience.

In all the above cases, a lot is yet to be done in creating an environment of awareness, preparedness and knowledge communication in the society. People's behaviour which is dependent on these fundamentals cannot be adequately pro-environmental unless training and education are redesigned over the prevailing ones. All components of the civil society will have to be involved in this participative process of environmental consciousness and sensitisation. The collective behavioural change will be possible only when every member is aware and endowed with the requisite knowledge and skill. These findings may act as inputs for framing the right set of policies for sustainable development in India where the trained, equipped and dedicated youth propagate pro-environmental behaviour to build their common sustainable future.

Acknowledgements The case studies presented here are based on the postgraduate dissertations of Shrishti Chaudhary, Sunny Singh and Shivam Dwivedy at the Department of Environmental Studies, University of Delhi, under the supervision of Dr. Anindita Roy Saha. The authors thank these students and all respondents of the various surveys.

References

Adiyoso, W., & Kanegae, H. (2013). Effectiveness of disaster-based school program on students' earthquake-preparedness. *Journal Disaster Research, 8*:1009–1017.https://doi.org/10.20965/jdr.2013.p1009

Aghaei, N., Seyedin, H., & Sanaeinasab, H. (2018). Strategies for disaster risk reduction education: A systematic review. *Journal Education Health Promotion, 7,* 1–8. https://doi.org/10.4103/jehp.jehp.

Belgrade Charter (1975). The Belgrade charter: A framework for environmental education. Retrieved from http://unesdoc.unesco.org/images/0001/000177/017772eb.pdf.

Billett, S. (2010). Dividing climate change: Global warming in the Indian mass media. *Climate Change, 99,* 1–16. https://doi.org/10.1007/s10584-009-9605-3.

Boykoff, M. T., & Boykoff, J. M. (2007). Climate change and journalistic norms: A case-study of US mass-media coverage. *Geoforum, 38,* 1190–1204. https://doi.org/10.1016/j.geoforum.2007.01.008.

Brown, R. (2015). Building children and young people's resilience: Lessons from psychology. *International Journal Disaster Risk Reduction, 14,* 115–124. https://doi.org/10.1016/j.ijdrr.2015.06.007.

Brundtland, G. H. (1987). Our common future: report of the world commission on environment and development. *Medicine Conflict Survive, 4*(1), 300. https://doi.org/10.1080/0748800880840 8783.

Census of India. (2011). Census of India.

Charatsari, C., & Lioutas, E. D. (2017). Environmental education in university schools : A study in a logistics faculty. *Applied Environmental Education Communications, 17,* 124–135. https://doi.org/10.1080/1533015X.2017.1366884.

Chawla, L., & Cushing, D. F. (2007). Education for strategic environmental behavior education for strategic environmental behavior. *Environmental Education Research, 13,* 437–452. https://doi.org/10.1080/13504620701581539.

Choudhary, S. (2017). *The role of compulsory environmental education in higher learning: A critical analysis.* Master's dissertation, Department of Environmental Studies, University of Delhi, (unpublished).

Choudhary, S., Saha, A.R., & Tiwary, N.K. (2019). The role of compulsory environmental education in higher learning: A study in the University of Delhi. *Applied Environmental Education Communications. 0,* 1–13. https://doi.org/10.1080/1533015X.2019.1605946

Cornforth, A. (2009). Behaviour change: Insights for environmental policy making from social psychology and behavioural economics. *Policy, 5,* 21–28. https://doi.org/10.1098/rstb.2007.0038.

Dunlap, R. E., & Van, L. K. D. (2008). The new environmental paradigm. *Journal Environment Educaation, 40,* 19–28. https://doi.org/10.1080/00139254.1971.10801578.

Dunlap, R. E., Van Liere, K. D., Mertig, A. G., & Jones, R. E. (2000). Measuring endorsement of the new ecological paradigm: A revised NEP scale. *Journal Sociology Issues, 56,* 425–442. https://doi.org/10.1111/0022-4537.00176.

Dwivedi, S. (2019). *Print media and Delhi'S environment coverage: A study of selected newspapers of Delhi.* Master's dissertation, Department of Environmental Studies, University of Delhi, (unpublished).

Frederiks, E. R., Stenner, K., & Hobman, E. V. (2015). Household energy use: Applying behavioural economics to understand consumer decision-making and behaviour. *Renewable and Sustainable Energy Reviews, 41,* 1385–1394. https://doi.org/10.1016/j.rser.2014.09.026.

Garcia-Sierra, M., van den Bergh, J. C. J. M., & Miralles-Guasch, C. (2015). Behavioural economics, travel behaviour and environmental-transport policy. *Transportation Research Part D Transport Environment, 41,* 288–305. https://doi.org/10.1016/j.trd.2015.09.023.

Goyal, E., & Gupta, M. (2014). Moving toward socially and environmentally responsible management education—A case study of Mumbai. *Applied Environmental Education Communications, 13,* 146–161. https://doi.org/10.1080/1533015X.2014.965802.

Hansen, A. (2011). Communication, media and environment: Towards reconnecting research on the production, content and social implications of environmental communication. *International Communications Gazette, 73,* 7–25. https://doi.org/10.1177/1748048510386739.

Huang, H. (2016). Media use, environmental beliefs, self-efficacy, and pro-environmental behavior. *Journal Business Research, 69,* 2206–2212. https://doi.org/10.1016/j.jbusres.2015.12.031.

Hungerford, H. R., & Volk, T. L. (1990). Changing learner behavior through environmental education. *Journal Environmental Education, 21,* 8–21. https://doi.org/10.1080/00958964.1990.10753743.

Indian Readership Survey (2019) Indian Readership Survey, Q1

Iyengar, R.N., Ghosh, S. (2004). Seismic hazard mapping of Delhi City. In 13th World conference on earthquake engineering. pp. 1–15.

Jickling, B. (2003). Environmental education and environmental advocacy: Revisited. *Journal Environmental Education, 34,* 20–27. https://doi.org/10.1080/00958960309603496.

Kesternich, M., Reif, C., & Rübbelke, D. (2017). Recent trends in behavioral environmental economics. *Environmental Resource Economics, 67,* 403–411. https://doi.org/10.1007/s10640-017-0162-3.

Kollmuss, A., & Agyeman, J. (2010). Mind the gap : Why do people act environmentally and what are the barriers to pro-environmental behavior ? Mind tge Gap : Why do people act environmentally and what are the barriers to. *Environment Education Research, 8,* 239–260. https://doi.org/10.1080/1350462022014540.

Kumar, K.J.A., Walia, A., Chaturvedi, S. (2011). India Disaster Report.

Lapeyre, R., Pirard, R., & Leimona, B. (2015). Payments for environmental services in Indonesia: What if economic signals were lost in translation? *Land Use Policy, 46,* 283–291. https://doi.org/10.1016/j.landusepol.2015.03.004.

Lowe, P., & Morrison, D. (1984). Bad news or good news: Environmental politics and the mass media. *Sociology Review, 32,* 75–90. https://doi.org/10.1111/j.1467-954X.1984.tb00780.x.

Ministry of Urban Development. (1997). Vulnerability Atlas of India.

Peek, L. (2008). Children and disasters: understanding vulnerability, developing capacities, and promoting resilience—an introduction. *Child Youth Environment, 18,* 1–29.

Pfefferbaum, B., Pfefferbaum, R.L., & Van Horn, R.L. (2018). Involving children in disaster risk reduction: the importance of participation. *European Journal Psychotraumatology* 9https://doi.org/10.1080/20008198.2018.1425577.
Ronan, K. R., Crellin, K., & Johnston, D. (2010). Correlates of hazards education for youth: A replication study. *Natural Hazards, 53,* 503–526. https://doi.org/10.1007/s11069-009-9444-6.
Rupley, K. H., Brown, D., & Marshall, R. S. (2012). Governance, media and the quality of environmental disclosure. *Journal of Accounting and Public Policy, 31,* 610–640. https://doi.org/10.1016/j.jaccpubpol.2012.09.002.
Samson, A. (2014). In The behavioral economics guide
Sánchez, M. J., & Lafuente, R. (2010). Defining and measuring environmental consciousness. *International Review of Sociology, 68,* 731–755. https://doi.org/10.3989/ris.2008.11.03.
Sarvothaman, H., & Kumar, A. K. J. (2013). *Disaster management: Engineering and environmental aspects.* Delhi: Asiatech Publishers Inc.
Schwartz, S. H. (1977). Normative influences on altruism. *Advances in Experimental Social Psychology, 10,* 221–279. https://doi.org/10.1016/S0065-2601(08)60358-5.
Shephard, K., Mann, S., Smith, N., & Deaker, L. (2009). Benchmarking the environmental values and attitudes of students in New Zealand's post-compulsory education. *Environment Education Research, 15,* 571–587. https://doi.org/10.1080/13504620903050523.
Shimray, C. (2016). In *Teaching environmental education: Trends and practices in India.* SAGE Publications.
Singh, S. (2019). *Disaster risk preparedness and awareness among children: A study of selected government schools of Delhi.* Master's dissertation, Department of Environmental Studies, University of Delhi, (unpublished).
Tbilisi Declaration. (1977). Tbilisi Declaration. Retrieved from, http://www.gdrc.org/uem/ee/tbilisi.html.
Torani, S., Majd, P. M., Maroufi, S. S., Dowlati, M., & Sheikhi, R. A. (2019). The importance of education on disasters and emergencies: A review article. *Jounal of Education Health Promotion, 8,* 1–7. https://doi.org/10.4103/jehp.jehp.
Valatin, G., Moseley, D., & Dandy, N. (2016). Insights from behavioural economics for forest economics and environmental policy: Potential nudges to encourage woodland creation for climate change mitigation and adaptation? *For Policy Economics, 72,* 27–36. https://doi.org/10.1016/j.forpol.2016.06.012.
Van Liere, K. D., & Dunlap, R. E. (1981). Environmental concern: Does it make a difference how it's measured? *Environmental Behaviour, 13,* 651–676. https://doi.org/10.1177/0013916581136001.
Wesley Schultz, P., & Zelezny, L. (1999). Values as predictors of environmental attitudes: Evidence for consistency across 14 countries. *Journal of Environmental Psychology, 19,* 255–265. https://doi.org/10.1006/jevp.1999.0129.

Uncertainty and Causality in Public Policy: The Cases of Heart Disease and Climate Change

Vikram Dayal

1 Introduction

The president of the United States of America often makes decisions that affect not just Americans but all who live on earth. President Trump has questioned the need for action to reduce the impacts of climate change. In an interview with (Stahl, 2018) President Trump said that "I don't wanna give trillions and trillions of dollars. I don't wanna lose millions and millions of jobs". Responding to Stahl saying that in Greenland we can see huge chunks of ice falling into the ocean, President Trump said, "And you don't know whether or not that would have happened with or without man. You don't know". President Trump in this interview is asserting that actions to check climate change will result in economic losses and saying that even though chunks of ice in Greenland are falling into the ocean, we do not *know* that this is because of human activity.

The Intergovernmental Panel on Climate Change (IPCC) has a different view from President Trump. Anyone can check the IPCC's (2018) Special Report on the Internet: Global Warming of 1.5 degrees centigrade, Summary for Policymakers. The report is (p. 4) "based on the assessment of the available scientific, technical and socio-economic literature relevant to global warming of 1.5 °C".

The IPCC report solemnly declares (p. 4): "Human activities are estimated to have caused approximately 1.0 °C of global warming above pre-industrial levels, with a *likely* range of 0.8–1.2 °C. Global warming is *likely* to reach 1.5 °C between 2030 and 2052 if it continues to increase at the current rate. (*high confidence*)". The report is a solemn declaration of an *estimate* of the *likely* effects of a *cause*, which is expressed with a high degree of *confidence*. Thus depending on how you look at it, once we assess the evidence we may be confident that we know what is *likely* but do not *know* for certain, or we know though we acknowledge the uncertainty. And perhaps our

V. Dayal (✉)
Institute of Economic Growth, University of Delhi Enclave, Delhi, India
e-mail: vikday@iegindia.org

P. Dasgupta et al. (eds.), *Sustainable Development Insights from India*,
India Studies in Business and Economics,
https://doi.org/10.1007/978-981-33-4830-1_20

uncertainty is personal, perhaps the authors of the report agreed to a statement, but had somewhat different perceptions of that uncertainty. And despite the differences in perceptions of the uncertainty, they were convinced that action with respect to climate change is important.

Powerful presidents have to deal with not just the health of the planet, but their own health. The future health of the planet will be affected by the decisions they make while in office but their own current health is influenced by the history of the personal decisions they made in their own lives, such as what they ate and how regularly they exercised. Former President of the United States of America, Bill Clinton, had quadruple bypass surgery in 2004 when he was 58 years old (Altman, 2004). Besides the surgical interventions that he has undergone, President Clinton has worked with two physicians who are well known for advocating changes in diet to reduce the risk of heart disease, though their views differ, Dr. Dean Ornish and Dr. Mark Hyman. Dr. Dean Ornish not only has worked with patients, he also did an experimental study of his approach. Dr. Mark Hyman is an author of several books, which engage with research studies in detail. Some years before his surgery in 2004, President Clinton had taken a statin, Zocor, for a while, but had stopped taking it. Why he stopped taking was not clear, though apparently it was not on account of side-effects. After the surgery, President Clinton started taking statins again.

Probability is a language that helps us express ideas along the lines of: this event is likely to happen 8 out of 10 times. A distinction is often made between risk, where probabilities are known, and uncertainty. In statistics, scholars of probability have different views of whether probability is objective or subjective. Some scholars regard probability as subjective, but conditional on knowledge, and capable of being updated. But in making decisions and taking actions, we are not just interested in questions such as will there be climate change or will I have a heart attack, but we are keen on questions such as should we be taking steps to tackle climate change and should we take statins. Thus, we consider both uncertainty and causality.

Our analytical framework (Sect. 2) begins with uncertainty and moves to causality. We often use a normative decision framework to think about issues involving uncertainty, indeed, such a framework may be quite influential in framing our attitude to the issue. We may have to decide in ignorance, though that may not imply a difficult decision. Our decision framework may initially emphasize economic considerations but these on closer inspection may be revealed to be about the uncertainty in physical impacts (Sect. 3). Researchers often explicitly aim at making causal inferences; this involves issues of study design and statistical analysis, within frameworks of causal inference (Sect. 4). Section 5 briefly discusses beliefs, communication and literacy.

2 Analytical Framework and Remarks

The analytical framework is presented as a narrative to intuitively communicate some basic ideas. This is followed by some interpretive remarks.

2.1 Analytical Framework

The analytical framework presents basic results and their interpretation drawing on (Lindley, 2006; Pearl, 2009) that will be built on in the discussion in this paper. Probability is a natural language of uncertainty. The style is relatively informal and intuitive, uses a narrative to hopefully make it less tedious, and a simulation is presented.

2.1.1 Seeing

I own a chemist shop and I find that some of my customers buy medicines for headaches. I do not keep track of all this very carefully, so there is some uncertainty. I have conversations with them, and from those impressions I believe that about half of them have a high sensitivity to headaches, (represented by variable *Sens*, and its high value by 1 and low value by 0), and half have a low sensitivity; over time I can see it on their faces! The rest are happily not sensitive. This belief can be expressed as a probability:

$$Pr(Sens = 1) \approx 0.5 \tag{1}$$

Professor Lindley would point out that this belief, and any such probabilistic belief, is implicitly based on, or conditional on, some knowledge, so if we are explicit about it we would express it as, using | to denote "given":

$$Pr(Sens|knowledge) \approx 0.5 \tag{2}$$

What is knowledge may itself be regarded as a kind of belief! But getting back to beliefs about "Sens", I did not have any beliefs about "Sens" in the days before I had my chemist shop, how could I have had the knowledge or experience about it? We will continue without explicitly using "knowledge".

I also believe that approximately 2/3 of those who are sensitive to headaches buy medicines (*Med*), so that

$$Pr(Med = 1|Sens = 1) \approx 2/3 \tag{3}$$

I am treating "Med" as either being bought (1) or not (0), and when bought it is used. Those who are not sensitive to headaches are less likely to buy "Med":

$$Pr(Med = 1|Sens = 0) \approx 1/3 \tag{4}$$

My son is studying epidemiology, and I will let him take the account further.

The purchase of medicines is not independent of sensitivity, $Med \not\perp Sens$. Independence is a key consideration when we study the effects of one variable on another.

We can see how many people buy medicines and have sensitivity by:

$$Pr(Med, Sens) = Pr(Med|\, Sens)Pr(Sens) \tag{5}$$

Those who come in with that "Sens" look are more likely to buy medicines; that I can vouch for!

The following also holds true,

$$Pr(Med, Sens) = Pr(Sens|\, Med)Pr(Med) \tag{6}$$

Professor Lindley tells me that I can use one of the most important equations, Bayes rule, to work out $Pr(Sens|\, Med)$, the probability of someone being sensitive to headaches if they bought medicines, by using

$$Pr(Sens|\, Med) = Pr(Med|\, Sens)Pr(Sens)/Pr(Med) \tag{7}$$

You can test positive for a rare disease, and yet, your probability of having the disease may be low. One of the customers in my father's shop was quite concerned when he tested positive for a rare but scary disease, but luckily for him the disease was subsequently ruled out. He is always muttering about medical tests now. I tried to tell him something about Bayes rule, but it is hard to communicate the idea in a conversation. I remember how I too struggled with Bayes rule initially.

2.1.2 Doing

I was interested in exploring how the medicine might affect the headache, "Ache". Generally, the customers are satisfied with the medicine, so I think we can say that Med does affect Ache. Sens also affects Med and probably affects Ache. Professor Pearl has developed an analytical tool called directed causal graphs or causal Bayesian networks. If a variable affects another, we represent this in a graph. I put my beliefs about the causal effects between Sens, Med and Ache in Fig. 1. Sens affects Med and Ache, and Med affects Ache.

A causal graph represents the flow of information. We can write the joint probability distribution of the variables in Fig. 1 as follows:

$$Pr(Sens, Ache, Med) = Pr(Sens)Pr(Med|\, Sens)Pr(Ache|\, Med, Sens) \tag{8}$$

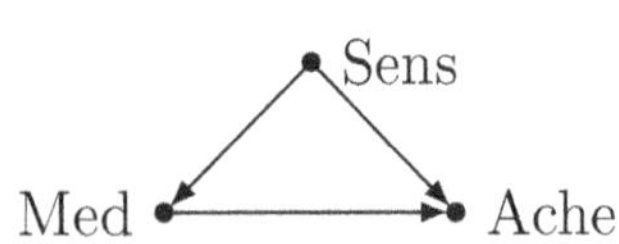

Fig. 1 Causal graph for seeing: Sens, Med and Ache

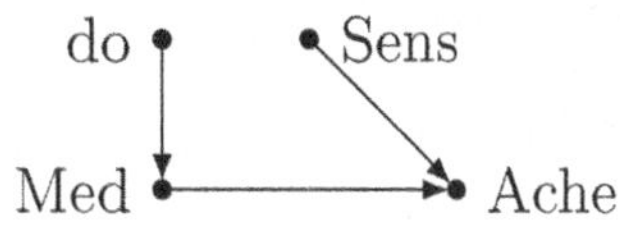

Fig. 2 Causal graph for doing: do(Med), Ache, Sens

Since Sens is a common cause of Ache and Med, it can act as a confounder. Or to see it another way, Med is not independent of Sens, $Med \not\perp Sens$.

The philosopher (Woodward, 2004) has developed an interventional theory of cause, consistent with Pearl's view of causal inference. Pearl builds on this view of what cause is and develops a "do" calculus, a calculus that helps us work with issues of causality. Here our intervention is medicine, and we can randomly assign whether medicine is taken or not, we "do", with symbol: do(Med). This breaks the causal link from Sens to Med; Sens does not influence Med now. We have moved from a world where we were only seeing to a world where we are intervening, and we are doing. We have a new conditional distribution; $Med \perp Sens$ now.

We can write the joint probability distribution of the variables in Fig. 2 as follows:

$$Pr(Sens, Ache, Med) = Pr(Sens)Pr(Med)Pr(Ache| Med, Sens) \quad (9)$$

2.1.3 Seeing World Simulation

To make all this numerically specific, I carried out a simulation incorporating some of the information above and making some assumptions. This allows us to see visual presentations of probability distributions corresponding to the causal graphs in Figs. 1 and 2.

So I assumed that Ache was given by the following equation:

$$Ache = 10 + 5\,Sens - 3\,Med \quad (10)$$

When we see, we only observe (Fig. 1). We can generate data in R that is consistent with Fig. 1 and Eqs. 1, 3, 4 and 10.

Equation 8 states that in the seeing world we can view the joint probability distribution in terms of specific conditional probability distributions, presented in Figs. 3, 4 and 5.

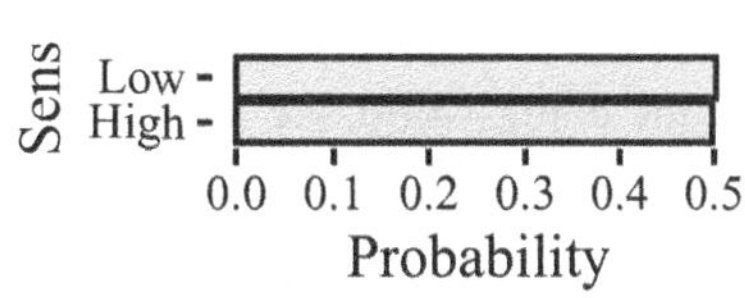

Fig. 3 Probability distribution of Sens, Pr(Sens)

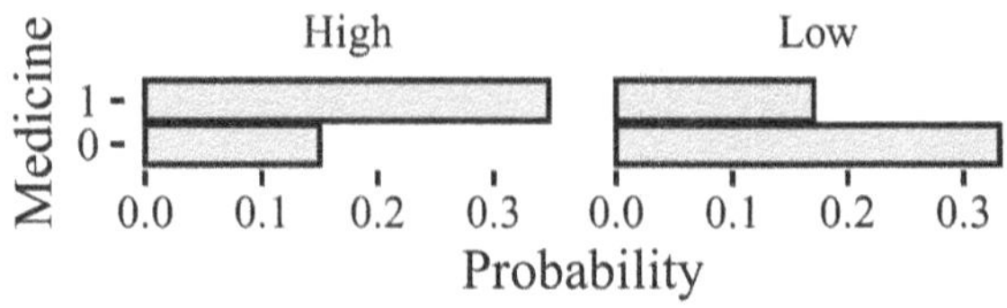

Fig. 4 Conditional probability for Med, Pr(Med|Sens)

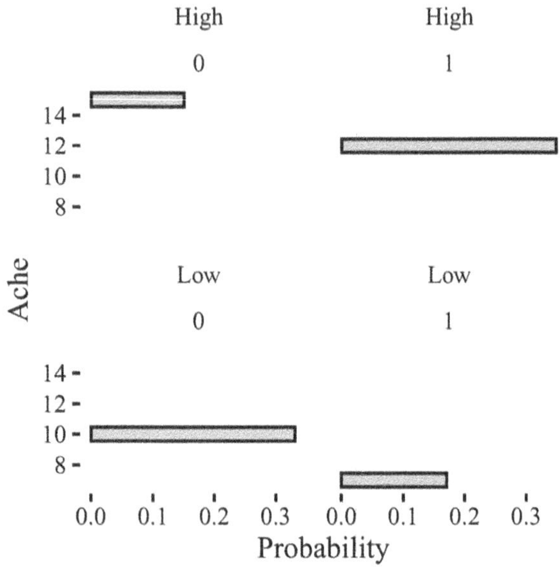

Fig. 5 Conditional probability distribution for Ache, Pr(Ache| Med, Sens)

Table 1 Conditional means for Ache

Med	mean_Ache	Number
0	11.56	0.48
1	10.35	0.52

We can look at the conditional means (Table 1); the difference between means of Ache for those taking Med and not is misleading about the effect of Med on Ache (The true effect is 3, we know because we generated the synthetic data).

2.1.4 Doing World Simulation

In the doing world, we are actively intervening (Fig. 2). The do-operator sets the value of Med. We assume now that

$$Pr(do(Med = 1)) = 0.5 \tag{11}$$

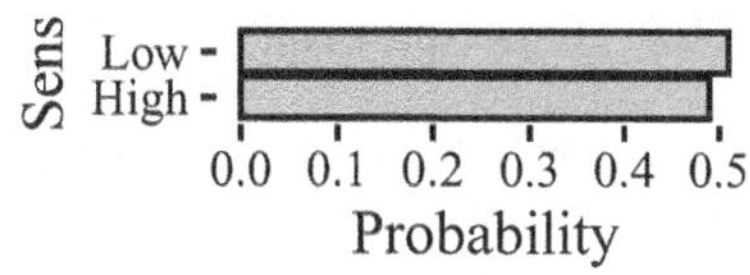

Fig. 6 Probability distribution of Sens, Pr(Sens)

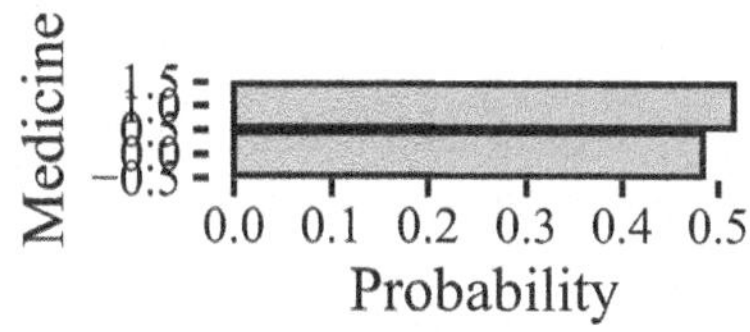

Fig. 7 Probability for Med, Pr(Med)

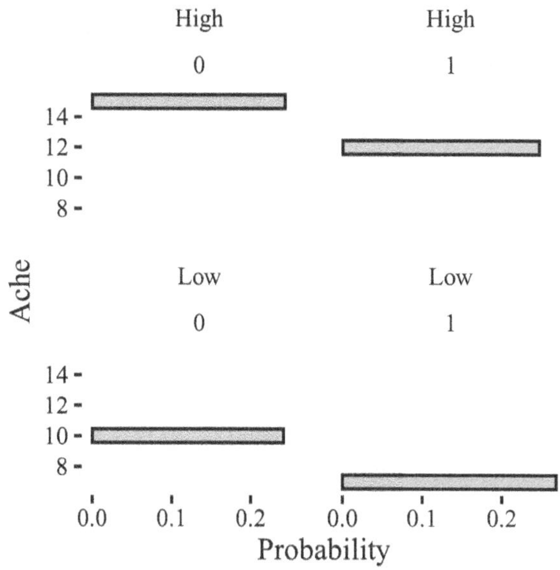

Fig. 8 Conditional probability distribution for Ache, Pr(Ache| Med, Sens)

Half the people get Med and half do not|Med is randomly assigned. Equation 11 replaces Eqs. 3 and 4. The probability distributions corresponding to those on the right hand side of Eq. 9 are in Figs. 6, 7 and 8.

Now the difference between means of those taking Med and not gives us an accurate estimate of the effect of Med on Ache (Table 2).

Table 2 Conditional means for Ache

Med	Mean_Ache	Number
0	12.51	0.48
1	9.39	0.52

2.1.5 Expected Utility

Faced with two states of the world, A, B and utility U in each state, the expected utility EU is

$$EU = Pr(A)U_A + Pr(B)U_B \tag{12}$$

If x is an action that can affect an outcome y, then what Professor Pearl calls "commonsensical" and others call causal decision theory "instructs rational agents to choose the option that maximizes expected utility". We should try to maximize the following (Pearl p. 108):

$$U(x) = \Sigma_y Pr(y|do(x))u(y) \tag{13}$$

We consider the expected utility of doing an action in terms of the expected utility of the effects of this cause on the outcome we care about, i.e. in the expression above we have probabilities with do-operators $Pr(y|do(x))$.

2.2 *Interpretive Remarks*

2.2.1 Probability

Probability has several interpretations—objective or subjective. What is regarded as subjective may be considered personal in Lindley's way of looking at things. If we are looking at future climate change, most of us will agree that this aligns more naturally with the subjective view. In fact, the IPCC's (2010) Uncertainty Guidance Note has recommendations about the reporting of uncertainty. This note has recommendations for reporting uncertainty, so for example, a probability of 90–100% is "very likely". Also, such probability levels are accompanied by statements of confidence, based on the agreement level and the amount and quality of evidence.

(Lindley, 2006) also says that we should think of the probability of an event A, Pr(A), as being the belief in A, as implicitly conditioning on a knowledge base: $Pr(A|K)$. In his example, the event A may be rain tomorrow, and a person may have a personal probability of rain tomorrow being 0.3. After watching the weather forecast, the person may have a personal probability of rain tomorrow being 0.8.

In their book Medical Decision Making, (Sox et al., 2013) recommend the use of probability as a language to express uncertainty. Uncertainty is ever present in medical practice, according to the authors (p. 21): "No clinical finding has this perfect, one-to-one correspondence with a disease. Therefore, clinicians are seldom, if ever, certain what a finding implies about the patient's true state. They must recognize the following bleak truth: The true state of the patient lies locked within the body, inaccessible to direct observation. The clinician must use external, imperfect cues to infer the patient's true state". Their advocacy of probability may surprise even a probability enthusiast (p. 22): "Clinicians who use words to communicate their uncertainty may feel secure that they have conveyed their meaning. In fact, words are the enemy of clarity in expressing uncertainty . When words are mapped onto a probability scale, the ranges of probabilities that correspond to different words overlap so much that the words do not have unique meanings. Probability , a quantitative means for expressing uncertainty, avoids this ambiguity". Of course, this avoidance of ambiguity may also bring out starkly the different personal assessments of different clinicians.

The combination of personal belief about events in the world expressed as probability, which are then revised and updated with data and evidence, characterizes the Bayesian view of probability (Pearl, 2009). Bayes rule expresses formally how we can revise our beliefs based on prior belief and evidence.

2.2.2 Causality

Judea Pearl is the winner of the Turing Award in artificial intelligence, for "fundamental contributions to artificial intelligence through the development of a calculus for probabilistic and causal reasoning". In an essay (Pearl, 2001), Pearl says that he became a Bayesian in 1971. In the essay, he says that he is now only a "half-Bayesian". According to him, scientific enquiry is about combining prior knowledge with data, but this requires a language to combine both of them, and most human knowledge is organized around causal relationships. The causal language he has developed builds on probabilistic concepts.

Pearl (2009, p. 1) writes: "Causality connotes lawlike necessity, whereas probabilities connote exceptionality, doubt, and lack of regularity. Still, there are two compelling reasons for starting with, and in fact stressing, probabilistic analysis of causality; one is fairly straightforward, the other more subtle.... The simple reason rests on the observation that causal utterances are often used in situations that are plagued with uncertainty .... The more subtle reason concerns the fact that even the most assertive causal expressions in natural language are subject to exceptions, and those exceptions may cause major difficulties if processed by standard rules of deterministic logic".

A basic insight from Pearl is that statistical and causal concepts are distinct, and we require a distinct mathematical framework for causality. In causal inference, we rely on doing, not only seeing. When we randomize, set the value of the treatment, now the arrows from other variables into the treatment are wiped out, and in Pearl's language, we use the "do-operator" on the treatment variable. Since this is really critical in Pearl's framework, we state this on a separate line.

The do-operator: we denote an intervention on a variable X by setting X to some value x by $do(X = x)$.

This changes the joint probability distribution, and we see this on comparing the causal DAGs before and after the intervention. This is like wiping out an equation in a structural model, an idea he traces to the econometricians (Strotz and Wold, 1960).

Pearl maintains and in his book discusses how the potential outcomes framework is consistent with the causal graph framework that we can translate from one to another. Rubin, who developed the potential outcomes framework, building on work by Neyman, demonstrated in a formal Bayesian framework that treatment assignment needs to be considered while determining the effects of a treatment. Randomization made the analysis easier and more credible; in the absence of randomization, the Bayesian would have to model the mechanisms through which units received the treatment in question. According to Rubin, in causal inference, design trumps analysis and even observational studies should be carefully designed (Rubin, 2008).

2.2.3 Expected Utility

An early derivation showing the desirability of maximizing expected utility was by (Ramsey, 1926) who had a subjective view of probability. In this approach, utility is not taken as given, but probability and utility emerge together from the thought experiment.

There have been philosophical debates about causal decision theory that are beyond the scope of this paper. (Sloman, 2009) provides an intuitive argument for heeding causal effects while deciding. Smoking can change the colour of teeth and lung cancer. If we consider two states of having lung cancer and not, we do have a large utility for not experiencing lung cancer. Our expected utility would depend on the probabilities of having lung cancer or not. If we consider the action of whitening our teeth, and use only associational probabilities, it would make sense to whiten our teeth. However, this does not make sense because teeth whitening will not affect lung cancer. Hence, we need causal probabilities, i.e. probabilities with the do-operator, as in Eq. 13.

3 Uncertainty and Decisions

In our analytical framework (Eqs. 12 and 13), we see that our expected utility depends on both utility and probability. In some novel situations, probability may be hard to assess, as in the case of the first person to have a heart transplant. We will see that an economic framework that considers well-being over time points to the importance of an assessment of the physical impacts and that leads to the importance of the uncertainty of such impacts. We then look at an example of an application of Bayesian networks to practically implement the idea of assessing expected utility in the case of wind energy in Mexico.

3.1 Heart Disease

In his book on decision theory, Peterson (2009, p. 6) presents the decision problem faced by the first person to experience a heart transplant, Louis Washkansky. Since this was the first time, a heart transplant was being conducted on a human being, there was ignorance, i.e. the probability of the operation being successful was not known. However, since Louis Washkansky was dying of severe heart disease anyway, the decision was not difficult to make, and he agreed to the heart transplant. Though the operation was successful, Louis Washkansky did not live long and died of pneumonia.

Although this was the first time that a heart transplant was being conducted, according to (Gigerenzer, 2002) Washkansky's wife did ask Barnard: What chance did he give Washkansky? Barnard replied that he gave him an eighty percent chance. We could interpret this as his subjective probability.

Often diet as a consideration for heart patients will arise as something they consider as a decision variable once they have encountered a heart issue themselves or through the experience of relatives. A close relative of mine had a heart blockage and was all set to get operated, but changed his mind (personal communication). He opted for Dean Ornish's diet plan. We will discuss Ornish's plan later in the paper. But if indeed diet affects blockages in arteries, such blockages are the result of a gradual process over the life of the patient. In this respect, it is somewhat like climate change. But unlike climate change, one person's heart blockage only affects that person in a direct physical sense. The issue of climate change these days is related to events around us, and there is widespread acceptance that it is here.

3.2 Climate Change

The framing of the economics of climate change often draws on intergenerational welfare economics, which was established by Ramsey (Dasgupta, 2001). Drawing on the prior normative theory by Ramsey and others, Dasgupta considers social well-being to be given by

$$V_t = \sum_{t}^{\infty}[1/(1+\delta)]^{\tau-t}U(C_\tau),$$

summed over time t, where U is well-being, and C is aggregate consumption.

Here well-being is the numeraire, and δ is the social discount rate of discount in well-being units. In assessing climate change, economists make estimates of future consumption streams and discount those. If the consumption rate of interest is ρ, Dasgupta shows that it relates to δ as follows:

$\rho_t = \delta + \eta(C_t)g(C_t)$.

Here η is the elasticity of marginal well-being and is a measure of the curvature of U, and g is the growth rate.

How future costs and benefits are discounted has been the key factor in different conclusions reached by economists about how much action we need to take (Dasgupta, 2008). We list below the values assumed by different authors ((Dasgupta, 2008), p. 150).

Cline (1992) $\delta = 0$, $\eta = 1.5$
Stern (2006) $\delta = 0.1$ percent a year, $\eta = 1$
Nordhaus (1994) $\delta = 3$ percent a year, $\eta = 1.5$.

Dasgupta (2008) notes that Cline and Stern urged immediate and strong action on climate change, while Nordhaus argued for a more gradual approach with increasing actions over time.

With the discount rate, the basic point is that the present value today of say a loss of 1000 consumption units 50 years from now on account of climate change is $[1/(1+\rho)]^{50}1000$. Once framed this way, the choice of the discount rate is critical. And the discount rate is an economic feature. Is the moral of the story not to do much about climate change if the information from the workings of the economy tells you to discount future costs so they are small?

Dasgupta asks us to pause. What if the physical impacts of climate change in 50 years are as some physical scientists believe, going to be catastrophic? What if because of such catastrophic climate change g is negative, then ρ will be negative, with different effects on the calculation. For example, $[1/(1+\rho)]^{50}1000 \approx 370$ when $\rho = 2$ and ≈ 2700 when $\rho = -2$.

So the economics of potentially catastrophic climate change depends on the assessment by physical scientists of the possibilities of catastrophe due to climate change. The economy environment link in climate change is in this simplified chain: emissions $\rightarrow$ concentration $\rightarrow$ temperature $\rightarrow$ damages. Weitzman (2011) forcefully brought in considerations of uncertainty in the economic discourse on climate change. Weitzman (p. 275) wrote: "I believe that the most striking feature of the economics of climate change is that its extreme downside is nonneglible. Deep structural uncertainty about the unknown unkowns of what might go very wrong is coupled with essentially unlimited liability on possible planetary damages".

Weitzman's first point was that CO_2 concentrations at the time he wrote were over 390 ppm; well over the pre-industrial level of 280 ppm and the level in the 180,000 years before that. So if we stabilize CO_2 concentrations at 700 ppm, we are in uncharted territory.

How would global average surface warming respond to such a doubling in global CO_2 concentrations? Weitzman cites the IPCC: the "equilibrium climate sensitivity" was likely to be in the range 2–4.5 degrees centigrade. The key point is that this does not rule out values more than 4.5 degrees centigrade. How likely such values are depends on the probability distribution.

Weitzman presents estimates of probabilities of exceeding increases in global mean surface temperatures assuming that the probability distribution is a fat-tailed Pareto distribution and a thin-tailed normal distribution for different levels of stationary greenhouse gas concentrations (G, CO_2 equivalent). Here, we only consider the values for G = 500; in this case the median temperature increase would be 2.5 degrees. The probability of exceeding a temperature increase of 5 degree centigrade is 6.5% for a fat-tailed Pareto distribution and 2% for a thin-tailed normal distribution. The probability of exceeding a temperature increase of 10 degree centigrade is 0.83% for a fat-tailed Pareto distribution and 10^{-10}% for a thin-tailed normal distribution.

Weitzman next criticizes the use of quadratic damages functions that weight increases in temperature (T) with a damages multiplier, $\alpha T^2/(1+\alpha T^2)$, as "cavalier". This implies that for an increase in temperature of 10 degree centigrade, the corresponding loss in world output is 19 degrees centigrade. But what the damages function should be at such great increases is highly uncertain, (p. 281): "There is just too much structural uncertainty and too much heterogeneity to put trustworthy bound on the unprecedented, almost unimaginable, changes to planetary welfare that would result from average global temperatures increasing by ten degrees centigrade".

Some parts of the climate puzzle are relatively well known. One of the key elements that is uncertain is highlighted in Weitzman's writings, the equilibrium climate sensitivity. A non-scientist citizen of earth may wonder why it is so uncertain, and since I count as one of those, I found a useful account on a website (Hausfather 2018). I will assume that it is a reasonably accurate account of the different studies done. As early as 1979, the environmental climate sensitivity was estimated to be between 1.5 and 4.5 degrees centigrade, quite close to the value cited in (Weitzman, 2011), of 2–4.5 degrees centigrade.

Figure 9 uses the data available from (Hausfather, 2018). It shows the estimates of climate sensitivity by studies that use a method called "constrained models" only and the not other types of study mentioned in the article. Nor do we get into what the meaning of "constrained models" is. Each dot shows an estimate by a study, plotted along with the range of possible sensitivity values estimated by each study. From the perspective of this paper, Figure 9 makes a key point about uncertainty that remains and does not disappear even though a number of studies by highly skilled researchers using different methods are deployed. The details are beyond the scope

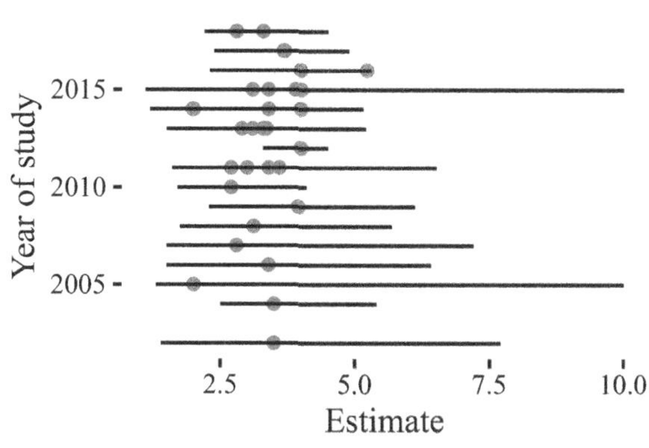

Fig. 9 Studies estimating environmental climate sensitivity, data from (Hausfather, 2018)

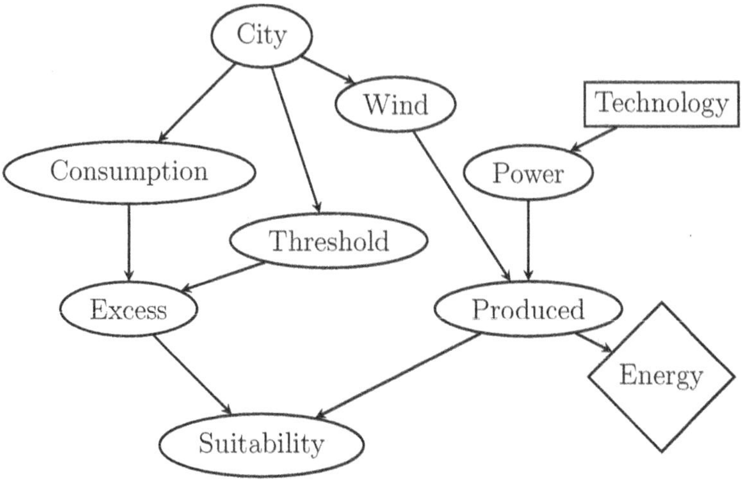

Fig. 10 Schematic diagram of Bayesian network for wind energy in Mexico, used by Borunda et al. 2020

of the paper, though it is apparent that the range varies across studies but does not appear to come down across time. Possibly, though there is better understanding over time, uncertainty persists.

We have seen that there is a chain of uncertainty in the global climate system (Weitzman, 2011). An important response to climate change is using renewable energy sources such as wind. (Borunda et al., 2020) use a Bayesian network and the Netica software to provide a decision support system for wind energy in Mexico. Figure 10 shows a schematic of the elements of the decision network. The rectangle represents the decision to opt for small-scale wind technology (SSWT), the ellipses represent different variables that have probability distributions, and the diamond represents the utility from the small-scale wind technology. A feature of residential electricity pricing in Mexico was that the prices depended on consumption; when consumption exceeded a threshold, the price went up, so SSWT could be used to reduce the total expenditure. As the figure shows, different cities will be located differently and experience different distributions of wind and will have different distributions of electricity consumption by consumers. Software implementations (here using Netica) use algorithms that estimate conditional probabilities of detailed and large networks. Uncertainties in the different variables are represented by probability distributions and can be particularly useful when there is a great spread or skewness, in contrast to making calculations that are based on averages or expected values of variables. Software implementations also facilitate improvements and incorporation of details over time.

4 Causal Inference from Data

Heart disease and climate change have one important difference: there are millions of people who had and will have heart disease, but there is one earth. The earth has a long history though. Experiments are an important way of studying causal effects, and in the case of heart disease a lot of experimental studies have been conducted.

In our analytical framework we saw that we can represent an experimental intervention in terms of a causal graph. In modern medicine, evidence is often generated by randomized control trials, and so many are now conducted that the information from several experiments is analysed in a "meta-analysis". In climate change, researchers may use an instrumental variable to overcome the presence of feedbacks while estimating causal effects ($Instrumental\ variable \rightarrow variable\ X \longleftrightarrow variable\ Y$).

4.1 *Heart Disease*

One of the outstanding features of modern medicine is the close interweaving of practice and research, with much of the research being based on experiments. Practising doctors often participate in research. New treatments are tested.

In the field of heart disease Dr. Dean Ornish is a well-known doctor. (Ornish et al., 1998) published their paper titled "Intensive Lifestyle Changes for Reversal of Coronary Heart Disease" in JAMA, the Journal of the American Medical Association. Forty-eight people who were suffering from heart disease were assigned to a treatment group or a control group where they would get typical care. The treatment was a combination of a low fat vegetarian diet, aerobic exercise, stress management training, giving up smoking and group support over five years. Thirty-five of the people in the study completed the five year follow-up coronary arteriography. The result was that coronary heart disease was reversed in the treatment group as indicated by the arteriography (p. 2001): "In the experimental group, the average percent diameter stenosis at baseline decreased 1.75 absolute percentage points after 1 year ... and by 3.1 absolute percentage points after 5 years ...In contrast, the average percent diameter stenosis in the control group increased by 2.3% points after 1 year ... and by 11.8% points after 5 years". The key point was that for the experimental group, the average percent diameter stenosis at baseline *decreased.*

From the perspective of this paper, it is interesting that Dr. Ornish combines roles as we have said before: medical practitioner, participant in research and communicator. Dr. Ornish has published several non-technical books. We now examine the interpretation of Dr. Ornish's work by two other doctors, who work with patients and have also written books, Dr. Joel Fuhrman and Dr. Mark Hyman, and see where they agree and disagree with Dr. Ornish.

Dr. Fuhrman is a family physician and nutritional researcher. Fuhrman (2018) is forthright in his advocacy of a dietary approach (p. 184): "Only a diet consisting predominantly of whole plant foods has been scientifically demonstrated to reverse heart disease and potentially remove the risk of future cardiac events, as documented in numerous peer-reviewed journals (discussed and referenced in this chapter)". Note the clear reference to journal papers. The broad agreement with Dr. Ornish on the importance of diet is also backed up by Dr. Fuhrman's work with thousands of patients, and in his book he illustrates with case histories of individual patients. One difference Dr. Fuhrman used to have with Dr. Ornish was that Dr. Fuhrman advocated eating nuts and seeds. Dr. Ornish over time incorporated the evidence accumulating about the benefits of nuts and seeds and included them in his recommended diet.

Dr. Mark Hyman is a family physician and a best-selling author. Hyman's (2016) book is carefully referenced. Dr. Mark Hyman is outspoken in his book, which may explain why his books have sold well. Hyman provides a sophisticated discussion of the strengths of different kinds of studies, which is rather impressive for a practising physician who works with patients.

Hyman agrees with Fuhrman's broad assessment of Ornish's work; a whole foods plant-based diet can be effective. Hyman then proceeds to raise some issues with the (Ornish et al., 1998) study: small sample size coupled with a complex treatment, so we do not know which elements of the treatment resulted in the outcome. Hyman also says that Ornish improved on the standard nutrient-poor American diet, but possibly one can improve it further. Hyman also does the reader a service by listing components of a healthy diet that few nutrition experts dispute, for example, vegetables and fruits. He also lists food that are controversial among nutrition experts, for example, dairy and grains.

In a recent review paper, (Freeman et al., 2017) take stock of the knowledge about nutrition science and cardiovascular disease and make recommendations on that basis. They also take stock of different research designs. Randomized controlled trials do provide evidence in this area, but there are limits, for example, limited duration and sample sizes. Prospective cohort studies are the strongest observational study design, but they too have some limits like measurement of diets and residual confounding. Also funding by the private sector complicates things.

(Freeman et al., 2017) provide a clear table of what evidence they are basing their recommendations on. Further, their central illustration provides a summary of recommendations in three categories of foods: (1) evidence of harm, limit or avoid, (2) inconclusive evidence and (3) evidence of benefit and recommended. Category 3 includes extra virgin olive oil, blueberries and strawberries, 30 g serving of nuts/day, green leafy vegetables and plant-based proteins. In several cases, the recommendations draw on evidence that is not only from randomized control trials but from a meta-analysis, which combines evidence from several studies.

One frequently debated topic related to heart disease is about the efficacy of statins. Both (Hyman, 2016) and (Fuhrman, 2018) have observations about statins. Hyman questions the benefits of statins, asking, "what does the science really prove?". At this point, it is interesting to point out two words that he uses in his argument: *science* and *prove*. Different scientists tend to agree and disagree, both about the mechanisms and about the evidence. If we are thinking about evidence, *prove* seems an inappropriate word, given uncertainty and that data-based statistical inference essentially provides estimates that are interpreted, not proof in a strict sense.

Hyman argues that inflammation and oxidative stress are bigger causes of heart disease than cholestrol. He argues that statins have an effect not because they affect cholestrol but because they affect inflammation and oxidative stress. Hyman also cites statistical studies questioning the efficacy of statins. Fuhrman also questions the use of statins, saying that diet is the key intervention, and cites a meta-analysis to support his view that the benefits of statins are doubtful. Here, we note the use of evidence by a medical practitioner, who is citing a meta-analysis that builds on several randomized control trials. Ray et al. (2010) indeed conclude: "this literature-based meta-analysis did not find evidence for the benefit of statin therapy or all-cause mortality in a high-risk primary prevention set-up".

However, Koskinas et al. (2018, p. 1172) conclude about statins and major vascular events (MVEs): "Reduction of MVE is proportional to the magnitude of LDL-C lowering across a broad spectrum of on-treatment levels in secondary prevention. Statin intensification and add-on treatment with PCSK9 inhibitors or ezetmibe are associated with significant reduction of cardiovascular morbidity in this very high-risk population".

There are differences between the two meta-analyses: one deals with primary prevention, the other with secondary intervention; one is studying mortality, the other morbidity. Meta-analyses have become very important as the number of randomized experiments conducted in medicine has grown greatly.

We look at a part of the Koskinas et al. meta-analysis, in which they compare statin as an intervention with no statin as a control. One of the randomized control trials they include was SPARCL. In the intervention group, 334 out of 2365 people experience a major vascular event. In the control group, 407 out of 2366 people experienced a vascular event. Hence, the risk ratio was 0.82. Eight other trials were considered for this comparison (statin versus no statin). Figure 11 shows the result of the meta-analysis. The 95% confidence intervals for each trial are plotted graphically along with the estimated risk ratio. We can see the SPARCL trial on the top. Some statisticians advocate using confidence intervals because they show estimates of effects and the uncertainty in the estimates and do not dichotomize evidence into significant and not significant. The results of the studies are broadly consistent. The width of the confidence intervals is an indicator of the precision with which each risk ratio is estimated. At the bottom, we have the result of using a random effects model to estimate an overall risk ratio (and its confidence interval)—0.77 (0.71–0.83). Had we looked only at a trial such as GISSI-P we might have used the p-value to decide that the estimated effect of statins was insignificant.

4.2 *Climate Change*

We now consider some cases of causal inference studies in climate change. Montamat and Stock (2020), use a quasi-experimental approach to estimate the transient climate response (TCR). The TCR is defined as (Montamat and Stock 2020, pp. 1–2) "the

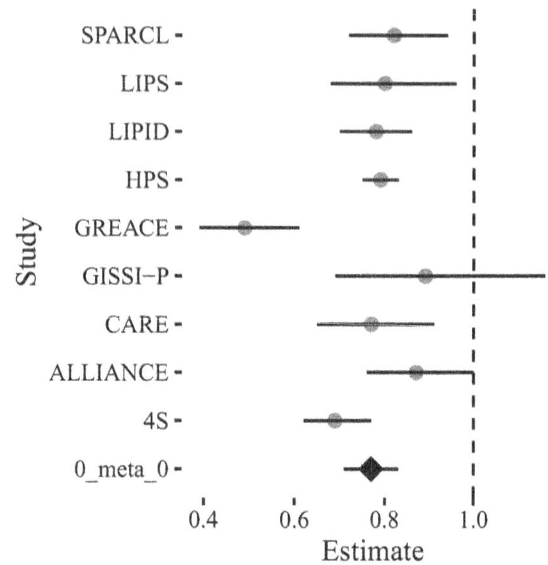

Fig. 11 Meta-analysis of statins by (Koskinas et al., 2018), comparing statin and no statin (part of their results)

change in the global mean temperature at the time of a doubling of atmospheric CO_2 concentration increasing at a rate of 1% per year".

Taking a horizon denoted by h, Montamat and Stock take a linear approximation and write the following equation linking change Δ in temperature (Temp) and change in radiative forcing (RF) over a horizon h:

$$\Delta_h Temp_t = \beta_h \Delta_h RF_t + u_t$$

Figure 12 shows the data on global mean temperature in the top row and aggregate radiative forcing in the bottom row. We can see that they are correlated.

Radiative forcing has several components, including a carbon dioxide component.

$$RF_t = RF_t^{Solar} + RF_t^{CO_2} + RF_t^{N_2O} + RF_t^{CH_4} + RF_t^{SO_2} + RF_t^{CFCs}$$

The causal effect of radiative forcing on temperature is given by β_h, and because of feedbacks in the climate system, the authors use instrumental variables to estimate this, and from β_h, the TCR. Their estimate using all five instrumental variables of (p. 8) the "20-year TCR (normalized to 70 years) …is 1.56 degrees centigrade (95% confidence interval = (0.95, 2.17)), and of the 30-year TCR is 1.49 degrees centigrade (95% confidence interval = (0.88, 2.10))". Their estimates are in line with the IPCC-AR5 range of 1–2.5 degrees centigrade for the 70 year TCR; the IPCC-AR5 results are based on climate models.

Increasingly, there is interest in attributing weather events to climate change. In August 2003, Western Europe experienced a severe heat wave, and thousands died. Can such a heat wave be attributed to climate change?

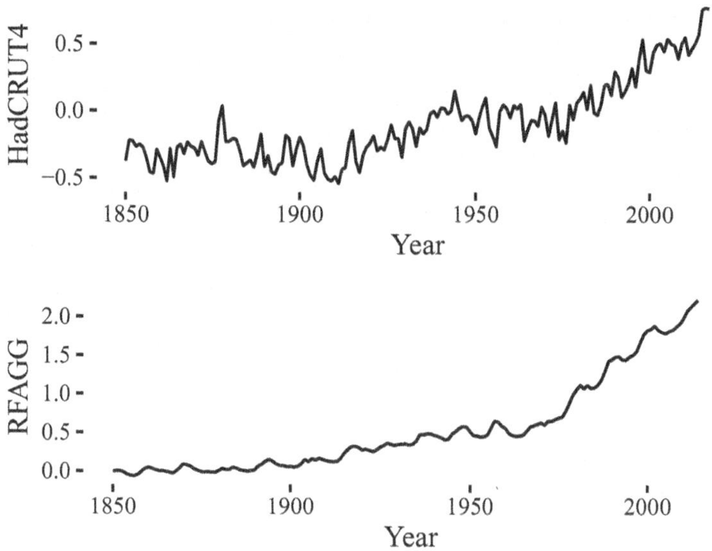

Fig. 12 Global mean temperature (top row) and aggregate radiative forcing (bottom row), data from authors of (Montamat and Stock 2019)

It is worth getting precise about what exactly the question is and then attempt to answer it as best as possible. Pearl's (2009) work has aimed to make intuition about causality precise and transparent. When we are asking such a question, we are working backwards from the event (heat wave) to the cause (climate change). We will use Y for the event and X for the cause and Y = 1 is the event happens and X = 1 is the cause was present.

There are two important concepts worked out and applied by (HannArt et al., 2016). PN, the probability of necessity, which is the probability of observing the outcome Y = 0, (Y did not happen), in a world where X = 0, given that we observed Y = 1 and X = 1. Another concept is PS, the probability of sufficiency. We imagine a world where Y = 0 and X = 0, and then ask, in such a world, how likely is it that if X = 1, Y would be 1? (HannArt et al., 2016) present formulae for PS and PN.

The counterfactual quantities are estimated "in silico" through runs of the simulation model of the climate system. (HannArt et al., 2016) estimate that PN was 0.9 and PS was 0.0072 in the case of the 2003 European heat wave; CO_2 emissions were very likely a necessary but not a sufficient cause of the 2003 European heat wave.

5 Beliefs, Communication and Literacy

In our analytical framework, we had pointed out that $Pr(A)$, the probability of A occurring, is implicitly conditional on a knowledge base, K, which we can make explicit by writing $Pr(A|K)$. The subjective view of probability admits of personal assessments, but implicitly assumes, in my view, careful reflection. Probabilities also must cohere, i.e. must obey rules. The rules of probability also point to how we can update prior beliefs in the light of new evidence. In practice, people often have remarkably good intuitive causal knowledge in some domains and beliefs and opinions that are not always grounded either on careful reflection or consideration of the evidence. Moreover, researchers and non-specialists may have beliefs and opinions on what constitutes K, the knowledge base.

5.1 Beliefs

Surveys help us gauge beliefs related to an issue in a population. (Leiserowitz et al., 2010) reported results of a survey to check knowledge of climate change by Americans. 63% of Americans thought that global warming was occurring, but did not understand why. Only 45% understood that carbon dioxide traps heat from the Earth's surface. However, American citizens recognized that they were not well informed about global warming.

(O'Halloran and Slattery, 2017) asked young people in South Dublin about their knowledge of cardiovascular disease. They found that age, level of education and having a relative with cardiovascular disease were associated with knowledge of cardiovascular disease. The most important sources of information were the family (18%) and the Internet (17%).

A similar study (Awad, 2014) conducted in Kuwait found similar associations with CVD knowledge. Also, they report: "nearly one-fifth are smokers, about two-thirds are either overweight or obese; almost three-quarters reported to exercise 0–2 times/week or do not eat healthy food regularly; and about one-third are very stressful or stressful. This may be attributed to that respondents did not consider themselves at risk and did not want to change their lifestyle and to take preventive measures".

The sociologist (Rydgren, 2011) points out that we all form beliefs, they are not always wrong nor always right. We rely on different ways to form beliefs. Beliefs are partly social, with a reliance on epistemic authorities and one's social group. In the analytical framework, we had mentioned $Pr(Event|K)$, so in many cases, it can be represented by $Pr(Event|EA, S)$, where EA and S are epistemic authorities and social groups.

In a New York Times, blog (North, 2015) wrote that some politicians portrayed the science on climate change as inconclusive. She disagrees, citing a review by (Cook et al., 2013) of about 12,000 scientific papers and their position on anthropogenic global warming (AGW). Cook et al. concluded: "66.4% of abstracts expressed no position on AGW, 32.6% endorsed AGW, 0.7% rejected AGW and 0.3% were uncertain about the cause of global warming. Among abstracts expressing a position on AGW, 97.1% endorsed the consensus position that humans are causing global warming". If people were made aware of this agreement of scientists about climate change, it would change people's beliefs, and North cites another study to support this view. This change in beliefs would be across supporters of different political parties.

5.2 *Communication and Literacy*

Something like climate change is uncertain but few deny the phenomenon entirely; one aspect of climate change is increased melting of glaciers. However, unguarded speculative comments can get reported in the media. In 1999, a glaciologist said that all the glaciers in the Central and Eastern Himalayas could disappear by 2035 (Pearce, 2010). This statement rose up the ladder of credibility from the New Scientist to a WWF report in 2005, ending up in the IPCC fourth assessment report published in 2007. Other experts contested the claim and questioned its inclusion in the IPCC report. Such a lapse is costly in terms of a loss of trust in experts and is a distraction from a complex issue.

Professor Spiegelhalter works on risk communication. In an online video (undated), he unpacks a newspaper story that said that a new statin drug taken every day would reduce the risk of a heart attack or stroke over the next 10 years by 40%, and this is something that is personally relevant to him. The newspaper reports the relative risk reduction. It is difficult to think about a percentage reduction in a percentage. Spiegelhalter says that he first needs to see what the absolute risk is that he will have a heart attack or stroke over the next 10 years. He found out that people with his characteristics have a baseline absolute risk of about 10%. To understand the information, his solution is to think of 100 S, where S is a person like him, Spiegelhalter. In ten years, 10 S of 100 S will have a heart attack or stroke without the statin; with the statin this will come down 6 S of 100 S experiencing a heart attack or stroke. The information is clearer in natural frequencies, and at this point it is up to Spiegelhalter to decide to take the statin or not, after thinking about the issue in the light of the information.

Gigerenzer (2011) argues that risk literacy is a key skill: "I believe that the answer to modern crises is not simply more laws, more bureaucracy, or more money, but, first and foremost, more citizens who are risk literate. This can be achieved by cultivating statistical thinking …. Simply stated, statistical thinking is the ability to understand and critically evaluate uncertainties and risks. Yet 76

Arguably, causal graphs can help researchers communicate their assumptions and be used for causal literacy (see (Swanson, 2015)). Although the specific form that causal literacy should take may be debated, advancement of risk literacy can also help appreciation of issues in causality.

6 Conclusion

Our analytical framework contains the kernel of key ideas that can help us think about uncertainty and causality. We start with probability, then move to conditional probability and see how new information helps us revise prior beliefs. We can have a network of conditional probabilities that represents our belief about the causal structure that links the variables we are interested in. Interventions can be brought into causal graphs, helping clarify the distinction between seeing and doing. Given information about the effects of different actions, we can decide which actions to take.

Though we may not *know* for certain, we can be convinced by a variety of evidence provided by the IPCC and climate science that climate change is a serious issue requiring serious efforts, despite the uncertainty. We may choose to adopt several actions, or change our lifestyles to prevent, delay or reduce heart disease, again based on a variety of evidence and information. We can use the language of probability and causal graphs to better understand an uncertain and complex world.

References

Altman, L. K. (2004, September 21). *The Doctor's world: Heart-health lessons from the Clinton case*. The New York Times. Retrieved on July 28, 2020, from https://www.nytimes.com/2004/09/21/health

Awad, A., & Al-Nafisi, H. (2014). Public knowledge of cardiovascular disease and its risk factors in Kuwait: a cross-sectional study. *BMC Public Health, 14*, 1471–2458

Borunda, M., Cruz, J., Garduno-Ramirez, R., & Ann Nicholson, A. (2020). Technical assessment of small-scale wind power for residential use in Mexico: A Bayesian intelligence approach. *PLoS ONE, 15*(3), e0230122. https://doi.org/10.1371/journal.pone.0230122

Cook, J., Nuccitelli, D., Green, S. A., Richardson, M., Winkler, B., Painting, R., Way, R., Jacobs, P.,& Skuce, A. (2013). Quantifying the consensus on anthropogenic global warming in the scientific literature. *Environmental Reseach Letter, 8*, 024024 (pp. 7).

Dasgupta, P. (2001). *Human well-being and the natural environment*. New Delhi: Oxford University Press.

Dasgupta, P. (2008). Discounting climate change. *Journal of Risk and Uncertainty, 37*(2/3), 141–169.

Freeman, A. M., Morris, P. B., Barnard, N., Esselstyn, C. B., Ros, E., Agatston, A., et al. (2017). Trending cardiovascular nutrition controversies. *Journal of the American College of Cardiology, 69*(9), 1172–1187.

Fuhrman, J. (2018). *The end of heart disease* (Kindle ed.). HarperCollins.

Gigerenzer, G. (2002). *Reckoning with risk: Learning to live with uncertainty*. New Delhi: Penguin Books Ltd.

Gigerenzer, G. (2011). *What scientific concept would improve everybody's cognitive toolkit?*. Retrieved on July 29, 2019, from https://www.edge.org/response-detail/10624

Hausfather, Z. (2018). *Explainer: How scientists estimate 'climate sensitivity'*. Retrieved on July 28, 2020, from https://www.carbonbrief.org/explainer-how-scientists-estimate-climate-sensitivity

HannArt, A., Pearl, J., Otto, F. E. L., Naveau, P., & GHil, M. (2016). *Bulletin of the American Meteorological Society, 97*(1), 99–110D.

Hyman, M. (2016). *Eat fat get thin: Why the fat we eat is the key to sustained weight loss and vibrant health*. Yellow Kite.

IPCC. (2010). guidance note for lead authors of the ipcc fifth assessment report on consistent treatment of uncertainties. Retrieved on July 28, 2020, fromhttps://www.ipcc.ch/site/assets/uploads/2017/08.

IPCC. (2018). Summary for Policymakers. In V. Masson-Delmotte, P. Zhai, H.-O. Pörtner, D. Roberts, J. Skea, P.R. Shukla, A. Pirani, W. Moufouma-Okia, C. Péan, R. Pidcock, S. Connors, J.B.R. Matthews, Y. Chen, X. Zhou, M.I. Gomis, E. Lonnoy, T. Maycock, M. Tignor, & T. Waterfield (Eds.), *Global warming of 1.5 degrees C. An IPCC special report on the impacts of global warming of 1.5 degrees C above pre-industrial levels and related global greenhouse gas emission pathways, in the context of strengthening the global response to the threat of climate change, sustainable development, and efforts to eradicate poverty*. World Meteorological Organization, Geneva, Switzerland, 32 pp. Retrieved on July 28, 2020 from https://www.ipcc.ch/site/assets/uploads/sites/2/2019/05

Koskinas, K. C., Siontis, G. C. M., Piccolo, R., Mavridis, D., Raber, L., Mach, F., et al. (2018). Effect of statins and non-statin LDL-lowering medications on cardiovascular outcomes in secondary prevention: A meta-analysis of randomized trials. *European Heart Journal*, *39*, 1172–1180.

Leiserowitz, A., Smith, N., & Marlon, J. R. (2010). *Americans' knowledge of climate change*. New Haven, CT: Yale Project on Climate Change Communication, Yale University. http://environment.yale.edu/climate/files/ClimateChangeKnowledge2010.pdf

Lindley, D. (2006). *Understanding uncertainty*. New Jersey: Wiley.

Montamat, G., & Stock, J. H. (2020). Quasi-experimental estimates of the transient climate response using observational data. *Climatic Change*, *160*, 361–371.

North, A. (2015). *Why misleading Americans about climate change is dangerous*. The New York Times. https://takingnote.blogs.nytimes.com/2015/08/11/why-misleading-americans-about-climate-change-is-dangerous/?searchResultPosition=4

O'Halloran, L., & Slattery, M. (2017). Assessing the knowledge of cardiovascular disease among young people in south Dublin. *Cardiol Cardiovascmed*, *1*(4), 187–194.

Ornish, D., Scherwitz, L. W., Billings, J. H., Gould, K. L., Merritt, T. A., Sparler, S., et al. (1998). Intensive lifestyle changes for reversal of coronary heart disease. *JAMA*, *280*(23), 2001–2007.

Pearce, F. (2010). *Debate heats up over IPCC melting glaciers claim*. Retrieved on July 29, 2020, from https://www.newscientist.com/article/dn18363-debate-heats-up-over-ipcc-melting-glaciers-claim/?ignored=irrelevant

Pearl, J. (2001). Baysianism and causality, or, why i am only a half-Bayesian. In: D. Corfield & J. Williamson (Eds.) *Foundations of Bayesianism, Kluwer applied logic series* (Vol. 24, pp. 19–36). Kluwer Academic Publishers.

Pearl, J. (2009). *Causality: Models, reasoning, and inference*. New York: Cambridge University Press.

Peterson, M. (2009). *An introduction to decision theory*. Cambridge: Cambridge University Press.

Ramsey, F. P. (1926). Truth and probability. In R. B. Braithwaite (Ed.), *Ramsey, 1931, the foundations of mathematics and other logical essays* (Chap. VII, pp. 156–198). Kegan, Paul, Trench, Trubner and Co., London.

Ray, K. K., Seshasai, S. R., Erqou, S., Sever, P., Joukema, J. W., Ford, I., et al. (2010). Statins and all-cause mortality in high- risk primary prevention: A meta-analysis of 11 randomized controlled trials involving 65,229 participants. *Archives on Internal Medicine*, *170*(12), 1024–31.

Rubin, D. B. (2008). For objective causal inference, design trumps analysis. *The Annals of Applied Statistics*, *2*(3), 808–840.

Rydgren, J. (2011). Beliefs. In P. Bearman, P. Hedstrom (Eds.), *The Oxford handbook of analytical sociology* (pp. 72–93). Oxford University Press, Oxford.

Sloman, S. (2009). *Causal models: How people think about the world and its alternatives*. Oxford: Oxford University Press.

Sox, H. C., Higgins, M. C., Owens, D. K. (2013). *Medical decision making* (p. 21). Wiley, Chichester.

Spiegelhalter, D. (undated). *Statins and risk*. University of Cambridge. https://nrich.maths.org/12165

Stahl, L. (2018). *Interview with Donald Trump*. Retrieved on July 28, 2020, from https://www.cbsnews.com/news/donald-trump-full-interview-60-minutes-transcript-lesley-stahl-2018-10-14/

Strotz, R. H., & Wold, H. O. A. (1960). Recursive versus nonrecursive systems: An attempt at synthesis. *Econometrica, 28*(2), 417–427.

Swanson, S. A. (2015). Communicating causality. *European Journal of Epidemiology*, *30*, 1073–1075.

Weitzman, M. L. (2011). *Review of Environmental Economics and Policy*, *5*(2), 275–292.

Woodward, J. (2004). *Making things happen: A theory of causal explanation*. Oxford: Oxford University Press.

Unbundling Air Pollution Concerns: A Closer Look at Socio-economic Factors

Purnamita Dasgupta and Kavitha Srikanth

1 Introduction

Air pollution has wide-ranging impacts on economic activity, human health and well-being, with accumulating evidence for India on the adverse implications (Kandlikar & Ramachandran, 2000; Balakrishnan et al., 2019; Spears et al., 2019). To cite from a recent tribunal order: "*Violation of laid down air pollution levels resulting in large number of deaths and diseases needs to be addressed expeditiously*" (para ix, Pg. 32, National Green Tribunal (NGT) order 21.08.2020) (NGT 2020a). The adverse impacts of air pollution are widespread on agricultural yields (Burney & Ramanathan, 2014; Gupta et al., 2017), labour productivity (Zivin & Neidell, 2012; Adhvaryu et al., 2016), cognitive functioning and health of children and older people (Power et al., 2011; Suglia et al., 2008; Jones, 2020), institutional functioning (Kountouris, 2020), increased healthcare costs and reduced profits to employers to name a few. The adverse health impacts from air pollution are a grave concern, especially for India, where air pollution has been on the rise for several decades now. We motivate the discussion by presenting here some data on air pollution and the health losses attributable to air pollution in India.

Air quality in Indian cities has been observed to be among the poorest in the world (WHO, 2018). Many Indian cities such as Kanpur, Varanasi, Faridabad, Delhi, Gaya, Patna, Lucknow, Muzzafarpur, Agra and Jaipur ranked among the top globally polluted cities in 2016. To motivate the discussion, we present some information on

P. Dasgupta (✉) · K. Srikanth
Institute of Economic Growth, University of Delhi Enclave, Delhi, India
e-mail: purnamita.dasgupta@gmail.com

K. Srikanth
e-mail: kavithasrikanth02@gmail.com

P. Dasgupta
International Centre for Integrated Mountain Development (ICIMOD), Kathmandu, Nepal

P. Dasgupta et al. (eds.), *Sustainable Development Insights from India*,
India Studies in Business and Economics,
https://doi.org/10.1007/978-981-33-4830-1_21

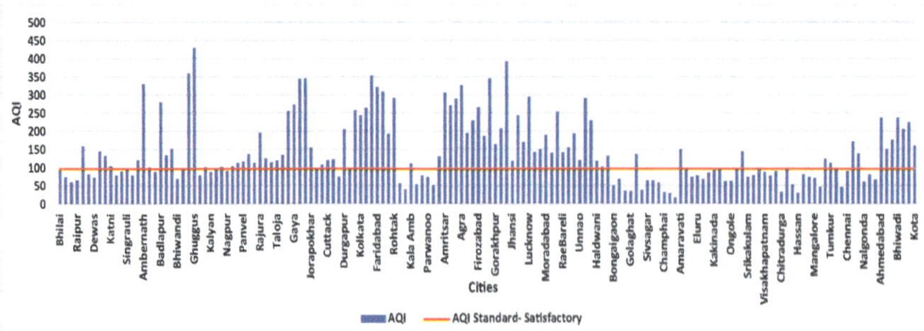

Fig. 1 Snapshot of AQI across some cities.
Source CPCB (n.d-a), APPCB (n.d.), KSPCB (n.d.), TNPCB (n.d.), MPCB (n.d.), CECB (n.d.), UPCB (n.d.), UPPCB (n.d.)

the air quality in India with the familiar index known as the air quality index (AQI). The air quality index AQI is a measure of the weighted values of various air pollutants (Central Pollution Control Board (CPCB), 2014) with a higher AQI denoting worse air quality (and vice versa). Figure 1 provides a snapshot of the extent to which this index (average of three months with the highest AQI in the year) has tended to exceed the limits for some cities during the three months with the highest AQIs in the year. A preliminary examination of the average AQI between May 2017 and March 2018 reveals that majority of the cities, namely 60%, have an AQI greater than the designated satisfactory limit which is set at 100.

The daily data indicates that in many cities, the AQI was beyond the satisfactory level for all the days in a month for several months during the year, indicating that the air quality was poor for a major part of the year (Fig. 2). This is a matter of grave concern as it indicates that the cities have been continually exposed to poor air quality for prolonged periods of time. For instance, by this measure, Delhi has consistently had air quality at worse than satisfactory levels for 5 months from

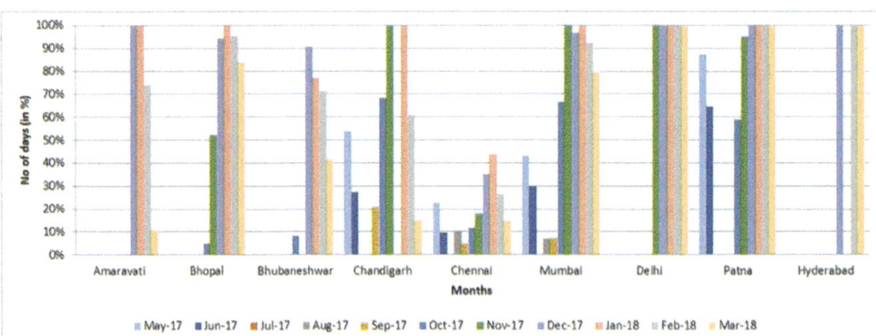

Fig. 2 Percentage of days where AQI exceeds the satisfactory limits in major cities.
Source CPCB (n.d-a), APPCB (n.d.), KSPCB (n.d.), TNPCB (n.d.), MPCB (n.d.), CECB (n.d.), UPCB (n.d.), UPPCB (n.d.)

November to March. Figure 2 captures the significant variation in the AQI across cities and seasonal variations in the air quality levels.

The relationship between air quality and health is well established, especially in relation to particulate matter (Johnson et al., 2011). We use particulate matter concentrations for the rest of our empirical analysis. Disability-adjusted life year (DALY)-based measurements are a convenient way of presenting the impact of air pollution on health. As Fig. 3 reveals, recent DALYs estimate (Balakrishnan et al., 2019) suggest that there is substantial variation across states in India. The columns represent DALYs attributable to overall air pollution (ambient particulate matter, household air pollution, ambient ozone pollution), while the orange and blue lines map DALYs attributable to household air pollution from exposure to $PM_{2.5}$ due to use of solid cooking fuels and the exposure to ambient particulate matter pollution based on $PM_{2.5}$ concentration level respectively. We note at the outset the importance of this differentiation between household and ambient pollution since policy instruments to deal with these two sources would be different. In terms of overall air pollution, Rajasthan, Uttar Pradesh, Haryana, Madhya Pradesh, Bihar and Chhattisgarh have some of the highest DALY rates per 1 lakh population. Uttar Pradesh, Haryana, Rajasthan, Bihar and Madhya Pradesh have high levels of DALYs attributable to both ambient and household pollutions, while DALYs for states like Delhi, Punjab and Maharashtra are primarily due to ambient pollution.

In addition to differentiation based on the source of pollution, air pollution can vary based on the kind of pollutant and also the economic activity that underlies the pollution source. Although the AQI is commonly used to obtain an idea of the air quality, it suffers from limitations as it masks concentration levels and movements in individual pollutants. Each pollutant originates from definite sources and has unique impacts, and accordingly, air pollution reduction policies and measures are needed.

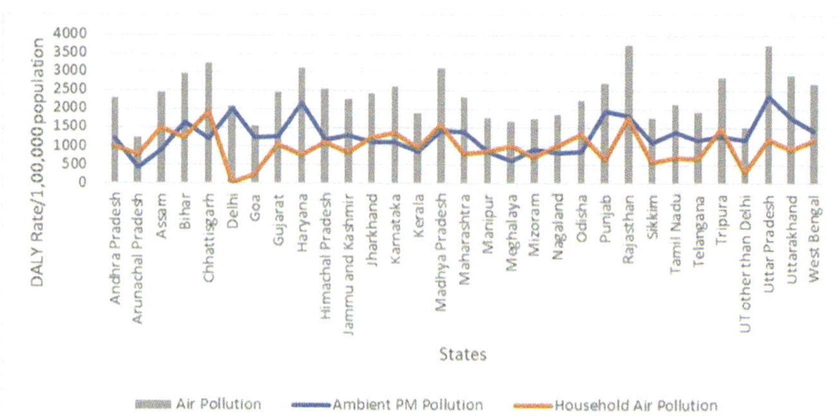

Fig. 3 DALY rate per 1 lakh population.
Source Based on data in (Balakrishnan et al., 2019); Data is for the year 2017 and has an uncertainty interval of 95%

For the rest of this paper, we therefore focus on individual pollutant concentrations. The ability to manage pollution effectively would depend on a host of interdependent factors, including supply-side and demand-side variables, and drivers that are technological, social or economic in nature. This study examines the relationship of PM_{10} with income and other socio-economic factors at the state level and provides some policy insights that could be considered for addressing the air pollution concerns.[1]

The paper is organized as follows. Section 2 contains the rationale and methods used in the analysis, Sect. 3 discusses some relevant insights from the literature, and Sect. 4 presents the results from an empirical analysis. Section 5 concludes with a discussion and suggestions based on potential synergies with the existing policies.

2 Rationale, Methods and Data

2.1 Rationale and Methods

The study examines the importance of socio-economic characteristics for air pollution management in cities and states in India, by analysing available data and information in the public domain. Three approaches are adopted to explore various dimensions of the problem, namely a desk review, a graphical analysis and an econometric exercise. We discuss these in some detail below.

2.1.1 Desk Review

A detailed literature review was carried out to understand the importance of various aspects of managing air pollution. These include studies concerning the types of air pollutants and their implications for health and socio-economic well-being, the sources of pollution and source apportionment studies that examine the causes and variations in these, the socio-economic determinants of air pollution and policies and instruments for managing air pollution. Both international literature and studies undertaken for India were consulted. Intensive efforts were also made to understand the data and information aspects of attempting an empirical exploration and its contextualization.

2.1.2 Descriptive and Graphical Analysis

Trends in air pollutant concentration levels are studied over time and across states to understand the patterns that emerge in the data through two-way tables and graphical

[1]Data on $PM_{2.5}$ is not available consistently at the same level of detail over time for all the cities/states. This is partially at least attributable to the fact that $PM_{2.5}$ monitoring was only started around 2009 and its coverage is being expanded.

representations. This facilitates an understanding of the heterogeneity across states in India and in the pollutant concentrations in these. An analysis of the changes in pollutant concentration levels of PM_{10} and $PM_{2.5}$ pre- and post-COVID-19 pandemic control measures provides some insights on the potential for reduction in pollution levels. The income–pollution relationship is also examined in some detail with this approach, using state-level Gross State Domestic Product (GSDP) and PM_{10} concentration as an indicator of air pollution.

2.1.3 Econometric Model

A rigorous econometric exercise is conducted to understand the associations between socio-economic characteristics of states and the observed pollution levels in terms of PM_{10}. A panel data regression model is used, with data for states pertaining to a period of 5 years. The rationale for the explanatory variables chosen for this estimation to understand the linkages with air pollution is briefly explained here.

Urbanization: Based on the existing understanding and evidence on urbanization, we introduce the share of urban population as a proportion of total population as an explanatory variable in our analysis, expecting an increase in urbanization to adversely impact emission levels of particulate matter.

Income: In the present study, we use the variable of total gross domestic product to capture the income effect with the expectation that there will be a positive relationship between income and pollutant concentrations given that the states in the Indian economy are various stages of development. India classified as a low middle-income country in global rankings.

Industrialization: The share of the secondary sector's contribution in the total income or GSDP of the states is included in the analysis to capture its relationship with pollution concentration given that this has had a significant impact in other countries.

Energy consumption: Given that total energy consumption data at a sub-national level is not directly compiled by one source or method across states, we introduce per capita electricity consumption as a potential indicator that influences air pollution. On one hand, electricity being a source of clean energy should have a negative relationship with pollution, and India has initiated several programmes to encourage renewable energy, clean technology for coal-based power plants and even introduced a coal cess. However, since the bulk of India's electricity production comes from coal, it is equally true that this could be a source of air pollution. Therefore, it is of interest to see how this variable behaves in the current context.

Social Development: States differ substantially in terms of outcomes on social sector indicators, depending on the indicator chosen. We use social sector expenditure to proxy for the impact of awareness and social development in general on outcomes observed with pollution. The expectation would be that of a negative relationship.

Green Cover: The analysis also uses the total forest cover of the state as a proportion of its total geographical area. This variable can play a crucial role in managing air pollution as the existing evidence seems to indicate.

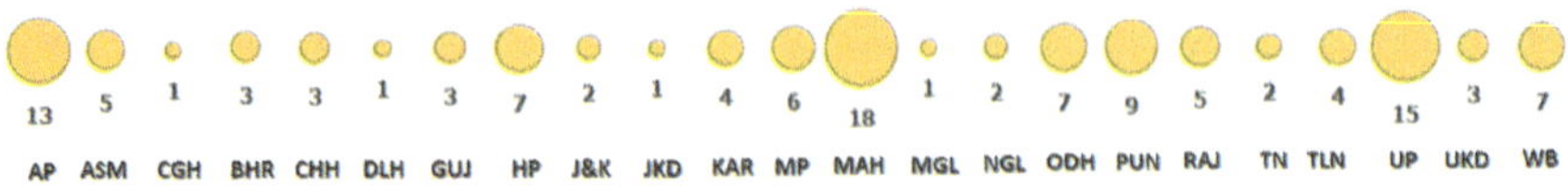

Fig. 4 Number of non-attainment cities under the NCAP in each state.
Source Authors' compilations based on MoEFCC 2019a and NGT 2019a. *Legend* State names: DLH—Delhi, UP—Uttar Pradesh, JKD—Jharkhand, RAJ—Rajasthan, HAR—Haryana, J&K—Jammu & Kashmir, UKD—Uttarakhand, NGL—Nagaland, PUN—Punjab, BHR—Bihar, GUJ—Gujarat, CGH—Chandigarh, WB—West Bengal, MAH—Maharashtra, ODH—Odisha, MP—Madhya Pradesh, CHH—Chhattisgarh, ASM—Assam, AP—Andhra Pradesh, TLN—Telangana, HP—Himachal Pradesh, KAR—Karnataka, MGL—Meghalaya, TN—Tamil Nadu

2.2 *Scale of Analysis*

In India, there has so far been an emphasis on considering cities as the appropriate level of analysis for understanding the causes of and managing air pollution. This has its own merits in terms of the extent of population that is exposed, the concentration of pollutants observed in cities, the availability of data from monitoring sites in cities and the causes which conventionally have for the most part been associated with the growth of economic activities centred around cities. We conduct some analysis at the city level to illustrate a few points.

However, it is increasingly observed that for large parts of the country, air pollution is often contiguous across rural, peri-urban and urban areas and administrative boundaries defined by cities and states, as are some of the pollution sources which are distributed on the cities' peripheries and hinterlands. Further, for economic decision-making, including setting targets for annual economic activity (production, logistics, etc.) and funding allocations, the state is the first level of decision-making, after the Centre. Given the spill overs across city boundaries, both the central planner and the state leadership can take care of inter-state externalities. The state in turn can take care of intra-state externalities and provide the requisite funds. At a practical level, most data on socio-economic characteristics is available consistently over time and across all states at the state level. For these reasons, we use the state as the preferred unit of analysis for most of our study.

It may be noted that the cities that we chose to examine are from the states of Delhi, Gujarat, Haryana, Maharashtra, Punjab, Rajasthan and Uttar Pradesh, which are among the most polluted. Most of these cities form part of the non-attainment cities[2] listed under the National Clean Air Programme (NCAP) (more details are available in Sect. 3.3.1). Figure 4 contains the number of non-attainment cities under the NCAP in each state as represented by the area of the circle and totals up to 122 cities. Except for Delhi which is a city-state and Haryana, the majority of these cities are located in the states of Maharashtra, Uttar Pradesh, Andhra Pradesh, Punjab—all of which are part of the state-level analysis.

---

[2]Non-attainment cities refer to cities where the National Ambient Air Quality Standards (NAAQS) were exceeded and were identified based on 2011–2015 air quality data and the WHO air quality update of 2018 (MoEFCC 2019a).

2.3 *Variables and Data Sources*

This study uses data for 32 states and union territories over a 5-year period from 2012–2013 to 2016–2017. Annual averages of PM_{10} concentrations were obtained at the location level in every city from manual monitoring data under the National Ambient Air Quality Monitoring Programme (NAMP) from Central Pollution Control Board (CPCB) sources (n.d.-b). City-level and state-level averages were computed. Data on PM_{10} annual averages was originally given based on the calendar year period. In order to facilitate comparison with other socio-economic variables, the corresponding financial years were identified. The choice of year was based on ensuring a maximum overlap in the number of months. For example, the calendar year of 2013 for PM_{10} was matched with financial year 2013–14 and similarly identified for the other years. Real-time monitoring data across various pollutants- PM_{10}, $PM_{2.5}$, NO_x and CO during the complete lockdown period in India due to the coronavirus pandemic was compiled from continuous ambient air quality monitoring stations (CPCB 2020).

Information on socio-economic variables was collected from various sources. Data on gross state domestic product (GSDP), per capita GSDP and value added from the secondary sector was based on Ministry of Statistics and Programme Implementation (MoSPI) data (MoSPI n.d.). Data on social sector expenditure was collected from reports on state finances (RBI 2019). Per capita electricity consumption data was collected from a Rajya Sabha Question answered by the Ministry of Power (2017). Proportion of urban population (projected) to total population was obtained from the estimates recently made available through the report of the technical group on population projections (MoHFW 2019). Ratio of total forest cover as a proportion of geographical area in the state was calculated from data sourced from the State of Forest reports given by the Forest Survey of India (2013, 2015, 2017, 2019). Total forest cover data is given at an interval of two years, so data for the years in between was interpolated on the assumption that the changes in the intervening period were uniformly distributed over time. Details of data sources and definitions are provided in Appendix A1.

3 Key Insights from the Desk Review

3.1 *Causes of Air Pollution*

Causes of air pollution vary, depending upon the meteorological factors, geographical factors such as terrain and elevation, rural or urban nature of areas. At an over-arching level, the relationship between economic growth and pollution has been extensively researched, especially for developing countries. Evidence on the interaction between sub-categories of pollution, such as outdoor and indoor pollution, has also been mounting, with indoor air pollution being recognized as a major cause of ambient air pollution (Chafe et al., 2014). For instance, in India, as in several other developing countries, cooking with biomass on cookstoves with inefficient combustion, has been seen as a prevalent concern for quite some time now (Bruce et al., 2000). Research on the adverse health impacts and ways to manage this pollution has increased exponentially over the last couple of decades (for instance, Zahnos et al., 2020; Lewis & Pattanayak, 2012, Hanna & Olivia, 2015). The Lancet Commission on pollution and health provides a recent assessment of the causes and implications of air pollution (Landrigan et al., 2017).

For a defined geographical area, how the sources contributing to air pollution in an area combine and evolve over time is important for understanding impacts and designing corrective measures. Information on the sources that contribute to air pollution over a demarcated area becomes a critical input in designing programmes and policies to control pollution. Source apportionment studies have therefore increasingly been recognized as an important step for designing contextually appropriate and cost-effective policies (Johnson et al., 2011). The variation in the sources and underlying causes contributing to air pollution is evident from studies conducted for Indian cities. This information is helpful in deciding which sectors need to be targeted for control measures. For example, transport, industry and dust from construction and roads contribute majorly to PM_{10} and $PM_{2.5}$ pollution in Delhi (ARAI and TERI 2018) and to $PM_{2.5}$ pollution in Mumbai and Ahmedabad. Local sources of $PM_{2.5}$ pollution are important for Varanasi, including cooking, lighting and heating, apart from dust from roads and burning of open waste (Guttikunda et al., 2019; Dasgupta & Srikanth, 2020).[3]

Across studies, it is observed that for most cities, air pollution was also clearly attributable to transboundary sources, beyond city boundaries. In the case of some cities, this has become an increasingly important factor, especially in the northern and western parts of the country. Airsheds with high pollutant concentration levels can stretch from within cities constituting an urban air shed, to cross parts of a state, covering both rural and urban areas such as in the Delhi NCR, and even cross-state boundaries as seen in the Indo-Gangetic Plain. This has in turn raised calls for an air shed management approach for controlling air pollution.[4]

A common contributor to air pollution levels in many Indian cities is emissions from dust caused by varied sources like construction, roads etc., which has been observed in several developing countries (Johnson et al., 2011). As some evidence indicates, a way out is through encouraging vegetative cover (MoRTH, 2015; Johnson et al., 2011). For example, the Green Highways (Plantation and Maintenance) Policy of 2015 in India can potentially contribute to this purpose (MoRTH, 2015).

---

[3]Sources of information: Delhi—ARAI and TERI (2018), year 2016; Mumbai and Ahmedabad—Ganguly et al. (2020), year 2018; Varanasi—Guttikunda et al. (2019), year 2015.

[4]https://www.worldbank.org/en/events/2019/10/21/air-quality-management-in-india-learning-from-international-experiences; https://www.downtoearth.org.in/news/air/join-the-dots-for-clean-air-67779.

3.2 *Socio-Economic Determinants of Air Pollution*

Various socio-economic determinants have been examined by scholars to enhance the understanding of the underlying associations with air pollution. Some socio-economic factors considered include population, population density, income and income proxies, energy efficiency and energy intensity-related measures, urbanization and built-up area, patterns of sectoral contribution to the national income, transportation and education-related indicators. Some key insights that are of relevance to India are discussed below.

3.2.1 Population-Related Indicators: Population, Population Density, Urban Population and Urbanization

Population and population density were seen to have a positive relationship with $PM_{2.5}$ in China's case by some authors, for example (Luo et al., 2018; Ma et al., 2016). In the Indian case, population and pollution were seen to have positive relationships for SO_2, NO_2 and PM (Holian, 2014), while the relationship of population density and environmental productivity was negative for NO_2, SO_2 and PM (Managi & Jena, 2008).

Urban population is a critical factor in relation to air pollution and climate change, especially when taking into account the growing energy requirements in India (Imam & Banerjee, 2016). As per one study, the relationship of urban population with $PM_{2.5}$ was found to be U-shaped for India (Han et al., 2016). Scholars use different approaches for characterizing the causal relationship. Luo et al. (2018) and Managi and Jena (2008) consider urbanization as the share of urban population in total population, with the objective of capturing movement of people to urban areas, while Xu and Lin (2018) consider urbanization with the additional argument that movement to urban areas will also cause an increase in purchase of motor vehicles which would have impacts on pollution. Luo et al. (2018) find a negative relationship of urbanization with $PM_{2.5}$ concentrations and justify it saying that rural area's energy consumption contributes a lot to $PM_{2.5}$ in China's case. For India, Managi and Jena (2008) found a negative relationship with environmental productivity. Fang et al. (2015) construct an urbanization index for China with many factors including urban population, secondary sector contribution, private vehicles and area and found that it had a negative impact on air quality.

3.2.2 Income and Income Proxies

The relationship between income and pollution has been examined by many authors, particularly by exploring the concept of the Environmental Kuznets Curve (EKC) (e.g. (Grossman & Krueger, 1994). The EKC curve depicts the relationship between levels of environmental pollutant and income. The relationship is theoretically hypothesized to be inverted U-shape, meaning that an increase in income leads to an increase in environmental pollutant until a point after which pollution is expected to decrease with an increase in income. Empirically, the inverted U-shape is contested and does not necessarily hold for all pollutants. While specifications have differed, most scholars have used a measure of gross domestic product (GDP) and/or consumption expenditure to capture income. Luo et al. (2018), Xu et al. (2016) and Managi and Jena (2008) consider per capita GDP guided by the EKC argument, while Holian (2014) considers two indicators, namely the district-level domestic product and the monthly consumption expenditure per capita, for measuring socio-economic development for India. Luo et al. (2018) find the relationship with income to be important, but opine that the nature of development, (namely the industrial sector's contribution) is more important for the case of China, while Xu et al. (2016) find an inverted U-shaped EKC relationship between $PM_{2.5}$ and economic growth in China. Holian (2014) estimates the relationship between development (measured through income, income proxies and literacy rate) and air pollution (Particulate Matter, SO_2 and NO_2) for Indian cities between 2006 and 2011, controlling for various other socio-economic factors with a regression. They find that development is negatively related to PM and positively to NO_2, and that manufacturing-centric cities also have higher pollution. Managi and Jena (2008) examine the relationship between environmental productivity and income for NO_2, SO_2 and PM using regression methods for Indian states for the period 1991–2003. They find that environmental productivity falls more in states with higher income in relation to states with lower income after taking into account some socio-economic variables. Sinha and Bhattacharya (2017) undertook an EKC analysis for SO_2 emissions in India and found the conventional inverted U curve applicable in industrial areas, while Sinha and Bhatt (2017) found a N-shaped EKC curve for NO_x in India.

3.2.3 Sectoral Contribution: Industrial Sector and Related Measures

The relationship between pollution and income is also conditional on how much that income is contributed to by various categories of economic activities, namely through primary, secondary and tertiary sectors. In relation to air pollution, both the composition and the size of the manufacturing sector are important considerations in determining the impacts (Cole, 2000). Some studies find that the tertiary sector can also contribute to air pollution (Luo et al., 2018), possibly due to factors like transportation (Xu et al., 2016). However, most scholars who have analysed the case of China find that a critical factor in relation to $PM_{2.5}$ pollution is the share and/or size of the industrial sector in the economy (Luo et al., 2018; Liu et al., 2019; Wang et al., 2018). The same holds true for India, with a positive relationship being observed between manufacturing sector and pollution (see Holian, 2014 for instance).

3.2.4 Energy-Related Indicators: Energy Intensity, Energy Efficiency, Electricity

Energy intensity and energy efficiency have been used to understand the implications for pollution in various ways. It has been used as a measure of technology, for instance (Xu & Lin, 2018). Most commonly, it has been calculated as a proportion of coal consumption and energy consumption in GDP, (Luo et al., 2018; Xu et al., 2016; Xu & Lin, 2018). Findings have varied. While Luo et al. (2018) find the relationship with energy intensity negatively significant for China, Xu et al. (2016) find a U-shaped relationship with $PM_{2.5}$. Beijing, in China, introduced subsidies and discounts for households to encourage movement to electricity or natural gas, along with incentives for greener transportation (Lu et al., 2020). China used technology to curb SO_2 and NO_2 pollution through installation of devices in coal and thermal power industries, along with financial incentives and penalties to industries and accountability of local political leaders (Lu et al., 2020; Guan et al., 2014).

In general, it has been observed that electricity consumption levels are closely associated with socio-economic development (Abdoli et al., 2015; Bayar, 2014; Sengupta, 2016). In India, the per capita electricity consumption is well below international standards, and hence, this is an important variable to plan for as it is associated with clean energy as well as overall well-being (Dasgupta & Chaudhuri, 2020). The per capita annual electric power consumption was 804.5 kwh per capita in 2014 in India, as compared to 3927 kwh per capita in China and 12,997.4 kwh per capita in USA (World Bank, 2019). SDG 7 encompasses the access to electricity as an essential part of affordable, sustainable and modern energy for all (UN, 2015).

3.2.5 Social Development Indicators: Education, Health

In studies for India, Managi and Jena (2008) and Holian (2014) consider education-related variables, namely those who have passed matriculation level schooling and literacy rate respectively. The former study suggests a positive relationship with environmental productivity caused possibly by increased awareness. The latter study indicates an inverted U-shaped relationship between education and pollution. In general, a case has also been made for having contextually appropriate pollution control policies at various local and regional levels. For example, China has had differential regional $PM_{2.5}$ pollution targets matching the developmental level of the area (Lu et al., 2020).

3.2.6 Forest Cover

Forest cover, in addition to contributing to carbon sequestration, can also help remove pollutants like SO_2, NO_2, PM_{10} etc., from the air (Imam & Banerjee, 2016). Green spaces and vegetation around high pollution industrial areas, highways and other urban areas can help reduce dust and pollutant concentrations (MoRTH, 2015;

Johnson et al., 2011). India has various national and international commitments on forestry and green cover. The Nationally Determined Contribution (NDC) target is to create an additional carbon sink for 2.5–3 billion tons of carbon equivalent (GoI, 2015). Several states in the country have sizeable share of their land area under forests. In 2017–18, some of the states that had a high share of their geographical area under forests included Arunachal Pradesh, Mizoram and Meghalaya (FSI, 2019).

3.3 Key Aspects of Some Recent Programmes and Initiatives

3.3.1 NCAP

The National Clean Air Programme (NCAP) is the most comprehensive policy initiative in India for air quality management which was launched in 2019 and now covers 122 cities, described as the non-attainment cities (see Footnote 2, MoEFCC 2019a). Among noteworthy points for our analysis, the NCAP mentioned a goal of causing a 20–30% fall in $PM_{2.5}$ and PM_{10} emissions by 2024. The cities included in the NCAP were to make city action plans with the National Green Tribunal requiring them to undertake carrying capacity assessments (NGT 2019b). As of now, carrying capacity and source apportionment studies in non-attainment cities have either been conducted or are in the process of being undertaken in 80 cities in 22 states (NGT 2020b). The city action plans for the most part comprise actions in relation to road dust, agricultural and waste burning, transportation and vehicular emissions, industrial emissions, construction, and use of domestic fuels. It is important to note that the NCAP recognizes that for many cities and states especially in the Indo-Gangetic plains, a significant part of the air pollution originates outside their boundaries, and hence, it is important to have comprehensive local and coordinated regional plans to tackle air pollution. An institutional and regulatory framework to facilitate matters is called for to introduce integrated DSM and SSM options. Further, guidelines and tool kits are required for ensuring reliable baseline and continuous monitoring and data collection. Initiatives for best practices documentation should be done and made available to all states drawing upon the experiences from both within and outside India.

3.3.2 Funding Initiatives

The 15th Finance Commission has provided funding through a grant of Rs. 4400 crores for the year 2020–21, for cities with population above a million for whom air pollution is a concern (GoI, 2019). The first instalment allows usage of funds to improve monitoring, infrastructure and capacities and to undertake source apportionment studies and so on. The disbursement of the second instalment of funds would be conditional on achieving improvements in air quality. In case there is failure to improve the air quality, this portion of the fund is to be redistributed among cities which show improvements in air quality and to cities whose population is less than a million (GoI, 2019).

The Ministry of Environment and Climate Change (MoEFCC) is to provide around Rs.10 crores in funds for cities with population of more than a million and above a specified PM_{10} standard of 90 $\mu g/m^3$. This fund is for the purpose of building capacities and various pollution-reducing measures in these cities; while for cities with lesser population, funding of Rs. 10 lakhs for each city (if population is less than 5 lakhs) or Rs. 20 lakhs for each city (if population is between 5 and 10 lakhs) is to be given (MoEFCC, 2019b).

3.3.3 Role of the National Green Tribunal

The role of the courts in protecting the environment has been much discussed in the Indian context. Specifically, with regard to air pollution management, significant orders have been passed by the NGT, starting from 2018. Recent ones include orders passed by the Tribunal dated 16.01.2019, 15.03.2019, 06.08.2019, 20.11.2019, 11.03.2020 and the latest, 21.08.2020. The enforcement of the principle of sustainable development and the Public Trust doctrine and the interests of public health have been emphasized in these orders. The CPCB has been regularly reporting on the status, (latest dated 18.08.2020) and the NGT has provided directions, including in its most recent order dated 21.08.2020. Directions have been provided to various state governments and agencies accordingly, with regard to preparing and executing action plans for controlling air pollution. These have included functioning of monitoring stations, undertaking source apportionment and carrying capacity studies, review of master plans in the light of such studies, development of action plans and graded response action plans and emergency response systems, information on execution of action plans and reduction in pollution loads if any, and evaluation of the existing air quality monitoring systems.

3.3.4 Energy Sector

On the energy front, the Indian government has various programmes which link up well with increasing electricity access and improving energy efficiency, and these should be integrated to the extent feasible. These range from permits for energy efficiency under the PAT programme for energy-intensive industries to subsidies for LED bulbs under the Ujjwala programme for households, to renewable energy certificates-based trading for the renewables sector. With regard to directly impacting air pollution, an emissions trading scheme is being piloted in the state of Gujarat (GPCB, 2019). However, most of these schemes and programmes operate under independent targets and mandates, and as of date, there has been some emphasis on measuring the potential and actual impacts in terms of greenhouse gas emissions. The same holds true for programmes across sectors that seek to incentivize the use of e-vehicles for transportation, or the targets fixed under various national missions. A range of initiatives to strengthen the infrastructure in the power sector, increase competition in the electricity sector, establishment of power exchanges and trading forums, evolution of legal and institutional frameworks (Electricity Act, 2003, the Energy Conservation Act, 2001, Integrated Energy Policy (IEP), 2005 and the National Mission for Enhanced Energy Efficiency (NMEEE), 2008) have worked well alongside the demand-side initiatives mentioned above (PAT, UJALA, ECBC, Star Ratings, etc.) in ensuring electricity access alongside promoting energy efficiency and clean energy. There are important lessons to be learnt here on introducing complementary regulatory and market mechanisms for effectively managing air pollution.

In fact, research indicates that India has been reasonably successful in reducing energy intensity of its GDP and achieving energy savings. Going forward, India may be able to achieve relatively high growth rates transitioning to a middle-income country while maintaining per capita electricity consumption at about 50% of the levels observed among developed countries currently (Dasgupta & Chaudhuri, 2020). This should be expected to have beneficial implications for air pollution, even given a high growth rate and a growing population.

4 Findings from Data Analysis

The initial discussion on AQI in Sect. 1 provides a glimpse into the substantial differences in air pollution levels across cities and states in India. As set out in Sect. 2, we conduct a set of empirical exercises to further probe the issue, drawing upon some of the insights from the desk review highlighted in Sect. 3. The findings from the empirical analysis are presented below.

4.1 Trends in Air Pollution

Mapping AQI and DALY values across states in Sect. 1 provided a glimpse into the variation that exists across cities and states both in relation to levels of pollution and exposure to pollution. We examine in more detail the data by first mapping the trends in PM_{10} over the last few years, just short of a decade, from 2011–2012 to 2018–2019.

Figure 5 plots the annual average PM_{10} concentration over the years for different states. Most of the states have consistently exceeded the NAAQS. NAAQS for PM_{10} is 60ug/m^3 (CPCB, 2009). We compute the exceedance factor for these states. The exceedance factor ratio is obtained by dividing the annual average pollutant concentrations by the respective pollutant standards. Ratio values between 1 and 1.5 are categorized as "high pollution", and ratio values above 1.5 are categorized as "critical pollution" (CPCB, 2016). The calculations for 2018–19 indicate that 88% of states fall under the categories of "high pollution" and "critical pollution". Delhi has

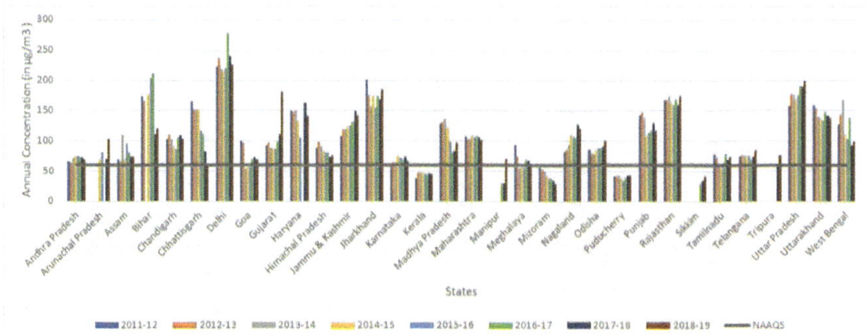

Fig. 5 Annual PM10 concentration state-wise, 2011–12 to 2018–19.
Source Authors' calculations based on data from national ambient air quality monitoring programme (NAMP), CPCB (n.d-b)

consistently had the highest exceedance factor value in comparison with the other states during these 8 years with the ratio within the range of 3.6–4.6. There are only a few states, such as Kerala, Puducherry and Sikkim that have consistently not exceeded the NAAQS in any year.

Combining the PM_{10} data across regions and comparing the concentration levels across these regions, Fig. 6 reveals substantial differences between regions, with the north and east regions consistently having higher pollution in comparison with the other regions. The southern region experiences relatively lower pollution in comparison with the other regions, since it does not exceed the NAAQS for most of the years. The North East has the second lowest pollution out of all the regions over the period, since it only slightly exceeds the NAAQS in most years.

The comparison across states confirms the significant heterogeneity in pollutant concentrations that exists between various states, traceable for the most part to various economic and social conditions in the state. The current COVID-19 situation has proved to be a great leveller with concentration levels coming down across regions, due to the restrictions placed on economic activities, including lockdowns. This in turn has provided an opportunity to understand the potential for reducing pollution across India. We next examine this contrasting situation.

4.2 *Air Quality During COVID-19 Lockdown Period*

In order to control the spread of the coronavirus, the Indian government imposed varying degrees of restrictions on economic activities over different phases of lockdown and unlock of the economy. The most stringent measures were imposed during a four-week period from March to April covering transportation, manufacturing and construction, followed by a gradual easing of restrictions in stages each lasting for a few weeks at a time. It is reasonable to presume that the halting of activities in major sectors of the economy would lead to reduction in pollution attributable to these

Fig. 6 Annual PM10 concentration region-wise, 2011–12 to 2018–19.
Source Authors' calculations based on data from National Ambient Air Quality Monitoring Programme (NAMP), CPCB n.d-b. Regional classification of States: Central—Chhattisgarh, Madhya Pradesh; East—Bihar, Jharkhand, Odisha, West Bengal; North- Chandigarh, Delhi, Haryana, Himachal Pradesh, Jammu and Kashmir, Punjab, Uttar Pradesh, Uttarakhand, North East—Arunachal Pradesh, Assam, Manipur, Meghalaya, Mizoram, Nagaland, Sikkim, Tripura; South—Andhra Pradesh, Karnataka, Kerala, Puducherry, Tamil Nadu, Telangana; West—Goa, Gujarat, Maharashtra, Rajasthan

activities. A comparison of the levels of pollution with and without such restrictions on economic activities can help to infer the extent to which interventions targeted at these sectors can lead to the abatement of pollution.

Researchers have noted that pollution across various cities changed markedly during the first phase of near complete lockdown (Dasgupta & Srikanth, 2020; Sharma et al., 2020; ICIMOD, 2020). Building on these earlier analyses, for the present exercise, we select a few cities which are representative of some of the highly polluted cities located within some of the most polluted states in India, for which there was comparable and consistent data publicly available. The cities included in the analysis are: Delhi, Ahmedabad, Gurugram, Hisar, Chandrapur, Mumbai, Jalandhar, Jaipur, Ghaziabad and Varanasi in the states of Delhi, Gujarat, Haryana, Maharashtra, Punjab, Rajasthan and Uttar Pradesh, respectively. Most of these cities come under the NCAP and are classified as non-attainment cities. As noted in Dasgupta and Srikanth (2020) ,a comparison of the daily concentrations of pollutants[5] such as PM_{10}, NO_x, $PM_{2.5}$ and CO over the lockdown period with corresponding levels during the same period in the previous year reveals that there are marked declines in the levels of most pollutants.

[5]Real-time monitoring data obtained from continuous ambient air quality monitoring stations from CPCB: https://app.cpcbccr.com/ccr/#/caaqm-dashboard-all/caaqm-landing.

Table 1 Change in pollutant concentrations between 2020 and 2019 (March–April).

Name of state	Name of city	PM10	PM2.5	NOx /NO2	CO
Delhi	Delhi				
Gujarat	Ahmedabad				
Haryana	Gurugram				
Haryana	Hisar				
Maharashtra	Chandrapur				
Maharashtra	Mumbai				
Punjab	Jalandhar				
Rajasthan	Jaipur				
Uttar Pradesh	Ghaziabad				
Uttar Pradesh	Varanasi				

Source Authors' calculations based on data from CPCB (2020).
Note Data for Jalandhar on NOx corresponds to NO_2 data; *Legend* Decrease in concentration levels are represented in green, increases in red.

For this analysis, we consider in particular the data on PM_{10} and $PM_{2.5}$ concentrations. The percentage change in PM_{10} indicates a decrease from 11 to 68%. $PM_{2.5}$ values across most cities except Mumbai also decreased, with percentage decreases over the previous year values ranging from 6 to 63%. Table 1 summarizes the change in pollutant concentration levels between COVID-19 and pre-COVID-19 levels in the previous year. The data is suggestive of the extent to which a decrease in pollution is possible in most cities, especially for PM_{10} and $PM_{2.5}$ if sources of pollution (i.e. pollution contributing economic activities) were adequately managed.

4.3 Policy Instruments for the Pollution–Income Relationship

We examine the relationship between income and pollution with state-level data on GSDP and particulate matter. Figure 7 represents annual per capita GSDP on the x-axis and annual average concentrations of PM_{10} on the y-axis. The red lines separate the states into four quadrants. The horizontal line depicts the all-India average per capita GSDP, while the vertical line represents the NAAQS annual standards for PM_{10}, which is at 60 $\mu g/m^3$. We also examine the relationship between total GSDP and PM_{10}. Expectedly five heavily populated but larger states shift from the left income quadrant to the right, into the higher GSDP group of states. Controlling for population has the advantage of linking more directly with development, since most policy measures and financing to support programmes for development consider population to be an important criterion for decision-making.

Air pollution has differential impacts in different states. Irrespective of whether one considers the total or the per capita income levels, only five states have pollution

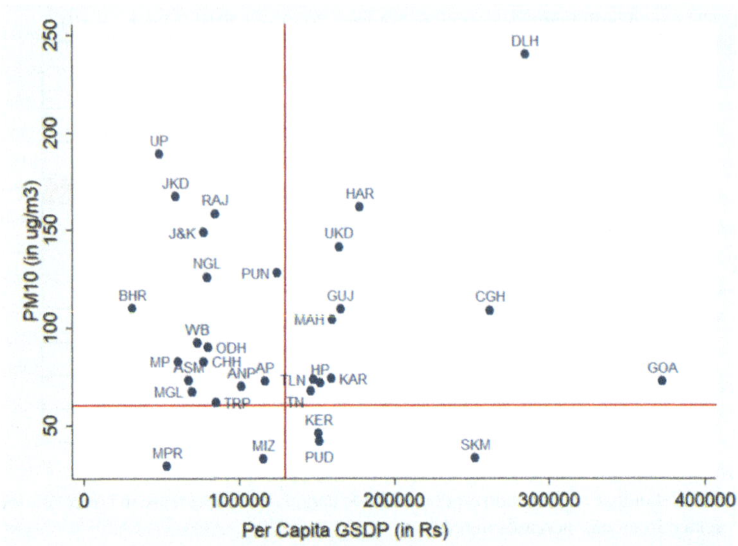

Fig. 7 Relationship between PM_{10} and PCGSDP.
Source Authors calculations based on data from CPCB (n.d.-b) and MoSPI (n.d.). *Legend* DLH—Delhi, UP—Uttar Pradesh, JKD—Jharkhand, RAJ—Rajasthan, HAR—Haryana, J&K—Jammu & Kashmir, UKD—Uttarakhand, NGL—Nagaland, PUN—Punjab, BHR—Bihar, GUJ—Gujarat, CGH—Chandigarh, WB—West Bengal, MAH—Maharashtra, ODH—Odisha, MP—Madhya Pradesh, CHH—Chhattisgarh, Goa—Goa, ASM- Assam, ANP—Arunachal Pradesh, AP—Andhra Pradesh, TLN—Telangana, HP—Himachal Pradesh, KAR—Karnataka, MGL—Meghalaya, TRP—Tripura, TN—Tamil Nadu, MPR—Manipur, MIZ—Mizoram, KER—Kerala, PUD—Puducherry, SKM—Sikkim

below the prescribed limit as per this particular indicator. These are the states of Sikkim, Puducherry, Kerala, Mizoram and Manipur. In general, among states in the upper right-hand quadrant which have high pollution and income levels, the scatter is skewed towards pollution, with the exception of two (Chhattisgarh and Goa), and a cluster of four states which hover around the cut-offs. These states are the ones which enjoy more privileged positions in terms of their income levels. High income states that have options to generate surpluses should actively consider introducing selective instruments such as taxes on pollution-generating activities. The introduction of permits trading for specific sectors would also be appropriate such as for the energy sector, setting up cross-boundary trading mechanisms. Gujarat has started a pilot, and this could provide valuable insights on developing a robust permits trading system.

The upper left quadrant has states which are heavily populated and in some instances also are not the typical high-income states (for instance, Rajasthan), challenging the standard idea of the positive relationship between income and pollution, even when considered in terms of the total GSDP. These are the states that need to be supported with direct funding (such as fiscal transfers) to support developmental programmes that facilitate the decoupling of economic growth with air pollution.

A targeted subsidy on green infrastructure would encourage investment in greener alternatives and move the states on a more sustainable growth pathway.

There is an urgent need for source apportionment studies in states with high pollution levels, and to that extent, the policy focus (NCAP, NGT) on such studies for the non-attainment cities (NACs) is welcome. A focus on specific cities however alone may not suffice where transboundary pollution sources are significant such as for states like Delhi. Many of these states are also clustered, and it may be feasible to have common regional regulatory bodies. States that have high per capita incomes may be well placed to raise some resources on their own through innovative market-based instruments. While command and control type of instruments which prescribe technology and performance standards are necessary and must be coupled with fines and penalties associated with non-compliance, market-based economic instruments have to be actively considered. Delhi, Haryana, Uttarakhand and Chandigarh belong to the northern region, and similarly, Maharashtra, Gujarat and Goa are all states in the western region. Many cities in these regions like Mumbai, Ahmedabad and Delhi have pollution sources outside their boundaries, which can also be governed better with the presence of a common regional regulatory body. The regulator can take into account the damage caused by the particular state on its neighbouring states and decide on fines and penalties proportional to the total social cost of such negative externalities. For instance, if spatial heterogeneity is addressed through the use of an emissions trading scheme, the cost of the permit must be high enough to encourage abatement and adoption of cleaner technology in the region and the incentivization accordingly designed.

States with air quality that falls within the limit and per capita incomes lower than average need to be supported actively with funding to ensure green growth. Handholding is necessary to ensure that these states can lead the way in sustainable development. A nation-wide enforceable tax or permits system encourage states with high income and pollution levels to abate, while utilizing the additional revenue to facilitate cleaner development in these low-income states. States with air quality better than the standard and per capita incomes higher than average (e.g. Kerala, Sikkim, Puducherry) must be incentivized to retain their position.

4.4 Socio-economic Determinants of PM_{10} Pollution

To probe the role played by various socio-economic factors, an econometric analysis was conducted. A panel dataset was compiled with data for 32 states and union territories, for a period of 5 years from 2012–13 to 2016–17. Apart from PM_{10} concentrations, the factors considered were income (gross state domestic product), urbanization, (proportion of urban population to total population), energy (per capita electricity consumption), secondary sector contribution (share of secondary sector in GSDP), social development (proxied by social sector expenditure), green cover (share of forest cover in geographical area of state) and transportation (total number of registered motor vehicles).

The number of observations varies from 142 to 160 across variables. While there is substantial variation across states in PM_{10} levels, within-state variation is much lower. Per capita electricity consumption increases over time in most states and also varies substantially across states. The share of forest cover in the geographical area also varies widely over states, but not much over time.

Expectedly, there is significant (5%) and positive correlation of PM_{10} with GSDP, social sector expenditure, transportation and significant negative correlation of PM_{10} with the share of forest cover. Correlations among the regressors were also significant in certain cases. The transportation variable is very highly and significantly correlated with GSDP and was therefore dropped from the analysis. Among the other variables, there are correlations though the coefficients are not high, such as between GSDP and the share of the secondary sector's contribution or between per capita electricity consumption and urbanization. The secondary sector GSDP is not significantly correlated with GSDP but is correlated with per capita electricity consumption. This is probably explained by the fact that India's economic transition was to move directly from agriculture to services. Social sector expenditure is significantly correlated with GSDP and with the share of forest cover in the state.

Statistical tests on alternative specifications were run to select the most appropriate regression model for the dataset, between random effects, fixed effects and pooled OLS options. The estimates from the selected specifications are presented in Table 2. The BP-LM test suggested that random effects were more appropriate than pooled OLS (Chi value: 202.34, $p = 0.00$), while the Hausman test indicated use of a random effects model rather than a fixed effect model (Chi value: 2.47, $p = 0.65$). Table 2 reports two specifications, both having PM_{10} concentration levels as the dependent variable.

Specification 1 is the estimation with all the variables. The coefficients suggest that these are all correctly signed as per expectations, with income, urbanization, share of the secondary sector having a positive impact on PM_{10} pollution, while electricity consumption and forest cover have a negative impact on PM_{10} levels. Unfortunately though, given the correlations among the regressors, the significance levels for some variables are low. This prompted a re-estimation of the model by dropping some of the variables based on the correlation matrix. Several alternative estimations were done. It was interesting to note that the results across alternative estimations were fairly consistent with regard to two key variables, namely share of forest cover and per capita electricity consumption. The results after dropping social sector expenditure and share of secondary sector due to their high correlations with GSDP and per capita electricity consumption, respectively, are reported in specification 2. This specification meets the criteria for a good specification. In specifications 1 and 2, per capita electricity consumption and share of forest cover in the geographical area of the state are significant explanatory variables. Per capita electricity consumption is negatively related with PM_{10} suggesting that ceteris paribus, increases in per capita electricity consumption are associated with a fall in PM_{10}. This is in line with the reasoning that electricity is a cleaner fuel. Although ideally one would like to control for the source of power, there are data limitations in conducting such an analysis. Diagnostics suggest that the growth rate of non-fossil installed capacity has been

Table 2 Regression estimates- Socio-economic determinants of PM_{10} pollution

Dependent variable	Independent variables	No of obs	Estimated coefficient
Estimation 1: PM_{10}	ln(GSDP)	135	8.4 (9.46)
	Per capita electricity consumption	135	(−)0.02** (0.01)
	Proportion of urban population to total population	135	10.98 (73.2)
	Social sector expenditure	135	(−)1.05e − 06 (2.50e-06)
	Share of secondary sector in GSDP	135	4.46 (45.87)
	Share of total forest cover in geographical area	135	(−)82.53* (42.62)
Estimation 2: PM_{10}	ln(GSDP)	140	5.22 (6.47)
	Per capita electricity consumption	140	(−)0.02** (0.01)
	Proportion of urban population to total population	140	5.09 (56.58)
	Share of total forest cover in geographical area	140	(−)91.39*** (31.59)

Note All regressions are run with a constant term. ***Significant at 1% level, **Significant at 5% level; *Significant at 10% level. Robust standard errors given in parentheses

higher than fossil during this period. An increase in forest cover area in relation to the geographical area of the state causes a decrease in PM_{10} concentration, which is consistent with the understanding that forests can play an important role in air pollution management .

A principal component analysis leads to three components with eigenvalues of 2.64, 1.62 and 0.99, significant at the 5% level. Component 1 and 2 cumulatively account for 71% of the variation with component 1 explaining 44% of the variation. 87% of the variation is cumulatively explained when component 3 is added. The principal components or eigenvectors suggest that the most important variables for component 1 were GSDP, proportion of forest cover in geographical area for the state, with social sector expenditure playing a limited role. For component 2, major drivers were per capita electricity consumption and the secondary sector's contribution to GSDP. For component 3, urban population as a proportion of total population was a major contributor with the share of the secondary sector in GSDP contributing to a limited extent.

The results clearly indicate the importance of the share of forest cover and per capita electricity consumption as determinants of PM_{10} concentration levels.

5 Conclusion

When policies are in place, the most important determinant of whether action proposed will be implemented successfully lies in the ground realities. This means that all actors need to be on-boarded: state and non-state. Supply-side measures supported by public sector resources alone cannot solve the problem, nor can a sole focus on technology-driven big ticket solutions. An understanding of the socio-economic determinants and explicitly factoring these implies that the demand-side measures can be brought into play.

There is a need to generate more information and fill the data and research gaps that persist. More research is required to map and evaluate the full impacts of air pollution in India and the costs to the economy. While efforts to expand monitoring stations in cities are ongoing, these need to be set up in rural and peri-urban areas as well. It is perhaps time to also integrate across sectors and define policies to incentivize air pollution management, and to measure, monitor and evaluate over time the success in terms of reduced air pollution outcomes. The use of population as a criterion for determining eligibility for funding air pollution reduction (as in the Finance Commission grant) or the extent of funding might disadvantage cities with severe pollution problems but with lower population, and there is a need to research on how best to incorporate relevant socio-economic factors that could influence the city and the state's ability to tackle air pollution. For instance, 76 out of the 122 non-attainment cities have population below a million.

While the government's role is critical in ensuring that the right policies are in place and public investment takes place in enabling the policies, environmental stewardship lies with all actors in the economy. In fact, it is the citizens who have to demand action from each other and the state to manage air pollution for their health and well-being. This requires adequate information and communication, which moves the science and technology (physical and social) from the domain of experts to that of citizens. Air pollution has relationships with many Sustainable Development Goals and is directly mentioned in Sustainable Development Goal 3 (Good health and well-being) in relation to reducing diseases and deaths caused through hazardous quality of air and in Goal 11 (Sustainable Cities and communities) in relation to decreasing the cities' adverse environmental impact per capita due to air quality. There is much that can be done in this regard to nudge behaviour in the right direction.

There is scope for addressing air pollution through enhanced cooperation among actors and across states in the country. In November 2019, the AQI in Delhi increased to severe levels repeatedly, leading popular media to report it as an air emergency. This corresponded to a period when the stubble burning was reducing in neighbouring states, while Delhi and surrounding areas continued to suffer from the accumulated stock of pollutants from this source along with other causes of air pollution. While wind speed and direction maybe beyond immediate control, institutional structures that support regional cooperation in a connected economy can play a major role.

While drawing up city action plans is a very welcome step, the role of small towns, peri-urban areas and rural areas in terms of understanding the sources of air pollution and designing policy for undertaking abatement measures needs to be paid more attention. An airshed management approach is called for. This approach was followed in Beijing through planning, monitoring and defining unified targets for contiguous areas. Typically, resources at the state level tend to be allocated across sectors and programmes based on sectoral priorities and targets. Environmental concerns may or may not find a place in these allocation decisions unless it is explicitly mandated. These mandates in the Indian federal system have tended to emanate from the Centre, whether in terms of target requirements or in terms of funds devolved for meeting specific targets. An exception in recent times has been the devolution of funds on the forestry head through fiscal transfers by the 14th and 15th Finance Commissions as part of the horizontal devolution. Studies reveal that when funds compensate for fiscal disability arising from environmental conservation (forests in this case), these do not guarantee fund flows to the sector in question (Dasgupta and Srikanth, 2021). Formal agreements, institutional structures and policies at sub-national levels, are called for to tackle abatement across state boundaries that are beneficial either to one or more states.

Our findings indicate that policies that tap into synergies between air pollution reduction and climate mitigation can have a substantial impact on particulate matter-related pollution. Expanding green cover and ensuring access to higher consumption of clean energy have the most significant impacts on air pollution. When these goals are pursued, it helps in achieving multiple SDGs as well as the commitments made under India's NDCs. The co-benefits of climate mitigation policies have substantial and significant impact for India. Economic instruments that exploit the synergies would be best placed to serve both interests.

Legislative and regulatory mechanisms need to be put in place so that a range of mechanisms at sub-national level can be conceptualized for supporting the cause. While some may require public support such as in procuring products based on energy-efficient technologies or pollution abatement technologies from the private sector, others may call for outright public investment in clean investment such as in infrastructure and renewable power generation. Experience from other countries suggests that economic instruments can be effective in controlling pollution. The role of fiscal and non-fiscal instruments, market and non-market instruments has to be acknowledged and mainstreamed.

Behavioural change among consumers and producers for a more sustainable lifestyle can blend well with the air pollution management strategy. Communications, outreach and knowledge management are important components for impacting air pollution. Reaching communities actively through risk-based communications for instance has not been pursued thus far. Over-dependence on government agencies and courts has created a narrative where the consumer consumes, the producer produces, and it becomes solely the public sector (agencies) responsibility to do the clean-up primarily through command and control-type approaches, supported by imposition of fines and penalties and levying compensation for environmental degradation. There is a need to move away from this conventional typecast, where air pollution management continues to be largely framed in terms of an unavoidable consequence of economic growth, attributable to urbanization and industrialization.

Air pollution management needs to be pursued as a priority for achieving sustainable development, with integrated management across sectors and spatial dimensions. Technological solutions will work best only when policies factor in the socio-economic determinants and both the supply side and the demand side are taken care of through appropriate market and non-market instruments.

Appendix: Data Sources and Definitions

Variable	Data source	Unit of measurement	Definition
PM_{10}	Manual monitoring data under national ambient air quality monitoring programme from CPCB (n.d-b.)	μg/m^3	–
PM_{10}, $PM_{2.5}$, CO, NO_x	Real-time data under continuous ambient air quality monitoring stations from CPCB (2020)	PM_{10} and $PM_{2.5}$: μg/m^3, CO: mg/m^3; NO_x: ppb	–
Air quality index	Air quality data from CPCB, (n.d.-a), state pollution control boards for Andhra Pradesh, Karnataka, Tamil Nadu, Maharashtra, Chhattisgarh, Uttarakhand, Uttar Pradesh	ratio	The air quality index (AQI) is a measure of the weighted values of various air pollutants (CPCB 2014) with a higher AQI denoting worse air quality (and vice versa)
Gross state domestic product	Constant prices, base year 2011–12. Data collected from MoSPI (n.d.) website	INR lakh	–
Per capita gross state domestic product		INR	–
Gross state value added from secondary sector		INR lakh	Secondary sector includes value added from manufacturing, electricity, water supply, gas and other utility services and construction (MoSPI n.d.)

(continued)

(continued)

Variable	Data source	Unit of measurement	Definition
Social sector expenditure	Reports on state finances (RBI 2019)	INR lakh	Social sector expenditure includes expenditure on "social services, rural development, and food storage and warehousing" (RBI 2019)
Per capita electricity consumption	Rajya Sabha question answered by MoP (2017)	kwh	"Per capita consumption = (gross energy generation + net import)/mid-year population" (MoP 2017)
Proportion of urban population (projected) to total population	As on 1st March, as estimated in the report of the technical group on population projections (MoHFW 2019)	Ratio	–
Total forest cover/geographical area	State of forest reports, FSI (2013,2015,2017,2019)	Ratio (variables measured in km^2)	Forest cover: "all lands more than one hectare in area with a tree canopy of more than 10%, irrespective of land use, ownership and legal status" (FSI 2017)

References

Abdoli, G., Farahani, Y. G., & Dastan, S. (2015). Electricity consumption and economic growth in OPEC countries: A cointegrated panel analysis. *OPEC Energy Review, 39*(1), 1–16. https://doi.org/10.1111/opec.12038.

Adhvaryu, A., Kala, N., & Nyshadham, A. (2016). Management and shocks to worker productivity. *International Growth Centre (IGC) Working Paper F-35143-INC-1*. https://www.theigc.org/wp-content/uploads/2017/01/Adhvaryu-et-al-2016-Working-paper.pdf

APPCB (Andhra Pradesh Pollution Control Board). (n.d.) Ambient air quality. https://appcb.ap.nic.in/ambient-air-quality-monitoring/

ARAI and TERI (The Automotive Research Association of India, The Energy and Resources Institute). (2018). Source Apportionment of PM2.5 & PM10 of Delhi NCR for Identification of Major Sources. https://www.teriin.org/sites/default/files/2018-08/Report_SA_AQM-Delhi-NCR_0.pdf

Balakrishnan, K., Dey, S., Gupta, T. et al. (2019). The impact of air pollution on deaths, disease burden, and life expectancy across the states of India: The Global Burden of Disease Study 2017. *The Lancet Planetary Health, 3*(1), e26–e39. https://doi.org/10.1016/S2542-5196(18)30261-4

Bayar, Y. (2014). Electricity consumption and economic growth in emerging economies. *Journal of Knowledge Management, Economics and Information Technology, IV*(2), 1–18. https://citeseerx.ist.psu.edu/viewdoc/download?doi=10.1.1.656.9349&rep=rep1&type=pdf

Bruce, N., Perez-Padilla, R., & Albalak, R. (2000). Indoor air pollution in developing countries: A major environmental and public health challenge. *Bulletin of the World Health Organization, 78*(9), 1078–1092. https://www.who.int/bulletin/archives/78(9)1078.pdf

Burney, J., & Ramanathan, V. (2014). Recent climate and air pollution impacts on Indian agriculture. *PNAS, 111*(46), 16319–16324. https://doi.org/10.1073/pnas.1317275111.

CECB (Chhattisgarh Environment Conservation Board). (n.d). Environmental data. https://enviscecb.org/data.htm

Chafe, Z. A., Brauer, M., Klimont, Z., et al. (2014). Household cooking with solid fuels contributes to ambient PM2.5 air pollution and the burden of disease. *Environmental health perspectives, 122*(12), 1314–1320.https://doi.org/10.1289/ehp.1206340

Cole, M. (2000). Air pollution and 'dirty' industries: How and why does the composition of manufacturing output change with economic development? *Environmental and Resource Economics, 17,* 109–123. https://doi.org/10.1023/A:1008388221831.

CPCB (Central Pollution Control Board). (n.d-a). National Air Quality Index. https://app.cpcbccr.com/AQI_India/

CPCB (Central Pollution Control Board). (n.d.-b). Manual Monitoring Data. Central Pollution Control Board. Retrieved on August 2020, from https://cpcb.nic.in/manual-monitoring/

CPCB (Central Pollution Control Board). (2009). National Ambient Air Quality Standards. New Delhi: Government of India. https://app.cpcbccr.com/ccr_docs/Air_quality_standards.pdf

CPCB (Central Pollution Control Board). (2014). National Air Quality Index. Central Pollution Control Board.

CPCB (Central Pollution Control Board). (2016). Air pollution in Delhi: An analysis. ENVIS Centre CPCB. https://cpcbenvis.nic.in/envis_newsletter/Air%20pollution%20in%20Delhi.pdf

CPCB (Central Pollution Control Board). (2020). Central Control Room for Air Quality Management—All India. https://app.cpcbccr.com/ccr/#/caaqm-dashboard-all/caaqm-landing

Dasgupta, P., & Chaudhuri, C. (2020). Environment and economic development: An analysis of electricity demand projections for India. In Aggarwal et al. (Ed.), *Accelerators of India's Growth.* Springer Nature, Springer. https://doi.org/10.1007/978-981-32-9397-7

Dasgupta, P., & Srikanth, K. (2020). Reduced air pollution during COVID 19: Learnings for sustainability from Indian cities. *Global Transitions, 2*(2020), 271–282. https://doi.org/10.1016/j.glt.2020.10.002.

Dasgupta, P., & Srikanth, K. (2021). Achieving the climate goal with intergovernmental transfers to the forestry sector: insights from the Indian experience. *Climatic Change, 164*(45). https://doi.org/10.1007/s10584-021-03016-0.

Fang, C., Liu, H., Li, G., Sun, D., & Miao, Z. (2015). Estimating the impact of urbanization on air quality in china using spatial regression models. *Sustainability, 7*(11), 15570–15592. https://doi.org/10.3390/su71115570.

FSI (Forest Survey of India). (2013). State of Forest Report. https://www.fsi.nic.in/forest-report-2013

FSI (Forest Survey of India). (2015). State of Forest Report. https://www.fsi.nic.in/forest-report-2015

FSI (Forest Survey of India). (2017). State of Forest Report. https://fsi.nic.in/forest-report-2017

FSI (Forest Survey of India). (2019). India State of Forest Report 2019. https://fsi.nic.in/isfr-volume-i?pgID=isfr-volume-i

Ganguly, T., Kurinji, L., & Guttikunda, S. (2020). How robust are urban India's clean air plans? An assessment of 102 cities. New Delhi: Council on Energy, Environment and Water. https://www.ceew.in/publications/how-robust-are-urban-india%E2%80%99s-clean-air-plans

GoI (Government of India). (2015). India's intended nationally determined contribution: working towards climate justice. https://www4.unfccc.int/sites/submissions/INDC/Published%20Documents/India/1/INDIA%20INDC%20TO%20UNFCCC.pdf

GoI (Government of India). (2019). XV Finance Commission: Report for the year 2020–21. Government of India. https://fincomindia.nic.in/ShowContent.aspx?uid1=3&uid2=0&uid3=0&uid4=0

GPCB (Gujarat Pollution Control Board). (2019). Circular: Pilot emissions trading scheme for selected industries in Surat, Gujarat. https://gpcb.gujarat.gov.in/uploads/GPCB_ETS_CIRCULAR_19112019.pdf

Grossman, G., & Krueger, A. (1994). Economic growth and the environment. *NBER Working Paper No. 4634*. https://www.nber.org/papers/w4634.pdf

Guan, D., Su, X., Zhang, Q., Peters, G., Liu, Z., & Lei, Y. (2014). The socioeconomic drivers of China's primary PM2:5 emissions. *Environmental Research Letters, 9*(2), 024010. https://doi.org/10.1088/1748-9326/9/2/024010.

Gupta, R., Somanathan, E., & Dey, S. (2017). Global warming and local air pollution have reduced wheat yields in India. *Climatic Change, 140,* 593–604. https://doi.org/10.1007/s10584-016-1878-8.

Guttikunda, S., Nishadh, K., & Jawahar, P. (2019). Air pollution knowledge assessments (APnA) for 20 Indian cities. *Urban Climate, 27,* 124–141. https://doi.org/10.1016/j.uclim.2018.11.005.

Han, L., Zhou, W., Pickett, S., Li, W., & Li, L. (2016). An optimum city size? The scaling relationship for urban population and fine particulate (PM2.5) concentration. *Environmental Pollution 208 (Part A)*, 96–101. https://doi.org/10.1016/j.envpol.2015.08.039

Hanna, R., & Oliva, P. (2015). Moving up the energy ladder: The effect of an increase in economic well-being on the fuel consumption choices of the poor in India. *American Economic Review, 105*(5), 242–246. https://doi.org/10.1257/aer.p20151097.

Holian, M. (2014). The effect of social and economic development on air pollution in Indian cities. *Environment and Urbanization Asia, 5*(1), 1–15. https://doi.org/10.1177/0975425314521536.

ICIMOD (International Centre for Integrated Mountain Development). (2020). COVID-19 impact and policy responses in the Hindu Kush Himalaya, International Centre for Integrated Mountain Development, Kathmandu, Nepal. Retrieved on July 2020, from https://www.preventionweb.net/publications/view/72631

Imam, A., & Banerjee, U. (2016). Urbanisation and greening of Indian cities: Problems, practices, and policies. *Ambio, 45,* 442–457. https://doi.org/10.1007/s13280-015-0763-4.

Johnson, T. M., Guttikunda, S., Wells, G. et al. (2011). Tools for improving air quality management: A review of top-down source apportionment techniques and their application in developing countries. Washington, USA: Energy Sector Management Assistance Program-The World Bank Group. https://openknowledge.worldbank.org/bitstream/handle/10986/17488/817400ESM0ESMA0Box0379844B00PUBLIC0.pdf

Jones, B. A. (2020). After the dust settles: The infant health impacts of dust storms. *Journal of the Association of Environmental and Resource Economists, 7*(6), 1005–1032. https://doi.org/10.1086/710242.

Kandlikar, M., & Ramachandran, G. (2000). The causes and consequences of particulate air pollution in urban India: A synthesis of the science. *Annual Review of Energy and the Environment, 25*(1), 629–684. https://doi.org/10.1146/annurev.energy.25.1.629.

Kountouris, Y. (2020). Ambient PM2.5 influences productive activities in public sector bureaucracies. *Environmental Research Communications, 2*(4), 041003. https://doi.org/10.1088/2515-7620/ab78cb

KSPCB (Karnataka State Pollution Control Board). (n.d.). *Ambient Air Quality*. https://kspcb.gov.in/ambient_air_quality.html

Landrigan, P. J., Fuller, R., Acosta, N. J. R., et al. (2017). The Lancet Commission on pollution and health. *The Lancet, 391*(10119), 462–512. https://doi.org/10.1016/S0140-6736(17)32345-0.

Lewis, J. J., & Pattanayak, S. K. (2012). Who adopts improved fuels and cookstoves? *A Systematic Review. Environmental Health Perspectives, 120*(5), 637–645. https://doi.org/10.1289/ehp.1104194.

Liu, Q., Wang, S., Zhang, W., Li, J., & Dong, G. (2019). The effect of natural and anthropogenic factors on PM2.5: Empirical evidence from Chinese cities with different income levels. *Science of the Total Environment, 653,* 157–167. https://doi.org/10.1016/j.scitotenv.2018.10.367.

Lu, X., Zhang, S., Xing, J., Wang, Y., Chen, W., Ding, D., et al. (2020). Progress of air pollution control in china and its challenges and opportunities in the ecological civilization era. *Engineering.* https://doi.org/10.1016/j.eng.2020.03.014.

Luo, K., Li, G., Fang, C., & Sun, S. (2018). PM2.5 mitigation in China: Socioeconomic determinants of concentrations and differential control policies. *Journal of Environmental Management, 213,* 47–55. https://doi.org/10.1016/j.jenvman.2018.02.044.

Ma, Y.-R., Ji, Q., & Fan, Y. (2016). Spatial linkage analysis of the impact of regional economic activities on PM2.5 pollution in China. *Journal of Cleaner Production, 139,* 1157–1167. https://doi.org/10.1016/j.jclepro.2016.08.152.

Managi, S., & Jena, P. R. (2008). Environmental productivity and Kuznets curve in India. *Ecological Economics, 65*(2), 432–440. https://doi.org/10.1016/j.ecolecon.2007.07.011.

MoEFCC (Ministry of Environment, Forest and Climate Change). (2019a). *National Clean Air Programme.* Government of India. https://moef.gov.in/wp-content/uploads/2019/05/NCAP_Report.pdf

MoEFCC (Ministry of Environment, Forest and Climate Change). (2019b). Lok Sabha Starred Question No. 262. Government of India. https://164.100.24.220/loksabhaquestions/annex/172/AS262.pdf

MoHFW (Ministry of Health and Family Welfare). (2019). Population Projections for India and states 2011–2036. Report of the technical group on population projections. Census of India 2011. https://nhm.gov.in/New_Updates_2018/Report_Population_Projection_2019.pdf

MoP (Ministry of Power). (2017). Rajya Sabha: Starred Question Number 164-Growth in electricity generation vis-a-vis demand. Government of India. https://powermin.nic.in/sites/default/files/uploads/RS31072017_Eng.pdf

MoRTH (Ministry of Road Transport and Highway). (2015). *Green highways: plantation, transplantation, beautification & maintenance policy 2015.* New Delhi: Government of India. https://morth.nic.in/sites/default/files/Green_Highways_Policy.pdf

MoSPI (Ministry of Statistics and Programme Implementation). (n.d.) Data. Retrieved on August 2020, from, https://www.mospi.gov.in/data

MPCB (Maharashtra Pollution Control Board). (n.d). https://mpcb.gov.in/envtdata/demoPage1.php#station1

NGT (National Green Tribunal). (2019a). Original Application No. 681/2018. Dated: 14.11.2019.

NGT (National Green Tribunal). (2019b). Significant interventions of the national green tribunal in March 2019. https://greentribunal.gov.in/sites/default/files/important_orders/SignificantinterventionsNationalGreenTribunalinMarch2019.pdf

NGT (National Green Tribunal). (2020a). Original Application No. 681/2018. Item No. 4. Date of hearing: 21.08.2020.

NGT (National Green Tribunal). (2020b). Original Application No. 681/2018. Dated: 06.03.2020.

Power, M. C., Weisskopf, M. G., Alexeeff, S. E., Coull, B. A., Spiro, A., III., & Schwartz, J. (2011). Traffic-related air pollution and cognitive function in a cohort of older men. *Environmental Health Perspectives, 119*(5), 682–687. https://doi.org/10.1289/ehp.1002767.

Rajya Sabha. (2020). *Demands for Grants (2020–21) of the Ministry of Environment, Forest and Climate Change (Demand No. 25).* New Delhi: Rajya Sabha Secretariat. https://rajyasabha.nic.in/rsnew/Committee_site/Committee_File/ReportFile/19/126/331_2020_3_15.pdf

RBI (Reserve Bank of India). (2019). *State finances: A study of budgets 2019–20.* Reserve Bank of India. Retrieved on August 2020, from, https://www.rbi.org.in/scripts/annualpublications.aspx?head=state%20finances%20:%20a%20study%20of%20budgets

Sharma, S., Zhang, M., Anshika, G. J., Zhang, H., & Kota, S. H. (2020). Effect of restricted emissions during COVID-19 on air quality in India. *Science of the Total Environment, 728,* 138878. https://doi.org/10.1016/j.scitotenv.2020.138878.

Sengupta, R. P. (2016). Challenges of transition from fossil fuels to green regimes. *Asian Institute of Transport Development: Economic Issues, 12.* https://www.aitd.net.in/pdf/monograph/1.%20Challenges%20of%20Transition%20from%20Fossils%20Fuel%20to%20Green%20Regimes.pdf

Sinha, A., & Bhatt, M. (2017). Environmental Kuznets Curve for CO_2 and NOx emissions: A case study of India. *European Journal of Sustainable Development, 6*(1), 267–276. https://doi.org/10.14207/ejsd.2017.v6n1p267

Sinha, A., & Bhattacharya, J. (2017). Estimation of environmental Kuznets curve for SO2 emission: A case of Indian cities. *Ecological Indicators, 72,* 881–894. https://doi.org/10.1016/j.ecolind.2016.09.018.

Spears, D., Dey, S., Chowdhury, S., Scovronick, N., Vyas, S., & Apte, J. (2019). The association of early-life exposure to ambient PM2.5 and later-childhood height-for-age in India: an observational study. *Environmental Health, 18*(62). https://doi.org/10.1186/s12940-019-0501-7

Suglia, S. F., Gryparis, A., Wright, R. O., Schwartz, J., & Wright, R. J. (2008). Association of black carbon with cognition among children in a prospective birth cohort study. *American Journal of Epidemiology, 167*(3), 280–286. https://doi.org/10.1093/aje/kwm308.

TNPCB (Tamil Nadu Pollution Control Board). (n.d). https://www.tnpcb.gov.in/

UN (United Nations). (2015). Sustainable development goals. https://sustainabledevelopment.un.org/?menu=1300

UPCB (Uttarakhand Pollution Control Board). (n.d). *Air quality data.* https://ueppcb.uk.gov.in/pages/display/95-air-quality-data

UPPCB (Uttar Pradesh Pollution Control Board) (n.d). *Air quality data.* https://www.uppcb.com/ambient_quality.htm

Wang, X., Tian, G., Yang, D., Zhang, W., & Lu, D. (2018). Responses of PM2.5 pollution to urbanization in China. *Energy Policy, 123,* 602–610. https://doi.org/10.1016/j.enpol.2018.09.001.

WHO (World Health Organization). (2018, April). *Ambient Air Quality Database.* World Health Organization. Retrieved on August 15, 2020, from https://www.who.int/airpollution/data/cities/en/

World Bank. (2019). *World Development Indicators*, World Bank. https://databank.worldbank.org/reports.aspx?source=2&series=EG.USE.ELEC.KH.PC&country

Xu, B., & Lin, B. (2018). What cause large regional differences in PM2.5 pollutions in China? Evidence from quantile regression model. *Journal of Cleaner Production, 174,* 447–461. https://doi.org/10.1016/j.jclepro.2017.11.008.

Xu, B., Luo, L., & Lin, B. (2016). A dynamic analysis of air pollution emissions in China: Evidence from nonparametric additive regression models. *Ecological Indicators, 63,* 346–358. https://doi.org/10.1016/j.ecolind.2015.11.012.

Zahnos, M., Michaelowa, K., Dasgupta, P., & Sachdeva, I. (2020). Health awareness and the transition towards clean cooking fuels: Evidence from Rajasthan. *PLoS ONE, 15*(4), e0231931. https://doi.org/10.1371/journal.pone.0231931.

Zivin, J. G., & Neidell, M. (2012). The impact of pollution on worker productivity. *The American Economic Review, 102*(7), 3652–3673. https://doi.org/10.1257/aer.102.7.3652.

Modelling Production of Bad Outputs: Theory and Empirics

Surender Kumar

1 Introduction

Sustainable production is at the core of sustainable development. During the production processes, it is not only the production of intended (desired) outputs is generated but also we end up producing unintended outputs such as environmental pollution, i.e. environmental externalities are generated in the presence of market failures. Increasing environmental problems call for an urgency of enacting appropriate regulations and policies for containing environmental pollution, and devising incentives for promotion of sustainable development is a centrepiece of environmental policy. The internalization of social costs arising from pollution externalities is at the centre stage of modelling bad outputs.[1]

The generation of by-products or unintended outputs is an inherent characteristic of almost all production processes. For example, a coal-fired thermal power plant inherently produces various air pollutants while generating electricity; the use of fertilizers and pesticides not only increases yields of agricultural crops but also generates leachings and run-offs. A failure to model the production of by-products not only precludes a policymaker or researcher to give credit for lesser generation and/or abatement of bad outputs but also makes the estimates of the desirable production process itself unreliable and susceptible (Kumbhakar & Malikov, 2018).

Modelling of production technologies has a long history. Conventional modelling of production activities considers only the production of marketed commodities and services and ignores the production of undesired outputs. This approach assumes free disposability of bad outputs similar to the free disposability of desired outputs and

[1]The words environmental pollution, unintended output, bad output and undesired output are used interchangeably throughout the chapter.

S. Kumar (✉)
Department of Economics, Delhi School of Economics, University of Delhi, Delhi, India
e-mail: skumar@econdse.org

P. Dasgupta et al. (eds.), *Sustainable Development Insights from India*,
India Studies in Business and Economics,
https://doi.org/10.1007/978-981-33-4830-1_22

inputs. This assumption is not reasonable in the presence of increasing environmental problems as it does not credit for environmental pollution abatement. The abatement involves the use of production inputs, i.e. inputs are diverted from the production of desirable outputs to abatement of undesirable outputs. Appropriate modelling of undesirable outputs will be advantageous in designing economic incentives that support in internalizing the production externalities.

This chapter provides an overview of the modelling of environmental pollution-generating production technologies in economics.[2] The rest of the chapter is divided into three sections. Section 2 provides a conceptual or theoretical description of various modelling approaches. We first define bad outputs (Sect. 2.1). Bad outputs are those outputs that are preferred less to more by a representative consumer. Since less of these outputs make the consumer better off. In the case of good outputs, more outputs are preferred by a consumer to be better off. In Sect. 2.2, an overview of the general production axioms is provided. Section 2.3 includes a description on modelling of bad outputs as inputs and joint outputs but weakly disposable which is detailed in Sect. 2.4. Section 2.5 provides an overview of production technologies in a network framework rather than considering them as black-box production technologies. Section 2.6 briefly introduces the by-production approach of modelling emission-generating production technologies. The by-production approach is of the view that emission-generating production technologies cannot be appropriately modelled in a reduced-form single-equation framework, but requires a multi-equation approach.

Followed by the conceptual discussion, in Sect. 3, we present a discussion on various empirical approaches. This section describes a way of representing production technologies using directional output distance function (DODF) (Sect. 3.1). The emission-generating production technologies can be estimated parametrically or non-parametrically. Parametric approaches involve both deterministic and stochastic techniques. Section 3.2 discusses parametric estimation approaches and discussion on non-parametric approaches as given in Sect. 3.3. An overview of some select empirical applications of production technologies involving both stochastic and non-stochastic is provided in Sect. 4. We discuss empirical applications that use Indian data from various production sectors. Note that the objective of this section is to illustrate the usefulness of modelling approach for environmental policy. The chapter closes with some concluding remarks (Sect. 5).

[2]For recent review of the literature on environmental pollution-generating production technologies, please refer to Dakpo et al. (2017) and Depko and Ang (2019). Murty and Russell (2017) provide an excellent detailed overview of these technologies.

2 Conceptual Framework

2.1 Good Versus Bad Output

During the production process, a firm producing marketed outputs also produces unintended outputs as by-products. These by-products may be desirable or undesirable. For example, a thermal power plant producing electricity by burning fossil fuels also produces air pollutants such as SO_2 and NO_X as by-products, which adversely affect human health. Similarly, a beekeeper producing honey also provides pollination services to apple growers as a by-product. In the first example, the by-product is an undesirable output, whereas, in the second example, it is a desirable unintended output.

To identify good and bad outputs systematically, we begin with the preferences of a representative consumer. Let the representative consumer have well-defined preferences $\succcurlyeq$ over two vector of outputs, $y \in \Re_{+}^{M}$ and $b \in \Re_{+}^{J}$. Let y be a vector of good or desirable outputs if the consumer prefers more of y to less of y, as long as there is no change in the level of b, i.e.

$$y' \geq y \rightarrow \left(y', b\right) \succcurlyeq (y, b) \tag{1}$$

Similarly, we can say b is a vector of bad or undesirable output if

$$b' \leq b \rightarrow \left(y, b'\right) \succcurlyeq (y, b) \tag{2}$$

i.e. if the consumer prefers less of b to more of it given the level of y. We can say more of undesirable output or less of desirable output which reduces the utility of the consumer. The case of a single good and a single bad output is illustrated in Fig. 1.

In Fig. 1, the indifference curve is upward sloping and increasing to the northwest representing a case of a single good and a single bad output. Bundle (y, b) is on the indifference curve I-I; bundle (y', b) is preferred over the bundle (y, b) since it is on a higher indifference curve II-II, which is in the north of bundle (y, b). Similarly, bundle (y, b') is also preferred over the bundle (y, b) as it is also on the indifference curve II-II, and it is in the west of bundle (y, b). This can be illustrated with the example of electricity (good output) and emissions (bad output) generation. For a given level of emission, more electricity is preferred over less. Similarly, for a given level of electricity, less emissions over more are preferred by the representative consumer. It is worth noting that if the unintended output is desirable, then the shape of the indifference curves is the standard textbook shape.

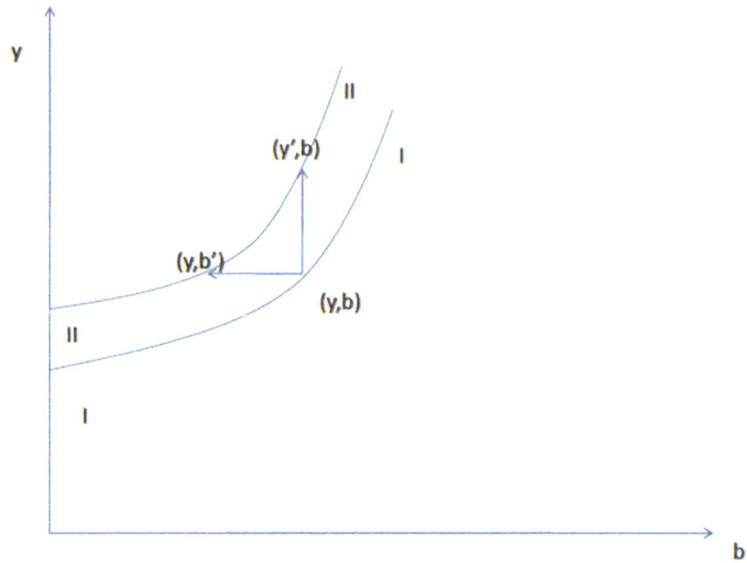

Fig. 1 Good and bad output preferences. *Source* Färe and Grosskopf (2013)

2.2 Production Technology

Consider a firm producing marketed outputs, $y = (y_1, \ldots, y_m) \in \Re_+^m$ using inputs, $x = (x_1, \ldots, x_n) \in \Re_+^n$ (e.g. labour, capital, renewable energy). The technology set, T, for a given production process is defined as:

$$T = \{(x, y) \in \Re_+^{m+n} : x \text{ can produce } y\} \tag{3}$$

Alternatively, technology T can be represented in terms of an output set,

$$P(x) = \{y : x \text{ can produce } y\}, x \in \Re_+^n \tag{4}$$

or an input requirement set,

$$L(y) = \{x : x \text{ can produce } y\}, y \in \Re_+^m \tag{5}$$

The production technology is supposed to satisfy the following axioms:

(i) $(x^j, y^j) \in T(j = 1, 2, \ldots, N)$
(ii) $(x, y) \in T \wedge \overline{x} > x \Rightarrow (\bar{x}, y) \in T$
(iii) $(x, y) \in T \wedge \overline{y} < y \Rightarrow (x, \bar{y}) \in T$
(iv) $(x^1, y^1) \in T \wedge (x^2, y^2) \in T \wedge 0 \leq \lambda \leq 1\{\lambda(x^1, y^1) + (1 - \lambda)(x^2, y^2)\} \in T$

The axiom (i) implies that every observed input–output bundle is feasible by default. Axioms (ii) and (iii) assume that technology satisfies the free disposability of outputs and inputs. Axiom (ii) states that the use of additional quantities of inputs is costless, i.e. additional use of inputs does not reduce the production of outputs. Similarly, axiom (iii) implies that for a given level of inputs, the output can be reduced arbitrarily. The last axiom, axiom (iv), shows that the production possibility set is convex. Moreover, the traditional production models satisfy the axioms of completeness, compact and inactivity.

These axioms are consistent with and useful for modelling the traditional neoclassical model. The laws of thermodynamics state that when we produce some good output using inputs, there is inevitably some production of intended bad output. Baumgartner et al. (2001, p. 365) state '*…the production of wanted goods gives rise to additional unwanted outputs…*'. To account for the production of bad outputs, these traditional models are required to be modified and some additional assumptions specific to the case to be added.

2.3 Bad Outputs as Inputs

In the early modellings of bad outputs, the treatment of these outputs in the production framework was very simple. Earlier authors such as Baumol and Oates (1975, 1988) and Cropper and Oates (1992) included bad outputs in the production modelling by treating them as conventional inputs. Similar to conventional inputs, the free disposability of bad outputs were considered. The logic behind treating bad outputs as inputs is the empirically observed positive association between the production of good and bad outputs: as a producer increases the production of good output, the production of bad output increases. For example, in a fossil fuel plant, as we produce more electricity, more pollutants are produced. This literature relates bad outputs to the waste disposal capacity of the environment. It considers waste disposal capacity as an economic input into the production process. In this framework, bad outputs are considered standard economic inputs with free disposability conditions; there is a non-negative trade-off between good and bad outputs (Murty & Russell, 2017).

To justify the treatment of bad outputs as conventional inputs, the proponents have invoked abatement activities. They argued that abatement activities involve the use of economic resources, and a firm producing bad output has to divert economic resources from the production of desired output to abatement activities, and as a result, less of both good and bad outputs is produced. Førsund (1998, 2009) shows that considering bad outputs as inputs is unreasonable as it is not revealing the underlying abatement activities. Abatement activities are implicitly assumed, and this approach fails to show the process of abatement explicitly.

Moreover, Murty and Russell (2002) and Murty et al. (2012) show that the treatment of bad outputs as inputs produces unacceptable implications for production trade-offs. These studies reveal that treating bad outputs as inputs results in a non-positive trade-off between emissions and emission causing inputs. It is counter-intuitive as it implies a non-positive relationship between the increasing use of coal and CO_2 emissions, for example. These studies also reveal that the positive association between emissions and emission causing inputs is in contradiction to the free disposability assumption of the emission causing inputs.

2.4 Bad Outputs as Weakly Disposable Joint Outputs

The assumption of free disposability of bad outputs conflicts with the notion of rationality. For the given quantities of inputs and marketed outputs, if it is possible to produce a lower quantity of bad outputs, it is irrational to produce any positive quantity of these bad outputs. As pointed out by Førsund (2009), the assumption of free disposability with respect to bad outputs gives '*...nonsensical result that zero bads can be achieved at no costs...*'.

In the literature, free disposability assumption in the context of bad outputs is modified in two alternative ways: weak disposability and costly disposability. Färe et al. (1986) modify the production technology for the bad outputs. They assume that bad outputs produced as joint products of good outputs producing technology should satisfy the following two axioms: the axioms of *null-jointness* between marketed and bad outputs, and good and bad outputs are jointly weakly disposable. The by-production approach considers the costly disposability of the bad outputs.

The axiom of *null-jointness* implies that the generation of good outputs necessarily produces bad outputs. For example, a coal-fired thermal power plant inevitably generates CO_2 emissions, when it generates electricity, i.e. this plant cannot generate electricity without generating CO_2 emissions:

$$if (y, b) \in P(x) \text{ and } b = 0, \quad \text{then } y = 0 \tag{6}$$

Similarly, the axiom of weak disposability of bad outputs implies that if a firm wants to reduce bad outputs, it can do so only by incurring costs either in terms of reducing the production of good output or using more inputs to produce the same level of good output. A reduction in bad output by reducing good output implies that the firm is diverting resources from production of desired output to abatement of bad outputs, i.e. reduction in bad outputs requires a simultaneous proportional reduction in the marketed or good output:

$$if (y, b) \in P(x) \text{ and } 0 \leq \alpha \leq 1, \quad \text{then } (\alpha y, \alpha b) \in P(x) \tag{7}$$

However, a reduction in good output without reducing bad outputs is possible:

$$if (y, b) \in P(x), \text{ then for } y_0 \leq y, (y_0, b) \in P(x) \tag{8}$$

A production technology producing both good and bad outputs can be represented using a conventional production function also. Again, consider a case of a firm producing a single good and a single bad output. Believing $y \in \Re_+^M$, an environmental production function is defined as:

$$F(x; b) = \max\{y : (y, b) \in P(x)\} \tag{9}$$

The production function $F(x; b)$ exists since $P(x)$ is non-empty and compact. Moreover, $F(x; b)$ is non-decreasing in inputs since inputs are freely disposable. The axioms of weak disposability of emissions and *null-jointness* imply that an environmental production function should satisfy the following conditions:

$$ify \leq F(x; b) \text{ and } 0 \leq \alpha \leq 1, \text{ then } \alpha y \leq F(x; \alpha b) \tag{10}$$

and

$$F(x; 0) = 0 \tag{11}$$

Equation (10) implies a proportional reduction in good and bad outputs. Equation (11) shows the essentiality of bad outputs in the production of good output, i.e. good and bad outputs are *null-jointness*, $ify = F(x; b)$ and $b = 0$, then$y = 0$.

Good output, y, is feasible since it is freely disposable, $y \leq F(x; b)$. Under this condition, the output set is reclaimed as:

$$P(x) = \{(y, b) : y \leq F(x; b)\} \tag{12}$$

An environmental production function is a complete characterization of a single good output environmental production technology (Färe et al., 2007). It seeks to maximize the production of good output for an observed level of inputs and bad outputs.[3] However, contrary to the environmental directional distance function, the environmental production function does not directly credit a producer for a reduction in emissions.

2.5 Network Production Technology

A reduced-form neoclassical production function approach presents a black-box framework of production structure. In the black-box framework, a producer uses inputs and produces outputs including bad outputs without knowing the underlying mechanism of inputs conversion into outputs. The assumption of weak disposability states that for a given level of inputs, reduction in a bad output involves a reduction

[3]Directional output distance is defined and discussed in the Sect. 3.

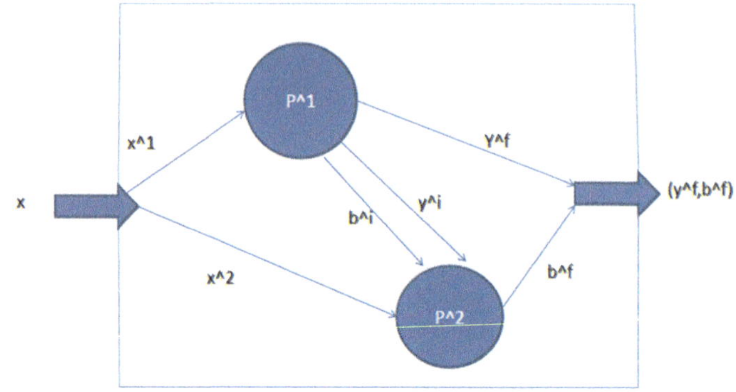

Fig. 2 Network joint production technology with abatement activities. *Source* Färe and Grosskopf (2013)

in good output. Reduction in a good output might be happening due to the diversion of resources from the production of good output to abatement activities.

Färe et al. (2013) discuss the network framework within the weak disposability postulate of production structure. The network framework looks inside the box. It explicitly introduces an abatement activity into the production process. Inside the box, subtechnologies are specified which are linked into a network. For example, in a coal-fired electricity generation plant, there are two technologies: one producing electricity and particulate matters, and abatement subtechnology for reducing particulate matters. A set-up of the network framework is illustrated in Fig. 2.

The network technology, P, involves two subtechnologies: P^1 and P^2. Subtechnology P^1 consists of the use of inputs such as labour, capital and raw materials for producing good and bad outputs. Subtechnology P^2 uses inputs such as labour and capital and outputs of subtechnology P^1 as inputs. This subtechnology abates emissions and releases final bad outputs into the ambient environment. Färe et al. (2013) referred to it as a source entering the black box and a sink with final products exiting the black box.

In the network framework, the exogenous inputs $\{x = (x^1 + x^2)\}$ are allocated into two subtechnologies, and the sink sums up final good and bad outputs (y^f, b^f). The good output y can either be a final output y^f or an intermediate input y^i in subtechnology P^2, $y = (y^f + y^i)$, within the black box. The subtechnology P^2, abatement process, has (y^i, b^i) as intermediate inputs and x^2 as exogenous input, and its output is the final bad output b^f. Therefore, in a network framework, the final outputs are (y^f, b^f). The network technology can be written as follows:

$$P(x) = \{(y^f, b^f) : (y, b^i) \in P^1(x^1), \\ y = y^f + y^i, b^f \in P^2(x^2, y^i, b^i), x \geq (x^1 + x^2)\} \quad (13)$$

Optimization over technology $P(x)$ yields optimal allocation of x into (x^1, x^2) and optimal allocation of y into (y^i, y^f).

2.6 By-Production Technology

The material balance conditions reveal that generation of emissions is related to the use of emission causing inputs, i.e. the production process of marketed output requires the use of emission causing inputs such as fossil fuels. These emission-causing inputs are not completely converted to desired outputs, and some amount of these inputs is transmitted into bad outputs (e.g. emissions). The quantity of emissions might not remain unchanged if the use of emission-causing inputs is increased. However, it is possible to produce the same amount of bad outputs with a lesser quantity of these inputs. This restriction is opposite to the standard axiom of free disposability of inputs. It implies costly disposability of bad outputs or joint disposability of bad outputs and emission causing inputs (Ray et al., 2018). It is essential to reduce the use of emissions-causing inputs to reduce emissions, which, in turn, also reduces marketed outputs.[4] Murty et al. (2012) termed it as costly disposability of bad outputs, rather than weak disposability of bad outputs. According to them, bad outputs are an unavoidable by-product of the production process of marketed output rather than joint products, and they call it a "by-production approach of modelling production of bad outputs. Moreover, Førsund (2009) and Murty et al. (2012) depict that joint production modelling of good and bad outputs with null jointness and weak disposability assumption fails to account for material balance conditions.

Consider a production plant producing marketed outputs, $y = \left(y_1, \ldots, y_M\right) \in \Re_+^M$ and bad outputs (e.g. CO_2 emissions), $b = (b_1, \ldots, b_J) \in \Re_+^J$, employing emission causing inputs (e.g. fossil fuels), $c = (c_1, \ldots, c_L) \in \Re_+^L$ and non-emission causing inputs, $x = (x_1, \ldots, x_N) \in \Re_+^N$ (e.g. labour, capital, renewable energy).

The production technology is divided into two parts: a production technology generating marketed output (T_1) and a production technology leading to the generation of emissions (T_2). By-production technology (T_{BP}) can be represented as an intersection of two technologies, i.e. $T_{BP} = T_1 \cap T_2$;

Technology T_1 used for good output production assumes that:

$$
\begin{aligned}
&(i) \quad (c, x; y, b) \in T_2 \wedge \overline{c} \leq c \Rightarrow (\overline{c}, x; y, b) \in T_2 \\
&(ii) \quad (c, x; y, b) \in T_2 \wedge \overline{b} \geq b \Rightarrow \left(c, x; y, \overline{b}\right) \in T_2 \\
&(iii) \quad (c, x; y, b) \in T_2 \wedge \overline{y} \neq y \wedge \overline{x} \neq x \Rightarrow (c, \overline{x}; \overline{y}, b) \in T_2
\end{aligned} \tag{14}
$$

Equation (14) states that in the production of good output, all inputs including emission generating inputs and good outputs are assumed to be freely disposable.

Production technology producing bad outputs T_2 assumes that:

$$
\text{(i)} \quad (c, x; y, b) \Rightarrow (\overline{c}, x; y, b) \in T_1
$$

[4] Another option for reducing bad outputs without reducing polluting inputs is abatement activities conducted as end-of-pipe treatment. In the end-of-pipe treatment, non-polluting inputs are diverted from main production process to abatement activities to reduce bad outputs that lead to a reduction in marketed output.

$$\text{(ii)}\quad (c, x; y, b) \in T_1 \wedge \overline{x} > x \Rightarrow (c, \overline{x}; y, b) \in T_1$$
$$\text{(iii)}\quad (c, x; y, b) \in T_1 \wedge \overline{y} < y \Rightarrow (c, x; \overline{y}, b) \in T_1 \tag{15}$$

Equation (15) implies that arbitrary changes in the production of marketed outputs and the use of non-emission causing inputs do not affect bad outputs generation, and the quantity of bad outputs is restricted by the use of emission causing inputs.

3 Empirical Framework

3.1 Directional Output Distance Function

In the preceding section, we described the axioms of production technology that suitably model generation of unindented by-products or emissions. The axioms are useful from a conceptual point of view, but they are not of much help from an empirical computational point of view. To bring these axioms into empirical applications, we need technology functions that can suitably represent a production technology of a multi-output framework satisfying these axioms. Directional output distance function (DODF) could be one suitable representation that accommodates bad output production and is consistent with the axioms described in Sect. 2.

DODF is defined as the maximal distance between the actual input–output vector and the frontier of the output set in a given directional vector $g \equiv \left(g_y, -g_b\right)$ (Färe et al., 2005), i.e.

$$\vec{D}_O\left(x, y, b; g_y, -g_b\right) = \sup\{\beta : \left(y + \beta g_y, b - \beta g_b\right)\} \in P(x) \tag{16}$$

where β is non-negative, scaled to reach the boundary of the output set $P(x)$. DODF seeks to simultaneously maximal expansion of good outputs and maximal contraction in bad outputs. This function gets its properties from the output set P(x) (Fare et al., 2005). These properties are:

i. $\vec{D}_O\left(x, y, b; g_y, -g_b\right) \geq 0$, if and only if $(y, b) \in P(x)$
ii. $\vec{D}_O\left(x, y', b; g_y, -g_b\right) \geq \vec{D}_O\left(x, y, b; g_y, -g_b\right)$, for $(y', b) \leq (y, b) \in P(x)$
iii. $\vec{D}_O\left(x, y, b'; g_y, -g_b\right) \geq \vec{D}_O\left(x, y, b; g_y, -g_b\right)$, for $(y, b') \geq (y, b) \in P(x)$
iv. $\vec{D}_O\left(x, \theta y, \theta b; g_y, -g_b\right) \geq 0$, for $(y, b) \in P(x)$ and $0 \leq \theta \leq 1$.
v. $\vec{D}_O\left(x, y, b; g_y, -g_b\right)$, is concave in $(y, b) \in P(x)$

The first property states that it is an additive measure of inefficiency in a given direction g. A zero value of DODF implies full efficiency, and a positive value of β implies inefficiency. Its value lies between 0 and 1. It could be considered as a measure of technical and environmental inefficiency since a producer simultaneously increasing good outputs and decreasing bad outputs is considered more technically efficient. Property (ii) is related to free (strong) disposability of good outputs. It states that if a firm using the same amount of inputs, but producing more good outputs and the same amount of undesirable output, inefficiency will not increase. Similarly, property (iii) shows that an increase in bad outputs, holding inputs and desirable outputs constant, does not decrease inefficiency. Joint weak disposability of good and bad outputs is reflected from the property (iv). The last property implies that this function is jointly concave in good and bad outputs and non-negative and non-increasing in good outputs and non-decreasing in bad outputs and inputs. It also satisfies translation property.

$$\vec{D}_O\left(y + \omega g_y, b - \omega g_b, x; g_y, -g_b\right) = \vec{D}_O\left(y, b, x; g_y, -g_b\right) - \omega \tag{17}$$

where ω is an arbitrary scaling factor. This property implies that if good outputs are expanded by ωg_y and bad outputs are reduced by ωg_b then, the resulting value of DODF gets reduced by ω.

The function, DODF, can be estimated either parametrically or non-parametrically. The parametric estimation can be again either deterministic or stochastic. Each of the estimation approaches has its pros and cons.

3.2 *Parametric Estimation*

3.2.1 Determinstric Parametric Estimation

The advantage of estimating the DODF parametric yields differentials of it with respect to input and output factors. A DODF can be estimated either using linear programming (LP) approach or stochastic frontier analysis (SFA) to recover its parameters. The LP approach, of being a deterministic approach, is free from the problems of the uncertainty of the distributional assumptions and facilitates modelling of DODF properties. Monotonicity properties of DODF with respect to good and bad outputs can be imposed through inequality constraints in the deterministic approach.

Deterministic DODF using the LP algorithm was introduced by Aigner and Chu (1968) in the production function context and extended by Färe et al. (2005) in the context of DODF.[5] Moreover, the quadratic form of DODF is more generalized and outperforms relative to translog or linear forms (Färe et al., 2010). It accommodates translation property (Färe et al., 2005).[6] The quadratic form of DODF is expressed as:

[5]For details on deterministic parametric estimation of distance functions, please refer to Murty and Kumar (2002), Kumar and Rao (2003), Murty et al. (2006) and Jain and Kumar (2018). Murty and Kumar (2002) and Kumar and Rao (2003) estimate output distance function, Murty (2006) estimates input distance function, and Jain and Kumar (2018) estimate DODF.

[6]Translation property is used while estimating DODF using stochastic frontier analysis (SFA) (Kumar et al., 2015).

$$\vec{D}_o^{kt}(y_{kt}, b_{kt}, x_{kt}; 1, -1) = \alpha_0 + \sum_{n=1}^{N} \alpha_n x_n^{kt} + \beta_1 y_1^{kt} + \gamma_1 b_1^{kt} + \frac{1}{2}\sum_{n=1}^{N} \alpha_{nn'} x_n^{kt} x_{n'}^{kt}$$
$$+ \sum_{n=1}^{N} \delta_{n1} x_n^{kt} y_1^{kt} + \sum_{n=1}^{N} \eta_{n1} x_n^{kt} b_1^{kt} + \frac{1}{2}\beta_{11} y_1^{kt} y_1^{kt}$$
$$+ \mu_{11} y_1^{kt} b_1^{kt} + \frac{1}{2}\gamma_{11} b_1^{kt} b_1^{kt} + \sum_{t=1}^{T-1} d_t year^t \tag{18}$$

where $\vec{D}_O(.)$ is the DODF for firm k in year t; y_1^{kt} is good output at firm k in year t; b_1^{kt} is the bad output at firm k in year t; and x_n^{kt} is the nth input use at firm k in year t. Year dummies capture the effect of external common changes that are happening over the period of time. The parameters of quadratic DODF can be retrieved solving the following linear programme:

$$\min \sum_{kt=1}^{KT} [\vec{D}_o^{kt}(y_{kt}, b_{kt}, x_{kt}; 1, -1) - 0]$$

Subject to

(i) $\vec{D}_o^{kt}\left(y_{kt}, b_{kt}, x_{kt}; g_y, -g_b\right) \geq 0, kt = 1, 2, \ldots, KT;$

(ii) $\partial \vec{D}_o^{kt}\left(y_{kt}, b_{kt}, x_{kt}; g_y, -g_b\right)/\partial x_n \geq 0; kt = 1, 2, \ldots, KT; n = 1, 2, 3;$

(iii) $\partial \vec{D}_o^{kt}\left(y_{kt}, b_{kt}, x_{kt}; g_y, -g_b\right)/\partial y_1 \leq 0; kt = 1, 2, \ldots, KT;$

(iv) $\partial \vec{D}_o^{kt}\left(y_{kt}, b_{kt}, x_{kt}; g_y, -g_b\right)/\partial b_1 \geq 0; kt = 1, 2, \ldots, KT;$

(v) $\beta_1 - \gamma_1 = -1; \beta_{11} - \mu_{11} = 0; \mu_{11} - \gamma_{11} = 0; \sum_{n=1}^{N} \delta_{n1} - \sum_{n=1}^{N} \eta_{n1} = 0; n = 1, 2, 3$

(vi) $\alpha_{nn'} = \alpha_{n'n}; n = 1, 2, 3$

Condition (i) ensures that none of the firms produces good and bad outputs that are not included in the output set $P(x)$. Conditions (ii) to (iv) impose monotonicity conditions for all inputs, good output and bad output, respectively. Conditions (v) and (vi) are related to translation property and symmetry conditions of the parameters. Condition (v) ensures the expansion of good output and contraction of bad output.

3.2.2 Stochastic Parametric Estimation

Though the LP approach is free from the distributional assumptions with respect to inefficiency and error terms and facilitates modelling of DODF properties, it confounds inefficiency term with the error term. However, an econometric or stochastic approach allows for appropriate treatment of measurement errors and random shocks, and tests for several statistical hypotheses, such as the significance of parameters, separability between outputs and inputs and between good and bad outputs, and monotonicity properties of distance functions.[7] To estimate parameters of DODF stochastically, we again use its quadratic form satisfying symmetric conditions and translation property.[8] The stochastic specification of DODF takes the form:

$$\vec{D}_o^{kt} = f(y_{kt}, b_{kt}, x_{kt}; 1, -1, t) + v \tag{19}$$

where v is an error term, $v \sim N(0, \sigma_v^2)$.

To estimate Eq. (19), we utilize the translation property of the DODF expressed in Eq. (17) since $\vec{D}_o^{kt}$ is unobservable. By substituting $f(y + \omega g_y, b - \omega g_b, x; g_y, -g_b, t) + \omega$ for $\vec{D}_o^{kt}(y_{kt}, b_{kt}, x_{kt}; 1, -1, t)$ in Eq. (19) and taking ω to the left-hand side, one can obtain:

$$-\omega = f(y + \omega g_y, b - \omega g_b, x; g_y, -g_b, t) + v - u \tag{20}$$

where $f(y + \omega g_y, b - \omega g_b, x; g_y, -g_b, t)$ is the quadratic form given by (16) with ω added to y and subtracted from b; and $u = \vec{D}_o^{kt}$ is a one-sided error term, $u \sim N^+(0, \sigma_u^2)$. Therefore, there is a variation in the left-hand side variable that we get by choosing ω that is specific to each observation. One of the outputs can be chosen as ω and estimate Eq. (20) using the stochastic frontier framework.

3.3 Non-parametric Estimation

The advantage of using non-parametric approaches is that we need not impose a functional form a-priori on the function to be estimated. For the non-parametric estimation of a multi-output framework in the presence of bad outputs that are weakly disposable, here we use the case of an environmental production function, rather than a directional distance function. We are illustrating the case for environmental production function to have a variety. The DODF can also be similarly estimated using the non-parametric framework with some modifications in the objective function.[9]

[7]However, the stochastic methods have their own disadvantages such as distributional assumptions for the inefficiency and error terms, and the problem of imposing nonlinear monotonicity constraints in the estimation process.

[8]For detailed application using the stochastic estimation of output distance function, please refer to Murty and Kumar (2003) and Kumar and Kumar (2015), and stochastic estimation of directional output distance function, please read Murty et al. (2007), Kumar and Managi (2011), Kumar et al. (2015) and Kumar and Jain (2019).

[9]Details on the non-parametric estimation of environmental production function using DEA can be obtained in Kumar et al. (2020) and Kumar and Jain (2020). Kumar (2006), Kumar and Managi

The environmental production function can be estimated parametrically or non-parametrically. Here, we illustrate data envelopment analysis (DEA), a non-parametric approach, for the estimation of the production function. Suppose there are $k = 1, 2, \ldots, K$ observations of inputs, good output and bad outputs, i.e. $\left(y^k, b^k, x^k\right)k = 1, 2, \ldots, K$. We consider a regulated production function for observation $k^{'}$ as assuming weak disposability of bad outputs:

$$
\begin{aligned}
& F\left(x^{k'}; b^{k'}\right) = \max \sum_{k=1}^{K} z_k y_k \\
& \text{Subject to} \quad \sum_{k=1}^{K} z_k b_{kj} = b_{k'j}, j = 1, 2, \ldots, J \\
& \sum_{k=1}^{K} z_k x_{kn} \leq x_{k'n}, n = 1, 2, \ldots, N \\
& \sum_{k=1}^{K} z_k \geq 0, k = 1, 2, \ldots, K
\end{aligned}
\tag{21}
$$

where $z_k(k = 1, 2, \ldots, K)$ are the weights assigned to each observation in the construction of production possibility frontier. We assume constant returns to scale for the sake of simplicity in the illustration.

The objective function shows the maximum quantity of the good output constructed from the observations taken. The first constraint of equality imposes the weak disposability of bad outputs. The second constraint in the linear programme is with respect to the inputs. There is a separate constraint for each of the N inputs used by a producer. The right-hand side of the constraint represents the observed amount of inputs used by a producer, and the left-hand side of the constraint represents the theoretical amount of inputs used by an efficient producer. The inequality sign shows that the inputs used by a theoretical producer must be less than or equal to the inputs employed by an observed producer, i.e. the inputs are freely disposable. Moreover, to ensure *null-jointness* in good and bad outputs, the following conditions are imposed:

$$
\sum_{j=1}^{J} b_{kj} > 0, k = 1, 2, \ldots, K
$$

$$
\sum_{k=1}^{K} b_{kj} > 0, j = 1, 2, \ldots, J
$$

(2009), Khanna and Kumar (2011), Kumar and Managi (2012), Kumar and Managi (2016) and Shetty and Kumar (2017) applied DEA technique for estimation of DODF.

That is, each row and column has at least one positive element of bad output in firm-level bad outputs (i.e. each producer produces at least one bad output and each bad output is produced by at least one firm). The *null-jointness* can be reflected by the selection $b_{k'j} = 0$ in Eq. (21). In this case, all the weights assigned are equal to zero, implying that in the absence of bad outputs, there is no good output, i.e. *there is no fire without smoke.*

4 Empirical Applications

A cost-effective environmental policy requires estimates of environmental costs and benefits. Note that these by-products are generally non-marketed outputs. Internalization of production of bad outputs asks for taxing polluters for the environmental damages incurred by them. Environmental benefits are measured in terms of the economic value of foregone damages accruing to society when the production of bad outputs is reduced. Environmental costs are measured by measuring costs borne by the producers for abating or preventing emissions by improving their production practices.

In the last three decades, many studies across countries, at different levels of aggregation, have attempted to estimate the efficiency and productivity of production units using the modelling approaches described in the above sections. These studies credit producers in measuring productivity and efficiency not only for the production of desirable output but also for the abatement/reduction of bad outputs. The abatement of bad outputs involves the use of production inputs and is a costly process. Since the production of good and bad outputs and abatement of bad outputs takes place simultaneously, these models are also used for estimating the shadow prices of the pollutants.

In this section, we provide a discussion on the estimates of some recent studies that have estimated the shadow prices of bad outputs and provide estimates of productivity and efficiency using data of the thermal power sector. Moreover, note that these applications are using either parametric or non-parametric approaches and either deterministic or stochastic specifications. Here, we discuss four studies.[10] The first two studies use a parametric estimation approach, and the later two studies involve non-parametric estimation of the objective function. In the studies using the parametric estimation approach, one study follows a deterministic approach, while the other is based on a stochastic estimation of directional output distance function.

Studies estimating the shadow price of carbon emissions in India are limited. To our knowledge, only two studies have estimated the shadow prices of CO_2 emissions (Gupta, 2006; Jain & Kumar, 2018). Gupta (2006) estimates the shadow price of

---

[10]The four studies are: Jain and Kumar (2018), Kumar and Jain (2019), Kumar and Jain (2020) and Kumar et al. (2020). Jain and Kumar (2018) apply deterministic parametric approach for estimating DODF, whereas Kumar and Jain (2019) use SFA for recovering parameters of a quadratic DODF. Kumar and Jain (2020) and Kumar et al. (2020) estimate environmental production functions using non-parametric DEA approach.

CO_2 emissions using output distance function, a radial measure of efficiency. Jain and Kumar (2018) estimate the shadow prices for the period of 2000–2013 using DODF. Both the studies use a parametric linear programming approach for estimating output distance function and DODF, respectively. DODF models non-proportional changes in outputs and allows good outputs to be expanded while bad outputs to be contracted in any chosen direction (Chambers et al., 1998; Färe et al., 2005). This function provides unambiguous welfare results contrary to output and input distance functions (Murty et al., 2007).

Moreover, from the related literature, it can be inferred that the shadow price of a pollutant is sensitive to the chosen direction of the directional vector in the estimation of distance functions (Vardanyan & Noh, 2006; Lee et al., 2002). Jain and Kumar (2018), rather than arbitrarily choosing any particular directional vector, choose three different directional vectors in the estimation of environmental efficiency and shadow prices of CO_2 emissions. These directional vectors are: positive for both good and bad outputs, positive only for the good output and positive for good output and negative for bad output.

Jain and Kumar (2018) find that CO_2 emissions could be reduced and electricity production could be enhanced if the thermal power plants improve their technical and environmental efficiency. The sample plants have the potential to reduce carbon emission and increase electricity production by about 18%, 19% and 13%, respectively, for the chosen three different directional vectors. The average shadow price of a tonne of CO_2 emissions is US$ 2.61, 14.54 and 18.68, respectively, for the selected three mitigation strategies with high standard deviations. Heterogeneity in the estimates of shadow price calls for an incentive-based environmental policy that could be cost-effective relative to the existing command and control (CAC) system.

Kumar and Jain (2019) use the multi-output framework described above for measuring carbon-sensitive meta-efficiency and productivity. They exploit a unique data set for 56 thermal power plants over the period of 2000–2013. They stochastically estimate meta-DODF. The meta-distance function is estimated in two steps, and they apply the SFA approach in both the steps. Meta-frontier analysis recognizes technological or other heterogeneity across groups.

In Kumar and Jain (2019), thermal power plants are grouped into two categories based on ownership: state sector and central sector plants. They find that the state sector plants have a higher potential to increase electricity generation and reduce carbon emission in comparison with the central sector plants relative to the meta-frontier. The potential in the state sector plants is the combination of both within-group inefficiency and technology gap. However, in the central sector, though there is no heterogeneity in inefficiency within the group, there exists a technology gap. All the plants under consideration could have reduced the CO_2 emissions of about 98 million tons during 2000–2013. Productivity growth in the sector is governed by the green innovation effect, though the green productivity growth in the central sector is higher than the state sector. We should recognize the fact that state sector plants are older than central sector plants. However, it should be noted that the productivity growth curve is of concave shape. This implies that further growth in green productivity is relatively difficult or more costly.

Kumar and Jain (2020) estimate carbon mitigation cost (CMC) and decompose it into the factors determining the change in the CMC. They use data of 45 coal-fired thermal power stations over the period of 2008–2012. They estimate an environmental production function. They use DEA under weak and strong disposability conditions. They apply the axioms of null jointness in the production of electricity and CO_2 emissions and weak disposability of the emissions in the estimation of the environmental production function. They defined the carbon mitigation cost (CMC) index as a ratio of the maximum output of electricity under weak disposability and strong disposability conditions. They decompose the change in the index into technical change, input change and undesirable output change indexes.

Kumar and Jain (2020) find that 32 plants produce more electricity under strong disposability condition relative to weak disposability condition scenario implying that reducing CO_2 emissions in the Indian thermal power sector is costly. These results reveal that the Indian thermal power sector has to forego the electricity output by about 3% per year. Moreover, they observe that there is a positive association between mitigation cost and carbon productivity in the sector. This implies that regulatory stringency and scale of operation are the determinants of mitigation cost. They also find that the decomposition of the change in mitigation cost reflects that technical progress favours decline in mitigation cost, but the changes in the scale of operation and CO_2 emissions offset the benefits of technical progress.

Moreover, variation in the mitigation cost across the plants reveals that the Indian thermal power sector can reduce the emissions cost-effectively by providing economic incentives to the polluters. The presence of technical inefficiencies in the production of electricity and reduction in CO_2 emissions reflects the scope for environmental and managerial improvement. The possibilities of a faster shift in the regulated frontier relative to the unregulated frontier show that a properly designed climate policy may produce more electricity with lesser CO_2 emissions.

Emission trading and taxation are the ways of putting a price on pollution. Market-based instruments such as emission trading accomplish the targeted emission levels cost-effectively by equalizing marginal abatement costs across the polluters (Carlson et al., 2000). An emission trading programme offers an opportunity to high abatement cost thermal power plants to realize regulatory compliance by purchasing a right to emit CO_2 emission from the plants facing a lower abatement cost. Moreover, inter-temporal trading of emissions equalizes marginal abatement cost not only spatially but also inter-temporally and further lowers the abatement costs.

The formulation of cost-effective environmental policy and pricing pollution requires estimates of opportunity abatement cost of reducing emissions. Kumar et al. (2020) use a joint production framework with the assumption of weak disposability of bad outputs for estimating unrealized gains of foregone trades. They use the same data set which is used by Kumar and Jain (2020). They estimate the technical efficiency of power plants under different nested and non-nested models. Non-nested estimates of technical efficiency provide an idea about the potential increase in electricity production in a scenario when the thermal power plants were not reducing the emissions. The nested models estimate technical efficiency under different policy scenarios such as CAC, spatial trading of emissions, and spatial and temporal trading of emissions. A comparison of the potential increase in electricity production under nested and non-nested models provides an idea about the abatement cost of reducing carbon emissions under different policy scenarios.

Kumar et al. (2020) find that the power plants under study are paying US$ 3.23 billion to have the emissions at the observed level relative to a scenario if they were not reducing the emissions at all. However, the plants could have accomplished the observed level of the emissions at an abatement cost of US$ 1.05 billion and US$ 0.55 billion if they were allowed to trade the emissions spatially and spatially and temporally. The results reflect the need for designing an effective carbon market in the country and potential costs saving for realizing the Paris Agreement targets.

These applications reflect that the appropriate modelling of bad output does not only provide reliable estimates of the underlying production technology but also useful in designing incentive compatible environmental policy.

5 Concluding Remarks

Emission generating technologies has been recognized as an important area in the analysis of market externalities and policy formulations aimed at efficient mitigation of inimical effects on the social welfare of the production of bad outputs. The joint production models reflect that emission generation is a joint production process and the production of marketed output cannot be separated from pollution abatement activities. These models have been used to assess the effect of regulation in terms of reduction in marketed output while reducing the pollutants. These models differentiate between regulated and unregulated technologies. Regulated technologies assume that the reduction in pollution is costly, either in terms of reduced marketed output or employment of more inputs, while the unregulated technologies consider that pollution can be disposed of in free. For the regulatory scenario, the disposability of pollutants involves two approaches: weak disposability and by-production. The weak disposability approach, propounded by Rolf Färe and his colleagues in the mid-1980s, is more popular in the literature. According to this approach, good and bad outputs are null joint, and the bad outputs are weakly disposable. However, the weak disposability approach fails to satisfy the materials balance conditions. Assuming free disposability for emission causing inputs (e.g. fossil fuels) may be questionable, and the bad outputs are the unavoidable by-products of the production process of marketed output, rather than the joint products. The empirical applications of the modelling of bad output framework reflect that it not only provides reliable estimates of the production processes but also provides useful information on various public policy parameters.

References

Aigner, D. J., & Chu, S.-F. (1968). On estimating the industry production function. *American Economic Review, 58*(4), 826–839.

Baumgartner, S., Dyckhoff, H., Faber, M., Proops, J. L. R., & Schiller, J. (2001). The concept of joint production and ecological economics. *Ecological Economics, 36*(3): 365–372.

Baumol, W. J., & Oates, W. E. (1988), *The Theory of Environmental Policy* (2nd eds.). Cambridge University Press.

Carlson, C., Burtraw, D., Cropper, M., & Palmer, K. (2000). SO_2 control by electric utilities: What are the gains from trade? *Journal of Political Economy, 108*(6), 1292–1326.

Chambers, R. G., Chung, Y. F. R. (1998). Profit, distance functions and Nerlovian efficiency. *Journal of Optimization: Theory and Applications, 98*(2), 351–364.

Cropper, M. L., & Oates, W. E. (1992). Environmental economics: A survey. *Journal of Economic Literature, 30,* 675–740.

Dakpo, K. H., Jeanneaux, P., & Latruffe, L. (2017). Modelling pollution-generating technologies in performance benchmarking: Recent developments, limits and future prospects in the nonparametric framework. *European Journal of Operational Research, 250,* 347–359.

Dakpo, K. H., & Ang, F. (2019). Modelling environmental adjustments of production technologies: A literature review. In T. Raa & W. H. Greene (Eds.), *The Palgrave handbook of economic performance analysis* (pp. 601–657). Springer.

Färe, R., Grosskopf, S., & Pasurka, C. (1986). Effects on relative efficiency in electric power generation due to environmental controls. *Resource Energy, 8,* 167–184.

Färe, R., Grosskopf, S., & Pasurka, C. (2013). Joint production of good and bad outputs with a network application. In J. F. Shogren (Ed.), *Encyclopedia of energy, natural resource, and environmental economics* (Energy) (Vol. 1, pp. 109–118). Elsevier.

Färe, R., & Grosskopf, S. (1983). Measuring output efficiency. *European Journal of Operational Research, 13,* 173–179.

Färe, R., Grosskopf, S., & Pasurka, C. A. (2007). Environmental production functions and environmental directional distance functions. *Energy, 32,* 1055–1066.

Färe, R., Martins-Filho, C., & Vardanyan, M. (2010). On functional form representation of multi-output production technologies. *Journal of Productivity Analysis, 33,* 81–96.

Färe, R., Grosskopf, S., Noh, D.-W., & Weber, W. (2005). Characteristics of a polluting technology: Theory and practice. *Journal of Econometrics, 126,* 469–492.

Førsund, F. R. (2009). Good modelling of bad outputs: Pollution and multiple-output production. *International Review of Environmental and Resource Economics, 3*(1), 1–38.

Førsund, F. (1998). Pollution modeling and multiple-output production theory. Discussion Paper #D-37/1998, Department of Economics and Social Sciences, Agricultural University of Norway.

Gupta, M. (2006). Costs of reducing greenhouse gas emissions: A case study of India's power generation sector. FEEM Working Paper No. 147.

Jain, R. K., & Kumar, S. (2018). Shadow price of CO_2 emissions in Indian thermal power sector. *Environmental Economics and Policy Studies.*

Khanna, M., & Kumar, S. (2011). Corporate environmental management and environmental efficiency. *Environmental and Resource Economics, 59*(2), 227–242.

Kumar, S., & Jain, R. K. (2019). Carbon-sensitive meta-productivity growth and technological gap: An empirical analysis of indian thermal power sector. *Energy Economics, 81,* 104–116.

Kumar, S., & Jain, R. K. (2020) Cost of CO_2 mitigation and its decomposition: Evidence from coal fired thermal power sector in India. *Empirical Economics.*

Kumar, S., & Kumar, S. (2015). Does modernization improve performance: Evidence from Indian police. *European Journal of Law and Economics, 39,* 57–77.

Kumar, S., & Rao, D. N. (2002). Estimating Marginal Abatement Costs of SPM: An Application to Thermal Power Sector in India. *Energy Studies Review, 11*(1), 76–92.

Kumar, S. & Rao, D. N. (2003). Environmental Regulation and Production Efficiency: A Case Study of Thermal Power Sector in India. *Journal of Energy and Development, 29*(1), 81–94.

Kumar, S. (2006, Febraury 15). Environmentally sensitive productivity growth: A global analysis using Malmquist-Luenberger index. *Ecological Economics, 56*(2), 280–293.

Kumar, S., & Managi, S. (2009) Energy Price-Induced and Exogenous Technological Change: Assessing the Economic and Environmental Outcomes. *Resource and Energy Economics, 31*(4), 334–353.

Kumar, S., & Managi, S. (2010). Environment and productivities in developed and developing countries: The case of carbon dioxide and sulfur dioxide. *Journal of Environmental Management, 91*(07), 1580–1592.

Kumar, S., & Managi, S. (2010). Sulfur dioxide allowances: Trading and technological progress. *Ecological Economics, 69*(10), 623–631.

Kumar, S., Fujii, H., & Managi, S. (2015). Substitute or complement? Assessing renewable and non-renewable energy in OECD countries. *Applied Economics*.

Kumar, S., Managi, S., & Jain, R. K. (2020). CO_2 mitigation policy for Indian thermal power sector: potential gains from trade. *Energy Economics, 86,* 1–11.

Kumar, S., & Managi, S. (2016). Carbon sensitive productivity, climate and institutions. *Environment and Development Economics*.

Kumar, S., & Managi, S. (2011). Separability and substitutability among water pollutants: Evidence from India. *Environment and Development Economics, 16*(6), 709–733.

Kumbhakar, S., & Malikov, E. (2018). Good modeling of bad outputs: Editors' introduction. *Empirical Economics, 54,* 1–6.

Lee, J.-D., Park, J.-B., & Kim, T.-Y. (2002). Estimation of the shadow prices of pollutants with production/environment inefficiency taken into account: A nonparametric directional distance function approach. *Journal of Environmental Management, 64,* 365–375.

Murty, S., & Russell, R. (2017). Bad Outputs. *Discussion Paper in Economics, Centre for International Trade and Development*, School of International Studies, Jawaharlal Nehru University, New Delhi.

Murty, S., Russell, R. R., & Levkoff, S. B. (2012). On modeling pollution-generating technologies. *Journal of Environmental Economics and Management, 64*(1), 117–135.

Murty, M. N., & Kumar, S. (2002). Measuring cost of sustainable industrial development in India: A distance function approach. *Environment and Development Economics, 7,* 467–486.

Murty, M. N., & Kumar, S. (2003). Win-win opportunities and environmental regulation: Testing the porter hypothesis for Indian manufacturing industries. *Journal of Environmental Management, 67*(2), 139–144.

Murty, M. N., Kumar, S., & Dhavala, K. K. (2007). Measuring environmental efficiency of industry: A case study of thermal power generation. *Environmental and Resource Economics, 38,* 31–50.

Murty, M. N., Kumar, S., & Paul, M. (2006). Environmental regulation, productive efficiency and cost of pollution abatement: A case study of sugar industry in India. *Journal of Environmental Management, 79*(1), 1–9.

Murty, S., & Russell, R. R. (2002). *On modeling pollution-generating technologies, Department of Economics* (pp. 02–14). Riverside, Discussion Papers Series, No: University of California.

Ray, S. C., Mukherjee, K., Venkatesh, A. (2018). Nonparametric measures of efficiency in the presence of undesirable outputs: a by-production approach. *Empirical Economics, 54*(1): 31–65.

Shetty, S., & Kumar, S. (2017). Are voluntary environmental programs effective in improving the environmental performance: Evidence from polluting indian industries. *Environmental Economics and Policy Studies*.

Vardanyan, M., & Noh, D.-W. (2006). Approximating pollution abatement costs via alternative specifications of a multi-output production technology: A case of the US electric utility industry. *Journal of Environmental Management, 80,* 177–190.

The manufacturer's authorised representative in the EU is Springer Nature Customer Service Centre GmbH, Europaplatz 3, 69115 Heidelberg, Germany. If you have any concerns regarding our products, please contact ProductSafety@springernature.com

Printed and bound by CPI Group (UK) Ltd, Croydon, CR0 4YY
30/09/2026
02225289-0018